ATLA Monograph Series
edited by Don Haymes

1. Ronald L. Grimes. *The Divine Imagination: William Blake's Major Prophetic Visions.* 1972.
2. George D. Kelsey. *Social Ethics among Southern Baptists, 1917–1969.* 1973.
3. Hilda Adam Kring. *The Harmonists: A Folk-Cultural Approach.* 1973.
4. J. Steven O'Malley. *Pilgrimage of Faith: The Legacy of the Otterbeins.* 1973.
5. Charles Edwin Jones. *Perfectionist Persuasion: The Holiness Movement and American Methodism, 1867–1936.* 1974.
6. Donald E. Byrne, Jr. *No Foot of Land: Folklore of American Methodist Itinerants.* 1975.
7. Milton C. Sernett. *Black Religion and American Evangelicalism: White Protestants, Plantation Missions, and the Flowering of Negro Christianity, 1787–1865.* 1975.
8. Eva Fleischner. *Judaism in German Christian Theology Since 1945: Christianity and Israel Considered in Terms of Mission.* 1975.
9. Walter James Lowe. *Mystery & the Unconscious: A Study in the Thought of Paul Ricoeur.* 1977.
10. Norris Magnuson. *Salvation in the Slums: Evangelical Social Work,1865–1920.* 1977.
11. William Sherman Minor. *Creativity in Henry Nelson Wieman.* 1977.
12. Thomas Virgil Peterson. *Ham and Japheth: The Mythic World of Whites in the Antebellum South.* 1978.
13. Randall K. Burkett. *Garveyism as a Religious Movement: The Institutionalization of a Black Civil Religion.* 1978.
14. Roger G. Betsworth. *The Radical Movement of the 1960s.* 1980.
15. Alice Cowan Cochran. *Miners, Merchants, and Missionaries: The Roles of Missionaries and Pioneer Churches in the Colorado Gold Rush and Its Aftermath, 1858–1870.* 1980.

16. Irene Lawrence. *Linguistics and Theology: The Significance of Noam Chomsky for Theological Construction.* 1980.
17. Richard E. Williams. *Called and Chosen: The Story of Mother Rebecca Jackson and the Philadelphia Shakers.* 1981.
18. Arthur C. Repp, Sr. *Luther's Catechism Comes to America: Theological Effects on the Issues of the Small Catechism Prepared in or for America prior to 1850.* 1982.
19. Lewis V. Baldwin. *"Invisible" Strands in African Methodism.* 1983.
20. David W. Gill. *The Word of God in the Ethics of Jacques Ellul.* 1984.
21. Robert Booth Fowler. *Religion and Politics in America.* 1985.
22. Page Putnam Miller. *A Claim to New Roles.* 1985.
23. C. Howard Smith. *Scandinavian Hymnody from the Reformation to the Present.* 1987.
24. Bernard T. Adeney. *Just War, Political Realism, and Faith.* 1988.
25. Paul Wesley Chilcote. *John Wesley and the Women Preachers of Early Methodism.* 1991.
26. Samuel J. Rogal. *A General Introduction of Hymnody and Congregational Song.* 1991.
27. Howard A. Barnes. *Horace Bushnell and the Virtuous Republic.* 1991.
28. Sondra A. O'Neale. *Jupiter Hammon and the Biblical Beginnings of African-American Literature.* 1993.
29. Kathleen P. Deignan. *Christ Spirit: The Eschatology of Shaker Christianity.* 1992.
30. D. Elwood Dunn. *A History of the Episcopal Church in Liberia.* 1992.
31. Terrance L. Tiessen. *Irenaeus on the Salvation of the Unevangelized.* 1993.
32. James E. McGoldrick. *Baptist Successionism: A Crucial Question in Baptist History.* 1994.
33. Murray A. Rubinstein. *The Origins of the Anglo-American Missionary Enterprise in China, 1807–1840.* 1996.
34. Thomas M. Tanner. *What Ministers Know: A Qualitative Study of Pastors as Information Professionals.* 1994.

35. Jack A. Johnson-Hill. *I-Sight: The World of Rastafari: An Interpretive Sociological Account of Rastafarian Ethics.* 1995.
36. Richard James Severson. *Time, Death, and Eternity: Reflections on Augustine's "Confessions" in Light of Heidegger's "Being and Time."* 1995.
37. Robert F. Scholz. *Press toward the Mark: History of the United Lutheran Synod of New York and New England, 1830–1930.* 1995.
38. Sam Hamstra, Jr. and Arie J. Griffioen. *Reformed Confessionalism in Nineteenth-Century America: Essays on the Thought of John Williamson Nevin.* 1996.
39. Robert A. Hecht. *An Unordinary Man: A Life of Father John LaFarge, S.J.* 1996.
40. Moses Moore. *Orishatukeh Faduma: Liberal Theology and Evangelical Pan-Africanism, 1857–1946.* 1996.
41. William Lawrence. *Sundays in New York: Pulpit Theology at the Crest of the Protestant Mainstream.* 1996.
42. Bruce M. Stephens. *The Prism of Time and Eternity: Images of Christ in American Protestant Thought from Jonathan Edwards to Horace Bushnell.* 1996.
43. Eleanor Bustin Mattes. *Myth for Moderns: Erwin Ramsdell Goodenough and Religious Studies in America, 1938–1955.* 1997.
44. Nathan D. Showalter. *The End of a Crusade: The Student Volunteer Movement for Foreign Missions and the Great War.* 1997.
45. Durrenda Onolehmemhen and Kebede Gessesse. *The Black Jews of Ethiopia: The Last Exodus.* 1998.
46. Thomas H. Olbricht and Hans Rollmann. *The Quest for Unity, Peace, and Purity in Thomas Campbell's* Declaration and Address, *Text and Studies.* 2000.

The Quest for Christian Unity, Peace, and Purity in Thomas Campbell's *Declaration and Address*: Text and Studies

Edited by Thomas H. Olbricht
and Hans Rollmann

ATLA Monograph Series, No. 46

The Scarecrow Press, Inc.
Lanham, Maryland, and London
2000

SCARECROW PRESS, INC.

Published in the United States of America
by Scarecrow Press, Inc.
4720 Boston Way, Lanham, Maryland 20706
http://www.scarecrowpress.com

4 Pleydell Gardens, Folkestone
Kent CT20 2DN, England

British Library Cataloguing in Publication Information Available

Library of Congress Cataloging-in-Publication Data
The quest for Christian unity, peace, and purity in Thomas Campbell's Declaration and address : text and studies / edited by Thomas H. Olbricht and Hans Rollmann.
p. cm. — (ATLA monograph series ; no. 46)
Includes bibliographical references and index.
ISBN 0-8108-3842-7 (hardcover : alk. paper) — ISBN 0-8108-3843-5 (pbk : alk. paper)
1. Campbell, Thomas, 1763–1854. Declaration and address of the Christian Association of Washington. 2. Restoration movement (Christianity) I. Olbricht, Thomas H. II. Rollmann, Hans, 1948– III. Campbell, Thomas, 1763–1854. Declaration and address of the Christian Association of Washington. IV. Series.
BX7321.C33 Q47 2000
286.6—dc21 00-032947

∞™ The paper used in this publication meets the minimum requirements of American National Standard for Information Sciences—Permanence of Paper for Printed Library Materials, ANSI/NISO Z39.48–1992.
Manufactured in the United States of America.

This book is dedicated to the memory of

Hiram J. Lester (1933–1998)   Jim Cook (1953–1998)

valued contributors to this reassessment of

the *Declaration and Address*.

Contents

Preface

This book emerges from an electronic seminar that convened an international assembly of scholars and students around a virtual table on the Internet for more than six months in 1997–98. These unusual, indeed unique, circumstances necessitate a brief yet threefold introduction. First we must discuss some of the technical aspects of the seminar and then examine its focus—that is, Thomas Campbell and his *Declaration and Address*. Finally, we must say something about the members of the seminar and their unique contributions, with particular attention to two scholars—Hiram J. Lester and Jim Cook—who did not live to see the end of it.

The *Declaration and Address* Internet Seminar

Essays now published in this book were first presented as papers in an Internet seminar convened on the Stone-Campbell History List (stone-campbell@bible.acu.edu), as an experiment in sustained, formal investigation and conversation on a topic of historical and theological interest. Each paper appeared on the List at approximately one-week intervals from November 1997 to May 1998, generating discussion from those committed to the seminar as well as from anyone subscribing to the Stone-Campbell List. Insights from suggestions and criticisms offered in the seminar have been incorporated into the essays that we now publish. As each paper was presented in the seminar it was added to a specially designated section of a website devoted to the literature and history of the Restoration Movement and maintained by Hans Rollmann of the Department of Religious Studies at Memorial University, St. John's,

Newfoundland, Canada, one of the seminar leaders and a coeditor of this volume. The website also allowed another means of entering into the scholarly discussion through an electronic mailbox and offered during the duration of the seminar a searchable log of the entire discussion, which was daily updated.

The site also includes various textual versions of Thomas Campbell's *Declaration and Address* prepared by Ernest Stefanik, as well as the first complete edition of all known publications and unpublished manuscripts attributed to Thomas Campbell. The text of the *Declaration and Address* (hereinafter *D&A*) commended to the seminar and printed in this volume is Mr. Stefanik's carefully edited, electronic rendering of the first edition,[1] accompanied by a collation of textual variants and an index to biblical references and allusions prepared by Christopher Roy Hutson.

The text of the *D&A* is produced page-for-page without any emendations. To ease future citation of the edition, the lines of the text have been numbered. The text "has been reconstructed from the Facsimile Edition (1908) and compared to the second edition (1861). Where text is obliterated or obscured by the autograph corrections, or where characters are not fully impressed in the Facsimile Edition, the latest and best printing of the Centennial Edition (designated 'Thirtieth Thousand' and bearing the imprint 'Centennial Bureau, 203 Bissell Block, Pittsburgh, Pennsylvania') has been consulted for the reading. This version, then, attempts to preserve all the features of the first edition, including the typographical errors and inconsistencies in word forms (spelling, punctuation, capitalization, word division, and typography). Inasmuch as the second edition of the book (as edited by Alexander Campbell) contains some 2,760 emendations, of which only 115 might be attributed to the author, only the first edition clearly reveals the author's intentions."[2] A more detailed discussion of the text and its history can be found in the introduction to the collation and the paper by Ernie Stefanik.

The website also features a photographic exhibit related to the historical surroundings in which the *D&A* originated, as well as the major body of secondary literature on Thomas Campbell and his *D&A*, including the *Memoirs of Elder Thomas Campbell* by his son Alexander, a commentary on the *D&A* by Frederick D. Kershner, and the Thomas Campbell biography by William Herbert Hanna. Hans Rollmann's website continues to offer many other important primary documents and commentaries relating to the so-called Stone-Campbell Movement and can be reached online through the Universal Resource Locator http://www.mun.ca/rels/restmov/index.html.

The Stone-Campbell History List commenced in August 1994 and is based at Abilene Christian University, Abilene, Texas. Its purpose is to explore items relating to the history of an American movement to restore New Testament Christianity and thereby to bring about unity among Christians. In recent years this movement, which began in the early nineteenth century in Virginia, Kentucky, Ohio, New England, and Pennsylvania, has been designated the Stone-Campbell Movement because of the early leadership of Barton W. Stone (1772–1844) and Thomas (1763–1854) and Alexander Campbell (1788–1866). Three major wings of the movement now exist: the Disciples of Christ, the Independent Christian Churches, and the Churches of Christ. The Stone-Campbell List has been active, often generating more than fifty messages a day. Complete archives of the List may be consulted online. Though many topics have been discussed at some depth on the List, the *Declaration and Address* Seminar is the only formal consultation of its kind to date.

Thomas Campbell and His *Declaration and Address*

Thomas Campbell's *Declaration and Address*, published in 1809, is one of the founding documents of the American Stone-Campbell Movement and a landmark in the history of American Christianity. It has been discussed widely by many leaders in the various wings of the movement through the years. These authors have commonly perceived it as an initiating and fundamental vision for the movement as indicated in several essays in this book.

Thomas Campbell (1763–1854, hereinafter TC), the principal author of the *Declaration and Address*, was born in County Down, Ireland.[3] His father had converted from Roman Catholicism to the Anglican Church. TC graduated from the University of Glasgow in 1786 and became a minister of the Seceder Presbyterian Church of Scotland. He then attended the theological school maintained by the Antiburgher branch of the Seceder church at Whitburn, Scotland, completing his five-year course in 1791. Since the theological program took up only a few months of the year, TC was also employed as a teacher. On completing his theological course he moved to Ballymena in Country Antrim, continuing to teach but also to preach in small, nearby Seceder congregations. In 1798 he accepted a call to be minister for a newly founded congregation in

Ahorey, not far from Armagh, famous as a center of operations for St. Patrick centuries earlier.

As the eighteenth century drew to a close, Northern Ireland was ravaged by religious and ethnic strife between Protestants and Roman Catholics. The churches of TC's involvement were wracked by constant wrangling. TC was tolerant in spirit and deeply troubled by the narrowness and bigotry of Christians in his time. He therefore worked for unity and magnanimity at all levels and especially in an effort to bring together the Burghers and Antiburghers among the Seceders. Though he played a significant role in the remerger efforts, TC did not see his hopes realized until some years after he migrated to America. He was also involved in an effort to establish an ecumenically oriented Evangelical Society of Ulster for the purpose of distributing Bibles and sending itinerant preachers into sparsely inhabited regions. This society set out to involve church persons across confessional lines. But TC was charged not to participate by his Seceder Association.

Weary of the Ulster scene and knowing several persons from Northern Ireland who had migrated to the region south of Pittsburgh in Pennsylvania, TC left Londonderry on 1 April 1807 for Philadelphia in the company of a relative of General Thomas Acheson, the cosigner of the *D&A*. By June he was in Washington, Pennsylvania, with an assignment from the Chartiers Presbytery to preach at several Antiburgher churches in the region. To TC's surprise he found the Presbyterian factions from the British Isles even more intolerant of each other in their new setting. He soon found himself under suspicion for perceived discrepancies from the declared views of the Presbytery. On a preaching assignment to Cannamaugh above Pittsburgh, TC invited all church persons present, regardless of alignment, to participate in the Lord's Supper. This action set in motion a series of Association investigations of TC both in Pittsburgh and Philadelphia with the outcome that by May 1809 he had withdrawn from the Association. By that time the rest of his large family was on the way from Scotland to America.

TC was now free from his ties with the Antiburgher Presbyterians, but he remained eager, along with several of his acquaintances who had migrated, to continue meeting in the name of the Lord. He and his friends, not being disposed to found a new church, met at the farm home of Abraham Altars early in the summer to discuss how they could promote the cause of Christ. They agreed to form an association, much like the British evangelical associations, for the purpose of distributing Bibles, supporting itinerant preachers, and encouraging the cooperation of the various denominations in these common efforts. They called their new community "The Christian Association of Washington." TC, as the only trained minister in the group, was commissioned to draw up a declaration and an address, which he did, presenting it to the Association on 7 September 1809. TC's manuscript was unanimously approved, and before the year was out it was printed and distributed to various Christian leaders in the surrounding region. The common reaction of most churchmen was that the proposed association would not so much promote unity but would likely result in still another distinct group of Christians. Despite their wishes not to found churches, in a few years TC and his friends did just that, with the result that now at the beginning of the third millennium almost four million spiritual heirs of TC may be found, scattered throughout the world, though the majority are in North America. For almost two hundred years now the *D&A* has been admired and respected among these people.

The *D&A,* just like any other document, is subject to interpretation regarding intention and basic import. The essays in this book represent different perspectives and responses to its fundamental vision. TC's document in these essays likewise has been approached with varying traditional and modern methodologies which in turn cast on it divergent lights. A brief characterization, however, may assist our understanding.

The *D&A* offered a challenge to the increasing denominationalism of American Protestantism. It was commissioned and approved by laypersons from southwest Pennsylvania who had migrated from Scotland and Northern Ireland, TC being the singular ordained churchman involved. The document did not call for a new denomination, but rather for the organization of evangelical societies that would solicit the support of believers across confessional lines in making Bibles available and promoting itinerant, evangelical preaching. TC and his cohorts hoped that these new societies might break down the walls of denominationalism, resulting in a new form of Christendom exhibiting genuine unity in sentiment and purpose.

This new vision for Christendom was underpinned by eschatological expectations that certain signs on the horizon heralded the dawning of a new day—the inbreaking of the long-anticipated millennium. It would be a new age of unity, peace, and purity. Proponents of the *D&A* believed that these changes would come about if Christians were to forego wrangling, develop a new sense of forbearance, and permit time for nascent believers to mature in the faith. Unity was to be achieved through a new respect for and loyalty to the teachings of the New Testament. These were to be ascertained through the express terms and approved precedents that could be found in the New Testament text. The goal was to recreate original Christianity through a rigorous perusal of the foundational documents.

The barriers to unity, peace, and purity lay not only in the dispositions of church persons, but also in the means through which the basic guidelines of the Christian faith were determined. One method of determining doctrinal conformity discussed in the *D&A* was through composition of creedal instruments. While TC believed that creeds could be helpful in orienting new believers, or in addressing heresies, he charged that they wreaked havoc on Christendom when employed as a means of creating walls that separated believers. Likewise, he thought that inferences as employed by clergymen and theologians were highly harmful to unity and fellowship. These inferences, much like creeds, might be of some help in providing guidelines, but they often alienated Christians from each other. TC maintained a high vision of the authoritative status of Scripture, arguing that whatever is stated in Scripture must receive the complete approbation of believers. He argued against trying to separate levels of belief as they relate to opinions. If a guideline is laid out in Scripture it is to be followed. If a guideline is not found in Scripture, it should not be bound on any believer nor used as a test for worthiness and fellowship.

TC therefore issued a clarion call for a church at peace and unified for the goal of recreating original Christianity in its faith and purity of life. He clearly did not envision a separate movement of people who perceived themselves as the true church and who distanced themselves from all other forms of Christendom. In fact, though he sought to restore original Christianity, he proposed to do it through the cooperation of believers across denominational lines in the hopes that these lines would eventually disappear. At the same time, he did not envision large structures for ecumenicity or ecumenical projects. He was disposed, because of his experiences in both Northern Ireland and America with larger church associations, to be wary of massive organizational mechanisms. What he favored was a grassroots movement of minimal organizational proportions that, empowered by the Spirit of the living God, would usher in the dawning of a new day for all Christian believers.

The Seminar Contributors and Their Work

Scholars from all three primary branches of the Restoration Movement contributed to the seminar; they came from North Pole, Alaska, in the north to Abilene, Texas, in the south, and from Malibu, California, in the west to the easternmost city of the continent, St. John's, Newfoundland. While several of the participants had met each other professionally before, the discussion took place entirely on the Internet, without any face-to-face contact. Their awareness of personal community was, however, amplified through the death of two participants: Hiram J. Lester, a retired professor of New Testament from Bethany College and Restoration Movement scholar, and Jim Cook, an anthropologist of religion, who ministered to a Church of Christ at North Pole, Alaska. The loss of these two active participants in our electronic seminar was experienced by their seminar colleagues with the same sense of loss felt in the communities where the two men lived and worked.

While this is not the place to provide a précis of the papers, a few words should be said about the scope of the seminar, although the order of papers has been slightly modified in this book. The seminar papers addressed initially the "Backgrounds" of the *D&A* and did so by studying the continental Reformation heritage that fed the *D&A* theologically (Olbricht), as well as its philosophical and intellectual roots in Scottish philosophy and thought (Berryhill).

Next, the "Text and Form" of the *D&A* were examined by the creator of the electronic edition and its collation (Stefanik), and its form-critical character was probed by the late Hiram J. Lester. In the case of the text, the first and second editions as well as the printed facsimile proofs for the second edition were used. We were not able, however, to examine the original of the proofs at Bethany College. In his study of the form and function of the *D&A*, Lester summarized for the seminar his previous studies about the Irish historical context and the continental missionary society charters that—according to Lester—had served as models for the Christian Association of Washington's *D&A*.

The major portion of the seminar focused on the "Thought" of the *D&A*. Here the hermeneutic and logical argumentation employed by TC and the theology of the document were examined. TC's exegetical style was explored (Hutson) as well as the implied hermeneutic reconstructed (Olbricht) and its use of logic and inference examined (Casey). A Scripture index (Hutson) of quotations and allusions greatly facilitated work on the *D&A*'s use of Scripture. A modern comparative examination of the rhetoric of the *D&A* (Hobbs) employed the methodology of Kenneth Burke. The thematic theological foci of the *D&A* that received special attention concerned its notion of unity (Straughn, Cook), forbearance (Snyder), God, Christ, and soteriology (Flynn) as well as its eschatology (Rollmann).

The final major division of the seminar explored the *D&A*'s "Influence and Assessment." It did so by examining the reception history in all three wings of the historic movement: (1) among two prominent Disciples who were strongly affected by the founding document in their own theology, namely Frederick D. Kershner and William Robinson (Blowers); (2) in the noninstrumental Churches of Christ (Foster); and (3) among the Independent Christian Churches (Dull). Two concluding reflections probed the *D&A*'s "countercultural agenda" (Haymes) and confronted its tacit Enlightenment assumptions with questions posed by contemporary Postmodernism (Nutter).

Notes

1. Thomas Campbell, *Declaration and Address of the Christian Association of Washington* (Washington, Pa.: Brown & Sample, 1809).

2. According to the editor's concluding note about the on-line edition: http://www.mun.ca/rels/restmov/texts/tcampbell/da/DA-1ST.HTM#About. During the reading of the final proofs of this volume, Paul Dover, Nottingham, has kindly brought to our attention a first edition of the *D&A*, kept in the archives of the Church of Christ Historical Society, Orchard Learning Resource Centre, University of Birmingham, U.K., which, however, could not be taken into account for this edition.

3. The two major works on Thomas Campbell are: Alexander Campbell, *Memoirs of Elder Thomas Campbell, Together with a Brief Memoir of Mrs. Jane Campbell* (Cincinnati: H. S. Bosworth, 1861), and Lester G. McAllister, *Thomas Campbell: Man of the Book* (St. Louis: Bethany Press, 1954).

Acknowledgments

We are deeply indebted to our colleagues who produced these essays and entered into weighing and sifting the various statements and observations in essays other than their own. In addition, we are profoundly grateful to Memorial University of Newfoundland and Abilene Christian University for providing the electronic means through which these papers were first presented, discussed, and displayed. Many individuals have made these efforts possible, and their silent contributions should be properly acknowledged. Special gratitude, however, is expressed to Don Haymes, who gave invaluable editorial advice and care to this project. The production of the manuscript was aided through the Publication Subventions Program of Memorial University of Newfoundland, and the expert technical and editorial services of Ms. Mary Walsh are herewith gratefully recorded.

The Text of the *Declaration and Address*

Declaration and Address.

by THOMAS CAMPBELL.

First Edition, 1809.

DECLARATION

AND

ADDRESS

OF THE

CHRISTIAN ASSOCIATION

OF

WASHINGTON.

WASHINGTON, (Pa.)

PRINTED BY BROWN & SAMPLE.

AT THE OFFICE OF "THE REPORTER."

1809.

AT a meeting held at Buffaloe, August 17, 1809, consisting of persons of different religious denominations; most of them in an unsettled state as to a fixed gospel ministry; it was unanimously agreed upon, the considerations, and for the purposes herein after declared, to form themselves into a religious association, titled as above—which they accordingly did, and appointed twenty-one of their number to meet and confer together; and, with the assistance of Mr. Thomas Campbell, minister of the gospel, to determine upon the proper means to carry into effect the important ends of their association: the result of which conference was the following declaration and address, agreed upon and ordered to be printed at the expence and for the benefit of the society. September 7, 1809.

DECLARATION, &C.

FROM the series of events which have taken place in the churches for many years past, especially in this western country, as well as from what we know in general of the present state of things in the christian world; we are persuaded that it is high time for us not only to think, but also to act for ourselves; to see with our own eyes, and to take all our measures directly and immediately from the Divine Standard; to this alone we feel ourselves divinely bound to be conformed; as by this alone we must be judged. We are also persuaded that as no man can be *judged* for his brother, so no man can *judge* for his brother: but that every man must be allowed to judge for himself, as every man must bear his own judgment;—must give account of himself to God—We are also of opinion that as the divine word is equally binding upon all so all lie under an equal obligation to be bound by it, and it alone; and not by any human interpretation of it: and that therefore no man has a right to judge his brother, except in so far as he manifestly violates the express letter of the law. That every such judgment is an express violation of the law of Christ, a daring usurpation of his throne, and a gross intrusion upon the rights and liberties of his subjects. We are therefore of opinion that we should beware of such things; that we should keep at the utmost distance from every thing of this nature; and, that, knowing the judgment of God against them that commit such things; we should neither do the same ourselves, nor have pleasure in them that do them. Moreover, being well aware, from sad experience, of the heinous nature, and pernicious tendency of religious controversy among christians; tired and sick of the bitter jarrings and janglings of a party spirit, we would desire to be at rest; and, were it possible, we would also desire to adopt and recommend such measures, as would give rest to our brethren throughout all the churches;—as would restore unity, peace, and purity, to the whole church of God. This desirable rest, however, we utterly despair either to find for ourselves, or to be able to recommend to our brethren, by continuing amidst the diversity and rancour of party contentions, the veering uncertainty and clashings of human opinions: nor, indeed, can we reasonably expect to find it any where, but in Christ and his simple word; which is the same yesterday, and to-day, and for ever. Our desire, therefore, for ourselves and our brethren would be, that rejecting human opinions and the inventions of men, as of any authority, or as having any place in the church of God, we might forever cease from farther contentions about such things; returning to, and holding fast by, the original standard; taking the divine word alone for our rule: The Holy Spirit for our teacher and guide, to lead us into all truth; and Christ alone as exhibited in the word for our salvation—that, by so doing, we may be at peace among ourselves, follow peace with all men, and holiness, without which no man shall see the Lord.—Impressed with these sentiments, we have resolved as follows:

I. That we form ourselves into a religious association under the denomination of the Christian Association of Washington—for the sole purpose of promoting simple evangelical christianity, free from all mixture of human opinions and inventions of men.

II. That each member, according to ability, cheerfully and liberally subscribe a certain specified sum, to be paid half yearly, for the purpose of raising a fund to support a pure Gospel Ministry, that shall reduce to practice that whole form of doctrine, worship, discipline, and government, expressly revealed and enjoined in the word of God. And also for supplying the poor with the Holy Scriptures.

III. That this society consider it a duty, and shall use all proper means in its power, to encourage the formation of similar associations; and shall for this purpose hold itself in readiness, upon application, to correspond with, and render all possible assistance to, such as may desire to associate for the same desirable and important purposes.

IV. That this society by no means considers itself a church, nor does at all assume to itself the powers peculiar to such a society; nor do the members, as such, consider themselves as standing connected in that relation: nor as at all associated for the peculiar purposes of church association;—but merely as voluntary advocates for church reformation; and, as possessing the powers common to all individuals, who may please to associate in a peaceable and orderly manner, for any lawful purpose: namely, the disposal of their time, counsel, and property, as they may see cause.

V. That this society, formed for the sole purpose of promoting simple evangelical christianity, shall, to the utmost of its power, countenance and support such ministers, and such only, as exhibit a manifest conformity to the original standard in conversation and doctrine, in zeal and diligence;—only such as reduce to practice that simple original form of christianity, expressly exhibited upon the sacred page; without attempting to inculcate any thing of human authority, of private opinion, or inventions of men, as having any place in the constitution, faith, or worship, of the christian church—or, any thing, as matter of christian faith, or duty, for which there cannot be expressly produced a thus saith the Lord either in express terms, or by approved precedent.

VI. That a standing committee of twenty-one members of unexceptionable moral character, inclusive of the secretary and treasurer, be chosen annually to superintend the interests, and transact the business, of the society. And that said committee be invested with full powers to act and do, in the name and behalf of their constituents, whatever the society had previously determined, for the purpose of carrying into effect the entire object of its institution—and that in case of any emergency, unprovided for in the existing determinations of the society, said committee be empowered to call a *pro re nota* meeting for that purpose.

VII. That this society meet at least twice a year, viz. On the first Thursday of May, and of November, and that the collectors appointed to receive the half yearly quotas of the promised subscriptions, be in readiness, at or before each meeting, to make their returns to the treasurer, that he may be able to report upon the state of the funds. The next meeting to be held at Washington on the first Thursday of November next.

VIII. That each meeting of the society be opened with a sermon, the constitution and address read, and a collection lifted for the benefit of the society—and that all communications of a public nature be laid before the society at its half yearly meetings.

IX. That this society, relying upon the all-sufficiency of the Churches Head; and, through His grace, looking with an eye of confidence to the generous liberality of the sincere friends of genuine christianity; holds itself engaged to afford a competent support to such ministers, as the Lord may graciously dispose to assist, at the request, and by invitation of, the society, in promoting a pure evangelical reformation, by the simple preaching of the everlasting gospel, and the administration of its ordinances in an exact conformity to the Divine Standard as aforesaid—and, that therefore, whatever the friends of the institution shall please to contribute towards the support of ministers in connexion with this society who may be sent forth to preach at considerable distances, the same shall be gratefully received and acknowledged as a donation to its funds.

ADDRESS, &C.

To all that love our Lord Jesus Christ, in sincerity, throughout all the Churches, the following Address is most respectfully submitted.

DEARLY BELOVED BRETHREN,

THAT it is the grand design, and native tendency, of our holy religion, to reconcile and unite men to God, and to each other, in truth and love, to the glory of God, and their own present and eternal good, will not, we presume, be denied, by any of the genuine subjects of christianity. The nativity of its Divine Author was announced from heaven, by an host of angels, with high acclamations of "glory to God in the highest, and, on earth, peace and good will towards men." The whole tenor of that divine book which contains its institutes, in all its gracious declarations, precepts, ordinances, and holy examples, most expressly and powerfully inculcates this. In so far, then, as this holy unity and unanimity in faith and love is attained; just in the same degree, is the glory of God, and the happiness of men, promoted and secured. Impressed with those sentiments, and at the same time grievously affected with those sad divisions which have so awfully interfered with the benign and gracious intention of our holy religion, by exciting its professed subjects to bite and devour one another; we cannot suppose ourselves justifiable, in withholding the mite of our sincere and humble endeavours, to heal and remove them.

What awful and distressing effects have those sad divisions produced! what aversions, what reproaches, what backbitings, what evil surmisings, what angry contentions, what enmities, what excommunications, and even persecutions!!! And, indeed, this must in some measure, continue to be the case so long as those schisms exist, for, saith the Apostle, where envying and strife is, *there* is confusion and every evil work. What dreary effects of these accursed divisions are to be seen, even in this highly favored country, where the sword of the civil magistrate has not as yet learned to serve at the altar. Have we not seen congregations broken to pieces, neighbourhoods of professing christians first thrown into confusion by party contentions, and, in the end, entirely deprived of gospel ordinances; while, in the mean time, large settlements, and tracts of country, remain to this day entirely destitute of a gospel ministry; many of them in little better than a state of heathenism: the churches being either so weakened with divisions, that they cannot send them ministers; or, the people so divided among themselves, that they will not receive them. Severals at the same time who live at the door of a preached gospel, dare not in conscience go to hear it, and, of course, enjoy little more advantage in that respect, than if living in the midst of heathens.—How seldom do many in those circumstances enjoy the dispensation of the Lord's Supper, that great ordinance of unity and love. How sadly, also, does this broken and confused state of things interfere with that spiritual intercourse amongst christians, one with another, which is so essential to their edification and comfort, in the midst of a present evil world;—so divided in sentiment, and, of course, living at such distances, that but few of the same opinion, or party, can conveniently and frequently assemble for religious purposes; or enjoy a due frequency of ministerial attentions. And even where things are in a better state with respect to settled churches, how is the tone of discipline relaxed under the influence of a party spirit; many being afraid to exercise it with due strictness, lest their people should leave them, and, under the cloak of some spurious pretence, find refuge in the bosom of another party; while, lamentable to be told, so corrupted is the church, with those accursed divisions, that there are but few so base, as not to find admission into some professing party or other. Thus, in a great measure, is that scriptural purity of communion banished from the church of God; upon the due preservation of which, much of her comfort, glory, and usefulness depends. To complete the dread result of our woeful divisions, one evil yet remains, of a very awful nature: the divine displeasure justly provoked with this sad perversion of the gospel of peace, the Lord withholds his gracious influential presence from his ordinances; and not unfrequently gives up the contentious authors and abettors of religious discord to fall into grievous scandals; or visits them with judgments, as he did the house of Eli. Thus while professing christians bite and devour one another they are consumed one of another, or fall a prey to the righteous judgments of God: Meantime the truly religious of all parties are grieved, the weak stumbled; the graceless and profane hardened, the mouths of infidels opened to blaspheme religion; and thus, the only thing under heaven, divinely efficacious to promote and secure the present spiritual and eternal good of man, even the gospel of the blessed Jesus, is reduced to contempt; while multitudes deprived of a gospel ministry, as has been observed, fall an easy prey to seducers, and so become the dupes of almost unheard of delusions. Are not such the visible effects of our sad divisions, even in this otherwise happy country.—Say, dear brethren, are not these things so. Is it not then your incumbent duty to endeavour, by all scriptural means, to have those evils remedied. Who will say, that it is not? And does it not peculiarly belong to *you*, who occupy the place of gospel ministers, to be leaders in this laudable undertaking. Much depends upon *your* hearty concurrence and zealous endeavours. The favorable opportunity which Divine Providence has put into your hands, in this happy country, for the accomplishment of so great a good, is in itself, a consideration of no small encouragement. A country happily exempted from the baneful influence of a civil establishment of any peculiar form of christianity—from under the direct influence of the anti-christian hierarchy—and, at the same time, from any formal connexion with the devoted nations, that have given their strength and power unto the beast; in which, of course, no adequate reformation can be accomplished, until the word of God be fulfilled, and the vials of his wrath poured out upon them. Happy exemption, indeed, from being the object of such awful judgments. Still more happy will it be for us, if we duly esteem and improve those great advantages, for the high and valuable ends, for which they are manifestly given; —and sure where much is given, much also will be required. Can the Lord expect, or require, any thing less, from a people in such unhampered circumstances—from a people so liberally furnished with all means and mercies, than a thorough reformation, in all things civil and religious, according to his word? Why should we suppose it? And would not such an improvement of our precious privileges, be equally conducive to the glory of God, and our own present and everlasting good? The auspicious phenomena of the times, furnish collateral arguments of a very encouraging nature, that our dutiful and pious endeavours shall not be in vain in the Lord. Is it not the day of the Lord's vengeance upon the anti-christian world; the year of recompences for the controversy of Zion? Surely then the time to favour her is come; even the set time. And is it not said that Zion shall be built in troublous times? Have not greater efforts been made, and more done, for the promulgation of the gospel among the nations, since the commencement of the French revolution, than had been for many centuries, prior to that event? And have not the churches both in Europe and America, since that period, discovered a more than usual concern for the removal of contentions, for the healing of divisions, for the restoration of a christian and brotherly intercourse one with another, and for the promotion of each others spiritual good; as the printed documents, upon those subjects, amply testify? Should *we* not, then, be excited, by these considerations, to concur with all our might, to help forward this good work; that what yet remains to be done, may be fully accomplished. And what! Tho' the well meant endeavours after union, have not, in some instances, entirely succeeded to the wish of all parties, should this dissuade us from the attempt. Indeed, should christians cease to contend earnestly for the sacred articles of faith and duty once delivered to the saints, on account of the opposition, and scanty success, which, in many instances, attend their faithful and honest endeavours; the divine cause of truth and righteousness might have, long ago, been relinquished. And is there any thing more formidable in the Goliah schism, than in many other evils, which christians have to combat? Or, has the Captain of Salvation sounded a desist from pursuing, or proclaimed a truce with, this deadly enemy, that is sheathing its sword in the very bowels of his church, rending and mangling his mystical body into pieces. Has he said to his servants, let it alone? If not, where is the warrant for a cessation of endeavours to have it removed? On the other hand, are we not the better instructed by sage experience, how to proceed in this business; having before our eyes the inadvertencies, and mistakes of others, which have hitherto, in many instances, prevented the desired success? Thus taught by experience, and happily furnished with the accumulated instructions of those that have gone before us; earnestly labouring in this good cause; let us take unto ourselves the whole armour of God; and, having our feet shod with the preparation of the gospel of peace, let us stand fast by this important duty, with all perseverance. Let none that love the peace of Zion be discouraged, much less offended, because that an object of such magnitude does not, in the first instance, come forth recommended by the express suffrage of the mighty or the many. This consideration, if duly weighed, will neither give offence, nor yield discouragement, to any, that considers the nature of the thing in question, in connexion with what has been already suggested. Is it not a matter of universal right, a duty equally belonging to every citizen of Zion, to seek her good. In this respect, no one can claim a preference above his fellows, as to any peculiar, much less exclusive obligation. And, as for authority, it can have no place in this business; for surely none can suppose themselves invested with a divine right, as to any thing peculiarly belonging to them, to call the attention of their brethren to this dutiful and important undertaking. For our part, we entertain no such arrogant presumption; nor are we inclined to impute the thought to any of our brethren, that this good work should be let alone, till such time as they may think proper to come forward, and sanction the attempt, by their invitation and example. It is an open field, an extensive work, to which all are equally welcome, equally invited.

Should we speak of competency, viewing the greatness of the object, and the manifold difficulties which lie in the way of its accomplishment; we would readily exclaim, with the Apostle, who is sufficient for these things!—But, upon recollecting ourselves, neither would *we* be discouraged; persuaded with him, that, as the work in which we are engaged, so likewise, *our* sufficiency, is of God. But after all, both the mighty and the many are with us. The Lord himself, and all that are truly his people, are declaredly on our side. The prayers of all the churches; nay, the prayers of Christ himself, John 17, 20, 23, and of all that have ascended to his heavenly kingdom, are with us. The blessing out of Zion is pronounced upon our undertaking. Pray for the peace of Jerusalem, they shall prosper that love thee. With such encouragements as these, what should deter us from the heavenly enterpize; or render hopeless the attempt, of accomplishing, in due time, an entire union of all the churches in faith and practice, according to the word of God. Not that we judge ourselves competent to effect such a thing; we utterly disclaim the thought: But we judge it our bounden duty to make the attempt, by using all due means in our power to promote it; and also, that we have sufficient reason to rest assured that our humble and well-meant endeavours, shall not be in vain in the Lord.

The cause that we advocate is not our own peculiar, nor the cause of any party, considered as such; it is a common cause, the cause of Christ and our brethren of all denominations. All that we presume, then, is to do, what we humbly conceive to be *our* duty, in connexion with our brethren; to each of whom it equally belongs, as to us, to exert themselves for this blessed purpose. And as we have no just reason to doubt the concurrence of our brethren, to accomplish an object so desirable in itself, and fraught with such happy consequences, so neither can we look forward to that happy event, which will forever put an end to our hapless divisions, and restore to the church its primitive unity, purity and prosperity; but, in the pleasing prospect of their hearty and dutiful concurrence.

Dearly beloved brethren, why should *we* deem it a thing incredible, that the church of Christ, in this highly favored country, should resume that original unity, peace, and purity, which belongs to its constitution, and constitutes its glory? Or, is there any thing that can be justly deemed necessary for this desirable purpose, but to conform to the model, and adopt the practice, of the primitive church, expressly exhibited in the New Testament? Whatever alterations this might produce in any or all of the churches, should, we think, neither be deemed inadmissible nor ineligible. Surely such alteration would be every way for the better, and not for the worse; unless we should suppose the divinely inspired rule to be faulty, or defective. Were we, then, in our church constitution and managements, to exhibit a complete conformity to the Apostolick church, would we not be in that respect, as perfect as Christ intended we should be? And should not this suffice us?

It is, to us, a pleasing consideration that all the churches of Christ, which mutually acknowledge each other as such, are not only agreed in the great doctrines of faith and holiness; but are also materially agreed, as to the positive ordinances of Gospel institution; so that our differences, at most, are about the things in which the kingdom of God does not consist, that is, about matters of private opinion, or human invention. What a pity, that the kingdom of God should be divided about such things!! Who, then, would not be the first amongst us, to give up with human inventions in the worship of God; and to cease from imposing his private opinions upon his brethren; that our breaches might *thus* be healed? Who would not willingly conform to the original pattern laid down in the New Testament, for *this* happy purpose? Our dear brethren, of all denominations, will please to consider, that we have our educational prejudices, and particular customs to struggle with as well as they. But this we do sincerely declare, that there is nothing we have hitherto received as matter of faith or practice, which is not expressly taught and enjoined in the word of God, either in express terms, or approved precedent, that we would not heartily relinquish, that so we might return to the original constitutional unity of the christian church; and, in this happy unity, enjoy full communion with all our brethren, in peace and charity. The like dutiful condescension we candidly expect of all, that are seriously impressed with a sense of the duty they owe to God, to each other, and to their perishing fellow-brethren of mankind. To this we call, we invite, our brethren, of all denominations, by all the sacred motives which we have avouched as the impulsive reasons of our thus addressing them.

You are all, dear brethren, equally included as the objects of our love and esteem. With you all we desire to unite in the bonds of an entire christian unity—Christ alone being the head, the centre, his word the rule—an explicit belief of, and manifest conformity to it, in all things—*the terms*. More than this, you will not require of us; and less we cannot require of you; nor, indeed, can we reasonably suppose, any would desire it; for what good purpose would it serve? We dare neither assume, nor propose, the trite indefinite distinction between essentials, and non-essentials, in matters of revealed truth and duty; firmly persuaded, that, whatever may be their comparative importance, simply considered, the high obligation of the Divine Authority revealing, or enjoining them, renders the belief, or performance of them, absolutely essential to us, in so far as we know them. And to be ignorant of any thing God has revealed, can neither be our duty, nor our privilege. We humbly presume, then, dear brethren, you can have no relevant objection to meet us upon this ground. And, we again beseech you, let it be none, that it is the invitation but of a few; by your accession we shall be many; and whether few, or many, in the first instance, it is all one with respect to the event, which must ultimately await the full information, and hearty concurrence, of all. Besides, whatever is to be done, must begin—sometime—somewhere; and no matter where, nor by whom, if the Lord puts his hand to the work, it must surely prosper. And has he not been graciously pleased, upon many signal occasions, to bring to pass the greatest events from very small beginnings, and even by means the most unlikely. Duty then is ours: but events belong to God.

We hope, then, what we urge, will neither be deemed an unreasonable nor an unseasonable undertaking. Why should it be thought unseasonable? Can any time be assigned, while things continue as they are, that would prove more favorable for such an attempt, or what could be supposed to make it so? Might it be the approximation of parties to a greater nearness, in point of public profession and similarity of customs? Or might it be expected from a gradual decline of bigotry? As to the former, it is a well known fact, that where the difference is least, the opposition is always managed with a degree of vehemence, inversely proportioned to the merits of the cause. With respect to the latter, tho' we are happy to say, that in some cases and places, and we hope, universally, bigotry is upon the decline: yet we are not warranted, either by the past or present, to act upon that supposition. We have, as yet, by this means, seen no such effect produced; nor indeed could we reasonably expect it; for there will always be multitudes of weak persons in the church, and these are generally most subject to bigotry; add to this, that while divisions exist, there will always be found interested men, who will not fail to support them:—nor can we at all suppose, that Satan will be idle to improve an advantage, so important to the interests of his kingdom. And, let it be farther observed upon the whole, that, in matters of similar importance to our secular interests, we would, by no means, content ourselves, with such kind of reasoning. We might farther add that the attempt here suggested not being of a partial, but of general nature, it can have no just tendency to excite the jealousy, or hurt the feelings, of any party. On the contrary, every effort towards a permanent scriptural unity amongst the churches, upon the solid basis of universally acknowledged, and self-evident truths, must have the happiest tendency to enlighten and conciliate; by thus manifesting to each other, their mutual charity, and zeal for the truth:–"Whom I love in the truth, saith the Apostle, and not I only, but also all they that have known the truth; for the truth's sake, which is in us, and shall be with us forever. Indeed if no such divine and adequate basis of union, can be fairly exhibited, as will meet the approbation of every upright and intelligent christian: nor such mode of procedure adopted in favour of the weak, as will not oppress their consciences, then the accomplishment of this grand object upon principle, must be forever impossible.—There would, upon this supposition, remain no other way of accomplishing it, but merely by voluntary compromise, and good natured accommodation. That such a thing however will be accomplished, one way or other, will not be questioned by any that allow themselves to believe, that the commands and prayers of our Lord Jesus Christ will not utterly prove ineffectual. Whatever way, then, it is to be effected; whether upon the solid basis of divinely revealed truth; or the good natured principle of christian forbearance and gracious condeseension; is it not equally practicable, equally eligible to us, as ever it can be to any; unless we should suppose ourselves destitute of that christian temper and discernment, which is essentially necessary to qualify us to do the will of our gracious Redeemer; whose express command to his people is, that there be no divisions among them; but that they all walk by the same rule, speak the same thing, and be perfectly joined together in the same mind, and in the same judgment? We believe then it is as practicable, as it is eligible. Let us attempt it.

"Up, and be doing, and the Lord will be with you."

Are we not all praying for that happy event, when there shall be but one fold, as there is but one chief shepherd. What! shall we pray for a thing, and not strive to obtain it!! not use the necessary means to have it accomplished!! What said the Lord to Moses upon a piece of conduct somewhat similar? "Why criest thou unto me? Speak unto the children of Israel that they go forward, but lift thou up thy rod, and stretch out thine hand." Let the ministers of Jesus but embrace this exhortation, put their hand to the work, and encourage the people to go forward upon the firm ground of obvious truth, to unite in the bonds of an entire christian unity; and who will venture to say, that it would not soon be accomplished? "Cast ye up, cast ye up, prepare the way, take up the stumbling block out of the way of my people," saith your God. To you, therefore, it peculiarly belongs, as the professed and acknowledged leaders of the people, to go before them in this good work—to remove human opinions and the inventions of men out of the way; by carefully separating this chaff, from the pure wheat of primary and authentic revelation;—casting out that assumed authority, that enacting and decreeing power, by which those things have been imposed and established. To the ministerial department, then, do we look with anxiety. Ministers of Jesus, we can neither be ignorant of, nor unaffected with, the divisions and corruptions of his church. His dying commands, his last and ardent prayers, for the visible unity of his professing people, will not suffer you to be indifferent in this matter. You will not, you cannot, therefore, be silent, upon a subject of such vast importance to his personal glory and the happiness of his people—consistently you cannot; for silence gives consent. You will rather lift up your voice like a trumpet to expose the heinous nature, and dreadful consequences of those unnatural and anti-christian divisions, which have so rent and ruined the church of God. Thus, in justice to your station and character, honored of the Lord, would we hopefully anticipate your zealous and faithful efforts to heal the breaches of Zion; that God's dear children might dwell together in unity and love—But if otherwise— * * * * we forbear to utter it. See Mal. 2, 1—10.

Oh! that ministers and people would but consider, that there are no divisions in the grave; nor in that world which lies beyond it: there our divisions must come to an end! we must all unite there!—Would to God, we could find in our hearts to put an end to our short-lived divisions here; that so we might leave a blessing behind us; even a happy and united church. What gratification, what utility, in the meantime, can our divisions afford either to ministers or people? Should they be perpetuated, 'till the day of judgment, would they convert one sinner from the error of his ways, or save a soul from death? Have they any tendency to hide the multitude of sins that are so dishonorable to God, and hurtful to his people? Do they not rather irritate and produce them? How innumerable and highly aggravated are the sins they have produced, and are at this day, producing, both amongst professors and profane. We entreat, we beseech you then, dear brethren, by all those considerations, to concur in this blessed and dutiful attempt—What is the work of all, must be done by all. Such was the work of the tabernacle in the wilderness. Such is the work to which you are called; not by the authority of man; but by Jesus Christ and God the

Father, who raised him from the dead. By this authority are you called to raise up the tabernacle of David, that is fallen down amongst us; and to set it up upon its own base. This you cannot do, while you run every man to his own house, and consult only the interests of his own party. Till you associate, consult, and advise together; and in a friendly and christian manner explore the subject, nothing can be done. We would therefore, with all due deference and submission, call the attention of our brethren to the obvious and important duty of association. Unite with us in the common cause of simple evangelical christianity—In this glorious cause we are ready to unite with you—United we shall prevail. It is the cause of Christ, and of our brethren throughout all the churches, of catholic unity, peace, and purity—a cause that must finally prosper in spite of all opposition. Let us unite to promote it. Come forward then, dear brethren, and help with us. Do not suffer yourselves to be lulled asleep by that syren song of the slothful and reluctant professor, "The time is not yet come—the time is not come—saith he,—the time that the Lord's house should be built." Believe him not.—Do ye not discern the signs of the times? "Have not the two witnesses arisen from their state of political death, from under the long proscription of ages? Have they not stood upon their feet, in the presence, and to the consternation and terror of their enemies? Has not their resurrection been accompanied with a great earthquake? Has not the tenth part of the great city been thrown down by it? Has not this event aroused the nations to indignation? Have they not been angry, yea very angry? Therefore, O Lord, is thy wrath come upon them, and the time of the dead that they should be avenged, and that thou shouldest give reward to thy servants, the Prophets, and to them that fear thy name, both small and great; and that thou shouldest destroy them that have destroyed the earth. Who amongst us has not heard the report of these things—of these lightnings and thunderings, and voices; of this tremendous earthquake and great hail; of these awful convulsions and revolutions that have dashed and are dashing to pieces the nations, like a potter's vessel? Yea, have not the remote vibrations of this dreadful shock been felt even by us, whom Providence has graciously placed at so great a distance? What shall we say to these things? Is it time for us to sit still in our corruptions and divisions, when the Lord, by his word and providence, is so loudly and expressly calling us to repentance and reformation? "Awake, awake; put on thy strength, O Zion, put on thy beautiful garments, O Jerusalem, the holy city; for henceforth there shall no more come unto thee the uncircumcised and the unclean. Shake thyself from the dust, O Jerusalem; arise, loose thyself from the *bands* of thy neck, O captive daughter of Zion"—Resume that precious, that dear bought liberty, wherewith Christ has made his people free; a liberty from subjection to any authority but his own, in matters of religion. Call no man father, no man master upon earth;—for one is your master, even Christ, and all ye are brethren. Stand fast therefore in this precious liberty, and be not entangled again with the yoke of bondage. For the vindication of this precious liberty have we declared ourselves hearty and willing advocates. For this benign and dutiful purpose have we associated, that by so doing, we might contribute the mite of our humble endeavours to promote it, and thus invite our brethren to do the same. As the first fruits of our efforts for this blessed purpose we respectfully present to their consideration the following propositions—relying upon their charity and candour that they will neither despise, nor misconstrue, our humble and adventurous attempt. If they should in any measure serve, as a preliminary, to open up the way to a permanent scriptural unity amongst the friends and lovers of truth and peace throughout the churches, we shall greatly rejoice at it. We by no means pretend to dictate: and could we propose any thing more evident, consistent, and adequate, it should be at their service. Their pious and dutiful attention to an object of such magnitude will induce them to communicate to us their emendations; and thus what is sown in weakness, will be raised up in power—For certainly the collective graces that are conferred upon the church, if duly united and brought to bear upon any point of commanded duty, would be amply sufficient for the right and successful performance of it. For to one is given by the spirit the word of wisdom; to another the word of knowledge by the same spirit; to another faith by the same spirit; to another the discerning of spirits: but the manifestation of the spirit is given to every man to profit withal. As every man, therefore, hath received the gift, even so minister the same one to another as good stewards of the manifold grace of God. In the face then of such instructions, and with such assurances of an all-sufficiency of divine grace, as the church has received from her exalted Head, we can neither justly doubt the concurrence of her genuine members; nor yet their ability, when dutifully acting together, to accomplish any thing that is necessary for his glory, and their own good; and certainly their visible unity in truth and holiness, in faith and love, is, of all things, the most conducive to both these, if we may credit the dying commands and prayers of our gracious Lord. In a matter, therefore, of such confessed importance, our christian brethren, however unhappily distinguished by party names, will not, cannot, withhold their helping hand. We are as heartily willing to be their debtors, as they are indispensably bound to be our benefactors. Came, then, dear brethren, we most humbly beseech you, cause your light to shine upon our weak beginnings, that we may see to work by it. Evince your zeal for the glory of Christ, and the spiritual welfare of your fellow-christians, by your hearty and zealous co-operation to promote the unity, purity, and prosperity of his church.

Let none imagine that the subjoined propositions are at all intended as an overture towards a new creed, or standard, for the church; or, as in any wise designed to be made a term of communion;—nothing can be farther from our intention. They are merely designed for opening up the way, that we may come fairly and firmly to original ground: upon clear and certain premises: and take up things just as the Apostles left them.—That thus disentangled from the accruing embarrassments of intervening ages, we may stand with evidence upon the same ground on which the church stood at the beginning—Having said so much to solicit attention and prevent mistake, we submit as follows.

PROP. 1. THAT the church of Christ upon earth is essentially, intentionally, and constitutionally one; consisting of all those in every place that profess their faith in Christ and obedience to him in all things according to the scriptures, and that manifest the same by their tempers and conduct, and of none else as none else can be truly and properly called christians.

2. That although the church of Christ upon earth must necessarily exist in particular and distinct societies, locally separate one from another; yet there ought to be no schisms, no uncharitable divisions among them. They ought to receive each other as Christ Jesus hath also received them to the glory of God. And for this purpose, they ought all to walk by the same rule, to mind and speak the same thing; and to be perfectly joined together in the same mind, and in the same judgment.

3. That in order to this, nothing ought to be inculcated upon christians as articles of faith; nor required of them as terms of communion; but what is expressly taught, and enjoined upon them, in the word of God. Nor ought any thing be admitted, as of divine obligation, in their church constitution and managements, but what is expressly enjoined by the authority of our Lord Jesus Christ and his Apostles upon the New Testament church; either in express terms, or by approven precedent.

4. That although the scriptures of the Old and New Testament are inseparably connected, making together but one perfect and entire revelation of the Divine will, for the edification and salvation of the church; and therefore in that respect cannot be separated; yet as to what directly and properly belongs to their immediate object, the New Testament is as perfect a constitution for the worship, discipline and government of the New Testament church, and as perfect a rule for the particular duties of its members; as the Old Testament was for the worship discipline and government of the Old Testament church, and the particular duties of its members.

5. That with respect to the commands and ordinances of our Lord Jesus Christ, where the scriptures are silent, as to the express time or manner of performance, if any such there be; no human authority has power to interfere, in order to supply the supposed deficiency, by making laws for the church; nor can any thing more be required of christians in such cases, but only that they so observe these commands and ordinances, as will evidently answer the declared and obvious end of their institution. Much less has any hu-

man authority power to impose new commands or ordinances upon the church, which our Lord Jesus Christ has not enjoined. Nothing ought to be received into the faith or worship of the church; or be made a term of communion amongst christians, that is not as old as the New Testament.

6. That although inferences and deductions from scripture premises, when fairly inferred, may be truly called the doctrine of God's holy word: yet are they not formally binding upon the consciences of christians farther than they perceive the connection, and evidently see that they are so; for their faith must not stand in the wisdom of men; but in the power and veracity of God—therefore no such deductions can be made terms of communion, but do properly belong to the after and progressive edification of the church. Hence it is evident that no such deductions or inferential truths ought to have any place in the churchs's confession.

7. That although doctrinal exhibitions of the great system of divine truths, and defensive testimonies in opposition to prevailing errors, be highly expedient; and the more full and explicit they be, for those purposes, the better; yet, as these must be in a great measure the effect of human reasoning, and of course must contain many inferential truths, they ought not to be made terms of christian communion: unless we suppose, what is contrary to fact, that none have a right to the communion of the church, but such as possess a very clear and decisive judgment; or are come to a very high degree of doctrinal information; whereas the church from the beginning did, and ever will, consist of little children and young men, as well as fathers.

8. That as it is not necessary that persons should have a particular knowledge or distinct apprehension of all divinely revealed truths in order to entitle them to a place in the church; neither should they, for this purpose, be required to make a profession more extensive than their knowledge: but that, on the contrary, their having a due measure of scriptural self-knowledge respecting their lost and perishing condition by nature and practice; and of the way of salvation thro' Jesus Christ, accompanied with a profession of their faith in, and obedience to him, in all things according to his word, is all that is absolutely necessary to qualify them for admission into his church.

9. That all that are enabled, thro' grace, to make such a profession, and to manifest the reality of it in their tempers and conduct, should consider each other as the precious saints of God, should love each other as brethren, children of the same family and father, temples of the same spirit, members of the same body, subjects of the same grace, objects of the same divine love, bought with the same price, and joint heirs of the same inheritance. Whom God hath thus joined together no man should dare to put asunder.

10. That division among christians is a horrid evil, fraught with many evils. It is anti-christian, as it destroys the visible unity of the body of Christ; as if he wcre divided against himself, exclu-

ding and excommunicating a part of himself. It is anti-scriptural, as being strictly prohibited by his sovereign authority; a direct violation of his express command. It is anti-natural, as it excites christians to contemn, to hate and oppose one another, who are bound by the highest and most endearing obligations to love each other as brethren, even as Christ has loved them. In a word, it is productive of confusion, and of every evil work.

11. That, (in some instances,) a partial neglect of the expressly revealed will of God; and, (in others,) an assumed authority for making the approbation of human opinions, and human inventions, a term of communion, by introducing them into the constitution, faith, or worship, of the church; are, and have been, the immediate, obvious, and universally acknowledged causes, of all the corruptions and divisions that ever have taken place in the church of God.

12. That all that is necessary to the highest state of perfection and purity of the church upon earth is, first, that none be received as members, but such as having that due measure of scriptural self-knowledge described above, do profess their faith in Christ and obedience to him in all things according to the scriptures; nor, 2dly, that any be retained in her communion longer than they continue to manifest the reality of their profession by their tempers and conduct. 3dly, that her ministers, duly and scripturally qualified, inculcate none other things than those very articles of faith and holiness expressly revealed and enjoined in the word of God. Lastly, that in all their administrations they keep close by the observance of all divine ordinances, after the example of the primitive church, exhibited in the New Testament; without any additions whatsoever of human opinions or inventions of men.

13. Lastly. That if any circumstantials indispensably necessary to the observance of divine ordinances be not found upon the page of express revelation, such, and such only, as are absolutely necessary for this purpose, should be adopted, under the title of human expedients, without any pretence to a more sacred origin —so that any subsequent alteration or difference in the observance of these things might produce no contention nor division in the church.

From the nature and construction of these propositions, it will evidently appear, that they are laid in a designed subserviency to the declared end of our association; and are exhibited for the express purpose of performing a duty of previous necessity—a duty loudly called for in existing circumstances at the hand of every one, that would desire to promote the interests of Zion—a duty not only enjoined, as has been already observed from Is. 57, 14, but which is also there predicted of the faithful remnant as a thing in which they would voluntarily engage. "He that putteth his trust in me shall possess the land, and shall inherit my holy mountain; and shall say, cast ye up, cast ye up, prepare the way; take up the stumbling block out of the way of my people." To prepare tho way for a permanent scriptural unity amongst christians, by calling up to their consideration fundamental truths, directing their attention to first principles, clearing the way before them by removing the stumbling blocks—the rubbish of ages which has been thrown upon it, and fencing it on each side, that in advancing towards the desired object, they may not miss the way through mistake, or inadvertency, by turning aside to the right hand or to the left—is, at least, the sincere intention of the above propositions. It remains with our brethren, now to say, how far they go towards answering this intention. Do they exhibit truths demonstrably evident in the light of scripture and right reason; so that to deny any part of them the contrary assertion would be manifestly absurd and inadmissible? Considered as a preliminary for the above purpose, are they adequate; so that if acted upon, they would infallibly lead to the desired issue—If evidently defective in either of these respects, let them be corrected and amended, till they become sufficiently evident, adequate, and unexceptionable. In the mean time let them be examined with rigor, with all the rigor that justice, candour, and charity will admit. If we have mistaken the way, we shall be glad to be set right;—but if, in the mean time, we have been happily led to suggest obvious and undeniable truths, which if adopted and acted upon, would infallibly lead to the desired unity, and secure it when obtained; we hope it will be no objection, that they have not proceeded from a general council. It is not the voice of the multitude, but the voice of truth, that has power with the conscience—that can produce rational conviction, and acceptable obedience. A conscience that awaits the decision of the multitude, that hangs in suspence for the casting vote of the majority, is a fit subject for the man of sin. This we are persuaded is the uniform sentiment of real christians of every denomination. Would to God that all professors were such—then should our eyes soon behold the prosperity of Zion; we should soon see Jerusalem a quiet habitation. Union in truth has been, and ever must be, the desire and prayer of all such—Union in Truth is our motto. The Divine Word is our Standard; in the Lord's name do we display our banners. Our eyes are upon the promises; "So shall they fear the name of the Lord from the west, and his glory from the rising of the sun." When the enemy shall come in like a flood the spirit of the Lord shall lift up a standard against him." Our humble desire is to be his standard bearers—to fight under *his* banner, and with *his* weapons, "which are not carnal; but mighty through God to the pulling down of strong holds;" even all these strong holds of division, those partition walls of separation; which, like the walls of Jericho, have been built up, as it were, to the very heavens, to separate God's people, to divide *his* flock and so to prevent them from entering into their promised rest, at least in so far as it respects this world. An enemy hath done this; but he shall not finally prevail;–"for the meek shall inherit the earth, and shall delight themselves in the abundance of peace." And the kingdom and dominion, even the greatness of the kingdom under the whole heaven, shall be given to the people of the saints of the Most High, and they shall possess it forever." But this cannot be in their present broken and divided state; "for a kingdom, or an house, divided against itself cannot stand; but cometh to desolation." Now this has been the case with the church for a long time. However, "the Lord will not cast off his people, neither will he forsake his heritage; but judgment shall return unto righteousness, and all the upright in heart shall follow it " To such, and such alone, are our expectations directed. Come, then, ye blessed of the Lord, we have your prayers, let us also have your actual assistance. What, shall we pray for a thing and not strive to obtain it!

We call, we invite you again, by every consideration in these premises. You that are near, associate with us; you that are at too great a distance, associate as we have done—Let not the paucity of your number in any given district, prove an insuperable discouragement. Remember him that has said, "if two of you shall agree on earth as touching any thing that they shall ask, it shall be done for them of my Father which is in heaven: for where two or three are gathered together in my name, there am I in the midst of them." With such a promise as this, for the attainment of every possible and promised good, there is no room for discouragement. Come on, then, "ye that fear the Lord keep not silence, and give him no rest till he make Jerusalem a joy and a praise in the earth." Put on that noble resolution dictated by the prophet, saying, "for Zion's sake will we not hold our peace, and for Jerusalem's sake we will not rest, until the righteousness thereof go forth as brightness, and the salvation thereof as a lamp that burneth."—Thus impressed, ye will find means to associate at such convenient distances, as to meet, at least, once a month, to beseech the Lord to put an end to our lamentable divisions; to heal and unite his people, that his church may resume her original constitutional unity and purity, and thus be exalted to the enjoyment of her promised prosperity—that the Jews may be speedily converted, and the fullness of the Gentiles brought in. Thus associated, you will be in a capacity to investigate the evil causes of our sad divisions; to consider and bewail their pernicious effects; and to mourn over them before the Lord—who hath said, "I will go and return to my place, till they acknowledge their offence and seek my face." Alas! then, what reasonable prospect can we have of being delivered from those sad calamities, which have so long afflicted the church of God; while a party spirit, instead of bewailing, is every where justifying, the bitter principle of these pernicious evils; by insisting upon the right of rejecting those, however unexceptionable in other respects, who cannot see with them in matters of private opinion, of human inference, that are no where expressly revealed or enjoined in the word o. God.—Thus associated, will the friends of peace, the advocates for christian unity, be in a capacity to con nect in larger circles, where several of those smaller societies may meet semi-annually at a convenient centre; and thus avail themselves of their combined exertions for promoting the interests of the common cause. We hope that many of the Lord's ministers in all places will volunteer in this service, forasmuch as they know, it is his favorite work, the very desire of his soul.

Ye lovers of Jesus, and beloved of him, however scattered in this cloudy and dark day, ye love the truth as it is in Jesus, (if our hearts deceive us not) so do we. Ye desire union in Christ with all them that love him; so do we. Ye lament and bewail our sad divisions; so do we. Ye reject the doctrines and commandments of men, that ye may keep the law of Christ; so do we. Ye believe the alone sufficiency of his word; so do we. Ye believe that the word itself ought to be our rule and not any human explication of it; so do we. Ye believe that no man has a right to judge, to exclude, or reject, his professing christian brother; except in so far as he stands condemned, or rejected, by the express letter of the law:—so do we. Ye believe that the great fundamental law of unity and love ought not to be violated to make way for exalting human opinions to an equality with express revelation, by making them articles of faith and terms of communion—so do we. Ye sincere and impartial followers of Jesus, friends of truth and peace, we dare not, we cannot, think otherwise of you;—it would be doing violence to your character; —it would be inconsistent with your prayers and profession, so to do. We shall therefore have *your* hearty concurrence. But if any of our dear brethren, from whom we should expect better things, should, through weakness or prejudice, be in any thing otherwise minded, than we have ventured to suppose; we charitably hope, that, in due time, God will reveal even this unto them:—Only let such, neither refuse to come to the light; nor yet, through prejudice, reject it, when it shines upon them. Let them rather seriously consider what we have thus most seriously and respectfully submitted to their consideration; weigh every sentiment in the balance of the sanctuary, as in the sight of God, with earnest prayer for, and humble reliance upon, his spirit; and not in the spirit of self-sufficiency and party zeal;—and, in so doing, we rest assured, the consequence will be happy, both for their own, and the church's peace. Let none imagine, that in so saying, we arrogate to ourselves a degree of intelligence superior to our brethren, much less superior to mistake—so far from this, our confidence is entirely founded upon the express scripture and matter of fact evidence, of the things referred to; which may, nevertheless, through inattention, or prejudice, fail to produce their proper effect;—as has been the case, with respect to some of the most evident truths, in a thousand instances.—But charity thinketh no evil: and we are far from surmising, though we must speak. To warn, even against possible evils, is certainly no breach of charity, as to be confident of the certainty of some things, is no just argument of presumption. We by no means claim the approbation of our brethren, as to any thing we have suggested for promoting the sacred cause of christian unity; farther than it carries its own evidence along with it: but we humbly claim a fair investigation of the subject; and solicit the assistance of our brethren for carrying into effect what we have thus weakly attempted. It is our consolation, in the mean time, that the desired event, as certain as it will be happy and glorious, admits of no dispute; however we may hesitate, or differ, about the proper means of promoting it. All we shall venture to say as to this, is, that we trust we have taken the proper ground, at least, if we have not, we despair of finding it elsewhere. For if holding fast in profession and practice whatever is expressly revealed and enjoined in the divine standard does not, under the promised influence of the divine spirit, prove an adequate basis for promoting and maintaining unity, peace and purity, we utterly despair of attaining those invaluable privileges, by adopting the standard of any party. To advocate the cause of unity while espousing the interests of a party would appear as absurd, as for this country to take part with either of the belligerents in the present awful struggle, which has convulsed and is convulsing the nations, in order to maintain her neutrality and secure her peace. Nay, it would be adopting the very means, by which the bewildered church has, for hundreds of years past, been rending and dividing herself into fractions; for Christ's sake, and for the truth's sake; though the first and foundation truth of our christianity is union with him, and the very next to it in order, union with each other in him–"that we receive each other, as Christ has also received us, to the glory of God." For this is his commandment that we believe in his son Jesus Christ, and love one another, as he gave us commandment. And he that keepeth his commandments dwelleth in him, and he in him—and hereby we know that he dwelleth in us, by the spirit which he hath given us"—even the spirit of faith, and of love, and of a sound mind. And surely this should suffice us. But how to love, and receive our brother; as we believe and hope Christ has received both him and us, and yet refuse to hold communion with him, is, we confess, a mystery too deep for us. If this be the way that Christ hath received us, then woe is unto us. We do not here intend a professed brother transgressing the express letter of the law, and refusing to be reclaimed.—Whatever may be our charity in such a case, we have not sufficient evidence that Christ hath received him, or that he hath received Christ as his teacher and Lord. To adopt means, then, apparently subversive of the very end proposed, means which the experience of ages has evinced successful only in overthrowing the visible interests of christianity; in counteracting, as far as possible, the declared intention, the express command of its Divine Author; would appear in no wise a prudent measure for removing and preventing those evils. To maintain unity and purity has always been the plausible pretence of the compilers and abettors of human systems; and we believe in many instances their sincere intention:

but have they at all answered the end? Confessedly, demonstrably, they have not—no, not even in the several parties which have most strictly adopted them—much less to the catholic professing body. Instead of her catholic constitutional unity and purity, what does the church present us with, at this day, but a catalogue of sects and sectarian systems; each binding its respective party by the most sacred and solemn engagements, to continue as it is to the end of the world; at least this is confessedly the case with many of them. What a sorry substitute these, for christian unity and love. On the other hand, what a mercy is it, that no human obligation that man can come under is valid against the truth. When the Lord the healer, descends upon his people, to give them a discovery of the nature and tendency of those artificial bonds, wherewith they have suffered themselves to be bound, in their dark and sleepy condition: they will no more be able to hold them in a state of sectarian bondage; than the withs and cords with which the Philistines bound Sampson were able to retain him their prisoner; or, than the bonds of anti-christ were, to hold in captivity the fathers of the reformation. May the Lord soon open the eyes of his people to see these things in their true light; and excite them to come up out of their wilderness condition—out of this Babel of confusion—leaning upon their beloved, and embracing each other in him; holding fast the unity of the spirit in the bond of peace. This gracious unity and unanimity in Jesus would afford the best external evidence of their union with him; and of their conjoint interest in the Father's love. By this shall all men know that ye are my disciples, saith he, if ye have love one to another. And "this is my commandment that ye love one another as I have loved you; that ye also love one another." And again, "Holy Father, keep through thine own name, those whom thou has given me that they may be one as we are," even "all that shall believe in me—that they all may be one; as thou Father art in me and I in thee, that they also may be one in us; that the world may believe that thou hast sent me. And the glory which thou gavest me, I have given them, that they may be one, even as we are one: I in them and them in me, that they may be made perfect in me; and that the world may know that thou hast sent me, and has loved them, as thou hast loved me." May the Lord hasten it in his time. Farewell.

Peace be with all them that love our Lord Jesus Christ in sincerity. Amen.

THOS. CAMPBELL, Secretary.
THOS. ACHESON, Treasurer.

APPENDIX.

TO prevent mistakes, we beg leave to subjoin the following explanations. As to what we have done—our reasons for so doing —and the grand object we would desire to see accomplished—all these, we presume, are sufficiently declared in the foregoing pages. As to what we intend to do in our associate capacity, and the ground we have taken in that capacity, tho' expressly and definitely declared; yet, these, perhaps, might be liable to some misconstruction.— First, then, we beg leave to assure our brethren, that we have no intention to interfere, either directly, or indirectly, with the peace and order of the settled churches, by directing any ministerial assistance, with which the Lord may please to favour us, to make inroads upon such; or, by endeavouring to erect churches out of churches—to distract and divide congregations. We have no nostrum, no peculiar discovery of our own to propose to fellow-christians, for the fancied importance of which, they should become followers of us. We propose to patronize nothing but the inculcation of the express word of God—either as to matter of faith or practice;—but every one that has a Bible, and can read it, can read this for himself.—Therefore we have nothing new. Neither do we pretend to acknowledge persons to be ministers of Christ, and, at the same time, consider it our duty to forbid, or discourage people to go to hear them, merely because they may hold some things disagreeable to us; much less to encourage their people to leave them on that account;—and such do we esteem all, who preach a free unconstitutional salvation through the blood of Jesus to perishing sinners of every description; and who manifestly connect with this a life of holiness, and pastoral diligence in the performance of all the duties of their sacred office according to the scriptures; even all, of whom, as to all appearance, it may be truly said to the objects of their charge, "they seek not *yours*, but *you*." May the good Lord prosper all such, by whatever name they are called; and fast hasten that happy period, when Zion's watchmen shall see eye to eye, and all be called by the same name. *Such* then have nothing to fear from our association, were our resources equal to our utmost wishes. But all others we esteem as hirelings, as idol shepherds; and should be glad to see the Lord's flock delivered from their mouth, according to his promise. Our principal and proper design, then, with respect to ministerial assistants, such as we have described in our fifth resolution, is to direct their attention to those places where there is manifest need for their labours; and many such places there are; would to God it were in our power to supply them. As to creeds and confessions, although we may appear to our brethren to oppose them, yet this is to be understood only in *so far* as they oppose the unity of the church, by containing sentiments not expressly revealed in the word of God; or, by the way of using them, become the instruments of a human or implicit faith: or, oppress the weak of Gods heritage: where they are liable to none of those objections, we have nothing against them. It is the *abuse* and not the *lawful use* of such compilations that we oppose. See PROP. 7, page 17. Our intention therefore, with respect to all the churches of Christ is perfectly amicable. We heartily wish their reformation; but by no means their hurt or confusion. Should any affect to say, that our coming forward as we have done, in advancing and publishing such things, have a manifest tendency to distract and divide the churches, or to make a new party; we treat it as a confident and groundless assertion: and must suppose they have not duly considered, or at least, not well understood the subject.

All we shall say to this at present, is, that if the divine word be not the standard of a party—Then are we not a party, for we have adopted no other. If to maintain its alone sufficiency be not a party principle: then are we not a party—If to justify this principle by our practice, in making a rule of it, and of *it alone*; and not of our own opinions, nor of those of others, be not a party principle—then are we not a party—If to propose and practice neither more nor less than it expressly reveals and enjoins be not a partial business, then are we not a party. These are the very sentiments we have approved and recommended, as a society formed for the express purpose of promoting christian unity, in opposition to a party spirit. Should any tell us that to do these things is impossible without the intervension of human reason and opinion. We humbly thank them for the discovery. But who ever thought otherwise? Were we not rational subjects, and of course capable of understanding and forming opinions; would it not evidently appear, that, to us, revelation of any kind would be quite useless; even suppose it as evident as mathematicks. We pretend not, therefore, to divest ourselves of reason, that we may become quiet, inoffensive, and peaceable christians; nor yet, of any of its proper and legitimate operations upon divinely revealed truths. We only pretend to assert, what every one that pretends to reason must acknowledge; namely, that there is a manifest distinction betwixt an express scripture declaration, and the conclusion or inference which may be deduced from it—and that the former may be clearly understood, even where the latter is but imperfectly, if at all perceived; and that we are, at least, as certam of the declaration, as we can be of the conclusion, we draw from it—and that, after all, the conclusion ought not to be exalted above the premises, so as to make void the declaration for the sake of establishing our own conclusion—and that, therefore, the express commands to preserve and maintain inviolate christian unity and love, ought not to be set aside to make way for exalting our inferences above the express authority of God. Our inference, upon the whole, is, that where a professing christian brother opposes or refuses nothing either in faith or practice, for which there can be expressly produced a "thus saith the Lord": that we ought not to reject him because he cannot see with our eyes as to matters of human inference—of private judgment. "Through thy knowledge shall the weak brother perish? How walketh thou not charitably? Thus we reason, thus we conclude, to make no conclusion of our own, nor of any other fallible fellow creature, a rule of faith or duty to our brother. Whether we refuse reason, then, or abuse it, in our so doing, let our brethren judge. But, after all, we have only ventured to suggest, what, in other words, the Apostle has expressly taught; namely, that the strong ought to bear with the infirmities of the weak, and not to please themselves. That we ought to receive him that is weak in the faith, because God hath received him. In a word, that we ought to receive one another, as Christ hath also received us to the glory of God. We dare not therefore, patronize the rejection of Gods dear children, because they may not be able to see alike in matters of human inference—of private opinion; and such we esteem all things, not expressly revealed and enjoined in the word of God. If otherwise, we know not what private opinion means. On the other hand, should our peaceful and affectionate overture for union in truth, prove offensive to any of our brethren; or occasion disturbances in any of the churches; the blame cannot be attached to us. We have only adventured to persuade, and, if possible, to excite to the performance of an important duty—a duty equally incumbent upon us all. Neither have we pretended to dictate to *them*, what *they* should do. We have only proposed, what appeared to *us* most likely to promote the desired event; humbly submitting the whole premises to their candid and impartial investigation: to be altered, corrected, and amended, as they see cause; or any other plan adopted that may appear more just and unexceptionable. As for ourselves, we have taken all due care, in the meantime to take no step, that might throw a stumbling block in the way; that might prove now, or at any future period, a barrier to prevent the accomplishment of that most desirable object; either by joining to support a party; or by patronizing any thing as articles of faith or duty, not expressly revealed and enjoined in the divine standard; as we are sure, whatever alterations may take place, *that* will stand. And that considerable alterations must and will take place, in the standards of all the churches, before that glorious object can be accomplished, no man, that duly considers the matter, can possibly doubt. In so far then, we have, at least, endeavoured to act consistently; and with the same consistency would desire to be instrumental in erecting as many churches as possible, throughout the desolate places of God's heritage, upon the same catholic foundation; being well persuaded, that every such erection will, not only in the issue, prove an accession to the general cause; but will also, in the mean time, be a step towards it; and of course, will reap the first fruits of that blissful harvest, that will fill the face of the world with fruit. For, if the first christian churches walking in the fear of the Lord, in holy unity and unanimity, enjoyed the comforts of the Holy Ghost, and were increased and edified; we have reason to believe, that walking in their footsteps will every where, and at all times, ensure the same blessed privileges. And it is in an exact conformity to their recorded and approved example, that we through grace, would be desirous to promote the erection of churches: and this we believe to be quite practicable, if the legible and authentic records of *their* faith and practice be handed down to *us*, upon the page of New Testament scripture: but if otherwise, we cannot help it—Yet even in this case, might we not humbly presume, that the Lord would take the will for the deed; for if there be first a willing mind, we are told, it is accepted, according to what a man hath, and not according to what he hath not. It would appear, then, that sincerely and humbly adopting this model, with an entire reliance upon promised grace, we cannot, we shall not, be disappointed. By this at least, we shall get rid of two great evils, which we fear, are at this day, grievously provoking the Lord to plead a controversy with the churches; we mean the taking, and giving, of unjust offences; judging and rejecting each other, in matters wherein the Lord hath not judged; in a flat contradiction to his expressly revealed will. But according to the principle adopted, we can neither take offence at our brother for his private opinions, if he be content to hold them as such; nor yet offend him with ours, if he do not usurp the place of the lawgiver; and even suppose he should, in this case we judge him, not for his *opinions*, but for his *presumption*. "There is one lawgiver, who is able to save, and to destroy: who art thou that judgest another?" But farther, to prevent mistakes, we beg leave to explain our meaning in a sentence or two, which might possibly be misunderstood. In page first, we say, that no man has a right to judge his brother; except in so far as he manifestly violates the express letter of the law. By the law here, and elsewhere, when taken in this latitude, we mean that whole revelation of faith and duty, expressly declared in the divine word, taken together, or in its due connexion, upon every article: and not any detached sentence. We understand it as extending to all prohibitions, as well as to all requirements. "Add thou not unto his words, lest he reprove thee, and thou be found a liar." We dare therefore neither do, nor receive any thing, as of divine obligation, for which there cannot be expressly produced a "thus saith the Lord" either in express terms, or by approved precedent. According to this rule we judge, and beyond it we dare not go. Taking this sentiment in connexion with the last clause of the fifth resolution; we are to be understood, of all matters of faith and practice, of primary and universal obligation; that is to say, of express revelation: that nothing be inculcated as such, for which there cannot be expressly produced a "thus saith the Lord" as above; without, at the same time, interfering directly or indirectly, with the private judgment of any individual, which does not expressly contradict the express letter of the law, or add to the number of its institutions. Every sincere and upright christian, will understand and do the will of God, in every instance, to the best of his skill and judgment: but in the application of the general rule to particular cases, there may, and doubtless will, be some variety of opinion and practice. This we see was actually the case in the apostolic churches, without any breach of christian unity. And if this was the case, at the erection of the christian church from amongst Jews and Gentiles, may we not reasonably expect, that it will be the same at her restoration, from under her long antichristian and sectarian desolations?

With a direct reference to this state of things; and, as we humbly think, in a perfect consistency with the foregoing explanations, have we expressed ourselves in page 10th; wherein we declare ourselves ready to relinquish, whatever we have hitherto received as matter of faith or practice, not expressly taught and enjoined in the word of God; so that we, and our brethren, might, by this mutual condescension, return together to the original constitutional unity of the christian church; and dwell together in peace and charity. By this proposed relinquishment, we are to be understood, in the first instance, of our manner of holding those things, and not simply of the things themselves: for no man can relinquish his opinions or practices, till once convinced that they are wrong; and this he may not be immediately, even supposing they were so. One thing, however, he may do, when not bound by an express command, he need not impose them upon others, by any wise requiring their approbation; and when this is done, the things, to them, are as good as dead; yea, as good as buried too; being thus removed out of the way. Has not the Apostle set us a noble example of this, in his pious and charitable zeal for the comfort and edification of his brother, in declaring himself ready to forego his rights (not indeed to break commandments) rather than stumble, or offend, his brother? And who knows not, that the Hebrew christians abstained from certain meats, observed certain days—kept the passover, circumcised their children, &c. &c.—while no such things were practised by the Gentile converts:—and yet no breach of unity, while they charitably forbore one with the other. But had the Jews been expressly prohibited, or the Gentiles expressly enjoined, by the authority of Jesus, to observe these things; could they, in such a case, have lawfully exercised this forbearance? But where no express law is, there can be no formal, no intentional transgression; even although its implicit and necessary consequences had forbid the thing, had they been discovered. Upon the whole, we see one thing is evident; the Lord will bear with the weaknesses, the involuntary ignorances, and mistakes, of his people; though not with their presumption. Ought they not, therefore, to bear with each other–"t o preserve the unity of the spirit in the bond of peace; forbearing one with another in love"—What saith the scripture? We say, then, the declaration referred to, is to be thus understood, in the first instance; though we do not say, but something farther is intended. For certainly we may lawfully suspend both declaration and practice upon any subject, where the law is silent: when to do otherwise must prevent the accomplishment of an expressly commanded, and highly important duty: and such, confessedly, is the thing in question. What saith the Apostle? "All things are lawful for me; but all things are not expedient. All things are lawful for me; but all things edify not." It seems, then, that amongst lawful things, which might be forborne; that is, as we humbly conceive, things not expressly commanded; the governing principle of the Apostle's conduct was the edification of his brethren—of the church of God. A divine principle this, indeed! May the Lord God infuse it into all his people. Were all those nonpreceptive opinions and practises, which have been maintained and exalted to the destruction of the church's unity, counterbalanced with the breach of the express law of Christ, and the black catalogue of mischiefs which have necessarily ensued; on which side, think you, would be the preponderance? When weighed in the balance with this monstrous complex evil, would they not all appear lighter than vanity? Who then would not relinquish a cent to obtain a kingdom! And here let it be noted, that it is not the renunciation of an opinion or practice as sinful, that is proposed or intended; but merely a cessation from the publishing or preaching of it, so as to give offence; a thing men are in the habits of doing every day, for their private comfort, or secular emolument; where the advantage is of infinitely less importance. Neither is there here any clashing of duties; as if to forbear was a sin; and also to practise was a sin; the thing to be forborne being a matter of private opinion; which, though not expressly forbidden, yet are we, by no means, expressly commanded to practise,—Whereas we are expressly commanded to endeavor to maintain the unity of the spirit in the bond of peace. And what saith the Apostle to the point in hand? "Hast thou faith, saith he, have it to thyself before God. Happy is the man, that condemneth not himself, in the thing which he alloweth."

It may be farther added, that a still higher and more perfect degree of uniformity is intended, though neither in the first nor second instance, which are but so many steps towards it; namely, the utter abolition of those minor differences, which have been greatly increased, as well as continued, by our unhappy manner of treating them; in making them the subject of perpetual strife and contention. Many of the opinions which are now dividing the church, had they been let alone, would have been, long since, dead and gone: but the constant insisting upon them, as articles of faith and terms of salvation, have so beat them into the minds of men, that, in many instances, they would as soon deny the Bible itself, as give up with one of those opinions. Having thus embraced contentions, and preferred divisions to that constitutional unity, peace and charity, so essential to christianity: it would appear, that the Lord, in righteous judgment, has abandoned his professing people to the awful scourge of those evils; as, in an instance somewhat similar, he formerly did his highly favored Israel. "My people, saith he, would not hearken to my voice. So I gave them up to their own hearts lusts, and they walked in their own counsels." "Israel hath made many altars to sin: therefore altars shall be unto him to sin." Thus, then, are we to be consistently understood, as fully and fairly intending, on *our* part, what we have declared and proposed to our brethren, as, to *our* apprehension, incumbent upon *them* and *us*, for putting an end forever, to our sad and lamentable schisms. Should any object and say, that after all, the fullest compliance with every thing proposed and intended, would not restore the church to the desired unity, as there might still remain differences of opinion and practice. Let such but duly consider, what properly belongs to the unity of the church, and we are persuaded, this objection will vanish. Does not the visible scriptural unity of the christian church consist in the unity of her public profession and practice; and, under this, in the manifest charity of her members, one towards another; and not in the unity of the private opinion and practice of every individual? Was not this evidently the case in the Apostles' days, as has been already observed? If so, the objection falls to the ground. And here, let it be noted, (if the hint be at all necessary,) that we are speaking of the unity of the church considered as a great visible professing body, consisting of many co-ordinate associations; each of these, in its aggregate or associate capacity, walking by the same rule, professing and practising the same things. That this visible scriptural unity be preserved, without corruption, or breach of charity, throughout the whole; and in every particular worshipping society, or church; is the grand desideratum—the thing strictly enjoined, and greatly to be desired. An agreement in the expressly revealed will of God, is the adequate and firm foundation of this unity; ardent prayer, accompanied with prudent, peaceable, and persevering exertion, in the use of all scriptural means for accomplishing it, are the things humbly suggested, and earnestly recommended to our brethren. If we have mistaken the way, their charity will put us right: but if otherwise, their fidelity to Christ and his cause will excite them to come forth speedily, to assist with us in this blessed work.

After all, should any impeach us with the vague charge of Latitudinarianism (let none be startled at this gigantic term) it will prove as feeble an opponent to the glorious cause in which we, however weak and unworthy, are professedly engaged, as the Zamzummins did of old, to prevent the children of Lot from taking possession of their inheritance. If we take no greater latitude than the divine law allows, either in judging of persons, or doctrines—either in profession, or practice (and this is the very thing we humbly propose and sincerely intend) may we not reasonably hope, that such a latitude will appear to every upright christian, perfectly innocent and unexceptionable? If this be Latitudinarianism, it must be a good thing—and therefore the more we have of it the better; and may be it is, for we are told, "the commandment is exceeding broad;" and we intend to go just as far as it will suffer us, but not one hair's breadth farther—so, at least, says our profession. And surely it will be time enough to condemn our practice, when it appears manifestly inconsistent with the profession, we have thus precisely and explicitly made. We here refer to the whole of the foregoing premises. But were this word as bad as it is long: were it stuffed with evil from beginning to end; may be, it better belongs to those, that brandish it so unmercifully at their neighbors; especially if they take a greater latitude than their neighbours do; or than the divine law allows. Let the case, then, be fairly submitted to all that know their Bible—to all that take upon them to see with their own eyes—to judge for themselves. And here let it be observed once for all, that it is only to such we direct our attention in the foregoing pages. As for those that either cannot, or will not see and judge for themselves, they must be content to follow their leaders, till they come to their eyesight; or determine to make use of the faculties, and means of information, which God has given them: with such, in the mean time, it would be useless to reason; seeing that they either confessedly cannot see; or have completely resigned themselves to the conduct of their leaders; and are therefore determined to hearken to none but them. If there be none such, however, we are happily deceived: but, if so, we are not the only persons that are thus deceived; for this is the common fault objected by almost all the parties to each other, viz. that they either cannot, or will not see; and it would be hard to think, they were all mistaking: the fewer there be, however, of this description, the better. To all those, then, that are disposed to see and think for themselves, to form their judgment by the divine word itself, and not by any human explication of it—humbly relying upon, and looking for, the promised assistance of divine teaching; and not barely trusting to their own understanding.—To all such, do we gladly commit our cause; being persuaded, that, at least, they will give it a very serious and impartial consideration; as being truly desirous to know the truth. To you, then, we appeal, in the present instance, as we have also done from the beginning. Say, we beseech you, to whom does the charge of Latitudinarianism, when taken in a bad sense (for we have supposed it may be taken in a good sense) most truly and properly belong. Whether to those that will neither add nor diminish any thing, as to matter of faith and duty; either to, or from, what is expressly revealed and enjoined in the holy scriptures: or to those who pretend to go farther than this; or to set aside some of its express declarations and injunctions to make way for their own opinions, inferences, and conclusions? Whether to those who profess their willingness to hold communion with their acknowledged christian brethren, when they neither manifestly oppose nor contradict any thing expressly revealed and enjoined in the sacred standard: or to those who reject such, when professing to believe and practise whatever is expressly revealed and enjoined therein; without, at the same time, being *alledged*, much less *found* guilty, of any thing to the contrary: but instead of this, asserting and declaring their hearty assent and consent to every thing, for which there can be expressly produced a "thus saith the Lord," either in express terms, or by approved precedent. To which of these, think ye, does the odious charge of Latitudanarianism belong? Which of them takes the greatest latitude? Whether those that expressly judge and condemn where they have no express warrant for so doing; or those that absolutely refuse so to do? And we can assure our brethren, that such things are, and have been done, to our own certain knowledge; and even where we least expected it: and that it is to this discovery, as much as to many other things, that we stand indebted for that thorough conviction of the evil state of things in the churches, which has given rise to our association. As for our part, we dare no longer give our assent to such proceedings: we dare no longer concur in expressly asserting, or declaring, any thing in the name of the Lord, that he has not expressly declared in his holy word. And until such time as christians come to see the evil of doing otherwise, we see no rational ground to hope, that there can be either unity, peace, purity or prosperity, in the church of God. Convinced of the truth of this, we would humbly desire to be instrumental in pointing out to our fellow christians, the evils of such conduct And, if we might venture to give our opinion of such proceedings, we would not hesitate to say, that they appear to include three great evils—evils truly great in themselves, and at the same time productive of most evil consequences.

First, to determine expressly, in the name of the Lord, when the Lord has not expressly determined, appears to us a very great evil: see Deut. xviii—20. "The prophet that shall presume to speak a word in my name, which I have not commanded him to speak—even that prophet shall die." The Apostle Paul, no doubt, well aware of this, cautiously distinguishes betwixt his own judgment and the express injunctions of the Lord; See 1st Cor. 7. 25. and 40. Though at the same time, it appear that he was as well convinced of the truth and propriety of his declarations, and of the concurrence of the holy spirit with his judgment, as any of our modern determiners may be; for "I think saith he that I have the spirit of God:" and we doubt much, if the best of them would honestly say more than this: yet we see, that with all this, he would not bind the church with his conclusions; and for this very reason, as he expressly tells us, because, as to the matter on hand, he had no commandment of the Lord. He spoke by permission and not by commandment, as one that had obtained mercy to be faithful—and therefore would not forge his master's name by affixing it to his own conclusions; saying, "The Lord saith, when the Lord had not spoken."

A second evil is, not only judging our brother to be absolutely wrong, because he differs from our opinions; but, more especially, our judging him to be a transgressor of the law in so doing: and of course treating him as such, by censuring, or otherwise exposing him to contempt; or, at least, preferring ourselves before him in our own judgment; saying, as it were, stand by, I am holier than thou.

A third and still more dreadful evil is, when we not only, in this kind of way, judge and set at nought our brother; but, moreover, proceed as a church, acting and judging in the name of Christ; not only to determine that our brother is wrong, because he differs from our determinations: but also in connexion with this, proceed so far as to determine the merits of the cause by rejecting him, or casting him out of the church, as unworthy of a place in her communion;—and thus, as far as in our power, cutting him off from the kingdom of heaven. In proceeding thus, we not only declare, that, in our judgment, our brother is in an error; which we may sometimes do in a perfect consistence with charity: but we also take upon us to judge, as acting in the name and by the authority of Christ, that his error cuts him off from salvation; that continuing such he has no inheritance in the kingdom of Christ and of God. If not, what means our refusing him—our casting him out of the church, which is the kingdom of God in this world? For certainly if a person have no right, according to the Divine Word, to a place in the church of God upon earth, (which we say, he has not, by thus rejecting him) he can have none to a place in the church in heaven—unless we should suppose, that those whom Christ by his word rejects here, he will nevertheless receive hereafter. And surely it is by the word that every church pretends to judge; and it is by this rule, in the case before us, that the person in the judgment of the church stands rejected. Now is not this to all intents and purposes determining the merits of the cause? Do we not conclude that the person's error cuts him off from all ordinary possibility of salvation, by thus cutting him off from a place in the church, out of which there is no ordinary possibility of salvation? Does he not henceforth become to us as a heathen man and a publican? Is he not reckoned amongst the number of those that are without, whom God judgeth? If not, what means such a solemn determination? Is it any thing, or is it nothing, for a person to stand rejected by the church of God? If such rejection confessedly leave the man still in the same safe and hopeful state, as to his spiritual interests; then, indeed, it becomes a matter of mere indifference; for as to his civil and natural privileges, it interferes not with them. But the scripture gives us a very different view of the matter; for there, we see, that those that stand justly rejected by the church on earth, have no room to hope for a place in the church of heaven. "What ye bind on earth shall be bound in heaven" is the awful sanction of the churches judgment, in justly rejecting any person. Take away this, and it has no sanction at all. But the church rejecting, always pretends to have acted justly in so doing; and, if so, whereabouts does it confessedly leave the person rejected, if not in a state of damnation; that is to say, if it acknowledge itself to be a church of Christ, and to have acted justly. If after all, any particular church acting thus, should refuse the foregoing conclusion, by saying, we meant no such thing concerning the person rejected—we only judged him unworthy of a place amongst *us*; and therefore put him away; but there are other churches that may receive him. We would be almost tempted to ask such a church, if those other churches be churches of Christ; and if so, pray what does it account itself? Is it any thing more or better than a church of Christ? And, whether if those other churches do their duty, as faithful churches, any of them would receive the person it had rejected? If it be answered, that, in acting faithfully, none of those other churches either could, or would receive him; then, confessedly, in the judgment of this particular church, the person ought to be universally rejected: but, if otherwise, it condemns itself of having acted unfaithfully, nay, cruelly towards a christian brother, a child of God; in thus rejecting him from the heritage of the Lord; in thus cutting him off from his father's house, as the unnatural brethren did the beloved Joseph. But even suppose some one or other of those unfaithful churches should receive the outcast, would their unfaithfulness in so doing nullify, in the judgment of this more faithful church, its just and faithful decision in rejecting him? If not, then, confessedly, in its judgment, the person still remains under the influence of its righteous sentence, debarred from the kingdom of heaven: that is to say, if it believe the scriptures, that what it has righteously done upon earth, is ratified in heaven. We see no way, that a church acting *thus*, can possibly get rid of this *awful conclusion*; except it acknowledge, that the person it has rejected from its communion, still has a right to the communion of the church; but if it acknowledge *this*—whereabouts does it leave itself, in thus shutting out a fellow-christian, an acknowledged brother, a child of God!! Do we find any parallel for such conduct in the inspired records, except in the case of Diotrephes, of whom the Apostle says, "who loveth to have the pre-eminence among them, receiveth us not—prating against us with malicious words, and not content therewith, neither doth he himself receive the brethren, and forbiddeth them that would, and casteth them out of the church."

But farther, suppose another church should receive this castaway, this person, which this faithful church supposed itself to have righteously rejected: would not, the church so doing, incur the displeasure, nay, even the *censure*, of the church that had rejected him? and, we should think, justly too, if he deserved to be rejected. And would not this naturally produce a schism betwixt the churches? Or, if it be supposed that a schism did already exist, would not this manifestly tend to perpetuate and increase it? If one church receiving those, whom another puts away, will not be productive of schism, we must confess, we cannot tell what would. That church, therefore, must surely act very schismatically—very unlike a church of Christ, which necessarily pre-supposes, or produces schism, in order to shield an oppressed fellow-christian, from the dreadful consequences of its unrighteous proceedings. And is not this confessedly the case with every church, which rejects a person from its communion, while it acknowledges him to be a fellow-christian; and in order to excuse this piece of cruelty, says, he may find refuge some place else; some other church may receive him? For as we have already observed, if no schism did already exist, one church receiving those whom another has rejected, must certainly make one. The same evils also will as justly attach to the conduct of an individual, who refuses, or breaks communion with a church, because it will not receive, or make room for, his private opinions, or self-devised practices, in its public profession and managements.—For, does he not, in this case, actually take upon him to judge the church, which he thus rejects, as unworthy of the communion of christians? And is not this to all intents and purposes declaring it, in his judgment, excommunicate; or at least worthy of excommunication?

Thus have we briefly endeavored to shew our brethren, what evidently appears to us to be the heinous nature and dreadful consequences of that truly latitudinarian principle and practice, which is the bitter root of almost all our divisions; namely, the imposing of our private opinions upon each other, as articles of faith or duty; introducing them into the public profession and practice of the church, and acting upon them, as if they were the express law of Christ, by judging and rejecting our brethren that differ with us in those things; or, at least, by *so* retaining them in our public profession and practice, that our brethren cannot join with us, or we with them, without becoming actually partakers in those things, which they, or we, cannot, in conscience approve; and which the word of God no where expressly enjoins upon us. To cease from all such things, by simply returning to the original standard of christianity—the profession and practice of the primitive church, as expressly exhibited upon the sacred page of New Testament scripture, is the only possible way, that we can perceive, to get rid of those evils. And we humbly think that a uniform agreement in *that* for the preservation of charity would be infinitely preferable to our contentions and divisions: nay, that such a uniformity is the very thing that the Lord requires, if the New Testament be a perfect model—a sufficient formula for the worship discipline and government of the christian church. Let *us* do, as we are there expressly told *they* did, say as *they* said: that is, profess and practise as therein expressly enjoined by precept and precedent, in every possible instance, after *their* approved example; and in so doing we shall realize, and exhibit, all that unity and uniformity, that the primitive church possessed, or that the law of Christ requires. But if after all, our brethren can point out a better way to regain and preserve that christian unity and charity expressly enjoined upon the church of God, we shall thank them for the discovery, and cheerfully embrace it.

Should it still be urged, that this would open a wide door to latitudinarianism, seeing all that profess christianity, profess to receive the holy scriptures; and yet differ so widely in their religious sentiments. We say, let them profess what they will, their difference in religious profession and practice originates in their departure from what is expressly revealed and enjoined; and not in their strict and faithful conformity to it—which is the thing we humbly advise for putting an end to those differences. But you may say, do they not already all agree in the letter, though differing so far in sentiment? However this may be, have they all agreed to make the letter their rule; or rather to make it the subject matter of their profession and practice? Surely no; or else they would all profess and practise the same thing. Is it not as evident as the shining light, that the scriptures exhibit but one and the self same subject matter of profession and practice; at all times, and in all places;—and, that therefore, to say as it declares, and to do as it prescribes, in all its holy precepts, its approved and imitable examples, would unite the christian church in a holy sameness of profession and practice, throughout the whole world? By the christian church throughout the world, we mean the aggregate of such professors, as we have described in props. 1 and 8th, page 7th; even all that mutually acknowledge each other as christians, upon the manifest evidence of their faith, holiness, and charity. It is such only we intend, when we urge the necessity of christian unity. Had only such been all along recognized, as the genuine subjects of our holy religion, there would not, in all probability, have been so much apparent need for human formulas, to preserve an external formality of professional unity, and soundness in the faith: but artificial and superficious characters need artificial means to train and unite them. A manifest attachment to our Lord Jesus Christ in faith, holiness, and charity, was the original criterion of christian character—the distinguishing badge of our holy profession—the foundation and cement of christian unity. But now, alas! and long since, an external name—a mere educational formality of sameness in the profession of a certain standard, or formula of human fabric, with a very moderate degree of, what is called, morality; forms the bond and foundation—the root and reason, of ecclesiastical unity. Take away from such the technia of their profession—the shiboleth of party; and what have they more? What have they left to distinguish, and hold them together? As for the Bible, they are but little beholden to it; they have learned little from it; they know little about it; and therefore depend as little upon it. Nay, they will even tell you, it would be of no use to them without their formula; they could not know a Papist from a Protestant by *it*; that merely by *it*, they could neither keep themselves nor the church right for a single week: you might preach to them what you please; they could not distinguish truth from error. Poor people! it is no wonder they are so fond of their formula. Therefore they that exercise authority upon them, and tell them what they are to believe, and what they are to do, are called benefactors. These are the reverend, and right reverend authors, upon whom they *can*, and *do*, place a more entire and implicit confidence, than upon the holy Apostles and Prophets; those plain, honest, unassuming men, who would never venture to say, or do, any thing, in the name of the Lord, without an express revelation from heaven; and, therefore, were never distinguished by the venerable titles of rabbi, or reverend; but just simple Paul, John, Thomas, &c. *These* were but servants. They did not assume to legislate; and therefore neither assumed, nor receiv-ed, any honorary titles amongst men: but merely such as were de-scriptive of their office. And how, we beseech you, shall this gross and prevalent corruption be purged out of the visible professing church, but by a radical reform; but by returning to the original simplicity, the primitive purity, of the christian institution; and, of course, taking up things just as we find them upon the sacred page. And, who is there, that knows any thing of the present state of the church, who does not perceive, that it is greatly overrun with the aforesaid evils? Or, who that reads his Bible, and receives the impressions, it must necessarily produce upon the receptive mind, by the statements it exhibits; does not perceive, that such a state of things is as distinct from genuine christianity, as oil is from water?

On the other hand, is it not equally as evident, that not one of all the erroneous tenets, and corrupt practices, which have so defamed and corrupted the public profession and practice of christianity, could ever have appeared in the world, had men kept close by the express letter of the divine law—had they thus held fast that form of sound words contained in the holy scriptures, and considered it their duty so to do:—unless they blame those errors and corruptions upon the very form and expression of the scrip-tures; and say, that, taken in their letter and connexion, they immediately, and at first sight, as it were, exhibit the picture they have drawn. Should any be so bold as to assert this, let them pro-duce their performance, the original is at hand; and let them shew us line for line; expression for expression; precept and precedent for practice; without the torture of criticism, inference, or conjec-ture; and then we shall honestly blame the whole upon the Bible; and thank those that will give us an expurged edition of it; call it constitution, or formula, or what you please; that will not be liable to lead the simple unlettered world into those gross mistakes, those contentions, schisms, excommunications and persecutions, which have proved so detrimental and scandalous to our holy religion.

Should it be farther objected, that even this strict literal unifor-mity would neither infer, nor secure unity of sentiment.—It is gran-ted, that, in a certain degree, it would not; nor, indeed, is there any thing, either in scripture, or the nature of things, that should induce us to expect an entire unity of sentiment, in the present imperfect state. The church may, and we believe will, come to such a scriptural unity of faith and practice, that there will be no schism in the body; no self-preferring sect of professed and acknowledged christians, rejecting and excluding their brethren. *This* cannot be, however, till the offensive and excluding causes be removed; and every one knows what *these* are. But that all the members should have the same identical views of all divinely revealed truths; or that there should be no difference of opinion among them, appears to us morally impossible, all things considered. Nor can we conceive, what desirable purpose such a unity of sentiment would serve; except to render useless some of those gracious, self-denying, and compassionate precepts of mutual sympathy and forbearance, which the word of God enjoins upon his people. Such, then, is the imperfection of our present state.—Would to God it might prove, as it ought, a just and humbling counterbalance to our pride! Then, indeed, we would judge one another no more about such matters. We would rather be conscientiously cautious to give no offence; to put no stumbling block, or occasion to fall, in our brother's way. We would then no longer exalt our own opinions and inferences to an equality with express revelation, by condemning and rejecting our brother, for differing with us in those things.

But although it be granted, that the uniformity we plead for, would not secure unity of sentiment; yet we should suppose, that it would be as efficacious for that purpose, as any human expedient, or substitute whatsoever. And here we would ask, have all, or any, of those human compilations been able to prevent divisions, to heal breaches, or to produce and maintain unity of sentiment, even amongst those who have most firmly, and solemnly, embraced them? We appeal for this to the history of all the churches, and to the present divided state of the church at large. What good then have those devisive expedients accomplished, either to the parties that have adopted them, or to the church universal; which might not have been as well secured, by holding fast in profession and practice, that form of sound words, contained in the divine standard; without, at the same time, being liable to any of those dangerous and destructive consequences, which have necessarily ensued upon the present mode? Or will any venture to say, that the scriptures thus kept in their proper place, would not have been amply sufficient, under the promised influence of the divine spirit, to have produced all that unity of sentiment, which is necessary to a life of faith and holiness; and also to have preserved the faith and worship of the church as pure from mixture and error, as the Lord intended; or as the present imperfect state of his people can possibly admit? We should tremble to think that any christian should say, that they would not. And if to use them thus, would be sufficient for those purposes; why resort to other expedients—to expedients, which, from the beginning to this day, have proved utterly insufficient; nay, to expedients, which have always produced the very contrary effects, as experience testifies. Let none here imagine that we set any certain limits to the Divine intention, or to the greatness of his power when we thus speak, as if a certain degree of purity from mixture and error were not designed for the church in this world, or attainable by his people upon earth; except in so far as respects the attainment of an angelic or unerring perfection: much less, that we mean to suggest, that a very moderate degree of unity and purity should content us. We only take it for granted, that such a state of perfection is neither intended, nor attainable in this world, as will free the church from all those weaknesses, mistakes, and mismanagements, from which she will be completely exempted in heaven;—however sound and upright she may now be in her profession, intention, and practice. Neither let any imagine, that we here, or elsewhere suppose, or intend to assert, that human standards are intentionally set up in competition with the Bible; much less, in opposition to it. We fairly understand and consider them as human expedients, or as certain doctrinal declarations of the sense in which the compilers understood the scriptures; designed, and embraced, for the purpose of promoting and securing, that desirable unity and purity, which the Bible alone, without those helps, would be insufficient to maintain and secure. If this be not the sense of those that receive and hold them, for the aforesaid purpose, we should be glad to know what it is. It is, however, in this very sense that we take them up, when we complain of them, as not only unsuccessful, but also as unhappy expedients; producing the very contrary effects. And even suppose it were doubtful, whether or not those helps have produced divisions; one thing at least is certain, they have not been able to prevent them; and now that divisions do exist, it is as certain, that they have no fitness nor tendency to heal them; but the very contrary, as fact and experience clearly demonstrate. What shall we do then to heal our divisions? We must certainly take some other way than the present practice, if they ever be healed; for it expressly says, they must, and shall, be perpetuated forever. Let all the enemies of christianity say amen. But let all christians, continually say, forbid it, O Lord. May the good Lord subdue the corruptions, and heal the divisions of his people. Amen and amen.

After all that has been said, some of our timid brethren may possibly still object, and say; we fear, that without the intervention of some definite creed or formula, you will justly incur the censure of latitudinarianism; for how, otherwise, detect and exclude Arians, Socinians, &c. &c? To such we would reply, that if to profess, inculcate, and practise, neither more nor less, neither any thing else nor otherwise, than the Divine Word expressly declares respecting the entire subject of faith and duty; and simply to rest in *that*, as the expression of our faith, and rule of our practice; will not amount to the profession, and practical exhibition, of Arianism, Socinianism, &c. &c. but merely to one and the self same thing, whatever it may be called; then is the *ground* that we have taken, the *principle* that we advocate, in nowise chargeable with latitudinarianism. Should it be still farther objected that all these sects, and many more, profess to receive the Bible, to believe it to be the word of God; and therefore will readily profess to believe and practise whatever is revealed and enjoined therein; and yet each will understand it his own way, and of course practise accordingly: nevertheless, according to the plan proposed, you receive them all. We would ask, then, do all these profess, and practise, neither more, nor less, than what we read in the Bible—than what is expressly revealed and enjoined therein? If so they all profess and practise the same thing; for the Bible exhibits but one and the self-same thing to all. Or, is it their own inferences and opinions that they, in reality, profess and practise? If so, then upon the ground that we have taken, they stand rejected, as condemned of themselves; for thus professing one thing, when in fact and reality they manifestly practice another. But perhaps you will say, that although a uniformity in profession, and it may be in practice too, might thus be produced; yet still it would amount to no more than merely a uniformity in words, and in the external formalities of practice; while the persons, thus professing and practising, might each entertain his own sentiments, how different soever these might be. Our reply is, if so, they could hurt no body but himself; besides, if persons thus united, professed and practised all the same things, pray, who could tell, that they entertained different sentiments; or even in justice suppose it, unless they gave some evident intimation of it? which, if they did, would justly expose them to censure; or to rejection, if they repented not; seeing the offence, in this case, must amount to nothing less than an express violation of the expressly revealed will of God—to a manifest transgression of the express letter of the law; for we have declared, that except in such a case, no man, in our judgment, has a right to judge, that is, to condemn, or reject, his professing brother.—Here, we presume, there is no greater latitude assumed, or allowed, on either side, than the law expressly determines. But we would humbly ask, if a professed agreement in the terms of any standard be not liable to the very same objection? If, for instance, Arians, Socinians, Arminians, Calvinists, Antinomians, &c. &c. might not all subscribe the Westminster Confession, the Athenasian Creed, or the doctrinal articles of the Church of England. If this be denied, we appeal to historical facts; and, in the mean time, venture to assert, that such things are, and have been done. Or will any say, that a person might not with equal ease, honesty, and consistency, be an Arian, or a Socinian, in his heart, while subscribing the Westminster Confession, or the Athenasian Creed, as while making his unqualified profession to believe every thing that the scriptures declare concerning Christ? to put all that confidence in him; and to ascribe all that glory, honor, thanksgiving, and praise to him, professed, and ascribed to him, in the Divine Word? If you say not, it follows of undeniable consequence, that the wisdom of men, in those compilations, has affected, what the Divine Wisdom either could not, would not, or did not do, in that all-perfect and glorious revelation of his will, contained in the holy Scriptures. Happy emendation! Blessed expedient! Happy, indeed, for the church, that Athenasius arose in the fourth century, to perfect what the holy apostles and prophets had left in such a rude and unfinished state. But if, after all, the Divine Wisdom did not think proper to do any thing more, or any thing else, than is already done in the Sacred Oracles, to settle and determine those important points; who can say that he determined such a thing should be done afterwards? Or has he any where given us any intimation of such an intention?

Let it here be carefully observed that the question before us is about human standards designed to be subscribed, or otherwise solemnly acknowledged, for the preservation of ecclesiastical unity and purity; and therefore of course, by no means applies to the many excellent performances, for the scriptural elucidation and defence of divinely revealed truths, and other instructive purposes. These, we hope, according to their respective merit, we as highly esteem, and as thankfully receive, as our brethren. But farther, with respect to unity of sentiment, even suppose it ever so desirable, it appears highly questionable, whether such a thing can at all be secured, by any expedient whatsoever; especially if we consider, that it necessarily pre-supposes in so far, a unity or sameness of understanding. Or, will any say, that, from the youth of seventeen to the man of fourscore—from the illiterate peasant, up to the learned prelate; all the legitimate members of the church entertain the same sentiments under their respective formulas? If not, it is still but a mere verbal agreement, a mere shew of unity. They say an amen to the same forms of speech, or of sound words, as they are called; without having, at the same time, the same views of the subject; or, it may be, without any determinate views of it at all. And what is still worse, this profession is palmed upon the world, as well as upon the too credulous professors themselves, for unity of sentiment; for soundness in the faith: when, in a thousand instances, they have, properly speaking, no faith at all: that is to say, if faith necessarily pre-supposes a true and satisfactory conviction of the scriptural evidence and certainty of the truth of the propositions we profess to believe. A cheap and easy orthodoxy this, to which we may attain by committing to memory a catechism; or professing our approbation of a formula, made ready to our hand; which we may, or may not have once read over; or even if we have, yet may not have been able to read it so correctly and intelligently, as to clearly understand one single paragraph from beginning to end; much less to compare it with, to search and try it by, the holy Scriptures; to see if these things be so. A cheap and easy orthodoxy this, indeed, to which a person may thus attain, without so much as turning over a single leaf of his Bible; whereas Christ knew no other way of leading us to the knowledge of himself, at least has prescribed no other, but by searching the Scriptures, with reliance upon his holy Spirit. A person may, however, by this short and easy method, become as orthodox as the Apostle Paul (if such superficial professions, such mere hearsay verbal repetitions, can be called orthodoxy) without ever once consulting the Bible; or so much as putting up a single petition for the Holy Spirit to guide him into all truth; to open his understanding to know the Scriptures; for, his form of sound words truly believed, if it happen to be right, must, without more ado, infallibly secure his orthodoxy. Thrice happy expedient! But is there no latitudinarianism in all this? Is not this taking a latitude, in devising ways and means for accomplishing divine and saving purposes, which the Divine law has no where prescribed; for which the Scriptures no where afford us, either precept or precedent? Unless it can be shewn, that making human standards to determine the doctrine, worship, discipline, and government, of the church, for the purpose of preserving her unity and purity; and requiring an approbation of them as a term of communion; is a Scripture institution. Far be it from us, in the mean time, to alledge, that the church should not make every scriptural exertion, in her power, to preserve her unity and purity; to teach and train up her members in the knowledge of all divinely revealed truth; or to say, that the evils, above complained of, attach to all that are in the habits of using the aforesaid helps; or that this wretched state of things, however general, necessarily proceeds from the legitimate use of such; but rather, and entirely, from the abuse of them; which is the very and only thing, that we are all along opposing, when we allude to those subordinate standards.—(An appellation this, by the bye, which appears to us highly paradoxical, if not utterly inconsistent, and full of confusion.)

But however this may be, we are by no means to be understood as at all wishing to deprive our fellow-christians of any necessary and possible assistance to understand the scriptures: or to come to a distinct and particular knowledge of every truth they contain;—for which purpose the Westminster Confession and Catechisms, may, with many other excellent performances, prove eminently useful. But, having served ourselves of these, let our profiting appear to all, by our manifest acquaintance with the Bible; by making our profession of faith and obedience, by declaring its divine dictates, in which we acquiesce as the subject matter and rule of both—in our ability to take the Scripture in its connexion upon these subjects, so as to understand one part of it by the assistance of another—and in manifesting our self knowledge, our knowledge of the way of salvation, and of the mystery of the christian life, in the express light of divine revelation; by a direct and immediate reference to, and correct repetition of, what it declares upon these subjects.—We take it for granted, that no man either knows God, or himself, or the way of salvation, but in so far, as he has heard and understood his voice upon those subjects, as addressed to him in the Scriptures; and that, therefore, whatever he has heard and learned of a saving nature, is contained in the express terms of the

Bible. If so, in the express terms, in and by which, "he hath heard and learned of the Father," let him declare it. This by no means forbids him to use helps: but, we humbly presume, will effectually prevent him from resting either in them or upon them; which is the evil so justly complained of—from taking up with the directory instead of the object to which it directs. Thus will the whole subject of his faith and duty, in so far as he has attained, be express-ly declared, in a "thus saith the Lord." And, is it not worthy of remark, that, of whatever use other books may be, to direct and lead us to the Bible; or to prepare and assist us to understand it; yet the Bible never directs us to any book but itself. When we come forward then as christians to be received by the church, which, properly speaking, has but one book, "For to it were committed the oracles of God;" let us hear of none else. Is it not upon the credible profession of our faith in, and obedience to, its divine contents, that the church is bound to receive applicants for admis-sion? And does not a profession of our faith and obedience, neces-sarily pre-suppose a knowledge of the dictates we profess to believe and obey? Surely, then, we can declare them; and as surely, if our faith and obedience be divine, as to the subject matter, rule, and reason of them, it must be a "thus saith the Lord;" if otherwise, they are merely human; being taught by the precept of men. In the case then before us, that is, examination for church member-ship, let the question no longer be what does any human system say of the primitive or present state of man; of the person, offices, and relations of Christ, &c. &c. or of this, that, or the other duty; but what says the Bible? Were this mode of procedure adopted, how much better acquainted with their Bibles would christians be? What an important alteration would it also make in the education of youth? Would it not lay all candidates for admission into the church under the happy necessity of becoming particularly acquainted with the holy Scriptures? whereas, according to the present practice, thousands know little about them.

One thing still remains that may appear matter of difficulty or objection to some; namely, that such a close adherence to the express letter of the Divine word, as we seem to propose, for the restoration and maintenance of christian unity; would not only interfere with the free communication of our sentiments one to another, upon religious subjects; but must, of course, also neces-sarily interfere with the public preaching and expounding of the Scriptures, for the edification of the church. Such as feel disposed to make this objection, should justly consider that one of a similar nature, and quite as plausible, might be made to the adoption of human standards; especially when made as some of them confess-edly are, "the standard for all matters of doctrine, worship, disci-pline, and government." In such a case it might, with as much justice, at least, be objected to the adopters; you have now no more use for the Bible; you have got another book which you have adopted as a standard for all religious purposes—you have no farther use for explaining the Scriptures, either as to matter of faith or duty; for this you have confessedly done already in your standard, wherein you have determined all matters of this nature. You also profess to hold fast the form of sound words, which you have thus adopted; and therefore you must never open your mouth upon any subject in any other terms than those of your standard. In the mean time, would any of the parties, which has thus adopted its respective standard, consider any of these charges just? If not, let them do as they would be done by. We must confess, however, that for our part, we cannot see how, with any shadow of consistency, some of them could clear themselves, especially of the first; that is to say, if words have any determinate meaning; for certainly it would appear almost, if not altogether, incontrovertible; that a book adopted by any party as its standard for all matters of doctrine, worship, discipline, and government; must be considered as the Bible of that party. And after all that can be said in favor of such a performance, be it called Bible, standard, or what it may; it is neither any thing more nor better, than the judgment, or opinion of the party composing or adopting it; and therefore wants the sanction of a Divine authority; except in the opinion of the party which has thus adopted it. But can the opinion of any party, be it ever so respectable, give the stamp of a Divine authority to its judgments? If not, then every human standard is deficient in this leading, all-important, and indispensable property of a rule, or standard, for the doctrine, worship, discipline, and government of the church of God. But without insisting farther upon the intrinsic and irremediable deficiency of human standards, for the above purpose, (which is undeniably evident, if it be granted that a Divine authority is indispensably necessary to constitute a standard, or rule for divine things: such as is the constitution, and managements; the faith, and worship of the christian church)—we would humbly ask would any of the parties consider as just, the foregoing objections, however conclusive and well founded, all or any of them may appear? We believe they would not. And may we not with equal consistency hold fast the expressly revealed will of God, in the very terms in which it is expressed in his Holy Word, as the very expression of our faith, and express rule of our duty; and yet take the same liberty that they do, notwithstanding their professed and stedfast adherence to their respective standards? We find they do not cease to expound, because they have already expounded, as before alledged; nor yet do they always confine themselves to the express terms of their respective standards; yet they acknowledge them to be their standards, and profess to hold them fast. Yea, moreover, some of them profess, and, if we may conclude from facts, we believe each of them is disposed to defend, by occasional vindications (or testimonies, as some call them,) the sentiments they have adopted, and engrossed in their standards; without, at the same time, requiring an approbation of those occasional performances, as a term of communion. And what should hinder us, or any, adopting the Divine Standard, as aforesaid, with equal consistency to do the same; for the vindication of the divine truths expressly revealed and enjoined therein? To say that we cannot believe and profess the truth; understand one another; inculcate and vindicate the faith and law of Christ; or do the duties incumbent upon christians, or a christian church, without a human standard; is not only saying, that such a standard is quite essential to the very being of christianity, and of course must have existed before a church was, or could be formed: but it is also saying, that without such a standard, the Bible would be quite inadequate, as a rule of faith and duty; or rather, of no use at all; except to furnish materials for such a work—whereas the church of Ephesus, long before we have any account of the existence of such a standard, is not only mentioned, with many others, as in a state of existence; and of high attainments too; but is also commended for her vigilance and fidelity, in detecting and rejecting false apostles. "Thou hast tried them which say they are apostles, and are not, and hast found them liars." But should any pretend to say, that although such performances be not essential to the very being of the church, yet are they highly conducive to its well being and perfection. For the confutation of such an assertion, we would again appeal to church history, and existing facts, and leave the judicious and intelligent christian to determine.

If after all that has been said, any should still pretend to affirm, that the plan we profess to adopt and recommend, is truly latitudinarian, in the worst and fullest sense of the term; inasmuch as it goes to make void all human efforts to maintain the unity and purity of the church, by substituting a vague and indefinite approbation of the Scriptures as an alternative for creeds, confessions, and testimonies; and thereby opens a wide door for the reception of all sorts of characters and opinions into the church. Were we not convinced by experience, that notwithstanding all that has been said, such objections would likely be made; or that some weak persons might possibly consider them as good as demonstration; especially when proceeding from highly influential characters (and there have not been wanting such in all ages to oppose, under various plausible pretences, the unity and peace of the church) were it not for these considerations, we should content ourselves with what we have already advanced upon the whole of the subject, as being well assured, *that* duly attended to, there would not be the least room for such an objection: but to prevent if possible such unfounded conclusions; or if this cannot be done, to caution and assist the too credulous and unwary professor, that he may not be carried away all at once with the high-toned confidence of bold assertion;—we would refer him to the overture for union in truth contained in the foregoing address. Union in truth, amongst all the manifest subjects of grace and truth, is what we advocate. We carry our views of union no farther than *this*; nor do we presume to recommend it upon any other principle than truth alone.

Now surely truth is something certain and definite; if not, who will take upon him to define and determine it? This we suppose God has sufficiently done already in his Holy Word. That men therefore truly receive and make the proper use of the Divine word for walking together in truth and peace, in holiness and charity, is, no doubt, the ardent desire of all the genuine subjects of our holy religion. This we see, however, they have not done, to the awful detriment, and manifest subversion of, what we might almost call, the primary intention of christianity. We dare not therefore follow their example, nor adopt their ruinous expedients. But does it therefore follow, that christians may not, or cannot, take proper steps to ascertain that desirable and preceptive unity, which the Divine word requires, and enjoins? Surely no—at least we have supposed no such thing;—but, on the contrary, have overtured to our brethren, what appears to us undeniably just, and scripturally evident; and which, we humbly think, if adopted and acted upon, would have the desired effect—adopted and acted upon, not indeed as a standard for the doctrine, worship, discipline, and government of the church; for it pretends not to determine these matters; but rather supposes the existence of a fixed and certain standard of divine original; in which every thing that the wisdom of God saw meet to reveal and determine, for *these*, and all other purposes, is expressly defined and determined; betwixt the christian and which, no medium of human determination ought to be interposed. In all this, there is surely nothing like the denial of any lawful effort, to promote and maintain the churches unity; though there be a refusal of the unwarrantable interposition, of an unauthorized and assuming power.

Let none imagine, that we are here determining upon the merits of the overture, to which, in the case before us, we find it necessary to appeal, in our own defence, against the injustice of the supposed charge above specified. To the judgment of our brethren have we referred that matter; and with them we leave it. All we intend, therefore, is to avail ourselves so far, of what we have done, as to shew, that we have no intention whatsoever of substituting a vague indefinite approbation of the Scriptures, as an alternative for creeds, confessions, and testimonies; for the purpose of restoring the church to her original constitutional unity and purity. In avoiding Sylla we would cautiously guard against being wrecked upon the Charybdis. Extremes we are told are dangerous. We therefore suppose a middle way; a safe way; so plainly marked out by unerring wisdom, that, if duly attended to under the Divine direction, the wayfaring men, though fools, need not err therein; and of such is the kingdom of God; "for he hath chosen the foolish things of the world to confound the things that are wise." We therefore conclude, it must be a plain way, a way most graciously and most judiciously adapted to the capacity of the subjects; and consequently not the way of subscribing, or otherwise approving human standards, as a term of admission into his church; as a test and defence of orthodoxy; which even the compilers themselves are not always agreed about; and which nineteen out of twenty of the Lord's people cannot thoroughly understand. It must be a way very far remote from logical subtilties, and metaphysical speculations; and as such we have taken it up, upon the plainest and most obvious principles of divine revelation, and common sense—the common sense, we mean, of christians, exercised upon the plainest and most obvious truths and facts, divinely recorded for their instruction. Hence we have supposed in the first place, the true discrimination of christian character to consist in an intelligent profession of our faith in Christ and obedience to him in all things according to the Scriptures; the reality of which profession is manifested by the holy consistency of the tempers and conduct of the professors, with the express dictates, and approved examples of the Divine word. Hence we have humility, faith, piety, temperance, justice, charity, &c. professed and manifested in the first instance, by the persons' professing with self-application the convincing, humbling, encouraging, pious, temperate, just and charitable doctrines and precepts of the inspired volume, as exhibited and enforced in its holy and approved examples; and the sincerity of this profession evidently manifested, by the consistency of the professor's temper and conduct with the entire subject of his profession; either by an irreproveable conformity like good Zachariah and Elizabeth, which is of all things most desirable; or otherwise, in case of any visible failure, by an apparently sincere repentance, and evident reformation. Such professors, and such only, have we supposed to be, by common consent, truly worthy the christian name. Ask from the one end of heaven to the other, the whole number of such intelligent and consistent professors as we intend, and have described, and, we humbly presume, there will not be found one dissenting voice. They will all acknowledge with one consent, that the true discrimination of christian character consists in these things; and that the radical, or manifest want, of any of the aforesaid properties, completely destroys the character.

We have only here taken for granted, what we suppose no rational professor will venture to deny; namely, that the Divine Word contains an ample sufficiency upon every of the foregoing topics to stamp the above character; if so be, that the impressions which its express declarations are obviously calculated to produce, be truly received; for instance, suppose a person profess to believe, with application to himself, that whole description of human depravity and wretchedness which the Scriptures exhibit of fallen man, in the express declarations and dismal examples of human wickedness therein recorded; contrasted with the holy nature, the righteous requirements, and inflexible justice of an infinitely holy, just, and jealous God; would not the subject matter of such a profession, be amply sufficient to impress the believing mind with the most profound humility, self-abhorrence, and dreadful apprehension of the tremendous effects of sin? Again, should the person profess to believe, in connexion with this, all that the Scriptures declare of the sovereign love, mercy, and condescension of God, towards guilty, depraved, rebellious man, as the same is manifested in Christ, and in all the gracious declarations, invitations, and promises, that are made in and through him, for the relief and encouragement of the guilty, &c. would not all this, taken together, be sufficient to impress the believing mind with the most lively confidence, gratitude, and love? Should this person, moreover, profess that delight and confidence in the Divine Redeemer—that voluntary submission to him—that worship and adoration of him, which the Scriptures expressly declare to have been the habits and practice of his people; would not the subject matter of this profession be amply sufficient to impress the believing mind with that dutiful disposition, with that gracious veneration, and supreme reverence, which the word of God requires? And should not all this taken together satisfy the church, in so far, in point of profession? If not, there is no alternative but a new revelation; seeing that to deny this, is to assert, that a distinct perception, and sincere profession, of whatever the Word declares upon every point of faith and duty, is not only insufficient, as a doctrinal means, to produce a just and suitable impression in the mind of the believing subject; but is also insufficient to satisfy the church, as to a just and adequate profession:—if otherwise, then it will necessarily follow, that not every sort of character, but that one sort only, is admissible upon the principle we have adopted; and, that by the universal consent of all, that we, at least, dare venture to call christians, *this* is acknowledged to be, exclusively, the true christian character. Here then we have a fixed point, a certain description of character, which combines in every professing subject, the scriptural profession, the evident manifestation, of humility, faith, piety, temperance, justice, and charity; instructed by, and evidently answering to, the entire declaration of the Word, upon each of those topics; which, as so many properties, serve to constitute the character. Here, we say, we have a fixed, and at the same time sweeping distinction; which, as of old, manifestly divides the whole world, however other ways distinguished, into but two classes only. "We know," said the Apostle, evidently speaking of such, "that we are of God, and the whole world lieth in wickedness."

Should it be enquired concerning the persons included in this description of character, whether they be Arminians, or Calvinists, or both promiscuously huddled together? It may be justly replied, that, according to what we have proposed, they can be nominally neither, and of course not both; for we call no man master on earth; for one is our master, even Christ and all we are brethren—are christians by profession: and, as such, abstract speculation and argumentative theory make no part, either of our profession, or practice. Such professors, then, as we intend, and have described, are just what their profession and practice make them to be; and this we hope has been scripturally, and, we might add, satisfactorily defined; in so far, at least, as the limits of so brief a performance would admit. We also entertain the pleasing confidence, that the plan of procedure which we have ventured to suggest, if duly attended to, if fully reduced to practice, would necessarily secure to the professing subject all the advantages of divinely revealed truth, without any liability to conceal, to diminish, or to misrepresent it; as it goes immediately to ascribe every thing to God respecting his sovereignty, independence, power, wisdom, goodness, justice, truth, holiness, mercy, condescension, love and grace, &c. which is ascribed to him in his word; as also to receive whatever it declares concerning the absolute dependence of the poor, guilty, depraved, polluted creature, upon the Divine will, power, and grace, for every saving purpose: a just perception and correspondent profession of which, according to the Scriptures, is supposed to constitute that fundamental ingredient in christian character, true evangelical humility. And so of the rest. Having thus, we hope, scripturally and evidently determined the character with the proper mode of ascertaining it, to the satisfaction of all concerned: we next proceed to affirm with the same scriptural evidence, that amongst such, however situated, whether in the same or similar associations, there ought to be no schisms, no uncharitable divisions; but that they ought all mutually to receive, and acknowledge each other as brethren. As to the truth of this assertion, they are all likewise agreed without one dissenting voice. We next suggest that for this purpose they ought all to walk by the same rule, to mind and speak the same thing, &c. and that this rule is, and ought to be, the Divine Standard. Here again we presume there can be no objection, no, not a single dissenting voice. As to the rule itself, we have ventured to alledge that the New Testament is the proper and immediate rule, directory, and formula, for the New Testament church, and for the particular duties of christians; as the Old Testament was for the Old Testament church, and for the particular duties of the subject under that dispensation; at the same time by no means excluding the old as fundamental to, illustrative of, and inseparably connected with, the new; and as being every way of equal authority, as well as of an entire sameness with it, in every point of moral natural duty; though not immediately our rule, without the intervention and coincidence of the new; in which our Lord has taught his people, by the ministry of his holy Apostles, all things whatsoever they should observe and do, till the end of the world. Thus we come to the one rule, taking the Old Testament as explained and perfected by the new, and the new as illustrated and enforced by the old; assuming the latter as the proper and immediate directory for the christian church, as also for the positive and particular duties of christians, as to all things whatsoever they should observe and do. Farther, that in the observance of this Divine rule—this authentic and infallible directory, all such may come to the desirable coincidence of holy unity and uniformity of profession and practice; we have overtured that they all speak, profess, and practise, the very same things, that are exhibited upon the sacred page of New Testament Scripture, as spoken and done by the Divine appointment and approbation; and that this be extended to every possible instance of uniformity, without addition or diminution; without introducing any thing of private opinion, or doubtful disputation, into the public profession or practice of the church. Thus and thus, have we overtured to all intents and purposes, as may be clearly seen by consulting the overture itself; in which, however, should any thing appear not sufficiently explicit, we flatter ourselves it may be fully understood, by taking into consideration what has been variously suggested, upon this important subject, throughout the whole of these premises; so that if any due degree of attention be paid, we should think it next to impossible, that we could be so far misunderstood, as to be charged with Latitudinarianism in any usual sense of the word. Here we have proposed but one description of character as eligible, or indeed as at all admissible to the rights and privileges of christianity. This description of character we have defined by certain and distinguishing properties, which not only serve to distinguish it from every other; but in which all the real subjects themselves are agreed, without one exception: all such being mutually and reciprocally acknowledged by each other, as legitimate members of the church of God. All these moreover agreeing in the indispensable obligation of their unity; and in the one rule by which it is instructed—and also in the preceptive necessity of an entire uniformity in their public profession and managements for promoting and preserving this unity—that there should be no schism in the body; but that all the members should have the same care one for another—yet in many instances unhappily, and, we may truly say, involuntarily differing through mistake and mismanagement; which it is our humble desire and endeavour to detect and remove, by obviating every thing that causeth difference; being persuaded that as truth is one and indivisible wherever it exists; so all the genuine subjects of it, if disentangled from artificial impediments, must and will necessarily fall in together, be all on one side, united in one profession, acknowledge each other as brethren, and love as children of the same family. For this purpose we have overtured a certain and determinate application of the rule, to which we presume there can be no reasonable objection, and which, if adopted and acted upon, must, we think, infallibly produce the desired effect; unless we should suppose that to say and do, what is expressly said and done before our eyes upon the sacred page, would offend the believer; or that a strict uniformity, an entire scriptural sameness in profession and practice, would produce divisions and offences amongst those, who are already united in one spirit, one Lord, one faith, one baptism, one hope of their calling, and in one God and father of all, who is above all, and through all, and in them all; as is confessedly the case with all of this character throughout all the churches. To induce to this we have also attempted to call their attention to the heinous nature and awful consequences of schism, and to that evil anti-scriptural principle from which it necessarily proceeds. We have likewise endeavored to shew, we humbly think with demonstrable evidence, that there is no alternative, but either to adopt that scriptural uniformity we have recommended, or else continue as we are, bewildered in schisms, and overwhelmed with the accursed evils inseparable from such a state. It remains now with our brethren to determine upon the whole of these premises; to adopt, or to reject, as they see cause: but, in the mean time, let none impeach us with the latitudinarian expedient of substituting a vague indefinite approbation of the Holy Scriptures, as an alternative for the present practice of making the approbation of human standards a term of communion; as it is undeniably evident that nothing can be farther from our intention. Were we to judge of what we humbly propose and urge as indispensably necessary for the reformation and unity of the church, we should rather apprehend, that there was reason to fear a charge of a very different nature; namely, that we aimed at too much strictness, both as to the description of character which we say ought only to be admitted, and also as to the use and application of the rule. But should this be the case, we shall cheerfully bear with it; as being fully satisfied, that not only the common sentiment of all apparently sincere, intelligent and practical christians is on our side; but that also the plainest and most ample testimonies of the inspired volume sufficiently attest the truth and propriety of what we plead for, as essential to the scriptural unity and purity of the christian church; and this we humbly presume is what we should incessantly aim at. It would be strange, indeed, if in contending earnestly for the faith once delivered to the saints, we should overlook those fruits of righteousness—that manifest humility, piety, temperance, justice and charity—without which faith itself is dead being alone. We trust we have not so learned Christ: if so be, we have been taught by him, as the truth is in Jesus, we must have learned a very different lesson indeed. While we would therefore insist upon an entire conformity to the Scriptures in profession, that we might all believe and speak the same things, and thus be perfectly joined together in the same mind and in the same judgment; we would, with equally scrupulosity, insist upon, and look for, an entire conformity to them in practice, in all those whom we acknowledge as our brethren in Christ. "By their fruits ye shall know them." "Not every one that saith unto me, Lord, Lord, shall enter into the kingdom of heaven: but he that doeth the will of my father which is in heaven. Therefore whosoever heareth those sayings of mine, and doeth them not, shall be likened unto a foolish man which built his house upon the sand. Woe unto you scribes and pharisees, hypocrites, for ye say and do not." We therefore conclude, that t oadvocate unity alone, howevery desirable in itself without at the same time purging the church of apparently unsanctified characters—even of all that cannot shew their faith by their works, would be, at best, but a poor, superficial, skin-deep reformation. It is from such characters, then, as the proposed reformation, if carried into effect, would entirely deprive of a name and a place in the church, that we have the greatest reason to apprehend a determined and obstinate opposition. And alas! there are very many of this description; and in many places, of considerable influence.—But neither should this discourage us, when we consider the expressly revealed will of God upon this point, Ezek. 44, 6—9, with Math. 13, 15—17, I Cor. 5, 6—13, with many other Scriptures. Nor, in the end, will the multitude of unsanctified professors, which the proposed reformation would necessarily exclude, have any reason to rejoice in the unfaithfulness of those, that either through ignorance, or for filthy lucre sake, indulged them with a name and place in the church of God. These unfaithful stewards—these now mistaken friends, will one day be considered by such, as their most cruel and treacherous enemies. These, then, are our sentiments, upon the entire subject of church reformation; call it latitudinarianism, or puritanism, or what you please: and *this* is the reformation for which we plead. Thus, upon the whole, have we briefly attempted to point out those evils, and to prevent those mistakes, which we earnestly desire to see obviated for the general peace, welfare, and prosperity of the church of God. Our dear brethren, giving credit to our sincere and well meant intention, will charitably excuse the imperfections of our humble performance; and by the assistance of their better judgment correct those mistakes, and supply those deficiencies, which in a first attempt of this nature may have escaped our notice. We are sorry, in the mean time, to have felt a necessity of approaching so near, the borders of controversy, by briefly attempting to answer objections which we plainly foresaw would, through mistake or prejudice, be made against our proceedings; controversy making no part of our intended plan. But such objections and surmises having already reached our ears from different quarters, we thought it necessary to attend to them; that, by so doing, we might not only prevent mistakes, but also save our friends the trouble of entering into verbal disputes in order to remove them; and thus prevent, as much as possible, that most unhappy of all practices sanctioned by the plausible pretence of zeal for the truth;—religious controversy amongst professors. We would therefore humbly advise our friends to concur with us in our professed and sincere intention to avoid this evil practice. Let it suffice to put into the hands of such as desire information what we hereby publish for that purpose. If this, however, should not satisfy, let them give in their objections in writing: we shall thankfully receive, and seriously consider, with all due attention, whatever comes before us in this way; but verbal controversy we absolutely refuse. Let none imagine, that, by so saying, we mean to dissuade christians from affording all the assistance they can to each other as humble enquirers after truth. To decline this friendly office would be to refuse the performance of an important duty. But certainly there is a manifest difference between speaking the truth in love for the edification of our brethren; and attacking each other with a spirit of controversial hostility, to confute, and prove each other wrong.

We believe it is rare to find one instance of this kind of arguing, that does not terminate in bitterness. Let us therefore cautiously avoid it. Our Lord says, Math. 18, 7, woe unto the world because of offences. Scott in his incomparable work lately published in this country, called his Family Bible, observes in his notes upon this place, 'that our Lord here intends all these evils within the 'church, which prejudice men's minds against his religion, or any 'doctrines of it. The scandalous lives, horrible oppressions, cru- 'elties, and iniquities of men called christians; their divisions and 'bloody contentions; their idolatries and superstitions, are, at this 'day, the *great offences* and *causes of stumbling*, to Jews, Mahome- 'tans, and Pagans, in all the four quarters of the globe; and they 'furnish infidels of every description, with their most dangerous 'weapons against the truth. The acrimonious controversies, agi- 'tated amongst those who agree in the principle doctrines of the 'gospel, and their mutual contempt and revilings of each other, 'together with the extravagant notions and wicked practices found 'among them, form the grand prejudice in the minds of multitudes 'against evangelical religion; and harden the hearts of hereticks, 'pharisees, disguised infidels, and careless sinners, against the 'truths of the gospel. In these and numberless other ways, it may 'be said, "woe be to the world because of offences;" for, the devil, 'the sower of these tares, makes use of them in deceiving the na- 'tions of the earth, and in murdering the souls of men. In the 'present state of human nature it must needs be, that such offences 'should intervene; and God has wise and righteous reasons for 'permitting them; yet we should consider it as the greatest of 'evils, to be accessary to the destruction of souls; and an awful 'woe is denounced against every one, whose delusions or crimes 'thus stumble men, and set them against the only method of salva- 'tion." We conclude with an extract from the Boston Anthology, which, with too many of the same kind that might be adduced, furnish a mournful comment upon the text—we mean, upon the sorrowful subject of our woful divisions and corruptions. The following reply to the Rev. Mr. Cram, missionary from Massachusetts to the Senecas, was made by the principle chiefs and warriors of the six nations in council assembled at Buffaloe creek, state of New-York, in the presence of the agent of the United States for Indian affairs, in the summer of 1805. 'I am come, brethren,' said the missionary, 'to enlighten your minds, and to instruct you how to 'worship the Great Spirit, agreeably to his will; and to preach to 'you the gospel of his son Jesus Christ. There is but one way to 'serve God, and if you do not embrace the right way you cannot be 'happy hereafter.' To which they reply, 'Brother, we understand 'that your religion is written in a book. You say that there is but 'one way to worship and serve the Great Spirit. If there be but 'one religion, why do you white people differ so much about it? 'Why not all agree as you can all read the book? Brother, we do 'not understand these things. We are told your religion was given 'to your forefathers; we also have a religion which was given to 'our forefathers. It teaches us to be *thankful* for all the favors we 'receive—to *love* one another, and to be *united*. We never quarrel 'about religion. We are told you have been preaching to the white 'people in this place. Those people are our neighbors; we are 'acquainted with them. We will wait a little to see what effect 'your preaching has upon *them*. If we find it does them good, 'makes them *honest*, and *less* disposed to cheat Indians; we will 'then consider again of what you have said.' Thus closed the conference! Alas! poor people! how do our divisions and corruptions stand in your way? What a pity that you find us not upon original ground, such as the Apostles left the primitive churches! Had we but exhibited to you their unity and charity; their humble, honest, and affectionate deportment towards each other, and towards all men; you would not have had those evil and shameful things to object to our holy religion, and to prejudice your minds against it. But your conversion, it seems, awaits our reformation—awaits our return to primitive unity and love. To this may the God of mercy speedily restore us, both for your sakes and our own; that *his way* may be known upon earth, and his saving health among all nations. Let the people praise thee, O God; let all the people praise thee. Amen and amen.

POSTSCRIPT.

THE publication of the foregoing address has been delayed much longer than was at first expected, through an unforeseen difficulty of obtaining paper of the quality intended. This difficulty and detention has also interfered with the publication of the discourse delivered at the first general meeting of the society, held in Washington, November 2d, in pursuance of the 7th resolution; (see page 4th) which discourse the committee has requested Mr. Campbell to have published, as soon as conveniency may serve for that purpose. At the first monthly meeting of the committee, December 14, (see resolution 6th, page 4,) the following considerations and proposals for the better carrying into effect the highly interesting and comprehensive object of the foregoing address, were submitted, and received with approbation, viz. That considering the very extensive and important design for which we have associated, as specified in the foregoing pages; wherein we propose and urge the necessity of a thorough reformation in all things civil and religious according to the word of God, as a duty of indispensable obligation upon all the highly favored subjects of the gospel; and especially in this country, where the Lord has been graciously pleased to favor his professing people with such ample opportunities, for the prosecution and accomplishment of those blessed and desirable purposes; it behoves us, in so doing, to exert our utmost energies, in every possible direction that may conduce to render successful, this arduous and important undertaking.

Besides what has been already agreed upon, and recommended in the foregoing pages, there yet remains two things of apparently great importance for promoting the grand object of our association; which this committee would do well to consider, as they seem to fall within the prescribed limits of its operation; and also as it appears to be within the compass of its power to take effectual steps for ascertaining the advantages, which the things intended, if duly executed, would appear obviously calculated to produce. The first of these is a catechetical exhibition of the fulness and precision of the holy scriptures upon the entire subject of christianity—an exhibition of that complete system of faith and duty expressly contained in the sacred oracles; respecting the doctrine, worship, discipline, and government of the christian church. The second thing intended is a periodical publication, for the express purpose of detecting and exposing the various anti-christian enormities, innovations and corruptions, which infect the christian church; which counteract and oppose the benign and gracious tendency of the gospel—the promotion and establishment of the Redeemer's kingdom upon earth; by means of which an infinitely good and gracious God has designed to bless the nations—to ameliorate as much as possible the present wretched and suffering state of mankind; upon the success and establishment of which depends the spiritual and temporal welfare of every individual of the human family. Whatever therefore has a tendency to undermine, or in anywise to counteract and oppose the interests of this benign and gracious institution of infinite goodness and mercy, becomes an evil of no small magnitude, how trifling soever it might otherwise appear. "Take us the foxes, the little foxes that spoil our vines; for our vines have tender grapes." Cant 2, 15. Such a publication from the nature and design of it, might with propriety be denominated The Christian Monitor.

The former of these, namely, a catechetical exhibition of the fulness and precision of the sacred scriptures upon the entire subject of faith and duty would, if duly executed, demonstrably evince their perfect sufficiency independent of human inference—of the dictates of private judgment; and would, at the same time, inevitably lead the professing subject to learn every thing, respecting his faith and duty, at the mouth of God, without any reference to human authority—to the judgment or opinions of men. This would, at once, free the great majority of professing christians from that perplexing uncertainty and implicit faith, to which so many of them are unhappily subjected, by the interposition of human definitions and opinions between them and the Bible; many of which are erroneous; and also many of which they are unable to understand, so as to determine certainly, whether they be just and scriptural, or not. By such an exhibition, therefore, would professed christians be delivered, not only from these perplexing and dangerous evils ("their faith," by this means, "no longer standing in the wisdom of men, but in the power of God; not in the words which man's wisdom teacheth, but which the Holy Ghost teacheth,") but they would also become better acquainted with the scriptures of truth—with that all-important word which shall judge them in the last day:—and, at the same time, would come to possess a much more ample and enlarged view of the alone sufficiency and perfection of the scriptures themselves: advantages these of no small moment to the interests of christianity. A performance of this nature might, with apparent propriety, be called the Christian Catechism.

In consequence of these considerations it is proposed and intended, with the approbation and under the patronage of the Christian Association of Washington, to forward as fast as possible the publication of the works above described, viz. To publish in numbers monthly by subscription, commencing with the year 1810—a work entitled the Christian Monitor, each number to consist of 24 pages, stitched in blue, price 12½ cents, type and paper as in the foregoing address. The numbers to be delivered to the subscribers at the respective places appointed for distribution. The execution of this work to commence as soon as 500 annual subscribers can be obtained. It is to be understood, that a number for each month will be duly delivered; though it is probable that the first two or three numbers may come together, as it is not likely, that the number of subscribers above specified can be obtained in time to commence the publication in the month of January, now so near at hand.

Also to prepare for the press and proceed to publish as soon as a competent number of subscribers can be obtained, a work entitled the Christian Catechism, to consist of upwards of one hundred pages, type and paper as above, price 50 cents. There will be prefixed to this work a dissertation upon the perfection and sufficiency of the holy scriptures; in which care will be taken to detect and expose, that unhappy ingenuity, which has been so frequently exerted to pervert and wrest them, from the obvious purpose for which they were graciously designed.

ERRATA—Page 2, line 5, the comma point should be after agreed, and not after upon.

Do. line 7, for titled read designated.

Page 7, line 15, for spurious read specious.

Page 18, line 3, for grounds read ground.

Page 29, line 23, for preaching read practising.

Page 32, line 39, for would read could.

A Collation of the *Declaration and Address:* Textual Variants in the First and Second Editions

Ernest C. Stefanik

The following critical apparatus catalogues and classifies the emendations to the text of the first edition of Thomas Campbell's *Declaration and Address* (Washington, Pa.: Washington Christian Association, 1809) as published in the second edition, in Alexander Campbell's *Memoirs of Elder Thomas Campbell* (Cincinnati: H. S. Bosworth, 1861). That only one edition of the book was published in the author's lifetime does not obviate the need for such an analysis of the text. The Facsimile Edition (Pittsburgh, Pa.: Centennial Committee, 1908), containing TC's autograph corrections, indicates that the author recognized the need for revision in the word forms, though not in the structure and sense of this work. After a half century, Alexander Campbell (hereinafter AC) was not content to merely reprint the *D&A.* With his considerable editorial skills, he left his own imprint on the work as he attempted to resolve matters that he considered problematical in the text. This is not to suggest that AC attempted to reshape the content with editorial hammer strokes; however, he certainly did apply a coat of editorial polish as he presented this foundational work to a second generation of Disciples. Perhaps the collation reveals more about editorial preferences than authorial intentions.

In categorizing the variants I have, in general, followed the classes advanced by Sir Walter Greg in his theory of proof-texts. The *substantives* (words as meaningful units, or diction) include substitution of one word for another; alteration in word order; addition or deletion of words; change in number, case, or tense (himself-themselves, churches-church's, came-come); expansion of abbreviations; homonyms and near-homonyms (principal-principle, idol-idle, affect-effect). Misspellings and probable typographical errors are classified not as substantives, but as accidentals. The *accidentals* (forms that words take) include spelling, punctuation, capitalization, and typography. In the category of spelling are archaic to modern spelling (hath-has, ye-you, thou-you, amongst-among, betwixt-between, shew-show); British and American conventions (endeavour-endeavor, centre-center); probable typographical errors or misspellings (fraction-faction, howevery-however, Gods-God's); words with accepted variants (toward-towards, farther-further, beat-beaten); compounds (any where-anywhere, good will-good-will); contractions (tho'-though); and changes in Scripture reference notations. A summary of the textual variants in the two editions of the *D&A* reveals the following:

Legend	Category	Occurrences
{D}	Diction	94
{C}	Capitalization	577
{P}	Punctuation	1,665
{S}	Spelling	410
{T}	Typography	14
	TOTAL	2,760

The publisher's note to the Facsimile Edition states:

> It shows a few corrections made with a quill pen by its author and many more revision marks at the hand of his illustrious son, when he gave it to the printers to republish in his *Life of Thomas Campbell*. Each compositor of that work was immortalized by having his name written in pencil on the margin opposite the beginning of his "take."

Unfortunately, the publisher does not indicate the source of the assertion that TC made only "a few corrections" while AC made "many more revision marks." I have serious doubts about the accuracy of the statement since there are approximately 115 corrections in TC's copy, whereas this collation reveals 2,760 variants in the second edition of the *D&A*. If AC did not include *all* of his emendations in his father's copy of the book for the printer, why should we assume that he included a fraction (less than 5 percent) of them there? Certainly a few of the revision marks are non-authorial, as they relate to insertion points for the editorial notes of the second edition and notes for the compositors. It remains for an expert in manuscripts to examine the copy held at Bethany College and determine who was responsible for the corrections. In the meantime, my working hypothesis is that the autograph corrections for the substantives and accidentals are, with few exceptions, those of TC, and that AC made his emendations on the proof-sheets. While it is also possible that the alterations were the work of an editor at H. S. Bosworth, or of Robert Richardson as his father-in-law's assistant in the project, AC as editor of the *Memoirs of Elder Thomas Campbell* would have approved the editorial choices. Whatever the resolution of this matter, I have identified the autograph corrections by the markers (TC) and (AC).

Grateful acknowledgement is made to Hans Rollmann for his suggestions, criticisms, and encouragement. His interest in this project has helped to shape the collation and to improve its utility as a critical tool for the study of the *D&A*. Thanks also to Mary Walsh for her careful proofreading of the first edition against the facsimile edition.

Page.Line 1st Ed.		Page.Line 2nd Ed.	First Edition [Second Edition
2.1	|	25.1	AT [[AT {P}{T}
2.1	|	25.1	Buffaloe, [Buffalo, {S}
2.3	|	25.2	denominations; [denominations, {P}
2.4	|	25.3	gospel [Gospel {C}
2.4	|	25.3	ministry; [ministry, {P}
2.5	|	25.3	agreed [agreed, {P} (TC)
2.5	|	25.3	upon, [upon {P} (TC)
2.6	|	25.4	herein after [hereinafter {S}
2.7	|	25.5	titled [designated {D} (TC)
2.7	|	25.5	above— [above, {P}
2.9	|	25.7	together; [together, {P}
2.10	|	25.7	Mr. [Elder {D} (TC)
2.11	|	25.8	gospel, [Gospel, {C}
2.13	|	25.9	association: [Association; {C}{P}
2.14	|	25.10	declaration [Declaration {C}
2.15	|	25.10	address, [Address, {C}
2.15	|	25.11	printed [printed, {P}
2.16	|	25.11	expence [expense, {S}{P}
2.17	|	25.12	September [—SEPTEMBER {T}{P}
2.17	|	25.12	1809. [1809.] {P}
3.T	|	25.T	&C. [ETC. {S} (AC)
3.2	|	25.14	churches [Churches {C}
3.2	|	25.14	western country [Western country {C} (TC) [1]
3.4	|	25.16	christian [Christian {C}
3.4	|	25.16	world; [world, {P}
3.5	|	26.1	act [act, {P} (TC)
3.7	|	26.3	Standard; [standard; {C}
3.8	|	26.3	divinely [Divinely {C}
3.8	|	26.4	conformed; [conformed, {P}
3.10	|	26.6	brother: [brother; {P}
3.10	|	26.6	but that every [every {D} (TC)
3.12	|	26.8	judgment;— [judgment— {P}
3.12	|	26.8	God—We [God. We {P}
3.13	|	26.9	divine [Divine {C}
3.13	|	26.10	all [all, {P}
3.15	|	26.12	it: [it; {P}
3.15	|	26.12	that [that, {P}
3.15	|	26.12	therefore [therefore, {P}
3.20	|	26.17	are [are, {P}

Page.Line 1st Ed.		Page.Line 2nd Ed.	First Edition [Second Edition
3.20	|	26.17	therefore [therefore, {P}
3.22	|	26.19	every thing [everything {S}
3.22	|	26.19	and, [and {P}
3.23	|	26.21	things; [things, {P}
3.24	|	26.22	have [take {D} (TC)
3.26	|	26.23	nature, [nature {P}
3.27	|	26.24	christians; [Christians; {C}
3.29	|	26.27	measures, [measures {P}
3.30	|	27.2	churches;— [Churches: {C} {P}
3.31	|	27.2	purity, [purity {P}
3.31	|	27.3	church [Church {C}
3.34	|	27.5	amidst [amid {S}
3.34	|	27.6	rancour [rancor {S}
3.36	|	27.8	any where, [anywhere {S} {P}
3.37	|	27.9	word; [word, {P}
3.37	|	27.9	and to-day, [to-day, {D} (TC)
3.38	|	27.9	for ever. [forever. {S}
3.39	|	27.11	that [that, {P}
4.1	|	27.11	men, [men {P}
4.2	|	27.12	church [Church {C}
4.2	|	27.13	God, [God {P}
4.2	|	27.13	farther [further {S}
4.3	|	27.14	to, [to {P}
4.3	|	27.14	by, [by {P}
4.4	|	27.15	divine [Divine {C}
4.4	|	27.15	rule: [rule; {P}
4.4	|	27.15	The [the {C}
4.6	|	27.17	alone [alone, {P}
4.6	|	27.17	word [word, {P}
4.6	|	27.18	salvation— [salvation; {P}
4.8	|	27.20	Lord.— [Lord. {P}
4.11	|	27.24	Washington— [Washington, {P}
4.12	|	27.25	christianity, [Christianity, {C}
4.16	|	27.30	Ministry, [ministry, {C}
4.19	|	27.32	And [And, {P}
4.19	|	27.33	also [also, {P}
4.19	|	27.33	Holy [holy {C}
4.21	|	27.34	society [Society {C}
4.27	|	28.6	society [Society {C}
4.27	|	28.7	church, [Church, {C}

Page.Line 1st Ed.		Page.Line 2nd Ed.	First Edition [Second Edition
4.30	|	28.9	relation: [relation; {P}
4.31	|	28.10	church [Church {C}
4.31	|	28.11	association;— [associa- tion; {P}
4.32	|	28.11	church [Church {C}
4.34	|	28.14	purpose: [purpose, {P}
4.36	|	28.16	society, [Society, {C}
4.37	|	28.17	christianity, [Christianity, {C}
4.40	|	28.20	diligence;— [diligence; {P}
4.41	|	28.22	christianity, [Christianity, {C}
4.42	|	28.23	any thing [anything {S}
4.44	|	28.25	christian [Christian {C}
4.45	|	28.25	church— [Church, {C} {P}
4.45	|	28.26	or, [or {P}
4.45	|	28.26	any thing, [anything {S} {P}
4.45	|	28.26	christian [Christian {C}
4.45	|	28.26	faith, [faith {P}
4.46	|	28.27	cannot [can not {S}
4.46	|	28.27	thus ["Thus {P} {C}
4.46	|	28.27	Lord [Lord, {P}
4.47	|	28.28	precedent. [precedent." {P}
4.48	|	29.1	standing [Standing {C}
4.48	|	29.1	committee [Committee {C}
5.2	|	29.4	business, [business {P}
5.2	|	29.4	society. [Society. {C}
5.2	|	29.5	committee [Committee {C}
5.4	|	29.7	society [Society {C}
5.5	|	29.8	institu- tution— [institution, {S} {P}
5.7	|	29.10	society, [Society, {C}
5.7	|	29.10	committee [Committee {C}
5.8	|	29.11	*pro re nota* [special {D} (TC)
5.9	|	29.12	society [Society {C}
5.9	|	29.12	viz. [viz.: {P}
5.9	|	29.13	On [on {C}
5.11	|	29.14	half yearly [half-yearly {S}
5.16	|	29.20	society [Society {C}
5.18	|	30.2	society— [Society; {C} {P}
5.19	|	30.3	society [Society {C}
5.19	|	30.4	half yearly [half-yearly {S}
5.20	|	30.5	society, [Society, {C}
5.21	|	30.6	Churches [Church's {D} (TC)

Page.Line 1st Ed.	Page.Line 2nd Ed.	First Edition [Second Edition
5.21	30.6	His [his {C}
5.23	30.8	christianity; [Christianity; {C}
5.24	30.9	ministers, [ministers {P}
5.25	30.11	of, [of {P}
5.25	30.11	society, [Society, {C}
5.27	30.12	gospel, [Gospel, {C}
5.28	30.14	Standard [standard {C}
5.28	30.14	aforesaid— [aforesaid; {P}
5.28	30.14	and, that [and that, {P}
5.30	30.16	towards [toward {S}
5.30	30.16	connexion [connection {S}
5.30	30.17	society [Society, {C} {P}
6.T	30.T	&c. [ETC. {S} (AC)
6.4	30.22	BRETHREN, [BRETHREN: {P} AC)
6.5	30.23	THAT [That {T}
6.5	30.23	design, [design {P}
6.5	30.23	tendency, [tendency {P}
6.6	30.24	religion, [religion {P}
6.9	30.27	christianity. [Christianity. {C}
6.9	30.28	Author [author {C}
6.11	30.29	"glory ["Glory {C}
6.11	31.1	and, on [and on {P}
6.11	31.1	earth, [earth {P}
6.11	31.1	good will [good-will {S}
6.12	31.1	towards [toward {S}
6.12	31.2	divine [Divine {C}
6.14	31.4	expressly [expressively {D}
6.16	31.6	attained; [attained, {P}
6.16	31.6	degree, [degree {P}
6.17	31.7	God, [God {P}
6.17	31.7	men, [men {P}
6.18	31.8	and [and, {P}
6.18	31.9	time [time, {P}
6.21	31.12	another; [another, {P}
6.22	31.12	cannot [can not {S}
6.22	31.13	justifiable, [justifiable {P}
6.23	31.14	endeavours, [endeavors {S} {P}
6.27	31.18	persecutions!!! [persecution!!! {D}
6.27	31.19	must [must, {P}
6.29	31.20	exist, [exist; {P}

Page.Line 1st Ed.		Page.Line 2nd Ed.	First Edition [Second Edition
6.29	|	31.20	Apostle, [apostle, {C}
6.30	|	31.22	these [those {D}
6.34	|	31.26	neighbourhoods [neighborhoods {S}
6.34	|	31.26	christians [Christians {C}
6.36	|	31.28	gospel [Gospel {C}
6.36	|	31.28	settlements, [settle- ments {P}
6.37	|	31.29	country, [country {P}
6.38	|	31.30	gospel [Gospel {C}
6.38	|	31.30	ministry; [ministry, {P}
6.38	|	31.31	hea- thenism: [heathenism, {P}
6.39	|	31.31	churches [Churches {C}
6.39	|	31.32	divisions, [divisions {P}
6.40	|	31.32	cannot [can not {S}
6.40	|	31.32	ministers; [min- isters, {P}
6.40	|	31.33	or, [or {P}
6.41	|	31.33	themselves, [themselves {P}
6.41	|	31.34	Severals [Several, {S} {P}
6.42	|	31.34	time [time, {P}
6.42	|	32.1	gospel, [Gospel, {C}
7.1	|	32.2	ad- vantage [advantage, {P}
7.1	|	32.3	heathens.— [heathens. {P}
7.2	|	32.4	dispensa- tions [dispensa- tion {D}
7.5	|	32.7	amongst [among {S}
7.5	|	32.8	christians, [Christians, {C}
7.7	|	32.9	world;— [world; {P}
7.10	|	33.1	purposes; [purposes, {P}
7.12	|	33.4	churches, [Churches, {C}
7.15	|	34.1	spurious [specious {D} (TC)
7.15	|	34.1	pretence, [pretense, {S}
7.16	|	34.3	church, [Church {C} {P}
7.17	|	34.4	base, [base {P}
7.19	|	34.6	scriptural [Scriptural {C}
7.20	|	34.7	church [Church {C}
7.20	|	34.7	God; [God, {P}
7.20	|	34.8	which, [which {P}
7.22	|	34.9	woeful [woful {S}
7.23	|	34.10	divine [Divine {C}
7.24	|	34.12	gospel [Gospel {C}
7.25	|	34.13	ordinances; [ordinances, {P}
7.27	|	34.15	scandals; [scandals, {P}

Page.Line 1st Ed.		Page.Line 2nd Ed.	First Edition [Second Edition
7.28	|	34.16	Thus [Thus, {P}
7.28	|	34.16	christians [Chris- tians {C}
7.29	|	34.17	another [another, {P}
7.30	|	34.18	God: [God; {P}
7.30	|	34.19	Meantime [meantime, {C} {P}
7.31	|	34.20	stumbled; [stumbled, {P}
7.33	|	34.21	religion; [religion, {P}
7.33	|	34.22	heaven, [heaven {P}
7.35	|	34.24	gospel [Gospel {C}
7.35	|	34.24	contempt; [contempt, {P}
7.36	|	34.25	multitudes [multitudes, {P}
7.36	|	34.25	gospel [Gospel {C}
7.38	|	34.27	unheard of [unheard-of {S}
7.39	|	35.2	country.— [country. {P}
7.40	|	35.2	so. [so? {P} (TC)(AC)
7.41	|	35.3	endeavour, [endeavor, {S}
7.41	|	35.3	scriptural [Scrip- tural {C}
7.42	|	35.4	say, [say {P}
7.43	|	35.6	gospel [Gospel {C}
7.44	|	35.7	undertaking. [undertaking? {P}
7.45	|	35.8	endeavours. [endeavors. {S}
7.47	|	35.11	is [is, {P}
8.1	|	35.13	christianity— [Christianity; {C} {P}
8.1	|	35.14	anti-christian [antichristian {S}
8.2	|	35.14	hierarchy— [hierarchy; {P}
8.2	|	35.15	connexion [connection {S}
8.3	|	35.16	nations, [nations {P}
8.8	|	35.21	us, [us {P}
8.9	|	35.23	ends, [ends {P}
8.9	|	35.23	given; — [given, {P}
8.11	|	35.25	any thing [anything {S}
8.11	|	35.25	less, [less {P}
8.13	|	35.27	reformation, [reform- ation {P}
8.14	|	35.28	things [things, {P}
8.16	|	35.30	privileges, [privileges {P}
8.18	|	35.32	times, [times {P}
8.19	|	35.34	endeavours [endeavors {S}
8.20	|	36.1	anti-christian [anti- christian {S}[2]
8.21	|	36.2	world; [world— {P}
8.21	|	36.2	recompences [recompenses {S}

Page.Line 1st Ed.		Page.Line 2nd Ed.	First Edition [Second Edition
8.22	|	36.3	Surely [Surely, {P}
8.22	|	36.3	then [then, {P}
8.22	|	36.3	favour [favor {S}
8.25	|	36.6	gospel [Gospel {C}
8.26	|	36.8	centuries, [centuries {P}
8.27	|	36.9	churches [Churches, {C} {P}
8.30	|	36.12	christian [Christian {C}
8.31	|	36.13	others [other's {S}
8.31	|	36.13	good; [good, {P}
8.32	|	36.14	documents, [documents {P}
8.32	|	36.14	subjects, [subjects {P}
8.33	|	36.15	excited, [excited {P}
8.33	|	36.15	considerations, [considerations {P}
8.35	|	36.18	what! [what {P}
8.35	|	36.18	Tho' [though {C} {S}
8.35	|	36.18	well meant [well-meant {S}
8.36	|	36.18	endeavours [endeavors {S}
8.36	|	36.18	union, [union {P}
8.38	|	36.20	attempt. [attempt! {P} (TC)
8.38	|	36.21	christians [Christians {C}
8.40	|	36.23	opposition, [opposition {P}
8.40	|	36.23	success, [success {P}
8.41	|	36.25	endeavours; [endeavors; {S}
8.41	|	36.25	divine [Divine {C}
8.42	|	36.26	have, [have {P}
8.42	|	36.26	ago, [ago {P}
8.43	|	36.26	any thing [any- thing {S}
8.44	|	36.28	evils, [evils {P}
8.44	|	36.28	christians [Christians {C}
8.46	|	36.30	with, [with {P}
8.46	|	36.30	enemy, [enemy {P}
8.47	|	36.31	church, [Church, {C}
8.48	|	36.32	pieces. [pieces? {P}
8.48	|	36.33	let [Let {C}
8.49	|	36.34	endeavours [endeavors {S}
9.2	|	37.2	business; [business, {P}
9.3	|	37.3	inadvertencies, [inadvertencies {P}
9.6	|	37.6	us; [us, {P}
9.6	|	37.7	labouring [laboring {S}
9.7	|	37.7	cause; [cause, {P}

Page.Line 1st Ed.	Page.Line 2nd Ed.	First Edition [Second Edition
9.7	37.8	armour [armor {S}
9.8	37.8	God; [God, {P}
9.9	37.9	gospel [Gospel {C}
9.9	37.10	duty, [duty {P}
9.14	37.15	offence, [offense, {S}
9.14	37.15	discouragement, [discourage- ment {P}
9.15	37.16	any, [any one {P} {D}
9.15	37.17	question, [question {P}
9.15	37.17	connexion [connection {S}
9.18	37.19	good. [good? {P}
9.20	37.22	for [for, {P}
9.20	37.23	surely [surely, {P}
9.21	37.23	divine [Divine {C}
9.21	37.24	any thing [anything {S}
9.26	37.29	alone, [alone {P}
9.26	37.30	forward, [for- ward {P}
9.32	38.2	Apostle, [apostle, {C}
9.33	38.2	who [Who {C}
9.33	38.2	things!— [things? {P}
9.35	38.4	so [so, {P}
9.35	38.5	suffi- ciency, [sufficiency {P}
9.36	38.5	But [But, {P}
9.38	38.8	churches; [Churches, {C} {P}
9.39	38.9	John 17, 20, 23, [(John xvii: 20, 23,) {S} {P}
9.41	38.11	Pray ["Pray {P}
9.42	38.12	Jerusalem, [Jerusalem; {P}
9.42	38.12	thee. [thee." {P}
9.44	38.14	enterpize; [enterprise, {S}
9.44	38.14	attempt, [attempt {P}
9.45	38.16	churches [Churches {C}
9.46	38.17	God. [God? {P}
9.48	38.18	thought: [thought; {P}
9.48	38.18	But [but {C}
10.3	38.22	endeavours, [endeavors {S} {P}
10.4	38.23	peculiar, [peculiar cause, {D} (TC)
10.7	38.26	do, [do {P}
10.8	38.27	connexion [connection {S}
10.9	38.29	themselves [himself {D} (TC)

Page.Line 1st Ed.		Page.Line 2nd Ed.	First Edition [Second Edition
10.10	|	38.30	brethren, [brethren {P}
10.13	|	38.33	event, [event {P}
10.14	|	38.34	church [Church {C}
10.14	|	39.1	purity [purity, {P}
10.14	|	39.1	prosperity; [prosperity, {P}
10.14	|	39.1	but, [but {P}
10.16	|	39.4	incredi- ble, [incredible, {P}
10.17	|	39.4	church [Church {C}
10.18	|	39.5	purity, [purity {P}
10.19	|	39.7	any thing [anything {S}
10.20	|	39.8	but [both {D} (TC)
10.21	|	39.8	model, [model {P}
10.21	|	39.9	practice, [practice {P}
10.22	|	39.9	church, [Church, {C}
10.23	|	39.11	or all [or in all {D} (TC)
10.23	|	39.11	churches, [Churches, {C}[3]
10.26	|	39.14	worse; [worse, {P}
10.26	|	39.14	divinely inspired [divinely-inspired {S}
10.27	|	39.16	church [Church {C}
10.28	|	39.16	Aposto- lick [apostolic {C} {S} (TC)[4]
10.29	|	39.17	church, [Church, {C}
10.29	|	39.17	be [be, {P}
10.31	|	39.20	churches [Churches {C}
10.32	|	39.21	Christ, [Christ {P}
10.33	|	39.22	holiness; [holi- ness, {P}
10.34	|	39.22	agreed, [agreed {P}
10.37	|	39.26	opinion, [opinion {P}
10.38	|	39.27	pity, [pity {P}
10.38	|	39.28	things!! [things! {P}
10.39	|	39.29	amongst [among {S}
10.39	|	39.29	us, [us {P}
10.39	|	39.29	up with human [up human {D}
10.40	|	39.30	God; [God, {P}
10.41	|	39.31	brethren; [brethren, {P}
10.44	|	39.34	brethren, [brethren {P}
10.44	|	39.34	denominations, [denominations {P}
10.44	|	40.34	consider, [con- sider {P}
10.45	|	40.1	prejudices, [prejudices {P}
10.46	|	40.2	with [against {D} (TC)
10.48	|	40.4	practice, [practice {P}

Page.Line 1st Ed.	Page.Line 2nd Ed.	First Edition [Second Edition
10.49	40.6	terms, [terms {P}
11.1	40.8	christian [Christian {C}
11.1	40.8	church; [Church; {C}
11.3	40.11	all, [all {P}
11.5	40.13	fellow-brethren [brethren {D} (TC)
11.6	40.14	brethren, [brethren {P}
11.11	40.19	christian [Christian {C}
11.11	40.20	head, [*head,* {T}
11.11	40.20	centre, [center, {S}
11.12	40.20	rule— [*rule;* {T} {P}
11.14	40.22	cannot [can not {S}
11.15	40.23	suppose, [suppose {P}
11.15	40.24	it; [it, {P}
11.16	40.25	assume, [assume {P}
11.16	40.25	propose, [propose {P}
11.17	40.26	essentials, [essentials {P}
11.20	40.29	Authority [authority {C}
11.21	40.30	belief, [belief {P}
11.21	40.30	them, [them {P}
11.23	40.32	any thing [anything {S}
11.23	40.33	duty, [duty {P}
11.24	40.33	presume [presume, {P}
11.26	41.2	none, [known {D}
11.26	41.2	but of a few; [of but few; {D}
11.28	41.4	event, [event {P}
11.29	41.5	information, [information {P}
11.30	41.5	concurrence, [concurrence {P}
11.31	41.6	begin— [begin, {P}
11.31	41.6	sometime— [some time, {S} {P}
11.36	41.12	ours: [ours; {P}
11.37	41.13	urge, [urge {P}
11.44	41.21	well known [well-known {S}
11.46	41.23	vehemence, [vehemence {P}
11.47	41.25	tho' [though {S}
11.48	41.26	and [and, {P}
11.49	41.26	decline: [decline; {P}
12.2	41.28	means, [means {P}
12.4	41.31	church, [Church, {C}
12.6	41.33	men, [men {P}

Page.Line 1st Ed.	Page.Line 2nd Ed.	First Edition [Second Edition
12.6	41.33	them:— [him; {D} {P}
12.7	41.34	suppose, [suppose {P}
12.7	42.1	advan- tage, [advantage {P}
12.9	42.2	farther [further {S}
12.10	42.4	would, [would {P}
12.10	42.4	means, [means {P}
12.10	42.4	our- selves, [ourselves {P}
12.11	42.5	farther [further {S}
12.11	42.5	add [add, {P}
12.14	42.8	feelings, [feelings {P}
12.14	42.9	towards [toward {S}
12.15	42.9	scriptural [Scriptural {C}
12.15	42.9	amongst [among {S}
12.15	42.9	churches, [Churches, {C}
12.16	42.10	acknowledged, [acknowledged {P}
12.17	42.12	conciliate; [conciliate, {P}
12.18	42.12	other, [other {P}
12.18	42.13	charity, [charity {P}
12.19	42.13	truth:— [truth: {P}
12.19	42.14	truth, [truth," {P}
12.19	42.14	Apostle, [apostle, {C}
12.19	42.14	and ["and {P}
12.21	42.16	forever. [forever." {P} (TC)
12.21	42.16	Indeed [Indeed, {P}
12.22	42.17	divine [Divine {C}
12.22	42.17	union, [union {P}
12.23	42.19	chris- tian: [Christian, {C} {P}
12.24	42.19	favour [favor {S}
12.24	42.20	weak, [weak {P}
12.26	42.21	principle, [principle {P}
12.26	42.22	impossible.— [impossible. {P}
12.28	42.24	good natured [good-natured {S}
12.29	42.25	thing [thing, {P}
12.29	42.25	however [however, {P}
12.31	42.27	believe, [believe {P}
12.33	42.29	effected; [effected, {P}
12.34	42.30	divinely revealed [Divinely-revealed {C} {S}
12.34	42.30	truth; [truth, {P}
12.34	42.30	good natured [good-natured {S}
12.34	42.31	christian [Christian {C}

Page.Line 1st Ed.		Page.Line 2nd Ed.	First Edition [Second Edition
12.35	|	42.31	condeseension; [condescension, {S} {P}
12.37	|	42.34	christian [Christian {C}
12.38	|	42.34	discernment, [discernment {P}
12.39	|	43.1	Redeemer; [Redeemer, {P} (TC)
12.40	|	43.2	no ["no {P} (TC)
12.42	|	43.5	judgment? [judgment?" {P} (TC)
12.43	|	43.6	practicable, [practicable {P}
12.44	|	43.7	you." [us." {D} (TC)
12.46	|	43.9	shepherd. [Shepherd? {C} {P}
13.5	|	43.19	chris- tian [Christian {C}
13.6	|	43.19	say, [say {P}
13.8	|	43.21	stumbling block [stumbling-block {S}
13.11	|	43.24	work— [work, {P}
13.12	|	43.25	way; [way, {P}
13.12	|	43.26	chaff, [chaff {P}
13.13	|	43.27	revelation;— [revelation; {P}
13.14	|	43.28	power, [power {P}
13.16	|	43.31	we [you {D} (TC)
13.17	|	43.31	ignorant of, [ignorant of {P}
13.17	|	43.31	with, [with {P}
13.18	|	43.32	church. [Church. {C}
13.18	|	43.33	prayers, [prayers {P}
13.20	|	44.1	cannot, [can not, {S}
13.21	|	44.1	silent, [silent {P}
13.22	|	44.3	cannot; [can not; {S}
13.24	|	44.5	nature, [nature {P}
13.25	|	44.6	anti-christian [antichristian {S}
13.26	|	44.7	church [Church {C}
13.29	|	44.11	love— [love; {P}
13.29	|	44.11	But [but {C}
13.30	|	44.12	* * * * [* * * {P}
13.30	|	44.12	See Mal. 2, 1—10. [(See Mal. ii: 1-10.) {S} {P}
13.31	|	44.13	Oh! [O! {S}
13.31	|	44.13	consider, [consider {P}
13.32	|	44.14	grave; [grave, {P}
13.32	|	44.15	it: [it! {P}
13.33	|	44.16	there!— [there! {P}
13.34	|	44.16	God, [God {P}

<table>
<tr><th>Page.Line
1st Ed.</th><th></th><th>Page.Line
2nd Ed.</th><th>First Edition [Second Edition</th></tr>
<tr><td>13.36</td><td>|</td><td>44.19</td><td>church. [Church. {C}</td></tr>
<tr><td>13.37</td><td>|</td><td>44.20</td><td>meantime, [mean time, {S}</td></tr>
<tr><td>13.38</td><td>|</td><td>44.21</td><td>perpetuated, [perpetuated {P}</td></tr>
<tr><td>13.38</td><td>|</td><td>44.21</td><td>‘till [till {P}</td></tr>
<tr><td>13.44</td><td>|</td><td>44.27</td><td>day, [day {P}</td></tr>
<tr><td>13.44</td><td>|</td><td>44.28</td><td>amongst [among {S}</td></tr>
<tr><td>13.45</td><td>|</td><td>44.30</td><td>attempt— [attempt. {P}</td></tr>
<tr><td>13.48</td><td>|</td><td>44.33</td><td>called; [called, {P}</td></tr>
<tr><td>13.49</td><td>|</td><td>44.33</td><td>man; [man, {P}</td></tr>
<tr><td>13.49</td><td>}</td><td>44.34</td><td>Christ [Christ, {P}</td></tr>
<tr><td>14.3</td><td>|</td><td>45.2</td><td>amongst [among {S}</td></tr>
<tr><td>14.3</td><td>|</td><td>45.2</td><td>us; [us, {P}</td></tr>
<tr><td>14.3</td><td>|</td><td>45.3</td><td>cannot [can not {S}</td></tr>
<tr><td>14.5</td><td>|</td><td>45.5</td><td>Till [Until {D}</td></tr>
<tr><td>14.6</td><td>|</td><td>45.6</td><td>together; [together, {P}</td></tr>
<tr><td>14.6</td><td>|</td><td>45.6</td><td>christian [Christian {C}</td></tr>
<tr><td>14.10</td><td>|</td><td>45.11</td><td>christianity— [Christianity; {C} {P}</td></tr>
<tr><td>14.10</td><td>|</td><td>45.11</td><td>In [in {C}</td></tr>
<tr><td>14.11</td><td>|</td><td>45.12</td><td>you— [you. {P}</td></tr>
<tr><td>14.13</td><td>|</td><td>45.13</td><td>churches, [Churches, {C}</td></tr>
<tr><td>14.13</td><td>|</td><td>45.14</td><td>purity— [purity; {P}</td></tr>
<tr><td>14.15</td><td>|</td><td>45.16</td><td>forward [forward, {P}</td></tr>
<tr><td>14.16</td><td>|</td><td>45.18</td><td>syren [siren {S}</td></tr>
<tr><td>14.17</td><td>|</td><td>45.18</td><td>professor, [professor: {P}</td></tr>
<tr><td>14.17</td><td>|</td><td>45.19</td><td>come— [come, {P}</td></tr>
<tr><td>14.18</td><td>|</td><td>45.19</td><td>come— [come, {P}</td></tr>
<tr><td>14.18</td><td>|</td><td>45.19</td><td>he,— [he; {P}</td></tr>
<tr><td>14.19</td><td>|</td><td>45.21</td><td>not.— [not. {P}</td></tr>
<tr><td>14.20</td><td>|</td><td>45.21</td><td>“Have [Have {P}</td></tr>
<tr><td>14.26</td><td>|</td><td>45.29</td><td>yea [yea, {P}</td></tr>
<tr><td>14.29</td><td>|</td><td>45.32</td><td>servants, [servants {P}</td></tr>
<tr><td>14.29</td><td>|</td><td>45.32</td><td>Prophets, [prophets, {C}</td></tr>
<tr><td>14.31</td><td>|</td><td>46.1</td><td>amongst [among {S}</td></tr>
<tr><td>14.32</td><td>|</td><td>46.1</td><td>things— [things, {P}</td></tr>
<tr><td>14.32</td><td>|</td><td>46.2</td><td>thunderings, [thunderings {P}</td></tr>
<tr><td>14.37</td><td>|</td><td>46.7</td><td>Providence [God {D} (TC)</td></tr>
<tr><td>14.37</td><td>|</td><td>46.8</td><td>distance? What [distance? ¶ What {T} (TC)</td></tr>
<tr><td>14.45</td><td>|</td><td>46.16</td><td>Zion”— [Zion.” {P}</td></tr>
<tr><td>14.46</td><td>|</td><td>46.17</td><td>dear bought [dear-bought {S}</td></tr>
</table>

Page.Line 1st Ed.		Page.Line 2nd Ed.	First Edition [Second Edition
14.49	|	46.20	upon [on {D}
14.49	|	46.20	earth;— [earth; {P}
15.1	|	46.21	fast [fast, {P}
15.1	|	46.21	therefore [therefore, {P}
15.5	|	46.26	doing, [doing {P}
15.6	|	46.27	endeavours [endeavors {S}
15.7	|	46.28	first fruits [first-fruits {S}
15.8	|	46.30	propo- sitions— [propositions, {P}
15.9	|	46.30	candour [candor {S}
15.10	|	46.31	despise, [despise {P}
15.10	|	46.31	misconstrue, [misconstrue {P}
15.12	|	46.34	scriptural [Scriptural {C}
15.12	|	46.34	amongst [among {S}
15.13	|	47.1	churches, [Churches, {C}
15.14	|	47.2	dictate: [dictate, {P}
15.18	|	47.7	weakness, [weakness {P}
15.19	|	47.7	power— [power. {P}
15.20	|	47.9	church, [Church, {C}
15.22	|	47.11	For ["For {P} (TC)
15.23	|	47.12	spirit [Spirit {C}
15.24	|	47.13	spirit; [Spirit; {C}
15.24	|	47.14	spirit; [Spirit; {C}
15.25	|	47.15	spirit [Spirit {C}
15.28	|	47.18	God. [God." {P} (TC)
15.28	|	47.18	face [face, {P}
15.28	|	47.18	then [then, {P}
15.29	|	47.19	di- vine [Divine {C}
15.30	|	47.20	church [Church {C}
15.33	|	47.23	any thing [anything {S}
15.37	|	47.28	christian [Christian {C}
15.39	|	47.30	cannot, [can not, {S}
15.41	|	47.32	Came, [Come, {D} (TC)
15.44	|	48.2	fellow-christians, [fellow-Christians, {C}
15.46	|	48.4	church. [Church. {C}
15.48	|	48.6	towards [toward {S}
15.48	|	48.6	creed, [creed {P}
15.48	|	48.6	standard, [standard {P}
15.48	|	48.7	church; [Church, {C} {P}
15.49	|	48.7	or, [or {P}

Page.Line 1st Ed.		Page.Line 2nd Ed.	First Edition [Second Edition
15.49	|	48.8	communion;— [communion; {P}
16.1	|	48.8	farther [further {S}
16.3	|	48.10	ground: [ground {P} (TC)
16.3	|	48.11	premises: [premises, {P}
16.4	|	48.12	Apostles [apostles {C}
16.4	|	48.12	them.— [them; {P}
16.4	|	48.12	That [that {C}
16.6	|	48.14	church [Church {C}
16.7	|	48.15	beginning— [beginning. {P}
16.8	|	48.16	follows. [follows: {P}
16.9	|	48.17	THAT [That {T}
16.9	|	48.20	church [Church {C}
16.12	|	48.20	scriptures, [Scriptures, {C}
16.13	|	48.22	else [else; {P} (TC)
16.14	|	48.23	christians. [Christians. {C}
16.15	|	48.24	church [Church {C}
16.17	|	48.26	another; [another, {P}
16.19	|	48.28	them [them, {P}
16.20	|	48.29	purpose, [purpose {P}
16.24	|	48.34	christians [Christians {C}
16.25	|	49.1	communion; [communion, {P}
16.25	|	49.1	taught, [taught {P}
16.26	|	49.2	them, [them {P}
16.26	|	49.2	any thing [anything {S}
16.26	|	49.3	be admitted, [to be admitted, {D} (TC)
16.27	|	49.3	divine [Divine {C}
16.27	|	49.3	church [Church {C}
16.29	|	49.5	Apostles [apostles {C}
16.29	|	49.6	church; [Church; {C}
16.30	|	49.6	terms, [terms {P}
16.30	|	49.7	approven [approved {S} (TC)
16.31	|	49.8	scriptures [Scriptures {C}
16.31	|	49.8	Testament [Test- aments {D}
16.34	|	49.11	church; [Church, {C} {P}
16.34	|	49.12	cannot [can not {S}
16.37	|	49.14	discipline [discipline, {P}
16.37	|	49.15	church, [Church, {C}
16.38	|	49.16	members; [members, {P}
16.39	|	49.17	worship [worship, {P}

Page.Line 1st Ed.		Page.Line 2nd Ed.	First Edition [Second Edition
16.39	|	49.17	discipline [discipline, {P}
16.40	|	49.18	church, [Church, {C}
16.43	|	49.21	scriptures [Scriptures {C}
16.43	|	49.21	silent, [silent {P}
16.44	|	49.23	be; [be, {P}
16.45	|	49.24	de- ficiency, [deficiency {P}
16.46	|	49.25	church; [Church; {C}
16.46	|	49.25	any thing [anything {S}
16.47	|	49.25	christians [Christians {C}
16.48	|	49.27	ordinances, [ordinances {P}
17.2	|	49.30	church, [Church, {C}
17.3	|	49.32	church; [Church, {C} {P}
17.4	|	49.32	amongst [among {S}
17.4	|	49.32	christians, [Chris- tians, {C}
17.6	|	49.34	scripture [Scripture {C}
17.8	|	50.2	word: [word, {P}
17.9	|	50.3	christians [Christians {C}
17.11	|	50.5	men; [men, {P}
17.11	|	50.6	God— [God. {P}
17.11	|	50.6	therefore [Therefore, {C} {P}
17.13	|	50.8	church. [Church. {C}
17.13	|	50.9	Hence [Hence, {P}
17.15	|	50.10	churchs's [Church's {C} {S}
17.16	|	50.13	divine [Divine {C}
17.18	|	50.14	expedient; [expedient, {P}
17.18	|	50.15	be, [be {P}
17.22	|	50.18	christian [Christian {C}
17.22	|	50.18	communion: [communion; {P}
17.23	|	50.20	church, [Church, {C}
17.24	|	50.21	judgment; [judgment, {P}
17.25	|	50.22	church [Church {C}
17.29	|	50.26	divinely revealed [Divinely-revealed {C} {S}
17.30	|	50.28	church; [Church; {C}
17.32	|	50.29	knowledge: [knowledge; {P}
17.33	|	50.31	scriptural [Scriptural {C}
17.34	|	50.32	practice; [practice, {P}
17.35	|	50.33	thro' [through {S}
17.36	|	50.34	in, [in {P}
17.36	|	50.34	things [things, {P}

Page.Line 1st Ed.		Page.Line 2nd Ed.	First Edition [Second Edition
17.38	|	51.2	church. [Church. {C}
17.39	|	51.3	enabled, [enabled {P}
17.39	|	51.3	thro' [through {S}
17.39	|	51.3	grace, [grace {P}
17.42	|	51.7	father, [Father, {C}
17.43	|	51.7	spirit, [Spirit, {C} (TC)
17.44	|	51.9	divine [Divine {C}
17.45	|	51.10	joint heirs [joint-heirs {S}
17.47	|	51.12	among [among the {D}
17.47	|	51.12	christians [Christians {C}
17.48	|	51.13	anti-christian, [antichristian, {S}
17.49	|	51.14	wcre [were {S} (TC)
17.49	|	51.15	exclo- ding [excluding {S} (TC)[5]
18.1	|	51.16	anti-scriptural, [antiscriptural, {S}
18.3	|	51.18	anti-natural, [antinatural, {S}
18.4	|	51.18	christians [Christians {C}
18.4	|	51.19	hate [hate, {P}
18.7	|	51.22	confusion, [confusion {P}
18.8	|	51.23	That, [That {P}
18.8	|	51.23	instances,) [instances) {P}
18.9	|	51.24	God; [God, {P}
18.9	|	51.24	and, [and {P}
18.9	|	51.24	others,) [others) {P}
18.10	|	51.25	opinions, [opinions {P}
18.10	|	51.26	inventions, [inventions {P}
18.12	|	51.27	worship, [worship {P}
18.12	|	51.28	church; [Church, {C} {P}
18.13	|	51.29	universally acknowledged [universally-acknowledged {S}
18.14	|	51.30	church [Church {C}
18.17	|	51.32	church [Church {C}
18.18	|	51.33	members, [members {P}
18.18	|	51.34	scriptural [Scriptural {C}
18.20	|	52.2	scriptures; [Scriptures; {C}
18.21	|	52.2	2dly, [secondly, {S}
18.22	|	52.4	tempers [temper {D} (TC)
18.23	|	52.5	3dly, [Thirdly, {S}
18.23	|	52.5	scripturally [Scripturally {C}
18.27	|	52.9	divine [Divine {C}
18.28	|	52.10	church, [Church, {C}

Page.Line 1st Ed.	Page.Line 2nd Ed.	First Edition [Second Edition
18.31	52.14	divine [Divine {C}
18.33	52.16	purpose, [purpose {P}
18.33	52.16	adopted, [adopted {P}
18.34	52.17	pretence [pretense {S}
18.34	52.18	origin— [origin, {P}
18.37	52.20	church. [Church. {C}
18.41	52.25	necessity— [necessity, {P}
18.42	52.26	one, [one {P}
18.43	52.27	Zion— [Zion; {P}
18.44	52.28	Is. 57, 14, [Isaiah lvii: 14, {S} {P}
18.48	52.32	cast [Cast {C}
18.49	52.33	stumbling block [stumbling-block {S}
18.49	52.34	prepare tho [prepare the {S}
19.1	52.34	scriptural [Scriptural {C}
19.1	52.34	amongst [among {S}
19.1	53.1	christians, [Christians, {C}
19.4	53.3	stumbling blocks— [stumbling-blocks— {S}
19.4	53.4	ages [ages, {P}
19.5	53.5	towards [toward {S}
19.6	53.5	object, [object {P}
19.6	53.6	mistake, [mistake {P}
19.7	53.7	left— [left, {P}
19.9	53.9	brethren, [brethren {P}
19.9	53.9	towards [toward {S}
19.11	53.11	scripture [Scripture {C}
19.11	53.11	reason; [reason, {P}
19.14	53.14	adequate; [adequate, {P}
19.15	53.16	issue— [issue? {P}
19.18	53.20	candour, [candor, {S}
19.20	53.21	right;— [right; {P}
19.21	53.23	which [which, {P}
19.23	53.24	obtained; [ob- tained, {P}
19.23	53.25	objection, [objection {P}
19.24	53.26	general [General {C}
19.24	53.26	council. [Council. {C}
19.25	53.28	con- science— [conscience; {P}
19.26	53.28	conviction, [conviction {P}
19.28	53.30	suspence [suspense {S} (TC)
19.29	53.31	This [This, {P}

Page.Line 1st Ed.	Page.Line 2nd Ed.	First Edition [Second Edition
19.29	53.32	persuaded [persuaded, {P}
19.30	53.32	christians [Christians {C}
19.31	53.34	such— [such, {P}
19.34	54.3	such— [such; {P}
19.34	54.3	Union ["Union {P}
19.34	54.3	Truth [Truth" {P}
19.35	54.3	Word [word {C}
19.35	54.4	Standard; [standard; {C}
19.36	54.5	promises; [promises, {P}
19.38	54.7	When ["When {P}
19.38	54.8	spirit [Spirit {C}
19.40	54.9	standard bearers— [standard-bearers, {S} {P}
19.41	54.11	carnal; [carnal, {P}
19.42	54.12	strong holds;" [strongholds;" {S}
19.42	54.12	strong holds [strongholds {S}
19.43	54.13	separation; [separation, {P}
19.47	54.17	this; [this, {P}
19.48	54.18	prevail;— [prevail; {P}
19.49	54.20	And ["And {P}
20.3	54.23	cannot [can not {S}
20.4	54.24	kingdom, [kingdom {P}
20.4	54.24	an house, [a house {D}
20.5	54.25	cannot [can not {S}
20.6	54.26	church [Church {C}
20.9	54.30	it " [it." {P}
20.16	55.2	done— [done. {P}
20.18	55.4	him [Him {C}
20.18	55.5	"if ["If {C}
20.19	55.6	any thing [anything {S}
20.20	55.7	which [who {D}
20.24	55.11	on, [on {P}
20.24	55.11	Lord [Lord; {P}
20.27	55.14	"for ["For {C}
20.29	55.17	burneth."— [burneth." {P}
20.30	55.18	ye [you {S}
20.31	55.19	meet, [meet {P}
20.31	55.19	least, [least {P}
20.33	55.21	church [Church {C}
20.35	55.23	pros- perity— [prosperity, {P}

Page.Line 1st Ed.	Page.Line 2nd Ed.	First Edition [Second Edition
20.39	55.28	said, [said: {P}
20.40	55.29	offence [offense {S}
20.43	55.32	church [Church {C}
20.43	55.33	every where [everywhere {S}
20.46	56.2	cannot [can not {S}
20.47	56.3	no where [nowhere {S}
20.48	56.4	word o. [word of {S}
20.48	56.4	God.— [God. {P}
20.49	56.5	christian [Christian {C}
21.2	56.8	centre; [center; {S}
21.5	56.11	know, [know {P}
21.7	56.13	Ye [You {S} (TC)
21.8	56.14	ye [you {S} (TC)
21.8	56.15	Jesus, [Jesus; {P}
21.9	56.15	Ye [You {S} (TC)
21.10	56.17	Ye [You {S} (TC)
21.11	56.18	Ye [You {S} (TC)
21.12	56.19	ye [you {S} (TC)
21.12	56.19	Ye [You {S} (TC)
21.13	56.20	Ye [You {S} (TC)
21.14	56.21	rule [rule, {P}
21.15	56.22	Ye [You {S} (TC)
21.15	56.23	re -ject, [reject {P}
21.16	56.23	christian [Chris- tian {C}
21.16	56.24	brother; [brother, {P}
21.17	56.24	condemned, [condemned {P}
21.17	56.25	rejected, [rejected {P}
21.17	56.25	law:— [law; {P}
21.18	56.25	Ye [You {S} (TC)
21.21	56.29	communion— [communion; {P}
21.21	56.30	Ye [You {S} (TC)
21.22	56.31	cannot, [can not {S} {P}
21.23	56.32	you;— [you; {P}
21.23	56.32	character;— [character; {P}
21.24	56.33	profession, [profession {P}
21.27	57.3	any thing [anything {S}
21.28	57.3	minded, [minded {P}
21.28	57.3	suppose; [suppose, {P}
21.28	57.4	hope, [hope {P}
21.29	57.5	them:— [them; {P}

Page.Line 1st Ed.		Page.Line 2nd Ed.	First Edition [Second Edition
21.29	|	57.5	Only [only {C}
21.30	|	57.5	such, [such {P}
21.30	|	57.6	light; [light, {P}
21.31	|	57.6	reject it, [reject it {P}
21.35	|	57.11	spirit; [Spirit, {C} {P} (TC)
21.36	|	57.12	zeal;— [zeal; {P}
21.37	|	57.14	own, [own {P}
21.38	|	57.14	church's [Church's {C}
21.39	|	57.16	brethren, [brethren; {P}
21.40	|	57.16	mistake— [mistake. {P}
21.40	|	57.16	so [So {C}
21.41	|	57.18	scripture [Scripture {C}
21.41	|	57.18	matter of fact [matter-of-fact {S}
21.42	|	57.18	evidence, [evidence {P}
21.43	|	57.19	inattention, [inattention {P}
21.44	|	57.20	effect;— [effect, {P}
21.44	|	57.21	case, [case {P}
21.45	|	57.22	instances.— [instances. {P}
21.46	|	57.22	evil: [evil; {P}
21.48	|	57.25	things, [things {P}
22.1	|	57.27	brethren, [brethren {P}
22.1	|	57.27	any thing [anything {S}
22.2	|	57.28	christian [Christian {C}
22.2	|	57.28	unity; [unity, {P}
22.2	|	57.28	farther [further {S}
22.3	|	57.29	it: [it; {P}
22.4	|	57.30	subject; [subject, {P}
22.7	|	57.34	dispute; [dispute, {P}
22.7	|	57.34	hesitate, [hesitate {P}
22.7	|	57.34	differ, [differ {P}
22.9	|	58.2	this, [this {P}
22.10	|	58.3	ground, [ground; {P}
22.11	|	58.4	For [For, {P}
22.12	|	58.6	divine [Divine {C}
22.13	|	58.7	divine [Divine {C}
22.13	|	58.7	spirit, [Spirit, {C} (TC)
22.14	|	58.8	peace [peace, {P}
22.16	|	58.10	unity [unity, {P}
22.17	|	58.11	party [party, {P}
22.17	|	58.11	absurd, [absurd {P}

Page.Line 1st Ed.	Page.Line 2nd Ed.	First Edition [Second Edition
22.21	58.16	means, [means {P}
22.22	58.16	church [Church {C}
22.23	58.17	fractions; [factions, {S} {P}
22.24	58.19	christianity [Christianity {C}
22.27	58.22	For ["For {P}
22.27	58.22	commandment [commandment: {P}
22.27	58.23	that [That {C}
22.28	58.23	son [Son {C}
22.30	58.25	him— [him; {P}
22.31	58.26	spirit [Spirit {C}
22.31	58.27	us"— [us," {P}
22.33	58.28	love, [love {P}
22.33	58.29	brother; [brother, {P}
22.38	58.34	reclaimed.— [reclaimed. {P}
22.40	59.2	Christ hath [Christ has {S}
22.40	59.3	he hath [he has {S}
22.44	59.6	christianity; [Christianity, {C} {P}
22.45	59.8	Author; [author, {C} {P}
22.48	59.11	pretence [pretense {S}
22.49	59.12	systems; [systems, {P}
22.49	59.12	believe [believe, {P}
22.49	59.12	instances [in- stances, {P}
22.49	59.13	intention: [intention; {P}
23.2	59.14	not— [not; {P}
23.3	59.16	them— [them; {P}
23.5	59.18	church [Church {C}
23.6	59.19	systems; [systems— {P}
23.6	59.20	party [party, {P}
23.8	59.21	least [least, {P}
23.9	59.22	these, [these {P}
23.9	59.23	christian [Christian {C}
23.10	59.23	love. [love! {P}
23.10	59.24	it, [it {P}
23.12	59.25	healer, [healer {P}
23.13	59.27	bonds, [bonds {P}
23.14	59.28	bound, [bound {P}
23.15	59.29	condition: [condition, {P}
23.16	59.30	bondage; [bondage {P}
23.16	59.30	withs [withes {S}
23.17	59.31	Sampson [Samson {S}

Page.Line 1st Ed.		Page.Line 2nd Ed.	First Edition [Second Edition
23.18	|	59.32	prisoner; [prisoner, {P}
23.18	|	59.32	or, [or {P}
23.18	|	59.32	anti-christ [Antichrist {C} {S}
23.18	|	59.32	were, [were {P}
23.19	|	59.33	reformation. [Reformation. {C}
23.20	|	59.34	see these things [see things {D}
23.20	|	59.34	light; [light, {P}
23.21	|	60.1	condition— [condition, {P}
23.22	|	60.2	confusion— [confusion, {P}
23.22	|	60.2	beloved, [Beloved, {C}
23.23	|	60.3	him; [him, {P}
23.25	|	60.6	him; [him, {P}
23.26	|	60.7	"By [By {P}
23.27	|	60.7	ye [you {S} (TC)
23.27	|	60.8	disciples, [disciples," {P}
23.27	|	60.8	saith [says {S}
23.27	|	60.8	if ["If {P} {C}
23.27	|	60.8	ye [you {S} (TC)
23.27	|	60.8	another. [another." {P}
23.28	|	60.9	"this ["This {C}
23.28	|	60.9	commandment [commandment, {P}
23.28	|	60.9	that [That {C}
23.28	|	60.9	ye [you {S} (TC)
23.29	|	60.10	ye [you {S} (TC)
23.30	|	60.11	name, [name {P}
23.30	|	60.12	has [hast {S}
23.31	|	60.12	me [me, {P}
23.31	|	60.12	one [one, {P}
23.31	|	60.12	are," [are;" {P}
23.32	|	60.13	me— [me; {P}
23.32	|	60.14	thou [thou, {P}
23.32	|	60.14	Father [Father, {P}
23.33	|	60.15	us; [us: {P}
23.35	|	60.17	them, [them; {P}
23.35	|	60.17	one: [one, {P}
23.36	|	60.17	them [them, {P}
23.36	|	60.18	and them [and thou {D}
23.36	|	60.18	me; [one; {D}
23.37	|	60.19	has [hast {S}
23.38	|	60.20	them, [them {P}
23.S1	|	60.S1	THOS. [THOMAS {S} {T} (TC)

Page.Line 1st Ed.	Page.Line 2nd Ed.	First Edition [Second Edition
23.S1	60.S1	CAMPBELL, Secretary. [CAMPBELL, {T} {D} {P} (TC)
23.S2	60.S2	THOS. [THOMAS {S} {T} (TC)
23.S2	60.S2	ACHESON, Treasurer. [ACHESON {T} {D} {P} (TC)
24.1	60.24	TO [To {T}
24.2	60.25	done— [done, {P}
24.2	60.26	doing— [doing, {P}
24.3	60.26	accomplished— [accom- plished, {P}
24.6	61.2	tho' [though {S}
24.6	61.2	declared; [declared, {P}
24.7	61.2	yet, [yet {P}
24.7	61.3	misconstruction.— [misconstruction. {P}
24.8	61.4	brethren, [brethren {P}
24.9	61.5	directly [directly, {P}
24.9	61.5	in irectly, [indirectly, {S}
24.10	61.6	churches, [Churches, {C}
24.11	61.7	assistance, [assistance {P}
24.11	61.7	favour [favor {S}
24.12	61.8	or, [or {P}
24.12	61.8	endeavouring [endeavoring {S}
24.12	61.8	churches [Churches {C}
24.13	61.9	churches— [Churches, {C} {P}
24.14	61.11	fellow-chris- tians, [fellow-Christians, {C}
24.15	61.11	which, [which {P}
24.17	61.13	God— [God, {P}
24.18	61.14	practice;— [practice; {P}
24.19	61.15	himself.— [himself. {P}
24.19	61.15	Therefore [Therefore, {P}
24.21	61.18	forbid, [forbid {P}
24.24	61.20	account;— [account. {P}
24.24	61.21	and [And {C}
24.24	61.21	all, [all {P}
24.25	61.21	free [free, {P}
24.25	61.21	unconstitutional [unconditional {D} (TC)
24.26	62.2	description; [description, {P}
24.27	62.3	holiness, [holiness {P}

Page.Line 1st Ed.		Page.Line 2nd Ed.	First Edition [Second Edition
24.28	|	62.4	office [office, {P}
24.28	|	62.4	scrip- tures; [Scrip- tures, {C} {P}
24.29	|	62.5	even [of even {D} (TC)
24.29	|	62.5	all, [all {P}
24.30	|	62.6	charge, [charge: {P}
24.30	|	62.6	"they ["They {C}
24.32	|	62.8	called; [called, {P}
24.32	|	62.8	fast hasten [hasten {D}
24.32	|	62.8	period, [period {P}
24.33	|	62.10	*Such* [*Such,* {P}
24.34	|	62.10	then [then, {P}
24.36	|	62.12	idol [idle {D}
24.36	|	62.12	shepherds; [shepherds, {P}
24.41	|	62.18	labours; [labors; {S}
25.2	|	62.22	church, [Church, {C}
25.5	|	62.25	faith: [faith, {P}
25.5	|	62.25	or, [or {P}
25.5	|	62.25	Gods [God's {S}
25.5	|	62.25	heritage: [heritage. {P}
25.5	|	62.25	where [Where {C}
25.8	|	62.28	PROP. [Proposition {T} {D}
25.8	|	62.28	page 17. [page 50. {D}
25.8	|	62.29	intention [intention, {P}
25.9	|	62.29	churches [Churches {C}
25.10	|	62.30	reformation; [ref- ormation, {P}
25.11	|	63.1	say, [say {P}
25.12	|	63.2	have a [has a {S}
25.13	|	63.3	churches, [Churches, {C}
25.13	|	63.4	par- ty; [party, {P}
25.14	|	63.4	assertion: [assertion, {P}
25.15	|	63.5	or [or, {P}
25.17	|	63.7	divine [Divine {C}
25.18	|	63.8	party— [party, {P}
25.18	|	63.8	Then [then {C}
25.19	|	63.10	prin- ciple: [principle, {P}
25.20	|	63.10	party— [party. {P}
25.21	|	63.12	*alone;* [*alone,* {P}
25.22	|	63.13	principle— [principles, {D} {P}
25.23	|	63.13	party— [party. {P}
25.27	|	63.18	christian [Christian {C}

Page.Line 1st Ed.	Page.Line 2nd Ed.	First Edition [Second Edition
25.28	63.20	inter- vension [intervention {S}
25.29	63.20	opinion. [opinion, {P}
25.29	63.20	We [we {C}
25.32	63.23	opinions; [opinions, {P}
25.32	63.24	appear, [appear {P}
25.33	63.25	useless; [useless, {P}
25.33	63.25	ma- thematicks. [mathematics? {S} {P} (TC)[6]
25.35	63.27	christians; [Christians; {C}
25.36	63.29	divinely revealed [Divinely-revealed {C} {S}
25.38	63.30	acknowledge; [acknowledge, {P}
25.39	63.31	betwixt [between {S} (TC)
25.39	63.31	scripture [Scrip- ture {C}
25.40	63.33	it— [it; {P}
25.41	63.34	im- perfectly, [imperfectly {P}
25.42	64.1	are, [are {P}
25.42	64.1	least, [least {P}
25.42	64.1	certam [certain {S} (TC)
25.43	64.1	declaration, [decla- ration {P}
25.43	64.2	conclusion, [conclusion {P}
25.43	64.2	it— [it; {P}
25.46	64.5	conclusion— [conclusion; {P}
25.47	64.6	christian [Chris- tian {C}
26.2	64.10	christian [Christian {C}
26.4	64.12	"thus ["Thus {C}
26.4	64.12	Lord": [Lord," {P}
26.5	64.13	cannot [can not {S}
26.6	64.14	infer- ence— [inference, {P}
26.7	64.15	walketh [walkest {D} (TC)
26.7	64.16	charitably? [charitably?" {P}
26.9	64.17	fellow creature, [fellow-creature, {S}
26.12	64.20	sug- gest, [suggest {P}
26.12	64.21	Apostle [apostle {C}
26.14	64.23	themselves. [themselves; {P}
26.14	64.23	That [that {C}
26.15	64.24	hath [has {S} (TC)
26.17	64.26	not [not, {P}
26.18	64.27	Gods [God's {S}
26.20	64.29	things, [things {P}

Page.Line 1st Ed.		Page.Line 2nd Ed.	First Edition [Second Edition
26.23	|	64.33	truth, [truth {P}
26.23	|	64.33	brethren; [brethren, {P}
26.24	|	64.34	churches; [Churches, {C} {P}
26.24	|	64.34	cannot [can not {S}
26.25	|	65.1	adventured [ventured {D} (TC)
26.28	|	65.4	*them,* [*them* {P}
26.28	|	65.5	proposed, [proposed {P}
26.29	|	65.6	event; [event, {P}
26.30	|	65.7	inves- tigation: [investigation, {P}
26.31	|	65.8	cause; [cause, {P}
26.31	|	65.8	any other plan adopted [to adopt any other plan {D} (TC)
26.33	|	65.10	mean- time [mean time, {S} {P}
26.34	|	65.11	step, [step {P}
26.34	|	65.11	stumbling block [stumbling-block {S}
26.34	|	65.12	way; [way, {P}
26.36	|	65.14	object; [object, {P}
26.37	|	65.14	party; [party, {P}
26.37	|	65.15	any thing [anything {S}
26.38	|	65.15	duty, [duty {P}
26.38	|	65.15	expressly revealed and enjoined [expressly enjoined {D}
26.38	|	65.16	divine [Divine {C}
26.40	|	65.17	And that [That {D} {C} (TC)
26.41	|	65.19	churches, [sects, {D} (TC)
26.43	|	65.21	far [far, {P}
26.43	|	65.21	have [have, {P}
26.43	|	65.21	least [least, {P}
26.43	|	65.21	endeavoured [endeavored {S}
26.45	|	65.23	churches [Churches {C}
26.45	|	65.23	possible, [possible {P}
26.47	|	65.25	foundation; [foundation, {P}
26.47	|	65.25	persuaded, [persuaded {P}
26.47	|	65.26	will, [will {P}
26.48	|	65.26	issue, [issue {P}
26.48	|	65.27	cause; [cause, {P}
26.49	|	65.27	towards [to- ward {S}
26.49	|	65.28	it; [it, {P}
26.49	|	65.28	and [and, {P}
27.1	|	65.28	first fruits [first-fruits {S}

Page.Line 1st Ed.		Page.Line 2nd Ed.	First Edition [Second Edition
27.1	|	65.29	harvest, [harvest {P}
27.2	|	65.29	For, [For {P}
27.2	|	65.30	christian [Christian {C}
27.2	|	65.30	churches [Churches, {C} {P}
27.3	|	65.31	Lord, [Lord {P}
27.4	|	65.32	Ghost, [Spirit, {D} (TC)
27.4	|	65.32	edi- fied; [edified, {P}
27.5	|	65.33	believe, [believe {P}
27.6	|	65.33	every where, [everywhere {S} {P}
27.6	|	65.34	times, [times {P}
27.6	|	65.34	ensure [insure {S}
27.8	|	66.2	we [we, {P}
27.9	|	66.3	churches: [Churches; {C} {P}
27.11	|	66.5	*us,* [*us* {P}
27.11	|	66.6	scripture: [Scripture; {C} {P}
27.12	|	66.6	cannot [can not {S}
27.12	|	66.7	it— [it. {P}
27.12	|	66.7	Yet [Yet, {P}
27.13	|	66.7	presume, [presume {P}
27.13	|	66.8	deed; [deed? {P}
27.14	|	66.9	it ["it {P} (TC)
27.14	|	66.9	accepted, [accepted {P}
27.15	|	66.11	not. [not." {P} (TC)
27.17	|	66.13	cannot, [can not, {S}
27.18	|	66.13	this [this, {P}
27.19	|	66.14	which [which, {P}
27.19	|	66.15	day, [day {P}
27.20	|	66.16	churches; [Churches: {C} {P}
27.20	|	66.16	taking, [taking {P}
27.21	|	66.17	giving, [giving {P}
27.21	|	66.17	offences; [offenses; {S}
27.21	|	66.17	other, [other {P}
27.22	|	66.18	judged; [judged, {P}
27.23	|	66.19	expressly revealed [expressly-revealed {S}
27.23	|	66.19	But [But, {P}
27.24	|	66.20	offence [offense {S}
27.25	|	66.22	such; [such, {P}
27.28	|	66.25	lawgiver, [Lawgiver, {C}
27.28	|	66.25	save, [save {P}
27.29	|	66.26	farther, [further, {S}

Page.Line 1st Ed.		Page.Line 2nd Ed.	First Edition [Second Edition
27.31	|	66.29	page first, [the first page {D}{P}
27.32	|	66.30	brother; [brother, {P}
27.35	|	66.33	duty, [duty {P}
27.35	|	66.33	divine [Divine {C}
27.36	|	66.34	connexion, [connection, {S}
27.36	|	66.34	article: [article, {P}
27.39	|	67.4	dare [dare, {P}
27.40	|	67.4	therefore [therefore, {P}
27.40	|	67.4	do, [do {P}
27.40	|	67.4	any thing, [anything {P}{S}
27.40	|	67.5	divine [Divine {C}
27.40	|	67.5	obligation, [obligation {P}
27.41	|	67.6	"Thus ["thus {C}
27.42	|	67.6	Lord" [Lord," {P}
27.42	|	67.6	terms, [terms {P}
27.44	|	67.9	connexion [connection {S}
27.44	|	67.9	resolution; [resolution, {P}
27.46	|	67.11	revelation: [rev- elation; {P}
27.47	|	67.12	inculcated [inculcated, {P}
27.47	|	67.13	cannot [can not {S}
27.48	|	67.13	"thus ["Thus {C}
27.48	|	67.13	Lord" [Lord," {P}
27.48	|	67.14	above; [above, {P}
27.49	|	67.15	indirectly, [indi- rectly {P}
28.3	|	67.18	christian, [Christian {C}{P} TC)[7]
28.4	|	67.19	judgment: [judgment; {P} (TC)
28.5	|	67.20	cases, [cases {P}
28.7	|	67.22	This [This, {P}
28.7	|	67.22	see [see, {P}
28.7	|	67.23	churches, [Churches, {C}
28.8	|	67.23	christian [Christian {C}
28.8	|	67.23	unity. [unity; {P}
28.8	|	67.23	And [and {C}
28.8	|	67.24	case, [case {P}
28.9	|	67.24	christian [Christian {C}
28.9	|	67.24	church [Church {C}
28.9	|	67.25	amongst [among {S}
28.10	|	67.25	expect, [expect {P}
28.10	|	67.26	resto- ration, [restoration {P}
28.12	|	67.28	things; [things, {P}

Page.Line 1st Ed.	**Page.Line 2nd Ed.**	**First Edition [Second Edition**
28.14	67.30	page 10th; [the thirty-ninth page, {D} {P}
28.15	67.31	relinquish, [relinquish {P}
28.17	67.33	God; [God, {P}
28.17	67.34	we, [we {P}
28.17	67.34	brethren, [brethren {P}
28.18	67.34	condescension, [concession, {D}
28.19	68.1	christian [Christian {C}
28.19	68.2	church; [Church, {C} {P}
28.20	68.3	relinquishment, [relinquishment {P}
28.22	68.5	themselves: [themselves; {P}
28.23	68.6	practices, [practices {P}
28.25	68.8	do, [do: {P}
28.26	68.10	any wise [anywise {S}
28.28	68.11	dead; [dead, {P}
28.28	68.12	buried [buried, {P}
28.28	68.12	too; [too, {P}
28.29	68.13	Apostle [apostle {C}
28.30	68.13	this, [this {P}
28.33	68.17	not, [not {P}
28.33	68.18	christians [Christians {C}
28.34	68.19	days— [days, {P}
28.35	68.19	&c. &c.— [etc., etc., {S} {P}
28.36	68.20	practised [practiced {S}
28.36	68.20	converts:— [converts, {P}
28.36	68.21	unity, [unity {P}
28.39	68.24	things; [things, {P}
28.41	68.26	transgres- sion; [transgression, {P}
28.44	68.29	evident; [evident: {P}
28.45	68.30	mistakes, [mistakes {P}
28.45	68.30	people; [peo- ple, {P}
28.47	68.33	spirit [Spirit {C}
28.48	68.34	love"— [love?" {P}
28.48	68.34	saith [says {S}
28.48	68.34	scrip- ture? [Scripture? {C}
28.49	69.1	to, [to {P}
29.1	69.1	un- derstood, [understood {P}
29.1	69.2	say, [say {P}
29.2	69.2	farther [further {S}
29.3	69.5	silent: [silent; {P}

Page.Line 1st Ed.	**Page.Line 2nd Ed.**	**First Edition [Second Edition**
29.4	69.6	ex- pressly commanded, [expressly-commanded {S} {P}
29.5	69.6	highly important [highly-important {S}
29.5	69.6	duty: [duty; {P}
29.6	69.7	saith [says {S}
29.6	69.8	Apostle? [apostle? {C}
29.9	69.10	amongst [among {S}
29.9	69.10	things, [things {P}
29.9	69.11	forborne; [forborne— {P}
29.10	69.12	commanded; [commanded— {P}
29.11	69.13	Apostle's [apostle's {C} (TD)
29.11	69.13	breth- ren— [brethren {P}
29.12	69.14	church [Church {C}
29.12	69.14	divine [Divine {C}
29.14	69.16	practises, [practices {S} {P}
29.15	69.17	church's [Church's {C}
29.17	69.20	ensued; [ensued, {P}
29.20	69.23	Who [Who, {P}
29.20	69.23	then [then, {P}
29.22	69.25	sinful, [sinful {P}
29.22	69.25	intended; [intended, {P}
29.23	69.26	preaching of [practicing {D} (TC)
29.24	69.27	offence; [offense; {S}
29.24	69.27	habits [habit {D} (TC)
29.24	69.28	day, [day {P}
29.25	69.28	comfort, [comfort {P}
29.25	69.28	emolument; [emolument, {P}
29.27	69.30	duties; [duties, {P} (TC)
29.27	69.31	sin; [sin {P}
29.27	69.31	practise [practice {S}
29.27	69.31	a sin; [sin; {D}
29.28	69.32	opinion; [opinion, {P} (TC)
29.29	69.33	we, [we {P} (TC)
29.29	69.33	means, [means {P}
29.30	69.33	practise,— [to prac- tice; {S} {P} (TC)[8]
29.31	69.34	Whereas [whereas {C} (TC)
29.31	70.1	spirit [Spirit {C}
29.32	70.2	saith [says {S}
29.32	70.2	Apostle [apostle {C} (TC)

Page.Line 1st Ed.	**Page.Line 2nd Ed.**	**First Edition [Second Edition**
29.33	70.3	faith, [faith," {P}
29.33	70.3	saith [says {S}
29.33	70.3	he, [he; {P}
29.33	70.3	have ["have {P}
29.34	70.4	man, [man {P}
29.34	70.4	himself, [himself {P}
29.35	70.6	farther [further {S}
29.37	70.8	towards [toward {S}
29.37	70.9	namely, [namely: {P}
29.40	70.11	them; [them, {P}
29.41	70.13	church, [Church, {C}
29.42	70.14	have been, [have been {P}
29.42	70.14	since, [since {P}
29.42	70.14	gone: [gone; {P}
29.44	70.16	beat [beaten {S}
29.45	70.18	itself, [itself {P}
29.46	70.18	with one [one {D}
29.46	70.19	contentions, [contentions {P}
29.47	70.20	peace [peace, {P}
29.47	70.20	charity, [charity {P}
29.48	70.20	christianity: [Christianity, {C} {P}
29.48	70.21	appear, [appear {P}
30.2	70.24	highly favored [highly-favored {S}
30.2	70.24	people, [people," {P}
30.2	70.24	saith [says {S}
30.2	70.25	would ["would {P}
30.3	70.26	hearts [hearts' {S}
30.9	70.32	forever, [forever {P}
30.10	70.33	say, [say {P} (TC)
30.10	70.33	that [that, {P}
30.10	70.34	every thing [everything {S}
30.11	70.34	intended, [intended {P}
30.11	71.1	church [Church {C}
30.12	71.1	might still remain [might re- main {D}
30.13	71.2	practice. [practice; {P} (TC)
30.13	71.2	Let [let {C} (TC)
30.13	71.3	consider, [consider {P}
30.14	71.3	church, [Church, {C}
30.14	71.4	persuaded, [persuaded {P}

Page.Line 1st Ed.	Page.Line 2nd Ed.	First Edition [Second Edition
30.15	71.5	scriptural [Scriptural {C}
30.15	71.5	christian [Christian {C}
30.15	71.5	church [Church {C}
30.16	71.6	practice; [practice, {P}
30.17	71.7	towards [toward {S}
30.17	71.8	another; [another, {P}
30.18	71.8	of the private [of private {D}
30.19	71.10	Apostles' [apostles' {C}
30.21	71.11	here, [here {P}
30.22	71.13	church [Church {C}
30.22	71.13	great [great, {P}
30.22	71.13	visible [visible, {P}
30.25	71.16	practising [practicing {S}
30.26	71.17	scriptural [Scriptural {C}
30.26	71.17	preserved, [preserved {P}
30.27	71.18	whole; [whole, {P}
30.27	71.19	worshipping [worshiping {S}
30.28	71.19	society, [society {P}
30.28	71.19	church; [Church, {C} {P}
30.29	71.20	enjoined, [enjoined {P}
30.29	71.21	expressly revealed [expressly-revealed {S}
30.30	71.21	God, [God {P}
30.32	71.24	scriptural [Scriptural {C}
30.33	71.25	suggested, [suggested {P}
30.35	71.27	right: [right; {P}
30.38	71.31	Lati- tudinarianism [Latitudinarianism, {P}
30.39	71.31	term) [term,) {P}
30.44	72.2	divine [Divine {C}
30.44	72.3	persons, [persons {P}
30.45	72.3	profession, [profession {P}
30.45	72.3	practice [practice, {P}
30.46	72.5	intend) [intend,) {P}
30.46	72.5	hope, [hope {P}
30.47	72.6	appear [appear, {P}
30.47	72.6	christian, [Christian, {C}
30.49	72.8	thing— [thing, {P}
30.49	72.8	and [and, {P}
30.49	72.8	therefore [therefore, {P}

Page.Line 1st Ed.	Page.Line 2nd Ed.	First Edition [Second Edition
31.3	72.11	hair's breadth [hair-breadth {S}
31.3	72.11	farther— [further; {S} {P}
31.5	72.14	profession, [profession {P}
31.7	72.16	long: [long, {P} (TC)
31.8	72.17	end; [end, {P} (TC)
31.8	72.17	be, [be {P} (TC)
31.9	72.17	those, [those {P} (TC)
31.9	72.18	neighbors; [neighbors, {P}
31.10	72.19	neighbours [neighbors {S}
31.10	72.19	do; [do, {P} (TC)
31.11	72.20	divine [Divine {C} (TC)
31.12	72.21	Bible— [Bible, {P}
31.13	72.22	eyes— [eyes, {P}
31.15	72.25	cannot, [can not {S} {P}
31.17	72.26	leaders, [leaders {P}
31.17	72.27	eyesight; [eyesight, {P}
31.18	72.27	faculties, [faculties {P}
31.18	72.28	information, [information {P}
31.19	72.28	them: [them; {P}
31.20	72.29	reason; [reason, {P}
31.20	72.30	cannot [can not {S}
31.20	72.30	see; [see, {P}
31.21	72.31	leaders; [leaders, {P}
31.23	72.33	deceived: [deceived; {P}
31.25	73.2	viz. [namely, {D}
31.26	73.2	cannot, [can not {S} {P}
31.27	73.3	think, [think {P}
31.27	73.3	mistaking: [mistaken; {D} {P} (TC)
31.29	73.6	divine [Divine {C}
31.30	73.7	it— [it, {P}
31.31	73.7	upon, [upon {P}
31.31	73.8	for, [for {P}
31.31	73.8	divine [Divine {C}
31.31	73.8	teach- ing; [teaching, {P}
31.32	73.9	understanding.— [understanding— {P}
31.32	73.9	To all [to all {C}
31.33	73.10	such, [such {P}
31.33	73.10	cause; [cause, {P}
31.33	73.10	persuaded, [persuaded {P}
31.34	73.11	consideration; [con- sideration, {P}

Page.Line 1st Ed.		Page.Line 2nd Ed.	First Edition [Second Edition
31.38	|	73.16	sense [sense, {P}
31.39	|	73.16	sense) [sense,) {P}
31.39	|	73.17	belong. [belong, {P}
31.39	|	73.17	Whether [whether {C}
31.40	|	73.18	any thing, [anything {S} {P}
31.41	|	73.19	duty; [duty, {P}
31.41	|	73.19	to, [to {P}
31.41	|	73.19	from, [from {P}
31.42	|	73.20	scriptures: [Scriptures, {C} {P}
31.42	|	73.21	farther [further {S}
31.43	|	73.21	this; [this, {P}
31.43	|	73.22	in- junctions [injunctions, {P}
31.46	|	73.25	christian [Christian {C}
31.47	|	73.26	any thing [anything {S}
31.48	|	73.27	standard: [standard, {P}
31.49	|	73.28	practise [practice {S}
32.1	|	73.29	therein; [therein, {P}
32.2	|	73.29	*alledged,* [*alleged,* {S}
32.2	|	73.30	any thing [anything {S}
32.2	|	73.30	contrary: [contrary, {P}
32.3	|	73.31	this, [this {P}
32.4	|	73.32	every thing, [everything {S} {P}
32.4	|	73.33	"thus ["Thus {C}
32.5	|	73.33	terms, [terms {P}
32.5	|	73.34	precedent. [precedent? {P}
32.6	|	73.34	*ye,* [you, {S} {T} (TC)
32.6	|	74.1	Latitudan- arianism [Latitudinarianism {S}
32.9	|	74.4	doing; [doing {P}
32.10	|	74.5	are, [are {P}
32.11	|	74.6	knowledge; [knowledge, {P}
32.12	|	74.7	expected it: [expected it; {P}
32.14	|	74.9	churches, [Churches, {C}
32.16	|	74.11	proceedings: [proceedings; {P}
32.17	|	74.12	asserting, [asserting {P}
32.17	|	74.12	declaring, [declaring {P}
32.17	|	74.12	any thing [anything {S}
32.19	|	74.14	christians [Christians {C}
32.20	|	74.16	hope, [hope {P}
32.20	|	74.16	purity [purity, {P}

Page.Line 1st Ed.	**Page.Line 2nd Ed.**	**First Edition [Second Edition**
32.21	74.17	church [Church {C}
32.23	74.19	fellow christians, [fellow-Christians {S} {C} {P}
32.23	74.19	conduct [conduct. {P}
32.23	74.19	And, [And {P}
32.29	74.26	evil: [evil. {P}
32.30	74.26	see [(See {P} {C}
32.30	74.26	Deut. xviii—20. [(See Deut. xviii: 20:) {S} {P}
32.31	74.28	speak— [speak, {P}
32.32	74.29	Apostle [apostle {C}
32.33	74.30	betwixt [between {S} (TC)
32.34	74.31	Lord; [Lord. {P}
32.34	74.31	See [(See {P}
32.34	74.31	1st Cor. 7. 25. [1 Cor. vii: 25 {S} {P}
32.34	74.31	and 40. [and 40.) {P}
32.34	74.31	Though [Though, {P}
32.35	74.32	appear [appears {S}
32.37	74.34	holy [Holy {C}
32.37	74.34	spirit [Spirit {C}
32.38	75.1	think [think," {P}
32.38	75.1	saith [said {S}
32.38	75.1	he [he, {P}
32.38	75.1	that ["that {P}
32.38	75.2	spirit [Spirit {C}
32.38	75.2	God:" [God;" {P}
32.39	75.3	would [could {D} (TC)
32.39	75.3	this: [this; {P}
32.40	75.3	see, [see {P}
32.40	75.3	that [that, {P}
32.40	75.4	church [Church {C}
32.41	75.5	and [and, {P}
32.43	75.7	permission [permission, {P}
32.44	75.8	faithful— [faithful, {P}
32.45	75.9	master's [Master's {C}
32.45	75.10	conclusions; [conclusions, {P}
32.48	75.13	opinions; [opinions, {P}
32.48	75.13	but, [but {P}
32.49	75.15	doing: [doing, {P}
32.49	75.15	and [and, {P}

Page.Line 1st Ed.		Page.Line 2nd Ed.	First Edition [Second Edition
33.1	|	75.15	course [course, {P}
33.1	|	75.15	such, [such {P}
33.1	|	75.15	censuring, [censuring {P}
33.2	|	75.16	contempt; [contempt, {P}
33.3	|	75.17	judgment; [judgment, {P}
33.3	|	75.18	stand [Stand {C}
33.6	|	75.20	nought [naught {S}
33.6	|	75.20	brother; [brother, {P}
33.7	|	75.21	church, [Church, {C}
33.7	|	75.22	Christ; [Christ, {P}
33.8	|	75.23	wrong, [wrong {P}
33.9	|	75.23	determinations: [determinations, {P}
33.9	|	75.23	also [also, {P}
33.9	|	75.24	connexion [connection {S}
33.11	|	75.26	church, [Church, {C}
33.12	|	75.26	communion;— [communion, {P}
33.14	|	75.29	error; [error, {P}
33.15	|	75.30	charity: [charity, {P}
33.18	|	75.33	such [such, {P}
33.20	|	76.1	church, [Church, {C}
33.21	|	76.2	certainly [certainly, {P}
33.22	|	76.3	Word, [word, {C}
33.22	|	76.3	church [Church {C}
33.22	|	76.4	say, [say {P}
33.23	|	76.5	him) [him,) {P}
33.24	|	76.5	church [Church {C}
33.24	|	76.6	suppose, [suppose {P}
33.26	|	76.8	church [Church {C}
33.28	|	76.10	church [Church {C}
33.29	|	76.11	this [this, {P}
33.29	|	76.11	purposes [purposes, {P}
33.32	|	76.14	church, [Church, {C}
33.34	|	76.17	amongst [among {S}
33.36	|	76.19	any thing, [anything {S} {P}
33.37	|	76.20	church [Church {C}
33.39	|	76.22	state, [state {P}
33.39	|	76.22	interests; [interests, {P}
33.41	|	76.25	scripture [Scripture {C}
33.42	|	76.26	there, [there {P}
33.42	|	76.26	see, [see {P}
33.43	|	76.27	church [Church {C}

Page.Line 1st Ed.	Page.Line 2nd Ed.	First Edition [Second Edition
33.44	76.28	church [Church {C}
33.45	76.29	churches [Church's {C} {D}
33.47	76.31	church [Church {C}
33.48	76.32	doing; [doing, {P}
33.49	76.34	damna- tion; [damnation? {P}
34.1	77.1	church [Church {C}
34.2	77.1	If [If, {P}
34.3	77.2	church [Church {C}
34.3	77.2	thus, [thus {P}
34.3	77.3	saying, [saying: {P}
34.3	77.3	we [We {C}
34.4	77.4	rejected— [rejected; {P}
34.5	77.5	amongst [among {S}
34.5	77.5	*us;* [*us,* {P}
34.6	77.5	away; [away, {P}
34.6	77.6	churches [Churches {C}
34.6	77.6	him. [him;— {P}
34.7	77.7	We [we {C}
34.7	77.7	church, [Church, {C}
34.8	77.7	churches [Churches {C}
34.8	77.8	churches [Churches {C}
34.8	77.8	Christ; [Christ, {P}
34.9	77.9	any thing [anything {S}
34.9	77.9	church [Church {C}
34.10	77.10	And, [And {P}
34.10	77.10	whether [whether, {P}
34.10	77.10	churches [Churches {C}
34.10	77.10	duty, [duty {P}
34.11	77.11	churches, [Churches, {C}
34.12	77.12	answered, [answered {P}
34.13	77.13	churches [Churches {C}
34.13	77.13	could, [could {P}
34.13	77.14	him; [him, {P}
34.14	77.15	church, [Church, {C}
34.15	77.15	rejected: [rejected; {P}
34.15	77.15	but, [but {P}
34.16	77.16	nay, [nay {P}
34.16	77.17	cruelly [cruelly, {P}
34.16	77.17	towards [toward {S}
34.16	77.17	christian [Christian {C}

Page.Line 1st Ed.		Page.Line 2nd Ed.	First Edition [Second Edition
34.17	|	77.17	God; [God, {P}
34.18	|	77.18	Lord; [Lord, {P}
34.18	|	77.19	father's [Father's {C}
34.20	|	77.21	churches [Churches {C}
34.22	|	77.23	church, [Church, {C}
34.25	|	77.26	heaven: [heaven; {P}
34.26	|	77.27	scriptures, [Scriptures, {C}
34.26	|	77.28	earth, [earth {P}
34.27	|	77.29	way, [way {P}
34.27	|	77.29	church [Church {C}
34.27	|	77.29	*thus,* [*thus* {P}
34.28	|	77.30	*conclusion;* [*conclusion,* {P}
34.28	|	77.30	acknowledge, [acknowledge {P}
34.29	|	77.31	communion, [communion {P}
34.30	|	77.32	church; [Church; {C}
34.30	|	77.32	*this*— [*this,* {P}
34.30	|	77.32	wherea- bouts [where- about {P}
34.31	|	77.33	fellow-christian, [fellow- Christian, {C}
34.32	|	77.33	God!! [God? {P}
34.34	|	78.1	Apostle [apostle {C}
34.34	|	78.3	"who ["Who {C}
34.35	|	78.4	not— [not, {P}
34.36	|	78.4	words, [words: {P}
34.38	|	78.7	church." [Church." {C}
34.39	|	78.8	farther, [further, {S}
34.39	|	78.8	church [Church {C}
34.40	|	78.9	person, [person {P}
34.40	|	78.9	church [Church {C}
34.41	|	78.10	rejected: [rejected, {P}
34.41	|	78.10	not, [not {P}
34.41	|	78.10	church [Church {C}
34.41	|	78.11	doing, [doing {P}
34.42	|	78.11	*censure,* [*censure* {P}
34.42	|	78.11	church [Church {C}
34.43	|	78.12	too, [too {P}
34.44	|	78.14	betwixt [between {S} (TC)
34.44	|	78.14	churches? [Churches? {C}
34.46	|	78.16	church [Church, {C} {P}
34.47	|	78.17	those, [those {P}
34.48	|	78.18	confess, [confess {P}

Page.Line 1st Ed.		Page.Line 2nd Ed.	First Edition [Second Edition
34.48	|	78.18	cannot [can not {S}
34.48	|	78.19	church, [Church, {C}
34.49	|	78.19	schismatically— [schismatically, {P}
34.49	|	78.20	church [Church {C}
35.1	|	78.20	pre-supposes, [presupposes {S} {P}
35.1	|	78.21	schism, [schism {P}
35.2	|	78.21	fellow-christian, [fellow- Christian {C} {P}
35.4	|	78.24	church, [Church {C} {P}
35.5	|	78.24	communion, [communion {P}
35.5	|	78.25	fellow-christian; [fellow-Christian; {C}
35.6	|	78.25	and [and, {P}
35.6	|	78.26	says, [says {P}
35.7	|	78.27	else; [else, {P}
35.7	|	78.27	church [Church {C}
35.8	|	78.27	For [For, {P}
35.9	|	78.29	church [Church {C}
35.9	|	78.29	rejected, [rejected {P}
35.11	|	78.31	individual, [individual {P}
35.11	|	78.31	refuses, [refuses {P}
35.12	|	78.32	church, [Church {C} {P}
35.12	|	78.32	receive, [receive {P}
35.12	|	78.33	for, [for {P}
35.13	|	78.33	opinions, [opinions {P}
35.13	|	78.33	practices, [practices {P}
35.13	|	78.34	ma- nagements.— [managements; {P}
35.14	|	78.34	For, [for {C} {P}
35.14	|	79.1	church, [Church {C} {P}
35.15	|	79.2	rejects, [rejects {P}
35.16	|	79.2	christians? [Christians? {C}
35.16	|	79.3	this [this, {P}
35.16	|	79.3	pur- poses [purposes, {P}
35.17	|	79.4	excommunicate; [excommunicate, {P}
35.19	|	79.6	shew [show {S}
35.19	|	79.6	brethren, [brethren {P}
35.21	|	79.9	practice, [practice {P}
35.22	|	79.9	divisions; [divi- sions, {P}

Page.Line 1st Ed.	Page.Line 2nd Ed.	First Edition [Second Edition
35.23	79.11	other, [other {P}
35.23	79.11	duty; [duty, {P}
35.25	79.12	church, [Church, {C}
35.25	79.13	them, [them {P}
35.26	79.14	with us [from us {D} (TC)
35.27	79.15	or, [or {P}
35.27	79.15	least, [least {P}
35.28	79.16	practice, [practice {P}
35.28	79.16	cannot [can not {S}
35.29	79.18	things, [things {P}
35.30	79.18	they, [they {P}
35.30	79.18	we, [we {P}
35.30	79.18	cannot, [can not {S} {P}
35.30	79.18	approve; [approve, {P}
35.30	79.19	no where [nowhere {S}
35.31	79.21	christianity— [Christianity, {C} {P}
35.33	79.22	church, [Church, {C}
35.35	79.23	way, [way {P}
35.35	79.24	perceive, [perceive {P}
35.38	79.27	divisions: [divisions; {P}
35.39	79.28	requires, [requires {P}
35.40	79.29	model— [model, {P}
35.40	79.29	worship [worship, {P}
35.40	79.29	discipline [discipline, {P}
35.41	79.30	christian [Christian {C}
35.41	79.30	church. [Church. {C}
35.41	79.30	do, [do {P}
35.42	79.31	said: [said; {P}
35.42	79.32	prac- tise [practice {S}
35.45	79.34	realize, [realize {P}
35.45	79.34	exhibit, [exhibit {P}
35.45	80.1	uniformity, [uniformity {P}
35.46	80.1	church [Church {C}
35.47	80.2	if [if, {P}
35.48	80.4	christian [Christian {C}
35.49	80.5	church [Church {C}
36.1	80.7	urged, [urged {P}
36.2	80.8	christianity, [Christianity {C} {P}
36.3	80.9	scriptures; [Scriptures, {P}
36.4	80.10	sentiments. [sentiments, {P}

Page.Line 1st Ed.		Page.Line 2nd Ed.	First Edition [Second Edition
36.4	|	80.10	We [we {C}
36.7	|	80.13	enjoined; [enjoined, {P}
36.7	|	80.14	to it— [to it, {P}
36.9	|	80.15	do [Do {C}
36.11	|	80.18	rule; [rule, {P}
36.11	|	80.18	or [or, {P}
36.11	|	80.18	rather [rather, {P}
36.12	|	80.18	subject matter [subject- matter {S}
36.13	|	80.19	no; [not, {D} {P} (TC)[9]
36.13	|	80.20	practise [practice {S}
36.14	|	80.21	light, [light {P}
36.14	|	80.21	scriptures [Scriptures {C}
36.15	|	80.22	self same [self-same {S}
36.15	|	80.22	subject matter [subject-matter {S}
36.15	|	80.23	practice; [practice, {P}
36.16	|	80.23	times, [times {P}
36.16	|	80.23	places;— [places, {P}
36.16	|	80.23	and, [and {P}
36.16	|	80.23	that [that, {P}
36.17	|	80.24	prescribes, [prescribes {P}
36.18	|	80.26	christian [Christian {C}
36.18	|	80.26	church [Church {C}
36.19	|	80.27	practice, [practice {P}
36.20	|	80.27	christian [Christian {C}
36.20	|	80.27	church [Church {C}
36.21	|	80.28	professors, [professors {P}
36.21	|	80.29	props. [Propositions {D} {C}
36.22	|	80.29	8th, [8, {D}
36.22	|	80.29	page 7th; [pages 48 and 50, {D} {P}
36.23	|	80.30	christians, [Christians, {C}
36.24	|	80.32	intend, [intend {P}
36.25	|	80.32	christian [Chris- tian {C}
36.25	|	80.33	recognized, [recognized {P}
36.27	|	81.2	formulas, [formulas {P}
36.28	|	81.3	unity, [unity {P}
36.29	|	81.3	faith: [faith, {P}
36.29	|	81.3	superficious [superficial {D}
36.32	|	81.6	christian [Christian {C}
36.32	|	81.6	character— [char- acter, {P}
36.33	|	81.7	profession— [profession, {P}
36.33	|	81.8	christian [Christian {C}

Page.Line 1st Ed.		Page.Line 2nd Ed.	First Edition [Second Edition
36.34	|	81.9	name— [name, {P}
36.35	|	81.10	standard, [standard {P}
36.36	|	81.11	degree of, [degree of {P}
36.37	|	81.12	called, [called {P}
36.37	|	81.12	morality; [morality, {P}
36.37	|	81.12	foundation— [foundation {P}
36.38	|	81.13	reason, [reason {P}
36.38	|	81.14	technia [technicalness {D}
36.39	|	81.14	profession— [profession, {P}
36.39	|	81.14	shiboleth [shibboleth {S}
36.39	|	81.14	party; [party, {P}
36.40	|	81.15	distinguish, [distinguish {P}
36.41	|	81.17	to it; [to it, {P}
36.42	|	81.17	from it; [from it, {P}
36.42	|	81.18	about it; [about it, {P}
36.43	|	81.19	you, [you {P}
36.45	|	81.21	merely by *it,* [merely by *it* {P}
36.46	|	81.22	church [Church {C}
36.46	|	81.22	week: [week. {P}
36.46	|	81.22	you [You {C}
36.47	|	81.23	please; [please, {P}
36.48	|	81.24	people! [people, {P}
36.49	|	81.25	formula. [formula! {P}
36.49	|	81.26	them, [them {P}
37.1	|	81.26	believe, [believe {P}
37.2	|	81.28	the reverend, [the reverend {P}
37.3	|	81.28	*can,* [*can* {P}
37.3	|	81.29	*do,* [*do* {P}
37.4	|	81.29	confidence, [confidence {P}
37.4	|	81.30	Apostles [apostles {C}
37.4	|	81.30	Prophets; [prophets; {C}
37.6	|	81.31	say, [say {P}
37.6	|	81.31	do, [do {P}
37.6	|	81.31	any thing, [anything {S} {P}
37.6	|	81.32	Lord, [Lord {P}
37.7	|	81.33	heaven; [Heaven, {P} {C}
37.7	|	81.33	and, [and {P}
37.7	|	81.33	therefore, [therefore {P}
37.8	|	81.34	rabbi, [Rabbi {C} {P} (TC)

Page.Line 1st Ed.	Page.Line 2nd Ed.	First Edition [Second Edition
37.8	81.34	or reverend; [or Reverend, {C}{P} (TC)
37.9	82.1	&c. [etc. {S}
37.10	82.2	legislate; [legislate, {P}
37.10	82.2	and [and, {P}
37.10	82.2	therefore [therefore, {P}
37.10	82.2	assumed, [assumed {P}
37.10	82.2	receiv- ed, [received {P}
37.11	82.3	amongst [among {S}
37.11	82.3	men: [men, {P}
37.14	82.6	church, [Church {C}{P}
37.14	82.6	reform; [reform, {P}
37.15	82.7	purity, [purity {P}
37.15	82.7	christian [Chris- tian {C}
37.15	82.8	institution; [institution, {P}
37.17	82.9	And, [And {P}
37.17	82.9	there, [there {P}
37.17	82.10	any thing [anything {S}
37.18	82.10	church, [Church {C}{P}
37.18	82.11	perceive, [perceive {P}
37.19	82.12	Or, [Or {P}
37.20	82.12	impressions, [im- pressions {P}
37.20	82.14	mind, [mind {P}
37.21	82.14	exhibits; [exhibits, {P}
37.21	82.14	perceive, [perceive {P}
37.22	82.15	christianity, [Christianity {C}{P}
37.23	82.17	evident, [evident {P}
37.24	82.18	tenets, [tenets {P}
37.24	82.18	practices, [practices {P}
37.26	82.20	christianity, [Christianity, {C}
37.26	82.20	world, [world {P}
37.27	82.21	divine [Divine {C}
37.27	82.21	law— [law, {P}
37.28	82.23	scriptures, [Scriptures, {C}
37.29	82.23	do:— [do, {P}
37.30	82.25	scrip- tures; [Scriptures, {C}{P}
37.31	82.25	say, [say {P}
37.31	82.26	connexion, [connection, {S}
37.34	82.29	shew [show {S}
37.35	82.30	line; [line, {P}
37.35	82.30	expression; [expression, {P}

Page.Line 1st Ed.		Page.Line 2nd Ed.	First Edition [Second Edition
37.36	|	82.31	practice; [practice, {P}
37.36	|	82.31	conjec- ture; [con- jecture, {P}
37.37	|	82.33	Bible; [Bible, {P}
37.38	|	82.34	it; [it, {P}
37.39	|	83.1	please; [please, {P}
37.40	|	83.1	simple [simple, {P}
37.41	|	83.3	excommunications [excommunications, {P}
37.41	|	83.3	persecutions, [persecutions {P}
37.43	|	83.5	farther [further {S}
37.44	|	83.6	infer, [infer {P}
37.44	|	83.6	sentiment.— [sentiment; {P}
37.44	|	83.7	It [it {C}
37.44	|	83.7	gran- ted, [granted {P}
37.45	|	83.8	any thing, [anything {S} {P}
37.46	|	83.8	scripture, [Scripture {C} {P}
37.46	|	83.9	things, [things {P}
37.47	|	83.10	sentiment, [sentiment {P}
37.48	|	83.10	church [Church {C}
37.49	|	83.11	scriptural [Scriptural {C}
38.1	|	83.12	body; [body, {P}
38.2	|	83.13	christians, [Christians {C} {P}
38.3	|	83.14	cannot [can not {S}
38.5	|	83.17	divinely re- vealed [Divinely-re- vealed {C} {S}
38.6	|	83.18	truths; [truths, {P}
38.8	|	83.20	conceive, [conceive {P}
38.9	|	83.21	serve; [serve, {P}
38.11	|	83.23	forbearance, [forbearance {P}
38.12	|	83.25	state.— [state. {P}
38.16	|	83.29	offence; [offense; {S}
38.16	|	83.29	stumbling block, [stumbling-block {S} {P}
38.17	|	83.30	fall, [fall {P}
38.19	|	83.32	brother, [brother {P}
38.21	|	83.34	granted, [granted {P}
38.21	|	84.1	for, [for {P}
38.22	|	84.1	sentiment; [sentiment, {P}
38.22	|	84.1	suppose, [sup- pose {P}
38.23	|	84.2	purpose, [purpose {P}

Page.Line 1st Ed.		Page.Line 2nd Ed.	First Edition [Second Edition
38.23	|	84.3	expedient, [expedient {P}
38.24	|	84.4	ask, [ask: {P}
38.24	|	84.4	have [Have {C}
38.24	|	84.4	all, [all {P}
38.24	|	84.4	any, [any {P}
38.26	|	84.6	sentiment, [sentiment {P}
38.27	|	84.6	amongst [among {S}
38.27	|	84.7	firmly, [firmly {P}
38.27	|	84.7	solemnly, [solemnly {P}
38.28	|	84.8	churches, [Churches, {C}
38.29	|	84.9	church [Church {C}
38.29	|	84.9	good [good, {P}
38.29	|	84.9	then [then, {P}
38.31	|	84.11	church [Church {C}
38.31	|	84.11	universal; [universal, {P}
38.32	|	84.12	secured, [secured {P}
38.32	|	84.13	prac- tice, [practice {P}
38.33	|	84.13	words, [words {P}
38.33	|	84.14	divine [Divine {C}
38.33	|	84.14	standard; [standard, {P}
38.35	|	84.15	consequences, [consequences {P}
38.36	|	84.16	Or [Or, {P}
38.36	|	84.17	say, [say {P}
38.36	|	84.17	scriptures [Scriptures, {C} {P}
38.38	|	84.19	divine [Divine {C} (TC)
38.38	|	84.19	spirit, [Spirit, {C} (TC)
38.39	|	84.20	sentiment, [sentiment {P}
38.41	|	84.22	church [Church {C}
38.41	|	84.22	error, [error {P}
38.41	|	84.23	intend- ed; [intended, {P}
38.43	|	84.25	christian [Christian {C}
38.43	|	84.25	say, [say {P}
38.44	|	84.26	thus, [thus {P}
38.45	|	84.26	purposes; [purposes, {P}
38.45	|	84.27	other expedients— [other expedients; {P}
38.45	|	84.27	to expedients, [to expedients {P}
38.47	|	84.29	expedients, [expedients {P}
39.2	|	84.34	for the church [for the Church {C}
39.3	|	85.1	earth; [earth, {P}

Page.Line 1st Ed.		Page.Line 2nd Ed.	First Edition [Second Edition
39.4	|	85.2	per- fection: [perfection, {P}
39.5	|	85.2	less, [less {P}
39.5	|	85.2	suggest, [suggest {P}
39.7	|	85.4	granted, [granted {P}
39.7	|	85.5	intended, [intended {P}
39.8	|	85.6	church [Church {C}
39.9	|	85.7	mismanagements, [mismanagements {P}
39.10	|	85.8	heaven;— [heaven, {P}
39.12	|	85.9	imagine, [imagine {P}
39.12	|	85.10	here, [here {P}
39.12	|	85.10	suppose, [suppose {P}
39.12	|	85.10	assert, [assert {P}
39.14	|	85.12	Bible; [Bible, {P}
39.14	|	85.12	less, [less {P}
39.17	|	85.15	scriptures; [Scriptures, {C}
39.17	|	85.15	designed, [designed {P}
39.17	|	85.15	embraced, [embraced {P}
39.18	|	85.16	securing, [securing {P}
39.18	|	85.17	purity, [purity {P}
39.22	|	85.21	up, [up {P}
39.23	|	85.22	expe- dients; [ex- pedients, {P}
39.25	|	85.24	doubtful, [doubtful {P}
39.25	|	85.25	divisions; [divisions, {P}
39.26	|	85.25	thing [thing, {P}
39.26	|	85.25	least [least, {P}
39.27	|	85.26	now [now, {P}
39.27	|	85.27	certain, [certain {P}
39.28	|	85.28	them; [them, {P}
39.29	|	85.29	do [do, {P}
39.29	|	85.29	then [then, {P}
39.32	|	85.32	must, [must {P}
39.32	|	85.32	shall, [shall {P}
39.33	|	85.33	christianity [Christianity {C}
39.33	|	85.33	amen. [Amen; {C} {P}
39.33	|	85.33	But [but {C}
39.33	|	85.33	christians, [Christians {C} {P}
39.34	|	85.34	say, [say: {P}
39.34	|	85.34	forbid [Forbid {C}
39.34	|	86.1	corruptions, [corruptions {P}
39.35	|	86.2	Amen [Amen, {P}

Page.Line 1st Ed.	Page.Line 2nd Ed.	First Edition [Second Edition
39.36	86.4	may [may, {P}
39.37	86.4	possibly [possibly, {P}
39.37	86.4	and say; [and say: {P}
39.37	86.4	fear, [fear {P}
39.39	86.6	how, [how {P}
39.39	86.6	otherwise, [otherwise {P}
39.40	86.7	&c. &c? [etc? {S} {D}
39.41	86.8	practise, [practice {S} {P}
39.41	86.9	any thing [anything {S}
39.42	86.9	otherwise, [otherwise {P}
39.42	86.10	Word [word {C}
39.43	86.11	duty; [duty, {P}
39.44	86.12	faith, [faith {P}
39.44	86.12	practice; [practice, {P}
39.45	86.12	profession, [pro- fession {P}
39.45	86.13	exhibition, [exhibition {P}
39.46	86.14	&c. &c. [etc., {S} {D} {P}
39.46	86.14	self same [self-same {S}
39.47	86.15	called; [called, {P}
39.49	86.17	farther [further {S}
40.2	86.19	God; [God, {P}
40.2	86.19	and [and, {P}
40.2	86.19	therefore [therefore, {P}
40.3	86.20	practise [practice {S}
40.4	86.21	therein; [therein, {P}
40.4	86.22	practise [practice {S}
40.4	86.22	accordingly: [accordingly; {P}
40.6	86.24	profess, [profess {P}
40.6	86.24	practise, [practice {S}
40.7	86.24	more, [more {P}
40.7	86.24	less, [less {P}
40.8	86.26	so [so, {P}
40.9	86.26	practise [practice {S}
40.9	86.27	thing; [thing, {P}
40.11	86.29	practise? [practice? {S}
40.12	86.30	taken, [taken {P}
40.13	86.31	themselves; [themselves, {P}
40.13	86.31	thing, [thing {P}
40.16	86.34	produced; [produced, {P}
40.17	87.1	merely a [a mere {D}

Page.Line 1st Ed.		Page.Line 2nd Ed.	First Edition [Second Edition
40.18	|	87.2	practice; [practice, {P}
40.18	|	87.3	persons, [persons {P}
40.18	|	87.3	practising, [practicing {S} {P}
40.20	|	87.5	no body [nobody {S}
40.20	|	87.5	himself; [themselves. {D} {P}
40.21	|	87.6	besides, [Besides, {C}
40.21	|	87.6	practised [practiced {S}
40.22	|	87.7	pray, [pray {P}
40.22	|	87.7	tell, [tell {P}
40.22	|	87.8	senti- ments; [sentiments, {P}
40.25	|	87.10	censure; [censure {P}
40.26	|	87.11	offence, [offense, {S}
40.27	|	87.12	expressly revealed [expressly-revealed {S}
40.30	|	87.16	condemn, [condemn {P}
40.30	|	87.16	reject, [reject {P}
40.30	|	87.16	brother.— [brother. {P}
40.31	|	87.17	assumed, [assumed {P}
40.31	|	87.17	allowed, [allowed {P}
40.32	|	87.18	side, [side {P}
40.35	|	87.22	&c. &c. [etc., {S} {D} {P}
40.36	|	87.23	Athenasian [Athanasian {S}
40.39	|	87.25	assert, [assert {P}
40.39	|	87.26	are, [are {P}
40.39	|	87.26	Or [Or, {P}
40.41	|	87.28	Arian, [Arian {P}
40.41	|	87.28	Socinian, [Socinian {P}
40.41	|	87.28	heart, [heart {P}
40.42	|	87.29	Confession, [Confession {P}
40.42	|	87.29	Athenasian [Athanasian {S}
40.43	|	87.31	every thing [everything {S}
40.44	|	87.31	scriptures [Scriptures {C}
40.45	|	87.32	him; [him, {P}
40.46	|	87.33	professed, [professed {P}
40.46	|	87.34	him, [him {P}
40.47	|	87.34	Word? [word? {C}
40.47	|	87.34	follows [follows, {P}
40.48	|	88.2	affected, [effected {D} {P}
41.1	|	88.4	holy [Holy {C}
41.3	|	88.6	church, [Church {C} {P}

Page.Line 1st Ed.	**Page.Line 2nd Ed.**	**First Edition [Second Edition**
41.3	88.6	Athenasius [Athanasius {S}
41.3	88.7	century, [century {P}
41.6	88.9	do any thing [so anything {S}
41.6	88.10	or any thing [or anything {S}
41.6	88.10	else, [else {P}
41.7	88.10	Sacred [sacred {C}
41.7	88.11	Oracles, [oracles, {C}
41.8	88.11	points; [points, {P}
41.9	88.13	afterwards? [afterward? {S}
41.9	88.13	any where [anywhere {S}
41.14	88.18	purity; [purity, {P}
41.14	88.18	therefore [therefore, {P}
41.15	88.20	scriptural [Scriptural {C}
41.16	88.20	defence [defense {S}
41.16	88.20	divinely revealed [Divinely-revealed {C} {S}
41.18	88.23	farther, [further, {S}
41.20	88.25	questionable, [questionable {P}
41.21	88.26	whatsoever; [whatsoever, {P}
41.21	88.27	consi- der, [consider {P}
41.22	88.27	pre-supposes [presupposes {S}
41.22	88.27	far, [far {P}
41.23	88.28	that, [that {P}
41.25	88.30	prelate; [prelate— {P}
41.25	88.31	church [Church {C}
41.27	88.33	shew [show {S}
41.29	88.34	called; [called, {P}
41.31	89.3	And [And, {P}
41.33	89.5	sentiment; [sentiment, {P}
41.33	89.6	faith: [faith; {P}
41.34	89.7	all: [all; {P}
41.35	89.8	pre-supposes [presupposes {S}
41.36	89.8	scriptural [Scrip- tural {C}
41.38	89.11	catechism; [catechism, {P}
41.40	89.13	hand; [hand, {P}
41.40	89.13	may, [may {P}
41.42	89.15	intelligently, [intelligently {P}
41.43	89.16	end; [end, {P}
41.44	89.17	by, [by {P}
41.44	89.17	Scriptures; [Scriptures, {P}
41.46	89.20	Bible; [Bible, {P}

Page.Line 1st Ed.	Page.Line 2nd Ed.	First Edition [Second Edition
41.49	89.23	holy [Holy {C} (TC)
42.1	89.25	Apostle [apostle {C}
42.3	89.26	repetitions, [repetitions {P}
42.4	89.27	Bible; [Bible, {P}
42.5	89.29	truth; [truth, {P}
42.10	89.34	divine [Divine {C}
42.11	90.1	no where [nowhere {S}
42.11	90.1	prescribed; [prescribed, {P}
42.12	90.2	no where [nowhere {S}
42.12	90.2	us, [us {P}
42.13	90.3	shewn, [shown {S} {P}
42.14	90.5	government, [government {P}
42.14	90.5	church, [Church {C} {P}
42.15	90.6	purity; [purity, {P}
42.16	90.7	communion; [communion, {P}
42.17	90.8	alledge, [allege {S} {P}
42.18	90.8	church [Church {C}
42.18	90.9	scriptural [Scriptural {C}
42.18	90.9	exertion, [exertion {P}
42.18	90.9	power, [power {P}
42.20	90.11	divinely revealed [divinely-revealed {S}
42.20	90.11	say, [say {P}
42.21	90.12	evils, [evils {P}
42.21	90.12	of, [of {P}
42.21	90.13	habits [habit {D}
42.24	90.15	rather, [rather {P}
42.24	90.15	entirely, [entirely {P}
42.24	90.16	them; [them {P}
42.25	90.16	thing, [thing {P}
42.25	90.17	opposing, [opposing {P}
42.26	90.18	standards.— [standards. {P}
42.27	90.18	the bye, [the by, {D}
42.29	90.21	But [But, {P}
42.30	90.22	fellow-christians [fellow-Christians {C}
42.31	90.24	scriptures: [Scriptures, {C} {P}
42.32	90.25	contain;— [contain, {P}
42.33	90.26	Catechisms, [Catechisms {P}
42.37	90.30	obedience, [obedience; {P}

Page.Line 1st Ed.		Page.Line 2nd Ed.	First Edition [Second Edition
42.37	|	90.30	di- vine [Divine {C}
42.38	|	90.31	acquiesce [acquiesce, {P}
42.38	|	90.31	subject matter [subject-matter {S}
42.39	|	90.32	both— [both; {P}
42.39	|	90.32	connexion [con- nection {S}
42.41	|	90.34	another— [another; {P}
42.41	|	90.34	self knowledge, [self- knowledge, {S}
42.42	|	91.1	salvation, [salvation {P}
42.42	|	91.2	christian [Christian {C}
42.43	|	91.2	divine [Divine {C}
42.43	|	91.3	revelation; [revelation, {P}
42.44	|	91.4	of, [of {P}
42.44	|	91.4	these [those {D}
42.45	|	91.4	subjects.— [subjects. {P}
42.45	|	91.5	granted, [granted {P}
42.46	|	91.6	far, [far {P}
42.48	|	91.8	Scriptures; [Scriptures, {P}
43.1	|	91.11	which, [which {P}
43.3	|	91.12	helps: [helps, {P}
43.4	|	91.14	them; [them, {P}
43.5	|	91.15	of— [of; {P}
43.8	|	91.18	declared, [declared {P}
43.8	|	91.18	"thus ["Thus {C}
43.8	|	91.18	And, [And {P}
43.9	|	91.19	that, [that {P}
43.10	|	91.20	Bible; [Bible, {P}
43.10	|	91.21	it; [it, {P}
43.12	|	91.22	forward, [forward {P}
43.12	|	91.22	then [then, {P}
43.12	|	91.22	christians [Christians, {C} {P}
43.12	|	91.23	church, [Church, {C}
43.14	|	91.24	God;" [God," {P}
43.15	|	91.26	to, [to {P}
43.15	|	91.26	divine [Divine {C}
43.16	|	91.27	church [Church {C}
43.17	|	91.28	obedience, [obedience {P}
43.18	|	91.29	pre-supposes [presupposes {S}
43.19	|	91.30	them; [them, {P}
43.20	|	91.31	divine, [Divine, {C}
43.20	|	91.32	subject matter, [subject-matter, {S}

Page.Line 1st Ed.		Page.Line 2nd Ed.	First Edition [Second Edition
43.21	|	91.32	"thus ["Thus {C}
43.22	|	91.33	human; [human, {P}
43.22	|	91.34	precept [precepts {D} (TC)
43.23	|	92.1	church membership, [Church-membership, {C} {S}
43.24	|	92.2	be [be, {P}
43.24	|	92.2	what [What {C}
43.25	|	92.3	man; [man? {P}
43.26	|	92.4	&c. &c. [etc., etc.? {S} {P}
43.26	|	92.4	duty; [duty? {P}
43.27	|	92.4	but [but, {P}
43.27	|	92.5	what [What {C}
43.28	|	92.6	christians [Christians {C}
43.30	|	92.9	church [Church {C}
43.35	|	92.14	some; [some, {P}
43.37	|	92.16	christian [Christian {C}
43.37	|	92.17	unity; [unity, {P}
43.39	|	92.18	another, [another {P}
43.39	|	92.18	subjects; [subjects, {P}
43.41	|	92.20	Scriptures, [Scriptures {P}
43.41	|	92.21	church. [Church. {C}
43.44	|	92.24	standards; [standards, {P}
43.47	|	92.28	adopters; [adopters: {P}
43.47	|	92.28	you [You {C}
43.48	|	92.29	book [book, {P}
43.49	|	92.30	purposes— [purposes; {P}
43.49	|	92.30	farther [further {S}
44.2	|	92.31	duty; [duty, {P}
44.5	|	93.1	adopted; [adopted, {P}
44.7	|	93.3	parties, [parties {P}
44.10	|	93.7	cannot [can not {S}
44.13	|	93.10	altogether, [altogether {P}
44.13	|	93.10	incontrovertible; [incontrovertible, {P}
44.15	|	93.12	government; [government {P}
44.17	|	93.15	may; [may, {P}
44.18	|	93.15	any thing [anything {S}
44.18	|	93.16	better, [better {P}
44.18	|	93.16	judgment, [judgment {P}
44.19	|	93.17	it; [it, {P}

Page.Line 1st Ed.	Page.Line 2nd Ed.	First Edition [Second Edition
44.19	93.17	and [and, {P}
44.19	93.17	therefore [therefore, {P}
44.20	93.18	authority; [authority, {P}
44.24	93.23	rule, [rule {P}
44.25	93.23	standard, [standard {P}
44.26	93.24	church [Church {C}
44.26	93.25	But [But, {P}
44.26	93.25	farther [further {S}
44.27	93.26	standards, [standards {P}
44.28	93.27	evident, [evident {P}
44.29	93.28	standard, [standard {P}
44.30	93.29	divine [Divine {C}
44.30	93.29	things: [things, {P}
44.30	93.29	constitution, [constitution {P}
44.30	93.30	manage- ments; [managements, {P}
44.31	93.30	christian [Christian {C}
44.31	93.30	church)— [Church,) {C} {P}
44.32	93.31	ask [ask, {P}
44.32	93.31	would [Would {C}
44.32	93.32	just, [just {P}
44.33	93.33	founded, [founded {P}
44.35	94.1	expressly revealed [expressly-revealed {S}
44.36	94.2	Holy [holy {C}
44.36	94.2	Word, [word, {C}
44.37	94.3	faith, [faith {P}
44.37	94.3	duty; [duty, {P}
44.39	94.5	stedfast [steadfast {S}
44.41	94.7	alledged; [alleged, {S} {P}
44.42	94.9	standards; [standards, {P}
44.43	94.9	standards, [standards {P}
44.45	94.12	defend, [defend {P}
44.46	94.13	them,) [them) {P}
44.47	94.14	adopted, [adopted {P}
44.47	94.14	standards; [standards, {P}
44.48	94.14	without, [without {P}
44.48	94.15	time, [time {P}
44.49	94.15	performances, [per- formances {P}
45.1	94.17	Standard, [standard, {C}
45.2	94.18	same; [same {P}

Page.Line 1st Ed.	Page.Line 2nd Ed.	First Edition [Second Edition
45.2	94.19	divine [Divine {C}
45.4	94.20	cannot [can not {S}
45.4	94.20	truth; [truth, {P}
45.4	94.21	another; [another, {P}
45.5	94.22	Christ; [Christ, {P}
45.6	94.22	christians, [Christians {C}{P}
45.6	94.23	christian [Christian {C}
45.6	94.23	church, [Church {C}{P}
45.7	94.23	standard; [standard, {P}
45.7	94.23	saying, [say- ing {P}
45.8	94.25	christianity, [Christianity, {C}
45.8	94.25	and [and, {P}
45.8	94.25	course [course, {P}
45.9	94.26	church [Church {C}
45.9	94.26	was, [was {P}
45.9	94.26	formed: [formed, {P}
45.10	94.27	inadequate, [inadequate {P}
45.11	94.28	duty; [duty, {P}
45.11	94.28	or [or, {P}
45.11	94.28	all; [all, {P}
45.12	94.29	work— [work; {P}
45.12	94.29	church [Church {C}
45.14	94.32	existence; [existence, {P}
45.15	94.32	too; [too, {P}
45.16	94.33	fidelity, [fidelity {P}
45.18	95.2	say, [say {P}
45.19	95.3	church, [Church, {C}
45.20	95.4	well being [wellbeing {S}
45.22	95.6	church [Church {C}
45.22	95.6	history, [history {P}
45.23	95.7	christian [Christian {C}
45.24	95.9	affirm, [affirm {P}
45.25	95.9	recommend, [recommend {P}
45.26	95.11	term; [term, {P}
45.28	95.12	church, [Church, {C}
45.30	95.14	testimonies; [testimonies, {P}
45.31	95.16	church. [Church. {C}
45.33	95.18	made; [made, {P}
45.34	95.19	demonstration; [dem- onstration, {P}
45.35	95.21	characters [characters, {P}
45.37	95.22	pretences, [pretenses, {S}

Page.Line 1st Ed.		Page.Line 2nd Ed.	First Edition [Second Edition
45.37	|	95.23	church) [Church,) {C} {P}
45.40	|	95.26	assured, [assured {P}
45.41	|	95.27	objection: [objection; {P}
45.42	|	95.28	conclusions; [conclusions, {P}
45.42	|	95.28	cannot [can not {S}
45.45	|	95.31	assertion;— [assertion, {P}
45.46	|	95.33	amongst [among {S}
45.48	|	96.1	farther [further {S}
45.48	|	96.1	*this;* [*this,* {P}
46.1	|	96.2	Now [Now, {P}
46.1	|	96.3	surely [surely, {P}
46.3	|	96.5	Holy [holy {C}
46.3	|	96.5	Word. [word. {C}
46.7	|	96.9	This [This, {P}
46.8	|	96.10	detriment, [detriment {P}
46.8	|	96.11	of, [of {P}
46.9	|	96.11	call, [call {P}
46.9	|	96.12	christianity. [Christianity. {C}
46.9	|	96.12	not [not, {P}
46.10	|	96.12	therefore [therefore, {P}
46.11	|	96.14	follow, [follow {P}
46.11	|	96.14	christians [Christians {C}
46.11	|	96.14	cannot, [can not {S} {P}
46.12	|	96.15	unity, [unity {P}
46.13	|	96.16	requires, [requires {P}
46.13	|	96.16	no— [no; {P}
46.14	|	96.17	thing;— [thing; {P}
46.15	|	96.18	brethren, [brethren {P}
46.15	|	96.19	just, [just {P}
46.16	|	96.19	scripturally [Scripturally {C}
46.16	|	96.19	evident; [evident, {P}
46.17	|	96.21	effect— [effect; {P}
46.19	|	96.23	church; [Church, {C} {P}
46.20	|	96.24	matters; [matters {P}
46.21	|	96.25	divine [Divine {C}
46.21	|	96.25	original; [original, {P}
46.21	|	96.25	every thing [everything {S}
46.22	|	96.27	*these,* [*these* {P}
46.23	|	96.28	betwixt [between {S}
46.23	|	96.28	chris- tian [Christian {C}

Page.Line 1st Ed.	Page.Line 2nd Ed.	First Edition [Second Edition
46.25	96.29	this, [this {P}
46.26	96.30	effort, [effort {P}
46.26	96.31	churches [Church's {P} {D}
46.26	96.31	unity; [unity, {P}
46.27	96.32	interposition, [interposition {P}
46.29	96.34	imagine, [imagine {P}
46.30	97.1	overture, [overture {P}
46.31	97.2	appeal, [appeal {P}
46.31	97.2	defence, [defense {S} {P}
46.33	97.4	matter; [matter, {P}
46.34	97.6	far, [far {P}
46.35	97.6	shew, [show {S} {P}
46.36	97.8	Scriptures, [Scriptures {P}
46.37	97.9	testimonies; [testimonies, {P}
46.38	97.10	church [Church {C}
46.39	97.11	Sylla [Scylla {S}
46.40	97.12	upon the Charybdis. [upon Charybdis. {D} (TC)
46.40	97.12	Extremes [Extremes, {P}
46.40	97.12	told [told, {P}
46.41	97.13	middle way; [middle way, {P}
46.41	97.13	safe way; [safe way, {P}
46.42	97.14	that, [that {P}
46.43	97.16	therein; [therein, {P}
46.44	97.17	God; [God: {P}
46.44	97.17	"for ["For {C}
46.46	97.19	conclude, [conclude {P}
46.47	97.20	subjects; [subjects, {P}
46.48	97.21	subscribing, [subscribing {P}
46.49	97.22	standards, [standards {P}
46.49	97.22	church; [Church, {C} {P}
47.1	97.23	defence [defense {S}
47.1	97.23	orthodoxy; [orthodoxy, {P}
47.2	97.24	about; [about, {P}
47.3	97.25	cannot [can not {S}
47.4	97.27	subtilties, [subtilties {P}
47.4	97.27	specula- tions; [speculations, {P}
47.6	97.29	divine [Divine {C}
47.6	97.29	revelation, [revelation {P}
47.7	97.30	christians, [Christians, {C}

Page.Line 1st Ed.		Page.Line 2nd Ed.	First Edition [Second Edition
47.8	|	97.31	facts, [facts {P}
47.9	|	97.32	supposed [supposed, {P}
47.10	|	97.33	christian [Christian {C}
47.12	|	98.1	Scriptures; [Scriptures, {P}
47.14	|	98.3	professors, [professors {P}
47.14	|	98.3	dictates, [dic- tates {P}
47.16	|	98.6	&c. [etc., {S} {P}
47.16	|	98.6	manifested [manifested, {P}
47.17	|	98.7	persons' [persons {S}
47.20	|	98.10	examples; [examples, {P}
47.21	|	98.11	manifested, [manifested {P}
47.22	|	98.11	pro- fession; [profession, {P}
47.23	|	98.13	irreproveable [irreprovable {S}
47.23	|	98.14	conformity [conformity, {P}
47.24	|	98.14	Elizabeth, [Elisabeth, {S}
47.24	|	98.15	desirable; [desirable, {P}
47.25	|	98.16	repentance, [repentance {P}
47.27	|	98.18	christian [Christian {C}
47.29	|	98.21	intend, [intend {P}
47.31	|	98.22	acknowledge [ac- knowledge, {P}
47.32	|	98.24	christian [Christian {C}
47.33	|	98.24	things; [things, {P}
47.33	|	98.25	radical, [radical {P}
47.33	|	98.25	want, [want {P}
47.34	|	98.25	properties, [properties {P}
47.35	|	98.27	only here [here only {D} (TC)
47.35	|	98.27	granted, [granted {P}
47.36	|	98.28	namely, [namely: {P}
47.36	|	98.28	Word [word {C}
47.37	|	98.29	every of [every one of {D}
47.38	|	98.30	character; [character, {P}
47.38	|	98.30	be, [be {P}
47.39	|	98.32	produce, [produce {P}
47.44	|	99.3	recorded; [recorded, {P}
47.46	|	99.5	God; [God, {P}
47.46	|	99.5	subject matter [subject-matter {S}
47.46	|	99.6	profes- sion, [profession {P}
48.1	|	99.9	connexion [connection {S}
48.2	|	99.11	God, [God {P}
48.3	|	99.11	towards [toward {S}

Page.Line 1st Ed.		Page.Line 2nd Ed.	First Edition [Second Edition
48.4	|	99.13	pro- mises, [promises {P}
48.5	|	99.14	him, [him {P}
48.6	|	99.15	&c. [etc., {S}{P}
48.10	|	99.20	him, [him {P}
48.12	|	99.21	people; [people, {P}
48.12	|	99.22	subject matter [subject-matter {S}
48.14	|	99.24	veneration, [veneration {P}
48.14	|	99.24	reverence, [rever- ence {P}
48.16	|	99.26	church, [Church, {C}
48.18	|	99.28	assert, [assert {P}
48.18	|	99.28	perception, [per- ception {P}
48.18	|	99.29	pro- fession, [profession {P}
48.19	|	99.29	Word [word {C}
48.21	|	99.32	subject; [subject, {P}
48.22	|	99.33	church, [Church {C}{P}
48.23	|	99.33	profession:— [pro- fession; {P}
48.25	|	100.2	and, [and {P}
48.26	|	100.3	all, [all {P}
48.26	|	100.4	christians, [Christians, {C}
48.27	|	100.5	christian [Christian {C}
48.27	|	100.5	Here [Here, {P}
48.28	|	100.5	then [then, {P}
48.29	|	100.7	subject, [subject {P}
48.29	|	100.7	scriptural [Scriptural {C}
48.30	|	100.8	manifestation, [manifestation {P}
48.31	|	100.9	charity; [charity, {P}
48.31	|	100.9	to, [to {P}
48.32	|	100.10	Word, [word {C}{P}
48.32	|	100.10	topics; [topics, {P}
48.34	|	100.13	distinction; [distinction, {P}
48.36	|	100.14	other ways [otherwise {D}
48.37	|	100.15	Apostle, [apostle, {C}
48.39	|	100.18	enquired [inquired {S}
48.40	|	100.19	Arminians, [Arminians {P}
48.42	|	100.21	that, [that {P}
48.43	|	100.22	both; [both, {P}
48.44	|	100.23	earth; [earth, {P}
48.44	|	100.23	master, [Master, {C}
48.44	|	100.24	Christ [Christ, {P}
48.44	|	100.24	brethren— [brethren, {P}
48.45	|	100.24	christians [Christians {C}

Page.Line 1st Ed.		Page.Line 2nd Ed.	First Edition [Second Edition
48.45	|	100.24	profession: [profession; {P}
48.45	|	100.25	and, [and {P}
48.46	|	100.26	part, [part {P}
48.46	|	100.26	profession, [profession {P}
48.47	|	100.27	intend, [intend {P}
48.49	|	100.29	scripturally, [Scripturally, {C}
48.49	|	100.29	and [and, {P}
49.1	|	100.30	defined; [defined, {P}
49.2	|	100.32	confidence, [confidence {P}
49.5	|	101.1	divinely revealed [divinely-revealed {S}
49.7	|	101.2	it; [it, {P}
49.7	|	101.3	every thing [everything {S}
49.9	|	101.5	love [love, {P}
49.9	|	101.5	&c. [etc. {S}
49.10	|	101.6	word; [word, {P}
49.12	|	101.9	grace, [grace {P}
49.13	|	101.9	purpose: [purpose; {P}
49.15	|	101.12	christian [Christian {C}
49.15	|	101.12	character, [character: {P}
49.17	|	101.13	scripturally [Scripturally {C}
49.17	|	101.14	character [character, {P}
49.18	|	101.15	concerned: [concerned, {P}
49.19	|	101.16	affirm [affirm, {P}
49.19	|	101.16	scriptural [Scriptural {C}
49.20	|	101.17	amongst [among {S}
49.21	|	101.19	divisions; [divisions, {P}
49.22	|	101.19	receive, [receive {P}
49.24	|	101.21	agreed [agreed, {P}
49.26	|	101.24	&c. [etc., {S} {P}
49.27	|	101.25	Standard. [standard. {C}
49.28	|	101.26	objection, [objection; {P}
49.29	|	101.27	alledge [allege {S}
49.30	|	101.28	formula, [formula {P}
49.31	|	101.29	church, [Church, {C}
49.31	|	101.30	christians; [Christians, {C} {P}
49.32	|	101.31	church, [Church, {C}
49.34	|	101.33	old [Old {C}
49.35	|	101.34	with, [with {P}
49.35	|	101.34	new; [New, {C} {P}

Page.Line 1st Ed.		Page.Line 2nd Ed.	First Edition [Second Edition
49.37	|	102.1	it, [it {P}
49.37	|	102.2	duty; [duty, {P}
49.38	|	102.3	new; [New, {C} {P}
49.40	|	102.5	Apostles, [apostles, {C}
49.42	|	102.8	new, [New, {C}
49.42	|	102.8	new [New {C}
49.43	|	102.8	old; [Old; {C}
49.44	|	102.10	christian [Christian {C}
49.44	|	102.10	church, [Church, {C}
49.45	|	102.11	christians, [Christians {C} {P}
49.46	|	102.12	Farther, [Further, {S}
49.47	|	102.13	rule— [rule, {P}
49.49	|	102.15	practice; [practice, {P}
50.1	|	102.16	practise, [practice {S}
50.1	|	102.16	things, [things {P}
50.5	|	102.20	diminution; [diminution, {P}
50.5	|	102.21	any thing [anything {S}
50.6	|	102.21	opinion, [opinion {P}
50.6	|	102.21	disputation, [dis- putation {P}
50.7	|	102.22	church. [Church. {C}
50.7	|	102.23	thus, [thus {P}
50.9	|	102.25	any thing [anything {S}
50.10	|	102.26	understood, [understood {P}
50.11	|	102.27	suggested, [suggested {P}
50.12	|	102.28	subject, [subject {P}
50.14	|	102.30	impossible, [impossible {P}
50.14	|	102.31	misunderstood, [misunderstood {P}
50.15	|	102.31	Latitudinarianism [latitudinarianism {C}
50.16	|	102.33	or [or, {P}
50.17	|	102.33	indeed [indeed, {P}
50.17	|	102.34	christian- ity. [Christianity. {C}
50.20	|	103.3	other; [other, {P}
50.21	|	103.4	exception: [exception, {P}
50.22	|	103.5	other, [other {P}
50.23	|	103.6	church [Church {C}
50.23	|	103.6	these [these, {P}
50.23	|	103.7	moreover [moreover, {P}
50.24	|	103.7	unity; [unity, {P}
50.25	|	103.8	instructed— [instructed, {P}

Page.Line 1st Ed.		Page.Line 2nd Ed.	First Edition [Second Edition
50.27	|	103.11	unity— [unity, {P}
50.28	|	103.12	body; [body, {P}
50.29	|	103.13	another— [another, {P}
50.29	|	103.13	instances [instances, {P}
50.30	|	103.15	mismanagement; [mismanagement, {P}
50.31	|	103.15	endeavour [endeavor {S}
50.32	|	103.16	every thing [everything {S}
50.32	|	103.17	difference; [difference, {P}
50.33	|	103.18	exists; [exists, {P}
50.41	|	103.27	do, [do {P}
50.43	|	103.28	believer; [believer, {P}
50.43	|	103.29	scriptural [Scriptural {C}
50.45	|	103.30	offences [offenses {S}
50.45	|	103.31	amongst [among {S}
50.45	|	103.31	those, [those {P}
50.47	|	103.33	father [Father {C}
50.48	|	103.34	all; [all, {P}
50.49	|	104.1	churches. [Churches. {C}
51.2	|	104.3	anti-scriptural [anti- scriptural {S}
51.4	|	104.5	shew, [show, {S}
51.5	|	104.6	alternative, [alternative {P}
51.5	|	104.7	scriptural [Scriptural {C}
51.7	|	104.8	schisms, [schisms {P}
51.9	|	104.11	premises; [premises, {P}
51.9	|	104.11	adopt, [adopt {P}
51.10	|	104.12	cause: [cause; {P}
51.11	|	104.13	vague [vague, {P}
51.12	|	104.14	Holy [holy {C}
51.12	|	104.14	Scriptures, [Scriptures {P}
51.14	|	104.17	farther [further {S}
51.17	|	104.19	church, [Church, {C}
51.17	|	104.20	apprehend, [apprehend {P}
51.18	|	104.21	namely, [namely: {P}
51.22	|	104.25	it; [it, {P}
51.22	|	104.25	satisfied, [satisfied {P}
51.23	|	104.27	intelligent [intelligent, {P}
51.23	|	104.27	chris- tians [Christians {C}
51.24	|	104.27	side; [side, {P}
51.26	|	104.30	scriptural [Scriptural {C}

Page.Line 1st Ed.		Page.Line 2nd Ed.	First Edition [Second Edition
51.27	|	104.31	christian [Christian {C}
51.27	|	104.31	church; [Church, {C} {P}
51.27	|	104.31	this [this, {P}
51.27	|	104.31	presume [presume, {P}
51.29	|	104.33	if [if, {P}
51.30	|	104.34	righteousness— [righteousness, {P}
51.31	|	105.1	justice [justice, {P}
51.31	|	105.1	charity— [charity, {P}
51.32	|	105.2	dead [dead, {P}
51.33	|	105.3	Christ: [Christ; {P}
51.33	|	105.3	be, [be {P}
51.35	|	105.5	would [would, {P}
51.35	|	105.5	therefore [therefore, {P}
51.38	|	105.9	judgment; [judgment, {P}
51.38	|	105.9	equally [equal {D} (TC)
51.39	|	105.10	upon, [upon {P}
51.39	|	105.10	for, [for {P}
51.42	|	105.14	heaven: [heaven; {P}
51.43	|	105.14	father [Father {C}
51.46	|	105.18	pharisees, [Pharisees, {C}
51.47	|	105.19	conclude, [conclude {P}
51.47	|	105.19	t oadvocate [to advocate {S}
51.48	|	105.19	how- every [however {S}
51.48	|	105.20	itself [itself, {P}
51.49	|	105.21	church [Church {C}
51.49	|	105.21	characters— [characters, {P}
51.49	|	105.22	can- not [can not {S}
52.1	|	105.22	shew [show {S}
52.4	|	105.26	church, [Church, {C}
52.6	|	105.28	description; [description, {P}
52.7	|	105.29	influence.— [influence. {P}
52.8	|	105.30	expressly revealed [expressly-revealed {S}
52.9	|	105.31	Ezek. 44, 6—9, [Ezek. xliv: 6, 9, {S} {P}
52.9	|	105.31	Math. 13, 15—17, [Matt. xiii: 15, 17; {S} {P}
52.9	|	105.31	I. Cor. 5, 6—13, [1 Cor. v: 6, 13, {S} {P}
52.10	|	105.32	Scriptures. [scriptures. {C}

Page.Line 1st Ed.		Page.Line 2nd Ed.	First Edition [Second Edition
52.11	|	105.33	professors, [professors {P}
52.13	|	106.1	those, [those {P}
52.14	|	106.3	church [Church {C}
52.15	|	106.3	stewards— [stewards, {P}
52.16	|	106.5	such, [such {P}
52.17	|	106.6	sentiments, [sentiments {P}
52.17	|	106.6	church reformation; [Church-reformation; {C} {S}
52.18	|	106.7	puritanism, [Puritanism, {C}
52.19	|	106.8	please: [please; {P}
52.21	|	106.10	mistakes, [mistakes {P}
52.22	|	106.12	church [Church {C}
52.23	|	106.13	well meant [well-meant {S}
52.25	|	106.14	performance; [performance, {P}
52.26	|	106.16	deficiencies, [deficiencies {P}
52.29	|	106.19	near, [near {P}
52.34	|	106.25	them; [them, {P}
52.36	|	106.27	them; [them, {P}
52.38	|	106.29	pretence [pretense {S}
52.38	|	106.29	truth;— [truth— {P}
52.39	|	106.30	amongst [among {S}
52.39	|	106.30	would [would, {P}
52.39	|	106.30	there- fore [therefore, {P}
52.44	|	107.1	writing: [writing; {P}
52.47	|	107.4	imagine, [imagine {P}
52.47	|	107.4	that, [that {P}
52.47	|	107.5	christians [Christians {C}
52.49	|	107.6	enquirers [inquirers {S}
53.3	|	107.10	brethren; [brethren, {P}
53.4	|	107.11	confute, [confute {P}
53.5	|	107.13	arguing, [arguing {P}
53.6	|	107.14	us [us, {P}
53.6	|	107.14	therefore [therefore, {P}
53.7	|	107.15	Math. 18, 7, [Matt. xvii: 7: {S} {D} {P}[10]
53.7	|	107.15	woe ["Woe {P} {C}
53.8	|	107.16	offences. [offenses." {S} {P}
53.8	|	107.16	Scott [Scott, {P}
53.10	|	107.18	'that our Lord ["that our Lord {P}[11]
53.11	|	107.19	church, [Church {C} {P}

Page.Line 1st Ed.	Page.Line 2nd Ed.	First Edition [Second Edition
53.13	107.22	christians; [Christians; {C}
53.14	107.23	are, [are {P}
53.15	107.23	day, [day {P}
53.15	107.23	*offences* [*offenses* {S}
53.15	107.24	*stumbling,* [*stumbling* {P}
53.15	107.24	Mahome- tans, [Mohammedands, {S}
53.16	107.24	Pagans, [pagans {C} {P}
53.16	107.25	globe; [globe, {P}
53.17	107.26	description, [description {P}
53.18	107.27	controversies, [controversies {P}
53.19	107.28	amongst [among {S}
53.19	107.28	principle [principal {D}
53.20	107.29	gospel, [Gospel, {C}
53.23	107.32	religion; [religion, {P}
53.23	107.33	hereticks, [heretics, {S}
53.24	107.33	pharisees, [Pharisees, {C}
53.24	107.34	sinners, [sinners {P}
53.25	107.34	gospel. [Gospel. {C}
53.26	108.1	said, [said: {P}
53.26	108.1	"woe ['Woe {P} {C}
53.26	108.1	to [un- to {D}
53.26	108.2	offences;" [offenses,' {S} {P} {P}
53.26	108.2	for, [for {P}
53.28	108.4	earth, [earth {P}
53.29	108.5	nature [nature, {P}
53.29	108.5	be, [be {P}
53.29	108.5	offences [offenses {S}
53.30	108.6	intervene; [intervene, {P}
53.30	108.6	ri hteous [righteous {S}
53.32	108.8	evils, [evils {P}
53.32	108.8	accessary [accessory {S}
53.33	108.9	one, [one {S}
53.34	108.10	men, [men {P}
53.37	108.14	text— [text; {P}
53.40	108.17	principle [principal {D}
53.41	108.18	Buffaloe [Buffalo {S}
53.41	108.18	state [State {C}
53.41	108.19	New- York, [New York, {S}
53.43	108.20	'I ["I {P}
53.43	108.21	brethren,' [brethren," {P}
53.44	108.21	'to ["to {P}[12]

Page.Line 1st Ed.		**Page.Line 2nd Ed.**	**First Edition [Second Edition**
53.44	|	108.21	minds, [minds {P}
53.45	|	108.22	Spirit, [Spirit {P}
53.45	|	108.23	will; [will, {P}
53.46	|	108.23	gospel [Gospel {C}
53.46	|	108.23	son [Son {S}
53.47	|	108.25	embr ce [embrace {S}
53.47	|	108.25	ri ht [right {S}
53.47	|	108.25	way [way, {P}
53.47	|	108.25	cannot [can not {S}
53.48	|	108.25	hereafter.' [hereafter." {P}
53.48	|	108.26	reply, [reply: {P}
53.48	|	108.26	'Brother, ["Brother, {P}
54.5	|	108.32	we [we, {P}
54.5	|	108.32	also [also, {P}
54.6	|	108.33	forefathers. [forefathers; {P}
54.6	|	108.33	It [it {C}
54.7	|	108.34	receive— [receive; {P}
54.9	|	109.3	neighbors; [neighbors, {P}
54.12	|	109.6	Indians; [Indians, {P}
54.13	|	109.7	said.' [said." {P}
54.14	|	109.8	conference! [conference. {P}
54.14	|	109.8	Alas! [Alas, {P}
54.15	|	109.9	way? [way! {P}
54.16	|	109.10	Apostles [apostles {C}
54.16	|	109.11	churches! [Churches! {C}
54.18	|	109.13	deportment towards [deportment toward {S}
54.18	|	109.13	other, [each other {P}
54.18	|	109.13	and towards [and toward {S}
54.19	|	109.13	men; [men, {P}
54.21	|	109.16	reformation— [reformation; {P}
54.23	|	109.19	own; [own, {P}
54.26	|	109.21	Amen [Amen, {P}

Notes

1. Both "W" and "C" are raised to capitals in the correction.

2. The word is hyphenated in the first edition, but not in the second. See treatment at 8.1, 13.25.

3. In the first edition, the final "s" resembles an epsilon character.

4. The final letter is deleted, but the first remains a capital.

5. The letter preceding the hyphen is obliterated; since this letter has no ascender or descender, "o" is a reasonable guess. Whatever the letter in the first edition, the autograph correction is for a "u."

6. A strike-out marks the letter "k" for deletion; no change is indicated for the period.

7. The comma is marked for deletion; the "c" remains in lower case.

8. The punctuation is marked for change, but not the spelling.

9. The word "no" is changed to "not" in the margin; the punctuation is not marked for change.

10. The second edition erroneously changes the chapter in Matthew from "18" to "xvii."

11. In the first edition, lines 53.11-25 constitute an extended quotation that is framed with a single quotation mark at the beginning of each line. In the second edition, this passage (107.18-108.11) is not set off.

12. In the first edition, lines 53.44 through 54.13 constitute an extended quotation that is framed with a single quotation mark at the beginning of each line. In the second edition, this passage (108.21-109.7) is not set off.

Scripture Index to the *Declaration and Address*

Christopher R. Hutson

This third edition (December 1998) of the index is keyed to the page and line numbers of the first edition as printed in the present volume. I wish to acknowledge the comments of members of the *Declaration and Address* Seminar, which have helped me improve the quality of the index. I am especially grateful to Lee Snyder for sharing with me his own preliminary index to biblical references in the *D&A*, which included a number of references I had previously overlooked.

Scripture	**D&A**	**Text as it appears in the *D&A***
passim	4.46	a thus saith the Lord either in express terms, or by approved precedent.
passim	26.4	for which there can be expressly produced a "thus saith the Lord":
passim	27.41-42	for which there cannot be expressly produced a "thus saith the Lord" either in express terms, or by approved precedent.
passim	27.48	for which there cannot be expressly produced a "thus saith the Lord" as above,
passim	32.4-5	for which there can be expressly produced a "thus saith the Lord," either in express terms, or by approved precedent.

Scripture	***D&A***	**Text as it appears in the *D&A***
passim	43.8	expressly declared, in a "thus saith the Lord."
passim	43.21	it must be a "thus saith the Lord;"
passim	19.7	by turning aside to the right hand or to the left—
Gn 11:9	23.22	this Babel of confusion
Gn 37:12-36	34.18-19	as the unnatural brethren did the beloved Joseph.
Gn 41:51 cf. 46:31	34.18	in thus cutting him off from his father's house,
Ex 14:15-16	12.49-13.2	"Why criest thou unto me? Speak unto the children of Israel that they go forward, but lift thou up thy rod, and stretch out thine hand."
Ex 14:17	53.23	and harden the hearts of hereticks,
Dt 2:19-20	30.41-43	as the Zamzummins did of old, to prevent the children of Lot from taking possession of their inheritance.
Dt 4:32	47.28	Ask from the one end of heaven to the other,
Dt 18:20	32.30-32	see Deut. xviii—20. "The prophet that shall presume to speak a word in my name, which I have not commanded him to speak— even that prophet shall die."
Jos 2, 6	19.44	like the walls of Jericho,
Jgs 12:6	36.39	the shiboleth of party;
Jgs 16	23.16-18	withs and cords with which the Philistines bound Sampson were able to retain him their prisoner;
1 Sam 3:14	7.28	the house of Eli.
1 Chr 22:16	12.44	"Up, and be doing, and the Lord will be with you."
Neh 2:18	9.25	this good work

Scripture	***D&A***	**Text as it appears in the *D&A***
Jb 10:15	42.28	full of confusion.
Ps 2:9	14.35	like a potter's vessel?
Ps 20:5	19.35-36	in the Lord's name do we display our banners.
Ps 23:6	55.35 (PS)	of infinite goodness and mercy,
Ps 37:11	19.48-49	"for the meek shall inherit the earth, and shall delight themselves in the abundance of peace."
Ps 41:13	39.35	Amen and amen.
Ps 41:13	54.26	Amen and amen.
Ps 45:7	9.18-19	no one can claim a preference above his fellows,
Ps 60:2 cf. Am 9:11	38.25-26	to heal breaches,
Ps 62:9	29.19-20	would they not all appear lighter than vanity?
Ps 67.2-3	54.23-26	that *his way* may be known upon earth, and his saving health among all nations. Let the people praise thee, O God; let all the people praise thee.
Ps 81:11-12	30.2-4	"My people, saith he, would not hearken to my voice. So I gave them up to their own hearts lusts, and they walked in their own counsels."
Ps 94:14-15	20.7-9	"the Lord will not cast off his people, neither will he forsake his heritage; but judgment shall return unto righteousness, and all the upright in heart shall follow it "
Ps 95:11	19.46	to prevent them from entering into their promised rest,
Ps 102:13	8.22-23	the time to favour her is come; even the set time.
Ps 119:96	31.1-2	for we are told, "the commandment is exceeding broad;"
Ps 122:6	9.41-42	Pray for the peace of Jerusalem, they shall prosper that love thee.
Ps 122:9	9.17-18	to seek her good.
Ps 128:5 cf. 134:3	9.40-41	The blessing out of Zion
Ps 133:1	13.29	dwell together in unity

Scripture	*D&A*	Text as it appears in the *D&A*
Prv 3:5	31.32	and not barely trusting to their own understanding.
Prv 30:6	27.38-39	"Add thou not unto his words, lest he reprove thee, and thou be found a liar."
Song 2:15	55.36-38(PS)	"Take us the foxes, the little foxes that spoil our vines; for our vines have tender grapes." Cant 2, 15.
Song 8:5	23.22	leaning upon their beloved,
Is 13:10	15.42	cause your light to shine upon our weak beginnings,
Is 28:10	37.35	line for line; expression for expression; precept and precedent for practice;
Is 29:13	43.22	being taught by the precept of men.
Is 30:14	14.35	like a potter's vessel?
Is 33:20	19.31-33	then should our eyes soon behold the prosperity of Zion; we should soon see Jerusalem a quiet habitation.
Is 34:8	8.20	the day of the Lord's vengeance
Is 34:8	8.21-22	the year of recompenses for the controversy of Zion?
Is 35:8	46.43	the wayfaring men, though fools, need not err therein;
Is 40-66 passim	55.27-28	the Redeemer's kingdom upon earth;
Is 49:19	26.46	the desolate places of God's heritage,
Is 52:1-2	14.41-45	"Awake, awake; put on thy strength, O Zion, put on thy beautiful garments, O Jerusalem, the holy city; for henceforth there shall no more come unto thee the uncircumcised and the unclean. Shake thyself from the dust, O Jerusalem; arise, loose thyself from the *bands* of thy neck, O captive daughter of Zion"
Is 52:8	24.32-33	Zion's watchmen shall see eye to eye,
Is 57:13-14	18.46-49	"He that putteth his trust in me shall possess the land, and shall inherit my holy mountain; and shall say, cast ye up, cast ye up, prepare the way; take up the stumbling block out of the way of my people."

Scripture	*D&A*	Text as it appears in the *D&A*
Is 57:14	13.7-8	"Cast ye up, cast ye up, prepare the way, take up the stumbling block out of the way of my people,"
Is 57:14	18.44	already observed from Is. 57, 14,
Is 57:14	19.4	clearing the way before them by removing the stumbling blocks
Is 58:1	13.23-24	lift up your voice like a trumpet
Is 59:19	19.36-38	"So shall they fear the name of the Lord from the west, and his glory from the rising of the sun." ["]When the enemy shall come in like a flood the spirit of the Lord shall lift up a standard against him."
Is 60:22	23.38	May the Lord hasten it in his time. Fare-well.
Is 62:1	20.27-29	"for Zion's sake will we not hold our peace, and for Jerusalem's sake we will not rest, until the righteousness thereof go forth as brightness, and the salvation thereof as a lamp that burneth."
Is 62:6-7	20.24-26	"ye that fear the Lord keep not silence, and give him no rest till he make Jerusalem a joy and a praise in the earth."
Is 65:5	33.3-4	stand by, I am holier than thou.
Ez 22:28	32.45-46	saying, "The Lord saith, when the Lord had not spoken."
Ez 34:10	24.36-37	and should be glad to see the Lord's flock delivered from their mouth,
Ez 44:6, 9	52.9	when we consider the expressly revealed will of God upon this point, Ezek. 44, 6—9, with Math. 13, 15—17, I Cor. 5, 6—13, with many other Scriptures.
Dn 5:27	21.33-34	weigh every sentiment in the balance of the sanctuary,
Dn 7:18	20.3	and they shall possess it forever."
Dn 7:19	31.35	desirous to know the truth.
Dn 7:27	19.49-20.3	And the kingdom and dominion, even the greatness of the kingdom under the whole heaven, shall be given to the people of the saints of the Most High,
Dn 9:25	8.23	shall be built in troublous times?

Scripture	*D&A*	Text as it appears in the *D&A*
Dn 10:21	56.11	the scriptures of truth
Hos 5:15	20.39-40	"I will go and return to my place, till they acknowledge their offence and seek my face."
Hos 8:11	30.4-5	"Israel hath made many altars to sin: therefore altars shall be unto him to sin."
Am 9:11 cf. Ps 60:2	13.28	to heal the breaches of Zion;
Am 9:11	14.2	raise up the tabernacle of David, that is fallen down
Mi 6:2	27.19-20	the Lord to plead a controversy
Zep 3:9	47.31-32	They will all acknowledge with one consent,
Hg 1:2	14.17-19	"The time is not yet come—the time is not come—saith he,—the time that the Lord's house should be built."
Zec 5:11	14.3	and to set it up upon its own base
Zec 8:8	8.42	the divine cause of truth and righteousness
Zec 8:19	15.13	the friends and lovers of truth and peace
Zec 8:19	21.22	friends of truth and peace,
Mal 2:1-10	13.30	See Mal. 2, 1-10.
Mt 3:12 //Lk 3:17	13.12	separating this chaff, from the pure wheat
Mt 4:4 cf. 2 Chr 35:22	55.47	at the mouth of God,
Mt 7:12	44.8-9	let them do as they would be done by.
Mt 7:20	51.40-41	"By their fruits ye shall know them."
Mt 7:21	51.41-43	"Not every one that saith unto me, Lord, Lord, shall enter into the kingdom of heaven: but he that doeth the will of my Father which is in heaven.
Mt 7:26	51.43-45	Therefore whosoever heareth those sayings of mine, and doeth them not, shall be

Scripture	***D&A***	**Text as it appears in the *D&A***
		likened unto a foolish man which built his house upon the sand.

Mt 12:25
//Mk 3:24-26
//Lk 11:17-18
	20.4-6	"for a kingdom, or an house, divided against itself cannot stand; but cometh to desolation."

Mt 13:15, 17	52.9	when we consider the expressly revealed will of God upon this point, Ezek. 44, 6—9, with Math. 13, 15—17; I Cor. 5, 6—13, with many other Scriptures.
Mt 13:28	19.47	An enemy hath done this;
Mt 13:39	53.26-27	the devil, the sower of these tares,
Mt 15:9 // Mk 7:7	21.11-12	Ye reject the doctrines and commandments of men,
Mt 16:3	14.19	Do ye not discern the signs of the times?
Mt 16:19; 18:18	33.44-45	"What ye bind on earth shall be bound in heaven"
Mt 16:19; 18:18	34.26-27	what it has righteously done upon earth, is ratified in heaven.
Mt 18:7	53.7-8	Our Lord says, Math. 18, 7, woe unto the world because of offences.
Mt 18:7	53.26	"woe be to the world because of offences;"
Mt 18:7	53.29-30	it must needs be, that such offences should intervene;
Mt 18:17	33.33-34	Does he not henceforth become to us as a heathen man and a publican?
Mt 18:18; 16:19	33.44-45	"What ye bind on earth shall be bound in heaven"
Mt 18:19-20	20.18-22	"if two of you shall agree on earth as touching any thing that they shall ask, it shall be done for them of my Father which is in heaven: for where two or three are gathered together in my name, there am I in the midst of them."
Mt 19:6 //Mk 10:9	17.45-46	Whom God hath thus joined together no man should dare to put asunder.
Mt 23:9	48.43-44	for we call no man master on earth; for one is our master, even Christ and all we are brethren—
Mt 23:3	51.46-47	for ye say and do not."
Mt 23:8-10	14.48-15.1	Call no man father, no man master upon earth;—for one is your master, even Christ, and all ye are brethren.

Scripture	*D&A*	Text as it appears in the *D&A*
Mt 23:13, 14, 15, 25, 27, 29	51.46	Woe unto you scribes and pharisees, hypocrites,
Mt 24:23 //Mk 13:21	14.19	Believe him not.
Mt 25:34 cf. Gn 24:31	20.10-11	Come, then, ye blessed of the Lord,
Mt 28:20	49.40-41	all things whatsoever they should observe and do, till the end of the world.
Mk 12:42 //Lk 21:2	6.22	the mite of our sincere and humble endeavours,
Mk 12:42 //Lk 21:2	15.5	the mite of our humble endeavours
Lk 1:5-6	47.23-24	like good Zachariah and Elizabeth,
Lk 2:14	6.11-12	"glory to God in the highest, and, on earth, peace and good will towards men."
Lk 12:48	8.10	where much is given, much also will be required.
Lk 13:8	8.48	Has he said to his servants, let it alone?
Lk 22:25	36.49-37.2	Therefore they that exercise authority upon them, and tell them what they are to believe, and what they are to do, are called benefactors.
Lk 24:45	42.5-6	to open his understanding to know the Scriptures;
Jn 1:14	45.47	the manifest subjects of grace and truth,
Jn 3:20	21.30	come to the light;
Jn 5:39	41.47-49	Christ knew no other way of leading us to the knowledge of himself, at least has prescribed no other, but by searching the Scriptures,
Jn 6:45	43.1-2	"he hath heard and learned of the Father,"
Jn 10:12-13	24.35-36	as hirelings, as idol shepherds;
Jn 10:16	42.46-47	he has heard and understood his voice upon those subjects,
Jn 12:48	56.12(PS)	that all-important word which shall judge them in the last day:
Jn 13:34	23.28-29	"this is my commandment that ye love

Scripture	*D&A*	Text as it appears in the *D&A*
cf. 15:12		one another as I have loved you; that ye also love one another."
Jn 13:35	23.26-27	By this shall all men know that ye are my disciples, saith he, if ye have love one to another.
Jn 16:13	4.4-5	The Holy Spirit for our teacher and guide, to lead us into all truth;
Jn 16:13f	42.4-5	Holy Spirit to guide him into all truth;
Jn 17	13.18-19	His dying commands, his last and ardent prayers, for the visible unity of his profess-ing people,
Jn 17	15.36	the dying commands and prayers of our gracious Lord.
Jn 17:11	23.29-31	"Holy Father, keep through thine own name, those whom thou has given me that they may be one as we are,"
Jn 17:20, 23	9.39	the prayers of Christ himself, John 17, 20, 23,
Jn 17:20-23	23.31-38	"all that shall believe in me—that they all may be one; as thou Father art in me and I in thee, that they also may be one in us; that the world may believe that thou hast sent me. And the glory which thou gavest me, I have given them, that they may be one, even as we are one: I in them and them in me, that they may be made perfect in me; and that the world may know that thou hast sent me, and has loved them, as thou hast loved me."
Acts 9:31	27.3-5	walking in the fear of the Lord, in holy unity and unanimity, enjoyed the comforts of the Holy Ghost, and were increased and edified;
Acts 11:29	4.14	according to ability,
Acts 16:17	17.35	the way of salvation
Acts 16:17	42.42	the way of salvation,
Acts 17:11	41.43-44	to search and try it by, the holy Scriptures; to see if these things be so.
Acts 26:8	10.16-17	why should *we* deem it a thing incredible,

Scripture	*D&A*	Text as it appears in the *D&A*
Acts 26:18	23.19-20	May the Lord soon open the eyes of his people to see things in their true light;
Acts 26:22	18.24	none other things than those
Rom 1:2	31.42	in the holy scriptures:
Rom 1:2	36.3	the holy scriptures;
Rom 1:2	37.28	in the holy scriptures,
Rom 1:2	41.44	the holy Scriptures;
Rom 1:2	43.32	the holy Scriptures?
Rom 1:2	51.12	the Holy Scriptures,
Rom 1:2	55.19(PS)	the holy scriptures
Rom 1:2	56.38(PS)	the holy scriptures;
Rom 1:32	3.22-25	knowing the judgment of God against them that commit such things; we should neither do the same ourselves, nor have pleasure in them that do them.
Rom 2:5	7.30	the righteous judgments of God:
Rom 3:2	43.13-14	"For to it were committed the oracles of God;"
Rom 3:9	28.9	Jews and Gentiles,
Rom 4:3	28.48-49	What saith the scripture?
Rom 4:3	43.27	but what says the Bible?
Rom 4:15	28.40-42	But where no express law is, there can be no formal, no intentional transgression;
Rom 6:17	4.17	that whole form of doctrine,
Rom 8:17	17.45	joint heirs of the same inheritance.
Rom 8:31	14.37-38	What shall we say to these things?
Rom 10:15 cf. Eph 6:15	7.24	the gospel of peace,
Rom 11:25	20.35-36	the fullness of the Gentiles brought in.
Rom 12:18	4.7-8	follow peace with all men,
Rom 13:4	6.32	sword of the civil magistrate
Rom 14:1	50.6	doubtful disputation,
Rom 14:1, 3	26.14-15	to receive him that is weak in the faith, because God hath received him.
Rom 14:3, 10	3.9-10	as no man can be *judged* for his brother, so no man can *judge* for his brother: but that every man must be allowed to judge for himself,
Rom 14:10	3.16	to judge his brother,
Rom 14:10	21.15-16	no man has a right to judge, to exclude, or reject, his professing christian brother;

Scripture	*D&A*	Text as it appears in the *D&A*
Rom 14:10	33.6	judge and set at nought our brother;
Rom 14:12	3.12	give account of himself to God
Rom 14:13	26.34	might throw a stumbling block in the way;
Rom 14:13	38.14-15	we would judge one another no more
Rom 14:13	38.16-17	to put no stumbling block, or occasion to fall, in our brother's way.
Rom 14:15	26.7	How walketh thou not charitably?
Rom 14:22	29.32-34	"Hast thou faith, saith he, have it to thyself before God. Happy is the man, that condemneth not himself, in the thing which he alloweth."
Rom 15:1	26.13-14	the strong ought to bear with the infirmities of the weak, and not to please themselves.
Rom 15:7 cf. 2 Cor 1:20; 4:15	6.7	to the glory of God,
Rom 15:7	16.18-19	They ought to receive each other as Christ Jesus hath also received them to the glory of God.
Rom 15:7	22.26-27	"that we receive each other, as Christ has also received us, to the glory of God."
Rom 15:7	22.33-34	But how to love, and receive our brother; as we believe and hope Christ has received both him and us,
Rom 15:7	22.36	If this be the way that Christ hath received us,
Rom 15:7	26.16-17	receive one another, as Christ hath also received us to the glory of God.
Rom 16:16	10.17	the church of Christ,
Rom 16:16	16.9	the church of Christ
Rom 16:16	16.15	the church of Christ
Rom 16:16	25.9	the churches of Christ
Rom 16:16	34.8	churches of Christ;
1 Cor 1:10	12.40	our gracious Redeemer; whose express command to his people is, that there be no divisions among them; but that they
1 Cor 1:10	12.41-42	speak the same thing, and be perfectly joined together in the same mind, and in the same judgment?

Scripture	***D&A***	**Text as it appears in the *D&A***
1 Cor 1:10	16.21-22	speak the same thing; and to be perfectly joined together in the same mind, and in the same judgment.
1 Cor 1:10	49.21	no uncharitable divisions;
1 Cor 1:10	49.26	to mind and speak the same thing,
1 Cor 1:10	51.36-38	that we might all believe and speak the same things, and thus be perfectly joined together in the same mind and in the same judgment;
1 Cor 1:21 *et* passim	46.21-22	the wisdom of God
1 Cor 1:27	46.44-45	"for he hath chosen the foolish things of the world to confound the things that are wise."
1 Cor 2:5	40.48	the wisdom of men,
1 Cor 2:5	56.7-9(PS)	"their faith," by this means, "no longer standing in the wisdom of men, but in the power of God;
1 Cor 2:13	56.9-10(PS)	not in the words which man's wisdom teacheth, but which the Holy Ghost teacheth,"
1 Cor 3:5	37.9	*These* were but servants.
1 Cor 4:1 cf. 2 Cor 11:23	24.20	ministers of Christ,
1 Cor 4:2	52.15	These unfaithful stewards
1 Cor 5:6, 13	52.9-10	when we consider the expressly revealed will of God upon this point, Ezek. 44, 6—9, with Math. 13, 15—17; I Cor. 5, 6—13, with many other Scriptures.
1 Cor 5:13	33.35	those that are without, whom God judgeth?
1 Cor 6:19	17.43	temples of the same spirit,
1 Cor 6:20; 7:23	17.44-45	bought with the same price,
1 Cor 7:6	32.43	He spoke by permission and not by commandment,
1 Cor 7:25, 40	32.34	The Apostle Paul, no doubt, well aware of this, cautiously distinguishes betwixt his own judgment and the express injunctions of the Lord; See 1st Cor. 7. 25. and 40.
1 Cor 7:25	32.42	he had no commandment of the Lord.
1 Cor 7:40	32.38	"I think saith he that I have the Spirit of God:"
1 Cor 8:9	7.31	the weak stumbled;

Scripture	***D&A***	**Text as it appears in the *D&A***
1 Cor 8:9	53.15	and *causes of stumbling*, to Jews, Mahometans, and Pagans
1 Cor 8:9	53.34	against every one, whose delusions or crimes thus stumble men,
1 Cor 8:9-12	12.24-25	the weak, as will not oppress their consciences,
1 Cor 8-10	28.29-32	Has not the Apostle set us a noble example of this, in his pious and charitable zeal for the comfort and edification of his brother, in declaring himself ready to forego his rights (not indeed to break commandments) rather than stumble, or offend, his brother?
1 Cor 8:11	26.6-7	"Through thy knowledge shall the weak brother perish?
1 Cor 8:13 cf. 10:32	38.16	to give no offence;
1 Cor 8:13 cf. 10:32	53.15	are, at this day, the *great offences*
1 Cor 9:16	22.36-37	then woe is unto us.
1 Cor 9:21 cf. Gal 6:2	3.18	the law of Christ,
1 Cor 9:21	29.16	the express law of Christ,
1 Cor 9:21	35.25-26	the express law of Christ,
1 Cor 9:21	35.46	the law of Christ
1 Cor 9:21	45.5	the faith and law of Christ;
1 Cor 10:16	17.48-49	unity of the body of Christ;
1 Cor 10:23	29.6-8	"All things are lawful for me; but all things are not expedient. All things are lawful for me; but all things edify not."
1 Cor 12:7	15.25-26	but the manifestation of the spirit is given to every man to profit withal.
1 Cor 12:8-9a	15.22	For to one is given by the spirit the word of wisdom; to another the word of knowledge by the same spirit; to another faith by the same spirit;
1 Cor 12:10b	15.24-25	to another the discerning of spirits:
1 Cor 12:12	17.43	members of the same body,
1 Cor 12:25	16.17	yet there ought to be no schisms, no uncharitable divisions among them.
1 Cor 12:25	37.49-38.1	that there will be no schism in the body;
1 Cor 12:25	49.21	there ought to be no schisms,

Scripture	*D&A*	Text as it appears in the *D&A*
1 Cor 12:25	50.27-29	that there should be no schism in the body; but that all the members should have the same care one for another
1 Cor 13:5	21.45-46	charity thinketh no evil:
1 Cor 14:16	41.28	They say an amen to the same forms of speech,
1 Cor 15:3-4	16.12	according to the scriptures,
1 Cor 15:3-4	18.20	according to the scriptures;
1 Cor 15:3-4	24.28-29	according to the scriptures;
1 Cor 15:3-4	47.12	according to the Scriptures;
1 Cor 15:3-4	49.14	according to the Scriptures,
1 Cor 15:43	15.18-19	what is sown in weakness, will be raised up in power—
1 Cor 15:58	8.19-20	our dutiful and pious endeavours shall not be in vain in the Lord.
1 Cor 15:58	10.2-3	our humble and well-meant endeavours, shall not be in vain in the Lord.
2 Cor 1:20 cf. Rom 15:7	6.7	to the glory of God,
2 Cor 2:9	16.11-12	obedience to him in all things
2 Cor 2:9	17.36	and obedience to him, in all things
2 Cor 2:9	18.20	obedience to him in all things
2 Cor 2:9	47.11	and obedience to him in all things
2 Cor 2:16	9.33	who is sufficient for these things!
2 Cor 3:5	9.35-36	*our* sufficiency, is of God.
2 Cor 3:5	9.46-47	Not that we judge ourselves competent
2 Cor 4:15 cf. Rom 15:7	6.7	to the glory of God,
2 Cor 5:18-19	6.6	to reconcile and unite men to God,
2 Cor 8:12	27.14-15	it is accepted, according to what a man hath, and not according to what he hath not.
2 Cor 8:18	6.2	*throughout all the Churches*,
2 Cor 8:18	50.49	throughout all the churches.
2 Cor 8:23	15.43	the glory of Christ,
2 Cor 10:4	19.41-42	"which are not carnal; but mighty through God to the pulling down of strong holds;"
2 Cor 10:16	41.39-40	made ready to our hand;
2 Cor 11:23 cf. 1 Cor 4:1	24.20	ministers of Christ,
2 Cor 12:14	24.30	"they seek not *yours*, but *you*."

Scripture	***D&A***	**Text as it appears in the *D&A***
2 Cor 13:8	23.11	against the truth.
Gal 1:1	13.49-14.1	not by the authority of man; but by Jesus Christ and God the Father, who raised him from the dead.
Gal 1:4	7.7	present evil world;
Gal 5:1	14.46-47	liberty, wherewith Christ has made his people free;
Gal 5:1	15.1-2	Stand fast therefore in this precious liberty, and be not entangled again with the yoke of bondage.
Gal 5:15	6.21	bite and devour one another;
Gal 5:15	7.28-29	bite and devour one another they are consumed one of another,
Gal 6:2 cf. 1 Cor 9:21		the law of Christ
Gal 6:5	3.11-12	every man must bear his own judgment;
Eph 1:19	39.1	greatness of his power
Eph 1:22; 5:23	5.21	the Churches Head;
Eph 1:22; 5:23	11.11	Christ alone being the head, the centre,
Eph 1:22; 5:23	15.30	her exalted Head,
Eph 2:14	19.43	those partition walls of separation;
Eph 3:5	37.4	the holy Apostles and Prophets;
Eph 3:5	41.4	the holy apostles and prophets
Eph 4:3	23.23-24	holding fast the unity of the spirit in the bond of peace.
Eph 4:3, 2	28.47-48	"to preserve the unity of the spirit in the bond of peace; forbearing one with another in love"
Eph 4:3	29.31-32	to maintain the unity of the spirit in the bond of peace.
Eph 4:4-6	50.45-48	united in one spirit, one Lord, one faith, one baptism, one hope of their calling, and in one God and father of all, who is above all, and through all, and in them all;
Eph 4:15	53.2	speaking the truth in love
Eph 4:20	51.32-33	We trust we have not so learned Christ:
Eph 5:5	33.18-19	he has no inheritance in the kingdom of Christ and of God.
Eph 5:21	51.33-34	if so be, we have been taught by him, as the truth is in Jesus,

Scripture	*D&A*	Text as it appears in the *D&A*
Eph 5:30-32	8.47-48	his mystical body
Eph 6:13	9.7-8	the whole armour of God;
Eph 6:14	9.9	let us stand fast
Eph 6:15	7.24	gospel of peace,
Eph 6:15	9.8-9	and, having our feet shod with the preparation of the gospel of peace,
Eph 6:18	9.9-10	with all perseverance.
Eph 6:24	6.1	*To all that love our Lord Jesus Christ*,
Eph 6:24	21.9-10	with all them that love him;
Eph 6:24	23.40-41	Peace be with all them that love our Lord Jesus Christ in sincerity. Amen.
Phil 1:6	8.34-35	to help forward this good work; that what yet remains to be done, may be fully accomplished.
Phil 1:11	51.30	fruits of righteousness
Phil 3:15	21.27-28	be in any thing otherwise minded,
Phil 3:15	21.29	God will reveal even this unto them:
Phil 3:16	12.40-41	but that they all walk by the same rule,
Phil 3:16	16.20-21	they ought all to walk by the same rule, to mind and speak the same thing;
Phil 3:16	49.25	they ought all to walk by the same rule,
Phil 4:1	6.4	DEARLY BELOVED BRETHREN,
Phil 4:1	10.16	Dearly beloved brethren,
Col 2:6	22.40-41	hath received Christ as his teacher and Lord.
1 Thes 3:12	30.17	charity of her members, one towards another;
1 Thes 3:12	54.18-19	affectionate deportment towards each other, and towards all men;
1 Thes 4:1, 10	13.45	we beseech you then, dear brethren,
1 Thes 5:13	4.7	be at peace among ourselves,
2 Thes 2:3	19.29	the man of sin.
1 Tm 4:15	42.35-36	let our profiting appear to all,
2 Tm 1:7	22.31-32	even the spirit of faith, and of love, and of a sound mind.

Scripture	***D&A***	**Text as it appears in the *D&A***
2 Tm 1:13	37.27-28	they thus held fast that form of sound words
2 Tm 1:13	38.33	holding fast in profession and practice, that form of sound words,
2 Tm 1:13	42.6	his form of sound words truly believed,
2 Tm 1:13	44.4	You also profess to hold fast the form of sound words,
2 Tm 4:18	9.40	to his heavenly kingdom,
Ti 1:11	52.13	or for filthy lucre sake,
Ti 1:13 cf. 2:2	41.33	for soundness in the faith:
Heb 2:10	8.45	Captain of Salvation
Heb 3:11, 18; 4:3, 5, 11	19.46	to prevent them from entering into their promised rest,
Heb 4:14; 10:23	22.11	holding fast in profession
Heb 4:14; 10:23	38.32	holding fast in profession and practice, that form of sound words,
Heb 10:19 cf. 1 Jn 1:7	24.25	through the blood of Jesus
Heb 10:23	16.11	that profess their faith
Heb 10:23	17.35-36	profession of their faith
Heb 10:23	18.19	profess their faith
Heb 10:23	47.11	profession of our faith
Heb 12:14	4.7-8	follow peace with all men, and holiness, without which no man shall see the Lord.
Heb 12:15	35.22	bitter root
Heb 13:8	3.37-38	Christ and his simple word; which is the same yesterday, and to-day, and for ever.
Jas 2:17	51.31-32	without which faith itself is dead being alone.
Jas 2:18	52.1	not shew their faith by their works,
Jas 3:16	6.29-30	where envying and strife is, *there* is confusion and every evil work.
Jas 4:12	27.28-29	"There is one lawgiver, who is able to save, and to destroy: who art thou that judgest another?"
Jas 5:20	13.39-41	convert one sinner from the error of his ways, or save a soul from death? Have they any tendency to hide the multitude of sins

Scripture	*D&A*	Text as it appears in the *D&A*
1 Pt 3:8	17.42	love each other as brethren,
1 Pt 3:8	18.5-6	love each other as brethren,
1 Pt 4:10	15.26-28	As every man, therefore, hath received the gift, even so minister the same one to another as good stewards of the manifold grace of God.
1 Pt 5:3	25.5	Gods heritage:
1 Pt 5:3	26.46	God's heritage,
1 Jn 1:1	3.5-6	see with our own eyes,
1 Jn 1:1	17.26	from the beginning
1 Jn 1:7 cf. Heb 10:19	24.25	through the blood of Jesus
1 Jn 2:12-14	17.26-27	little children and young men, as well as fathers.
1 Jn 3:23-24	22.27-31	For this is his commandment that we believe in his son Jesus Christ, and love one another, as he gave us commandment. And he that keepeth his commandments dwelleth in him, and he in him—and hereby we know that he dwelleth in us, by the spirit which he hath given us"
1 Jn 5:19	48.36-38	"We know," said the Apostle, evidently speaking of such, "that we are of God, and the whole world lieth in wickedness."
2 Jn 1:1-2	12.19-21	"Whom I love in the truth, saith the Apostle, and not I only, but also all they that have known the truth; for the truth's sake, which is in us, and shall be with us forever.
2 Jn 1:2	22.23	for the truth's sake;
2 Jn 1:3	6.6-7	in truth and love,
3 Jn 9-10	34.34-38	Diotrephes, of whom the Apostle says, "who loveth to have the pre-eminence among them, receiveth us not—prating against us with malicious words, and not content therewith, neither doth he himself receive the brethren, and forbiddeth them that would, and casteth them out of the church."

Scripture	*D&A*	Text as it appears in the *D&A*
Jude 3	8.38	contend earnestly for the sacred articles of faith and duty once delivered to the
Jude 3	51.29	contending earnestly for the faith once delivered to the saints,
Rv 2:2	45.16-18	"Thou hast tried them which say they are apostles, and are not, and hast found them liars."
Rv 4:9	40.45-46	to ascribe all that glory, honor, thanks-giving, and praise to him,
Rv 11:3	14.20	the two witnesses
Rv 11:11	14.22	stood upon their feet,
Rv 11:13	14.24	a great earthquake? Has not the tenth part of the great city been thrown down by it?
Rv 11:18	14.25-31	aroused the nations to indignation? Have they not been angry, yea very angry? Therefore, O Lord, is thy wrath come upon them, and the time of the dead that they should be avenged, and that thou shouldest give reward to thy servants, the Prophets, and to them that fear thy name, both small and great; and that thou shouldest destroy them that have destroyed the earth.
Rv 11:19	14.32-33	lightnings and thunderings, and voices; of this tremendous earthquake and great hail;
Rv 13	8.4	the beast;
Rv 14:6	5.26-27	the everlasting gospel,
Rv 16:1	8.5-6	the vials of his wrath poured out upon them.
Rv 17:13	8.3-4	that have given their strength and power unto the beast;
Rv 17:17	8.5	until the word of God be fulfilled,
Rv 18:13	53.28	the souls of men.
Rv 20:8	53.16	in all the four quarters of the globe;
Rv 20:8	53.27-28	in deceiving the nations of the earth,

Studies on the *Declaration and Address*

Toward a Critical Edition of the *Declaration and Address*

Ernest C. Stefanik

The External History of the *Declaration and Address*

The history of the composition and publication of TC's *D&A* can be presented only in broad terms. A brief historical introduction appears at the beginning of the book:

> At a meeting held at Buffaloe, August 17, 1809, consisting of persons of different religious denominations; most of them in an unsettled state as to a fixed gospel ministry; it was unanimously agreed upon, the considerations, and for the purposes herein after declared, to form themselves into a religious association, titled as above—which they accordingly did, and appointed twenty-one of their number to meet and confer together; and, with the assistance of Mr. Thomas Campbell, minister of the gospel, to determine upon the proper means to carry into effect the important ends of their association: the result of which conference was the following declaration and address, agreed upon and ordered to be printed at the expence and for the benefit of the society. September 7, 1809.[1]

Although the precise date of publication is not known, we do know that the composition, printing, and publication of the book was accomplished within four or five months, by the end of 1809 or the beginning of 1810. Between 17 August and 7 September, in less than three weeks, TC had completed the writing of the document that has come to be regarded as a foundational statement of the Restoration Movement. Upon the approval of the steering committee, the publication was authorized on 7 September. Alexander Campbell writes in a footnote to the *D&A*, published in his *Memoirs of Elder Thomas Campbell*, that he had read "the proof-sheets of this 'Declaration,' as they issued from the press, immediately after [his] arrival in Washington, Pennsylvania, direct from Scotland."[2] This statement suggests that the type had been set and galley proofs pulled by Brown & Sample, "at the Office of 'The Reporter'" in Washington by the end of October. In the Postscript of the *D&A,* TC states that the "publication of the foregoing address has been delayed much longer than was at first expected, through an unforeseen difficulty of obtaining paper of the quality intended."[3] His mention in the third sentence of the "considerations and proposals" submitted at the meeting on 14 December fixes the earliest publication date as late December 1809. Thus, possibly by the end of the year or, more probably, at the beginning of 1810, the *Declaration and Address* was printed and bound by Brown & Sample, and then distributed by the Christian Association of Washington.

Facts concerning the distribution and reception of the book are practically nonexistent, except perhaps for Robert Richardson's general statement in his *Memoirs of Alexander Campbell*:

> The ministers of the different parties around, to whom copies were sent, received them apparently with silent acquiescence as to the principles laid down, not a single one of them venturing a public reply, though earnestly and repeatedly invited to consider carefully the propositions submitted, and to make any corrections or amendments which might occur to them, and assured that all objections presented in writing would be "thankfully received and seriously considered with all due attention."[4]

It is interesting to note that TC does not mention this work in his published writings until 1832, when he quotes a portion in his pamphlet *On Religious Reformation*. Later he briefly discusses the *Declaration and Address* in three articles in the *Millennial Harbinger* (June 1835; March 1839; May 1844). Possibly the first notice of the work as "the original plea for reformation" is Richardson's series "Reformation" in the *Millennial Harbinger* (1848: 696-701). This suggests that it was not until the second generation of Disciples that the *Declaration and Address* assumed a significance beyond the short-lived "Christian Association of Washington." By 1909 the date on which the Association approved the document and authorized publication (7 September 1809) had become the accepted birthdate of the Disciples of Christ; TC's copy of the book was displayed as the "chief exhibit" at the Centennial Convention in Pittsburgh.

It is doubtful whether facts concerning the publication of the book can be ascertained in any more detail. The paucity of information concerning the history of the book, however, does not present any significant hindrance in preparing a critical edition of the *D&A*, although the following printing history must be considered as tentative, pending a full examination of all printings of the *D&A*.

The Editions of the *Declaration and Address*

First Edition

The first edition of the *D&A*, as I have stated in the note on the external history of the book, is that seen through the publication process by TC in 1809. Perhaps the only copy of this edition available for examination by scholars is held in Special Collections, T. W. Phillips Memorial Library, Bethany College, Bethany, West Virginia. This copy, containing TC's autograph corrections (as well as notes by AC and instructions for the compositors), was used in the publication of the second edition and has been reproduced as the Facsimile Edition (see below). It was used for this report in photocopy by courtesy of the Disciples of Christ Historical Society, Nashville, Tennessee.

First Edition [1809]

Title Page: DECLARATION | AND | ADDRESS | OF THE | CHRISTIAN ASSOCIATION | OF | *WASHINGTON.* | [rule] | WASHINGTON, (Pa.) | [rule] | *Printed by BROWN & SAMPLE,* | AT THE OFFICE OF "THE REPORTER." | 1809.
Pagination: [1-4] 5 [6] 7-23 [24] 25-56
Contents: Title page, p. 1. Introductory note, p. 2. Declaration, &c;., pp. 3-5. Address, &c;., pp. 6-23. Appendix, pp. 24-54. Postscript, pp. 54-56. Errata, p. 56.
Typography: 49 lines/page; 3 5/8" x 6 1/4" text page. 8-pt. type with 1-pt. leading.

Note 1: Portions of the first edition were reprinted in TC's *On Religious Reformation* (ca. 1832). No other printings of this edition have been located.
Note 2: Information obtained from photocopy of facsimile edition.

Facsimile Edition [1908]

Cover Title: [within rule frame] DECLARATION | AND | ADDRESS | THOMAS CAMPBELL | CHRISTIAN BOARD OF PUBLICATION | ST. LOUIS.
Title Page: DECLARATION | AND | ADDRESS | OF THE | CHRISTIAN ASSOCIATION | OF | *WASHINGTON.* | [rule] | WASHINGTON, (Pa.) | [rule] | *Printed by BROWN & SAMPLE,* | AT THE OFFICE OF "THE REPORTER." | 1809.
Pagination: [i-ii] [1-4] 5 [6] 7-23 [24] 25-56 [57-58]
Contents: Note on facsimile edition, p. i. Title page, p. 1. Introductory note, p. 2. Declaration, &c;., pp. 3-5. Address, &c;., pp. 6-23. Appendix, pp. 24-54. Postscript, pp. 54-56. Errata, p. 56. Blank, pp. 57-58.
Typography: 49 lines/page; 3 5/8" x 6 1/4" text page. 8-pt. type with 1-pt. leading.
Note: Information obtained from photocopy of facsimile edition.

Centennial Edition [1909]

Cover title: [within rule frame] Declaration | and | Address | THOMAS CAMPBELL | CENTENNIAL | EDITION
Title page: [blackletter typeface] Declaration and Address | Thomas Campbell | [device] | Centennial Edition | Thirtieth Thousand | Centennial Bureau | 203 Bissell Block | Pittsburgh, Pennsylvania
Copyright page: This edition follows the original, | page for page, | line for line, letter for | letter. Even the type face dupli- | cates that of a hundred years ago | with remarkable exactness. | 1909 | RECORD PUBLISHING COMPANY | CORAPOLIS, PA.
Pagination: [i-vi] [1-3] 4-5 [6] 7-56 [57-58]
Contents: Blank, pp. i-ii. Frontispiece, portrait of Thomas Campbell, tipped in between pp. ii and iii. Title page, p. iii. Copyright page, p. iv. Centennial Introduction, pp. v-vi. Facsimile of first edition title page, p. 1. Introductory note, p. 2. Declaration, &c;., pp. 3-5. Address, pp. 6-23.

Appendix, pp. 25-54. Postscript, pp. 54-56. Errata, p. 56. Centennial Aims, p. 57. Blank, p. 58.
Typography: 49 lines/page; 3 5/8" x 6 3/4" text page. 8-pt. type with 2-pt. leading.
Note: The book as described above is not the first printing of this edition, but it is the only one available for examination as of this writing. According to the card catalog of the Disciples of Christ Historical Society, there are other printings of this edition. Another published by the Centennial Bureau (1908) has "Twentieth Thousand" imprinted on the title page (probably this is the first printing); another, by the Centennial Bureau (1909), "Twenty-fifth Thousand"; another published by the Western Pennsylvania Christian Missionary Society (1908), "Twentieth Thousand"; another published by the Centennial Department of the American Christian Missionary Society (Cincinnati, 1908), "Twenty-fifth Thousand." There may be others. Whether these copies are editions, printings, reprintings, or issues can be determined only by having access to the publishers' and/or printers' records.

Second Edition

The second edition of the *D&A* is that seen through the publication process by AC in 1861. This edition was first published as a contribution to another book, not as a separate publication. It incorporates TC's corrections and includes AC's notes and numerous corrections (principally of punctuation and capitalization). The most notable difference between the first and second editions is the absence of the Postscript in the second.

Second Edition [1861]

Title page: MEMOIRS | OF | ELDER THOMAS CAMPBELL | BY | ALEXANDER CAMPBELL, | OF BETHANY, VIRGINIA. | [rule] | CINCINNATI, O.: | PUBLISHED BY H. S. BOSWORTH, | COR. EIGHTH AND WALNUT STS. | 1861.
Pagination: 25-109.
Contents: DECLARATION AND ADDRESS | OF THE | CHRISTIAN ASSOCIATION OF WASHINGTON, PENN. | PUBLISHED A. D. 1809. Introductory note, p. 25. Declaration, Etc., pp. 25-30. Address, Etc., pp. 30-60. Appendix, pp. 60-109.

Note: According to the bibliography of TC's works published in *Discipliana* (1961), this edition was reprinted in 1871 by H. S. Bosworth and in 1954 by the Old Path Book Club.[5]

Young Edition [1904]

Title Page: Historical Documents | Advocating | Christian Union | Epoch-Making Statements by Leaders among | the Disciples of Christ for the Restora- | tion of the Christianity of the New | Testament—its Doctrines, its | Ordinances, and its | Fruits | Historical Introductions by | Charles Alexander Young | Managing Editor of THE CHRISTIAN CENTURY | [rule] | Chicago | The Christian Century Company | 1904
Pagination: 71-209.
Contents: [blackletter] Declaration and Address [Declaration], pp. 71-78. Address, Etc., pp. 79-128. Appendix, pp. 128-209.
Note 1: The text of the *D&A* in this edition omits the heading "Declaration, Etc." and the introductory note. A cursory examination of the text against the second edition has revealed several variants in punctuation and capitalization.
Note 2: This anthology also includes a historical introduction by Young (pp. 27-32) and an analysis by Errett Gates (pp. 33-69).

Notes

1. Thomas Campbell, *Declaration and Address of the Christian Association of Washington* (Washington, Pa.: Brown & Sample, 1809): 4.1-17.
2. Alexander Campbell, *Memoirs of Elder Thomas Campbell, Together with a Brief Memoir of Mrs. Jane Campbell* (Cincinnati: H. S. Bosworth, 1861), p. 28.
3. *D&A*, 54.27-29(PS).
4. Robert Richardson, *Memoirs of Alexander Campbell Embracing a View of the Origin, Progress and Principles of the Religious Reformation which he Advocated* (Philadelphia: J. B. Lippincot, 1868), 1:273.
5. An electronic edition with simultaneous access to the first, second, and facsimile editions plus collations can be accessed via the following URL: http://www.mun.ca/rels/restmov/texts/tcampbell/da/DA-1ST.HTM.

Continental Reformation Backgrounds for the *Declaration and Address*

Thomas H. Olbricht

All Protestants are to some degree indebted to the magisterial Reformers, and certainly this is also true of Thomas Campbell and his more famous son, Alexander. TC had no doubt studied the Reformation in his theological education at the University of Glasgow and the Anti-Burgher Seminary at Whitburn. The *Declaration and Address* discloses evidence of these studies—for example, in arguing that creeds do not prevent diversity of beliefs:

> If, for instance, Arians, Socianians, Arminians, Calvinists, Antinomians, &c. &c, might not all subscribe the Westminster Confession, the Athanasian Creed, or the doctrinal articles of the Church of England. If this be denied, we appeal to historical facts; and, in the mean time, venture to assert, that such things are and have been done. Or will any say, that a person might not with equal ease, honesty, and consistency, be an Arian or a Socinian in his heart while subscribing the Westminster Confession, or the Athanasian Creed, as while making his unqualified profession to believe everything that the Scriptures declare concerning Christ?[1]

But we have few other clues in this document as to how TC viewed the Reformation or Reformers.

How, then, do we bring the Continental Reformers to bear as background for the *D&A*? We should not presume that TC's earlier perspectives were the same as those later championed by his son, Alexander. Yet the way in which he envisioned the Reformers does not differ materially from that of AC found in the 1835 preface of *Christianity Restored*.[2] AC's line of argument is much like that of the *D&A* in that he suggested that previous efforts at reform have failed due to creeds, which in turn resulted in various sects rather than in the one body of Jesus Christ. The difference is that AC in *Christianity Restored* set out specifically the platforms of the Continental Reformers.

AC first mentioned the great apostasy, which he declared foretold by the prophets and apostles, and the attempts at reformation, beginning with Martin Luther. The result, he declared, was the most splendid era in the history of the world. These beneficent outcomes may be attributed to "the intelligence, faith, and courage of Martin Luther and his heroic Associates."[3] Luther's foremost accomplishment was that he restored the Bible to the world in A.D. 1534. When Luther died, however, he had no comparable successor:

> His tenets were soon converted into a new state religion, and the spirit of reformation which he excited and inspired, was soon quenched by the broils and feuds of the protestant princes, and the collisions of rival political interests both on the continent and islands of Europe.[4]

Those who aspired to control soon produced creeds and manuals, along with synods and councils, and shackled the minds of men.

Calvin, AC charged, renewed the speculative theology of Augustine. Disputes arose about forms and ceremonies, giving way to speculative strifes of opinion and the political and religious grounds for burning heretics. AC admitted, however, that "much light was elicited," and more headway would have been made had it not been for the wrangles. The results of the efforts, he declared, were more than major political or literary achievements. But because of extremes, unity did not ensue; Protestants would as soon worship with Catholics as with other Protestants. For AC these divisions were brought about by speculative theologies such as those based on Platonism and Egyptian mysticism, perhaps more so than by church practices. Protestant declarations often provoked opposition—for example, the five great dogmas of John Calvin were opposed by Jacob Arminius in 1591, while the five were affirmed by the Synod of Dort in 1618.

These three major perspectives—Lutheranism, Calvinism, and Arminianism—were, according to AC, imported to Britain, where they spawned another: Quakerism. Whereas Luther and Calvin had discovered *faith alone*, George Fox discovered *Spirit alone*. Furthermore, according to AC, remonstrants were found in all the northern European countries:

> the Pope and the Protestants;—the Lutherans and the Calvinists;—the Calvinists and the Arminians—the Bishops against the Presbyters, and the Presbyterians among themselves, until, by the potency of metaphysics and politics, they are now frittered down to numerous parties.[5]

Campbell highlighted earlier Reformers because in his opinion their failure to mold churches based on the Bible into one body of Christ left a window of opportunity. The new, superior effort at reform he promulgated would abandon creeds so as to restore primitive Christianity:

> Not until within the present generation did any sect or party in christendom unite and build upon the Bible alone. Since that time, the first effort known to us to abandon the whole controversy about creeds and reformations, and to *restore* primitive christianity, or to build alone upon the Apostles and Prophets, Jesus Christ himself the chief corner, has been made.[6]

This effort, according to AC, commenced with his father's publication of the *D&A*:

> A deep and an abiding impression that the power, the consolations and joys—the holiness and happiness of Christ's religion were lost in the forms and ceremonies, in the speculations and conjectures, in the feuds and bickerings of sects and schisms, originated a project many years ago for uniting the sects, or rather the *christians* in all the sects, upon a clear and scriptural bond of union; upon having a *thus saith the Lord*, either in express terms, or in approved precedents, "for every article of faith, and item of religious practice." This was offered in the year 1809, in the "Declaration and Address" of the Washington Association, Pennsylvania. It was first tendered to the parties that confessed the Westminster creed; but equally submitted to all protestants of every name, making faith in Christ and obedience to him, the only *test* of christian character, and the only bond of church union, communion, and co-operation. It was indeed approved by all, but adopted and practised by none; except the few, or part of the few, who made the overture.[7]

Taking up the lead provided by AC, in order to comprehend the Continental background for the *D&A,* we shall discuss not only the reforms of Luther and Calvin, but also the Swiss reforms, the views of Jacob Arminius, and of the various Continental heretics.

Martin Luther (1483–1546)

Though other Reformers preceded Martin Luther, he became a pivotal figure in Reformation history because, due to his excommunication and the support by German electors, a new, evangelical church emerged in Germany distinct from the Roman Catholic church. Luther focused on ways that Rome had departed from early Christianity and needed to heed once again the demands of the gospel. Guidelines for required changes were to come from the Scriptures. At Worms in 1521 Johann von der Ecken, chancellor of the bishop of Trier, demanded that Luther recant. Luther held his ground:

> Unless I am convinced by the testimony of the Holy Scriptures or by evident reason—for I can believe neither pope nor councils alone, as it is clear that they have erred repeatedly and contradicted themselves—I consider myself convicted by the testimony of Holy Scripture, which is my basis; my conscience is captive to the Word of God. Thus I cannot and will not recant, because acting against one's conscience is neither safe nor sound. God help me. Amen.[8]

At this stage Luther put aside neither Pope nor councils, but affirmed that they too must rise or fall under the scrutiny of Scripture. The result was a recovery of the Bible, which was now printed and shortly translated into modern languages—into German by Luther himself—and made available for the first time on a large scale to every literate believer. Biblical Christianity became the standard goal in northern Europe, along with a rejection of medieval accoutrements. More attention was now being given to the Scriptures by Continental Christian communities than for the past one thousand years.

In a disputation with Eck at Leipzig in 1519, Luther denied both the primacy of the Pope and the infallibility of the General Councils. This was 290 years before the 1809 publication of TC's *D&A*. TC carried the authority of the Scriptures a step further by pushing aside all councils and declaring the Scriptures alone (*sola scriptura*) the final court of appeals:

> [W]e are persuaded that it is high time for us not only to think, but also to act, for ourselves; to see with our own eyes, and to take all our

> measures directly and immediately from the Divine Standard; to this alone we feel ourselves Divinely bound to be conformed; as by this alone we must be judged.[9]

Luther early on discovered, in Romans and Galatians, that salvation is not of works but of faith. This led him to translate Romans 3:28, "*So halten wir nun dafür, daß der Mensch gerecht werde ohne des Gesetzes Werke, allein durch den Glauben.*" The last phrase in English may be translated "alone through faith." This was a great personal revelation for the young Luther, who struggled over his own efforts to achieve reconciliation on the grounds of his endeavor to comply with the regulations of his Augustinian order. The weight of the conviction that salvation is by faith *only* occurred as early as 1518 when Luther commenced teaching Romans.[10] The great Reformation principle, justification by faith, came to a culmination in 1519 when Luther reported the discovery. The famous Ninety-Five Theses, posted on the Castle Church door in Wittenberg on 31 October 1517 (or 1 November), focused almost entirely on justification by works, a major example of which was the sale of indulgences.[11] AC, in his Preface to *Christianity Restored*, cited Luther's "faith alone" perspective as an "extreme begot by extremes."[12]

John Calvin (1509–64)

John Calvin, born in France but a noted church leader in Geneva, Switzerland, experienced a conversion about 1530 and commenced entertaining reformation ideas. Though later and less flamboyant than Luther, his views and leadership were likely more influential in bringing especially the English-speaking world to Reformation views than were those of Martin Luther. While the Lutheran Reformation in Germany was called Evangelical, the heirs of both Calvin and Zwingli were designated "Reformed."

Calvin likewise insisted upon the supremacy of the Scriptures. While realizing that the Roman Catholic Church recognized the authority of the Scriptures, he asserted a crucial distinction:

> The difference between us and the papists is that they believe that the church cannot be the pillar of the truth unless she presides over the Word of God. We, on the other hand, assert that it is because she reverently subjects herself to the Word of God that the truth is preserved by her, and passed on to others by her hands.[13]

Calvin likewise fends off the charge of being a schismatic through laying the blame at the feet of others for the schisms in the church—on the one hand the Papists and on the other the Anabaptists. "We are assailed by two sects," Calvin wrote to Cardinal Sadolet in 1539,

> which seem to differ most widely from each other. For what similitude is there in appearance between the pope and the Anabaptists? . . . For when they boast extravagantly of the Spirit, the tendency certainly is to sink and bury the "Word of God," that they may make room for their own falsehoods. And you, Sadolet, by stumbling on the very threshold, have paid the penalty of that affront which you offered to the Holy Spirit, when you separated him from the Word. For, as if those who seek the way of God were standing where two ways meet, and destitute of any certain sign, you are forced to introduce them as hesitating whether it be more expedient to follow the authority of the church, or to listen to those whom you call the inventors of new dogmas. . . .[14]

> As to the charge of forsaking the church, which they were wont to bring against me, there is nothing of which my conscience accuses me, unless, indeed, he is to be considered a deserter, who, seeing the soldiers routed and scattered, and abandoning the ranks, raises the leader's standard, and recalls them to their posts.[15]

Calvin particularly influenced Reformed theology, including Scottish and Puritan, in regard to the doctrines of election and predestination. It was these doctrines to which the Campbells objected and which inflamed their ire as they reflected on the Westminster Confession (a 1643 Reformed statement for the English church), even though they could support most of the rest of the document. The doctrine of predestination, for which Calvin has been famous through history, was not, however, central to his theology, being rather an aspect of the doctrine of salvation. He did hold, however, that all are predestined, some to salvation and others to damnation, designated double election. On predestination, Calvin wrote in his *Instruction in Faith*, his own compendium of the much longer and more famous *Institutes of the Christian Religion*:

> For, the seed of the word of God takes root and brings forth fruit only in those whom the Lord, by his eternal election, has predestined to be children and heirs of the heavenly kingdom. To all others (who by the same counsel of God are rejected before the foundation of the world) the clear and evident preaching of truth can be nothing but an odor of death unto death. Now, why does the Lord use his mercy toward some and

> exercise the rigor of his judgment on the others? We have to leave the reason of this to be known by him alone. For, if he willed to ruin all mankind, he has the right to do it, and in those whom he rescues from perdition one can contemplate nothing but his sovereign goodness. We acknowledge, therefore, the elect to be recipients of his mercy (as truly they are) and the rejected to be recipients of his wrath, a wrath, however, which is nothing but just.[16]

In some circles in the twentieth century the chief characteristic of Calvinistic theology is perceived to be the conversion experience. But that again was not characteristic of Calvin. He professed such an experience but did not describe it, and therefore let it reside in the background. Emphasis on the conversion experience came about rather as the result of the Pietists (a late seventeenth- and early eighteenth-century movement in the Evangelical or Lutheran church) and the American awakenings (beginning in the middle of the eighteenth century), both of which were influenced by later Calvinist theology. The hardening of Calvinistic theology came about through the writings of Theodore Beza (1519–1605), who served as a professor in Calvin's academy in Geneva, and the Synod of Dort (1618–19), a Reformed conclave held in the Netherlands. Dort theologians were opposed to Arminianism, named for the celebrated Dutch theologian Jacob Arminius (1560–1609), and drew up the famous so-called fundamentals of Calvinism (sometimes subsumed by reordering under the acronym TULIP). The synod was, in effect, a council of the Reformed Churches, with delegates from England, Scotland, Switzerland, Hesse, and the Palatinate.[17] These five principles reflected in some measure the views of John Calvin, but more properly are characteristic of the later Calvinism that the Campbells and their heirs denigrated. The five sets of articles asserted (1) unconditional election, (2) a limited atonement, (3) the total depravity of man, (4) the irresistibility of grace, and (5) the final perseverance of the saints.

The Campbells theologically identified more clearly with the views of Arminius, but argued that he did not fully reflect the biblical message since his views were an extreme reaction to Calvinism. Arminius was schooled at Utrecht, Marburg, Leiden, and Geneva under Theodore Beza. As a minister in Amsterdam he gave special attention to the Epistle to the Romans and came to doubt the Calvinist doctrine of predestination.[18] He was charged with Pelagianism (named for Pelagius, a native of Britain who migrated to Rome in the early fifth century) and disloyalty to the confessions of his church. He was appointed professor at Leiden in 1603.

He tried, not altogether successfully, to revise the Belgic Confession and the Heidelberg Catechism. He insisted that Divine sovereignty was compatible with a genuine human free will and that common Calvinist views of predestination were unbiblical. He won over Hugo Grotius (1583–1645), another Dutch theologian whose federal or convenantal theology was greatly admired by AC, if not by TC.

The Swiss Reformers

The early Swiss Reform was possible because of the political climate, much like in Germany, in which the leading citizens were influenced by reforming doctrines and resisted the authority of the Bishop of Constance when he tried to interfere. The Swiss were interested in purging the church of statues, depictions, stained-glass windows, and vestiges of the Mass, that is, in restoring the simplicity of New Testament buildings and worship. Though direct influence is difficult to establish, the Swiss Reform proceeded in guiding motives similar to those of the Campbells, more than either the Lutheran or Calvinist reforms. Indirect influence is certainly present through the Scottish Reform, the Puritans, and various British Independents. Some aspects of the Swiss Reform predated the efforts of Luther but were later influenced by the work of Luther.[19] We shall look at three main leaders of the Swiss Reform.

Ulrich Zwingli (1484–1531)

Zwingli was educated at Berne, Vienna, and Basle, was ordained a priest in 1506, and was pastor at Glarus from 1506 to 1516. He became interested in the Christian humanism of Erasmus (1466–1536) and taught himself Greek and possibly Hebrew. In 1518 he was elected People's Preacher at Old Minster in Zurich. His first attacks on Catholic practices came in 1519 in sermons commenting on the New Testament in which he criticized purgatory, invocation of saints, and monasticism. By 1525 the Mass was suppressed in Zurich; Zwingli had married Anna Meyer in the cathedral the previous year.

During this period Zwingli commenced changing his views on the Eucharist, and by 1525 he held, over against Luther, a purely symbolic interpretation. Luther argued for a consubstantiation in which Christ was actually present at the time of the celebration, though not in the ingredients (transubstantiation), as held by the Roman Catholics. Zwingli argued that it is only in the communicant's faith that Christ is present when the Eucharist is celebrated. "I believe that in the Holy Eucharist, i.e, the supper of thanksgiving, the true body of Christ is present by the contemplation of faith," Zwingli wrote in *An Account of the Faith*:

> This means that they who thank the Lord for the benefits bestowed on us in His Son acknowledge that He assumed true flesh, in it truly suffered, truly washed away our sins by His blood; and thus everything done by Christ becomes as it were present to them by the contemplation of faith. But that the body of Christ in essence and really, i.e., the actual body itself, is either present in the supper or masticated with our mouth and teeth, as the Papists or some who look back to the fleshpots of Egypt assert, we not only deny, but constantly maintain to be an error, contrary to the Word of God.[20]

The differences among the Reformers over the manner in which Christ is present in the Lord's Supper, later reflected in the confessions, is indeed a case in point as to the manner in which, as the Campbells contended, the creeds preserved dissonances among the Protestants.

Martin Bucer (1491–1551)

Martin Bucer moved from Switzerland to Heidelberg in 1516, in 1518 heard Luther dispute, and by 1521 adopted a version of Lutheran teaching. His doctrine of the Eucharist was considered halfway between that of Luther and Zwingli, and he set out to serve as a mediator between the two groups.[21] After the death of Zwingli he became involved in several efforts to engage Catholics and the various Reformers in dialogue, but with limited success. In 1548 Bucer migrated to England at the invitation of Thomas Cranmer and was appointed Regius Professor of Divinity at Cambridge. He exercised considerable influence on the Anglican Ordinal for appointing and maintaining the priesthood.

Heinrich Bullinger (1504–75)

Bullinger was born in the Swiss Canton of Aarau and educated in Swiss monastic schools and the University of Cologne. About 1520 he commenced reading the writings of Luther, and in succession adopted Lutheranism and later Zwinglianism. In 1529 he became pastor of Bremgarten and married. In 1531 he succeeded Zwingli as chief pastor at

Zurich and continued in that role until his death. Bullinger was in some ways the progenitor of covenantal (federal) theology, which was further developed by Johannes Cocceius and Grotius. Federal theology influenced both theological thinking and governmental theory, as Charles McCoy and Wayne Baker have shown.[22] Bullinger's crucial work was *De testamento seu foedere Dei unico et aeterno* (1534). But unlike Cocceius and later Grotius, Bullinger argued for a single covenant throughout the whole Scriptures that was especially envisioned as the covenant with Abraham. Aside from Luther and Calvin, he was likely the most influential Reformer in his time. He helped draw up the Helvetic Confessions (First 1536; Second 1566) and the *Consensus Tigurinus* (1549), making the Reform more national. He battled the Lutheran doctrine of the Eucharist as well as the Anabaptists.

While the leaders of the Swiss Reform contributed to the movement that affirmed the Scriptures as the final authority for Christendom, they also brought about a fractured Christendom, as the Campbells argued.

The Anabaptists (Antinomians)

The final aspect of the Continental Reformation to be taken up here is that of the Anabaptists. The Anabaptists were fewer in number than the mainstream of the Reformation and often had to resort to clandestine meetings in the Rhineland, Switzerland, Holland, and England. At least seven major groups of Anabaptists may be identified. They not only battled with the magisterial reformers but with each other. Though the Campbells shared many points of view with these dissident groups, they seemed little interested in them—partly, no doubt, because "Anabaptist" became a pejorative designation, and even the Baptists, with whom the Continental Anabaptists had certain traditional ties, made a concentrated effort in the time of the Campbells to distance themselves from these groups. But Anabaptists certainly could be singled out (identified by TC under the label "antinomians") as evidence for the Campbellian charge that Protestantism had by and large produced schismatics.

The one common commitment of these varying Anabaptist groups was that baptism should be administered to adult believers and by immersion. They therefore opposed the baptism of infants and insisted that persons so baptized be immersed again as adults. For that reason they were designated "anabaptists"—that is, the baptizing again of those baptized as infants. As Owen Chadwick has summed up their predilections:

> For the most part they rejected the baptism of infants. They believed that the true Church was called out of the world and therefore most of them repudiated the idea that the magistrate should uphold the true Church. The so-called Anabaptist Confession of Schleitheim (1527), the document nearest to a confession agreed by the early Anabaptists, proclaimed adult baptism and separation from the world, including everything popish, and from attendance at parish churches and taverns. It condemned the use of force, or going to law, or becoming a magistrate, or the taking of oaths.[23]

We shall here discuss some of the major leaders.

Thomas Müntzer (1489–1525)

Thomas Müntzer was at the extreme left of the Anabaptists, goading the German peasants into the famous 1524 revolt in the region of Mühlhausen. He became increasingly convinced that the struggle of the saints in the last days had begun. Müntzer was a native of Stolberg and may have studied at Leipzig, thereafter taking a degree at Frankfurt on der Oder. He probed with great care the medieval mystics, especially Tauler and Suso. Probably on Luther's recommendation he took up a ministry in Zwickau in 1520. In 1521 he made his way to Prague and became convinced that the end of all things was at hand. In 1523 he became pastor in Allstedt, where he wrote much, attacking among other traditional doctrines infant baptism. Soon thereafter he placed himself at the head of local troops in a rebellion but his forces were defeated and he himself tortured and executed. Because of these uprisings, Anabaptists came to be feared all over the Continent and the major Reformers joined in the persecutions.

Balthasar Hubmaier (1485–1528)

Hubmaier was born in Germany and trained at Freiburg and Ingolstadt, becoming priest and professor at the latter. He then was appointed preacher at Regensburg Cathedral, and afterwards parish priest at Waldshut, where he came in contact with the Swiss Reformers and openly allied himself with Zwingli in 1523. By 1525 he rejected infant baptism and cast his lot with the Anabaptists. In the Peasants' War he fled to Zurich, where Zwingli forced him to adjure his views. The next year, however, he left Zurich and renounced his recantation. He now settled in

Nikolsburg in Moravia. The Austrians took him to Vienna and there burned him at the stake in March 1528.

Melchior Hoffman (1500–43)

Hoffman, a leather-dresser, became a lay preacher in Livonia in 1523. After coming into conflict with the city officials, he fled to Stockholm and there became more and more convinced of the approaching end of the world. In Denmark he entered into a dispute over the Lutheran view of the Lord's Supper and held that it was only a sign. Upon being banished from Denmark he went to Strasbourg, where he joined forces with the Anabaptists. From 1530 to 1533 he preached in East Friesland in the Netherlands, but in the latter year returned to Strasbourg, perceived as the New Jerusalem, to await the Last Day. He was imprisoned for life, but remained firm in his convictions and influenced many Anabaptists who developed into a party called the Melchiorites.

Menno Simons (1496–1561)

Menno Simons was a parish priest in Dutch Friesland who in 1536 renounced the Roman Catholic Church and joined the Anabaptists. Until his death he shepherded congregations. He emphasized adult baptism and a connectional type of church arrangement with local rights and responsibilities. He objected to believers participating in governments and favored non-resistance. Some branches of the Mennonites held Socinian views, and some objected to the developments of newer, mechanical ways of farming and of new clothing styles. The latter became known as Amish.

Socinus (Lelio Francesco Maria Sozini 1525–62; Fausto Paolo Sozzini 1539–1604)

Two Socinians were prominent, first the uncle and then his nephew Fausto. The elder of the two was born in Siena in Italy and trained as a lawyer, like his father. He soon discovered that theology was his real interest and made his way to Venice, the Protestant headquarters in Italy. From 1547 to 1550 he traveled to several European countries and was received by various Reformers, including Melancthon in Wittenberg. In 1554 he made his way to Geneva and was challenged on his views of the Trinity by John Calvin. He then settled in Zurich and found it easier to live in the same town with Bullinger. The nephew, Fausto, also grew up in Siena. In 1561 he moved to Lyons and published a work on the Gospel of John (1562) in which he denied the essential divinity of Christ. He was in the service of Isabella de' Medici from 1563 until 1574 and outwardly conformed to Catholicism. In 1578 he moved to Basle and in 1594 published *De Christo Servatore*, in which he opposed the Reformer's teachings on salvation. He moved then to Transylvania and later to Poland, where he spread a moderate unitarianism among the upper classes.

The Socinians were involved in the beginnings of a unitarian movement on the Continent which later became known among indigenous anti-Trinitarian groups in Great Britain and North America. Another northern Italian, Michael Servetus (1511–53), became famous after being burned at the stake in Geneva under the supervision of John Calvin. He argued in a 1531 treatise, *De Trinitatis Erroribus Libri VII*, that the term Trinity itself was unbiblical. His principal work, however, was *Christianismi Restitutio*, which he submitted to John Calvin. Servetus not only rejected the Trinity, but also professed that the Word of God was Jesus, who though Son of God existed only in his earthly life. The death of Servetus created heated controversy among Protestants as to whether heretics should be killed, the outcome of which was the rejection of capital punishment of heretics a century later.[24] The Campbells were sometimes charged with being Socinians because they questioned the Trinity as a biblical doctrine. In sentiment, however, they upheld Trinitarian views more than did Barton W. Stone, who may be described as an Arian (after Arius, d. 336).

Conclusions

With these insights into the Continental Reformers, it is clear that a case can be made, as TC did in the *D&A*, that though the Reformers are to be admired for making the Bible once again the standard for the Christian faith, very soon they, and especially their successors, multiplied sectarian positions and formalized them into creeds. The elder Campbell proposed that in order to break out of this syndrome, the Scripture must be studied most rigorously, theology criticized and sometimes rejected, and a genuine effort made to either do away with creeds or to subject them to the teachings of the Scriptures. Further evidence was found in the

Thirty Years' War (1618–48), in which the various religious groups on the Continent engaged in battle for the hegemony.

The Campbells were indebted to the magisterial Reformers for both the doctrine of *sola scriptura* and the ways of interpreting it. But they were convinced that the Reformers and especially their successors divided Christendom rather than moving ahead in a united front. The Campbells therefore not only proposed that religious persons turn away from past theological battles but also refrain from making governments the supporters of sectarian schisms. The Campbells believed that in the Scriptures alone they had located such a unifying force that might eventually bring about the Kingdom of God on earth.

Notes

1. Thomas Campbell, *Declaration and Address of the Christian Association of Washington* (Washington, Pa.: Brown & Sample, 1809), 40.34-44.
2. Alexander Campbell, *A Connected View of the Principles and Rules . . .* [Cover Title, *Christianity Restored*; later editions titled *The Christian System* (Bethany, Va.: McVay & Ewing, 1835)]. I shall give the pagination for this reprint (Rosemead, Calif.: Old Path Book Club, 1959).
3. AC, *Christianity Restored*, 3.
4. AC, *Christianity Restored*, 4.
5. AC, *Christianity Restored*, 5.
6. AC, *Christianity Restored*, 5, 6.
7. AC, *Christianity Restored*, 7.
8. Quoted in Heiko A. Oberman, *Luther: Man between God and the Devil* (New York: Doubleday, 1992), 39. Oberman did not include the famous line "Here I stand, I cannot do otherwise" before "God help me," since it is now thought to be a later addition.
9. *D&A*, 3.3-8.
10. Oberman, *Luther: Man between God*, 164 f.
11. I have read the version found in *Martin Luther: Selections from His Writings*, ed. John Dillenberger (Garden City: Anchor Books, 1961), 490-500.
12. AC, *Christianity Restored*, 4.
13. Quoted by Alister E. McGrath, *Reformation Thought: An Introduction* (Grand Rapids: Baker, 1993), 143.
14. John Calvin, "Letter to Cardinal James Sadolet," in *Great Voices of the Reformation*, ed. Harry Emerson Fosdick (New York: The Modern Library, 1952), 204, 205.
15. Calvin, "Letter to Cardinal James Sadolet," 212.

16. John Calvin, *Instruction in Faith*, trans. & ed. Paul T. Fuhman (Louisville: Westminster/John Knox, 1992), 222, 223.

17. Owen Chadwick, *The Reformation* (London: Penguin Books, 1990), 220, 221.

18. Peter Bertius, "An Oration on the Life and Death of that Reverend and Very Famous Man James Arminius," in *The Works of James Arminius*, trans. James Nichols (Grand Rapids: Baker Book House, 1992), 29-32.

19. Chadwick, *The Reformation*, 76, 77.

20. Ulrich Zwingli, "An Account of the Faith," in *Great Voices of the Reformation*, 189.

21. Chadwick, *The Reformation*, 81.

22. Charles S. McCoy and J. Wayne Baker, *Fountainhead of Federalism: Heinrich Bullinger and the Covenantal Tradition; with a translation of* De Testamento seu foedere Dei unico et aeterno (Louisville: Westminster/John Knox Press, 1991), 45-62.

23. Chadwick, *The Reformation*, 189.

24. Chadwick, *The Reformation*, 198, 199.

The Form and Function of the *Declaration and Address*[1]

Hiram J. Lester

A passion for Christian unity has characterized the Restoration Movement from its beginnings in the first decade of the nineteenth century.[2] For the several indigenous American reform movements that coalesced into this unique American reformation, and especially for Thomas and Alexander Campbell (and Barton W. Stone), Christian union was the "polar star" from the first.[3] Given the American propensity for sectarian fragmentation, this institutionalization of a concern for Christian unity represents a historic break from a normative sectarian past.

What are the historical sources of this revolutionary development? Both foundation documents—TC's *Declaration and Address of the Christian Association of Washington* (1809) and Stone's *Last Will and Testament of the Springfield Presbytery* (1804)[4]—are recognized as seminal documents in American ecumenism; each places heavy emphasis on Christian unity. How did these reformers, educated in a creedal, contentious Presbyterianism, independently decide that the needed reform was *unity*? This question, important to both the history of the Restoration Movement and that of the ecumenical movement, has never been explored critically.[5]

This essay, based on primary texts recently discovered in Northern Ireland and London, seeks to establish the historical source(s) for the form and function of the *D&A* and, perhaps thereby, to discover the bases of TC's passion for Christian unity. Since the *D&A* is his earliest known statement on the subject (after only two years in America), this essay will use it to trace his earlier ecumenical[6] relationships and then to describe briefly his ecumenical activity up to 1809.[7]

I shall first describe the formal characteristics of the document as a means of establishing a model that can be compared to similar documents elsewhere and, on the basis of that description of form, attempt to determine the function of the document. This process will highlight some of the historical problems in the *D&A* and the Christian Association of Washington that have been ignored by earlier studies. Next, I shall establish a historical model or precursor for TC's tract and also for the Christian Association. Finally, a brief account of TC's work with the precursor and the aftermath of that experience will demonstrate graphically the depth of TC's ecumenical passion and frustration.

Form and Function Analysis

The formal characteristics of the *D&A* are so obvious that it seems strange that no one appears to have ever asked the questions that naturally arise from such an analysis. The tract consists of two parts of unequal size: The initial section, denominated the Declaration, is much shorter and seems to be a charter or plan for an organization called the Christian Association of Washington. This observation seems to be confirmed when Item VIII of the Declaration calls for a reading of "the constitution and address" as a required item on the agenda at each meeting of the Christian Association.

If this first section is a constitution for the Association, then why is it called the Declaration? The answer is not immediately obvious. Certainly the basic American character of the *D&A* is assumed by most studies of the tract. For example, Donald H. Yoder summarized the tract's significance and its intentional break with the sectarian Christian past: "This document, one of the great milestones on the path of Christian unity in America, was a Declaration of Independence to all those on the frontier who desired to transcend the sectarian spirit."[8] Yoder's observation is more than a rhetorical flourish, for the first paragraph of the Declaration seems to be consciously reminiscent of Thomas Jefferson's earlier Declaration of Independence.[9] Perhaps this explains the choice of the title for this section.

The choice of title for the second part may be easier to explain. In its present form this section is a "general" epistle addressed "to all that love our Lord Jesus Christ, in sincerity, throughout all the churches." However, once we have established the precursor and traced its history, it will appear more likely that the Address is so denominated because it was read as an inaugural address at the first meeting of the Christian Association in Buffaloe, Pennsylvania, on 17 August 1809.

Furthermore, although the two parts of the document share some of the same ideas, the relationship between them is ambiguous. For example, the purposes of the Christian Association, as stated in the Declaration, and the primary burden of the rest of the document diverge significantly. The pervasive concern of the Address is Christian unity, and most of its content is devoted to that goal or, more precisely, to the perniciousness of the sin of sectarian division. Its justly famous phrase found at the center of the Address states that theme emphatically:

> Prop. 1. THAT the church of Christ upon earth is essentially, intentionally, and constitutionally one; consisting of all those in every place that profess their faith in Christ and obedience to him in all things according to the scriptures, and that manifest the same by their tempers and conduct, and of none else, as none else can be truly and properly called christians.[10]

In fact, the tract has so long been seen as "one of the great milestones on the path to Christian unity in America" that ecumenism is usually assumed to be the *raison d'etre* of the Christian Association.[11] The contemporary reader is surprised to discover that the association was not founded "to work for Christian unity," but rather to function as a voluntary, parachurch, missionary society and to encourage the forming of sister associations. The Declaration expresses that purpose in Article I:

> I. That we form ourselves into a religious association under the denomination of the Christian Association, *for the sole purpose of promoting simple evangelical Christianity*, free from all mixture of human opinions and inventions of men.[12]

Item II makes clear that the methods by which the association expected to accomplish its purpose were to be (1) the funding of commissioned itinerant ministers to preach at considerable distances and (2) the distribution of Bibles to the poor.[13] Strangely, the history of the Association does not indicate any implementation of this program. Although extant records furnish references to meetings of the Association, there are no indications that this group recruited any itinerants or distributed any Bibles.[14]

Since Christian unity is the focus of the Address, historians have usually read Item IV of the Declaration as evidence of that concern:

> IV. That this Society by no means considers itself a church, nor does at all assume to itself the powers peculiar to such a society; nor do the members, as such, consider themselves as standing in that relation; nor as at all associated for the peculiar purposes of church association;—but merely as voluntary advocates of church reformation; and, as possessing the powers common to all individuals, who may please to associate in a peaceable and orderly manner, for any lawful purpose, namely, the disposal of their time, counsel, and property, as they may see cause.[15]

In fact, Item IV has to do with the society's evangelical aim and must be properly read in the light of Item III:

> III. That this society considers it a duty . . . to encourage the formation of similar associations; and shall . . . hold itself in readiness . . . to correspond with, and render all possible assistance to, such as may desire to associate for the same desirable and important purposes.[16]

Item V sets forth the standards that shall be imposed in selecting the itinerant preachers who shall be supported by the semiannual membership dues, provided for in Item II. Item VI provides for the election of a standing committee of twenty-one who shall act for the Association between meetings. Item VII establishes the semiannual meeting dates and the dates when membership subscriptions are due. Item VIII gives the order of business to be followed at the semiannual meetings. Item IX affirms the Association's reliability under God to support an itinerant, evangelical ministry at distant points.

As the *D&A* makes clear, TC and the Christian Association saw themselves as a voluntary, parachurch, evangelical society and understood their mission in the context of such associations. Anyone who is aware of AC's later vituperative attacks on evangelical societies in the *Christian Baptist* (1823–30) must be struck by the irony of these beginnings. Thus, determining where TC got the idea of the Christian Association is probably necessary to discovering the roots of his ecumenical message.

The Second British Evangelical Awakening, Christian Unity, and the Association's Model

Since W. E. Garrison examined the sources of AC's theology, historians have generally assumed that the *D&A* derived its ecumenical emphasis from John Locke and the British rationalists.[17] Recently, Richard T. Hughes has argued that the natural tensions between AC's ecumenism, derived from Locke, and his restitutionism, derived from the Puritans, explain the major transition in AC's thought, which many historians locate in the 1830s.[18] That Locke influenced both Campbells is indisputable. However, an analysis of the *D&A* and its context in TC's life does not support the generally accepted assumption that Locke is the source of his ecumenism.

I am convinced that establishing a "form and function" description of the *D&A* and observing that the tract contains historical references, emphases, and plans that are both alien to its own 1809 American milieu and inconsistent with subsequent practices of the Campbells moves us closer to the sources of TC's ecumenism. Where did TC get the model for the Christian Association and the *D&A*? We can now establish from primary sources that the models for the Christian Association and its foundation tract are to be found in the evangelical missionary and Bible societies that first arose and proliferated in the United Kingdom between 1790 and 1820. These voluntary associations sought nothing less than the conversion of the world and the total reformation of the morals of human society. They are the most permanent legacy of the British evangelical renewal at the end of the eighteenth century and its ecumenical emphasis.

The renewal, which began about 1790 and ran its course in the next decades, differed from the First Revival in no way more markedly than in its emphasis on Christian unity. As the noted Calvinist, David Bogue, said in the founding sermon for the London Missionary Society in 1795, "Behold us here assembled with one accord to attend the funeral of bigotry."[19] As Donald Mathews has observed, "The Second Great Awakening was characterized by unity, as well as organization, and demonstrated the dynamics of a movement."[20] Although Lefferts A. Loetscher[21] and Roger H. Martin[22] have analyzed the ecumenical emphasis of the Second Awakening in America, the crucial role of evangelicalism as a source of contemporary ecumenism has been largely ignored by histories of the ecumenical movement.

Just why the Second British Awakening placed so much emphasis on Christian unity cannot be answered with precision. No doubt, Rowland Hill and other "young Turks" from the first revival remembered ruefully how the unity of that movement was shattered by the Calvinist Controversy of the 1770s.[23] However, the institutionalization of the Methodists with their alleged "Arminian" and "antinomian" tendencies had removed the strongly felt danger that this latitudinarian group would spoil the pure revival of the Calvinistic Wesleyans, Anglicans, Dissenters, Presbyterians, and Independents.

Second, a radically changed external situation provided strong motivation for a new ecumenical emphasis. The First Awakening confronted a spiritually decayed and complacent church. But to the incessant itinerants of the Second, the enemy was outside the church. The survival of Christendom seemed to be at stake as Deism and rationalism shook the very foundations of the faith. The social upheaval of the Atlantic community, resulting from the American and French Revolutions, confirmed Enlightenment ideas and seemed bent on spreading skepticism everywhere.

Freedom had been a big word to earlier dissenting British Protestants, and the France of His Most Catholic Majesty had been perceived as the very harbinger of the Antichrist. But, to the later dissenters' surprise, freedom had enthroned atheism in France instead of true religion. AC later observed that the triumph of unbelieving rationalism through democratic freedom would have driven him to unbelief if St. Paul had not foretold that the Apostasy would precede Jesus' return.[24]

In pulpits rife with millennial speculation, the American and French Revolutions were regularly portrayed as "the pouring out of vials of apocalyptic wrath on the Antichrist" and, therefore, as evidence of the near return of Jesus. TC was simply reflecting the common, Protestant, millennial understanding of the time when he said in the *D&A*:

> The auspicious phenomena of the times furnish collateral arguments of a very encouraging nature, that our dutiful and pious endeavors shall not be in vain in the Lord. Is it not the day of the Lord's vengeance upon the anti-christian world; the year of recompenses for the controversy of Zion? Surely, then, the time to favor her is come; even the set time. And is it not said that Zion shall be built in troublous times? Have not greater efforts been made, and more done, for the promulgation of the gospel among the nations, since the commencement of the French revolution, than had been for many centuries prior to that event?[25]

The divines knew that the millennium was to be initiated by the action of God. Nonetheless, on the basis of Scripture, theologians and preachers of the time affirmed that the millennium would not begin until the gospel had been preached in all nations under heaven. Thus, this happy result of divine governance could be hastened by preaching the gospel throughout the world. During the Second Awakening, European and American Protestants heard the missionary call for the first time.

A third, allied characteristic of the British Second Awakening, which was also related to the era's upheaval, was the birth of the great evangelical societies themselves. Escalating millennial speculations and widespread acceptance of the essential democratic presuppositions presumed by voluntary organizations seem to be the best explanation as to why these associations came into existence at this time and not earlier.[26] First in Europe and then in the United States voluntary missionary, education, and moral societies proliferated throughout Protestantism at this time.

The ecumenical thrust that characterized these evangelical societies is well demonstrated by the story of the Missionary Society. This association, later called the London Missionary Society (LMS hereafter), was the first of the great societies and the model for the later ones. At the organizational conference in Northampton Chapel in Spa Fields on 22–24 September 1795, which included more than two hundred ministers from several denominations, most of the sermons emphasized both unity and mission. The ecumenical excitement was palpable. "Such a scene was perhaps never before beheld in our world." There was:

> a visible union of ministers and Christians of all denominations, who, for the first time, forgetting their party prejudices and partialities, assembled in the same place, sang the same hymns, united in the same prayers, and felt themselves one in Christ.[27]

The climax was reached when David Bogue, a staunch Calvinist, preached his sermon on "The Funeral of Bigotry." Although the contribution of LMS to the church's world mission in the nineteenth and twentieth centuries is well known, nonetheless one cannot avoid asking what happened to its ecumenical dream of uniting the missionary efforts of the whole church.[28]

The hope of maintaining a continuing union of all Christians in mission failed, torpedoed by party pride. From the beginning, the Baptists had refused to bring their new missionary society into the ecumenical fellowship. In the next decade, the Anglicans decided that they had to have their own and so organized the Church Missionary Society. Was TC speaking of this result when he asked, "What though the well-meant endeavors after union have not, in some instances, entirely succeeded to the wish of all parties, should this dissuade us from the attempt?"[29]

The parallels between TC's Declaration and the LMS Plan of the Society are obvious. Article I of the LMS charter names the organization as "The Missionary Society"; Article II gives its purpose; Article III indicates that membership shall be by subscription. Succeeding articles designate the time of general meetings, the officers to be elected (a secretary and a treasurer, plus directors and collectors).[30]

The particular model of a Plan of the Society, with successive articles on the name, purpose, membership, subscription rate, meetings, secretary and treasurer, directors, provisions for correspondence with similar societies, etc., may be older than LMS, but the LMS Plan seems to have become the exemplar for a host of successors. Both the LMS archetype and the stereotypical charters that followed that model were bound together with the founding sermon or address and distributed.[31]

No historian known to me seems ever to have asked why the second part of the Campbell document is called the Address, or how the two parts of the document are related to each other. As indicated above, the relationship between the two parts is less than clear to the modern reader. Yet in both the *D&A* and the Plan of the Society, the first sections give organizational plan and purpose, while the second, called the sermon or the address, sets forth the necessary underlying presuppositions of the newly formed association.

Furthermore, other elements in TC's tract are clarified by comparison. For example, the emphasis on "supplying the poor with the holy Scriptures" conforms to the usual practice of these evangelical parachurch and church-related organizations. A quick perusal of *The Evangelical Magazine and Missionary Tidings* in its first two decades also demonstrates the importance that such societies attached to correspondence between societies; each felt an obligation to foster the development of sister societies in other population centers.

During the Second Awakening, a voluntary, parachurch infrastructure was proliferating throughout Europe and then America. These societies were to change permanently the character of Protestantism. When the *D&A* is compared to the British evangelical society charters, beginning with LMS in 1795, the identification of the Christian Association as a typical evangelical society of the Second Great British Awakening is confirmed. But the crucial question remains: Where did TC get the model? Had he had any previous personal experience with such a society?

The Connecting Link

When the Christian Association was formed in 1809, TC had been in America for only two years. Evangelical associations were still rare in the United States, and most American societies as of that date were denominational in character.[32] Furthermore, there is no evidence that TC knew any of the American agencies. Certainly the Antiburghers, who completely controlled the Associate Synod of North America, were adamantly opposed to intercourse with such groups because of the fear of latitudinarianism. If TC was acquainted with the missionary society model, he must have developed that familiarity in Ireland.

Is there evidence that TC knew such associations before emigrating from Ireland in 1807? The answer is an unequivocal "yes." In 1798, within months of his ordination as the Antiburgher pastor at Ahorey in County Armagh, TC joined a group of ministers and laymen (including Anglicans, Synod of Ulster Presbyterians, Burghers, and Antiburghers) to form the ecumenical Evangelical Society of Ulster (ESU hereafter). This Ulster association, dedicated to itinerant preaching, "clearly saw itself as a part of an international pan-evangelical movement."[33] It was related to LMS, but not an auxiliary of it. On a 1987 trip to Northern Ireland, I discovered the charter, founding sermon, list of original subscribers, official account of the society's beginnings, and some of ESU's correspondence, all of which supplements considerably the heretofore limited historical accounts of this association.[34]

In the midst of the violent aftermath of the United Irish Rebellion of 1798, a group of Burgher ministers and laypersons met in Armagh for a sacramental occasion.[35] The sermon by George Hamilton, pastor of Armagh's Burgher congregation, challenged the worshipers to assume evangelical responsibility, and the group decided to convene an organizational meeting during October.[36] In response, four other Burgher ministers joined Hamilton in inviting ministers and laypersons to an October meeting to assist "in forming a Society for the purpose of having the Gospel preached in those Towns and Villages which are destitute of it." Their letter reminded readers of successful revivals then in process "in America,—in England,—in Scotland,—and other parts of Europe." Although the letter noted that the group planned to form an evangelical society like those formed elsewhere, it makes no reference to other Irish societies. In spite of heavy rain, a large crowd—including thirteen ministers from four denominations—met in Armagh on Wednesday, 10 October 1798, to form ESU. In the ecumenical worship, TC prayed and Hamilton preached on "The Necessity of Itinerant Preaching." Afterward, the assembly voted unanimously to organize an evangelical society for the preaching of the Gospel and adopted "the sketch of a Plan" that George Hamilton had prepared. The majority of the elected officers were laymen, as required, but five ministers were also elected: George Hamilton (Burgher), George Maunsell (Anglican), William Henry (Burgher), Reed (Synod of Ulster), and Thomas Campbell (Antiburgher).

The Plan of ESU is obviously TC's literary connection to the LMS model. All three documents have the same patterns of form and substance. The first article states the name and the second the purpose, that is, "to make the Gospel known . . . by introducing the Preaching of the Word, setting up prayer meetings, distributing bibles and Evangelical tracts among the poor." The governing committee was to have a lay majority; ESU and the Christian Association also had the same officers. Meeting times were specified and provision was made for commissioning evangelical itinerants. Article Eighth provided for subscriptions and Article Ninth indicated ESU's intention to support and to correspond with "The Missionary Societies, formed in Great-Britain,[37] and elsewhere." The tenth authorized the employment of itinerants as soon as funds were available.[38] Furthermore, ESU's foundation sermon bears the same relationship to the Plan as the Address bears to the Declaration, that is, both were sermons that provided the necessary rationale for the ministry that the agency intended to undertake.[39] In each case the constitution was distributed with the sermon or address.

TC's Bitter Experience with the Model

Just why TC became so deeply involved with ESU cannot be established with certainty. He must have known the absolute stance against participation in evangelical societies taken recently by the General Synod of the Antiburgher church. Liberal laypersons at Ahorey may have encouraged him, but surely he knew that its radical origins made that congregation suspect. His action inevitably confirmed the doubts of those Antiburghers who were suspicious of his Glasgow education.

TC, however, also knew the price of sectarianism. His grandfather had lived and died a Roman Catholic in spite of the high costs of that profession in Ireland. His father had converted to Anglicanism as a young adult, but adamantly opposed TC's conversion to narrow Antiburgher Seceder Presbyterianism in late adolescence. His continued opposition delayed TC's preparation for the Antiburgher ministry by more than a year.

Furthermore, TC was rearing his growing family in a cauldron of socioeconomic and sectarian violence. A paranoid, determined Anglican ascendancy and an effectively organized but disenfranchised Presbyterian subculture, both committed to suppressing the overwhelming Catholic population, guaranteed that all issues would take on sectarian overtones. A nonsectarian brawl in a local pub might lead to guerrilla warfare, then to pitched battles, and finally to institutionalized sectarian enemies. In fact, it had come to this in TC's neighborhood when a Saturday afternoon fight led to months of guerrilla fighting in northeastern County Armagh, then to the pitched Battle of the Diamond on 21 September 1795, and finally to the permanent organization of the Orange Order and the Defenders.

Whatever his motives for joining ESU and accepting a leadership position in his first months at Ahorey, TC plunged into ESU's work with enthusiasm and found a satisfaction in that effort that lasted a lifetime.

In early 1799 Hamilton reported that much work had already been done. A substantial group of subscribers (115) had joined ESU, a regular supply of religious tracts had been procured for distribution among the poor, and LMS had promised them two itinerant preachers for the summer of 1799. Nonetheless, a dark shadow was already hanging over the project. "We are indeed sorry to state," Hamilton writes, "that a large number of those, who should be forward to every good work, still appear to stand at a distance, jealous of our association, and indulging many strange and ungrounded fears concerning it."[40]

Hamilton's reminder to the opponents that ESU had "disclaimed all intention of interfering directly, or indirectly, with the internal arrangements, or distinguishing peculiarities of any Christian denomination"[41] sounds remarkably like TC's repeated assurances in the *D&A* that the Christian Association was not a church, claimed none of the prerogatives of a church, and had no intentions of interfering with the denominational associations of its members.

The crisis came quickly and furiously. The Burgher synod met in Armagh on 2-4 July 1799,[42] a month after Cooper and Richards began their mission in central Ulster. From the opening, the argument raged fiercely as the opponents sought to excommunicate George Hamilton and William Henry for acting contrary to Presbyterian practice. Nonetheless, the ESU advocates had the skill, the zeal, and, above all, the numbers to defend themselves and the society. It took four years for the Burghers to force the ESU ministers either out of the denomination or into conformity.[43]

When the more unbending Antiburghers met in Belfast on 30 July 1799, the situation was markedly different. TC was the only Antiburgher minister in ESU's membership. On the evening of 31 July, the synod took up two overtures:

> Question 1. Is the Evangelical Society of Ulster constituted on Principles consistent with the Secession Testimony?
> Question 2. What shall be done with respect unto a Member of this court who took an Active part in forming that Society & promoting its Interests?[44]

The synod spent much time on the first question. The Clerk read aloud *The Address & Constitution of the Evangelical Society of Ulster* and other relevant papers. TC read long passages from the Address and explicated the other documents at great length. Then each synod member was asked his opinion about whether ESU was consistent with Secession principles. The group consensus showed:

> a Charitable Opinion of the Piety & Zeal [of ESU], but a conviction that its principles were completely latitudinarian and would tend to destroy the truth & power of the Gospel and to undermine the very Kingdom whose enlargement it sought.[45]

The synod then answered "No" to the first overture on a roll-call vote.

A committee, including William Drysdale, the representative of the General Associate Synod[46] in Scotland, was then appointed to confer with TC on his connection with ESU. (Church minutes always sound so orderly and rational!) The committee's report, presented on 1 August 1799, implies that the pressure applied had not produced a complete meeting of minds:

> Synod Called for the report of the Committee appointed to converse with Mr. Cample when Revd Henry Hunter Read the following Paper Drawn up & Subscribed by sd. Mr. Campble viz—
>
> I am willing to receive the Advice of the Synod respecting my Connexion with the Evangelical Society of Ulster to take it under my most Serious Consideration & to endeavour in all things to see Eye to Eye with the Revd Synod & in the meantime to desist from any official Intercourse with sd. Society only remaining a simple subscriber.
> Mr.Camble
>
> After some Conversation the foregoing Declaration was accepted as Satisfactory on the Occasion.[47]

The year 1800 was also one of near apocalyptic excitement in the ministry of ESU. William Gregory, one of the first LMS missionaries to the South Seas, excited great crowds with his vivid stories of mission work among the heathen, his militant anticatholicism, and his strong conversionist preaching.[48] Although the Church of Ireland (Anglican) parishes and the Synod of Ulster (Presbyterian) churches may have been more receptive, opposition among the Seceders hardened. And, by the 1800 synod, TC had conformed:

> On the motion of a member the minute of last Synod, concerning Mr Campbell's connexion with the Evangelical Society of Ulster was read. Mr Campbell gave full satisfaction as to his seeing eye to eye with the Synod in this matter, having even declared, that he had not paid the last year's subscription to that society.[49]

The Flame Does Not Die

Why had he changed? Was it the obvious pressure of Synod? TC felt strongly the essential bonds of denominational fellowship, and he indicated at other times in his life the lengths to which he was willing to go to avoid rupture. Did something happen in the ministry of ESU that caused him to doubt its ecclesiastical orthodoxy? We no longer possess the evidence to judge which alternative is correct, but we do know that his first euphoric experience in Christian unity kindled a flame in TC that the cold floods of sectarianism in Ireland and America could not quench.

TC remained in Ireland seven more years before health problems forced his emigration. They were years when the poverty of the countryside and the penuriousness of parishioners forced him to turn to farming and then to teaching to support his growing family. They were also years of important, unsuccessful work for ecumenism in Ireland, as well as years of constructive, but very frustrating, leadership in the Antiburgher Church at a time when acrimony grew exponentially. The newly discovered materials demonstrate clearly TC's constructive efforts to bring about change among the Seceders and the personal price exacted.

In 1803, in response to a Burgher initiative, the Antiburghers appointed TC, along with David Arrot of Markethill and William Laing of Newry, to an interdenominational committee to propose terms of reunion in Ireland.[50] Through four years of intricate negotiations, the joint committees sought a basis for coalescence of the two denominations. Again and again they were rebuffed by the timidity of the Irish Antiburghers and the vituperation of the General Synod in Scotland. But TC continued doggedly to pursue the ecumenical dream.

TC's frustrating search for a basis for uniting the Burghers and Antiburghers occurred in the midst of a twenty-year effort to update the Secession Testimony, adapting it to Ireland and seeking to make coalescence possible.[51] It was his own brethren, and not the distrusted Burghers, who repeatedly rejected the basis for merger that he had negotiated. Even more to the point, he was elected moderator in 1805, only after being defeated in 1802, 1803, and 1804, the only moderator in the thirty-year history of the Irish Antiburgher synod not to be elected moderator on the second attempt. He was also the only moderator to have the content of his synod sermon challenged officially. Perhaps Jesus promised, "Happy are the peacemakers for they shall be called the children of God," because he knew that the church would usually use other epithets for such persons.

It is difficult to know what TC expected to find in the churches of America, but what he actually found was a sectarianism more intransigent than any in Ireland. The process of his removal from the Associate Synod of North America began following a sacramental occasion at Cannamaugh, Pennsylvania, when he invited Presbyterians of all parties to share in the Table of the Lord. Even "occasional communion" with other Christians who had not affiliated formally with a Seceder congregation was forbidden by the Associate Synod of North America,[52] although permitted by the Antiburghers in both Scotland and Ireland.

Conclusion

In America TC found a response much like the one he had known in Ulster a decade earlier. Naturally, when he and his colleagues sought a model for "the purpose of having the Gospel preached in those Towns and Villages which are destitute of it," he turned to the model in his own experience, the Evangelical Society of Ulster.

Notes

1. I am grateful to the editors of *Encounter* for permission to update, expand, and revise my essay entitled "An Irish Precursor for Thomas Campbell's *Declaration and Address*," *Encounter* 50 (Summer 1989): 247-67.

2. My own research supports the conclusion of Anthony L. Dunnavant *Restructure: Four Historical Ideals in the Campbell-Stone Movement and the Development of the Polity of the Christian Church (Disciples of Christ)*, American University Studies, no. 85 (New York: Peter Lang, 1993), 9-36, that the Stone-Campbell movement rested at its beginnings on four basic ideals, i.e., unity, restoration, liberty, and mission. Although each of these ideals is reflected, at least in a nascent form, in each of the foundation documents of the Restoration Movement, I have chosen to focus the essay on Christian unity because that is the most surprising emphasis in TC's *D&A*, given what we know initially of its historical context.

3. Paul K. Conkin (*America Originals, Homemade Varieties of Christianity* [Chapel Hill: University of North Carolina Press, 1997], 7) is only the most recent scholar to observe that all the early reform movements which later coalesced to become the "Restoration Christianity" emphasized Christian unity.

4. Thomas Campbell, *Declaration and Address of the Christian Association of Washington* (Washington, Pa.: Brown & Sample, 1809). No first edition copy of *The Last Will and Testament of the Springfield Presbytery* (1804) is known to exist.

5. Donald H. Yoder ("Christian Unity in Nineteenth-Century America," in *A History of the Ecumenical Movement, 1517–1948*, ed. R. Rouse and S. C. Neill [London: SPCK, 1954], 237-39) comments at length on the unique contribution of TC's *D&A* to the American ecumenical movement.

6. The choice of synonyms for TC's view of "Christian union" in 1809 is fraught with difficulties. Some historians have used "non-denominational" to describe the efforts he was involved in. Neither TC nor his colleagues would have found that term acceptable, with its implied rejection of the denominations with which they were affiliated. Instead, they affirmed the value of their denominations and had great difficulty understanding why their denominations took such umbrage at their joint ministries beyond the usual denominational lines, especially

since these activities conformed to the truth affirmed by their denominations. "Interdenominational" also will not do, since it implies intentional cooperation between the structures of denominations, and at no time was interdenominational or even intercongregational activity assumed. Although "ecumenical" is also a loaded word, I have chosen to use it because, in its classical sense, it seems to best express what they seemed to believe about Christian unity, that is: (1) that there were Christians in every Protestant sect; (2) that the primary goal of the Church should be to win the entire world to Jesus Christ; (3) that sectarian "janglings" and bigotry were the chief impediments to the unity of the Church for which Jesus prayed and which would be necessary if the Church's mission were to be accomplished.

7. Lester G. McAllister, *Thomas Campbell: Man of the Book* (St. Louis: Bethany Press, 1954), is the best study of TC's career and significance (see 21-59 on TC in Scotland and Ireland). William Herbert Hanna, *Thomas Campbell: Seceder and Christian Union Advocate* (Cincinnati: Standard Publishing, 1935), treats TC's break with the American Seceders in detail. *Memoirs of Elder Thomas Campbell*, ed. Alexander Campbell (Cincinnati: H. S. Bosworth, 1861), provides few details regarding his Irish years, some of which do not seem to be chronologically accurate; AC makes no mention of the Evangelical Society of Ulster. See also Robert Richardson, *Memoirs of Alexander Campbell*, vol. 1 (Philadelphia: J. P. Lippincott & Co., 1868), chaps. 1-5.

8. Yoder, "Christian Unity," 237-39.

9. My earlier essays ("A Dream Still Lives," *Disciple* 12 [January 1985]: 12-14; and "The Disciple Birthday—A Disciple Passover," *Discipliana* 44 [Winter 1984]: 51-54) came close to claiming that the document was peculiarly American. See also TC, *Declaration and Address: 175th Anniversary Abridged Edition*, ed. Hiram J. Lester (Wellsburg, W.Va.: Privately printed, 1984). Only McAllister (*Thomas Campbell*, 100) and David M. Thompson have ever suggested that the Christian Association of Washington might have an Irish precursor. I received Thompson's essay ("The Irish Background to Thomas Campbell's Declaration and Address," *Discipliana* 46 [Summer 1986]: 23-27) after I had finished the first draft of this essay. Although Thompson did not have the ESU primary sources which I discovered in 1985, the conclusions that he surmised without that evidence are basically correct and supportive of the argument in this essay.

10. *D&A*, 16.9-14.

11. Most treatments of the Declaration begin with the assumption that the Christian Association of Washington was founded as a restorationist group to promote Christian unity and analyze the text with restorationism or Christian unity as the established goal. See, for example, Winfred Ernest Garrison and Alfred T. DeGroot, *The Disciples of Christ: A History* (St. Louis: Christian Board of Publication, 1948), 145-48; McAllister, *Thomas Campbell*, 105-10.

12. Italics added. This *raison d'etre* is reaffirmed in Items V and X.

13. The Declaration affirms the intention of each member of the Association to "subscribe a certain specified sum, to be paid half yearly, for the purpose of raising a fund to support a pure Gospel ministry. . . . And, also, for supplying the poor with the Holy Scriptures" (*D&A*, 4.15-20).

14. Given the paucity of Association records, the lack of extant lists of subscribers does not prove that the intended system of semi-annual subscriptions, collection agents, and accounting was never instituted. More serious, however, is the lack of any tradition which identifies any itinerant ministers in the society other than TC and AC. The absence of such a tradition is noteworthy because itinerant preaching was rapidly becoming the norm in the trans-Allegheny region where the Campbells were located.

15. *D&A*, 4.27-35.

16. *D&A*, 4.21-26.

17. McAllister (*Thomas Campbell*, 125-32) argues that John Locke provides the philosophical background for the *D&A*. See also W. E. Garrison, *Alexander Campbell's Theology: Its Sources and Historical Setting* (St. Louis: Christian Publishing, 1900), 23-114, and *Religion Follows the Frontier—A History of the Disciples of Christ* (New York: Harper & Brothers, 1931); William E. Tucker and Lester G. McAllister, *Journey in Faith: A History of the Christian Church (Disciples of Christ)* (St. Louis: Bethany Press, 1975), 92-102.

18. Richard T. Hughes, "The Role of Theology in the Nineteenth-Century Division of Disciples of Christ," in *American Religion: 1974 Proceedings*, ed. Edwin S. Gaustad (Tallahassee, Fla.: American Academy of Religion, 1974), 70-71 n. 23; and "From Primitive Church to Civil Religion: The Millennial Odyssey of Alexander Campbell," *Journal of the American Academy of Religion* 44 (March 1976), 92. See also Richard T. Hughes and C. Leonard Allen, *Illusions of Innocence: Protestant Primitivism in America, 1630–1875* (Chicago: University of Chicago Press, 1988), 177-78.

19. Richard Lovett, *The History of the London Missionary Society, 1795–1895* (London: H. Frowde, 1899), 35.

20. Donald G. Mathews, "The Second Great Awakening as an Organizing Process, 1780-1830," *American Quarterly* 21 (Spring 1969): 27.

21. Lefferts A. Loetscher, "The Problem of Christian Unity in Early Nineteenth-Century America," *Church History* 32 (March 1963): 3-16.

22. Roger H. Martin, *Evangelicals United: Ecumenical Stirrings in Pre-Victorian Britain, 1795-1830*, Studies in Evangelicalism, no. 4 (Metuchen, N.J.: Scarecrow Press, 1983), passim.

23. Martin, *Evangelicals United*, 2-3. In the earlier revival, the sense of denominational identity sat lightly on Whitefield and those of his Calvinistic milieu. In fact, Whitefield's unwillingness to ally himself with "the true Biblical Church" in Scotland was the express reason why the Erskines and the Seceders rejected Whitefield and vehemently attacked the Cambuslang revival. But the Wesleyans, especially the militant non-Calvinists among them, were a different problem. Not only did John Wesley insist on loyalty to the Anglican Church but

also increasingly he and his brother took strong stands for free will and against particular salvation.

24. Alexander Campbell and Robert Owen, *A Debate on the Evidences of Christianity; Containing an Examination of the "Social System," And of All the Systems of Scepticism of Ancient and Modern Times; Between Robert Owen, of New Lanark, Scotland, and Alexander Campbell, of Bethany, Virginia, with an Appendix Written by the Parties* (Bethany, Va.: A. Campbell, 1829).

25. *D&A*, 8.17-28.

26. After the American and French Revolutions, things were dramatically different. Ford Brown (*Father of the Victorians: The Age of Wilberforce* [Cambridge: Cambridge University Press, 1961], 333-41) indicates that only five voluntary societies for public good were established in the United Kingdom between 1750 and 1790. In contrast, Brown lists seven pages of such societies established between 1790 and 1830 (omitting generally the auxiliary branches of national societies and the associations formed by Dissenters, Quakers, and other non-Anglicans). See also Martin, *Evangelicals United*, 24-26; Charles Silvester Horne, *The Story of the L.M.S.: With an Appendix Bringing the Story Up to the Year 1904*, new ed. (London: London Missionary Society, 1908), chap. 1; *The Evangelical Magazine* 3 (January 1795); Lovett, *History*, 16.

27. *The Evangelical Magazine* quoted in Horne, *Story*, 12.

28. In 1796 Dr. Waugh, the influential London Presbyterian minister and officer of the society, explained the society's decision on a potentially divisive issue (*The Evangelical Magazine* quoted in Horne, *Story*, 16):

> As the union of Christians in various denominations, in carrying on this great work, is a most desirable object: so to prevent, if possible, any cause for future dissension, it is declared to be a fundamental principle of the Missionary Society, that its design is not to send Presbyterianism, Independency, Episcopacy, or any form of Church order and government (about which there may be difference of opinion among serious persons), but the glorious Gospel of the blessed God, to the heathen; and that it shall be left (as it ought to be left) to the minds of the persons whom God may call into the fellowship of his Son from among them to assume for themselves such form of Church government as to them shall appear most agreeable to the word of God.

As Thompson has noted ("Irish Background," 24), it may have been this action that led the General Associate Synod (Antiburgher) in 1796 to condemn the constitution of missionary societies with LMS in mind.

29. It is notable that AC's 1823 condemnation of American evangelical societies (after, of course, he and the Brush Run church had become the second largest supporter of the Baptist Missionary Society among the churches of the Redstone Baptist Association) was not made on a New Testament basis, but on the basis that such societies were calculated to strengthen the sect that created the

society.

30. Lovett, *History*, 30.

31. See, for example, *The Evangelical Magazine* 8 (1800): 256; or 10 (1802): 471. The same model still governed evangelical practice as late as 1850 when the American Bible Union was formed, although the address had become an artifice by that time.

32. Sydney E. Ahlstrom, *A Religious History of the American People* (New Haven: Yale University Press, 1972), 422-28.

33. David Hempton and Myrtle Hill, *Evangelical Protestantism in Ulster Society, 1740–1890* (London: Routledge, 1992), 39.

34. In addition to David Thompson, Lester McAllister, and Robert Richardson, already cited, see also Alan R. Acheson, "The Evangelicals in the Church of Ireland, 1784–1859" (Ph.D. diss., Queen's University, Belfast, 1967); Peter Brooke, "Controversies in Ulster Presbyterianism, 1790–1836" (Ph.D. diss., Queen's University, Belfast, 1980); David Stewart, *The Seceders in Ireland with Annals of Their Congregations* (Belfast: Presbyterian Historical Society, 1950); Joseph Thompson, "The Inter-relationship of the Secession Synod and the Synod of Ulster" (Ph.D. diss., Queen's University, Belfast, 1980); Thomas Whitherow, *Historical and Literary Memorials of Presbyterianism in Ireland (1731–1800)* (London: W. Mullan and Son, 1879–80), 310-12; and James Seaton Reid, *History of the Presbyterian Church in Ireland* (Belfast: William Mullan, 1867), 3:415-17. I am indebted to Professor Joseph Thompson for helping me to locate ESU materials in the library of the Presbyterian Historical Society in Belfast.

35. Marilyn Jeanne Westerkamp, "Triumph of the Laity: The Migration of Revivalism from Scotland and Ireland to the Middle Colonies, 1625–1760" (Ph.D. diss., University of Pennsylvania, 1984), passim.

36. George Hamilton, *The Great Necessity of Itinerant Preaching. A Sermon Deliver'd in the new Meeting-house in Armagh, at the formation of the Evangelical Society of Ulster, on Wednesday, 10th of Oct. 1798. With a short Introductory Memorial, respecting the Establishment and first Attempt of that Society* (Armagh: n.p., [1799?]), v-vi.

37. Hamilton, *Great Necessity*, vii-viii.

38. Hamilton, *Great Necessity*, x.

39. An initial reading has turned up only one sentence that is found in both documents, "Are we not told, that in troubleous times Zion shall be built up?" However, the concluding appeals of both documents are very similar, and both share many of the same emphases, for example, the unity of all Christians, an eschatological excitement about the new movements in the contemporary church, a conviction of the basic inadequacy and evil of attempting to do the work of the gospel for the sake of a particular party, a belief that the tumultuous times (no reference is made to the Irish situation) are an indication of the early return of Jesus, among others.

40. Hamilton, *Great Necessity*, xi.

41. Hamilton, *Great Necessity*, xii.

42. *Minute Book of the Associate Synod of Ireland* [Burgher] XXI (1799), 116-25. The 1799 meeting was the twenty-first convocation of the independent Irish Burgher synod. Because of the availability of the Minute Books of the two synods, the material which follows has received fuller treatment by Brooke, Scott, Stewart, David Thompson, Joseph Thompson, and others. The lack of personal narratives and other historical details, such as the new materials provide, have made it difficult to place the disputes in a full context of meaning.

43. I have not been able to find the evidence that justifies Peter Brooke's assertion ("Controversies," 47) that the Burghers originally approved of ESU, but in 1800 passed a resolution against certain of its key practices. Brooke's claim seems to be the basis of Thompson's statement ("Irish Background," 25) that Burgher suspicion of ESU intensified in the second year. What did take place was a vociferous attack that lasted until the ESU advocates either left or conformed.

44. *Minute Book of the Associate Synod of Ireland* [Antiburgher] (31 July 1799), 116. The different spellings of the name Campbell found on the following pages of this essay are those found at the cited points in the original manuscript.

45. *Minute Book* [Antiburgher] (1799), 117-18.

46. The Associate General Synod had just deposed the Reverend George Cowie of Huntly because he favored itinerant preaching. Thompson, "Irish Background," 24.

47. Thompson, "Irish Background," 119-20.

48. Hempton and Hill, *Evangelical*, 40. William Gregory, "Extracts of a Tour through the North of Ireland . . . in the Summer of 1800," typescript in the Linen Hall Library in Belfast.

49. *Minute Book of the Associate Synod of Ireland* [Antiburgher] (1800), 131-32.

50. *Minute Book* [Antiburgher] (1803), 162. There does not appear to be any evidence to support Thompson's claim ("Irish Background," 25) that renewed interest in coalescence was probably "a result of the cooperation in evangelical enterprise."

51. Stewart, *Seceders*, 99.

52. Thompson's observation ("Irish Background," 26) is on target: "What we see here is a clash between a conservative Seceder position in the U.S.A. which was already on the defensive in Ireland, and a representative of the new evangelical mood spreading throughout the British Isles."

Scottish Rhetoric and the *Declaration and Address*

Carisse Mickey Berryhill

That the *Declaration and Address* should be approached from a variety of perspectives is the fundamental assumption of the conversation of this volume. It is a product not only of Thomas Campbell's university education in Glasgow, but of his life: his early life, his theological and homiletic education, his experiences in Irish ministry and politics, and his American situation. This essay attempts to take into account what I know about Scottish thought, and about Scottish rhetoric in particular, in order to cast light on those features of the document which are due to this intellectual substrate in TC's life.[1]

When TC enrolled at Glasgow University in 1783, the great intellectual project of the late eighteenth century was fully underway: using powerful new technologies of knowledge to understand human behavior. What the scientific method had already been able to accomplish in the physical sciences promised that inductive methods would make it possible to understand human knowledge and human behavior better. Economics, sociology, and psychology were born as disciplines during this era. Excitement was intense. Real progress in human society seemed possible.[2]

At the same time, Scotland was the center of a great apologetic project to defend intelligent Christian faith from the challenges of skepticism. Could a reasonable person believe the miracle stories of the Bible? What assumptions about the nature of reality were warranted? Could the processes by which people gather, organize, and communicate knowledge support Christian faith? What constitutes satisfactory proof? What is the relationship between Revelation and Reason?

Neither of these two projects was being carried on without regard to the other. In many cases, the same men worked in both, since both are epistemological projects. George Campbell of Aberdeen, for example, wrote both *A Dissertation on Miracles* (a closely reasoned apologetic work) and *The Philosophy of Rhetoric* (the foundation document of modern communication psychology) as well as *Lectures on Pulpit Eloquence* (which applied those psychological principles to homiletic situations). Thomas Reid, the great philosopher, was also expert in botanical research. John Young, TC's Greek professor, was proficient in geology. But it was not simply a matter of multiple interests. The Scottish professors intended to "relate the principles of inductive reasoning and the Christian faith," as McAllister puts it.[3] Their task was to recontextualize Christian faith in a world forever changed by the philosophical shifts of the Enlightenment.

John Locke's *Essay Concerning Human Understanding* was almost one hundred years old when TC went to Glasgow. Locke's analysis of how human beings think had set the agenda for research and discussion for the century. When Locke destroyed the doctrine of innate ideas, he raised the corresponding problem of how the ideas we are aware of are related to reality. The resulting philosophical problem—"How can I test whether my senses are accurate?" or "Is anybody—or anything—out there?"—was answered theologically by Berkeley and skeptically by Hume. Neither answer satisfied the Scots. To accept Berkeley disabled science, which held so much promise for the advancement of learning; but to accept Hume disabled religion and morality, by dismissing both causation and the reality of the spiritual realm. The Scottish philosophers intended to have both, in a philosophically unified and reasonable world.[4]

At the time TC enrolled at Glasgow, the philosopher Thomas Reid was living there. His landmark work *Intellectual Powers* was published in 1785, during TC's Glasgow years. Reid's friend and student George Jardine taught Reid's views to TC as well as to three generations of Scottish leaders. Until 1763, Reid had lived in Aberdeen, Scotland, where he and George Campbell had formed a philosophical discussion group nicknamed the Wise Club. Along with George Skene, John Gregory, James Beattie, Alexander Gerard, and others, they prepared and discussed papers that criticized Hume and proposed new understandings of both religious and academic subjects.[5] Occasionally they corresponded with Hume over their differences, all the while preserving a gentlemanly eighteenth-century decorum.

Reid's solutions to the epistemological problems posed by Hume's interpretation of Locke were persuasive to the devout and pragmatic Scots. Reid's main concern was to develop a philosophically defensible and psychologically accurate model for how the human mind acquires and processes knowledge. He asserted that the human mind accepts its sensory impressions as effects of a cause. That is, we know reality exists because its signs are present to our minds as our sensations.[6] Even unwelcome sensations are admitted.[7]

The psychological capacity to accept sensations as signs of objective reality Reid called "Common Sense," with the meaning of *sensus communis*, a sense (or mental capacity) common to everyone. The term was not a synonym for "horse sense," or "school of hard knocks." It was a more technical and Latinate term, which has subsequently had an unfortunate trajectory in hermeneutic debates. What Reid mainly meant by it was that human beings universally believe their eyes, ears, noses, and skin unless they have good reason not to.

Although Reid followed Locke in rejecting innate ideas, he described cognitive and affective psychological processes, calling them "natural powers" or "faculties." People come equipped with hardwired ways to process the impressions they receive, we might say. His attempts to describe the structure of the mind could be compared to trying to reason out the motherboard design. Like a computer, the mind has an information-processing structure.

Reid's method of thinking these issues through attempted to be modern, that is to say, scientific. Observations could include the philosopher's knowledge of his own reasoning processes, as well as accounts by others. Strong emphasis was placed on the term "natural," because what was wanted was to recover an understanding of the basic processes common to all human beings. Rather than predicting what ought to happen from philosophical premises, Reid attempted to be a good Baconian philosopher by proceeding from actual observations of mental and linguistic behaviors. He built what we should call a general psychological model, though in those days his discipline was called Moral Philosophy.[8] In Reid's model, the mental powers, or faculties, function in a hierarchical sequence, each faculty specialized to receive and process input from a more fundamental one.

While Reid was able to formulate an epistemological foundation for philosophical realism, it fell to his Aberdeen Philosophical Society friends George Campbell and James Beattie to wield his arguments successfully in apologetics. Beattie was immensely popular as a defender of Christianity and a literary figure, but his abilities lay in popularization rather than in originality. George Campbell (1719–96), on the other hand, was able to make brilliant original applications of Reid's philosophical principles in apologetics, communication theory, literary criticism, and homiletics.

George Campbell, who spent his career associated with Marischal College in Aberdeen, published his *Dissertation on Miracles* in 1762, a work which was immediately hailed as the definitive answer to Hume's skeptical *Essay on Miracles*. The definitive point in Campbell's *Dissertation* was his doctrine of testimony, by which he countered Hume's arguments that miracles are incredible because they are contrary to human experience. Experience, Campbell pointed out, is a generalization based on a person's experiences. Experiences come to us directly through our senses, or indirectly through the testimony of others. Testimony is a report of someone's experiences (but not of their experience). The mind's native power to believe, which is analogous to its acceptance of sensory information, accepts the report as reliable unless good cause is presented to doubt it. This would mean that testimony would have a stronger effect on the mind than generalizations: "Testimony is more adequate evidence than any conclusions from experience."[9] The generalizations we call "experience" may have to be modified in the face of testimony.[10]

George Campbell is more admired today in academic circles for his *Philosophy of Rhetoric* (1776) than for his apologetic works. This is partly because of the preferences of modern secularism and partly because of the genuinely important nature of his understandings about human communication expressed in the *Philosophy of Rhetoric*, which can rightly be considered the first great modern rhetoric. In this work he described a message as composed of two parts, sense and expression, cooperating to achieve one of four ends: "to enlighten the understanding, to please the imagination, to move the passions, or to influence the will."[11]

Sense (that is, what the speaker has to say) is related to expression as a soul is to a body. This incarnational metaphor was very satisfying because it had the appeal of being "natural." It tied together the two great Scottish domains of scientific investigation and spiritual devotion. How satisfactory, to take as the model of human discourse the human being, an embodied soul!

Now thought embodied as expression moves purposefully toward one of the four ends just mentioned. These four ends of speaking are hierarchically arranged, according to the natural relationship of the mental faculties addressed by various kinds of discourse. What Reid called the "active powers" of attention and memory function globally, alongside the four main units, that is, the understanding, the imagination, the emotions, and the will. What the understanding comprehends is passed on to the imagination, which pictures it. The response of the emotions to the visualized situation is what motivates the will. As George Campbell wrote:

> . . . each preceding species, in the order above exhibited, is preparatory to the subsequent; [and] each subsequent species is founded on the preceding; and . . . thus they ascend in a regular progression. Knowledge, the object of the intellect, furnisheth materials for the fancy; the fancy culls, compounds, and by her mimic art, disposes these materials so as to affect the passions; the passions are the natural spurs to volition or action, and so need only to be right directed.[12]

Knowing the structure of the human mind, in other words, makes a scientific rhetoric possible. Different kinds of discourse can be adapted in their sense and expression to their ends. George Campbell explicitly applied these concepts in his *Lectures on Pulpit Eloquence* to his homiletics students. Lectures 5 through 12 discuss different types of sermons based on their ends.[13]

The faculty at Glasgow were deeply absorbed in the scientific and apologetic projects of the day when TC was there. No person was a better conduit of the Scottish admiration for Bacon and the ideas of Reid than George Jardine, the professor of Logic and *Belles Lettres*, who taught TC in 1763 and Alexander Campbell in 1808–09. Jardine taught the "first philosophy class" for fifty years, completely renovating it from a course in Aristotelian and Scholastic logic to a modern introduction to epistemology, cognitive psychology, and aesthetics. He not only remodeled the content of the course, but required daily oral examinations and written papers from his students. Indefatigable as an instructor, Jardine published his rationale, methods, and outline for the course in his *Outlines of Philosophical Education*.[14]

The course opened with a history and critique of the way logic had been studied and taught through the ages, and then launched into a description of Reid's analysis of the human mind. Jardine had studied under Reid, and he and Reid for many years had enjoyed "habits of most familiar friendship."[15] In Jardine's opinion, Reid surpassed Locke, Hutcheson, Hume, and Smith as an "intelligent" and "faithful" scholar of

Bacon in applying Bacon's inductive methods to the study of the human mind. Jardine admitted that his agreement and long familiarity with Reid had made it "extremely difficult to distinguish thoughts and sentiments suggested by that excellent person from those which may have been derived from other sources."[16] The most important feature of Jardine's course was its emphasis on inductive logic. The syllogistic reasoning, studied only briefly for historical purposes in the course, yielded to the inductively derived descriptions of how human beings acquire, appreciate, and communicate knowledge. There was so much new to learn, and so much confidence that people now had the tools to do it. Syllogistic procedures are excellent for testing the consistency of statements with received principles; but in this new era, no syllogism was adequate for the advancement of both society and learning.[17] What was required was the Baconian method, united with Reid's philosophical respect for human nature as the creation of God and revelation as the testimony of God.

The textbook for the class when AC took it in 1808–09 was the *Synopsis of Lectures on Logic and Belle Lettres: Read in the University of Glasgow*. AC's copy in the Campbell Collection at Bethany College is bound with the *Quaedam ex Logicae Compendiis Selecta*, a collection of Latin readings on logic compiled by Jardine for his students. The class card for the course, bearing George Jardine's signature, "Geo. Jardine L. P.," is also in the Campbell Collection at Bethany. AC's copies of the essays he wrote for Jardine's class are in Manuscript B, held by the Disciples of Christ Historical Society.[18] His notes on Jardine's lectures are in the Campbell Collection at Bethany in Manuscript L, titled "Lectures in Logick Delivered by Professor Jardan in the University of Glasgow, 1808."[19] Five years before his own death, AC commented that Jardine's discussion of the faculty of attention was "the most useful series of college lectures, of which I have any recollection."[20]

No documents from TC's enrollment are known to be extant, but it is clear from the *Outlines of Philosophical Education* that the course in 1763 was very similar to what Jardine taught in 1808. Jardine taught a second course, referred to in his *Synopsis* as comprising lectures "On the Powers of Communication" and "The Art of Improving them—or the Art of Rhetoric." He comments: "These heads form the subjects of the Lectures of a Separate Course.—[See *Synopsis of Rhetoric*.]"[21] The latter work is unknown, as is whether TC may have taken the course it summarized.

Glasgow must have been an exciting place to be between 1750 and 1800. The influence of Reid and his circle dominated the intellectual landscape. People must have felt that real progress was being made there, both intellectually and spiritually, while in their view the Continent and England sagged in skeptical despair and immorality. From Glasgow people could go forth and build a better world.

Certainly the optimism of better-world-building was on TC's mind in 1809 when he composed the *D&A*. More than once he exclaims on the unique opportunity for reform that the American situation, "this highly favored country," provides.[22] Both optimistic and pragmatic, the document offered its readers both the goal (Christian unity) and the means (associations) to promote the work of unity. There are obviously many important influences that participated in TC's personhood as uttered in this document. In order to carry out my part, I want to recapitulate certain distinctive ideas that can serve as indicators of Scottish intellectual and rhetorical influence. Then we will turn to a closer examination of the rhetorical characteristics of the document itself.

First, there is a typical Scottish way of knowing that is rooted in Baconian induction, which looks to data accepted from the senses. We might also be alert for any use of Reidian "sign language": of the function of sensations as signs of reality, of effects as signs of causes, and of words as signs of thought. Appeals to faculty psychology, or the specialization of the powers of the mind to particular functions, especially in a hierarchical sequence, are also good indicators. The role of reason is also distinctive in Scottish rhetoric. Reason examines whether testimony is sufficiently attested, but it cannot reject the content of sufficiently attested testimony as incredible by nature. Therefore, Scottish reason does not stand over revelation, but beside it. The doctrine of testimony is a direct link to the Scots. Furthermore, Scottish rhetoric prefers inductive proofs, and consequently appeals frequently to data gained by observation, introspection, and history, upon which deductions can be based. (Syllogistic sequences are reserved for testing the verbal consistency of propositions.) In Scottish thought there is a clear preference for realism and pragmatism, a clear bias in favor of data over against speculation. In sum, Scottish-rooted discourse has a hard-edged tang, the bite of realism. This realism is combined with a principled piety that takes the Bible seriously as an inspired record of actual events and with a literary/rhetorical sensibility that also recognizes the Bible as a collection of literary documents.

The *D&A* itself is a collection of documents. This multipart structure should be taken into account in the beginning of any consideration of its rhetoric. As the late Hiram J. Lester points out elsewhere in this volume, the document's charter/address form is derived from those that inaugurated evangelical associations TC had been involved with before emigrating to America. However, instead of a two-part constitution and address, as even the title would lead us to expect, the document has three parts; the Declaration, the Address, and the Appendix. Furthermore, the Appendix constitutes the bulk of the document, thirty-three of its original fifty-six pages. This anomaly of proportion is interesting in itself and suggests that we should begin by describing the rhetorical features of each section, to discover what each is designed to accomplish.

The first section, the Declaration, is relatively short—three pages of fifty-six. After a brief preamble, TC presents the nine resolutions by which the Christian Association has constituted itself. In the preamble the speakers are presented as "we," the members of the association. Three reasons for the formation of the association are given, two (in good Scots fashion) from observation and one from principle: (1) the condition of the churches, (2) the right and responsibility of individual judgment, and (3) the destructive effects of religious controversy.

A Scottish understanding of perception underlies one passage in particular. TC writes that the time has come "for us to see with our own eyes, and to take all our measures directly and immediately from the Divine Standard."[23] The language ordinarily applied to the processes of sensation, in which a stimulus directly impresses the receptive sense, is used here as an analogy. It is an extremely compact metaphor, but an important one. In Scottish thinking, Revelation has a direct impact on the moral and intellectual capacities that is as compelling as that of physical stimuli on the sensory parts of the nervous system. Here the language of psychological and philosophical realism is applied to the reader's encounter with Scripture. An "impression" in Scottish psychology is the imprint of a stimulus on an appropriate receptor. The analogy is of pressure, as in printing, or as in pressing a seal into wax. (Our common use of the term "impression" conveys almost the opposite. Where they were thinking of an exact image, we use the term to mean an approximation.) So when TC says they intend to "take all our measures directly and immediately from the Divine Standard," he means that reading the Bible will stamp into the reader's mind a replica of the idea signified. His word "immediate" carries a force similar to our "unmediated." This unmediated interaction with the text is his best hope for an exact duplication of the original community of the church.

The Declaration, with its informative catalogue of bylaws, is swiftly over, and TC launches into the Address, which is explicitly directed to "all that love our Lord Jesus Christ . . . throughout all the churches," referred to as "dearly beloved brethren," and clearly ministers from his appeal to their role.[24] The Address is chiefly remarkable for its urgent, motivational language in the opening and closing sections, framing the propositions that TC presents as the basis for discussion in the associations that he hopes his auditors will form to investigate, repent of, and remove the causes of divisions. With all the warmth and pathos he can muster TC pleads and beseeches, always assuming that his readers share his noble goals and his love for Jesus Christ. The language is full of intensives, of exclamations; it is rhythmic, colorful, emotional, and lofty. It depicts the evils of divisive strife, the noble call of duty, and the joys of reconciliation in vivid language. The Address concludes with a prayer for unity that quotes extensively from Jesus' prayer for unity in Jn 17. The last line is a blessing: "Peace be with all them that love our Lord Jesus Christ in sincerity. Amen."[25]

The propositions that form the core of the Address are a series of normative statements. TC states that their purpose is to clear away the "rubbish of ages" so that discussion can proceed.[26] They are rules of engagement, by which Christians of differing beliefs may discern the barriers that prevent unity. Occupying only three of the thirteen pages of the Address, the propositions are stated precisely, with qualifying statements where necessary, but without extended discussion or exemplification. Here TC's gifts in constructing sentences are apparent, for he is able to build elaborate periodic structures that express a high level of complexity and qualification, and also to round off such structures with rhythmic and conclusive statements, such as the one that concludes the tenth proposition: "In a word, it is productive of confusion, and of every evil work."[27] Compared with the language that frames them, the propositions are less emotional, though not without feeling, but they contain no exclamations. Clearly they must serve people as clear statements of principle from which to work.

The richness of TC's expressiveness in the beginning and end of the Address contrasts with the matter-of-fact tone of the Declaration and with the measured conceptual language of the Address's propositions. Here is a clear example of a Scottish "natural" rhetorical principle: adapting all aspects of the utterance to whether one is appealing to the hearer's cognitive, imaginative, emotional, or volitional capacities. The Declaration, for the most part, appeals to the understanding. Its main function is to relate the factual details of the Association's structure and purpose. The early and late parts of the Address appeal to the imaginative and emotional faculties, first to engage attention and sympathy, then to exhort and motivate. The propositions embedded in the heart of the Address appeal to a carefully balanced blend of the faculties, so that the listener, prepared to give a serious and sympathetic attention, will be presented with ideas that are both reasonable and forceful. Once this is accomplished, TC uses the noblest language, drawn heavily from Scripture, that will inspire his hearers and readers to take action. Intellectually and emotionally rich, this discourse is neither overly cerebral nor insubstantial. It is an excellent demonstration of the resourcefulness and range of the rhetorical training that TC had received.

This brings us to the Appendix, in which TC supplies a series of closely, even densely, reasoned defenses against objections he anticipates to the Association as an association, or as he puts it, "in our associate capacity."[28] Occupying thirty-one of the document's fifty-six pages, the Appendix is designed "to prevent mistakes" and to clarify points that "might be liable to some misconstruction."[29] It is organized according to the objections that it anticipates: that the Association intends to attack existing churches, ministers, or creeds; that its members are forming a new party; that they espouse latitudinarian principles; and that they discount legitimate religious study and discussion. Its tone, TC apologetically remarks toward its close, approaches "near the borders of controversy."[30] But, having already gotten wind that these objections are circulating, he attempts to make public dispute unnecessary.[31]

If anyone as kind and as fervently pious as TC can seem anxious, he seems so in this section. The length, the complexity, indeed the very existence of this portion of the document bear witness to the depth of the wounds that he had suffered in trying to reconcile religious strife in Ireland and in America. As the late Hiram J. Lester shows in his article in this volume, TC had been rebuked in 1799 by the Antiburgher synod in Belfast for his affiliation with the Evangelical Society of Ulster, whose principles, it charged, "were completely latitudinarian and would tend to destroy the truth and power of the gospel and to undermine the very Kingdom whose enlargement it sought."[32] Then, of course, in America he had recently been forced out of the Seceder ministry by criticisms from his presbytery and synod of his efforts to minister to Presbyterians of different parties.

As TC brings every rhetorical resource to bear on the problem, he turns again and again to two patterns of thought that are clearly Scottish. First, he frequently uses a Reidian psychology of perception to describe how the Bible interacts with the human mind. And second, he appeals to observable facts as conclusive.

We have already met TC's use of Scottish psychology in the discussion of the Declaration's first paragraph. To that we can add multiple examples from the Appendix. The Bible as the Divine Word of the Creator of the natural world is designed for human capacities— "graciously and most judiciously adapted" to its auditors, "calculated" to produce its effect.[33] It "exhibits but one and the self-same thing to all," "at all time, and in all places," because it speaks in the "plainest and most obvious" way, presenting "obvious truths and facts" to the "common sense . . . of christians," that is, to their universal and innate tendency to accept at face value the input of their senses, or, as here, the analogous capacity in the moral nature to accept the input of Revelation.[34] The Word creates an impression necessarily and immediately (that is, directly and without mediation), and between the Word and the Christian "no medium of human determination ought to be interposed."[35] Just as a seal shapes the clay into which it is pressed, the Word shapes, or "stamp[s]," the character of the auditor, which then replicates the impressing Word, "instructed by, and . . . answering to," or mirroring, the formative Word.[36] This line of argument is crucial to TC, because he is drawing a distinction between the Word itself and doctrines inferred from it. The Word is not to blame for divisions, since it functions reliably and uniformly to shape the essential Christian character. Human mediation, on the other hand, interposes opinions and deductions that, however well intended, inevitably produce disunity.

The Scottish preference for inductive proofs is apparent in the Appendix as well. Recourse to currently observable conditions or to the facts of history, whether personal history or church history, is the trump card for sequence after sequence. "This we see was actually the case in the apostolic churches," he concludes.[37] Or, "For the confutation of such an assertion, we would again appeal to church history, and existing facts, and leave the judicious and intelligent christian to determine."[38] Or again, "We appeal for this to the history of all the churches, and to the present divided state of the church at large."[39] In every case, when TC uses this line of argument, he treats it as conclusive: "our certain knowledge," "thorough conviction," "clearly demonstrate."[40] AC used the same line of reasoning in debating Robert Owen. Following the only syllogism he presented in the debate, he offered a piece of factual data "in proof of the syllogism."[41]

A special category of inductive evidence is experience (sing.), that cumulative expectation based on the patterns of experiences (pl.). Since it is a species of probability, it is not as strong as direct testimony of a single event, but it has predictive force: TC was "convinced by experience, that . . . such objections would likely be made."[42]

Other examples of both these two techniques can be given, but perhaps these selections are sufficient to establish that in this third and most polemical section of his document, TC is careful to reinforce his credibility, not only by anticipating and answering his opponents' arguments, but also by bringing to bear in that process the most modern and convincing tools of knowledge at his disposal, those he had learned in Scotland.

Consistent with his Scottish preference for data over speculation, and history over abstraction, TC concludes the Appendix with a historical anecdote from efforts to evangelize among the Seneca Indians.[43] The anecdote is dated, in a particular place, and two witnesses are given. After this poignant story of how the disunity of the Christians hindered efforts to evangelize the Indians, TC swiftly closes the Appendix with a fervent apostrophe to those unconverted Indians and a prayer.

So we see that in each section of the *D&A*, whether declarative, persuasive, or polemical, TC has adapted his discourse to the subject matter and to his relation to it and his hearers, using rhetorical skills and strategies that are clearly rooted in the Scottish philosophy of natural rhetoric.

Appendix A
The Structure of George Campbell's Rhetorical Theory

PhR = *The Philosophy of Rhetoric*
LPE = *Lectures on Pulpit Eloquence*

PhR I	LPE 2	**Sense** (or, Sentiment)
PhR I.4		Its parent art: natural logic
PhR I.5, I.6		Sources of evidence
		Intuitive
		Intellection
		Consciousness
		Common sense
		Deductive (rational)
		Experience
		Analogy
		Testimony
		Calculation of chances (probability)
PhR I.7, I.8		Audience analysis
		General characteristics
		Particular characteristics
PhR I.9		Speaker's reflexive image
		Sources of sympathy
		Influences on sympathy
PhR II, III	LPE 2	**Expression**
PhR I.4		Its parent art: grammar
	LPE 3	Elocution (style)
PhR II.1-II.4		Grammatical elocution: purity
		Rhetorical elocution
PhR II.5-II.9		Perspicuity
		Vivacity
		Elegance
		Animation
		Music
	LPE 4	Pronunciation
		Grammatical pronunciation: conventional signs
		Rhetorical pronunciation:

		natural signs
		Emphasis
		Gesture
		Modulation
PhR I.1-I.3	LPE 5-12	**Purpose** (ends)
		To enlighten the understanding
		To please the imagination
		To move the passions
		To influence the will

Appendix B
Course Outline
First Philosophy Class
University of Glasgow

From George Jardine's *Synopsis of the Lectures on Logic and Belles Lettres*

Object of the course: "To explain the methods of improving the powers or faculties of knowledge, of taste, and of communication by speaking or writing."

"The course consists of three parts, each part admitting of two general divisions."

Part I. The powers or faculties of knowledge.

A. Analysis of the powers of knowledge, illustrated by the principles of general grammar (pp. 1-58)
B. The art or method of improving the powers of knowledge, illustrated by the history of logic, and an explanation of the principal rules of that ancient art (pp. 59-84)

Part II. The powers of taste.

A. An analysis of the powers of taste, or reflex senses, illustrated by the principles of the fine arts (pp. 85-108)
B. The method of improving them, illustrated by the principles and rules of criticism (pp. 109-45)

Part III. The powers of communication.*

A. Analysis of the powers of forming and applying signs in communication
B. The art of improving them, illustrated by the principles of Rhetoric and Eloquence

*These heads for the subjects of the Lectures of a Separate Course. See *Synopsis of Rhetoric*, p. 145.

Notes

1. Thomas Campbell, *Declaration and Address of the Christian Association of Washington* (Washington, Pa.: Brown & Sample, 1809).

2. Lester McAllister's *Thomas Campbell: Man of the Book* (St. Louis: Bethany Press, 1964), 24-29, gives a very helpful overview of the situation at Glasgow University at the time of TC's enrollment. Clarence R. Athearn's excellent *Religious Education of Alexander Campbell* (St. Louis: Bethany Press, 1928) is very detailed. Wilbur Samuel Howell's *Eighteenth-Century British Logic and Rhetoric* (Princeton: Princeton University Press, 1971) is a magisterial study of its topic.

3. McAllister, *Thomas Campbell*, 25.

4. For a comprehensive discussion of the Scottish philosophers and their ideas in the eighteenth and nineteenth centuries, see William L. Davidson, "Scottish Philosophy," in *Encyclopaedia of Religion and Ethics*, ed. James Hastings (New York: Scribner's, 1955), 11:261-71. A valuable collection of essays on the Scottish intellectual environment is *The Origins and Nature of the Scottish Enlightenment*, ed. R. H. Campbell and Andrew S. Skinner (Edinburgh: John Donald, 1982).

5. Robert S. Rait, *The Universities of Aberdeen* (Aberdeen, 1895), 322-23.

6. Reid's theory of signs is most clearly articulated in manuscripts described and discussed by Eric Skopec in two articles: "Thomas Reid's Rhetorical Theory: A Manuscript Report," *Communication Monographs* 45, no. 3 (August 1978): 258-64, and "Thomas Reid's Fundamental Rules of Eloquence," *Quarterly Journal of Speech* 64, no. 4 (December 1978): 400-8.

7. As the dying monster remarks at the end of John Gardner's novel *Grendel*, "Grendel has had an accident. So may you all."

8. Reid held the chair of Moral Philosophy at Glasgow University from 1763 to 1780. His predecessor in that position had been Adam Smith, whose contributions to the scientific study of humans were more sociological than psychological.

9. George Campbell, *Philosophy of Rhetoric*, in *Landmarks in Rhetoric and Public Address*, ed. Lloyd Bitzer (Carbondale, Ill.: Southern Illinois University Press, 1963), 54.

10. George Campbell's exposition of experience, experiences, and testimony appears in the *Dissertation on Miracles*, 3d ed. (Edinburgh: Bell and Bradfute, 1797), 406-15; and in sections I.V.I and I.V.III of the *Philosophy of Rhetoric*, 52-56.

11. Campbell, *Philosophy of Rhetoric*, 1.

12. Campbell, *Philosophy of Rhetoric*, 2.

13. George Campbell, *Lectures on Systematic Theology and Pulpit Eloquence* (Boston: Wells and Wait, 1810).

14. George Jardine, *Outlines of Philosophical Education* (Glasgow: University Press, 1818; 2d ed., 1825).

15. Jardine, *Outlines*, 152.

16. Jardine, *Outlines*, 151.

17. This was George Campbell's criticism of syllogistic reasoning. See *Philosophy of Rhetoric*, I.IV, 61-70.

18. This manuscript was transcribed and published by Lester G. McAllister as *Alexander Campbell at Glasgow University, 1808-1809* (Nashville: Disciples of Christ Historical Society, 1971).

19. This spelling of Jardine's name probably reflects its pronunciation. In *Memoirs of Elder Thomas Campbell* (Cincinnati: H. S. Bosworth, 1861), Alexander Campbell spelled it "Jardane" (117).

20. AC, *Memoirs*, 267.

21. George Jardine, *Synopsis of Lectures on Logic and Belles Lettres: Read in the University of Glasgow* (Glasgow: Printed for James and Andrew Duncan, 1809), 145.

22. *D&A*, 10.17.

23. *D&A*, 1.5-7.

24. *D&A*, 6.1, 4; 7.43.

25. *D&A*, 23.41.

26. *D&A*, 19.4.

27. *D&A*, 18.6-7.

28. *D&A*, 24.5-6.

29. *D&A*, 24.1, 7.

30. *D&A*, 52.29.

31. *D&A*, 52.32-33.

32. *Minute Book of the Associate Synod of Ireland* [Antiburgher], 1 July 1799, 117-18.

33. *D&A*, 46.46-47; 47.39.

34. *D&A*, 40.9; 36.16; 47.5, 8; 47.7.

35. *D&A*, 37.20; 42.24; 46.24-25.

36. *D&A*, 47.37; 48.31.

37. *D&A*, 28.7-8.

38. *D&A*, 45.20-23.

39. *D&A*, 38.28-29.

40. *D&A*, 32.11, 13; 39.29.

41. *Debate on the Evidences of Christianity . . .; between Robert Owen . . . and Alexander Campbell* (Bethany, Va.: A. Campbell, 1829), 156.

42. *D&A*, 45.31-33.

43. *D&A*, 53.35-54.13.

Thomas Campbell's Use of Scripture in the *Declaration and Address*

Christopher R. Hutson

This study sketches the various ways Thomas Campbell appropriates Scripture in the *Declaration and Address*, surveys his choice of passages, and comments on his exegetical method. The final section discusses in more detail his appropriation of a crucial passage, Paul's discussion of "weak" and "strong" in Rom 14-15. The study should be read in consultation with the "Scripture Index to the *D&A*," elsewhere in this volume.

Forms of Reference

References to Scripture in the *D&A* fall into three categories. First, there are citations, that is, references to chapter and verse numbers only, without the actual words of Scripture, as, for example, "when we consider the expressly revealed will of God upon this point, Ezek. 44, 6—9, with Matt. 13, 15—17; I Cor. 5, 6—13, with many other Scriptures."[1] This is the smallest category of references in the *D&A*, consisting of only six examples.[2]

Second, there are quotations of the words of Scripture in such a way as to indicate that they are taken from Scripture. Quotations are marked as such by (a) use of quotation marks,[3] (b) a quotation formula such as, "saith the apostle,"[4] (c) citation of the chapter and verse reference in conjunction with the quotation,[5] or often by some combination of these.

Many of the apparent quotations in the *D&A*, however, are inexact or even paraphrases by which TC appropriates texts for his own purposes. For example, he quotes 1 Chr 22:16, which is David's exhortation to Solomon to launch the temple building project, and juxtaposes it with inexact quotations of 1 Cor 1:10 and Phil 3:16.[6] The effect is that the exhortation no longer applies to the task of temple-building but to a call for TC's audience to join in the task of nonsectarian evangelism.[7] In another example, within a single set of quotation marks clauses are stitched together from 1 Cor 12:8-9a, 10b, 7, and 1 Pt 4:10, as if it were a coherent quotation. It is sometimes difficult, therefore, to distinguish between quotations and allusions to Scripture in the *D&A*.

The third and largest category of Scripture references in the *D&A* is allusion, use of the words of the Bible without any explicit indication that they are taken from Scripture. Campbell may lift whole sentences or incorporate words or phrases into his own sentences. In some cases he likely assumes that his audience will recognize the words of Scripture and know the specific passages. In such cases, the allusions may have functioned the same as quotations or citations for the original audience.

On the other hand, Campbell seems to use some biblical phrases merely as a rhetorical device to set a mood. That is, he may intend for his words to sound Scripture-esque, but he cannot assume that his audience will know the specific passage(s) to which he alludes. This seems especially true when he creates a pastiche from snippets of several passages, as in the cases already noted. Similarly, when he says that the church of Christ on earth consists of "all those in every place that profess their faith in Christ and obedience to him in all things according to the scriptures, and that …,"[8] he cobbles together phrases from Heb 10:23; 2 Cor 2:9 and 1 Cor 15:3-4 in such a way that his assertion carries the ring of biblical authority without actually deriving from or commenting on any particular passage of Scripture.

This rhetorical effect is especially clear at pages 19-20, where in a very short space a cascade of allusions and quotations tumbles forth one upon another with little or no comment between. The stream begins at Is 33:20; flows on to Is 59:19, 2 Cor 10:4, Jos 2 (and/or Jos 6), Ps 95:11 (and/or Heb 3:11, etc.); at which point it becomes a torrent, flooding the text with Mt 13:28, Ps 37:11, Dn 7:27, 18, Mt 12:25 (and parallels), Ps 94:14-15, Mt 25:34, 18:19-20, Is 62:6-7, 1; after which the torrent slows again to a stream with Rom 11:25 and trickles out at Hos 5:15. No listener could be expected to catch every chapter and verse as references gush from the lips of the orator. Even readers of the printed text, aided by quotation marks, would not likely discern whether each quotation is exact or a paraphrase. This is not exposition but exhortation.[9] TC does not explain the passages to which he refers but assumes a general familiarity with the Bible, and he uses the words of Scripture freely to give his own words a prophetic ring.[10]

A sense of biblical authority derives also from TC's use of expressions such as "amen," "day of judgment," "far be it," "kingdom of God," "liberally/liberality," "word of God," "would to God," together with variations on "according to the word of the LORD," "heritage of the LORD," and so forth. Such turns of phrase do not allude to any particular passage, but they reflect the degree to which the speaker has so absorbed the language of the English Authorized Version that it becomes his own language.[11] Among these, "thus saith the Lord" is a key expression in the *D&A* and is included in the "Scripture Index." Although other such words and phrases are not indexed, readers should be alert to "biblical" turns of phrase that create an atmosphere of assumptions and vocabulary held in common by the speaker and his audience.

Choice of Texts

TC makes wide use of Scripture, referring in one way or another to no fewer than twenty-one books from the Old Testament and twenty-five from the New Testament, lacking only references to Philemon and 2 Peter.

In the Old Testament, TC makes particular use of the prophets, from whom he draws his oft-repeated "thus saith the Lord." He makes use of oracles of judgment against Israel and Judah to decry the sectarianism of his own time. Further, he makes use of oracles about the restoration of Jerusalem to anticipate a glorious outcome for the enterprise he is undertaking. For this purpose, he reads the prophets eschatologically, applying their language about Jerusalem to the church in the end times, which he identifies with his own day.[12]

After the prophets, TC refers most often to the Psalms, referring to verses that are for the most part similar to the prophetic oracles of judgment and restoration. He reads the Psalms as theological propositions rather than as prayers, so that his use of them differs little from his use of the prophets.

TC's use of the New Testament is wide-ranging. Although he makes use of all four gospels, he seems to favor Matthew, which he mines for language of judgment. But he also likes the Johannine commandment to "love one another," and he returns five times to the prayer for unity in John 17. Among the Pauline epistles, he draws most heavily from the Corinthian letters and Romans. He pays particular attention to the weak and strong in Rom 14-15, to the related discussion in 1 Cor 8-10, and to the unity of the body in 1 Cor 12. The theme of unity also accounts for the disproportionately high number of references to Ephesians, since four references to that letter are to 4:2-6. In addition, TC draws from Revelation, especially chapter 11, which reinforces his understanding of the oracles of judgment from the Old Testament.

Among the books that receive little notice in the *D&A*, it is interesting that Acts receives only eight references and 1 Timothy only one. Although the Index lists twelve references to Hebrews, there are none to the typologies in chapters 5-10, which would later become important for Restoration Movement ecclesiology. So there is little emphasis in this document on the forms and structures of worship, which would later become the focus of the peculiarly Campbellite brand of "restoration."[13]

Exegesis

There is nothing in the *D&A* that can be called "exegesis" in the technical sense of the word. That is, TC does not expound the meaning of any passage in a systematic way with attention to historical and literary context, vocabulary, grammar, and so forth. The *D&A* is, after all, a hortatory and not a didactic text.

This does not mean that TC is entirely unaware of the historical distance between himself and the texts, as, for example, at 29.46-30.9, where he draws on Ps 81 and Hos 8 to create an analogy between God's response to "his highly favored Israel" and his response to "us." There he is aware that the original referents of his texts were far removed from his own time.[14]

Nevertheless, TC does not typically make the historical gap explicit but applies the words directly, as if they were addressed to the contemporary situation. Nor does he typically distinguish among authors of various books. Though he occasionally identifies Paul as the source of a quotation,[15] he can just as easily refer to "the will of our gracious Redeemer, whose express command to his people is . . ." as he introduces the pastiche from 1 Corinthians and Philippians.[16] For the most part, TC reads Scripture on the flat, with no attention to historical context. As he says, "the scriptures of the Old and New Testament are inseparably connected, making together but one perfect and entire revelation of the Divine will."[17] The New Testament is all equally "the commands and ordinances of our Lord Jesus Christ."[18] It is the "law of Christ."[19] Since TC reads Scripture as an assortment of divinely inspired, propositional truths, it is easy for him to pluck snippets from disparate passages and combine them into his own statements of divine "Truth."

One final point: TC takes the Protestant canon to be the definitive Word of God for the Church. For example, he says, "the Bible never directs us to any book but itself," ignoring completely that the Letter of Jude, for example, quotes from non-canonical literature.[20] In the same context, he quotes Rom 3:2 as an assertion that the "oracles of God" were delivered to the Church![21] Thus for TC the historical context of any particular passage is subordinated to a dogmatic understanding of the whole.

Romans 14:1-15:13

Even though his exegesis is not explicit, we may ask what exegesis lies behind TC's application of a favorite text. I shall, therefore, trace his application of one programmatic passage, Paul's discussion of the "weak" and the "strong" in Rom 14:1-15:13. TC refers to it on the first page of the *D&A* and comes back to it repeatedly, so that the index lists nineteen entries from this passage. The opening paragraph of the Declaration includes the following:

> . . . we are persuaded that it is high time for us not only to think, but also to act for ourselves; *to see with our* own *eyes* [1 Jn 1:1], and to take all our measures directly and immediately from the Divine Standard; to this alone we feel ourselves divinely bound to be conformed; as by this alone we must be judged. We are also persuaded that as no man can be judged for his brother, so *no man can judge* for *his brother* [Rom 14:3,10]: but that every man must be allowed to judge for himself, as *every man must bear his own judgment* [Gal 6:5];—must *give account of himself to God* [Rom 14:12]—We are also of opinion that as the divine word is equally binding upon all so all lie under an equal obligation to be bound by it, and

> it alone; and not by any human interpretation of it: and that therefore no man has a right to *judge his brother* [Rom 14:10], except in so far as he manifestly violates the expresss letter of the law. That every such judgment is an express violation of *the law of Christ* [1 Cor 9:21], a daring usurpation of his throne, and a gross intrusion upon the rights and liberties of his subjects [cf. Gal 6:2]. We are therefore of opinion that we should beware of such things; that we should keep at the utmost distance from every thing of this nature; and, that, *knowing the judgment of God against them that commit such things*, we should neither *do the same ourselves, nor have pleasure in them that do them* [Rom 1:32].[22]

The initial allusion to Rom 14:3,10 is odd, because it alters the language of Paul in a strange way, so that we are not immediately certain of the allusion. Where Paul speaks of "judging" a brother, TC speaks of "judging for" and "being judged for" a brother. In the preceding sentence he speaks of "the Divine Standard" by which "we must be judged." There he means that Scripture is the standard by which each one will be judged at the Last Judgment. Then, by way of analogy, he asserts that (a) "as no man can be judged for his brother" (that is, at the Last Judgment), (b) "so no man can judge for his brother" (that is, judge the meaning of Scripture). Thus, (c) "every man must be allowed to judge for himself" (that is, judge the meaning of Scripture), (d) "as every man must bear his own judgment—must give account of himself to God" (that is, at the Last Judgment).

So the right of private interpretation of Scripture becomes for TC a basic principle pertaining to the Last Judgment. A few lines down, "no man has a right to judge his brother" is a closer allusion to the language of Rom 14:10, though still inexact. But when TC glosses "judgment" by saying that "every man must . . . give account of himself to God," he is clearly alluding to Rom 14:12. It is surprising that he does not cite Rom 14:5, "Let each man be fully persuaded in his own mind." Nevertheless, it is clear that he has sifted the particular historical issues in Rom 14-15 (dietary laws and observance of holy days) out of his argument, and has retained only the right of private interpretation as his nugget.

Near the end of the Address, TC draws on Rom 15:7:

> To advocate the cause of unity while espousing the interests of a party would appear as absurd, as for this country to take part with either of the belligerents in the present awful struggle, which has convulsed and is convulsing the nations, in order to maintain her neutrality and secure her peace. Nay, it would be adopting the very means, by which the bewil-

> dered church has, for hundreds of years past, been rending and dividing herself into fractions; for Christ's sake, and *for the truth's sake* [2 Jn 1:2]; though the first and foundation truth of our christianity is union with him, and the very next to it in order, union with each other in him—"that we receive each other, as Christ has also received *us, to the glory of God"* [Rom 15:7]. *For this is his commandment that we believe in his son Jesus Christ, and love one another, as he gave us commandment. And he that keepeth his commandments dwelleth in him, and he in him—and hereby we know that he dwelleth in us, by the spirit which he hath given us"* [1 Jn 3:23-24]—even the *spirit* of faith, *and of love, and of a sound mind* [2 Tim 1:7]. And surely this should suffice us. But how to love, and *receive* our brother; *as* we believe and hope *Christ has received* both him and *us* [Rom 15:7], and yet refuse to hold communion with him, is, we confess, a mystery too deep for us. If this be *the way that Christ hath received us*, then *woe is unto us* [Rom 15:7].[23]

Here Rom 15:7 is juxtaposed with the Johannine commandment to "love one another," taken from 1 Jn 3:23-24. Once again, TC does not mention the historical context—the exhortations concerning "strong" and "weak" in Rome. But it is clear that, like Paul, he is speaking to those who view themselves as "strong." Against sectarianism, he urges his audience to leave off "espousing the interests of a party" and instead to "practice whatever is expressly revealed and enjoined in the Divine standard." In other words, all claims to "strength" in the form of insistence on particular sectarian interpretations must be set aside on the basis of the simple common denominator that "we receive each other, as Christ also received us."[24]

TC explicitly ties Rom 15:7 to its context in the Appendix, where at last he relates the verse more explicitly to its context:

> Our inference, upon the whole, is, that where a professing christian brother opposes or refuses nothing either in faith or practice, for which there can be expressly produced a "*thus saith the Lord*": that we ought not to reject him because he cannot see with our eyes as to matters of human inference—of private judgment. "*Through thy knowledge shall the weak brother perish?* [1 Cor 8:11] *How walketh thou not charitably?*["] [Rom 14:15] Thus we reason, thus wé conclude, to make no conclusion of our own, nor of any other fallible fellow creature, a rule of faith or duty to our brother. Whether we refuse reason, then, or abuse it, in our so doing, let our brethren judge. But, after all, we have only ventured to suggest, what, in other words, the Apostle has expressly taught; namely, that *the strong ought to bear with the infirmities of the weak, and not to please them-*

> *selves* [Rom 15:1]. That we ought *to receive him* [Rom 14:1,3] that is weak in the faith, because God hath received him. In a word, that *we ought to receive one another, as Christ hath also received us to the glory of God* [Rom 15:7]. We dare not therefore, patronize the rejection of Gods dear children, because they may not be able to see alike in matters of human inference—of private opinion; and such we esteem all things, not expressly revealed and enjoined in the word of God. If otherwise, we know not what private opinion means. . . . As for ourselves, we have taken all due care, in the meantime to take no step, that might throw *a stumbling block in the way* [Rom 14:13]; that might prove now, or at any future period, a barrier to prevent the accomplishment of that most desirable object; either by joining to support a party; or by patronizing any thing as articles of faith or duty, not expressly enjoined in the divine standard; as we are sure, whatever alterations may take place, that will stand.[25]

TC reads Rom 14-15 side by side with the similar discussion in 1Cor 8-10.[26] Here again he is not concerned to expound the historical issues behind either letter, but he extracts from both his principle of the right of private interpretation. For TC, that right is essential to "that most desirable object," the uniting of all Christians that will precipitate the millennial kingdom. Failure to respect the private interpretation of any fellow believer on a matter "for which there can be expressly produced a 'Thus saith the Lord,'" constitutes throwing a "stumbling-block" in the way of a "weaker brother."[27] Here he defines the "weaker brother" from the viewpoint of the "strong," as anyone who "may not be able to see with our eyes in matters of human inference—of private opinion."[28]

For TC the right of private interpretation extends to the issue of the silence of Scripture. For instance, as he draws out the meaning of Paul's dictum that "all things are not expedient" (1 Cor 10:23), he applies Rom 14:22 to the question of practices that are neither explicitly condemned in the Bible nor explicitly commended:

> Neither is there here any clashing of duties; as if to forbear was a sin; and also to practise was a sin; the thing to be forborne being a matter of private opinion; which, though not expressly forbidden, yet are we, by no means, expressly commanded to practise,—Whereas we are expressly commanded to endeavor *to maintain the unity of the spirit in the bond of peace* [Eph 4:3]. And what saith the Apostle to the point in hand? *"Hast thou faith,* saith he, *have it to thyself before God. Happy is the man, that condemneth not himself, in the thing which he alloweth"* [Rom 14:22].[29]

Here TC presses his attack against those who view their sectarian opinions as "strong." All matters of private interpretation are between individual believers and God, whereas the expressed command is for unity. In a later passage, he returns to expound what it means to judge a brother:

> A third and still more dreadful evil is, when we not only, in this kind of way, *judge and set at nought our brother* [Rom 14:10]; but, moreover, proceed as a church, acting and judging in the name of Christ; not only to determine that our brother is wrong, because he differs from our determinations: but also in connexion with this, proceed so far as to determine the merits of the cause by rejecting him, or casting him out of the church, as unworthy of a place in her communion;—and thus, as far as in our power, cutting him off from the kingdom of heaven. In proceeding thus, we not only declare, that, in our judgment, our brother is in an error; which we may sometimes do in a perfect consistence with charity: but we also take upon us to judge, as acting in the name and by the authority of Christ, that his error cuts him off from salvation; that continuing such *he has no inheritance in the kingdom of Christ and of God* [Eph 5:5].[30]

Here TC specifies that the issue is not that it is wrong to disagree. One may determine that a brother is wrong in some matter of interpretation or practice. But to "judge and set at nought our brother" is to place oneself in the role of Christ in the Last Judgment by "casting him out of the church, as unworthy of a place in her communion." TC's language here is suggestive of his own experience with the Presbytery of Chartiers. On the other hand, a little later in the *D&A*, he takes pains to distance himself from charges of "latitudinarianism."[31] So it seems that the understanding of "judging" that he expounds here is for him a middle way between two extreme positions—either that everything is a matter of eternal salvation or that everything is a matter of indifference. For TC, the right of private interpretation does not mean that anything goes; rather, it implies that in all matters where the Scriptures are not explicit, one's interpretation is between oneself and God.[32] It is a matter for the Last Judgment and not for the judgment of any temporal, ecclesiastical court. This brings us back to TC's initial point that everyone must "give account of himself to God" (Rom 14:12).[33]

Throughout the *D&A*, TC avoids describing the historical issues that Paul addressed, although Paul's principles come through. This may be a deliberate strategy, since he also studiously avoids describing any particular historical issues under dispute among the churches of his own day. By highlighting the principles and not tying them to specific historical issues—whether ancient or modern—he gives the principles themselves maximal force. The principles of the unity of believers and the right of private interpretation cannot be circumscribed as if they applied only to this or that specific issue but must be applied anew by every believer.

This paper is by no means an exhaustive treatment of the use of Scripture in the *D&A*. Nevertheless, I hope that the observations sketched here, together with the "Scripture Index," will stimulate new discussion that will lead to greater understanding of this important topic.

Notes

1. Thomas Campbell, *Declaration and Address of the Christian Association of Washington* (Washington, Pa.: Brown & Sample, 1809), 52.9.

2. The others are Mal 2:10; Jn 17:20, 23; and 1 Cor 7:25, 40.

3. For example, *D&A*, 12.49-13.2; 19.36-38; 19.48-20.3. In a number of instances, an unmarked reference is converted into an explicit quotation by the addition of quotation marks in the second edition, as in the quotation of Ps 122:6 (*D&A*, 9.41-42).

4. For example, *D&A*, 6.29; 23.27; 26.12-14.

5. *D&A*, 18.44-49; 32.30-32; 53.7-8; and 55.36-38.

6. *D&A*, 12.40-44. Here TC seems to be quoting from memory and conflating two passages, perhaps because of the similarity between "speak the same thing" (1 Cor 1:10) and "mind the same thing" (Phil 3:16). Note that the clause he inserts from Phil 3:16 is from the Textus Receptus, and that the word "rule" and the phrase "mind the same thing" are not in the earliest and best mss. Since, therefore, modern versions have quite different readings, one must use the Authorized Version (KJV) in order to follow TC's use of Scripture.

7. On the task to which TC is exhorting his audience, see Hiram J. Lester, "The Form and Function of the *Declaration and Address,*" in this volume.

8. Prop. I, *D&A*, 16.10-12. Variations on this particular combination of phrases are found at *D&A*, 17.35-37; 18.19-20; and 47.11-12.

9. By contrast, when TC uses what he calls a "chain of quotations" in "To the Editor of the Christian Baptist," *Christian Baptist* 1 (7 June 1824): 65, he is engaged in a didactic exercise. There he cites chapter and verse for each reference, quoting whole sentences, as he assembles his biblical data on a particular point of doctrine.

10. On the use of Old Testament prophetic imagery in American public rhetoric, see James Darsey, *The Prophetic Tradition and Radical Rhetoric in America* (New York: New York University Press, 1997), chap. 2, who emphasizes

that the projection of a prophetic ethos is especially effective in times of cultural transition and major reform efforts.

11. Alexander Campbell commented on his father's style in his introduction to TC's "Synopsis of Christianity," *Millennial Harbinger* 1 (November 1844): 481:

> The apparent redundancy of quotations and proofs in all his essays is the effect of a seventy years' devout study of THE BOOK, until it has become part and parcel of the mind of the writer. Himself an old man, he is fond of the old style of expressing himself, as well as the ancient and commendable custom of dealing out liberal portions of the sacred documents in explanation as well as in confirmation of his views.

On the rhetorical value of such appropriation of classic texts, including the Bible, see Kathleen H. Jamieson, *Eloquence in an Electronic Age: The Transformation of Political Speechmaking* (New York: Oxford University Press, 1988), 24-30.

12. Paul D. Hanson, "Apocalypses and Apocalypticism: Introductory Overview," *Anchor Bible Dictionary* (New York & Toronto: Doubleday, 1992), 1:281, distinguishes between world-denying "apocalyptic eschatology" and the related but world-affirming "prophetic eschatology." TC would seem to favor the latter, which would explain why he makes but little use of Daniel. On TC's eschatology, see Hans Rollmann, "The Eschatology of the *Declaration and Address*," in this volume.

13. The Lord's Supper is mentioned only once and then simply as "that great ordinance of unity and love" (*D&A*, 7.3). The only mention of baptism is within a quotation from Eph 4 on unity (*D&A*, 50.46). Questions of church polity are not in view at all. One may, however, see a precursor of things to come at *D&A*, 43.14-19; 43.30-32, where correct knowledge of crucial passages becomes necessary for admission to the Church.

14. Compare also the reference to Ex 14:15-16 (*D&A*, 12.48-13.7).

15. TC cites Paul by name at *D&A*, 32.32; compare 42. Elsewhere, he sometimes credits "the Apostle" when introducing quotations from Paul (*D&A*, 26.12; 28.29; 29.32) or 3 Jn (*D&A*, 34.34).

16. *D&A*, 12.39.

17. Prop. 4, *D&A*, 16.31-33.

18. Prop. 5, *D&A*, 16.42-43.

19. *D&A*, 35.36-47.

20. *D&A*, 43.11. TC is familiar with Jude, of course, and refers to it at *D&A*, 8.38 and 51.29.

21. *D&A*, 43.13-14. Compare Prop. 4, that "the scriptures of the Old and New Testaments are inseparably connected" (*D&A*, 16.31-32).

22. *D&A*, 3.4-25.

23. *D&A*, 22.16-37.

24. Compare *D&A*, 16.18-19.

25. *D&A*, 26.1-40.

26. Since he is concerned only with Paul's underlying principles and not with the particular historical issues, TC easily moves between Rom 14-15 and 1 Cor 8-10 in his discussion of "weak" and "strong." Space does not permit me to examine each reference to the latter passage, but readers may easily find those references in the "Scripture Index to the *D&A*" in this volume.

27. Compare *D&A*, 38.16-17.

28. Compare the similar language in TC's address before the Associate Synod of North America, as recorded in Alexander Campbell, *Memoirs of Elder Thomas Campbell*, 12-13 (online at: http://www.mun.ca/rels/restmov/texts/acampbell/metc/metc01.htm#Doc2-): "And all this without any intention on my part, to judge or despise my Christian brethren who may not see with my eyes in those things, which, to me, appear indispensably necessary to promote and secure the unity, peace, and purity of the Church."

29. *D&A*, 29.26-34.

30. *D&A*, 33.5-19; see also 38.14-15.

31. *D&A*, 35.19-41.10.

32. Compare again TC's address before the Associate Synod of North America (*Memoirs*, 13-14):

> Is it for objecting to human standards? "Had they been necessary," says Dr. Doddridge, "the sacred oracles would have presented them, or, at least, have given directions for composing and enforcing them." As to the expediency of such, I leave every man to his own judgment, while I claim the same privilege for myself. This, I presume, I may justly do about a matter on which, according to the learned doctor, the Scriptures are silent; but when the having or wanting the approbation or disapprobation of such is magnified into the unjust importance of being made a positive article of sin or duty, or a term of communion—in which cases I dare neither acquiesce nor be silent—allegiance to Christ and fidelity to his cause and people constrain me to protest against making sins and duties which his word has nowhere pointed out. And if, in the mean time, my brethren should reject me, and cast out my name as evil for so doing, referring my case to the Divine tribunal, I would say: "By what authority do ye these things, and who gave you this authority?" As to human authority in matters of religion, I absolutely reject it—as that grievous yoke of antichristian bondage which neither we nor our fathers were able to bear.

But this ideal did not endure in the movement. On the gradual encroachment of "necessary inference" in Campbellite thinking, see Michael W. Casey, *The Battle over Hermeneutics in the Stone-Campbell Movement 1800–1870* (Lewiston, NY: Edwin Mellen Press, 1998).

33. *D&A*, 3.12, previously cited.

The Theory of Logic and Inference in the *Declaration and Address*[1]

Michael W. Casey

Thomas Campbell's ideas on logic and inference in the *Declaration and Address* stand in the Protestant "epistemological" and British Empiricist traditions. In addition, TC's ideas about inference were at the heart of his project for Christian unity in the *D&A*.

First, I shall explore the backgrounds to TC's theory of inference and opinion. While it is easily overlooked, it is not surprising, given TC's training and long career in the Seceder Presbyterians, that at the time he composed the *D&A* he mostly held to the theology of Westminster. In the Appendix of the *D&A* TC wrote that "of any necessary and possible assistance to understand the scripture . . . and knowledge of every truth they contain . . . the Westminster Confession and Catechisms may . . . prove eminently useful."[2]

While it is useful to locate the similarities between the Westminster Confession and TC's ideas, I want to focus on a relevant passage that echoes the *D&A*. The first chapter of the Confession in part VI sets out an important hermeneutic position:

> The whole counsel of God concerning all things necessary for his own glory, man's salvation, faith and life, is either expressly set down in Scripture, or by *good and necessary consequence may be deduced* from Scripture; unto which nothing at any time is to be added, whether by new revelations of the Spirit, or traditions of men.[3]

The similarity with TC's Proposition 3 found in the Address is striking:

> [N]othing ought to be inculcated upon Christians as articles of faith. . . . Nor ought any thing be admitted, as of divine obligation, in their church constitution and managements, but what is expressly enjoined by the authority of our Lord Jesus Christ and his Apostles upon the New Testament Church; either in express terms or approved precedent.[4]

While TC added a new category "approved precedent" and dropped "good and necessary consequence" he probably saw his project as generally congruent with Presbyterian thought. The main adjustment needed to occur with the authoritative nature of "good and necessary consequence." TC denied that inferences and deductions from Scripture were authoritative in Proposition 6:

> That although inferences and deductions from scripture premises, when fairly inferred, may be truly called doctrine of God's holy word; yet are they not formally binding upon the consciences of christians farther than they perceive the connection, and evidently see that they are so; for their faith must not stand in the wisdom of men; but in the power and veracity of God. . . . Hence it is evident that no such deductions or inferential truths ought to have a place in the Church's confession.[5]

The seventh proposition emphasized this denial even more by declaring that while doctrines of the "great system of Divine truths" (the Westminster Confession) are "highly expedient" since they are largely the products of human reasoning and contain "many inferential truths, they ought not to be made terms of Christian communion."[6]

Here TC clearly distanced himself from the Reformed tradition. The Reformed use of reason stands in what Theodore Dwight Bozeman calls the Protestant epistemology.[7] While Puritans attacked Anglicans because they gave reason an independent role in religion, Westminster Divines and Puritans made extensive use of reason as they subordinated its role to faith in Christ and the authority of Scripture.[8] The Puritans were university-educated men who argued that reason and other tools of learning were needed in order to interpret Scripture. They refused to trust in human reason alone but believed that regenerate reason guided by the Holy Spirit enabled one to find the religious authority that was present in Scripture.[9]

Although the Westminster Divines restricted the range of reason, at times they spoke well of Aristotle and frequently used Aristotelian terminology in their writing. They used Aristotelian arguments for the existence of God, and they believed that the intellect was the highest human capacity. Cornelius Burges spoke of "the mind, intellect, spirit" as the "supreme and most sublime faculty in man's soul." However, this Aristotelian emphasis was tempered by their restitutionist understanding that reason was ultimately subordinate to God and Scriptural authority.[10] The Westminster Divines believed that some doctrine necessary for a person's salvation could be determined only by a logical deduction from the express statements of Scripture. They vigorously defended this idea and tried to explain what it meant on numerous occasions. As Thomas Gataker asserted, "a conclusion necessarily deduced from Scripture is a *divine truth*, as well as that is expressly found in Scripture." Alexander Henderson illustrated a defense of a theological position by necessary inference in an argument directed to Charles I:

> *In my Answer to the first of your Majesties many arguments, I brought a Breviate of some Reasons to prove*, that a Bishop and a Presbyter, are one and the same in Scripture: from which by *necessary consequence, I did inferre the negative*; Therefore, *no difference in Scripture between a Bishop and a Presbyter.*[11]

The Westminster Divines distinguished between "good consequences" and "necessary consequences." According to Gillespie, necessary consequences were "strong and certain." They were the only conclusions possible. Good consequences, in contrast, "prove a suitableness or agreeableness of this or that to Scripture, though another thing may also be proved to be agreeable unto the same Scripture in the same or another place. This later sort are in divers things of very great use."[12]

Gillespie distinguished between necessary consequences drawn from a person's word and inferences drawn from God's word. He believed people may not always be consistent and their use of language can "ensnare them." In contrast:

> God being infinitely wise, it were a blasphemous opinion to hold that anything can be drawn by a certain and necessary consequence from his holy word which is not his will. This were to make the only wise God as foolish as man, who cannot foresee all things which will follow from his words. Therefore we must needs hold it is the mind of God which necessarily followeth from the word of God.[13]

God, in contrast to people, is completely self-consistent, so any deduction correctly drawn from the Scriptures (assumed to be wholly God's word) will correspond exactly to God's will. The Westminster Divines did not see this method as supplementing Scripture but as a means to help make the meaning of Scripture clearer. As Burges said:

> That I may more methodically proceed, the dispatch more speedily that which I have alledg out of the Scriptures, I must necessarily bind my selfe to the lawes of argumentation, wrapping up the force of my Arguments in some plaine *Syllogismes* (as I haue done in the former chapter,) and confirming the seuerall propositions that need proofe, by expresse scriptures, expounded by such learned expositors as mine adversaries pretend most respect vnto.[14]

With biblicism at the center of their theology, the Westminster Divines did not consider the use of syllogistic reasoning optional. The rejection of logic as an aid to Scripture interpretation would lead to dire consequences:

> Sure if *reason* be the eye of the soul, and *Logick* the *art* or *way*, or *methode* of *using reason aright*; they that would debar men of the use of *Logick*, would have them either put out or seal up their eyes, that being blind or blinded, they may lead tham as the Prophet did the *Syrian Troopers* smitten with blindnesse upon his prayer, or transfer and carry them as the *Falkner* doth the *Hawk* hood-winkt, whether themselves please.[15]

The Westminster Divines not only battled the Anglicans over the scope of reason, they opposed the Anabaptists and sectarians who wanted to use only express Scripture. The Westminster Divines considered the sectarians to be inconsistent because they would use inferences, but the sectarians refused to label their own inferences as inferences. The Divines believed that the sectarian arguments against the Presbyterians should proceed differently:

> If any man demande expresse Scriptures for the very terms, he will soone declare of what Spirit he is. But if by sufficient consequence the distinction be not clearly deduced thence, he shall then have cause to complaine. Let him view the foundation on which it is built and afterwards tell me his minde, if he remaine unsatisfied.[16]

The sectarians should have accepted logic and then argued about any flaws in the reasoning used to muster the Presbyterian conclusions. The Divines were completely confident in their argumentation.

As the Westminster Divines debated the legitimacy of using necessary consequences in Biblical authority when they wrote the Westminster Confession, they offered two justifications for using necessary consequence. First, they concluded that the examples or actions of the Apostles were part of the primitive church and binding on modern church practices:

> In all examples, as we have cause to believe that the fathers at the first had a command from God for those things whereof we now find only their example for the ground of their posterity's like practice for many generations, so likewise, though we believe that Christ, in the time that He conversed with His disciples before and after His resurrection, did instruct them in all things concerning the Kingdom of God, yet nothing is left recorded to show His will and appointment of the things instanced in, but the example and practice of the Apostles and churches in their time.[17]

Deductions could be drawn from these apostolic examples to determine modern church practices by Christians enlightened by the Holy Spirit. Therefore, the Westminster Divines believed that their conclusions would "correspond to the Word of God, originally given, but not fully recorded."[18] Regenerate reason could draw out everything implicit in Scripture.

The second justification was that necessary consequence was the only way to preserve many of the Reformed doctrines and practices. Gillespie argued this conclusion against the Arminian position of following only express Scripture:

> If embraced, we must renounce many necessary truths which the reformed churches hold against Arians, Antitrinitarians, Socinians, Papists, because the consequences and arguments from Scripture brought to prove them are not admitted as good by the adversaries."[19]

Gillespie also offered several examples of doctrines and practices maintained by necessary consequence: women taking communion, that the "late war" against the Catholics was right, that the solemn league and covenant was acceptable to God, and that fasting or thanksgiving could be done on special occasions.

Why would Campbell turn away from an idea that was so central to Westminster hermeneutics and theology? Here philosophical influences enter the picture. After 150 years of religious and civil unrest in an England filled with political intrigue, executions, and war, toleration came into vogue. John Locke and his empiricist philosophy undergirded British toleration. Locke wanted to reduce the number of the essentials of Christianity to a minimum to maximize the toleration of differences between Christians so that burning people at the stake, beheading, and war would cease. Locke based his principles of toleration on his epistemology.

For Locke, knowledge was limited to ideas that originate in experience, or through sensation and reflection. Locke defined faith as "the assent to any proposition, not thus made out by the deductions of reason, but upon the credit of the proposer as coming from God, in some extraordinary way of communication. This way of discovering truths to men we call *revelation*."[20] In Locke's scheme one cannot know everything that is believed to be true through his or her own experience but must rely on others' experience for many things. Therefore, faith is established in the testimony of others to what they have experienced. Faith, for Locke, is not as certain as knowledge; however, religious faith reaches the highest level of probability. "Whatever God hath revealed is certainly true: no doubt can be made of it. This is the proper object of *faith*." While human testimony may be false and thus cannot reach the same level as knowledge obtained by our own senses, the testimony of God, in contrast, is certain: "Whatsoever is divine *revelation*, ought to overrule all our opinions, prejudices, and interests, and hath a right to be received with full assent."[21] This position Locke more fully explained in *The Reasonableness of Christianity*.

According to Locke, the propositions of the Christian faith were "above reason"; that is, their truth could not be deduced from any ideas obtained by sensation and reflection. Reason alone could not produce the contents of the Christian faith; however, reason was used to determine what revelation meant: "It still belongs to *reason* to judge of the truth of its being a revelation and of the signification of the words wherein it is delivered."[22] Locke saw the Scriptures as historical, that is, as recording past events that were observed and then testified to by trustworthy witnesses. The Bible, then, was to be evaluated by the same standards by which all historical events are evaluated.[23]

Locke believed that by following the express commands of Scripture anyone would be able to see plainly what God required. Locke further distinguished between the positive commands of the old law and the new, concluding that the commands of the old were temporary.[24] Locke defined opinion (which he also called belief or assent) as "the admitting or receiving any proposition for true, upon arguments or proofs that are found to persuade us to receive it as true, without certain knowledge that it is so."[25] Opinion did not have the status of knowledge. Consistent with his epistemology, Locke objected to "sublime notions" and "mysterious reasoning," since such things made it difficult and impossible for the poor to understand the gospel. Whenever Scriptures were obscure, a person was not responsible for knowing them:

> If he had required more of us in those points, he would have declared his will plainer to us, and discovered the truth contained in those obscure, or seemingly contradictory places, as clearly and as uniformly as he did that fundamental article that we were to believe him to be the Messiah, our King.[26]

Locke also wrote that to be a Christian a person must have "an explicit belief of all the propositions, which he, according to the best of his understanding, really apprehends to be contained and meant in the Scripture," and an implicit belief of all the other propositions that God might in the future allow him or her to understand.[27]

In *A Letter Concerning Toleration*, Locke applied these principles to the question of Christian union and toleration: "Now nothing in worship or discipline can be necessary to the Christian communion, but what Christ our legislator, or the Apostles, by inspiration of the Holy Spirit, have commanded in express words."[28] Locke argued in *The Reasonableness of Christianity* that any truth that must be proved with an argument occupies a lower or secondary status to plainly stated truth.[29]

Locke's religious views are consistent with much of his philosophy found in *An Essay Concerning Human Understanding*. Locke claimed that "the immediate object of all our reasoning and knowledge is nothing but particulars."[30] Because of his inductive and atomistic approach to knowledge he did not like the syllogism. He considered it an artificial way to reason that could easily entangle the mind. Usually people used it to win victory in debate rather than as a means to discover truth. Locke believed that inference was a legitimate act of the rational faculty.

Humans saw connections between ideas in a proposition and drew new propositions from ones already laid down as true. Locke also realized that reason is limited. Sometimes human ideas will fail and at other times human ideas are obscure or confused. The mind mistakenly uses false principles as a starting point for its reasoning.[31] Most of the theological systems, and even the homiletic method, of Locke's day were scholastic in orientation and made use of deductive syllogisms. Locke aimed in his *Essay* to show that these forms of reasoning used in ecclesiastical circles rested on an inadequate base. It is no surprise that he made positive commands the basis upon which Christians should agree and dismissed the prevalent scholastic theology as having no authority.

TC in his *D&A* advocated almost the same position as Locke. He distinguished between the old law and the new, saying that the church was under the new law. He saw divisions in the church as a "horrid evil." Christian union would be attained by following the authority of God in "either express terms or by approved precedent." This proposal followed Locke except that TC added the category of example or the divinely approved actions of the apostles and first-century churches.[32] In harmony with Locke's idea that only scriptural commands should be authoritative, TC urged that those doctrines that were inferences and those deductions that were "fairly inferred from Scripture" should not be imposed upon other Christians, or "have any place in the Church's confession."[33] The way to Christian tolerance was to bind only express commands and move away from deductions made from Scripture. TC recognized that these inferential truths were the result of human reasoning and potentially unattainable to many people. TC also believed that a person did not have to make any doctrinal professions "more extensive than their knowledge."[34]

Locke's distrust of syllogistic reasoning continued in the British-Scottish empiricist tradition and the Scottish Common Sense philosophy as it was developed by Thomas Reid, George Campbell, and George Jardine. TC studied at Glasgow University during Reid's tenure and Common Sense Realism permeated the curriculum. TC studied under Jardine, the professor of Logic and *Belles Lettres* in 1783. Jardine's published works—*Outline of Philosophical Education* and *Synopsis of Lectures on Logic and Belle Lettres Read in the University of Glasgow*—along with Alexander Campbell's student notes of Jardine's course that he took in 1808, basically reflect the course content that TC would have received.[35] Jardine continued the "rehabilitation" of logic started under Bacon and continued by Locke and Reid. As Carisse Berryhill notes:

> The most important feature of Jardine's course was its emphasis on inductive logic. The syllogistic reasoning, studied only briefly for historical purposes in the course, yielded to the inductively derived descriptions of how human beings acquire, appreciate, and communicate knowledge. There was so much new to learn, and so much confidence that people now had the tools to do it. Syllogistic procedures are excellent for testing the consistency of statements with received principles; but in this new era, no syllogism was adequate for the advancement of both society and learning.[36]

The first part of Jardine's course on logic consisted of two sections: (1) an analysis of the powers of knowledge, and (2) the method of improving those powers, which Jardine illustrated by the history of logic and an "explanation of the principal rules of that ancient art."[37]

Jardine argued that the faculties of the mind could be studied by the Baconian method. Jardine's division of the faculties of the mind followed Locke closely, indicating that the Scottish Realists were conservative Lockeans. The powers of the mind consisted in the understanding and the will. The powers of understanding or of knowledge were: (1) the simple faculties where sensation and ideas were acquired by perception, attention, reflection, and abstraction; (2) the sensations and ideas which were preserved by memory and imagination; (3) the complex powers where agreements, disagreements, and relations among ideas were discerned by judgment, reasoning, invention, and genius. Jardine argued, with Locke, that the imagination cannot create new knowledge or sensations, but that it depends upon sensations previously received by the mind. "No act of will can call upon a sensation altogether new."[38]

The most important part of TC's study under Jardine, showing his training in the Baconian viewpoint, is the history of logic. Jardine distinguished between two forms of logic: natural logic and artificial logic. Natural logic was the means of improving the powers of judging and reasoning without the assistance of general rules. Natural logic was analogous to "natural culture." Culture, according to Jardine, was "an improvement or change performed on the original powers of anything, animated or inanimated." "Natural culture" was the natural means that "nature furnishes and applies without instruction, or the assistance of art." The effects of "natural culture" on humanity could be traced back to infancy, where habits were acquired that were "essentials to the future unfolding of the human powers."[39]

People learn more from society or "artificial culture," however, than natural culture. Artificial culture was "the art of training the faculties of man by the discipline of rules and precepts, instructions and example." Jardine placed in this category language and its artificial rules, interaction with other people, and the forming and maintaining of political unions. Analogous to this was "artificial logic," which Jardine defined as a system of rules and laws "which experience and sagacity have suggested and applied for the improvement of the powers of judging and reasoning." Jardine considered the "natural logician" to be superior to the "artificial logician."[40]

Jardine divided the history of logic into three periods. The first period included the time previous to Aristotle, but Aristotle was considered to be the first significant person in the history of logic. The second period covered the time of Aristotle to the revival of literature in Europe, and the third period ranged from the revival of literature to the present time.[41]

Jardine spent most of his time developing the second period in history, although closer to the end of this section he frequently referred to the third period and Bacon's ideas of logic. It would be easy to assume that Jardine looked favorably on the syllogism and Aristotelian logic because of his detail in describing the different types of syllogisms.[42] However, Thomas Reid described Jardine's attitude toward Aristotle and the syllogism in different terms:

> The present Professor [Jardine], after a short analysis of the powers of the understanding, and an explanation of the terms necessary to comprehend the subjects of his course, gives a historical view to the rise and progress of the art of reasoning, and particularly of the syllogistic method, which is rendered a matter of curiosity by the universal influence which for a long time it obtained over the learned world.[43]

Jardine's negative assessment of Aristotle and the syllogism was directly influenced by Thomas Reid, who considered the syllogism better suited for "scholastic litigation" than for "real improvement in knowledge." Its only importance was as "a venerable piece of antiquity," like the pyramids of Egypt or the Wall of China showing the extent of "human genius."[44] Neither Reid nor Jardine attempted to give an exact exegesis of the texts of Aristotle; rather, they focused on British scholastic thought that was labeled Aristotelian.[45] Reid, in his analysis of Aristotelian logic, argued that the concept of "necessary inference" came from scholastic logic, specifically the syllogism:

> A Syllogism is an argument, or reasoning consisting (always, explicitly or implicitly) of three propositions, the last of which, called the CONCLUSION, is (necessarily) inferred from the (very statement of the) two preceding, which are called the PREMISES.[46]

The method of syllogistic reasoning was the same construct as the "good and necessary consequences" found in the Westminster Creed.

Jardine, like Reid, rejected syllogistic reasoning and the scholastic philosophy. "The authority of Aristotle on every subject, previous to the revival of literature, was universal and despotic—The encomiums bestowed upon his logic are extravagant and ridiculous." Jardine pointed to Bacon as the one who laid aside the logic of Aristotle, which was "radically defective" as a mode of reasoning.[47] Here Jardine followed Reid who claimed that Bacon proposed induction as a more effectual method than the syllogism. Bacon, according to Jardine, brought about the greatest reform ever in the art of reasoning by completely overthrowing it and establishing a "new" method—induction—in its place.[48] Jardine claimed that Bacon really did not discover induction. "All men, the savage, the farmer and the huntsman and all make the use of this mode of Reasoning by induction." Bacon was simply the first person who applied it to the interpretation of Nature.[49] Jardine pointed to Bacon's *De Augmentis Scientiarum* and *Novum Organon* as the works which best explain induction. Reid claimed that the *Novum Organon* should be held as a most important addition to the ancient logic. In 1803 Jardine had an edition of the *Novum Organon* printed at the Glasgow University Press for use as a textbook in his class on logic.[50]

In his lectures Jardine lavishly praised the inductive method. He offered three proofs for the superiority of induction. First, he pointed to the numerous discoveries made since Bacon's works as opposed to the few discoveries made before Bacon. Second, he argued that Isaac Newton's discoveries and laws were founded upon the *Novum Organon*. And third, he stated that "the experience of nearly two centuries had convinced the learned that in Natural Philosophy, experiment and just induction alone are to be trusted."[51]

Jardine also said that Bacon's method had been improved by Locke, Hume, Reid, and Condillac. Their writings provided "more clear and distinct notions of the powers of knowledge—their operations and offices—their extent and limits." They had given the world correct "specimens of Synthesis and Analysis."[52]

Jardine concluded his section on the history of logic by saying that the art of reasoning was not learned by a set of rules but that it was learned in training the attention of the mind:

> 1. To a careful observation of immediate facts, the first principles of knowledge.
> 2. To the kinds and degrees of evidence by which truths are supported.
> 3. To the distinct and accurate methods of comparison and inference.
> 4. To a simple and regular process of analysis in the study of every subject.[53]

TC, with his Glasgow education and his affirmation of the British Empiricist tradition, broke with the Reformed tradition and Westminster theology over the role of inferences and deductions. By accepting the priority of inductive logic and the express statements of Scripture (along with approved examples) he believed he had found the key to solving the intractable divisions of Christianity that he found in both Ireland and America. The key to unity was grounded in the "cutting edge" philosophy of TC's day.

Now we turn to the *D&A* to see how central TC's view of inference was to his program of unity. In the Declaration, describing the formation of the Christian Association, TC desired rest from "the bitter jarrings and janglings of a party spirit," to "restore unity, peace, and purity to the whole Church of God." Yet he despaired because "the diversity and rancor of party contentions, the veering uncertainty and clashings of human opinions" seemed to make the problem of human opinion intractable. The only place to find freedom from religious division was "in Christ and his simple word, which is the same yesterday, to-day, and forever." He concluded, using the language of the British Empiricist tradition:

> Our desire, therefore, for ourselves and our brethren would be, that, rejecting human opinions and the inventions of men as of any authority, or as having any place in the Church of God, we might forever cease from

> further contentions about such things; returning to and holding fast by the original standard; taking the Divine word alone for our rule.[54]

Moved by these convictions, TC "resolved" two (of nine) propositions in the Declaration:

> I. That we form ourselves into a religious association under the denomination of the Christian Association of Washington--for the sole purpose of promoting simple evangelical christianity, free from all mixture of human opinions and inventions of men. . . .
>
> V. That this Society, formed for the sole purpose of promoting simple evangelical christianity, shall, to the utmost of its power, countenance and support such ministers, and such only, as exhibit a manifest conformity to the original standard in conversation and doctrine, in zeal and diligence;—only such as reduce to practice that simple original form of christianity, expressly exhibited upon the sacred page; without attempting to inculcate any thing of human authority, of private opinion, or inventions of men, as having any place in the constitution, faith, or worship, of the christian church, or any thing as matter of christian faith or duty, for which there cannot be expressly produced a thus saith the Lord, either in express terms, or by approved precedent.[55]

Hiram J. Lester saw the relationship between the Declaration and the Address to be "ambiguous" because purposes of each section "diverge significantly." The Address focused on Christian unity while the Declaration formed a society that was "to function as a voluntary, parachurch, missionary society and to encourage the forming of sister associations."[56] Lester's analysis of the history of the form of the Address clearly shows the ecumenical roots of the association concept. TC himself said in the Appendix that the "society [was] formed for the express purpose of promoting Christian unity, in opposition to a party spirit."[57] Additionally, as TC's concept that human inference or opinion was the root problem of division is understood, then items I and V clearly delineate an ecumenical understanding for the Association. Only those ministers who spread the unity of Christianity by following express Scripture of primitive Christianity (knowledge) and rejecting all human authority and inference (opinion) would be supported by the new society.

TC's theory of inference and opinion was also prominent in the Address, or the inaugural sermon for the new association. As previously noted, the absence of the authority of inference is prominent in Proposition 3 when it is compared with the Westminster Confession. Inference is also explicitly denied authority in Propositions 6 and 7. TC brought up the problem again in Propositions 11 and 12. In 11 he made explicit the central role of binding human inference in creating Christian division:

> 11. That, (in some instances,) a partial neglect of the expressly revealed will of God, and (in others) an assumed authority for making the approbation of human opinions, and human inventions a term of communion, by introducing them into the constitution, faith, or worship of the church; are, and have been, the immediate, obvious, and universally acknowledged causes, of all the corruptions and divisions that ever have taken place in the church of God.[58]

Then in Proposition 12 he proposed the obvious solution of adhering to express Scripture and eliminating human opinion.

> 12. That all that is necessary to the highest state of perfection and purity of the church upon earth is, first, that none be received as members but such as having that due measure of scriptural self-knowledge described above, do profess their faith in Christ and obedience to him in all things according to the scriptures; . . . 3rdly, that her ministers, duly and scripturally qualified, inculcate none other things than those very articles of faith and holiness expressly revealed and enjoined in the word of God. Lastly, that in all their administrations they keep close by the observance of all divine ordinances, after the example of the primitive church, exhibited in the New Testament; without any additions whatsoever of human opinions or inventions of men.[59]

In essence he repeated the same ideas of items I and V found in the Declaration.

TC restated these ideas in the Address in two passages before the thirteen propositions. He acknowledged an already existing agreement on express Scripture to establish a positive basis for his ecumenical proposal:

> It is, to us, a pleasing consideration that all the churches of Christ which mutually acknowledge each other as such, are not only agreed in the great doctrines of faith and holiness, but are also materially agreed as to the positive ordinances of the Gospel institution; so that our differences, at most, are about the things in which the kingdom of God does not consist, that is, about matters of *private opinion or human invention.*[60]

In hopes that his readers would agree with this proposition, TC pressed his hope that opinions, having no basis as knowledge or any real authority, can be surrendered for Christian unity:

> What a pity that the kingdom of God should be divided about such things!! Who, then, would not be the first amongst us to give up with human inventions in the worship of God, and *to cease from imposing his private opinions upon his brethren*, that our breaches might thus be healed? Who would not willingly conform to the original pattern laid down in the New Testament, for this happy purpose? Our dear brethren, of all denominations, will please to consider that we have our educational prejudices and particular customs to struggle against as well as they. But this we do sincerely declare, that there is nothing we have hitherto received as matter of faith or practice which is not expressly taught and enjoined in the word of God, either in express terms or approved precedent, that we would not heartily relinquish, that so we might return to the original constitutional unity of the christian Church; and, in this happy unity, enjoy full communion with all our brethren, in peace and charity. The like dutiful condescension we candidly expect of all, that are seriously impressed with a sense of the duty they owe to God, to each other, and to their perishing fellow-brethren of mankind.[61]

In another passage TC offered an emotional exhortation for ministers to press for unity by giving up opinions that divide Christians:

> Are we not all praying for that happy event, when there shall be but one fold, as there is but one chief shepherd? . . . To you, therefore, it peculiarly belongs, as the professed and acknowledged leaders of the people, to go before them in this good work,—*to remove human opinions and the inventions of men out of the way*, by carefully separating this chaff from the pure wheat of primary and authentic revelation;—casting out their assumed authority, that enacting and decreeing power by which those things have been imposed and established.[62]

In the Address, the lack of authority for human inference was prominent in the central propositions. TC pointed to the broad unity of all Christians and the recognition that private opinion was the source of division. He appealed to readers and ministers, essentially all rational religious people, to remove the "chaff" of human opinion to achieve unity.

In addition to the Declaration and the Address sections, TC continued his theory of inferences as the source of religious division in his Appendix, where he made lengthy explanations to "prevent mistakes" in understanding his proposal.[63] In the midst of several similar pleas, one crucial passage reiterated and summed up the essential need to exclude human opinion and inference as the basis of Christian unity:

> All we shall say to this at present, is, that if the divine word be not the standard of a party—Then are we not a party, for we have adopted no other. . . . These are the very sentiments we have approved and recommended, as a society formed for the express purpose of promoting christian unity, in opposition to a party spirit. Should any tell us that to do these things is impossible without the intervention of human reason and opinion. We humbly thank them for the discovery. But who ever thought otherwise? Were we not rational subjects, and of course capable of understanding and forming opinions, would it not evidently appear that, to us, revelation of any kind would be quite useless, even suppose it as evident as mathematicks? We pretend not, therefore, to divest ourselves of reason, that we may become quiet, inoffensive, and peaceable christians; nor yet, of any of its proper and legitimate operations upon divinely revealed truths. We only pretend to assert, . . . namely, that there is a manifest distinction betwixt an express scripture declaration, and the conclusion or inference which may be deduced from it—and that the former may be clearly understood, even where the latter is but imperfectly if at all perceived; and that we are, at least, as certain of the declaration as we can be of the conclusion we drew from it—and that, after all, the conclusion ought not to be exalted above the premises, so as to make void the declaration for the sake of establishing our own conclusion—and that, therefore, the express commands to preserve and maintain inviolate christian unity and love, ought not to be set aside to make way for exalting our inferences above the express authority of God. Our inference, upon the whole, is, that where a professing christian brother opposes or refuses nothing either in faith or practice, for which there can be expressly produced a "thus saith the Lord,": that we ought not to reject him because he cannot see with our eyes as to matters of human inference—of private judgment. "Through thy knowledge shall the weak brother perish? How walkest thou not charitably?" Thus we reason, thus we conclude, to make no conclusion of our own, nor of any other fallible fellow creature, a rule of faith or duty to our brother. Whether we refuse reason, then, or abuse it, in our so doing, let our brethren judge. . . . We dare not therefore, patronize the rejection of God's dear children, because they may not be able to see alike in matters of human inference—of private opinion; and

> such we esteem all things not expressly revealed and enjoined in the word of God. If otherwise, we know not what private opinion means.[64]

TC clearly did not reject reason, but he refused to put conclusions drawn by reason on an equal plane with express Scripture. This lengthy passage also linked the rejection of inference with Christian unity and toleration of persons who differed in their conclusions from Scripture.

TC believed that by rejecting the binding nature of human inferences and by agreeing with the simple positive or express ordinances of Scripture all division between Christians would disappear and unity would result. By adjusting Reformed theology and hermeneutics with the British empiricist theory of knowledge and inference, TC believed religious controversy should cease. While in retrospect such a project seems hopelessly naive, and his own reasoning in the *D&A* can be easily critiqued as self-contradictory, TC used the best thinking of his day to propose an elegant, simple, and persuasive appeal for unity. Such an effort is worthy for any era.

Notes

1. Some of the following material is adapted from my work: Michael W. Casey, "The Origins of the Hermeneutics of the Churches of Christ, Part One: The Reformed Tradition," *Restoration Quarterly* 31, no. 2 (1989): 75-91; "The Origins of the Hermeneutics of the Churches of Christ, Part Two: The Philosophical Background," *Restoration Quarterly* 31, no. 4 (1989): 193-206; and *The Battle Over Hermeneutics in the Stone-Campbell Movement, 1800–1870* (Lewiston, N.Y.: Edwin Mellen Press, 1998), 9-49.

2. Thomas Campbell, *Declaration and Address of the Christian Association of Washington* (Washington, Pa.: Brown & Sample, 1809), 42.30-35.

3. John Leith, *Creeds of the Churches: A Reader in Christian Doctrine from the Bible to the Present*, rev. ed. (Atlanta: John Knox Press, 1973), 195. Italics mine.

4. *D&A*, 16.23-24, 26-30.

5. *D&A*, 17.5-11, 13-15.

6. *D&A*, 17.16-18, 20-22.

7. Theodore Dwight Bozeman, *To Live Ancient Lives: The Primitivist Dimension in Puritanism* (Chapel Hill: University of North Carolina Pess, 1988).

8. This section relies heavily on Jack B. Rogers, *Scriptures in the Westminster Confession: A Problem of Historical Interpretation for American Presbyterianism* (Grand Rapids: William B. Eerdmans, 1967). Rogers's study is one of

the best and most thorough analyses of the Confession's positions on Scripture and its interpretation.

9. Rogers, *Scriptures*, 82, 83, 85, 86, 107, 109, 114, 115.

10. Rogers, *Scriptures*, 234-36, 224-27, 228.

11. Rogers, *Scriptures*, 334.

12. Rogers, *Scriptures*, 336.

13. Rogers, *Scriptures*, 336.

14. Rogers, *Scriptures*, 337.

15. Rogers, *Scriptures*, 338.

16. Rogers, *Scriptures*, 342.

17. Rogers, *Scriptures*, 345.

18. Rogers, *Scriptures*, 345.

19. Rogers, *Scriptures*, 346.

20. John Locke, *An Essay Concerning Human Understanding* (New York: Everyman's Library, 1978), IV.18.2.

21. Locke, *Essay*, IV.18.10. On Locke's concept of faith see Billy Doyce Bowen, "Knowledge, the Existence of God, and Faith: John Locke's Influence on Alexander Campbell's Theology" (Ph.D. diss., Michigan State University, 1978), 81-97.

22. Locke, *Essay*, IV.17.3; IV.18.8.

23. John Locke, *The Reasonableness of Christianity* (Stanford: Stanford University Press, 1958), 25, 71.

24. Locke, *Reasonableness*, 30, and John Locke, *A Second Vindication of the Reasonableness of Christianity, The Works of John Locke* 7 (1823; reprint, Aalen, Germany: Scientia Verlag, 1963), 228-29.

25. Locke, *Essay*, IV.15.2.

26. Locke, *Reasonableness*, 76-77, and Locke, *A Second Vindication*, 228-29.

27. Locke, *A Second Vindication*, 232.

28. John Locke, *A Letter Concerning Toleration, The Works of John Locke* 6 (1823; reprint, Aalen, Germany: Scientia Verlag, 1963), 58. Also see 15.

29. Locke, *A Second Vindication*, 322. "For whatsoever is brought as an argument to prove another truth, cannot be thought to be the principal thing aimed at, in that argumentation; though it may have so strong and immediate a connexion with the conclusion, that you cannot deny it, without even denying even what is inferred from it, and is therefore the fitter to be an argument to prove it."

30. Locke, *Essay*, IV.18.8.

31. Locke, *Essay*, IV.18.4.5.6.7.8; IV.18.9.

32. AC questioned his father's second category because he was not sure what it meant. See AC, "Anecdotes, Incidents, and Facts—No. 1," *Millennial Harbinger* (May 1848): 280.

33. Locke, *Letter*, 57, and *D&A*, 17.7, 15.

34. *D&A*, 17.32.

35. Carisse Mickey Berryhill, "Scottish Rhetoric and the *Declaration and Address*," in this volume, and "Lectures in Logic Delivered by Professor Jardan [*sic*] in the University of Glasgow, 1808," Manuscript C, John Barclay Family Papers, Alexander Campbell Archives, Bethany College, Bethany, W.Va. (microfilm, Disciples of Christ Historical Society, Nashville, Tenn.).

36. Berryhill, "Scottish Rhetoric."

37. George Jardine, *Synopsis of Lectures in Logic and Belles Lettres Read in the University of Glasgow* (Glasgow: Glasgow University Press, 1804), 3, 4.

38. Jardine, *Synopsis*, 8, 21, and "Lectures in Logic," 43.

39. Jardine, *Synopsis*, 62; "Lectures in Logic," 94; *Synopsis*, 60.

40. Jardine, *Synopsis*, 61, 62, 63.

41. "Lectures in Logic," 101, and Jardine, *Synopsis*, 62.

42. Lester G. McAllister, Introduction to *Alexander Campbell At Glasgow University, 1808–09* (Nashville: Disciples of Christ Historical Society, 1971), 4.

43. Thomas Reid, "A Statistical Account of the University of Glasgow," in Thomas Reid, *Philosophical Works*, ed. William Hamilton (Hildesheim, Germany: Georg Olms Verlagsbuchhandlung, 1967), 2:735.

44. Thomas Reid, "A Brief Account of Aristotle's Logic, with Remarks," in *Philosophical Works*, 2:711.

45. Wilbur Samuel Howell, *Eighteenth-Century British Logic* (Princeton: Princeton University Press, 1971), 381.

46. Reid, "Brief Account," 2:694.

47. Jardine, *Synopsis*, 78, 81-82.

48. Reid, "Brief Account," 2:712; Jardine, *Synopsis*, 79.

49. "Lectures in Logic," 164, and Jardine, *Synopsis*, 80.

50. Reid, "Brief Account," 2:712; Jardine, *Synopsis*, 81; and David Murray, *Memories of the Old College of Glasgow: Some Chapters in the History of the University* (Glasgow: Jackson, Wylie, 1927), 8.

51. Jardine, *Synopsis*, 81, and "Lectures in Logic," 166.

52. Jardine, *Synopsis*, 82, and "Lectures in Logic," 166-67.

53. Jardine, *Synopsis*, 84.

54. *D&A*, 3.27-28, 31-32, 34-39, and 4.1-4.

55. *D&A*, 4.10-13, 36-47.

56. Hiram J. Lester, "The Form and Function of the *Declaration and Address*," in this volume.

57. *D&A*, 25.26-27.

58. *D&A*, 18.8-15.

59. *D&A*, 18.16-20, 23-29.

60. *D&A*, 10.31-37. Italics mine.

61. *D&A*, 10.37-50, 11.1-6. Italics mine. TC appealed to identification with readers (lovers of Jesus) who agreed with him about express Scripture and human opinions in a passage after the thirteen propositions. See 21.7-25.

62. *D&A*, 12.45 and 13.9-15. Italics mine.

63. *D&A*, 24.1.

64. *D&A*, 25.17-19, 25-48, and 26.1-11, 17.22. For the other passages see 27.23-28, 29.26-49, 30.1-19, 31.28-45, 32.34-49, 33.1-4, 35.10-31, 37.23-49, 38.1-30, 40.6-14, and 50.1-15.

Hermeneutics and the *Declaration and Address*

Thomas H. Olbricht

The *Declaration and Address* of Thomas Campbell presupposes an implicit hermeneutic and one that is eminently serviceable for the driving motivation explicit in the document. TC was chiefly interested in reducing the frictions in Christendom through a recovery of the primitive church in its theology and practice. He believed that this recovery needed to be based upon the Scriptures, more specifically the New Testament. He further believed that certain interpretative or hermeneutical guidelines would be crucial in bringing the Scriptures to bear, in order that unity might result. This implicit hermeneutic drew on rules characteristic of TC's background, but which he tailored to be even more serviceable to the undertaking at hand. In this regard TC was not unique; hermeneutics are always constructed and modified according to the motivating drives of the individuals and groups that utilize them.

The Reformed Context

TC commenced the address by declaring the need to "take all our measures directly and immediately from the Divine Standard."[1] A human interpretation of that standard is, however, to be avoided. He therefore desired to set out guidelines that avoided human constructions:

> We are also of opinion that as the Divine word is equally binding upon all, so all lie under an equal obligation to be bound by it, and it alone; and

> not by any human interpretation of it: and that therefore no man has a right to judge his brother, except in so far as he manifestly violates the express letter of the law.[2]

Somewhat later, TC set forth a larger perspective for taking up the Scriptures so as to reject "human opinions and the inventions of men as of any authority." First, the Word alone is to be the rule. Second, the Holy Spirit is to be teacher and guide. Third, Christ alone, as exhibited in the Word, is the ground for salvation.[3] In this program may be recognized the larger agenda of the Reformation.[4] The first is the *sola scriptura* principle common to both Luther and Calvin.

The second is the Scripture along with the Holy Spirit principle again found in both Luther and Calvin. Since TC is from a Calvinistic background it is appropriate to quote Calvin:

> [W]e have no great certainty of the word itself, until it be confirmed by the testimony of the Spirit. For the Lord has so knit together the certainty of his word and his spirit, that our minds are duly imbued with reverence for the word when the Spirit shining upon it enables us there to behold the face of God; and, on the other hand, we embrace the Spirit with no danger of delusion when we recognise him in his image, that is, in his word.[5]

TC clearly believed that the Spirit worked in conjunction with the Word in bringing about a proper interpretation of the Scriptures, unlike some of his descendants who argued that the Spirit did not work separate and apart from the Word. Scripture must be searched to avoid a cheap orthodoxy obtained through "committing to memory a catechism, or professing our approbation of a formula, made ready to our hand, which we may or may not have once read over."[6] Yet right interpretation involves more than a careful reading, important as that is, since any

> person may . . . by this short and easy method [relying on catechetical or credal formulas] become as orthodox as the apostle Paul . . . without ever once consulting the Bible; or so much as putting up a single petition for the Holy Spirit to guide him into all truth; to open his understanding to know the Scriptures.[7]

TC believed that the Holy Spirit did not give the searcher an insight into the Word of God apart from reading the Scripture. In the *D&A*, however, he was not concerned to specify dangers inherent in claiming right interpretation because of the Spirit's presence.

TC's document is basically centered on the community of the faithful, but he wanted to make clear that Christ is Lord of the church and its savior: "and Christ alone as exhibited in the word for our salvation."[8] He returned to this theme later, but not often. "With you all," he wrote, "we desire to unite in the bonds of an entire christian unity—Christ alone being the *head*, the centre, his word the rule—an explicit belief of, and manifest conformity to it, in all things—*the terms*."[9]

TC likewise embraced another age-old rule of thumb that Scriptures are to be interpreted in the light of the whole of Scripture. Martin Luther exhibited a renewed interest in this rule:

> That is the true method of interpretation which puts Scripture alongside of Scripture in a right and proper way; the father who can do this best is the best among them. And all the books of the fathers must be read with discrimination, not taking their word for granted, but looking whether they quote clear texts and explain Scripture by other and clearer Scripture.[10]

TC argued that isolated texts should not be advanced to judge a brother, but that all the appropriate Scriptures should be brought to bear:

> In the page first, we say, that no man has a right to judge his brother; except in so far as he manifestly violates the express letter of the law. By the law here, and elsewhere, when taken in this latitude, we mean that whole revelation of faith and duty, expressly declared in the divine word, taken together, or in its due connection, upon every article: and not any detached sentence. We understand it as extending to all prohibitions, as well as to all requirements.[11]

TC did not incorporate in the *D&A* classical, detailed rules in regard to hermeneutics—and, in fact, that would have taken him too far afield. Later, his son Alexander became convinced that in order to carry out the program of unity, it was important to hold consensus agreements on "Principles of Interpretation."[12] He worked from the standard classic on hermeneutics by Johann August Ernesti (1707–81) as mediated by an American, Moses Stuart, who not only translated the work of Ernesti but also expanded it, as was customary in that time.[13] Neither did TC offer the standard claim that the Scriptures are to be interpreted in the same manner as any other work.

Express Terms and Approved Precedents

In the effort to bring Christians together, TC placarded the New Testament church as opposed to opinions and confessions. He soon disclosed his hermeneutical rules through highlighting express terms and approved precedents:

> V. That this Society, formed for the sole purpose of promoting simple evangelical christianity, shall, to the utmost of its power, countenance and support such ministers, and such only, as exhibit a manifest conformity to the original standard in conversation and doctrine, in zeal and diligence; —only such as reduce to practice that simple original form of christianity, expressly exhibited upon the sacred page; without attempting to inculcate anything of human authority, of private opinion, or inventions of men, as having any place in the constitution, faith, or worship, of the christian church—or, anything, as matter of christian faith, or duty, for which there can not be expressly produced a thus saith the Lord either in express terms, or by approved precedent.[14]

At this point in his edited version of the *D&A*, Charles Alexander Young inserted a footnote in which AC, on reading the document in proofs, is said to have told his father, "Then, sir, you must abandon and give up infant baptism, and some other practices for which it seems to me you cannot produce an express precept or an example in any book of the Christians' scriptures!"[15] One might conclude from this exclamation of AC that the proposed hermeneutic came as a surprise. If it did, however, it is not as if TC were the originator. We may take AC's reaction, therefore, to be his assertion of the ramifications of a rigorously applied, express terms, approved precedent hermeneutic.

I have not been able to discover the explicit roots of this hermeneutic. It may go back as far as the fathers of the church, but its more modern versions lie in the Reformation. In determining what specific matters were to be adapted, Ulrich Zwingli (1484–1531) wrote of both the commands of Christ and Biblical examples.[16] I have not as yet found, however, a statement in which Zwingli brought the two together as a clear hermeneutic principle. Edward Dering (1540–76), a Puritan, offered what may be one of the earliest written statements on commands, examples, and inferences, in arguing for the theological importance of inferences. He insisted that a conclusion based on Scripture and drawn from "proportion, or deduction, by consequence . . . is as well the Word of God, as that which is an express commandment or example."[17]

This tripartite formula is found in American Puritan, Baptist, and other circles. For example, Barnas Sears, one-time professor at Newton Theological Seminary and president of Brown University, wrote:

> (1) Popular and poetical language is to be translated, so far as may be, into the exact language of science. Hence it presupposes an exegetical training. Some subjects can be so well understood by us, as to enable us to determine with clearness how language must be understood; but on subjects beyond our comprehension a difficulty in interpreting language will always remain.
>
> (2) Subjects must be analyzed philosophically, so far as it is in our power to do it. Otherwise, their nature, their difference or agreement with others cannot be understood. E.G., repentance, faith, love regeneration, sanctification.
>
> (3) The relations of doctrines to each other must be so far ascertained as to preserve their harmony. The uncertain must conform to the certain; our inferences must not set aside divine testimony. Express and clear declaration of Scripture, and simple and necessary inferences, take the precedence of philosophical speculation and long concatenations of reasoning. Two doctrines fully established by independent evidence, must be allowed to stand, even when we cannot perceive the connection, which is most likely to occur on subjects which lie out of the sphere of human knowledge.
>
> The demands of theology, as a science, are exegetical and logical, the former furnishing the material, the latter the instruction.[18]

TC was working within a well-defined consensus perspective as to how Scripture is to be embraced. This is not to say, however, that he accepted conventional hermeneutics without modification. TC believed that in some versions this commended hermeneutic contributed to rifts rather than reducing them.

TC elaborated more fully on these guidelines in the propositions in the Address part of the document. He particularly addressed those items that bar believers from acceptance and from participating in the Lord's Supper. These should be based on "what is expressly taught and enjoined upon them in the word of God."[19] Without express biblical warrant these items likewise should neither be construed as divine obligation nor contained in church constitutions. The only items for inclusion should be "what is expressly enjoined by the authority of our Lord Jesus Christ and his apostles upon the New Testament Church; either in express terms or by approved precedent." The language is that of the logician, though tailored to hermeneutics by the Westminster Divines, if not earlier, as Michael W. Casey has shown in his essay on logic and inferences. Rather than highlighting commands and examples, terms widely employed later in the movement, TC wrote of express terms, a concept with much wider connotations and application than the more restricted word "commandments." "Express terms" specifies a clear statement on the matter, whatever the content of the utterance. "Approved precedents" narrows the examples to those receiving approbation in Scripture. The Scriptures contain numerous incidents that set forth actions counter to that which God desires. Only the approved examples or honorific actions are to be followed.

Not only must express terms and approved precedents be embraced, no license to believe or do what seems expedient is permitted where these are not found:

> 5. That with respect to the commands and ordinances of our Lord Jesus Christ, where the Scriptures are silent, as to the express time or manner of performance, if any such there be; no human authority has power to interfere, in order to supply the supposed deficiency, by making laws for the Church.[20]

While the slogan "We speak where the Bible speaks and are silent where it is silent" is not found in the *D&A*, TC clearly argued that silence limits rather than permits. Ulrich Zwingli worked from a similar premise. According to Geoffrey W. Bromiley, in the view of Zwingli the church must not retain "traditional forms or ceremonies simply on the ground that they were not actually forbidden by Scripture."[21] TC concluded, "Nothing ought to be received into the faith or worship of the church; or be made a term of communion amongst christians, that is not as old as the New Testament."[22]

Though in the final analysis TC's hermeneutics may have been reductionistic, he himself resisted this designation. He believed that his guidelines included everything of consequence from the standpoint of the Scripture. At the same time, in the Appendix he took umbrage at the charge of laditudinarianism. He contended that he was neither too limiting nor too permissive, but rather one who embraced the whole counsel of God:

> If we take no greater latitude than the divine law allows, either in judging of persons, or doctrines—either in profession, or practice (and this is the very thing we humbly propose and sincerely intend), may we not reasonably hope, that such a latitude will appear to every upright christian, perfectly innocent and unexceptionable? If this be Latitudinarianism, it must be a good thing—and therefore the more we have of it the better; and may be it is, for we are told, "the commandment is exceeding broad"; and we intend to go just as far as it will suffer us, but not one hair's breadth farther—so, at least, says our profession.[23]

In order to avoid reductionism, TC resisted the delineating of faith and opinion. He held that everything taught in Scripture should be practiced:

> We dare neither assume, nor propose, the trite indefinite distinction between essentials, and non-essentials, in matters of revealed truth and duty; firmly persuaded, that, whatever may be their comparative importance, simply considered, the high obligation of the Divine Authority revealing, or enjoining them, renders the belief, or performance of them absolutely essential to us, in so far as we know them.[24]

What is expressly taught in Scripture is essential. What is not expressly taught, only, falls into the category of opinion. Here TC gives sweeping latitude to what is essential, but he is always afraid that, by other rules, opinions will return through the back door, for example, especially through inferences. He rejects neither confessional, doctrinal, nor inferential conclusions as such, but he thinks they are to be clearly steered away from the category of "express terms" or "essentials." He fears most that they will become the grounds for "terms of Christian communion":

> 7. That although doctrinal exhibitions of the great system of divine truths, and defensive testimonies in opposition to prevailing errors, be highly expedient; and the more full and explicit they be, for those purposes, the better; yet, as these must be in a great measure the effect of human reasoning, and of course must contain many inferential truths, they ought not to be made terms of christian communion: unless we suppose, what is contrary to fact, that none have a right to the communion of the church, but such as possess a very clear and decisive judgment; or are come to a very high degree of doctrinal information.[25]

TC wants to apply his rules to be as accepting as Scripture, not to go beyond Scripture. Whether indeed his rules can attain this end, is discussible, but at least it is clear what he hoped to achieve with his hermeneutic. Much more can be written about inferences, but we need not say more here because of the fine work in this volume by Michael W. Casey.

Some argued—for example, Samuel Rogers—that the advantage of the TC proposal over the approach of the Christian Connexion was that opinions and essentials were to be separated.[26] Although it might appear that TC resisted such an effort, he recognized that opinions persist and was not so sanguine as to believe that they would disappear. But opinions were not to be determinative of the practice nor the fellowship boundaries of the church. Everything without explicit Scripture warrant is opinion. Nothing, however, within Scripture can be a matter of opinion:

> [F]or no man can relinquish his opinions or practices, till once convinced that they are wrong; and this he may not be immediately, even supposing they were so. One thing, however, he may do, when not bound by an express command, he need not impose them upon others, by any wise requiring their approbation; and when this is done, the things, to them, are as good as dead; yea, as good as buried too; being thus removed out of the way. Has not the Apostle set us a noble example of this, in his pious and charitable zeal for the comfort and edification of his brother, in declaring himself ready to forego his rights (not indeed to break commandments) rather than stumble, or offend, his brother? And who knows not, the Hebrew Christians abstained from certain meats, observed certain days—kept the passover, circumcised their children, &c,. &c.—while no such things were practiced by the Gentile converts:—and yet no breach of unity, while they charitably forbore one with the other. But had the Jews been expressly prohibited, or the Gentiles expressly enjoined, by the authority of Jesus, to observe these things; could they, in such a case, have lawfully exercised this forbearance? But where no express law is, there can be no formal, no intentional transgression; even although its implicit and necessary consequences had forbid the thing, had they been discovered.[27]

TC, having been brought up on creeds, attested to their usefulness, even the Westminster Confession, as long as these instruments were not employed for cutting asunder believers. He was not anti-creedal, at least in the *D&A,* as were his later descendants:

> [W]e are by no means to be understood as at all wishing to deprive our fellow-christians of any necessary and possible assistance to understand the scriptures: or to come to a distinct and particular knowledge of every truth they contain;—for which purpose the Westminster Confession and

> Catechisms, may, with many other excellent performances, prove eminently useful. But, having served ourselves of these, let our profiting appear to all, by our manifest acquaintance with the Bible; by making our profession of faith and obedience, by declaring its divine dictates, in which we acquiesce as the subject matter and rule of both. . . . This by no means forbids him to use helps: but, we humbly presume, will effectually prevent him from resting either in them or upon them; which is the evil so justly complained of—from taking up with the directory instead of the object to which it directs.[28]

Obviously, TC hoped to direct believers away from attachments either to opinions or to creeds so as to stand "upon the same ground on which the Church stood at the beginning."[29]

The Old and New Testaments

TC also launched a major hermeneutical strategy in specifying the New Testament rather than the Old as the basis for unity. This decision has precedents, but is a departure from basic Reformed doctrine. TC declared that all the Scriptures are normative, but the Old for the Old Testament church and the New for the New Testament church:

> 4. That although the Scriptures of the Old and New Testaments are inseparably connected, making together but one perfect and entire revelation of the Divine will, for the edification and salvation of the church; and therefore in that respect cannot be separated; yet as to what directly and properly belongs to their immediate object, the New Testament is as perfect a constitution for the worship, discipline and government of the New Testament church, and as perfect a rule for the particular duties of its members; as the Old Testament was for the worship, discipline and government of the Old Testament church, and the particular duties of its members.[30]

The more rigorous separation of the Old from the New is not as obvious in this statement as was later proposed by AC in his famous 1816 "Sermon on the Law," but it is clear that the express terms and approved precedents are to be drawn from the New Testament. Toward the end of the *D&A* TC addressed more directly the importance of the Old Testament even to Christian believers:

> [A]t the same time by no means excluding the old as fundamental to, illustrative of, and inseparably connected with, the new; and as being every way of equal authority, as well as of an entire sameness with it, in every point of moral natural duty; though not immediately our rule, without the intervention and coincidence of the new; in which our Lord has taught his people, by the ministry of his holy Apostles, all things whatsoever they should observe and do, till the end of the world. Thus we come to the one rule, taking the Old Testament as explained and perfected by the new, and the new as illustrated and enforced by the old.[31]

In fact, this relegation of the Old Testament to a nonauthoritative status for Christians, though not extreme, ran counter to the Reformed positions of Calvin, Zwingli, Knox, and the Puritans. Luther, in contrast, found employment for the Old Testament, but as a counterpoint to the gospel. AC rejected Luther's proposal, commenting pointedly, "There is no necessity for preaching the law in order to prepare men for receiving the gospel."[32]

TC's perspective on the three dispensations was indebted to the federal or covenantal theology of the Dutch scholars, especially Hugo Grotius (1583–1645) and Johannes Cocceius (1603–69).[33] Cocceius held that as the result of the failure of the covenant of works with Adam, God instituted the covenant of grace in three dispensations: the patriarchal, the Mosaic, and the Christian.[34] This dispensationalism not only established a groundwork for what is authoritative in each dispensation, but it also provided a means of relating the dispensations. In effect, it became a biblical theology, featuring promise and fulfillment. It is interesting that Cocceius essentially followed Calvin in suggesting that the covenant of grace begins not with the New Testament, but with Abraham in the Old.

Charles S. McCoy and J. Wayne Baker have taken Heinrich Bullinger's *A Brief Exposition of the One and Eternal Testament or Covenant of God* to be the formulative document for Reformed covenantal theology. It is interesting that, in view of what TC wrote in regard to the Old and New—that is, "Thus we come to the one rule"—his language sounded reminiscent of Bullinger, though likely as mediated through Cocceius and Grotius. The title of the document makes clear that Bullinger believed that there was one covenant and that it was eternal. In the discourse he wrote, "There is therefore one covenant and one church of all the saints before and after Christ, one way to heaven, and one unchanging religion of all the saints (Ps. 14 and 23)."[35] Bullinger went on to cite Mt 8:11-12 in regard to those who come from the east and west and sit down to eat with Abraham, Isaac, and Jacob. TC, too, emphasized the oneness of Scripture, but much more than Bullinger he was disposed to focus on the New Testament as the authoritative source of unity.

It would be a mistake to situate TC in a rigid covenantal or constitutional mode of theologizing. He was no doubt aware of covenantal theology from Bullinger to his time, and certainly the newly achieved interest in constitutional government in the United States was useful rhetorically for the program he announced in the *D&A*. TC obviously argued for a strict constructionist interpretation of the text in respect to express terms and approved precedents. But he was careful to avoid an arid legalism in which the constitution and law become the end of Christianity. It seems to me that he employed "constitution" more as a timely rhetorical metaphor than as a principle for constructing theology. TC was careful to reiterate his true interests toward the end of the *D&A*:

> It would be strange, indeed, if in contending earnestly for the faith once delivered to the saints, we should overlook those fruits of righteousness—that manifest humility, piety, temperance, justice and charity—without which faith itself is dead being alone. We trust we have not so learned Christ: if so be, we have been taught by him, as the truth is in Jesus, we must have learned a very different lesson indeed. While we would therefore insist upon an entire conformity to the Scriptures in profession, that we might all believe and speak the same things, and thus be perfectly joined together in the same mind and in the same judgment; we would, with equal scrupulosity, insist upon, and look for, an entire conformity to them in practice, in all those whom we acknowledge as our brethren in Christ. . . . We therefore conclude, that to advocate unity alone, however desirable in itself without at the same time purging the Church of apparently unsanctified characters—even of all that cannot shew their faith by their works, would be, at best, but a poor, superficial, skin-deep reformation.[36]

American dispensational counterparts may be located in various other quarters, for example, in the lectures of David Tappan (1752–1803), a moderate Calvinist and Hollis Professor at Harvard, on Jewish history.[37] Furthermore, Grotius emphasized the need to understand the Old Testament in its own right rather than whatever light it might shed on Christology. As David Steinmetz noted, this relegation of the Old Testament to its own context delimits its use by Christians.[38] Furthermore, the Campbells were no doubt influenced by Locke and heirs, who chiefly sought to root Christianity in the Gospels, and in a secondary manner to the letters of Paul. The Campbells, in contrast, focused on Acts and the epistles, especially Hebrews, rather than the Gospels.[39]

Conclusions

TC worked from implicit rules of hermeneutics that were widely accepted in his time and had been around since at least early in the Reformation. He modified these, however, in such a manner as to enhance the prospect of the unity of believers. He therefore denigrated an effort to distinguish the essential from the nonessential or from opinions. Likewise, he played down the significance of inferences and deductions from Scripture premises. He argued that interpreters should employ these rules in such a manner that those growing in the faith be permitted to mature, as Harold Kent Straughn has pointed out in his essay "Church Unity, Biblical Purity, and Spiritual Maturity" in this volume.

TC's hermeneutical rules were helpful for the task at hand, that is, to place in bold relief features of the New Testament church found ostensibly in the Scriptures. In efforts at reformation in the English-speaking world the church has perennially played a central role. From the time of Henry VIII (1491–1547), the focus of English Christianity had been on the church. The battles of Henry and his successors were the struggles of royalty and the ruling classes to define the contours of a specifically English Church over against a Christianity politically directed from Rome. Henry broke ties with Rome and became prince and defender of the church. He confiscated the church's lands, closed the monasteries, and declared the right of the English government to try church functionaries. For a growing group of church leaders, later designated Puritans, most of what Henry accomplished was simply a tinkering with the politics of the church. Under the influence of the Swiss Reform they wanted to go much further and purify the liturgy and life of the church. They demanded explicit scriptural warrant for all such matters, regarding whatever was without such as idolatrous, popish, and superstitious. The Puritans championed plain preaching and heralded simplicity of proclamation and life.

While the Campbells and other early Restoration leaders had no direct ties to Puritanism, they were heirs of many of its principles.[40] The Campbell movement grew rapidly in a country founded on Puritan principles. By TC's time in America, only the vestiges of a state church existed to rally against—and in Massachusetts that establishment was a

Puritan inheritance. Now multiple churches were visible on the scene. The Campbells championed a united church over against a warring Christendom. The question therefore became the contours of this united body. The solution as time went on was to reject all creeds and rebuild the Church of Jesus Christ, plank by plank, from the Oracles of God, the Scriptures, and especially the New Testament. The America of the Campbells was specifically one in which the denominations were organizing and testing their wings, as Jon Butler has argued in a recent book.[41]

The approach of TC was also useful since it was compatible with the Enlightenment predilection for establishing a case via the building-block method, by adding fact to fact, in TC's case, express terms and approved precedents.[42] These items focused on discrete exterior features. It is not as clear, should one be mostly concerned to ascertain God's steadfast love, mercy, and justice, how helpful the hermeneutic might be, though adaptation was obviously possible.

It would have been helpful for greater understanding of his hermeneutics had TC exhibited the application of these guidelines in concrete contexts. This he did only to a limited extent. Christopher Hutson has shown that TC's greatest employment of Scripture came about through allusions and not by the citation of express terms. TC did, however, establish the desirability of unity through express statements of Jesus and Paul. He also cited various items from the Scriptures to establish that the message of the Scripture is one, incorporating both Old and New Testaments.

However we may evaluate the implicit hermeneutic of TC in the *D&A*, it was tailored to and useful for his effort to bring about unity among those who believed in the God who appeared to Abraham, Isaac, and Jacob and who was the Father of the Lord Jesus Christ.

Notes

1. Thomas Campbell, *Declaration and Address of the Christian Association of Washington* (Washington, Pa.: Brown & Sample, 1809), 3.6-7.
2. *D&A*, 3.11-17.
3. *D&A*, 3.39-4.6.

4. The reformation produced a flowering of books on hermeneutics. Johann August Ernesti, the German scholar, cites nineteen Roman Catholic and twenty-three Protestant books on hermeneutics by 1761; see Moses Stuart, *Elements of Interpretation, Translated from the Latin of J. A. Ernesti, and Accompanied by Notes and an Appendix Containing extracts from Morus, Beck and Keil* (Andover: Flagg & Gould, 1822) [2nd ed. London, 1822; 3rd ed. Andover, 1838; 4th ed. Andover and New York, 1842]. Ernesti's work was titled *Institutio interpretis Novi Testament* (Leipsiae: Weidimann Reichium, 1775). Samuel Davidson published a history of interpretation in which he included a forty-page bibliography covering the category of hermeneutics; see Samuel Davidson, *Sacred Hermeneutics Developed and Applied, Including A History of Biblical Interpretation from the Earliest of the Fathers to the Reformation* (Edinburgh: Thomas Clark, 1843). This impressive succession of books set the style for instruction and works on hermeneutics that has prevailed, especially in conservative American circles.

5. John Calvin, *Institutes of the Christian Religion*, trans. Henry Beveridge (Grand Rapids: Eerdmans, 1957), I, ix, 3.

6. *D&A*, 41.38-40.

7. *D&A*, 41.49-42.6.

8. *D&A*, 4.6.

9. *D&A*, 11.11-13. For Calvin the Scripture itself is the authority for the believer, not a Christocentric interpretation of Scripture; see Robert M. Grant and David Tracy, *A Short History of the Interpretation of the Bible* (Philadelphia: Fortress Press, 1984), 96.

10. Martin Luther, "Answer to the Superchristian, Superspiritual, and Superlearned Book of Goat Emser," in *Works of Martin Luther* (St. Louis: Concordia Press, 1955–86), 3:334.

11. *D&A*, 27.31-38.

12. Alexander Campbell, *A Connected View of the Principles and Rules . . .* [Cover Title, *Christianity Restored*; later editions titled *The Christian System* (Bethany, Va.: McVay & Ewing, 1835)]. I shall give the pagination for this reprint (Rosemead, Calif.: Old Path Book Club, 1959), 15-99.

13. Stuart, *Elements of Interpretation*; see n. 4. On Stuart see John H. Giltner, *Moses Stuart: The Father of Biblical Science in America* (Atlanta: Scholars Press, 1988).

14. *D&A*, 4.36-47. Express terms and approved examples are mentioned several times throughout the document, sometimes together and sometimes separately; see *D&A*, 16-18, 21, 25, 27, 28, 31-33, 35-36, 37-38, 42-44, 47.

15. Charles Alexander Young, ed., *Historical Documents Advocating Christian Union* (Chicago: Christian Century, 1904), 76.

16. *Zwingli and Bullinger*, ed. G. W. Bromiley (Philadelphia: Westminster Press, 1963), 29.

17. Edward Dering, "The Praelections . . . upon . . . Hebrews," in Dering, *Workes*, 447-48, as quoted by Theodore Dwight Bozeman in *To Live Ancient Lives* (Chapel Hill: University of North Carolina Press, 1988), 70. This document was probably published in 1572.

18. Alvah Hovey, *Barnas Sears: A Christian Educator His Making and Work* (New York: Silver, Burdett, 1902), 72, 73.

19. *D&A*, 16.25-26.

20. *D&A*, 16.42-46.

21. *Zwingli and Bullinger*, 29.

22. *D&A*, 17.2-4.

23. *D&A*, 30.43-31.3.

24. *D&A*, 11.16-22. TC therefore took exception to the famous slogan of Peter Meiderlin, "We would be in the best shape if we kept in essentials, unity; in nonessentials, liberty; and in both charity." See Hans Rollmann, "In Essentials Unity: The Pre-History of a Restoration Movement Slogan," *Restoration Quarterly* 39, no. 3 (1997): 129-40.

25. *D&A*, 17.16-25.

26. *Autobiography of Samuel Rogers*, ed. John I. Rogers (Cincinnati: Christian Standard, 1880), 118.

27. *D&A*, 28.22-43.

28. *D&A*, 42.29-38; 43.2-6.

29. *D&A*, 16.6-7.

30. *D&A*, 16.31-41.

31. *D&A*, 49.33-43.

32. AC, "Sermon on the Law," in Young, *Historical Documents*, 263.

33. See especially Robert Frederick West, *Alexander Campbell and Natural Religion* (New Haven: Yale University Press, 1948). Also in regard to the role of these scholars in biblical criticism, Simon J. De Vries, *Bible and Theology in the Netherlands* (New York: Peter Lang, 1989), 5 ff.

34. "Johannes Cocceius," in John McClintock and James Strong, *Cyclopaedia of Biblical, Theological, and Ecclesiastical Literature* (New York: Harper and Brothers, 1895).

35. Charles S. McCoy and J. Wayne Baker, *Fountainhead of Federalism: Heinrich Bullinger and the Covenantal Tradition; with a translation of* De Testamento seu foedere Dei unico et aeterno (Louisville: Westminster/John Knox Press, 1991), 118.

36. *D&A*, 51.28-52.2.

37. David Tappan, *Lectures on Jewish Antiquities; Delivered at Harvard University in Cambridge, A.D. 1802 & 1803* (Cambridge: W. Hilliard and E. Lincoln, 1807).

38. David C. Steinmetz, "The Superiority of Precritical Exegesis," *Theology Today* 37 (April 1980): 27-38.

39. See the insightful article on the centers of AC's biblical studies, hence theology, by M. Eugene Boring, "The Formation of a Tradition: Alexander Campbell and the New Testament," *The Disciples Theological Digest* 2, no. 1 (1987): 5-54; and his book, M. Eugene Boring, *Disciples and the Bible: A History of Disciples Biblical Interpretation in North America* (St. Louis: Chalice Press, 1997). Also Thomas H. Olbricht, "Alexander Campbell as a Theologian," *Impact* 21 (1988): 22-37.

40. See Dwight Bozeman, "Alexander Campbell, Child of the Puritans?" in *Lectures in Honor of the Alexander Campbell Bicentennial, 1788–1988* (Nashville: Disciples of Christ Historical Society, 1988), 3-18.

41. Jon Butler, *Awash in a Sea of Faith: Christianizing the American People* (Cambridge, Ma.: Harvard University Press, 1992), 257, 258.

42. This compounding of the discrete is especially evident in the works of Lamar and Dungan. J. S. Lamar, *The Organon of Scripture* (Philadelphia: J.B. Lippincott, 1960); D. R. Dungan, *Hermeneutics* (1888; reprint, Cincinnati: The Standard Publishing, n.d.); compare J. D. Thomas, *We Be Brethren* (Abilene: Biblical Research Press, 1958).

A Pentadic Analysis of Two Pleas for Christian Unity

Jeffrey Dale Hobbs

The prayer for Christian unity began with Christ himself (Jn 1:21), and continues today. This essay proposes to examine two pleas for Christian unity using the rhetorical theory of Kenneth Burke. According to Em Griffin, "Kenneth Burke was the foremost rhetorician of the twentieth century. Burke wrote about rhetoric; other rhetoricians write about Burke."[1]

Burke's theory seems especially relevant to the study of pleas for unity because of his focus on identification; for Burke, rhetoric is identification. "You persuade a man only insofar as you can talk his language by speech, gesture, tonality, order, image, attitude, idea, identifying your ways with his."[2] Additionally, Burke equates identification with consubstantiality. "To identify A with B is to make A 'consubstantial' with B."[3]

The two calls for Christian unity to be analyzed are Thomas Campbell's *Declaration and Address* and E. Glenn Wagner's *The Awesome Power of Shared Beliefs*.[4] TC's *D&A* is important because of its historical significance. "This document, which calls for Christian unity through a return to the clear and unambiguous teachings of the New Testament, in many ways chartered the course for the movement the Campbells led."[5] Wagner's book is chosen because of the contemporary prominence of the Promise Keepers movement.

This essay will proceed by explaining relevant aspects of Kenneth Burke's works, including the methodology to be used, applying the methodology to the two pleas, and discussing the results.

Dramatism and the Pentad

Burke saw life as a drama played out in human language. By examining the words of a person, one can determine his or her motives. Motives are grammatical creations that explain "what people are doing and why they are doing it."[6] As Sonya K. Foss explains:

> We use rhetoric to constitute and present a particular view of our situation, just as the presentation of a play creates a certain world or situation inhabited by characters who engage in actions in a setting. Through rhetoric, we size up situations and name their structures and outstanding ingredients. How we describe a situation indicates how we are perceiving it, the choices we see available to us, and the action we are likely to take in our situation.[7]

The pentad is a tool used to investigate motives. Burke wrote that "any complete statement about motives will offer some kind of answer to these five questions: what was done (act), when or where it was done (scene), who did it (agent), how he did it (agency), and why (purpose)."[8] The pentad was not designed to be an exact instrument—it highlights rather than eliminates ambiguity.[9] In other words, multiple descriptions of motives may exist for the same situation. The nature of the situation, however, changes as the elements of the pentad are described in different terms.

Another term important in understanding the concept of motives is the notion of ratios. "A ratio is the pairing of two of the elements in the pentad in order to discover the relationship between them and the effect that each has on the other."[10] A ratio highlights the key or predominant term in a given pentad which helps specify the condition or nature of the situation.[11] "Discovery of the dominant term provides insight into what dimension of the situation the rhetor privileges or sees as most important."[12]

For example, David Ling argues that the language used in Senator Edward Kennedy's "Chappaquiddick" speech developed a pentad that emphasized a scene-agent ratio. Kennedy argued that he (the agent) should not be held accountable for failing to report the accident that led to the drowning of Mary Jo Kopechne (the act) because he, himself, was nearly drowned in the accident and he became exhausted and alarmed when his repeated attempts to rescue Mary Jo failed because of the "strong" and "murky" tide (the scene). Ling concludes that while the speech helped Kennedy achieve forgiveness from the people of Massachusetts, it ultimately hurt his chances to become President. According to Ling:

> Kennedy's description of the events of July 18th presented him as a normal agent who was overcome by an extraordinary scene. However, the myth that has always surrounded the office of the President is that it must be held by an agent who can make clear, rational decisions in an extraordinary scene.[13]

Additionally, Burke argues that identifying the predominant term in the pentad helps to identify the motive with a particular philosophy. Scene is associated with materialism, agent with idealism, agency with pragmatism, purpose with mysticism, and act with realism.[14]

One recurring drama for Burke is the language of victimage. He contends that language leads to guilt—language leads to guilt because of "the negative" and "being rotten with perfection."[15] It allows us to invent negatives or "shall nots," and since we are human, we break the commands and feel guilty. Language also allows us to imagine a perfect condition. Utopias exist only in words. Again, since we are human, we fail to reach perfection, which results in more guilt. We then seek ways to remove our guilt. Mortification is one method, but victimage or scapegoating is more common. The scapegoat is ritualistically loaded with "certain unwanted evils" and sacrificed,[16] performing the "role of vicarious atonement."[17]

With this theory in mind, it is time to apply the pentad to two pleas for Christian unity—first to TC's and then to Wagner's.

Thomas Campbell's *Declaration and Address*

Act:	Adopting one rule—the rule of Scripture
Scene:	The right time
Agent:	Real Christians of every denomination
Agency:	Searching the Scriptures for express terms and approved precedents

Purpose: To restore the Christian unity of the primitive church
Ratio: Agency-purpose

The act requested is for Christians to adopt one rule—the rule of Scripture. TC says that we should be "returning to and holding fast by, the original standard; taking the divine word alone for our rule."[18] Later he writes:

> . . . if the divine word be not the standard of a party—Then are we not a party, for we have adopted no other. If to maintain its alone sufficiency be not a party principle: then we are not a party—If to justify this principle by our practice, in making a rule of it, and of it alone; and not of our own opinions, nor of those of others, be not a party principle—then are we not a party—If to propose and practice neither more nor less than it expressly reveals and enjoins be not a partial business, then are we not a party.[19]

The scene is a set of circumstances that has led to the right time to act. TC asks, "Can the Lord expect, or require, any thing less, from a people in such unhampered circumstances—from a people so liberally furnished with all means and mercies, than a thorough reformation, in all things civil and religious according to his word?"[20] He continues, "The auspicious phenomena of the times, furnish collateral arguments of a very encouraging nature, that our dutiful and pious endeavors shall not be in vain in the Lord."[21] Finally, he asks, "And have not the churches both in Europe and America, since that period [the French Revolution], discovered a more than usual concern for the removal of contentions, for the healing of divisions . . . ?"[22]

TC describes a situation in which Christians of every denomination become the agent for action. He addresses "the truly religious of all parties,"[23] "Our dear Brethren, of all denominations," "every sincere and upright christian,"[24] and "all that know their Bible."[25] He says that "It is an open field, an extensive work, to which all are equally welcome, equally invited."[26]

The agency or means to achieve unity is to search the Scriptures for "the original pattern laid down in the New Testament."[27] One is to search for "express terms" (including commands) and "approved precedent" (or approved examples).[28] One is to avoid "human formulas"[29] and "creed(s)."[30] TC asks, "have all, or any, of those human compilations been able to prevent divisions, to heal breeches, or to produce and maintain unity of sentiment, even amongst those who have most firmly, and solemnly, embraced them?"[31]

The stated purpose is to "restore to the church its primitive unity, purity, and prosperity"[32] and "to adopt and recommend such measures . . . as would restore unity, peace, and purity to the whole church of God."[33]

The ratio is one of agency-purpose with agency being the predominant term of the pentad. In other words, the agent (Christians) cannot act (adopt the one rule) and achieve the purpose (unity) without having the agency (searching the Scriptures for express terms and approved precedents) to discover the rule of Scripture. The agency predominates because it is only through these means that unity may be achieved. There is no other way:

> For if holding fast in profession and practice whatever is expressly revealed and enjoined in the divine standard does not, under the promised influence of the divine spirit, prove an adequate basis for promoting and maintaining unity, peace, and purity, we utterly despair of attaining those invaluable privileges, by adopting the standard of any party.[34]

Later TC argues that "Christ knew no other way of leading us to the knowledge of himself, at least has prescribed no other, but by searching the Scriptures, with reliance upon his holy Spirit."[35]

The Awesome Power of Shared Beliefs

Act:	Promising—the sixth promise
Scene:	"Fort Misidentification" and friendly fire
Agent:	Men (males)—Promise Keepers
Agency:	A Creed—Promise Keepers Statement of Faith
Purpose:	To achieve unity in diversity
Ratio:	Agent-act

In *The Awesome Power of Shared Beliefs*, by E. Glenn Wagner, the desired act is for men (males) to, "Promise with me to be a man committed to unity."[36] Wagner is Promise Keepers' Vice-President of Ministry Advancement, and the sixth promise of a Promise Keeper is to be "committed to reaching beyond any racial and denominational barriers to demonstrate the power of biblical unity."[37]

The scene is one of chaos in which Christians are killing each other with friendly fire.[38] According to Wagner, ". . . in Fort Misidentification there is another battle going on, and it's all taking place within the four walls of the fort! No one is shooting at the real enemy; rather, everyone is shooting at each other."[39]

The agent of action is men (males). The "ideas shared" in the book "are specifically directed toward men—Christian men, both leaders and followers."[40] "It is a book to call men to action."[41] It is a book that "clarifies the mission statement that every man so desperately needs in life."[42] An abundance of war and sports metaphors provide additional evidence of the book's male focus.

The agency to achieving unity is the adoption of a creed. The "important" or "essential" elements of the faith are found in the Apostles' Creed and the Nicene Creed.[43] "[T]he Apostles' Creed and Nicene Creed are vital summaries of the truth."[44] In Wagner's view, "all that is necessary to add to the Apostle's Creed and the Nicene Creed is the issue of the inerrancy of Scripture. And I add that only because it was not an issue back then as it is today. The early church fathers accepted the Scriptures as inerrant. We do too."[45] With the inerrancy of Scripture added to these creeds, Wagner proposes five core beliefs on which to base unity: the Bible is revealed truth; God exists; Jesus Christ lived and died to provide us an example; the Holy Spirit enables us to live a Christian life; and because of our sinfulness, Jesus had to provide for "the redemption of man."[46] These five core beliefs correspond to the "Promise Keepers Statement of Faith."[47]

The purpose is to achieve "unity in diversity."[48] As Warner explains, "Don't think for a minute that because the emphasis of this book is on unity we have any intention of shortchanging the importance of diversity. It is of utmost importance to strive for unity, but it is diversity that enhances the unity."[49]

The ratio is one of agent-act with agent being the predominant term of the pentad. The agent predominates because "The awesome power of shared beliefs will only become reality when *we* come together, based on these beliefs, with a unity of purpose and witness to a lost world."[50]

Discussion and Conclusions

First, by comparing the two pentads, one can see that these two pleas for unity are not the same plea. They are distinct movements. TC and

E. Glen Wagner are not providing the same description of motives —identification is lacking. One of the most important differences to consider is in the element of agency. Wagner relies on a creed or "Statement of Faith" to achieve unity. TC abhors such an idea of a creed—one must return to the Scriptures.

Second, examining the pentad of the *D&A* reveals some interesting insights into the motives and difficulties of the Restoration Movement. With agency as the dominant term, the corresponding philosophy is pragmatism—the philosophy of means.[51] Burke argues that agency is symbolic of formative experiences "in the person of the mother" or "maternal care."[52] In other words, agency emphasizes the process of maturing. One is restoring, but never restored. One is becoming, but never being. One is placed in the task of achieving "perfect" unity, when one's method says that one must continue to search for the keys to unity. As TC himself notes:

> We only take it for granted, that such a state of perfection is neither intended, nor attainable in this world, as will free the church from all those weaknesses, mistakes, and mismanagements, from which she will be completely exempted in heaven;—however sound and upright she may now be in her profession, intention, and practice.[53]

The tendency to feel guilt and search for a scapegoat must be guarded against in such a situation. The most obvious scapegoat is anyone who criticizes the agency or means (express terms and approved precedents) to achieving unity by advancing a "new hermeneutic."

Third, examining the pentad of *The Awesome Power of Shared Beliefs* reveals some interesting insights into the motives and difficulties of the Promise Keepers movement. With agent as the dominant term, the corresponding philosophy is idealism.[54] According to Burke, in idealism the "ideal" created by the agent affects the agent's notion of reality, changing the "ideal" into the "real."[55] In other words, the agent's "ideals" are taken as the "real." In the case of Promise Keepers, there is the danger that "The Promise Keepers Statement of Faith" (the "ideal") becomes a substitute for the Scriptures (what's really real). Additionally, the emphasis on the agent as men/males rightfully opens the organization to charges of patriarchy and sexism. Finally, with the act of making promises, and knowing that promises "should not" be broken, comes the act of breaking promises. Again, one must be on guard to avoid the tendency to scapegoat. The most obvious scapegoats are those who refuse to make the "promise."

It is no small irony that pleas for unity can also create pressures for disunity.

Notes

1. Em Griffin, *A First Look at Communication Theory*, 3d ed. (New York: McGraw-Hill, 1997), 319.

2. Kenneth Burke, *A Rhetoric of Motives* (Berkeley: University of California Press, 1969), 55.

3. Burke, *Rhetoric*, 21.

4. E. Glenn Wagner, *The Awesome Power of Shared Beliefs: Five Things Every Man Should Know* (Dallas: Word Publishing, 1995), 28.

5. Richard T. Hughes, *Reviving the Ancient Faith: The Story of Churches of Christ in America* (Grand Rapids: William B. Eerdmans, 1996), 11.

6. Kenneth Burke, *A Grammar of Motives* (New York: George Braziller, 1955), x.

7. Sonya K. Foss, *Rhetorical Criticism: Exploration and Practice*, 2d ed. (Prospect Heights: Waveland Press, 1996), 456.

8. Burke, *Grammar*, x.

9. Burke, *Grammar*, xii-xiii.

10. Foss, *Rhetorical Criticism*, 460.

11. Burke, *Grammar*, 151.

12. Foss, *Rhetorical Criticism*, 460.

13. David A. Ling, "A Pentadic Analysis of Senator Edward Kennedy's Address to the People of Massachusetts, July 25, 1969," *Central States Speech Journal* 21, no. 2 (1970): 85-86.

14. Burke, *Grammar*, 128.

15. Kenneth Burke, *Language as Symbolic Action* (Berkeley: University of California Press, 1966), 16.

16. Kenneth Burke, *The Philosophy of Literary Form*, 3d ed. (Berkeley: University of California Press, 1973), 40-41.

17. Burke, *Grammar*, 406.

18. Thomas Campbell, *Declaration and Address of the Christian Association of Washington* (Washington, Pa.: Brown & Sample, 1809), 4.3-4.

19. *D&A*, 25.17-25.

20. *D&A*, 8.10-14.

21. *D&A*, 8.17-20.

22. *D&A*, 8.27-29.

23. *D&A*, 7.30-31.

24. *D&A*, 28.3.

25. *D&A*, 31.12.
26. *D&A*, 9.27-29.
27. *D&A*, 10.42-43.
28. *D&A*, 10.49; 47.14.
29. *D&A*, 36.27.
30. *D&A*, 39.38.
31. *D&A*, 38.24-27.
32. *D&A*, 10.14.
33. *D&A*, 3.29-32.
34. *D&A*, 22.11-16.
35. *D&A*, 41.47-49.
36. Wagner, *Shared Beliefs*, 28.
37. "The Seven Promises of a Promise Keeper," http://www.promisekeepers.org/faqs/core/faqscore24.htm.
38. Wagner, *Shared Beliefs*, 3-17.
39. Wagner, *Shared Beliefs*, 8.
40. Wagner, *Shared Beliefs*, xiv.
41. Wagner, *Shared Beliefs*, 43.
42. Wagner, *Shared Beliefs*, 175.
43. Wagner, *Shared Beliefs*, 36-37.
44. Wagner, *Shared Beliefs*, 39.
45. Wagner, *Shared Beliefs*, 38.
46. Wagner, *Shared Beliefs*, 42-43.
47. "Promise Keepers Statement of Faith," http://www.promisekeepers.org/faqs/core/faqscore22.htm.
48. Wagner, *Shared Beliefs*, v, xii.
49. Wagner, *Shared Beliefs*, xiii.
50. Wagner, *Shared Beliefs*, 186.
51. Burke, *Grammar*, 128.
52. Burke, *Grammar*, 283.
53. *D&A*, 39.6-11.
54. Burke, *Grammar*, 128.
55. Burke, *Grammar*, 174.

Church Unity, Biblical Purity, Spiritual Maturity: Theological Synthesis in the *Declaration and Address*

Harold Kent Straughn

When it comes to interpreting Thomas Campbell's *Declaration and Address*, one issue is indisputable: all branches of the Stone-Campbell Movement claim the *D&A* as a foundational document. As such it seeds the faith and identity of more than four million persons worldwide. In fact, the *D&A* is one of the most analyzed documents created by the Stone-Campbell Movement. Beyond this agreement as to its importance, however, opinions diverge dramatically as to its meaning.

One perspective, the one that has shaped the Christian Church (Disciples of Christ), views the *D&A* as a clarion call to institutional church unity, and, in fact, as a wellspring of the ecumenical movement. Thus, its value belongs not only to the direct heirs of Campbell and Stone but also to all of modern Protestantism and, indeed, to the world's religions.

A quite different view is often held among the two groups known as the Independent Christian Churches/Churches of Christ and the non-instrumental Churches of Christ. Here the conviction is that TC set in motion a biblically based restoration movement to clear away centuries of apostate faith and order, and to replace a corrupt tradition with the original one true church fully revealed in the New Testament.

According to both the ecumenical and restorationist views, the *D&A* inspired events of historic consequence. Yet we are left to wonder how one document could inspire such different religious visions. Could one of the views be a serious misreading? Is the *D&A* vision so complex and subtle that it proved impossible to hold the creative tension? Was the message so inconsistent that both sets of conclusions are faithful to the text?

I have attempted to explore TC's personal and cultural situation, to seek what might have impelled him to construct the *D&A* as he did, and to suggest a new explanation of how unity and restoration sometimes competed, sometimes dovetailed, and sometimes synthesized into something new.

Seceding from the Seceders: TC's Encounters with Unity and Purity Movements in America

It is difficult to know what TC expected to find in the churches of America. What he actually found was a sectarianism more intransigent than any he had faced in his early years as a minister in Ireland.

The process of his removal from the Associate Synod of North America began following a service he conducted at Cannamaugh, Pennsylvania, when he invited Presbyterians of all parties to participate in communion. Even "occasional communion" with other Christians who had not affiliated formally with a Seceder congregation was forbidden by the Associate Synod of North America, although it was permitted by its counterparts in both Scotland and Ireland.

The minutes of the Presbytery tell the story of TC's trial and reveal that more was involved than his ecumenical tendencies. TC clearly expressed serious reservations about his church's theology. The seven charges brought against him objected to his opposition to creeds as terms of communion; his sympathy for the lay ministry; his desire for fellowship with other churches; his idea that preachers do not need a divine call; and his view that believers can live in this world without sinning. He more or less admitted guilt to all of these except the last one, but insisted that he, rather than his peers, stood on scriptural ground.

After the Presbytery suspended him, TC appealed to the Synod in Philadelphia. His suspension was rescinded, but he was rebuked for his aberrations. Back in Western Pennsylvania, the Presbytery resented his reinstatement. It gave him no appointment, and finally suspended him again, this time for not submitting to its authority. By this time he was already out on his own, for about midway through the dispute TC had withdrawn from the Presbytery, left the Presbyterian ministry, and become in effect an independent.

The conflicts that resulted in TC's status as excommunicant when his family arrived have been told well elsewhere. I want only to emphasize two quotations that show how TC's passion for unity was influenced by the wounds he received from the Presbytery. "How great the injustice," he pleads with his accusers,

> how aggravated the injury will appear, to thrust out from communion a Christian brother, a fellow-minister, for saying and doing none other things than those which our Divine Lord and his apostles have taught and enjoined.[1]

TC's appeal to Scripture alone is both poignant and somewhat arrogant. Small wonder that he appears divisive from the Presbytery's point of view. In fact, they were correct in holding that TC is asserting a new right to individual liberty of interpretation, a view that, in effect, he alone may determine the meaning of Scripture, apart from a community consensus. "I absolutely refuse," he writes, "as inadmissible and schismatic, the introduction of human opinions and human inventions into the faith and worship of the Church."[2] He returned the fifty dollars the Presbytery gave him on his arrival in America. By the time he was deposed, he had already written the *D&A* and had organized the Christian Association.

His break with the Presbyterian Church placed TC in a grave crisis of both financial security and spiritual identity. While free from what he felt was a tradition-bound straitjacket, he was also outside the entire visible church of his time and place. TC found himself "alone with the word of God and the souls of men."

1810–1828: TC's Two Decades of Crisis of Security, Community, and Identity

In what James Cook[3] has described as TC's "betwixt and between" crisis, TC and his followers began to seek a new means for survival and identity. Cook's article on liminality, a contribution to this seminar, asserts that the *D&A* was a spontaneous expression of ideological *communitas* that attempted to sustain a feeling of transcendent power during a crisis when a group possesses no power or identity. Cook observes that the rereading of the *D&A* propositions at each meeting, and, presumably, study and discussion of its principles at intervening sessions, served to maintain the *communitas*. According to Cook's approach, this purpose helps explain the vital, spontaneous outburst of creative crisis theology that resulted in the *D&A*.

Indeed, for the next several years, this temporary bridge appeared to be precisely the fate of the *D&A*, for the Christian Association never grew beyond the circle of friends who followed TC out of the Seceders. Alexander Campbell says that his father succeeded in constituting two Christian congregations in 1810. For the next five years, TC ministered to the two churches, assisted by Elder James Foster.

By the end of 1810, however, TC saw the need to apply for admission to the Synod of Pittsburgh. The response to his petition was abrupt and severe, as we may see in the minutes of the Synod for the afternoon session of 4 October:

> After hearing Mr. Campbell at length, and his answers to various questions proposed to him, the Synod unanimously resolved, that however specious the plan of the Christian Association and however seducing its professions, as experience of the effects of similar projects in other parts has evinced their baleful tendency and destructive operations on the whole interests of religion by promoting divisions instead of union, by degrading the ministerial character, by providing free admission to any errors in doctrine, and to any corruptions in discipline, whilst a nominal approbation of the Scriptures as the only standard of truth may be professed, the Synod are constrained to disapprove the plan and its native effects.[4]

In short, the Synod charged that while TC spoke of unity, his message would create only division. The most divisive aspect was his rejecting creeds and other interpretations of Scripture in favor of Scripture alone. The comment years later by Robert Richardson likely preserves the sting felt by TC and his followers: "For a party to have admitted into their bosom those who were avowedly bent on the destruction of partyism would, of course, have been perfectly suicidal."[5] Still, the Synod's doubts would become part and parcel of the debates that eventually would result in breakdowns in unity among the heirs of the Campbells. One can only speculate whether the future would have been different if the Christian Association had succeeded as a parachurch organization similar to its

British models. Certainly TC had good reason, based on earlier experience, to envision the success of a movement in which unity could develop, traditions fall away, the Scriptures be exalted and studied, and the church expand and thrive.

TC's efforts during the next decade, from 1810 to 1820, tend to be overlooked in the history of the Stone-Campbell Movement, though they are the best place to look for TC's own understanding of what he expected the *D&A* to yield. In the autumn of 1813, TC moved to Guernsey County, Ohio, where he engaged in farming and conducted "an English mercantile academy," while he continued to press his vision for the Christian Association. He spoke frequently on the subject of "The Christian Institution" wherever he could find a hearing. Unfortunately, according to AC's remembrance fifty years later, "the religious mind of the community was so strongly attached to their respective church establishments" that his father labored with "but little apparent success."[6]

Finding so little response to his efforts, TC moved in the autumn of 1815 to Pittsburgh, where he again attempted "to constitute a worshiping congregation upon the foundation of the apostles and prophets." He opened another mercantile academy and used the school building for worship. Here again he made little impact on the community, failing to nurture a group large enough to support his work.

Two years later, in the fall of 1817, he moved again, this time to Kentucky. Here he worked more closely with existing Baptist churches and achieved more positive results. The biggest obstacle to his teaching was the Calvinist bent of the Baptists, from which TC had been gradually but inexorably moving away. He struggled with his understanding of the nature of conversion, which slowed his effectiveness in drawing new members. Although he gained more adherents in Kentucky than in Pennsylvania, he still was unable either to persuade congregations to follow his lead or to create one from scratch.

As a result, in the autumn of 1819 he moved back to Washington County, Pennsylvania, and made contact with the two congregations he had planted some ten years before. After being out of touch for most of the decade, TC discovered that these two congregations had drawn into their orbit six small congregations with about two hundred total members. These six churches, along with TC's two, in 1815 had united with the Redstone Baptist Association. Unlike the earlier union attempt with the Seceders, this time they had asked for and received agreement to be left free to be led into new directions by their search for a New Testament model for the church.

Their freedom came to a crisis, however, in the fall of 1816 when AC delivered his celebrated "Sermon on the Law," arguing against a religious practice unless it was authorized in the New Testament as well as the Old. Not surprisingly, since many Baptist and other Calvinist practices would come under challenge, enough opposition arose that the Campbells escaped excommunication only by withdrawing from the Redstone Association and uniting with the Mahoning Baptist Association on the Ohio Western Reserve.

It was not until 1828, when more than one thousand persons responded to the fiery evangelistic preaching of Walter Scott in the course of a year, that the Mahoning churches became strong enough to create their own independent association outside the Baptist orbit. With the launching of this independent movement the Christian Association of Washington County, Pennsylvania, at long last found its fulfillment.

Or, as those who held to its parachurch and nondenominational vision might have said, yet another defeat.

Unity, Purity, Maturity: Assessing the Message of the *D&A* in Its Own Time

In the original draft of the document, the *D&A* is divided into three sections. The first constitutes what was styled the Declaration, the second the Address, and the third the Appendix. The Appendix contains about 60 percent of the whole, as originally published, the Address about one-third, and the Declaration about one-sixteenth.

Unity: Work across Confessional Lines

Although the *D&A* calls ministers in all churches to discard their creeds and customs and come together upon a simple New Testament platform, it is hard to argue that TC thought that those who answered the call would have to separate from the denominations to which they belonged.

Nowhere does TC invite others to follow in his steps and withdraw from their church bodies. The Christian Association as TC envisioned it offered the security of staying in one's home church, the avoidance of opposition that could kill the work in its crib, and the opportunity to work in concert across confessional lines for causes with which all agreed. In so doing, the Christian Association might embody the unity TC sought even as it helped to influence existing bodies to narrow their differences.

The reality turned out to be quite different. Opponents and supporters of the idea of an association saw people begin to leave the existing churches, even as TC was insisting there was no new church for them to join. As F. D. Kershner has observed, "A condition so anomalous could not and did not exist for long."[7]

This "anomalous condition" is only part of the story.

Purity: No Biblical "Nonessentials"

TC presented the Bible as both authoritative and also to be interpreted freely in accordance with individual conscience and rational study. Unlike Earl Irvin West, I do not hear in TC any echoes of the Meldenius unity-liberty-charity distinction between essentials and nonessentials.[8]

In fact, for TC, there are no nonessentials in Scripture. There is biblical truth, and there are human interpretations that vary from it. Critics of TC in his time and ever since have argued that the one principle contradicts the other, and that the Scripture text and the personal judgment of the individual cannot both be authoritative. TC does not face the criticism directly, although it is possible to see why it never bothered him as it did later generations.

TC was quite capable of stressing obedience to the minutiae of Scripture. However, he tended to consider such details as the province of the more mature believers. Their responsibility certainly did not include separating from or excommunicating those who did not agree. Rather, they had an obligation to continue to discuss the points of disagreement until a consensus was reached, based on his confidence in the *sensus communis*.

Maturity: Leadership, Not Disfellowship

TC made a distinction based on what I should call the stages of spiritual maturity that readers brought to Scripture. In my analysis of TC's special fusion of church unity and biblical purity, I shall use the shorthand term "maturity" to capsule what I believe is unique about the *D&A*: TC's particular synthesis of unity and purity.

TC believed that the only legitimate reason for differences of opinion lay in the amount of a person's exposure to Scripture. *As a result, his issue was not what to do when two people disagreed over the meaning of Scripture, but rather what to do when a less spiritually mature person could not understand the full teaching that a more mature person might possess*. Thus, TC's greatest disagreement with creedal statements was not that they went beyond Scripture, or that they failed to summarize Scripture accurately, but rather that they imposed Scripture's teachings on believers prematurely, before people had a chance to discover it for themselves.

For TC, mature leaders had a responsibility to help the less mature, following the counsels of both Jesus and Paul for stronger believers to help the weaker, and for the rich in faith to help the poor. Creeds are wrong because they impose faith rather than nurture it. For TC, all believers eventually could come to agree on the truth of Scripture because that truth ultimately was both reasonable and consistent. There was no tension for him between the unity of the church and the purity of the Scriptures. Indeed, he was more Catholic than Protestant in holding that a united church preserved a pure Scripture and that a pure Scripture would create a united church.

While some have argued that TC failed to hold to a creative tension between private judgment and the authority of Scripture, I maintain that he does do so. In fact, I argue that the issue of this particular tension arose only considerably later, as his followers traveled further down separate paths, and sought to explain how it happened.

Maturity, Not Imposed Conformity, as the Proper Path to Unity

The primary contribution of TC to Christian unity lies in his attempt to furnish a definite and concrete proposal by which unity could be obtained. This effort went beyond the achievements of the evangelistic societies in his home country, where unity was a byproduct of their preaching and benevolence efforts. The Christian Association would be a way to convey to power-sensitive clergy the proper means of spiritual nurture: evangelism by means of patient nurture of individuals. Eventually new Christians might come to understand and affirm the great doctrines of the Bible and the creeds, rather than be required to accept them before they understood them.

TC cites "large tracts of country entirely destitute of a gospel ministry," as well as "churches so weakened" that they cannot send out missionaries, and the laity so divided that they "will not receive" those who by chance may come to them.

TC refers frequently to "our brethren of all denominations." Even so, this oft-repeated phrase, while an indication that TC regarded the members of existing churches as Christians, does not provide evidence that he affirmed the institutions themselves, or their teachings. This is particularly true of the way he felt that they used creeds as means for those in ecclesiastical power to coerce those whose consciences were still works in progress.

TC expresses his vision of Christian unity in two sentences:

> With you all we desire to unite in the bonds of an entire Christian unity—Christ alone being the head, the center, his word the rule—an explicit belief of, and manifest conformity to it, in all things—the terms. More than this, you will not require of us; and less we cannot require of you.[9]

Here TC seems to assume it is possible to know the will of God in all vital particulars and that it is also possible for this knowledge to be universally recognized for what it is. Agreement on right belief is possible, and so, in consequence, should agreement be possible on right action, taken together. His only caution is for the strong to be patient with the weak:

> If no such divine and adequate basis of union can be fairly exhibited as will meet the approbation of every upright and intelligent Christian: nor such mode of procedure adopted in favor of the weak, as will not oppress their consciences, then the accomplishment of this grand object upon principle, must be forever impossible.[10]

While his position makes any sort of compromise impossible, patience is another matter. TC allows not only the possibility but the requirement for "the good natured principle of Christian forbearance and gracious condescension."[11]

Perhaps the most important section of the *D&A* in regard to the issue of church unity and biblical purity is found in Proposition 6:

> That although inferences and deductions from Scripture premises, when fairly inferred, may be truly called the doctrine of God's holy word: yet are they not formally binding upon the consciences of Christians farther

> than they perceive the connection, and evidently see that they are so; for their faith must not stand in the wisdom of men; but in the power and veracity of God—therefore no such deductions can be made terms of communion, but do properly belong to the after and progressive edification of the church. Hence it is evident that no such deductions or inferential truths ought to have any place in the church's confession.[12]

I see in these statements the primary evidence of my contention that for TC the major distinction is not between essentials and nonessentials (which he calls "a trite indefinite distinction").[13] Nor is it between faith and opinion, much less between church unity and biblical purity. The issue is between those who see a biblical principle clearly and those who do not.

The responsibility of those who see an issue clearly is that of restraint—not to "bind upon the consciences of Christians further than they see the connection."[14] TC seems to be referring to creeds and those who bind them on humble followers who cannot understand their complex theology when he alludes to those who practice "the wisdom of men" rather than "the power and veracity of God." However, he also seems to be taking the issue a step further than creeds, and extending it to the idea of binding personal or collective "deductions" and "inferential truths" upon those who cannot follow the logic.

TC's fuller explication shows an appreciation of a certain validity to creeds, as is found in Proposition 7:

> That although doctrinal exhibitions of the great system of divine truths, and defensive testimonies in opposition to prevailing errors, be highly expedient; and the more full and explicit they be, for those purposes, the better; yet as these must be in a great measure the effect of human reasoning, and of course must contain many inferential truths, they ought not to be made terms of Christian communion; unless we suppose, what is contrary to fact, that none have a right to the communion of the church, but such as possess a very clear and decisive judgment; or are come to a very high degree of doctrinal information; whereas the church from the beginning did, and ever will, consist of little children and young men, as well as fathers.[15]

Here TC seems to give creeds the same value as that of works of systematic theology—they are fine for scholars, and are not necessarily wrong or unbiblical, and, indeed, may actually help some people come to a clearer view of scriptural truth. TC's primary problem with creeds is that people misuse them. Creeds cease being repositories of traditional theology and become weapons that the powerful use against the weak, and that mature believers use to intimidate the less mature.

What seems to be motivating TC's views both of church unity and of biblical purity, coming from his own scars from bouts with what he considers abuses of power and morality, is a vision of a more democratic process in church governance. He would open access in having a say in the life of the church to all those who meet the minimum requirements of faith—or so he implies in Proposition 8:

> That as it is not necessary that persons should have a particular knowledge or distinct apprehension of all divinely revealed truths in order to entitle them to a place in the Church; neither should they, for this purpose, be required to make a profession more extensive than their knowledge; but that, on the contrary, their having a due measure of Scriptural self-knowledge respecting their lost and perishing condition by nature and practice, and of the way of salvation through Jesus Christ, accompanied with a profession of their faith in and obedience to him, in all things, according to his word, is all that is absolutely necessary to qualify them for admission into his Church.[16]

I do not think TC is here trying to redefine the plan of salvation, or to reduce the basics of who is a Christian, or to reveal whether one can be a member of an existing church and carry out his vision for unity and purity. Rather, I think he is doing something far more radical. He is trying to upset the power structure of the existing churches by "entitling" all believers to have "a place in the church" so long as they follow the recognized Calvinist *ordo salutis*. Such persons would be free to exercise leadership at levels that heretofore were open only to those who satisfied the power structure that they would meekly acknowledge the authority of a creed they did not understand.

It seems clear that such an influx of new "nullificators" of the existing order would be more threatening to the established order than either withdrawing from the churches in a sectarian fashion or staying in them and merely working across ecclesiastical lines on projects of mutual interest. It seems equally clear that both TC and the Synod leaders understood to some degree the consequences of such a change.

Proposition 9 expresses what appears at first glance to be a more irenic and idealistic version of TC's vision:

> That all that are enabled through grace to make such a profession, and to manifest the reality of it in their tempers and conduct, should consider each other as the precious saints of God, should love each other as brethren, children of the same family and Father, temples of the same Spirit, members of the same body, subjects of the same grace, objects of the same Divine love, bought with the same price, and joint-heirs of the same inheritance. Whom God hath thus joined together no man should dare to put asunder.[17]

With this sevenfold repetition of the word "same," TC asserts not simply the rhetoric of unity, but also the rhetoric of equality. Later history seems to confirm that, even though the Christian Association failed to survive as a parachurch organization, this egalitarian aspect of TC's vision certainly survived, and thrived—and not only among those who came out of existing groups to join the Campbell-Stone Movement. The Baptist, Methodist, and Presbyterian bodies that lost thousands of freedom-seeking members to the Disciples did not lose them all; the ensuing Second Great Awakening and subsequent revivals and social reforms clearly show the relentless democratization of Protestantism.

What, then, shall we make of the statement often considered TC's most passionate attack on religious division, Proposition 10?

> That division among the Christians is a horrid evil, fraught with many evils. It is antiChristian, as it destroys the visible unity of the body of Christ; as if he were divided against himself, excluding and excommunicating a part of himself. It is antiscriptural, as being strictly prohibited by his sovereign authority; a direct violation of his express command. It is antinatural, as it excites Christians to contemn, to hate, and oppose one another, who are bound by the highest and most endearing obligations to love each other as brethren, even as Christ has loved them. In a word, it is productive of confusion and of every evil work.[18]

Here again I see an underlying thread of democratization of the ecclesiastically powerful and the spiritually weak, the more mature and the less mature. TC's use of the biblical imagery of the "body of Christ" is closely connected to references to the weak and the strong, as Christopher R. Hutson has pointed out elsewhere in this volume:

> Among the Pauline epistles, he draws most heavily from the Corinthian letters and Romans. He pays particular attention to the weak and strong in Rom 14-15, to the related discussion in 1 Cor 8-10, and to the unity of

> the body in 1 Cor 12. The theme of unity also accounts for the disproportionately high number of references to Ephesians, since four references to that letter are to 4:2-6.[19]

In Proposition 11, TC draws a similar connection between disunity and the illegitimate use of power over the spiritually weak and immature. He goes so far as to say that "assumed authority" is the "immediate, obvious, and universally acknowledged cause" of disunity:

> That (in some instances) a partial neglect of the expressly revealed will of God, and (in others) an assumed authority for making the approbation of human opinions and human inventions a term of communion, by introducing them into the constitution, faith, or worship of the Church, are, and have been, the immediate, obvious, and universally acknowledged causes, of all the corruptions and divisions that ever have taken place in the Church of God.[20]

Propositions 12 and 13 seem to me to be summaries of the principles articulated in the earlier ones, presented in a somewhat more programmatic fashion. Proposition 12 contains four features: (1) only professed believers who acknowledge the authority of the Scriptures should be received into church membership; (2) only those who live a Christian life should be retained in the church; (3) ministers are to preach nothing but what is expressly enjoined in Scripture; (4) church practices should be drawn from apostolic practice with no additions.[21] Here TC appears to be closing in on a more rigorist program, although the rhetoric itself would have been acceptable to most Protestant bodies. He might have intended to make certain that nobody would read his treatise as favoring latitudinarianism, which was his greatest fear, as his 18,000-word defense against the charge in the Appendix makes clear.

TC's final proposition, however, was read in later times as a "loophole" to any literalistic understanding of apostolicity, because of its focus on the role of expedient actions taken in the face of the silence of Scripture:

> Lastly. That if any circumstantials indispensably necessary to the observance of divine ordinances be not found upon the page of express revelation, such, and such only, as are absolutely necessary for this purpose should be adopted under the title of human expedients, without any pretense to a more sacred origin, so that any subsequent alteration or

> difference in the observance of these things might produce no contention nor division in the Church.[22]

One may wonder why TC uses so few words on the subject of "circumstantials" and the silence of Scripture, especially in light of the battles between the Lutheran tendency to favor them and the Calvinist tendency to restrict them. This may simply indicate that once again he is trying to state a principle generally accepted among Presbyterians and Baptists, and not intending to create a separatist, much less a restorationist, hermeneutic.

My conclusion, then, is that TC envisioned neither a program of organic unity of existing churches nor a restorationist church organizational program. Rather, he hoped for a parachurch method of working together in areas of interest where believers all agree, and where all can study and discover scriptural truth free from the imposition by creed or dogma of conclusions beyond their state of spiritual maturity.[23]

Maturity as the Path to Biblical Purity

Although TC began the *D&A* by declaring the need to "take all our measures directly and immediately from the Divine standard," his opposition to "human interpretations" was not that they were errant, but that they were enforced on people who could not, or at least did not yet, understand them. This was just as true of the commands of Scripture as of the teachings of creeds:

> We are also of opinion that as the Divine word is equally binding upon all, so all lie under an equal obligation to be bound by it and it alone; and not by any human interpretation of it; and that, therefore, no man has a right to judge his brother, except in so far as he manifestly violates the express letter of the law.[24]

This is not so much a plea for biblical authority as for the freedom and obligation of individuals to study Scripture and come to their own conclusions without being pressured by those who consider themselves more advanced in knowledge.

In claiming that the Spirit worked in conjunction with the Word in bringing about a proper interpretation of the Scriptures, TC is affirming what all Calvinists would agree on, unlike some of his descendants who argued that the Spirit did not work separate and apart from the Word.

Scripture is Campbell's defense against an imposed-from-above orthodoxy obtained through "committing to memory a catechism, or professing our approbation of a formula, made ready to our hand, which we may or may not have once read over."[25]

TC is opposing the efforts of clergy guardians of orthodoxy to emphasize assent without study over assent through study:

> A person may, however, by this short and easy method, become as orthodox as the apostle Paul . . . without ever once consulting the Bible, or so much as putting up a single petition for the Holy Spirit to guide him into all truth, to open his understanding to know the Scriptures.[26]

As Hutson has shown us, TC makes wide-ranging use of Scripture in the *D&A*, referring in one way or another to no fewer than twenty-one books from the Old Testament and twenty-five from the New Testament. Furthermore, he frequently used Scripture as a mood-setting rhetorical device for exhorting his readers with "a cascade of allusions and quotations" that "tumbles forth one upon another with little or no comment between." Such use of Scripture falls well outside the scrupulous logic of exegesis or carefully developed hermeneutic. I agree with Hutson that in many of TC's references to Scripture, "This is not exposition but exhortation . . . passages to which he refers but assumes a general familiarity with the Bible, and he uses the words of Scripture freely to give his own words a prophetic ring."

Still, it is not so much the hortatory quality of TC's use of Scripture that is important in understanding its power for him. It is the particular Scriptures that motivate him that matter more, as well as those that he does not emphasize, especially those that took on importance in later generations of his heirs.

In referring to the Old Testament, TC makes particular use of the prophets. Numerous times he repeats the prophetic phrase, "thus saith the Lord," and links it to the authority of Scripture with the phrases "express terms" and "approved precedents." But he also sees in the Old Testament a vast treasury of examples for Christians. He alludes to Joseph, Moses, Joshua, and Samson, as well as some numerous references to the Psalms, along with the prophets Isaiah, Jeremiah, Ezekiel, Daniel, Hosea, Amos, Micah, Haggai, Zechariah, and Malachi. Often he identifies himself with them as one called to proclaim a prophetic message. That message is both to decry the fallen state of the church in his day and to recapitulate the ancient restoration of Jerusalem.

It is significant that TC's use of Old Testament restoration imagery refers neither to a return to a well-developed view of New Testament church organization nor to a coming-together of existing churches. Instead, he evokes a general eschatological tone regarding the stirrings he is involved with in the church of his day. Even the four Gospels tend to be used to borrow Jesus' language of judgment rather than as models for individual or collective discipleship. The one exception is the Johannine material on the counsel to "love one another" and Jesus' prayer for unity, to which TC refers seven times.

What is most striking to me in terms of TC's favorite Scripture passages is his particular collection of citations from the Pauline epistles. Here his interest in the weak and the strong in Romans 14-15 (nine citations) and 1 Corinthians 8-10 (ten citations) supports his specific objections to creeds and church orders that allow the strong to impose their will on the weak. Similarly, he makes seven references to the spiritual unity of the body in 1 Corinthians 12 and four references to the same theme in Ephesians 4:2-6.

In contrast to later emphases, TC refers to Acts only twice; neither citation relates to the early church or early conversions. He cites Hebrews six times, to call for steadfastness and constancy, not, as in later generations, to illustrate the contrasts between Moses and Christ. The pastoral and general Epistles are cited for their exhortations to faithfulness, not for their treatment of church leadership. The Book of Revelation is used rhetorically in the same way he uses the Prophets, rather than for a vision of a particular end-time expectation.

In short, Hutson is correct when he concludes that

> . . . there is little emphasis in this document on the forms and structures of worship, which would later become the focus of the peculiarly Campbellite brand of "restoration."[27]

I would add that neither does TC use Scripture to urge a peculiarly Campbellite brand of organic church unity. Instead, he envisions a church united in love because the leaders properly nurture the followers.

Maturity: The Appropriate Approach to Cultural Renewal

It is these moral aspects of disunity—which he had experienced personally at the hands of the Seceder synod—that affected TC most profoundly. The litany of sorrows runs on: "grievous scandals," "visitations of judgment," "the weak are caused to stumble," the graceless and profane "are hardened," "the mouths of infidels opened to blaspheme religion," and the gospel of Jesus is "reduced to contempt."[28]

Accounts of the religious situation in the generation following the American Revolution have verified that these are not exaggerated claims. As Sydney Ahlstrom depicted it:

> By the end of the period, church membership had dropped both relatively and absolutely, so that not more than one person in twenty or possibly one in ten seems to have been affiliated; in many churches membership itself became increasingly nominal. Tory ministers fled; patriot ministers often had their labors interrupted. Most of the college faculties were scattered and their facilities appropriated for military use, disastrously affecting the recruitment and training of a clergy. "Enthusiasm" was widely spurned, and revivalism came to a temporary halt everywhere except in the remoter parts of the South.[29]

This period of moral and religious decline was reaching its lowest level just as TC arrived in America. Because of its sectarian divisions, the church was becoming more and more enfeebled and unable to cope with the moral evils of the time.

TC's concerns with the Old World situation at the time seem calculated to frame the American experience with global significance. The year of publication of the *D&A*, 1809, was the time when Napoleon's power was at its height. He had become emperor in 1804, had overthrown the Austrians and Russians at Austerlitz in 1805, and had completely crushed Prussia at Jena in 1806. In 1807 the Treaty of Tilset was signed, marking the highest point in Napoleon's career. The years following saw him as undisputed lord of Europe, intensely hated by peoples of other nations and especially by the English. The French emperor, in the eyes of many devout Christians, was clearly identified with the Beast spoken of in the Book of Revelation. This is undoubtedly the meaning of the reference TC makes to "the devoted nations that have given their strength and power unto the Beast." Otherwise, there is no particular sympathy with, or interest in, the European struggles. Evidently TC considers them as simply words of warning to Americans by which Americans should profit.

Maturity as Eschatology

Even with these few references to the subject, we can conclude that TC painted his appeal to Christian union in distinctly millenarian colors. His only citations from the Book of Revelation are to identify the events of current history with the predictions of the Apocalypse. In fact, he seems to have expected still greater convulsions on the European continent in accordance with Old Testament prophecy yet to be fulfilled. "No adequate reformation can be accomplished," he says, "until the word of God be fulfilled and the vials of his wrath poured out upon them [the European nations]."[30]

Along with this somber interpretation of the European scene, TC sounds a strikingly optimistic tone in his vision of a coming rebirth of Christianity in the New World. Here church and state are separated, so religious freedom is on the rise. Here no entangling alliances with foreign nations threaten political stability. TC sees the disestablishment of religion and isolation from Europe as opportunities for a new, unified, more biblical Christianity, if it could only complete the task of separating from the sectarian self-serving that had been imported from overseas.

Maturity as the Spiritual Quality to Be Restored

To what degree was TC's vision restorationist in a way that might dilute efforts to unite members of existing religious bodies? I find virtually no flavor of restorationism in TC, at least not in the Anabaptist sense of the radical restitution of a church that had all but disappeared following the rise of Constantine. His restorationism flowed from the Puritan sense of removing the elements of church government that benefitted the powerful over the poor and humble.

Union in Truth—The Motto of Campbell's Vision

The final words of the *D&A* are hortatory in style, but they express a subtlety of vision and a clear understanding that for TC no tension should exist between the ideal of unity and the ideal of biblical purity. Here is the core of his valedictory:

> Union in truth has been, and ever must be, the desire and prayer of all such; "Union in Truth" is our motto. The Divine word is our standard; in

> the Lord's name do we display our banners. Our eyes are upon the promises, "So shall they fear the name of the Lord from the west, and his glory from the rising of the sun." "When the enemy shall come in like a flood, the Spirit of the Lord shall lift up a standard against him." Our humble desire is to be his standard bearers, to fight under his banner, and with his weapons, "which are not carnal, but mighty through God to the pulling down of strongholds"; even all these strongholds of division, those partition walls of separation, which, like the walls of Jericho, have been built up, as it were, to the very heavens, to separate God's people, to divide his flock and so to prevent them from entering into their promised rest, at least in so far as it respects this world.[31]

With such passion TC perorates what is, after all, an invitation to those who are nearby to join the Washington County Association and to those who live elsewhere to organize similar associations of their own. In one sense, very few people joined the Washington County Association and practically no other associations were ever organized. Far-reaching as the *D&A* proved to be in later times, what befell it at first was a writer's worst fear, worse even than persecution. In Kershner's words, "People did not take the trouble to criticize it or oppose it for the simple reason that nobody read it."[32]

The Appendix, while far less frequently analyzed than the Declaration or the Address, is revealing for the nature of its defensiveness and its anticipation of criticism (which never came). Still, TC surely had no basis to expect such neglect. He had borne scars of injustice, scars which were still fresh and painful. One cannot help sensing that he is thinking of his treatment by the Presbytery of Chartiers when he writes:

> Is it anything or is it nothing for a person to stand rejected by the Church of God? 'What ye bind on earth shall be bound in heaven' is the awful sanction of the Church's judgment in justly rejecting any person. Take away this, and it has no sanction at all. But the Church rejecting, always pretends to have acted justly in so doing, and if so whereabouts does it confessedly leave the person rejected, if not in a state of damnation?[33]

Such rejection surely must have challenged TC's trust in God and in himself to the core. His very survival in the wilderness was threatened. Here he was, a man in ill health and with no means of employment in sight, now facing imminent family responsibilities when his wife and three sons arrive. Even so, he writes with clarity, insight, and courage about the issues that his followers will have to confront, now that they, too, are adrift from all the bodies of Christendom present where they lived. He is likely thinking of them and their plight when he writes:

> If, after all, any particular church acting thus should refuse the foregoing conclusion, by saying: we meant no such thing concerning the person objected; we only judged him unworthy of a place among us, and therefore put him away, but there are other churches that may receive him; we would be almost tempted to ask such a church if those other churches be Churches of Christ, and if so, pray what does it account itself? Is it anything more or better than a Church of Christ?[34]

TC pleads for more mature understanding. Think of the injustice, he writes, of expecting that when a believer is excluded from fellowship with one church body, the excommunication should extend to all other bodies, even those with whom the original group is out of fellowship. Think of the cruel irony, he says, of thinking that if one group receives somebody rejected by another group, they will be criticized by the first one and thereby deepen the schism between the churches. TC sarcastically shows the box that both groups put themselves in:

> That church, therefore, must surely act very schismatically, very unlike a Church of Christ which necessarily presupposes, or produces schism in order to shield an oppressed fellow-Christian from the dreadful consequences of its unrighteous proceedings. And is this not confessedly the case with every church which rejects a person from its communion while it acknowledges him to be a fellow-Christian; and in order to excuse this piece of cruelty, says he may find refuge some place else, some other church may receive him? For, as we have already observed, if no schism did already exist one church receiving those whom another has rejected must certainly make one.[35]

Such poignant statements make clear to me that church unity was not just a nice ideal of a prophetic visionary, nor was biblical purity merely a line in the sand drawn by a sectarian. What I see in the *D&A* is a life-and-death cry for help, that some persons, somewhere, might in conscience be inspired by the power of his vision and rescue him from disaster.

The temptation to self-serving interpretation on the part of historians and popularizers who have written about the *D&A* may have done as much to bury its original intent as TC's own long-winded style. The temptation to pick and choose either the church unity theme or the biblical purity theme has proved all but irresistible. The polarization has become all the more pronounced as the two groups of heirs have moved further apart. Many of the millions of adherents of the Stone-Campbell churches are continually surprised to hear that their neighbors who belong to the other groups once were family. The disputes have ceased, but so for the most part has serious dialogue, in the sense of trying to express each other's point of view in words the other would accept.

Toward a Fresh Understanding of the Lasting Impact of the *D&A*

As scholars from divided backgrounds begin to understand this document with its contemporary context as its most important guide, they are uncovering a message with unexpected power and relevance for today. TC's understanding of the stages of spiritual development deserve serious new study. So does his call for responsibility of the mature toward the immature, the powerful toward the weak, and the rich toward the poor. A more careful reading of the *D&A* might go a long way toward recovery of a biblical message free from sectarian impasses. It might renew a vision of church unity free from organizational impasses.

The challenge to the ecumenical heirs might be to lead in a rediscovery of biblical theology based on the best of scholarship and discipleship, while avoiding the older brittleness of Restoration scholasticism. The challenge to the restorationist descendants might be to develop a new, ecumenical vision based on celebrating the diversities of faith expressions, in contrast to older models of emphasizing similarities and suppressing differences.

Such a postmodern appreciation and adaptive reuse of the *D&A* would be a product of a hermeneutics of suspicion, an overcoming of one's biases by slanting both ways. This might well be the expected role of the current generations of our movement, a role that treats playfully, with an anticipation of discovery, rather than solemnly, with a sense of protectiveness, this priceless but frail document.

Notes

1. Thomas Campbell, "Protest and Appeal," in Alexander Campbell, *Memoirs of Elder Thomas Campbell, Together with a Brief Memoir of Mrs. Jane Campbell* (Cincinnati: H. S. Bosworth, 1861), 11.

2. TC, "Protest," 12.

3. Jim Cook, "The *Declaration and Address*: Betwixt and Between," in this volume.

4. Synod minutes quoted in Frederick D. Kershner, *The Christian Union Overture: An Interpretation of the Declaration and Address of Thomas Campbell* (St. Louis: Bethany, 1923), 35-37.

5. Robert Richardson, *Memoirs of Alexander Campbell* (Cincinnati: Standard Publishing, 1897), 1:330.

6. Alexander Campbell, "Remarks on the Declaration and Address," in *Memoirs*, 122. The passage cited here comes from a section of AC's introduction that was written by his brother Archibald Campbell.

7. Kershner, *Christian Union Overture*, 35.

8. Earl Irvin West, *The Search for the Ancient Order* (Nashville: Gospel Advocate, 1949), 1:49.

9. Thomas Campbell, *Declaration and Address of the Christian Association of Washington* (Washington, Pa.: Brown & Sample, 1809), 11.12.

10. *D&A*, 12.23.

11. *D&A*, 12.35.

12. *D&A*, 17.5.

13. *D&A*, 11.17.

14. *D&A*, 17.8.

15. *D&A*, 17.17.

16. *D&A*, 17.28.

17. *D&A*, 17.39.

18. *D&A*, 17.10.

19. Christopher R. Hutson, "The Use of Scripture in the *D&A*," in this volume.

20. *D&A*, 18.9.

21. *D&A*, 18.15-29.

22. *D&A*, 18.30-38.

23. Compare Lee Snyder, "Forbearance as a Means of Achieving Unity in *The Declaration and Address*," in this volume. Snyder correctly views growth in personal spirituality (which he calls *forbearance*) as the means for achieving unity. Snyder identifies the characteristics of TC's view of forbearance in several statements: ". . . a person is always responsible for obeying just what he or she knows." "Not only must one be willing to keep private opinions to oneself—one must go an extra mile and forfeit practices that, while perfectly lawful, nevertheless offend a weaker brother." ". . . the church will always contain many of the weak—that is, little children and young men—so forbearance must be exercised

in determining what are the terms of a congregation's communion." Snyder goes further and holds that TC's view of forbearance implies a style of leadership which Snyder calls "the tolerant advocate" of change, who can see more than one side and "can overlook immaturity and error for the sake of fellowship."

24. *D&A*, 3.14.

25. *D&A*, 41.38.

26. *D&A*, 42.1.

27. Hutson, "Use of Scripture."

28. *D&A*, 7.25-40.

29. Sydney Ahlstrom, *A Religious History of the American People* (New Haven: Yale University Press, 1972), 365-66.

30. *D&A*, 8.4. Compare Hans Rollmann,"The Eschatology of the *Declaration and Address*," in this volume. Rollmann explores the eschatological aspects of TC's theology, and demonstrates how pervasively his millennial hopes fueled his vision—as thoroughly as the more familiar Enlightenment rationalism and Scottish Calvinism. One of the most important of TC's millennial expectations was the new nation's constitutional guarantees of individual liberty. While clearly aware that many adherents of Calvinism would accuse him of "latitudinarianism," TC still relentlessly attacked creedalism as a barrier to both personal spirituality and church unity. Rollmann rightly concludes: "The *D&A* became thus for TC an eschatological action plan to suggest means to accomplish these ecclesiastical desiderata. By restoring to the church its original unity and purity, he hoped to create the irenic conditions for effective evangelization, which were eventually to prosper into a millennial Zion, when Jews would convert and the fullness of the Gentiles was to be completed." Before such a millennial Zion can appear, TC recognizes, rigid belief requirements for all people in all times and places must go.

31. *D&A*, 19.33. Along with "union in truth," TC employed a number of word clusters centered on "unity" and "union" in the *D&A*. Here are a few: "unity, peace, and purity" (3.32, 22.14); "holy unity and unanimity in faith and love" (6.15); "the Lord's Supper, that great ordinance of unity and love" (7.3); "restore to the church its primitive unity, purity and prosperity" (10.14); "original unity, peace, and purity" (10.18); "original constitutional unity" (11.1); "permanent scriptural unity amongst the churches" (12.15); "catholic unity, peace, and purity" (14.13); "visible unity in truth and holiness, in faith and love" (15.34); "unity, purity, and prosperity" (15.45); "a permanent scriptural unity amongst christians" (19.1); "original constitutional unity and purity" (20.34); "the great fundamental law of unity and love" (21.18); "catholic constitutional unity and purity" (23.4); "gracious unity and unanimity in Jesus" (23.24); "accomplishing, in due time, an entire union of all the churches in faith and practice" (9.45); "union in truth" (19.33, 19.34, 26.23, 45.45, 45.46); "union in Christ" (21.9); "union with him, and the very next to it in order, union with each other in him" (22.25); "holy unity and unanimity" (27.3); "constitutional unity, peace and charity" (29.47); "visible scriptural unity of the christian church" (30.15); "unity, peace, purity or

prosperity" (32.20); "all that unity and uniformity that the primitive church possessed" (35.45); "scriptural unity of faith and practice" (37.49); "unity of sentiment" (37.44, 37.47, 38.22, 38.26, 38.39, 41.19, 41.33); "ecclesiastical unity and purity" (41.13); "unity and purity" (22.47, 39.6, 39.18, 41.13, 42.15, 42.19, 45.27, 46.38, 51.26); "the unity and peace of the church" (45.37); "holy unity and uniformity of profession and practice" (49.49); "the reformation and unity of the church" (51.16); "unity and charity" (54.17); "our return to primitive unity and love" (54.22). The richness and variety of phrases TC employs strengthen my contention that something more than institutional union or biblical restoration lies at the heart of his vison. It embraces aspects that are spiritual, moral, ethical, liturgical, organizational, mystical, emotional, personal, universal, eschatological, and—most important of all in my judgment—pastoral.

32. Kershner, *Christian Union Overture*, 102.

33. *D&A*, 33.37.

34. *D&A*, 34.2.

35. *D&A*, 34.49.

The *Declaration and Address*: Betwixt and Between

Jim Cook

My purpose in this paper is to explore the connection between liminality and unity during the period Thomas Campbell produced the *Declaration and Address* and the Christian Association of Washington was formed. I shall briefly outline the concept of liminality and identify TC as a liminar who created a new identity with an agenda for unity via a clergy-laity status reversal.

Ritual and Liminality

Religious ritual, for Emile Durkheim and his followers, is a set of practices through which the participants relate to the sacred. Within the broad category of religious rites are several categories, that is, calendrical, life-crisis, status-reversal, and others. Arnold van Gennep noted that rituals that mark social transition—be it territorial, succession to office, or part of the life cycle—compose a general class, termed "rites of passage."[1] He further noted that passage from one status to another follows a fixed scheme of three phases—the separation from the old situation, the transition to the new status, and finally the readmittance into the society in the new status. The successive phases of the passage are combined with rites, and each phase has its typical symbolic expressions: the first phase with rites of separation, the second with rites of transition (*de marge*), and the last with rites of absorption. These phases have been given various labels. The separation phase is also known as preliminal or initiation phase, the transition phase as liminal (threshold, margin, betwixt and between), and the absorption phase as reintegration or aggregation.

Whereas van Gennep looked at the social aspects of the liminal state and saw in tripartite rites of passage the outward change of social status, Victor Turner focused on the inward, moral, and cognitive changes of deconstruction and reconstruction that he believed occur during the second, liminal phase. (Or to put it another way, van Gennep focused on the external changes of the first and third phase and Turner concentrated on the internal changes effectuated by the second.) Turner regarded symbols and actions as channels for communicating basic social and cultural values, and as channels for developing new moral and metaphysical insights that may subvert as well as support the established religious and social system.

Turner's theory of religious symbols and liminality first appeared in two accounts of his fieldwork on Ndembu initiation rites, *The Forest of Symbols* (1967) and *The Drums of Affliction* (1968). In *The Ritual Process* (1969), Turner further developed his theory of liminality, elaborating a host of contrasting liminal forms and applying his theory of liminality to help explain past religious and political movements up to the 1960s, including the Disciples. Liminality is found in both religious and secular situations. Turner used liminoid to represent the secular forms of art, sport, and performance. Among the liminal phenomena considered by Turner are not only rites of passages but also festivals, pilgrimages, and other kinds of public celebration.[2]

The establishment of a new identity is one of the most important features of the liminal phase. For Turner, it is in the ambiguity of the ritual experience, where everyday reality is transformed into a symbolic, "communitarian" experience that thereafter affects the individual's lived reality. Liminality is a moment of ritually generated limbo, an antistructural moment of reversal that is the creative fond for culture.[3]

Turner believed that ritual could be viewed as flow or process, as a psychophysical experience of involving oneself totally in an activity, providing the individual and the community with the opportunity to assess one's normal life, which can induce personal and social change.

As liminars—threshold people—cross the threshold, they temporarily exit from the status system and find themselves in immediate, nonhierarchical contact with their compadres. They belong neither to the community from which they have come, nor yet to a new community, hence they are "betwixt and between." Liminality is represented in various ways, including lack of possessions, passiveness, or humility. Most significant are the comradeship and egalitarianism that are promoted in this phase and that lead to a form of homogeneity that Turner has labeled *communitas,* the predominant element of the liminal phase. Turner defined communitas as the direct, egalitarian encounter and fellowship between people as people that characterizes both temporary ritual states and certain, more enduring, social groups. Communitas stands for a model of society or a modality of social relationship representing a rather unstructured and "undifferentiated community, or even communion of equal individuals who submit together to the general authority of the ritual elders." The liminal group is a community or comity and not a structure of hierarchically arrayed positions. The comradeship transcends distinctions of rank, age, kinship position, and sex.[4] This type of comradeship was a defining characteristic of the Christian Association of Washington and has been a central theme in the movement that emerged from it. Turner identifies several religious innovations as arising out of and extolling the comradeship and egalitarianism of the liminal phase, including the early Disciples of Christ.

In the Christian tradition, too, there have been innumerable founders of religious orders and sects who came from the upper half of the social cone, yet preached the style of life-crisis liminality as the path to salvation. As a minimal list, one might cite Saints Benedict, Francis, Dominic, Clare, and Teresa of Avila in the Catholic sphere; the Wesleys, with their "plain living and high thinking"; George Fox, founder of the Quakers; and (to cite an American example) Alexander Campbell, leader of the Disciples of Christ, who sought to restore primitive Christianity, and especially the primitive conditions of Christian fellowship, in the Protestant sphere. These Protestant leaders came from solid, middle-class backgrounds, yet sought to develop in their followers a simple, unostentatious lifestyle without distinctions of worldly status.[5]

Turner distinguished between three kinds of communitas: spontaneous or existential, normative, and ideological. Spontaneous communitas is likened to a 1960s "happening," often arising out of catastrophes or periods of crisis.[6] This type of communitas prevailed in the informal meetings of TC's friends and supporters that led to the decision to form the Christian Association of Washington. When, under the influence of time, the need exists to organize and mobilize resources, and also to realize social control among the members of the group in pursuit of these goals, the existential communitas is organized into a perduring, normative communitas. An ideological communitas applies to a variety of utopian models of society based on existential communitas. "It is an attempt to describe the outward form of an inward experience of existential communitas, and to spell out the optimal social conditions under which such experiences might be expected to flourish and multiply."[7] The Christian Association of Washington was an ideological communitas.

The temptation is to try to sustain the feeling of endless power generated by spontaneous communitas. The rereading of the Propositions at each meeting functioned to maintain the communitas. Yet the crucial difficulty of ideological communitas is that to endure it has to mobilize resources, and to mobilize resources it has to mobilize people, which requires social organization ultimately undermining the communitas. Inevitably, some must initiate and command, and others must respond and follow. TC became an elder, AC was ordained, a church building was built. But this power (of communitas) untransformed cannot readily be applied to the organizational details of social existence. It is no substitute for lucid thought and sustained will. On the other hand, structural action swiftly becomes arid and mechanical if those involved in it are not periodically immersed in the regenerative abyss of communitas. Wisdom is always to find the appropriate relationship between structure and communitas under the given circumstances of time and place, to accept each modality when it is paramount without rejecting the other, and not to cling to one when its present impetus is spent.[8]

Turner's significant contribution is to understand that society is "processual" rather than structural. An individual's, and a group's, social life is a process, or a multiplicity of processes, cycling through dialectical phases of communitas and structure.[9] It is during the liminal period, punctuated by communitas, that old elements are reformulated into new patterns. Liminality is the realm of primitive hypothesis where there is a certain freedom to juggle with the factors of existence, in a realm of pure possibility where novel configurations of ideas and relations may arise.[10]

It was inevitable that the Christian Association would either dissolve back into Presbyterianism or create a new sect. It was unlikely that TC would return to the Seceders, since he equated their adjudication of his unfitness to preach as unfitness for salvation.[11] A defining moment came in October 1810, when the attempt to seek union with the Synod of Pittsburgh failed. Lester G. McAllister observed that "no existing denomination could possibly shelter [TC] or his followers."[12] This was the case not just because of their beliefs but because the liminal process had changed them.

It was also inevitable that the Christian Association would experience a loss of communitas and a return to structure:

> It is the fate of all spontaneous communitas in history to undergo what most people see as a 'decline and fall' into structure and law. In religious movements of the communitas type, it is not only the charisma of the leaders that is 'routinized' but also the communitas of their first disciples and followers.[13]

Turner concludes his section on the Disciples by predicting the inevitable secularization of the movement:

> That their movements subsequently succumbed to "the world"—and, indeed, as Weber shows, throve in it—in no way impugns their pristine intents. In fact, as we have seen, the regular course of such movements is to reduce communitas from a state to a phase between incumbencies of positions in an ever developing structure.[14]

The spontaneity and immediacy of communitas can seldom be maintained for very long. "Communitas itself soon develops a structure, in which free relationships between individuals become converted into norm-governed relationships between social personae."[15]

Thomas Campbell as Liminar

TC was experiencing liminality on several fronts, inducing powerful forces for personal and social change that worked together to create in him a new identity. In the first place, his voyage to North America and early settlement in Washington County were liminal experiences. He was between countries, jobs, and homes—betwixt and between. TC was also in a liminal phase on another level, beginning with the Anderson affair in October 1808 and extending through his final break with the Associate Synod in May 1809, neither "in" nor "out" of the Seceders.

Previous papers in this series have explored some of the ideological factors—Scottish Common Sense philosophy, European missionary and evangelical alliances, British Enlightenment, and the Continental Reformation—that contributed to TC's decision to form the Christian Association and to compose the *D&A*. These factors may have determined the ideological base of the movement, but psychosocial factors, including TC's liminality, may have been more determinative of the "when" and the "how." This is not to diminish TC's contribution and convictions, but it must be acknowledged that he was a middle-aged man with a large family dependent on him in a new country, susceptible to the extraordinary strains and stresses of a life-changing move. TC had long been troubled by religious divisions and entertained notions of unity. What propelled him, at this point and this time, to the forefront and an eventual break with the Presbyterians?

TC provides some insight into this question, noting first the disestablishment of religion in the United States:

> A country happily exempted from the baneful influence of a civil establishment of any peculiar form of Christianity—from under the direct influence of the anti-christian hierarchy—and, at the same time, from any formal connexion with the devoted nations, that have given their strength and power unto the beast.[16]

Adding to the signs of the fullness of time TC points to the "greater efforts" that have been made "for the promulgation of the gospel among the nations, since the commencement of the French revolution" as well as the "well-meant endeavors after union."[17]

Other factors surely played a part, including the fertile and relatively safe territory of the American frontier, where one could plant new seeds free of denominational hegemony. Additionally, the frontier was a "preachers' market," affording great opportunity for enterprising ministers preaching a "simple" Christianity, accessible to the common person. TC arrived in America in May 1807, settling on the western Pennsylvania frontier and initially expecting his family to join him in the near future. His most pressing needs were pecuniary—finding work and establishing a home. Within days of his arrival he received his appointment to the Chartiers Presbytery and by 1 July he was booked through October. He was astounded at the grace God had bestowed on him through the safe voyage and rapid integration into American society. Surrounded by old friends and acquaintances and with four months of appointments, he found his primary needs met, and it appeared that he could successfully support his family in America.

By the end of October he was involved in a controversy with his fellow Seceder ministers over the Anderson matter. Even though he walked out of the meeting, it appears that he did not fear that his position was in jeopardy, nor was he dissuaded from remaining in America. Just four days prior to the January meeting of the Chartiers Presbytery, he wrote, encouraging his family to come as quickly as possible. According to Robert Richardson, they immediately began making preparations for the voyage.[18] Within a week the picture had changed and charges were levied against him, but two more months elapsed before he was suspended from preaching indefinitely. He could not believe the jealousies and politicking of the Chartiers Presbytery and filed a Protest and Appeal with the Associate Synod, which, in conjunction with petitions supporting him, created in him an expectation that they would resolve the issue in his favor.

TC's behavior during the synod in Philadelphia shows us a person of convictions, under great stress, acting out in a passive-aggressive manner. By late May he would have believed that his family had received his 1 January letter and might be already on their way to America. It has been suggested that one reason he remained in Philadelphia for two months after the synod was to await the imminent arrival of his family. It is possible that the Associate Synod wanted to keep him nearby for supervision purposes, but it seems more likely that he requested the extended stay in Philadelphia.[19] TC faced a dilemma. Just as he was expecting his family to arrive, his early success at finding work was now in jeopardy and it was too late to get word to them to delay their departure. TC did not believe he was in error, but he was economically dependent, to a degree, on the synod's decision. McAllister accounts for TC's reluctance to withdraw from the Associate Synod as due to his long connection with the Seceder fellowship.[20] This does not seem sufficient to explain the Remonstrance of 26 May, the following day's accusatory letter, its withdrawal, and TC's subsequent acceptance of censure with caveats. It seems that this set of actions may more properly be attributed to his dependent role in the proceedings, pressure of his family's imminent arrival, and his predisposition to a less confrontational (more passive) mode of disagreement.

This situation also helps to explain TC's ready acceptance of the delay caused by the shipwreck and AC's subsequent plan to remain in Glasgow.[21] It would give him more time to resolve the problems and establish a stable means of support. TC was "betwixt and between" in his relationship with the Presbyterians.

Although the synod had released TC from censure with a "rebuke and admonition," he was effectively banned from gainful employment by the

Chartiers Presbytery. TC was indignant at the failure of the synod to vindicate him. This indignation was not veiled as he pointed the finger of latitudinarianism at the synod.[22] It was TC's personal experience of perceived unjust treatment at the hands of the synod that thoroughly convinced him of "the evil state of things in the churches, which has given rise to our association. . . . we would humbly desire to be instrumental in pointing out to our fellow-christians the evils of such conduct."[23] The intensity of his anger and disappointment was increased by his expectation that things would be different in America and the bind the synod had put him in while his family was relocating.

Why didn't TC seek reassignment to another Presbytery? Or another denomination? Were his ties to the former parishioners and friends in Washington County too strong to move? Or, with his strong base of support, was he entertaining ideas of becoming independent? He was an entrepreneur: He identified the need, saw the market, had a loyal customer base, and models[24] were readily available to him. The frontier provided the market, Washington County provided the loyal customer base, and the late Hiram Lester has convincingly argued that the model for the Christian Association and the *D&A* are to be found in the European evangelical missionary and Bible societies with which TC was familiar.[25]

Notes

1. Arnold van Gennep, *The Rites of Passage* (Chicago: University of Chicago Press, 1960).
2. Victor W. Turner, "Betwixt and Between," in *Reader in Comparative Religion: An Anthropological Approach*, ed. William A. Lessa and Evon Z. Vogt (New York: Harper and Row, 1979); *From Ritual to Theater: The Human Seriousness of Play* (New York: Performing Arts Journal Publications, 1982).
3. Ronald L. Grimes, *Beginnings in Ritual Studies*, rev. ed. (Columbia: University of South Carolina Press, 1995), 151.
4. Turner, "Betwixt and Between," 238.
5. Victor W. Turner, *The Ritual Process: Structure and Anti-Structure* (New York: Aldine de Gruyter, 1969), 198.
6. Turner, *Ritual Process*, 148.
7. Turner, *Ritual Process*, 132.
8. Turner, *Ritual Process*, 139.
9. Turner, *Ritual Process*, 203.
10. Turner, "Betwixt and Between," 241, 236.

11. Thomas Campbell, *Declaration and Address of the Christian Association of Washington* (Washington, Pa.: Brown & Sample, 1809), 33-35.

12. Lester G. McAllister, *Thomas Campbell: Man of the Book* (St. Louis: Bethany Press, 1954), 144.

13. Turner, *Ritual Process*, 132-33.

14. Turner, *Ritual Process*, 199.

15. Turner, *Ritual Process*, 132.

16. *D&A*, 7.48-8.4.

17. *D&A*, 8.24-27.

18. Robert Richardson, *Memoirs of Alexander Campbell* (Cincinnati: Standard Publishing, 1897), 1:88-90.

19. Richardson, *Memoirs*, 1:95-97; McAllister, *Thomas Campbell*, 91.

20. McAllister, *Thomas Campbell*, 89.

21. Richardson, *Memoirs*, 1:148.

22. *D&A*, 30-32, 36.

23. *D&A*, 32.

24. *D&A*, 7-11.

25. Hiram J. Lester, "The Form and Function of the *Declaration and Address*," in this volume.

Forbearance as a Means of Achieving Unity in the *Declaration and Address*

Lewis Leroy (Lee) Snyder[1]

> Whatever way, then, it [Christian unity] is to be effected, whether upon the solid basis of Divinely revealed truth, or the good-natured principle of Christian forbearance and gracious condescension, is it not equally practicable, equally eligible to us, as ever it can be to any?
>
> Thomas Campbell[2]

The subject of this paper, "forbearance," is something different from "tolerance" and "toleration." In fact, those words do not appear in the *Declaration and Address* at all. According to the *Encyclopedia of Philosophy,* toleration suggests that one is in the presence of "something disliked or disapproved of."[3] One tolerates error, not truth. Toleration implies an attitude of condescension, for to tolerate "is first to condemn and then to put up with."[4] To "forbear," though, or "to bear with," as Thomas Campbell uses these terms, is to suppose that one who disagrees with me may be as conscientious as I am, may love God as much as I do, may be as wise as I think myself to be.

TC chose the best state in the United States in which to write about forbearance. Pennsylvania, called "America's first self-consciously plural society," was inhabited by a population that was, by 1790, one-third English, one-third German, and one-fifth Scottish and Scots-Irish.[5] The religious openness of the state, as much as its cultural diversity, had earlier made the colony of Pennsylvania a welcome home for TC's sect of Presbyterians. William Penn specifically had designed this American colony as an experiment in religious liberty, and the inhabitants made the experiment work. By the time TC emigrated to Pennsylvania, the first state constitution of 1776 had expanded Penn's concept of freedom of conscience, and the second constitution (1790) continued this enlargement.[6]

As a result of the unique ethnic and religious liberty enjoyed in Pennsylvania, the Seceder Presbyterians, including some of TC's old neighbors and friends from Ireland, found in western Pennsylvania a hospitable home. Hence, when TC initially appeared before the Synod in Philadelphia, he asked for and received assignment to Washington, Pennsylvania; his son would later settle in Bethany, Virginia, only twenty miles farther west.

The story of TC's conflicts with the Presbyterian governing bodies has been told often, as well as his subsequent formation of the Washington Association. This was a lofty name for a handful of neighbors who enjoyed TC's ministry. For them he prepared the *D&A*, setting forth, briefly, a program of service through a parachurch organization; then, more extensively, proposing a plan for Christian unity based on reformation and forbearance.

When treated as ends to be achieved, reformation and forbearance are competing and incompatible goals. When understood as processes for achieving a transcendent purpose, that of Christian unity, they become complementary strategies.

I hope, in this historical and rhetorical study, to prove three claims concerning the *D&A* and its influence. First, I argue that TC derived the principle of forbearance, an integral part of the program proposed in the *D&A,* from the Pauline doctrine of forbearance set forth primarily in Rom 14. Second, the *D&A*, including especially this principle of forbearance, had a direct influence on TC's prominent son, Alexander, who genuinely devoted himself to putting it into practice. Third, in following out the implications of this principle, TC (as well as AC) exemplified a rhetorical stance that I call the "gracious advocate," a stance which remains a vital element of the Stone-Campbell heritage.

Part One: Forbearance and Romans 14

To suffer tension between competing values is part of the human predicament. Even with the aid of dialectic and rhetoric, the balance between equally valid goals remains uneasy, always fluctuating. For example, the incompatibility of orthodoxy and unity was of recurring interest to TC.

Thomas H. Olbricht has pointed out that earlier Protestant reformers emphasized the importance of orthodoxy.[7] In contrast, TC began his reformation by emphasizing unity. Robert Richardson confirmed that this emphasis existed from the very outset of the Campbells' reformation:

> In the present efforts at reformation, it is this unity which has been chiefly urged upon the religious community. Christian union and intercommunion were the original and ruling thoughts with those with whom this movement began.[8]

Unity in itself, though, was not an adequate goal for TC. He envisioned that Christians might achieve "Union in Truth," referring to the truth of God's Word. His position in the *D&A* is similar to that of his son, who later posited two propositions on the subject:

> 1st. Nothing is essential to the conversion of the world but the union and co-operation of the Christians.
> 2d. Nothing is essential to the union of Christians but the Apostles' teaching or testimony.[9]

What this "truth" consisted of remains undefined by TC, beyond the following description: "We dare therefore neither do, nor receive any thing, as of divine obligation, for which there cannot be expressly produced a 'thus saith the Lord' either in express terms, or by approved precedent."[10] It is an act of wisdom that TC did not at this time spell out the elements of truth on which he thought all Christians could be united. In fact, by his principles, any such summary would be as extensive as the Word itself.[11]

Even a cursory reading of the *D&A* shows that, to TC, the Christian church of his day was handicapped by two dysfunctional characteristics. First, it was divided into hostile camps, instead of enjoying the glorious unity prophesied by Isaiah and prayed for by Jesus.[12] Second, it had encumbered the simple truth of the Bible with speculations, human doctrines, and creeds.[13] Many church members knew these creeds better than they knew the Bible. So, instead of unity in truth, the church suffered division in corruption.[14] To these two problems TC offered two cures: to undo the devotion to human doctrine, it was necessary to pursue truth by reforming the church on the basis of the Bible;[15] to undo the division, it was necessary to practice forbearance.[16]

Either of these processes could fail if it became an end in itself. TC was on guard against the danger of extremes; the virtue of the reformer easily becomes legalism and forbearance easily becomes "latitudinarianism" or liberalism.[17] Hence, TC attempts to balance these two healing impulses in the *D&A*.

Reformation has been a common topic of discussion in the Stone-Campbell Movement. The rest of this paper will concentrate instead on the more neglected practice of forbearance. TC drew his program for engaging in forbearance from Rom 14:1-15:7. (Some or all of the fifteenth chapter is generally treated by commentators and modern Bible versions as continuous with chapter fourteen.) Various scholars have exposed several layers of influences that shaped the *D&A*,[18] and TC's use of Rom 14 also has been discussed by Christopher Roy Hutson,[19] but I wish in this first section to emphasize its importance to the *D&A*.[20]

TC did not exposit Rom 14 as a text. His style was like that of his son's early sermons, some of which are recorded in his "Journal."[21] TC's discourse was not so much an exegesis of a text as a jazz riff on it, calling into service other passages that echoed in word and sense the main theme. This style of development apparently was an application of the inductive method of reasoning, for many verses (some quoted and some only alluded to) were called on to show that the proposition presented was true to the sense of the Bible. TC assumed that his readers already knew the Bible. Hence, by weaving the verses throughout the discourse (apparently his usual style of expression throughout his public life), he gave to his words a resonance that would invite the audience to feel a mental integration of formerly diverse strains of biblical thought; for example, he conflates apocalyptic verses from Is 34, Ps 102, and Dn 9, making them all refer to the same event, apparently the millennium.[22]

The principles set forth in Rom 14 provide the major part of TC's program for unity, though he buttresses this passage with references to other Pauline passages on forbearance—specifically 1 Cor 8-10 and Eph 4:1-3. At the beginning of the Declaration, TC posits the right of personal judgment, by quoting Rom 14:12, 10:

> We are also persuaded that as no man can be judged for his brother, so no man can judge for his brother: but that every man must be allowed to judge for himself, as every man must bear his own judgment;—must give account of himself to God—. . . [N]o man has a right to judge his brother, except in so far as he manifestly violates the express letter of the law.[23]

The last clause ("except") is TC's addition to Paul's words; perhaps he thought this addition was implied by Paul. Outside of this exception, judgment of a brother is "a daring usurpation of his [Christ's] throne, and a gross intrusion upon the rights and liberties of his subjects."[24] While not constituting an exact quotation, these verses echo Rom 14:4, 9, where Paul argues that to criticize another person's servant is to usurp rudely the owner's prerogative, a prerogative that Christ obtained for himself by his death.

This principle, that Christians are not responsible for judging others, is based on the presumption of liberty of conscience, which is essential to TC's doctrine of forbearance. Paul established the right of private interpretation and the sanctity of the individual conscience in Rom 14:2-6. There, those who were scrupulous about eating certain meat and observing certain days were praised by Paul for obeying their conscience, and so were their opposite colleagues who honored all meat and all days alike. Thus, Paul established a transcendent viewpoint from which apparently opposite modes of conduct could be seen as entirely harmonious; from this transcendent position, he explained that both camps of Christians were serving God by their behavior, as well as following the dictates of their diverse consciences. Transcendence has been defined by Kenneth Burke as "The adoption of another point of view from which [opposites] cease to be opposites," an appropriate definition in this case.[25]

Forbearance is a stance that entails a vision of transcendence. As mentioned earlier, transcendence is a rhetorical tool used to discover or create new ground on which opposites can meet. For TC, this ground is simply the Bible:

> Is it not as evident as the shining light, that the scriptures exhibit but one and the self same subject matter of profession and practice; at all times, and in all places;—and, that therefore, to say as it declares, and to do as it prescribes, in all its holy precepts, its approved and imitable examples, would unite the christian church in a holy sameness of profession and practice, throughout the whole world? But had the Jews been expressly prohibited, or the Gentiles expressly enjoined, by the authority of Jesus, to observe these things; could they, in such a case, have lawfully

> exercised this forbearance? But where no express law is, there can be no formal, no intentional transgression; even although its implicit and necessary consequences had forbid the thing, had they been discovered. Upon the whole, we see one thing is evident; the Lord will bear with the weaknesses, the involuntary ignorances, and mistakes, of his people; though not with their presumption. Ought they not, therefore, to bear with each other.[26]

In this paragraph is laid out in a nutshell the doctrine of forbearance. There is a ground on which people should be able to meet, but TC is not so naive as to think that there would be no disagreement about the nature of that ground. He expected that there would have to be discussion and reasoning, "for no man can relinquish his opinions or practices, till once convinced that they are wrong; and this he may not be immediately, even supposing they were so."[27] What is important is that all parties agree that the common ground exists and that they will earnestly seek that ground. In the face of disagreements, Christians must forbear with each other, recognizing that even God is forbearing, as long as his people are not presumptuous.

Here TC reasons from the greater to the lesser (as does Paul in the verse TC quoted so frequently, Rom 15:7). By arguing the forbearance of God and of Christ as models, TC takes away the sectarian's unbearable weight of having to be right (yet he does not remove at all the duty of *wanting* to be right). TC's argument also suggests that it would be only small-souled people who would refuse to bear with a fellow-believer, given God's forbearance toward them. Being accepted by Christ entails accepting others.

Accordingly, TC followed Paul by urging, in the fifth resolution of the Declaration, that the Association should send out ministers who would not attempt to "inculcate any thing of human authority, of private opinion, or inventions of men."[28] Like Paul, he found no fault with people for having private opinions and interpretations, as long as they did not try to bind them on others' consciences. The consistency between TC's doctrine and his practice on this point is shown by the Aylett Raines affair, which I shall discuss later.

Although one person's opinions cannot be bound upon another, still it is useful and edifying to discuss questionable problems with each other.[29] If, at any time, another person's reasoning persuades us that we are wrong, we are then responsible for living according to our new understanding. One principle, then, that emerges from TC's epistemology is that a person is always responsible for obeying just what he or she knows. TC's intriguing extension of Paul's teaching implicitly justifies all extrabiblical publication, so long as it is well intentioned. This extension allows room for the sharing of experience and testimony, so important, as Carisse M. Berryhill has pointed out, to Locke and to George Campbell as scientific tools of improvement. Otherwise, TC's other principles would compel the church to be nearly silent. There could be no catechisms, sermons, declarations, or addresses—nothing but the reading of the Bible without notes or comments.

When auxiliaries such as these are treated as though they are authoritative, division is at hand. But to hold private opinions only as private property (a principle that Paul urged in the verses already mentioned and in Rom 14:22) is to eliminate those matters that divide the kingdom: "[O]ur differences, at most, are about the things in which the kingdom of God does not consist, that is, about matters of private opinion, or human invention."[30]

At this point, it is necessary for both Paul and TC to extend the principle of forbearance. Not only must one be willing to keep private opinions to oneself—one must go an extra mile and forfeit practices that, while perfectly lawful, nevertheless offend a weaker brother. Paul mentions the right to eat meat or to drink wine in Rom 14:2; TC was not so specific, referring in general to "educational prejudices, and particular customs," which he was willing to relinquish for the sake of the unity of the church.[31]

If human interpretations and personal opinions are omitted as grounds for confessional unity, what is left is only that which is divine—Christ's Word. TC sanguinely expected of his readers that "more than this, you will not require of us."[32] He explicitly rejected the distinction between essentials and nonessentials as a basis for fellowship, knowing well the fatuity of such a distinction. Instead, whatever is revealed or enjoined by God must be believed and obeyed absolutely.[33]

Having presented these claims, TC next built upon them in some of the Propositions of the Address. Since the church is one, as the First Proposition states, then, says the Second, there should be no divisions among Christians. Instead, as TC quotes Romans again, they should "receive each other as Christ Jesus hath also received them to the glory of God."[34] The means of healing divisions is to practice forbearance—to require nothing of human origin as a term of communion other than "what is expressly taught, and enjoined" in the Bible.[35]

Inferences and deductions may be sound and true, supposes the Sixth Proposition, "yet are they not formally binding upon the consciences of christians farther than they perceive the connection, and evidently see that they are so."[36] Though not explicitly stated, this principle seems based on Paul's admonition in Rom 14:5, "Let every one be fully persuaded in his own mind." The Seventh Proposition is similar to the Sixth, and adds that the church will always contain many of the weak—that is, little children and young men—so forbearance must be exercised in determining what are the terms of a congregation's communion.[37]

In fact, for the desired state of a united church to be achieved, and for the millennium to dawn, forbearance must become universal. Three times TC cited Is 57:14, which he interpreted as a call to remove stumbling-blocks that stood in the way of harmony, preventing the accomplishment of that happy event, the union of God's people—apparently the millennial age.[38] To eliminate stumbling blocks, one simply removes human opinions by distinguishing them from God's primary revelation.[39] TC did not quote Rom 14 explicitly in this chain of reasoning, but he spoke earlier in this paragraph about weak brethren who tended to bigotry, surely a reference to the problem Paul mentioned in Rom 14:2, 3, and 15:1.[40] The reference to stumbling blocks also recalls Paul's admonition in Rom 14:13 against putting such obstacles in a brother's way.

TC again refers to Isaiah's prophecy in describing the removal of stumbling blocks as consisting in directing people's attention to first principles. Here he connects clearing the path with promoting the interests of Zion, a duty the faithful remnant would engage in, apparently as preparation for the millennium.[41] Although Rom 14:13 is in the shadows, it is not explicitly mentioned.[42] However, in the third set of TC's references to stumbling blocks, the connection is explicit. The day when the church has no schisms will come when offenses are removed.[43] Even then, people will have differing opinions, but these will not be obstacles when people "judge one another no more about such matters. We would rather be conscientiously cautious to give no offense; to put no stumbling block, or occasion to fall, in our brother's way."[44] This is a clear reference to Rom 14:13. Thus, the adoption of the forbearance principle of Rom 14 is connected in TC's mind to the dawning of the millennium.

Finally, Rom 14 reappears when TC presents his version of the two Great Commandments—be united with Christ and be united with each other.[45] Hutson has already discussed that location, the last reference to Romans in the Address itself.[46] What remains is the Appendix, which amplifies the points TC had already made and answers some objections. Romans is prominent in this part of the document as well.[47]

The point of the first part of this discussion is to argue that, among all the strata of TC's ideas already discussed in this volume of essays, Paul's own "declaration" in Rom 14 on the subject of forbearance is a primary source of the *D&A*. It was not something added to make TC's ideas sound more acceptable, but it was the very seedbed from which emerged many of the most important principles of the *D&A*. Specifically, TC borrowed directly from Paul the concepts of the right of private judgment; the leaving of judgment to God rather than to human authority; the illegitimacy of forcing opinions on others; the willingness to sacrifice the lawful for the sake of others; and the need for the strong to bear lovingly with the weak, thus bringing about a harmony in the church that would be better than uniformity.

TC then extended these principles, claiming that religious discussion is useful; that private opinions and even creeds may be edifying in their proper place; that offences against the express Word must not be treated with tolerance; and that people are responsible only for what they know. The whole matter may be summed up even more briefly. Because, to TC, Christian "faith" is belief in revealed facts in the New Testament, we may say that the *D&A* advocates this familiar unity program: "In faith, unity; in opinion, liberty; in all things, love."[48]

Part Two: The Influence of the *D&A*

Other essays in this volume discuss the long-term influence of TC's proposed program for unity on the three major branches of the Stone-Campbell Movement. It would be easy to conclude that, in the short term, it was not a successful program. He and his followers actually did what he had promised not to do, and they left undone what he had called on them to do. For though he began his Appendix by assuring other churches that he had no intention of proselytizing, of "endeavouring to erect churches out of churches—to distract and divide congregations," that was precisely the result.[49] Eventually, a new sect would be born and, later, three major "denominations" would emerge—not an auspicious outcome for a movement to unite Christians. On the other hand, the proposed projects of the Washington Association were not carried out, except insofar as they continued to have the meetings called for in the Declaration.[50] However, no evangelists were sent out under their auspices, no

Bibles given to the poor, no catechism developed (as recommended in the Postscript), and, if AC's *Christian Baptist* fulfilled the call for a new journal, the "*Christian Monitor*," it was seventeen years in coming.[51]

Ernest Stefanik argues that the *D&A* had no influence outside the Washington Association until the second generation of Disciples.[52] Even in the Washington Association, though, its influence and that of TC were limited. In 1810 only two congregations followed the principles of the *D&A*; by 1820 only four more had been added, totalling in all about two hundred members.[53] The program for unity excited so little respect that the Association was sternly rebuffed when it attempted to join the Synod of Pittsburgh.[54]

However, as my second major claim, I argue that the *D&A*, especially in its principle of forbearance, did have a significant impact on TC's son, Alexander, the most prominent and influential of all the pioneers of the Stone-Campbell Movement. After being exposed to its principles and program, AC thereafter followed it earnestly, though not perfectly.

Some support for the claim of this influence comes from the fact that AC's writing, speaking, and actions seem designed to carry out the principles and program set forth in the *D&A*. It has long been known that AC read the proof sheets of the *D&A* on his arrival in Washington, Pennsylvania, in October 1809, "straight from Scotland." He immediately informed his father that infant baptism would have to be abandoned, on the principle that only "express precept or example" was binding.[55] In another account, AC wrote that the phrase "express terms or by approved precedent" deeply impressed him, and he struggled for a year to resolve for himself the problem of infant baptism.[56] Clearly, then, AC read the document immediately and was affected by it. During the next year, while he preached for the Christian Association in Washington (among other locations), he worked out in his mind ramifications of it that even his father had not seen.

To prove that AC was directly influenced by TC's *D&A*, or to demonstrate that the influence did not come from AC's father through some other medium, could usually be a difficult task. However, a remarkable document survives that demonstrates that AC studied the *D&A* carefully and was strongly influenced by it. This document is the manuscript outline of young AC's twentieth sermon, one that he delivered before the Washington Association. It is preserved in part in Robert Richardson's *Memoirs*, and *in toto* still exists in AC's unpublished "Manuscript D."[57]

Though he first preached on 15 July 1810, his twentieth sermon is the first one recorded in the back pages of his diary, "A Journal of a Voyage to America."[58] This discourse, delivered on Thursday, 1 November 1810, is an apology for the Washington Association, setting forth its basic principles and answering objections that apparently had been offered against such principles. AC's richly detailed "skeleton" preserves the main ideas of a long sermon based on Is 57:14 "in connexion with" Is 62:10. TC had referred to Is 57:14 several times in the *D&A*. There are a number of other references to the *D&A*, including some noted by Hans Rollmann elsewhere in this volume.[59] I cite the most prominent references for the purposes of this paper. In the quotations taken from AC's manuscript, I follow his spelling, punctuation, and abbreviations as exactly as possible.

AC spoke of reformation and renewal of the church, treating them as matters of prophecy, as TC had. AC's tenth topic was, "The attempt made in this place [meaning Washington] for it." He spoke of a program for renewal that aimed to "disencumber the Scriptures" from human doctrines. He referred to the stumbling blocks Isaiah mentioned as "whatever prevents them from conforming to the Word of God in all things"—that is, human opinions. This application exactly follows that of his father.[60]

Under the second heading, AC noted to himself, "Shew that we have attempted to perform these duties." Afterward, he wrote that "the New Testament is as perfect a constitution for the worship, Discipline, and Gov. of the Ch. church and as perfect a rule for the particular duties of its members as the old T &." (This sentence is at the end of a page, so he did not have room to finish.) This is a direct quotation from the *D&A*.[61]

In a later part of the sermon, AC discussed a number of objections to the plan of reformation. As he put it, he tried to "obviate objections that may have been made through ignorance or willful opposition." The first one was, "That the principle and plan adopted has a tendency to increase divisions and terminates in a new party." In part of his reply, he wrote, "Address page 25-49." He added:

> If taking the new testament for our constitution be a party principle, then are we a party; If to make it the only rule be a party principle then are we a party. If to open the door of communion as wide as the gates of Heaven be a party principle then are we a party but on the same ground and in the same sense as the primitive church.

This is a close paraphrase, down to the periodic repetition of TC's words.[62] Another explicit reference came when AC discussed a third objection, relating to church discipline. He referred to "our Declaration, Prop. 7-8-12." Under the fourth objection, he wrote, "See appendix to 'Declaration and Address.'"[63]

Finally, there is an interesting discussion of the fifth objection: "That your principles exclude infant baptism." AC's treatment of this topic seems mature and gracious for a twenty-two-year-old preacher, especially considering that there were in the Washington Association only three members who had not been baptized as infants.[64] Here is part of AC's reply to this hypothetical objection:

> We dare not inculcate infant Baptism in the name of the Lord, as indispensably incumbent on Christians; because the Lord has no where expressly enjoined it. If any thing can be produced on this head expressly declared in the sacred scriptures, we should be glad to see it. Until this be done, we think it highly antiscriptural to make it a term of communion, for to do that is to make it a term of salvation. It is as much as to say except ye baptize your children you cannot be saved. . . .
> Sum all that has been said;—from the whole we conclude that it should be a matter of forbearance, as it is evident circumcision was in the prim. Ch. Church. By no means considering it a matter of indifference—it can never be a light thing to mistake the will of God. We look at baptism now in nearly the same point of view in which the primitive Church looked at circumcision, and consider the cases if not altogether yet nearly paralel, so far so, that we must either forbear or reject [all of vast (?)] numbers of God's dear children without his special command if not in express violation of his divine Command, "Him that is weak in the faith receive ye," receive ye one another as Christ has also received us to the Glory of God.

For AC at this time, infant baptism was a matter about which people should think carefully, yet not a matter of direct command. To treat as unsaved all who had not been baptized in infancy would violate God's express command to receive the weak in the faith (Rom 14:1). Here, then, AC applied his father's principles to a particularly personal case, and he began by referring to circumcision as a matter on which the primitive Christians exercised forbearance. This his father did also.[65] (In the third sentence of the excerpt above, he originally wrote in his manuscript, "we think it highly unscriptural," but he changed it to "antiscriptural." Perhaps he changed it because, if requiring infant baptism for church membership were only unscriptural—a matter of indifference—then the principle of forbearance would have required AC to bear with it.)

This manuscript, then, shows that AC was quite familiar with the *D&A*, so much so that a reference to its page numbers was adequate for his speaking outline. He imitated even its very sentence structure, applied similar verses in similar ways, and pragmatically extended its principle of forbearance.

Now that it is established that the *D&A* immediately became significant and a matter of intense contemplation to young AC, I shall make a larger inferential leap. I believe that the *D&A* contains the famous Lunenburg letter in embryo. In 1837, a reader in Lunenburg, Virginia, expressed surprise that AC had referred to "Christians" in other churches. If only the Reformers practiced scriptural baptism by immersion, then how could he speak of Christians in other denominations? In a brief, potent reply, AC made his position so clear that he alienated some strong supporters. He defined a Christian as "Every one that believes in his heart that Jesus of Nazareth is the Messiah, the Son of God; repents of his sins, and obeys him in all things according to his measure of knowledge of his will." He could not "make any one duty the standard of Christian state or character, not even immersion." Furthermore, if he should find a Presbyterian who was more spiritual and more devoted to God than a person who had been baptized according to AC's doctrine, "I could not hesitate a moment in giving the preference of my heart to him that loveth most."[66]

AC's bold answer caused a great stir. The immersion of adult believers was the most visible characteristic of the Stone-Campbell Movement, because the members believed baptism to be a divine ordinance and a part of the process of conversion. This belief made them obnoxious to the Baptists, who baptized believers because they had experienced conversion. Half of AC's four oral debates to that point were on the subject and meaning of baptism. Yet, in his reply to the Lunenburg letter, he asserted that there were members of other denominations who were Christians in spite of their failure to share his insight on baptism.

In his reply, AC was only being faithful to the statement he had read in his father's document a quarter-century before: Christian character consists "in an intelligent profession of our faith in Christ and obedience to him in all things according to the Scriptures."[67] Even more in the spirit of the *D&A* was the unusual forbearance AC showed, for he was one of the strongest and most implacable advocates of believers' immersion since the days of Paul; nevertheless, he advocated forbearance on the subject.[68]

We find another instructive example in AC's attitude toward Aylett Raines, whose case came up before the annual meeting of the Mahoning Association (in the Western Reserve) in 1828. Aylett Raines, a recent convert of Walter Scott, believed in Universalism, the doctrine that all people will be saved either before or after death. This doctrine was thoroughly unorthodox within the nascent Campbell movement. Inasmuch as Raines was doing some preaching for the Reformers, they were criticized for tolerating such heresy.

The day before Raines's case came up, AC addressed the Association from Rom 14, emphasizing the first verse.[69] He divided all subjects pertaining to Christianity into three headings, just as his father had: matters of knowledge (personal experience); matters of faith (based on testimony concerning scriptural facts); and matters of opinion. AC argued, as had his father, that the third category would become a source of division, unless Christians were willing to receive each other as Christ received them.

Nevertheless, the next day, there was serious debate about whether Raines could be allowed to fellowship with the Association, unless he publicly abandoned his belief. After questioning, he announced that he was not ready to change his opinion about the fate of the dead, but, since such opinions are not part of the gospel, he would not teach them publicly. Both Campbells supported Raines. TC even remarked that he would rather have his hand burned off than to raise it (in a vote, we may presume) against Raines.[70] Furthermore, AC expressed his opinion that, if no pressure were put on Raines to conform, he would eventually outgrow his heterodox opinions anyway. Raines became an effective preacher for the movement and AC's prediction proved to be right.[71]

For the sake of thoroughness, it should be noted that there were a few instances in AC's career when he did not show the forbearance that his father probably would have. This is especially evident in the case of a controversy with Jesse B. Ferguson, beginning in 1852.[72] Still, as a whole, AC showed in his words and his actions the spirit of the *D&A*, fulfilling the promise he had made to his father as a young man—that he "had determined to devote himself to the dissemination and support of the principles and views presented in the 'Declaration and Address.'"[73]

In summary of these first two sections, the *D&A* is a manifesto of forbearance, based on the primary Scripture concerning forbearance, and clearly shaping the religious world by leading AC to be a forbearing leader.

Part Three: TC's Stance

Students of rhetoric have sometimes discussed the "stance" of a speaker or writer, by which they mean the communicator's attitude toward the audience, the communication situation, and the message.[74] Wayne Booth has described the specific stances of the Pedant, the Advertiser, the Entertainer, and the Noble Lover.[75]

My third claim is that TC both taught and exemplified a stance I call "the gracious advocate."[76] This phrase appears to be oxymoronic, but it captures the tension of competing values that TC embodied and that I discussed at the beginning of the first section of this paper.

This stance requires skill in both argumentation and forbearance. The process of reforming the church demands the voice of a critic, wielded by a person who loves truth and is skilled in the traditional tools of persuasive rhetoric. This reformer speaks boldly, like Plato's noble lover, and advocates what is good for the audience.[77] To the degree that this reformer prevails, his or her social system becomes more pure.

On the other hand, the practice of forbearance demands a gracious change-agent—one who can see both sides, who is skilled in achieving identification with and between opponents, one who understands other worldviews without necessarily accepting them.[78] Pragmatically, this person is more concerned with winning people than debates, and can overlook immaturity and error for the sake of fellowship. To the extent that this peacemaker prevails, the system becomes more inclusive and loving.

The gracious advocate, though, combines both qualities. After arguing his or her position as strongly as possible, a gracious advocate can still treat the person who sincerely disagrees as a member of the family. I find this an intriguing and useful stance that suits the change-agent in the post-modern age. Today, our culture shares with TC's audience a romantic devotion to individual freedom, although fewer people now accept the idea of an authoritative document. The question of textual authority itself is under debate. But postmodernism has merely altered, not eliminated, the tasks of analyzing texts, making private judgments, arguing them publicly, and discovering common ground. Whether a new apologetics and evangelism will emerge from the present cauldron is still a moot question. If the progress of the causes of unity and reformation are to increase, though, gracious advocates must also increase.

Notes

1. The author thanks Thomas H. Olbricht and the late Hiram J. Lester for their helpful criticism of an earlier draft of this paper.

2. Thomas Campbell, *Declaration and Address of the Christian Association of Washington* (Washington, Pa: Brown & Sample, 1809), 12.32-36. This text is included in this collection.

3. Maurice Cranston, "Toleration," in *The Encyclopedia of Philosophy*, ed. Paul Edwards (New York: MacMillan and Free Press, 1967), 143.

4. Cranston, "Toleration," 143.

5. Sally Schwartz, *"A Mixed Multitude": The Struggle for Toleration in Colonial Pennsylvania*, The American Social Experience Series, ed. James Kirby Martin (New York: New York University Press, 1987), 1.

6. Schwartz, *"Mixed Multitude,"* 296.

7. Thomas H. Olbricht, "Continental Reformation Backgrounds for the *Declaration and Address*," in this volume.

8. Robert Richardson, "Reformation.—No. V," *Millennial Harbinger* (1848): 33. All references to the *Millennial Harbinger* refer to the undated reprint edition by College Press, Joplin, Mo. I cite the *Harbinger* only by year and page. Hiram J. Lester points out that the Stone-Campbell Movement's institutionalized program for unity was "a historic break from a normative sectarian past"; see Lester, "The Form and Function of the *Declaration and Address*," in this volume.

9. Alexander Campbell, *Christian System*, 2d ed. (Cincinnati: Standard Publishing, 1839), 107.

10. *D&A*, 27.39-42.

11. A brief summary of the elements of the Christian faith may be found in the undated pamphlet by Thomas Campbell, "Prospectus of a Religious Reformation," available online at: http://www.mun.ca/rels/restmov/texts/tcampbell/etc/porr.htm.

12. *D&A*, 19.49-20.3; 13.18-20.

13. *D&A*, 18.8-15.

14. *D&A*, 14.37-41.

15. *D&A*, 22.8-16.

16. *D&A*,12.32-44. On contemporary philosophical influences that encouraged toleration, see Michael W. Casey, "The Theory of Logic and Inference in the *Declaration and Address*," in this volume.

17. See Propositions Five through Eight against legalism, and *D&A*, 22.37-47; 30.38-32.10, against latitudinarianism. TC, having earlier been charged with the religious crime of latitudinarianism, made a rare joke, working into the same

sentence as this "gigantic" word an utterly irrelevant reference to the Zamzummins (*D&A*, 30:41-42).

18. See, in this volume, Lester, "Form"; Casey, "Theory"; Olbricht, "Continental"; Carisse Mickey Berryhill, "Scottish Rhetoric and the *Declaration and Address*; Hans Rollmann, "The Eschatology of the *Declaration and Address*." Also Leroy Garrett, "Bicentennial Notes on Restoration History: Thomas Campbell Writes His Declaration of Independence," *Restoration Review* 18 (1976): 244-47.

19. Christopher R. Hutson, "Thomas Campbell's Use of Scripture in the *Declaration and Address*," in this volume.

20. TC's free use of the Old Testament in the passages about to be quoted does not contradict his expressed belief that the Old Testament is the constitution of the Jewish nation alone. That the Law is no constitution for the church does not subtract from the validity of its history, poetry, prophecy, and general moral principles. See *D&A*, 49.28-46. His son shared this view; when criticized for his supposed rejection of the Old Testament, he replied, "I make more use of the Old Testament in my family, and in my public addresses, than any Baptist I know." See Alexander Campbell, "Letter to R. B. Semple—No. IV," *Millennial Harbinger* (1831): 201.

21. Alexander Campbell, "A Journal of a Voyage to America," Manuscript D, microfilm; used by permission of the Disciples of Christ Historical Society.

22. *D&A*, 8.20-24. On resonance, see Richard Weaver, "The Spaciousness of Old Rhetoric," in *The Ethics of Rhetoric* (Chicago: Henry Regnery, 1953), 164-85.

23. *D&A*, 3.9-17; 21.15-18.

24. *D&A*, 3.17-20.

25. Kenneth Burke, *Attitudes Toward History*, 3d ed. (Berkeley: University of California Press, 1984), 336.

26. *D&A*, 28.37-47. This necessity for a common ground explains why TC could later wage an argumentative campaign against the Mormons, without being inconsistent.

27. *D&A*, 28.22-24.

28. *D&A*, 4.42, 43.

29. *D&A*, 21.46-22.4.

30. *D&A*,10.35-37.

31. *D&A*, 10.45.

32. *D&A*, 11.1-14.

33. *D&A*, 11.16-22. TC was devoted to the private nature of personal opinions. When his son published a philosophical dialogue on the Holy Spirit in the first edition of the *Christian System*, TC rebuked him for his philosophical speculations; out of respect for his father's opinion, AC omitted the dialogue from the second edition. See Robert Richardson, *Memoirs of Alexander Campbell* (Indianapolis: Religious Book Service, n.d.), 2:355.

34. *D&A*, 16.18-19.

35. *D&A*, 16.25-26.
36. *D&A*, 17.8-10.
37. *D&A*, 17.25-27.
38. *D&A*, 13.7, 8; 12.45.
39. *D&A*, 13.11-13.
40. *D&A*, 12.3-5, 24-25.
41. *D&A*, 18.43-46. See Rollmann, "Eschatology."
42. *D&A*, 19.3, 4.
43. *D&A*, 37.48-38.1.
44. *D&A*, 38.14-17.
45. *D&A*, 22.26-27.
46. Hutson, "Use of Scripture."
47. See *D&A*, 26.6-15; 26.34; 29.32-34; 27.23-28; 27.31-33; 28.14-17; 33.6; 38.14-17; 40.30; and 50.5-6.
48. Earl Irvin West, *The Search for the Ancient Order* (Nashville: Gospel Advocate, 1957), 1:49, also cited in Douglas A. Foster, "The Understanding and Impact of the *Declaration and Address* among Churches of Christ," in this volume. On the origin of this motto, see Hans Rollmann, "In Essentials Unity: The Pre-History of a Restoration Movement Slogan," *Restoration Quarterly* 39, no. 3 (1997): 129-39.
49. *D&A*, 24.12-13.
50. Lester, "Form."
51. There are portions of catechisms in AC's writings, though he never compiled them into a book. For example, two hundred questions and answers are presented in catechistic format in his "Extra, No. 4," in *Millennial Harbinger* (1832): 337-66.
52. Ernest Stefanik, "Toward a Critical Edition of the *Declaration and Address*," in this volume.
53. Alexander Campbell, *Memoirs of Elder Thomas Campbell, Together with a Brief Memoir of Mrs. Jane Campbell* (Cincinnati: H. S. Bosworth, 1861), 130-31.
54. Lester G. McAllister, *Thomas Campbell: Man of the Book* (St. Louis: Bethany Press, 1954), 140-43.
55. *D&A*, 2d ed., in *Historical Documents Advocating Christian Union*, ed. Charles Alexander Young (Rosemead, Calif.: Old Path Book Club, 1955), 76 n; see also AC, "Anecdotes, Incidents and Facts," in *Millennial Harbinger* (1848): 280.
56. AC, "Anecdotes," 280, 281.
57. Richardson, *Memoirs*, 1:335-47.
58. The pages are unnumbered. The manuscript is available on microfilm from the Disciples of Christ Historical Society.
59. Rollmann, "Eschatology."
60. *D&A*, 13.7-15.
61. *D&A*, 16.36-41.

62. *D&A*, 25.17-23.

63. This is from Richardson's transcription, *Memoirs*, 1:344.

64. R[ichardson], R[obert], "Death of Joseph Bryant," in *Millennial Harbinger* (1867): 387.

65. *D&A*, 28.33-37.

66. AC, "Any Christians among Protestant Parties," in *Millennial Harbinger* (1837): 412.

67. *D&A*, 47.9-15; 17.28-38.

68. AC reconciled his forbearance and advocacy by a creative invention of "real" and "formal" remission of sins. See Richard T. Hughes and C. Leonard Allen, *Illusions of Innocence: Protestant Primitivism in America, 1630–1875* (Chicago: University of Chicago Press, 1988), 179.

69. Richardson, *Memoirs*, 2:244.

70. Richardson, *Memoirs*, 2:245.

71. Amos Sutton Hayden, *Early History of the Disciples in the Western Reserve, Ohio; with Biographical Sketches of the Principal Agents in Their Religious Movement* (Cincinnati: Chase and Hall, 1875), 161-70.

72. Brooks Major, "The Campbell-Ferguson Controversy," in *Explorations in the Stone-Campbell Traditions: Essays in Honor of Herman A. Norton*, ed. Anthony L. Dunnavant and Richard L. Harrison, Jr. (Nashville: Disciples of Christ Historical Society, 1995), 55-70.

73. Richardson, *Memoirs*, 1:274.

74. James L. Golden, Goodwin F. Berquist, and William E. Coleman, "The Communicator's Stance," in *The Rhetoric of Western Thought*, 5th ed. (Dubuque, Iowa: Kendall/Hunt, 1992), 352-62.

75. Wayne C. Booth, "The Rhetorical Stance," *College Composition and Communication* 14, no. 3 (October 1963): 139-45.

76. See Lewis L. Snyder, "Alexander Campbell as a Change-Agent in the Stone-Campbell Movement from 1830–1840" (Ph.D. diss., Ohio State University, 1986), 383. I originally called this the stance of "the tolerant advocate."

77. Golden, Berquist, and Coleman, "Communicator's Stance," 361.

78. On identification, see Kenneth Burke, *A Rhetoric of Motives* (Berkeley: University of California Press, 1969), 19-28.

God, Christ, and Soteriology in the *Declaration and Address*

Carl F. Flynn

This paper reflects on the theological claims of Thomas Campbell's *Declaration and Address* with an eye toward what it affirms about God, Christ, and salvation. This task immediately confronts one with a problem: the *D&A* makes few direct theological affirmations. Unlike the Nicene Creed, with its explicit claims about God and Christ, or the Westminster Confession, which delineates the particulars of salvation, the *D&A* only makes generic allusions to an implicit theology that lies somewhere in the subtext of the document.

In light of this dilemma, how should one approach the *D&A* in this analysis? On the one hand, one should not want to make the *D&A* something it was never cut out to be theologically. It is not a creed or systematically developed system of doctrine that expresses a clarified understanding of God, Christ, and salvation. Yet the *D&A* is a theological writing. TC's motivation in composing the *D&A* is to glorify God. His hope is that the Association created by this constitution will bring about the restoration of the intended unity of the church, with the chief end being the spread of the gospel to all the world and the final reunion with God in the resurrection. So I find myself, due to the nature of the *D&A* and the theological task before us, between a methodological rock and hard place.

The approach I shall take in this analysis does not solve the dilemma, but it gives priority to the *D&A* and the claims that it makes regarding

God, Christ, and soteriology. I shall first examine the claims of the text, and then make some theological connections with Scripture and theological traditions with which TC may have been familiar. This may, at the end of the day, help us to ground the theological perspective of the *D&A* within an overarching schema akin to the thought of the document, rather than making the document cohere within a particular theological framework from the outset.

Who Is God in the *D&A*?

We must first distinguish between God and Christ in the *D&A*. We cannot blame the confusion we encounter between the usage of God and Christ throughout the text solely on the lack of theological clarity in TC's writing. Christian theologians have struggled for centuries in their attempt to articulate the relationship between God and Christ in the doctrine of the Trinity. Classically rendered, this doctrine claims that the Holy One of Israel is expressed in three interrelated persons: God the Father, God the Son, and God the Holy Spirit. It is apparent that the *D&A*, while not delineating trinitarian relations, relies on an implicit trinitarian understanding of God.[1] As a result, there is ambiguity throughout the text as to the distinctions between God and Christ essential to our inquiry.

An example is the infamous Campbellian call for a "thus saith the Lord" to establish authority in matters of faith and practice. Is a "thus saith the Lord" part of the "law of Christ" or the "word of God?" In other words, is it a literal word from Jesus or does this phrase encompass the express will of God from the entirety of Scripture? The answer in this case is "Yes" to both questions. Throughout the *D&A*, "Lord" is used in reference to the person and work of God as well as to the historical person and work of Jesus Christ.[2] The conflation of God and Christ into "Lord" seems to be a theological claim that for TC the work of Jesus Christ is nothing less than the work of God the Son, according to trinitarian expression.[3]

This observation raises a second question: Could TC have meant something by his generic references to God and his more specific references to Father, Son, Holy Spirit, Christ, and Jesus? Do we have in TC an unwitting genius of trinitarian reflection? Sometimes it is evident that a distinction is being made, but it usually serves a different purpose and is not making any explicit theological claims. For example, in the midst of the Address, TC declares that the call to Christian unity comes not from man, "but by Jesus Christ, and God the Father, who raised him from the dead."[4] A distinction is made here, but his purpose is not to clarify the nuances of trinitarian doctrine. Rather, TC invokes Jesus Christ and God to emphasize the authoritative ground for the call to unity. While this claim certainly has implications for TC's understanding of the relationship between the Son and the Father, it is only an incidental effect of the argument.

Thus, in answer to my question, TC is not interested in making distinctions between, for example, the Jesus of history and the Christ of faith. When he uses the term "Jesus" he is not making an ontological distinction from the term "Christ." This is, frankly, too theologically erudite for TC, who is no systematician. These sorts of theological details are only incidental to his burning concern for a method by which the union of the saints can be brought about in accordance with the divine will. TC has years of empirical evidence that this union can only be built upon the foundation of the express word of God and not theological systems constructed by humans.[5]

Now, having dispensed with the questions of theological distinctions between God and Christ, we turn to TC's understanding of God in the *D&A*.

God as Providence

Before delving into this study, I thought, on the basis of the theological norm in my Restoration heritage, that TC conceived of God as no longer active among his people. In light of this false impression, it was a wonderful surprise to see throughout the *D&A* a commitment to God's providential care. TC has on his theological horizon a God who is the Lord of history and who is present with his church, calling it and encouraging it as it strives to fulfill the divine will.

Throughout the *D&A*, TC holds to the notion that God is the director of the events of history. As he declares in the Address, "Duty then is ours: but events belong to God."[6] By this, TC means that God is the Lord of the events of history; humans are only required to fall in behind the leading of God as he unfolds these events. In particular, TC believed that God unfolded the historical events that led to the establishment of the United States of America. Here was an environment in which Christian union had the possibility of becoming a reality since the civil government was not wedded to one particular form of Christianity.[7] To support this supposition, TC cites the prosperity of the gospel in the wake of the French Revolution and the greater union among Christian brothers and sisters in Europe as signal events showing God's intent to unify the church during his era on a broad scale.[8] TC must have also seen himself as one obediently falling in behind this historical leading of God, since he was forced by his health to come to America, the only place, so he seemed to think, where his vision for Christian unity could meet with some success.

All of this confidence in God's providential direction of history is part of TC's millennial concern. TC stands in a classic, prophetic tradition that sees a direct relationship between the events of history, the prophecies of Scripture, and the return of Christ.[9] In one section of the *D&A*, for example, TC cites several prophecies of Zion and relates them to events of his day that signal the end.[10] At one point, he even pleads with the reader with a phrase common among those with zeal for the millennium: "Do ye not discern *the signs of the times?*"[11] Two of these classic "signs of the times" were an increase in natural disasters (especially earthquakes) and the conversion of the world. Natural disasters were interpreted as signs of judgment, designed to give Christians an opportunity to proclaim the gospel around the world. Once all had the opportunity to hear the gospel, the end would bring salvation for the redeemed and destruction for the rest. TC saw the natural "signs of the times" as judgment not only against unbelievers, but also against the divided church.[12] Union of Christians, he argued, would perpetuate the proclamation of the gospel worldwide by giving integrity to the message, as well as through the sheer force of the church working in harmony. His hope was that the universal proclamation would take place before God, in his providence, would bring about the consummation of history.[13]

In sum, TC saw the signs of history indicating the coming end, and was motivated to fall in behind God's leading to bring about the union of Christians so that the gospel could be proclaimed to the ends of the earth. It was confidence in this pervasive providence of God that compelled TC to pursue so vigorously the task of the union of all Christians.

God as Judge

We have already noted that for TC the judgment of God was directed not against the unbeliever, but the divided church. The reason the church suffers the judgment of God is that it has replaced God as judge. As a result of this "usurpation" the church has alienated itself from other

Christians and hindered the spread of the gospel.[14] As TC decries, "Thus while professing christians bite and devour one another they are consumed one of another, or fall a prey to the righteous judgments of God . . . [and] even the gospel of the blessed Jesus, is reduced to contempt."[15]

In order to restore things to their proper order, TC encourages Christians to share his conviction that "as no man can be *judged* for his brother, so no man can *judge* for his brother."[16] The only trustworthy standard of judgment is "the express letter of the law" in Scripture.[17] As the Word of God, this divine standard "in all its gracious declarations, precepts, ordinances and holy examples" is the only firm foundation for judgment.[18] In Scripture, TC affirms, what we have is the expression of the divine will discernible in "express terms" or "approved precedents."[19] Thus, no judgment can be secured against another Christian "for which there cannot be expressly produced a 'thus saith the Lord.'"[20]

Therefore, God is judge in two senses. First, the authority of God that stands behind the express commands and examples in his Word allows God to judge through the pages of Scripture. By adhering to the "express terms" and "approved precedents" of Scripture, the church can be assured that God's judgment, rather than some "human interpretation," is being heard. TC is confident that if this approach to making judgments between Christians is followed, many of the existing divisions will be dissolved since they are more often than not rooted purely in human opinion.[21]

This approach to discerning God's judgment in Scripture has strong affinities in both form and motive with Chapter I, Article IV, of the Westminster Confession:

> The authority of the holy Scripture, for which it ought to be believed and obeyed, dependeth not upon the testimony of any man or church, but wholly upon God (who is truth itself), the Author thereof; and therefore it is to be received, because it is the Word of God.[22]

Allusions have already been made in other contributions to this volume to a possible influence of the Westminster theology on Campbell.[23] Here we see another occasion that supports this thesis. In form, the Scriptures are considered to be the final authority for both TC and the Confession. In addition, the motive of both the Confession and the *D&A* for holding to the express authority of Scripture is the same. TC asserts that by holding to the authority of the Bible, human opinions will be avoided in making judgments. The Westminster Confession does not have the same function in view, but asserts that an allegiance to the authority of

Scripture will help one to depend on God through the Bible, rather than on "the testimony of any man or church." Thus, we see a possible theological trajectory stretching from the views that triumphed in Westminster Assembly to the work of TC.

Second, God is judge in his present judgment against the church. This judgment is manifest in the Lord's withholding his "gracious influential presence from his ordinances," as well as in "not infrequently giv[ing] up the contentious authors and abettors of religious discord to fall into grievous scandals."[24] This direct judgment of God on the church, as we have seen, reflects TC's confidence that God is not distanced from his people, but present with them in both his providence and his judgment.

God as Gracious Lawgiver

As we have seen in our expositions of TC's understanding of God as Providence and Judge, the Word of God plays a pivotal role in the theology expressed in the *D&A*. In addition, I noted that TC holds to the authority of the Word of God in a way strikingly similar to that expressed in the Westminster Confession. For TC, however, biblical authority can only be established within a particular interpretive framework. The express commands and approved precedents of the Bible embody the authoritative Word of God in Scripture. This is clearly stated in the third proposition of the Address:

> Nor ought anything to be admitted, as of Divine obligation, in their church constitution and managements, but what is expressly enjoined by the authority of our Lord Jesus Christ and his apostles upon the New Testament church; either in express terms or by approved precedent.[25]

These commands ("terms") and precedents are the "express letter of the law" or the "Divine law" that emerge from the properly interpreted Word of God.[26] This law is the direct expression of the divine will that forms the basic foundation for Christian unity. It is contained, according to TC, in the New Testament Scriptures, which are superior to the Old Testament canon in authority. This view stems from TC's understanding that in divine providence, God divides history into different dispensations. As the Old Testament dispensation was authoritative for the ancient Hebrews, so the New Testament is the divine law for the church constituted by Jesus Christ.[27] This dispensational understanding of revelation goes hand in hand with TC's approach to the millennium previously discussed, as God makes his will evident from time to time in the course of human events. For TC these historical signs were beginning to point to the consummation of history, which began, as we have noted, with the conversion of the world. In conjunction with this view, TC held that if the unity of the church could be founded on the express law of the New Testament Scriptures, the gospel could be spread and this conversion would be made manifest.

For TC, therefore, God is the "Lawgiver" whose standard is the only basis on which judgments can be made among Christians.[28] TC believes that if Christians of all denominations will give allegiance to this divine law, which requires humbling oneself before the Lawgiver, unity will be the inevitable result. As we saw previously, TC places the blame for division on Christians who have turned away from the divine law and established their own standards. A return to the "Divine Standard" will reverse this process and restore the unity that the primitive church once enjoyed.[29] In the end, this great reversal has millennial implications.

Now, for TC, the fact that God as Lawgiver has clearly expressed his will in his Word for the union of the churches demonstrates that God is gracious. In fact, there is a sense pervading the entire *D&A* of the grace of God. The commands of Scripture are "gracious declarations."[30] God is "graciously pleased . . . to bring to pass the greatest events [in history] from very small beginnings."[31] The reformation proposed moves "with an entire reliance upon promised grace."[32] This graciousness of God is manifest in his "condescension . . . toward guilty, depraved, rebellious man."[33] In other words, grace is the only means by which humanity would have an opportunity to know and carry out the divine will. This approach to grace emphasizes the depravity of humanity and its "absolute dependence" on God to make a way out of the current dilemma they face.[34] This "way out," of course, is the divine law revealed in the express commands and precepts of the New Testament Scriptures.

The theology driving TC's vision has its roots in Augustine's notion of the absolute depravity of humanity. This theological tradition is perpetuated by Calvin and becomes a mainstay in Reformed theology. Thus, it comes as little surprise to find that the Westminster Assembly, composed of a number of Christians from the Reformed tradition, affirmed:

> Man, by his fall into a state of sin, hath wholly lost all ability of will to any spiritual good accompanying salvation; so as a natural man, being altogether averse from that good, and dead in sin, is not able, by his own

> strength to convert himself, or to prepare himself thereunto. . . . [B]y his grace alone, [God] enables him freely to will and to do that which is spiritually good; yet so as that, by reason of his remaining corruption, he doth not perfectly, nor only, will that which is good, but doth also will that which is evil.[35]

In addition, TC's dispensational scheme of revelation parallels the separation between the "covenant of works" and the "covenant of grace" established in the Westminster Confession.[36] Here we have another theological point of contact with the theology of Westminster, further grounding the possibility that TC was influenced by its insights before he ever returned to the Scriptures in order to restore the primitive unity of the church.

In sum, TC's God is a gracious Lawgiver. God is gracious in that he must provide a way for humanity to be restored to unity, since humans cannot do so on their own. He is a Lawgiver in that the medium for restoration God provides is the express letter of the law of the New Testament Scriptures.

Summary

There is much more that could be said about TC's doctrine of God from the *D&A*.[37] But these four emphases give a fairly well-rounded understanding of TC's theology and also provide some helpful connections to a broader theological context in which TC may be better understood. I now move to what will necessarily be a more abbreviated treatment of TC's Christology.

Who Is Christ in the *D&A*?

In my introductory comments to the previous section, I briefly discussed the difficulty of determining the roles of God and Christ in the *D&A*. I suggested that TC does not distinguish systematically between God and Christ on most points of theology. The activities of Father, Son (Christ) and Holy Spirit are consistently portrayed as the work of one God. In fact, throughout the *D&A*, it seems as if Father and Son are only used as titles. There is no trinitarian argument made to define their characters. The Father is the Father simply because Jesus Christ is his Son. And Jesus Christ is given the title "Son" because God is his Father. This falls in line with both a New Testament understanding of the relationship between the God of Israel and the Christian understanding of the fulfillment of God's promises in Jesus Christ, as well as with the classic creedal distinctions between God the Father and God the Son.[38] Interestingly, the Holy Spirit is given more press in the *D&A* as the trinitarian name given to the present activities of God among his people.

So where does this leave one in determining the role of Christ in the *D&A*? I can begin by affirming that the term "Christ" in the *D&A* refers both to the human existence of Jesus and to Christ as the subject of Christian faith.[39] It is also used generically throughout the text as a title, in the classic form "the Lord Jesus Christ." For TC, as we have noted, this is not a tripartite theological designation for Jesus. I suggest that TC simply carries over this formulation from Scripture and tradition. Aside from these primary uses, there are three other roles that Christ plays in the *D&A*: Savior, Lawbearer, and Head of the church.

Christ as Savior

I shall devote an entire section of this paper to soteriology, so my comments here will be as brief as possible. In the *D&A*, Christ is the means of God's gift of salvation. This comes as no surprise, since this has been a central affirmation of the Christian faith since its inception. For TC, Christ is known solely through the Bible.[40] When he is received in faith and obedience, the believer is saved and, as a result, is united with him. Thus, Christ becomes our sole authority as he is exhibited in the Word.[41] As our authority, Christ saves us from our depraved state of nature and calls us to honor the unity that is created in him with all believers.

Insofar as the role of Christ as Savior is concerned, this is all that the *D&A* gives us to go on. TC does not expend any substantial amount of time developing the theological nuances of the role of Jesus Christ as Savior. He has no interest in classic theories of the atonement or details about how Jesus saves; his primary concern is unity among Christians. Inasmuch as the role of Christ as Savior touches on this theme it is mentioned: as Christ unites believers in himself as Savior, we should maintain this unity peaceably. This is a significant theological theme, since Christ's role as Savior establishes not only the foundation and authority for Christian faith, but is also the primary medium for the unity of all Christians.

Christ as Lawbearer

One prominent phrase in the *D&A* that bears on TC's Christology is "the law of Christ."[42] This phrase carries the same meaning and functions in the same manner as "the express letter of the law." In addition, it is used interchangeably throughout the *D&A* with other statements, such as "Divine law." The specific significance of this "law" terminology is that while God is the Lawgiver, it is in Jesus Christ that the law is born. Thus, all of TC's "law" terminology, while finally grounded in God as Lawgiver, always has an essential point of contact with the incarnate Son of God, Jesus Christ. It is necessary, therefore, to hold in tension the two natures of Christ—the eternal nature of God the Son and the historical incarnation of God in Jesus Christ—in order to make sense of TC's approach to the "law of Christ" in the *D&A*.

TC's commitment to a dispensational understanding of revelation motivates him to separate the words of Christ and the apostles in the New Testament Scriptures as of greater authority than the express commands and precedents from Old Testament Scriptures.[43] This defines the parameters of the law of Christ on a historical basis: since the New Testament records the commands and examples of Jesus Christ and the church he constituted, it is prior to the Old Testament laws. On this foundation, TC narrowed the scope of biblical law that was essential to Christian faith. His plea was that if Christians could obey these commands and precepts of the "law of Christ," that is, God's will expressed to the full in the gracious dispensation in Jesus Christ, the ground for Christian union would be clearly established. Christ as Lawbearer, therefore, serves in TC's theology as the final, authoritative ground on which to assure the unity of Christians.

Once again, then, we see that all of theology undergirds the plea for Christian unity that resounds throughout the *D&A*.

Christ as the Churches' Head

The roles of Christ as Savior and Lawbearer are summed up in the absolute authority granted to Christ in the *D&A* as the Churches' Head. As we have seen, Christ is the Savior who unites believers in himself to one another through the express letter of the law of Christ. In other words, if believers obey the express commands of the New Testament Scriptures, they will enjoy the intended unity in Christ. Both of these activities take place under the authority and "all sufficiency" of the Churches' Head.[44]

The notion of Christ as head of the church comes directly from the New Testament and has been adopted in the creedal affirmations of the Christian faith.[45] It is no surprise, therefore, that TC takes it up in the *D&A*. As head of the church, Christ is the center of its authority who instructs the church as to its purpose by his Word.[46] As the church works to fulfill its purpose, it relies upon the head. As a result of the grace of the head, the church receives encouragement in its efforts.

One example of this is the hope, expressed in the *D&A*, that this newly formed society, "relying upon the all-sufficiency of the Churches' Head," would "afford a competent support to such ministers as the Lord may graciously dispose to assist."[47] TC hoped that the Association would be able to support, through donations, ministers to be sent out to "promote a pure evangelical reformation."[48] In his plea, however, he recognized the sovereignty of the will of the head as to whether or not his hope would become a reality. This affirms that for TC, Christ is in control of the operations of the church. Inasmuch as TC can assist in bringing about the unity of the church, he is willing to do so. Yet, he seems equally willing to have his plans fail if he is counteracting the will of the head. I think, however, that based on his reading of Scripture regarding the need to unify Christians, TC's confidence in his understanding of the will of the head is strong enough to encourage him that he is within the bounds of God's will in his plea for unity.

Here again we may see TC's emphasis on the absolute authority or sovereignty of God. This fundamental affirmation underlies all of the theological emphases I have identified in my analysis of the *D&A* thus far.

Summary

It is difficult, if not impossible, to construct a consistent Christology from the *D&A*. I have, however, suggested several affirmations about Christ from the *D&A*: the two natures of Christ, Christ as a new dispensation, Christ as Savior, Christ as bearer of the law, and Christ as the supreme authority of the church. Yet even these affirmations are finally subservient to TC's overriding concern for the unity of Christians. This, so it seems to TC, is the core of Christian theology.

What Is Salvation in the *D&A*?

In my explorations of God and Christ in the *D&A*, I have noted that TC is not attempting to treat theological affirmations systematically. We have had to read the *D&A* and, from the affirmations therein, move to more general statements as to its theology. As we approach the question of soteriology in the *D&A*, we find ourselves in a similar situation. In fact, the most that is positively affirmed in the *D&A* about salvation is that it is effected by no more than "a profession of faith in and obedience to [Christ], in all things according to his word."[49] The *D&A* does not enjoin any of the classic questions surrounding the understanding of soteriology. Baptism, which later becomes central to soteriology in the Restoration tradition, is only mentioned once in the *D&A*, and, in this instance, baptism has nothing to do with salvation, but with unity.[50] In addition, there is in the *D&A* no mention or discussion of the classic theories of atonement.

This leads me to affirm that in the *D&A* salvation is assumed. There is no need to develop a systematic approach to salvation, nor to spell out the details of salvation from Scripture because the *D&A* is only concerned with salvation, as with these other doctrines, as peripheral to the driving issue of the unity of the church. Once we are in this arena, however, there are several things that the *D&A* has to say about salvation. But outside of the question of unity, the *D&A* is generally silent in regard to soteriology.

Turning toward this arena, then, the first thing that I can affirm about soteriology in the *D&A* is that salvation is only available in the church.[51] TC held a literal view of Mt 16:19: "Whatever you bind on earth will be bound in heaven, and whatever you loose on earth will be loosed in heaven."[52] Therefore, if a church grants or withdraws salvation from a person on earth, it is likewise granted or withdrawn in heaven. This must be the case since a person cannot be placed outside of the Kingdom of God and still retain his "hopeful state."[53]

But what happens when a person is dismissed by one church and readily received into another? In TC's view, if the dismissing church was faithful to the Word of God in its express declarations, then the receiving church endangers its own existence as a church of Christ.[54] For TC, this dilemma clearly demonstrates the problem of the division of the churches. How can it be true that salvation is available only in the church when the church itself does not agree on the terms of salvation and damnation? This is why TC places such stress on determining how to get at the will of God expressed in his Word. If the terms of salvation can be clearly delineated in Scripture, then the churches will have a basis on which to mutually judge between the saved and the damned. It is at this point we see the convergence of soteriology and unity.

The obverse of this dilemma emphasizes another aspect of soteriology in the *D&A*. I have already mentioned that salvation is obtained by "Christ as exhibited in his word." TC contends that since the church has not been proclaiming a gospel informed by the Word of God—preferring to tout its own standards informed by human opinion—Christ has not been exhibited according to his own Word in evangelistic preaching. Therefore, the gospel is hindered and salvation is not available to those who are dying. "Should [our divisions] be perpetuated, 'till the day of judgment, would they convert one sinner from the error of his ways, or save a soul from death?"[55] TC's driving point here is that while the church remains divided, a number of people are perishing since the gospel is not being univocally proclaimed. Here we see that the witness of the church as it proclaims the gospel is one medium through which faith and salvation come about. This reemphasizes the notion of a Christian union on the Word of God that will overcome the confusion about the gospel that has arisen within a divided church.

In sum, salvation is an assurance from God received by faith in and obedience to Christ as he is exhibited in the Word of God. It can only be enjoyed within the context of the church and cannot be extended to anyone outside of its bounds. This approach to soteriology fits well with the affirmation in the Westminster Confession that "the principle acts of saving faith are accepting, receiving, and resting upon Christ alone for justification, sanctification, and eternal life, by virtue of the covenant of grace."[56] Thus, TC shows yet another aspect in which his theology is influenced by the theology of Westminster.

Concluding Reflections

In TC's *D&A*, the pivotal theological point is the union of all Christians on the foundation of the Word of God. As I have observed in my exposition of God, Christ, and soteriology in the *D&A*, every other theological category plays a subservient role to this first principle. Thus, God in the *D&A* is seen as the Lord of history who stands in judgment on the church because it has failed to live according to the express commands and precedents of the Word of God. Christ has a hand in God's judgment as the head of the church whose law requires the union of Christians in order to be effective for salvation rather than judgment. And this salvation is manifested in faith in and obedience to Christ inasmuch as he is known in the Word of God. TC worked within this theological perspective, calling the church of his day to rededicate itself to the Word of God so that the unity of the church could be restored. But restoration of primitive unity was not the sole end TC had in mind. TC's millennial anticipation saw this union of the saints as a step along the way to the conversion of the world and, soon thereafter, the consummation of history.

This theological vision is an extension of a Reformed theology best summarized in the Westminster Confession. From my analysis of the *D&A* in light of the Confession, I am compelled to think that the Westminster theology held a strong influence over TC before he ventured through the pages of the Bible. I would even be willing to go out on a limb and claim that a later version of the Westminster theology is the "implicit" theology that runs throughout the *D&A*. I only make two exceptions to the absolute consistency of the Westminster theology as the vision driving TC's theology in this document. First is the millennial concern of TC, which takes its influence from another tradition of thought not expressed in the Confession. Second is the ingenuity of TC as he sought the "express terms and examples" of the Word of God. TC probably kept much of the Westminster theology because it fit within his approach to Scripture, but that which conflicted with the express word or fell under the category of biblical silence may have been either unexpressed in the *D&A* or dropped from TC's theological horizon.

More work needs to be done along these lines in tracing out the theological trajectories that inform the *D&A*. I consider what I have done here only a beginning. I have spent a great deal of time mining the text of the *D&A* for its theological claims, and less time checking the broader theological horizon for possible influences. I see an in-depth study into the latter as something that would greatly enrich the theological self-understanding of the various Restoration traditions.

Notes

1. Thomas Campbell, *Declaration and Address of the Christian Association of Washington* (Washington, Pa.: Brown & Sample, 1809), 13.48-14.1; 41.44-49. [Line numbering throughout concurs with the on-line version of this edition arduously constructed by Ernie Stefanik.]

2. *D&A*, 22.39-41; 23.19-24.

3. I am not claiming here that TC adheres to a particular form of trinitarian doctrine. I am simply observing that functionally "Lord" denotes both the work of God and Christ for TC. This intends that there is some trinitarian framework at work in TC, though it is never made explicit, nor is it central to his argument in the *D&A*.

4. *D&A*, 13.48-14.1.

5. *D&A*, 46.7-9.

6. *D&A*, 11.35-36.

7. *D&A*, 7.47-8.6.

8. *D&A*, 8.24-32.

9. Many of these suggestions stem from research done for a paper I have written (unpublished) on the response of Restoration leaders to the Millerite movement. See Paul Boyer, *When Time Shall Be No More* (Cambridge, Ma.: Harvard University Press, 1992), and James Davidson West, *Logic of Millennial Thought* (New Haven: Yale University Press, 1977), for further background. Some notable figures in the tradition include Sir Isaac Newton and the founder of the Christian Adventist/Seventh-Day Adventist movement, who was a contemporary of the Campbells, William Miller (1782–1849).

10. *D&A*, 13.26-14.45.

11. *D&A*, 14.19. Emphasis mine.

12. *D&A*, 7.45-8.7; 13.31-15.7. Note especially the references in the *D&A* to earthquakes. These are not metaphorical earthquakes! "Sign watchers" were ever aware of the natural portents signaling the return of Christ.

13. *D&A*, 54.13-26.

14. *D&A*, 3.15-20.

15. *D&A*, 7.28-38.

16. *D&A*, 3.9-10.

17. *D&A*, 3.17.

18. *D&A*, 6.13-14.

19. *D&A*, 27.41-43.

20. *D&A*, 27.47-48.

21. *D&A*, 33.5-35.19.

22. "The Westminster Confession of Faith," Chapter I, Article 4 [http://www.gty.org/~phil/creeds/wcf.htm#chap1], June 2000.

23. Michael W. Casey, "The Theory of Logic and Inference in the *Declaration and Address*," in this volume.

24. *D&A*, 7.24-27.

25. *D&A*, 16.26-30.

26. *D&A*, 42.9-12. In this passage the relationship between command, precedent, and law is negatively stated.

27. *D&A*, 49.28-41.

28. *D&A*, 27.28 ff.

29. *D&A*, 35.31-47.

30. *D&A*, 6.12.

31. *D&A*, 11.33.

32. *D&A*, 27.17.

33. *D&A*, 48.2-3.

34. *D&A*, 49.11.

35. "Westminster Confession," Chapter IX, Articles 2-3.

36. "Westminster Confession," Chapter VII, Articles 2-3.

37. See *D&A*, 47.43-47; 48.1 ff.; 49.2 ff.

38. Thomas C. Oden (*Systematic Theology*, vol. 1, *The Living God* [San Francisco: HarperCollins, 1987]) calls the attempt of New Testament authors to wrestle with the revolutionary understanding of God revealed in Christ "proto-trinitarian" thought. Oden's position, with which I am in agreement, is that we do not have in the New Testament a systematic treatment of the Trinity. If this is the case, then any trinitarian conception that emerges from the New Testament relies either on a preconception of the Trinity informed by the later creedal affirmations, such as Nicaea, or on one's own deductive reasoning from the texts of Scripture. TC, in my estimation, could either be working from a deductive approach to the New Testament in his "implicit trinitarianism" or from the affirmations of Westminster and other historical creeds. It is impossible to tell from what we have in the *D&A* and, in the final analysis, is probably a combination of both approaches.

39. *D&A*, 9.39; 47.11.

40. *D&A*, 4.6.

41. *D&A*, 22.25-26; 14.47-48.

42. *D&A*, 3.17-20; 21.7 ff; 24.15-16; 35.45-47; 45.3-16.

43. *D&A*, 16.26-41.

44. *D&A*, 15.30.

45. Eph. 1:22, 4:15, 5:23; Col. 1:18, 2:19.

46. *D&A*, 15.29-36.

47. *D&A*, 5.20-26.

48. *D&A*, 5.25-26.

49. *D&A*, 17.35-37; see also 4.6; 42.45-43.1.

50. *D&A*, 50.46.

51. *D&A*, 33.13-26.

52. Cited in *D&A*, 33.44-45.

53. *D&A*, 33.36-41.

54. *D&A*, 34.48-35.3. This parallels the declaration in Chapter 25, Article 5, of the Westminster Confession: "Some [churches] have so degenerated as to become apparently no churches of Christ."

55. *D&A*, 13.38-40.

56. "Westminster Confession," Chapter XIV, Article 2.

The Eschatology of the *Declaration and Address*

Hans Rollmann

"Do ye not discern the signs of the times?" Eschatological Events as Signals for United Ecclesiastical Action

With most evangelicals of his day, Thomas Campbell shared the view of a pervasively evil world in need of salvation.[1] This black-and-white picture is, however, not the specific problem for which the *Declaration and Address* offers a solution; it rests rather with the state of the empirical churches—in particular, those of which TC and the Christian Association of Washington were members. He and his fellow Association members had been directly affected by ecclesiastical "divisions," "schisms," and "party contentions" in such a way that they viewed them as serious obstacles to a vigorous proclamation of the gospel and "spiritual intercourse among Christians."[2] The confessional and ecclesiastical barriers erected by his presbytery prohibited, among others, a wider fellowship during the Lord's Supper, "that great ordinance of unity and love."[3] TC's more inclusive attitude and practical ecumenism had become a divisive issue between him and his fellow Seceder clergy in western Pennsylvania within a year of his arrival.[4]

This *Sitz im Leben* is reflected in the apocalyptic passages of the *D&A* with a language that draws attention to the "awful and distressing effects" of ecclesiastical division. These divisions, according to TC, produced "reproaches," "backbitings," "evil surmisings," "angry contentions," "enmities," "excommunications," congregational discord, "confusion," ministerial and sacramental destitution and deprivation, interference in "spiritual intercourse among Christians," but also an all too "relaxed discipline" that churches were "afraid to exercise . . . with due strictness, lest their people should leave them, and, under the cloak of some spurious pretence, find refuge in the bosom of another party." Not only did the effects extend to churchgoing and committed Christians, but it had especially a devastating effect on those outsiders in need of the evangelical message. The result was that

> the weak stumbled; the graceless and profane hardened, the mouths of infidels opened to blaspheme religion; and thus, the only thing under heaven, divinely efficacious to promote and secure the present spiritual and eternal good of man, even the gospel of the blessed Jesus, is reduced to contempt; while multitudes deprived of a gospel ministry, as has been observed, fall an easy prey to seducers, and so become the dupes of almost unheard of delusions.[5]

Such had already been TC's European experience, which he now saw repeated in America, the "highly favored" or "happy country." When contrasting American opportunities for proclamation and fellowship with the Old World ecclesiastical situation, he viewed the European hierarchical and episcopal state churches as apocalyptic tools of the devil, a judgment shared by many evangelicals during his day. In the *D&A* TC can therefore speak of "the antichristian hierarchy," of "devoted nations that have given their strength and power unto the beast."[6] In consequence of this infernal pact they now experienced divine wrath. In contrast to America, the "happy country," Europe was experiencing "the Lord's vengeance upon the antichristian world."[7] In one passage this process is rendered explicit with the apocalyptic language of millennialism drawn from Revelation 11:

> Do ye not discern the signs of the times? Have not the two witnesses arisen from their state of political death, from under the long proscription of ages? Have they not stood upon their feet, in the presence, and to the consternation and terror of their enemies? Has not their resurrection been accompanied with a great earthquake? Has not the tenth part of the great city been thrown down by it? Has not this event aroused the nations to indignation? Have they not been angry, yea very angry? Therefore, O Lord, is thy wrath come upon them, and the time of the dead that they

> should be avenged, and that thou shouldest give reward to thy servants, the Prophets, and to them that fear thy name, both small and great; and that thou shouldest destroy them that have destroyed the earth. Who amongst us has not heard the report of these things—of these lightnings and thunderings, and voices; of this tremendous earthquake and great hail; of these awful convulsions and revolutions that have dashed and are dashing to pieces the nations, like a potter's vessel? Yea, have not the remote vibrations of this dreadful shock been felt even by us, whom Providence has graciously placed at so great a distance?[8]

In the absence of a detailed commentary by TC, explaining what he meant, it is difficult to match existing historical events and personalities with his apocalyptic language. While he presupposes a familiarity with the European events among his fellow Europeans in America to whom this address is directed, it is difficult to determine whether the apocalyptic images match historical individuals and natural events or signal, more generally, a wider symbolic correspondence. Among the eschatological specifics, some, such as the "vials of his wrath"[9] and the "two witnesses arisen from their state of political death," stand out.[10]

One way of dealing with the biblical imagery is to interpret it—as Kershner has done—as correlative events of the European Napoleonic wars. The "Two Witnesses" of Revelation 11 refer "to two of the nations liberated by the Napoleonic conquests of the early part of the century." Kershner identifies them with Poland and Egypt as well as other possible principalities, while the "great earthquake" may possibly mirror the earthquake of Lisbon (1755), and the anger of the nations refers to the convulsions shaking Europe in the wake of the Napoleonic conquests.[11]

While revolutionary Europe and the turmoil of the Napoleonic wars obviously furnish the context for TC's apocalyptic illustrations, it seems methodologically more sound to probe the meanings of his apocalyptic language, wherever possible, in the vicinity of those associated with the *D&A*. None of the remaining writings of TC shed light on the apocalyptic passages of the *D&A*, because he does not repeat the specific images and themes elsewhere. TC is clearly a millennialist, because throughout his life he "look[ed] for a Millennium of universal peace and prosperity, in which truth shall universally triumph,"[12] but his eschatology, apart from the *D&A*, remains nonspecific about apocalyptic particulars. Even in his "Synopsis of Christianity"—published in 1844, and according to its publisher, Alexander Campbell, representing a "grand outline, elements, and design of Christianity"—the focus on eschatology is largely paraenetic, assuring those who persist to the end divine inheritance and enjoyment.[13]

In reconstructing the apocalyptic views of TC at the time of the writing of the *D&A*, we are left with his own likely background and with views shared by his immediate coworkers, as well as with the question about his likely exposure to the thought-world of apocalyptic eschatology prior to the writing of the *D&A*.

David Thompson and Hiram J. Lester have pointed out how important are Irish matters for understanding the *D&A*.[14] In this connection Lester also draws attention to the fact of a shared eschatological emphasis in the *Address* of the London Missionary Society and that of the Evangelical Society of Ulster (ESU), of which TC was a charter member. In fact, the one sentence that the two addresses share *verbatim* represents an eschatological reference drawn from Dn 9:25, which also recurs in the *D&A*: "Are we not told, that in troublous times Zion shall be built up?"[15] Beyond citing a direct correspondence in words, Lester also observed that among the shared emphases of the ESU and London documents were

> the unity of all Christians, an eschatological excitement about the new movements in the contemporary church, a conviction of the basic inadequacy and evil of attempting to do the work of the gospel for the sake of a particular party, a belief that the tumultuous times . . . are an indication of the early return of Jesus, among others.[16]

While the *D&A* does not speak of the "early return of Jesus" as such and focuses its apocalyptic attention on the judgment of "the devoted nations, that have given their strength and power unto the beast," a united proclamation of the gospel is indeed central. Both of these elements were part of the eschatology of the Second Great Awakening. And the apocalyptic treatment of state religion, and of Roman Catholicism in particular, was a significant feature as well of Presbyterianism in Ireland during the revolutionary 1790s, when TC most likely became personally exposed to apocalyptic thought.

Peter Brooke, David Miller, and I. R. McBride have demonstrated in their studies on religion in revolutionary Ireland that the Presbyterians of Ulster were caught up in the apocalyptic fervor of the times.[17] The Secession, of which TC was a member, was in the 1790s the fastest growing part of the Presbyterian church in Ireland. Its preoccupation and quarrelsomeness in matters of church polity was balanced by an emphasis on grace in theology and an otherworldly evangelical piety.[18] Seceders were by no means resistant to the thought-world of apocalypticism. As McBride argues, Seceders and Covenanters

> fed on popular attachment to the militant Presbyterian programme set out in the Solemn League and Covenant of 1643, which called for the extirpation of popery and prelacy, and the extension of the Presbyterian revolution throughout the three kingdoms.[19]

Notably the French Revolution, the subsequent disestablishment of French Catholicism, and the eventual expulsion of the Pope from Rome were interpreted widely as the pouring out of the "vials" in Revelation. Already Robert Fleming had predicted the fall of the papacy in 1701 in his *Discourse on the Rise and Fall of the Papacy*, a book reprinted in the 1790s and even serialized in 1793 in the Belfast *Northern Star.*[20] Dickson, the moderator of the Presbyterian Synod of Ulster, predicted in the same year before the synod the "final overthrow of the Beast" as imminent.[21] Other apocalyptic tracts, among them John Owen's *The Shaking and Translation of Heaven and Earth* (1795) and James Bicheno's *The Signs of the Times: Or the Overthrow of Papal Tyranny in France* (1795), were published by the office of the *Northern Star.*[22] Both Owen and Bicheno drew the attention of the young AC, who excerpted copiously from their writings, including Bicheno's chronological speculations about the end-times.[23] An Antiburgher Seceder from Lyle Hill recalled later how the Reverend Isaac Patton had in his preaching related the Pope and the Turks to the figures of Antichrist and the Beast of Revelation.[24] Another theme that surfaced at the time, along with the destruction of the Turks and the papacy, was the conversion of the Jews, a notion that both TC and AC related to the church during the end-times.[25] Father and son Campbell had thus ample opportunities to be exposed to the apocalyptic currents of their day, which saw in the destruction of nations allied with the beast of Revelation—understood as the Roman Catholic Church—a divine judgment as well as a vindication of evangelical Christianity.

While a recreation of the wider European context may be helpful in establishing what TC was previously exposed to, the early unpublished manuscripts of AC, found in Australia, furnish more explicit knowledge about his apocalyptic awareness and interests.[26] It is the AC from 1809–1812 who interests us particularly. Already a cursory view of his notes and writings during that time exhibits his great interest in apocalyptic eschatology. In the absence of other evidence about eschatological particulars in TC, we can consider cautiously AC's apocalyptic interest as also the likely intellectual horizon of his father in those matters. Among the unpublished papers are some items that furnish specific information on eschatology: (1) an introductory fragment from his sermon at the anniversary meeting of the Christian Association of Washington in 1810, some apocalyptic passages of which are not included among the published excerpts in Robert Richardson's Campbell biography but deal with prophecies and their significance for the church; (2) a manuscript from ca. 1810, titled "Opinions and Conjectures on Prophecy: Extracts from Diverse Authors"; among the authors are James Bicheno and Enoch Shepherd, contemporary premillennialists; (3) a manuscript from the same period, titled "Hieroglyphic Dictionary," or "A Symbolic-Vocabulary," in which AC arranges prophetic symbols alphabetically and explains them from various authors, including such classics as Mede, Moore, John Owen, Vitringa, and others; later, in 1832, AC would publish this "dictionary" in a more developed form under the title "Prophetic Iconisms" in the *Millennial Harbinger*;[27] (4) several manuscripts dealing with fulfilled prophecies in the Bible, as well as one on "Important Eras for the Illustration of Prophecy." AC, at the time of the writing of the *D&A* and shortly thereafter, was keenly interested in apocalyptic thought, as those manuscripts demonstrate, a fact never properly appreciated in most of the literature about his eschatology. It seems that the development of an interest in eschatology in AC goes back to his formative years in America and most likely had its earliest roots in his exposure to such thought in Ireland, because some of the authors he is particularly aware of were also bestsellers in Ulster during the 1790s. The publication of his "Prophetic Iconisms" in the *Millennial Harbinger* also establishes a direct continuity between AC's views on eschatology in the 1830s and his apocalyptic interests around the time of the composition of the *D&A*.

If we use Irish apocalypticism and AC's contemporary awareness of apocalyptic literature as a guide, the reference to the pouring out of the vials of wrath on the "devoted nations," an image drawn from Revelation, will refer most likely to the judgment on Catholic and other nations whose state-church relations had so far prevented a thoroughgoing evangelical reform. In the interpretation of contemporaries, the "Beast," to whom, according to TC, the "devoted nations" paid their allegiance, is most likely the Two-Horned Beast of Revelation. Since Martin Luther, but especially since the time of Joseph Mede, it referred to ecclesiastical Rome—that is, the Roman Catholic Church—although in due time Protestant dissenters extended it to refer to any clerical, hierarchical system, including territorial Protestantism. The beast was contrasted by dissenters with an idealized church, the "heavenly woman," who was clothed with the sun and other celestial objects. This extended use of the beast may also be found in TC, who speaks—when contrasting America with Europe—of the "baneful influence of a civil establishment of any peculiar form of christianity" from under the direct influence of the anti-Christian hierarchy—and, at the same time, from any formal connection with "the devoted nations, that have given their strength and power unto the beast."[28] In a series on "Historic Prophecy" in the 1832 *Millennial Harbinger*, AC identifies the beast that arose from the sea with "Rome, in its *Papal* form, while the Papacy and all the clerical dynasties, Protestant and Papistical, are pictured out under the symbol of the *two horned* beast which arose out of the earth."[29]

Roman Catholicism as Babylon and Beast became a powerful image that AC considered antithetical not only to Protestantism but also to America.[30] TC does not spend any appreciable time speculating about how an evangelical reconstruction in the Old World might proceed after God's judgment. His commitment is largely to America, not to Europe. European hierarchies are only invoked as a contrast and incentive for evangelical action in America. Kershner already recognized this importance of America and the contrast with Europe in the thought of TC when he wrote that TC's isolationism was devoid of any "note of sympathy with, or interest in, the European struggles."[31]

The resurrection of the Two Witnesses of Revelation 11, an apocalyptic comeback story that originally had more likely Moses and Elijah in mind, was discussed much in the apocalyptic literature of the day. Interpreters were divided as to what contemporary events and persons they reflected. Kershner thinks that TC refers to "two of the nations liberated by the Napoleonic conquests of the early part of the century."[32] While any meaningful event corresponding to Revelation appears plausible, in August of 1809, when the *D&A* was being penned, two politico-ecclesiastical events had just occurred that might also fit into TC's frame of reference: Napoleon's defeat of the Roman Catholic Austrians and the imprisonment of the Pope, who had excommunicated Napoleon after the annexation of the Papal States in May of the same year.

But an immediate political interpretation is not the only possibility available to students of biblical prophecy at the time. The Two Witnesses can also refer, according to AC, to those who generally "plead for the political and religious rights of men, against the usurpations of priests and kings."[33] If we follow James Bicheno,[34] one of the more prominent late eighteenth- and early nineteenth-century interpreters of Revelation—one also copiously excerpted by AC during the time that the *D&A* was being written—the death of the Two Witnesses occurred in 1685 through Louis XIV, when the French King revoked the Edict of Nantes and set in motion the massive flight of Huguenots from France.[35] The resurrection of the Two Witnesses, after their "political death," is said to have taken place, according to the notes of AC, three-and-one-half lunar days later in 1789, with the French Revolution, when according to Bicheno, as excerpted by AC, "the final attack of the witnesses for civil and religious liberty upon the Errors, usurpations and Tyrannies, of the papal beast" began.[36]

The French Revolution is the starting point for most modern millennial thought and for a reconstruction of apocalyptic chronology, in that it provided a fixed point in the flux of history on which to base the timeline of apocalyptic events. Ernest R. Sandeen, a major modern interpreter of British and American millennialism, goes so far as to call it "a prophetic Rosetta stone."[37] Both TC and AC concur with this judgment in pointing out the significance of that event for the proclamation of the gospel but refrain from speculating on chronology. From the several excerpts of chronological schemes among the manuscripts of AC, no firm conclusion can be reached as to which one he favored. But that the French Revolution represented a milestone and even a turning point in the proclamation of the gospel is clearly stated by both Campbells. TC asks in the *D&A*, "Have not greater efforts been made, and more done, for the promulgation of the gospel among the nations, since the commencement of the French revolution, than had been for many centuries, prior to that event?"[38] AC repeated the same point in his anniversary address of October 1810 celebrating the founding of the Christian Association of Washington.[39]

In the absence of a clear commentary by TC himself, we can never be certain about how he understood the identity of the Two Witnesses. It is clear, however, that all of these intimations of divine judgment on the European continent serve mainly to highlight in a demonstrative manner the "troublous times" in which he and his contemporaries were living. All the other apocalyptic signs from the Bible—the Great Earthquake, lightning, thunderings, voices, and hail—can be interpreted either as natural events of symbolic value, such as the great earthquake of Lisbon in 1755, or as symbolic signifiers of historical and political events reshaping at the time the European continent and significantly affecting the ecclesiastical establishment. If we use AC's "Prophetic Iconisms" as a guide, the tenth part of the Great City can very well refer to "the European part of the Western Roman Empire;"[40] earthquakes to "the political and moral revolutions and convulsions of society;"[41] hail to "killing and destroying;"[42] and thunder and lightning to the "sudden and terrific dispersion and destruction of the forces of war."[43]

While these apocalyptic events were taking place beyond the ocean and were viewed by TC from a distance, they were for him signs of God's punitive judgment and rallying calls for action. As signals to Christians in America, the European events became beacons of hope and invitations to join forces ecclesiastically. For the evangelical "Zion"—so TC assured the readers of the *D&A* with the words of Daniel—will be "built in troublous times." This same assurance is also found earlier in the charter documents of the London Missionary Society and the Evangelical Society of Ulster. The signs, however, have relevance for evangelical America as well: "Yea, have not the remote vibrations of this dreadful shock been felt even by us, whom Providence has graciously placed at so great a distance?"[44] For the "auspicious phenomena of the times, furnish collateral arguments of a very encouraging nature, that our dutiful and pious endeavours shall not be in vain in the Lord."[45] That which eschatological thought of the nineteenth and twentieth centuries has interpreted predominantly as signs of an apocalyptic countdown toward Armageddon were for TC primarily signs of a hopeful beginning: a golden age of the proclamation of the gospel and a purified and unified church. He observed that since the French Revolution efforts toward evangelization had increased, as well as "a more than usual concern for the removal of contentions, for the healing of divisions, for the restoration of a christian and brotherly intercourse one with another, and for the promotion of each other's spiritual good."[46] We know through the research by Thompson and Lester that TC was personally involved in evangelical and ecumenical causes in Ireland, notably his participation in the Evangelical Society of Ulster and his attempts to heal the historic rifts among the Seceders.[47] Thus, the "signs of the times" became for TC once more hopeful reminders that God's *kairos* of evangelization and fellowship had dawned in America. In the *D&A* he exhorted his readers with specific reference to the apocalyptic signs of the times: "Do not suffer yourselves to be lulled asleep by that syren song of the slothful and reluctant professor, 'The time is not yet come—the time is not come—saith he,—the time that the Lord's house should be built.' Believe him not.—Do ye not discern the signs of the times?"[48]

For TC apocalyptic signs were thus signals for call and action, not chronological markers that invited end-time speculations. Advancement of "simple evangelical Christianity" became for him an eschatological action plan, indicated, illuminated, and urged by the "signs of the times." The relative restraint from speculations regarding the end is consistent throughout all of his writings and even increases as time goes on. Not even in periods of eschatological tension, such as the years of Mormon and Millerite excitement, did TC show any signs of a quickened apocalyptic pulse. Apocalyptic eschatology remained for him always directed toward and instrumental in proclamation, spiritual formation, and fellowship.

"The favorable opportunity which Divine Providence has put into your hands, in this happy country . . ." The *D&A* as Eschatological Action Plan

For TC America provided ecumenical opportunities for evangelization not realizable in Europe, as he had experienced personally when his involvement with the Evangelical Society of Ulster was criticized by his church, his objections to the revision of the "Narrative and Testimony" of the Secession Church were ignored, and the plan to unite Burgher and Antiburgher factions among the Seceder Presbyterians was rejected. As David Thompson has suggested, the opposition of the Antiburgher Seceders to the ecumenical ESU may have been motivated by political concerns that itinerant preaching fostered rebellion, and by its proximity to Haldane activities in Ireland.[49] TC's protest over the way in which the planned revision of Seceder polity would limit the liberty of conscience fell temporarily on deaf ears, but it did imply, as Thompson writes, "that he favoured greater liberty of conscience even than the new Testimony allowed."[50] The effort of arriving at an Irish solution for what originally had been Scottish problems and the healing of the Burgher and Antiburgher rift among the Seceders through the union of both parties were rejected by TC's Antiburgher faction while he was the moderator of the Irish Synod and arguing the case for union.[51] One cannot help but observe that TC's introductory remarks of 1804 to the resolutions, suggesting a union of the Burgher and Antiburgher factions, mirror much of the hortatory language with which he chides five years later the discord on the Pennsylvania frontier.[52]

Thus, on all three occasions that TC had championed public ecclesiastical causes in Ireland, he had either lost or been ignored. At the time he wrote the *D&A* he had experienced yet another, more recent, setback in overcoming divisions: the actions by the Chartiers Presbytery and Associate Synod in response to his efforts, among others, toward a more inclusive practice of communion in western Pennsylvania.

The events of churches in the "west" and the state of Christianity in general indicated for him a "high time" for gospel-based action. The reference to "the series of events which have taken place in the churches for many years past, especially in this western country"[53] that now called for decisive action refers presumably to the tension between practical religious needs and confessional obstructionism but also to the signal opportunities witnessed in the recent revivals in the west, which clashed with the Seceder ecclesiastical self-centeredness. America and the frontier offered great promise. TC notes particularly the separation of church and state: ". . . this highly favored country, where the sword of the civil magistrate has not as yet learned to serve at the altar."[54] It is a country without "the baneful influence of a civil establishment of any peculiar form of christianity." America lacked an episcopal system that was wedded to a state-church establishment, a situation that TC linked in apocalyptic terms with God's present-day judgment and the pouring out of the "vials of wrath" over the European nations.[55] God's favor had kept America relatively free from his punitive judgment, a fact TC regarded as a "happy exemption." Ruth Bloch, in her *Visionary Republic: Millennial Themes in American Thought, 1756–1800,* argues that in the wake of the resumption of the European wars in 1803, American evangelicals began to distinguish on a wider scale their own successful revivalistic initiatives more clearly from the European situation, which was beset with "politics, broils, and wars."[56]

And yet amidst such patent advantages and opportunities, ecclesiastical disunity persisted and inhibited the proclamation of the gospel as well as the fellowship and spiritual formation of the believers, which according to TC could be attributed to Satan himself, that "deadly enemy, that is sheathing its sword in the very bowels of his church, rending and mangling his mystical body into pieces."[57] While America was not subject to God's punitive judgments as Europe was, a serious consequence of such divisiveness was nevertheless the absence of divine grace and care from those who perpetuated discord. Moreover, division produced sin instead of removing it, because sinners remained unconverted while the "scriptural purity of communion" among believers was absent.[58] The eschatological action plan suggested in the *D&A* was designed to remedy such evil by overcoming divisions and establishing unity for the purpose of the uninhibited prosperous proclamation of the gospel. Divine Providence had predisposed America to be the place where such goals could be achieved.

Given the advantageous position of America, TC felt the need to "duly esteem and improve those great advantages, for the high and valuable ends, for which they are manifestly given."[59] For him, it was a religious opportunity that demanded undivided attention. He asked: "Can the Lord expect, or require, any thing less, from a people in such unhampered circumstances—from a people so liberally furnished with all means and mercies, than a thorough reformation, in all things civil and religious, according to his word?"[60] TC saw himself as part of a much larger enterprise of evangelization, in which the past could serve as teacher for present efforts. Consequently, the history of discord and unity furnished the "sage experience" needed "to proceed in this business, having before our eyes the inadvertancies and mistakes of others."[61]

The language of experience that informs action may very well have its origins in the inductive Common Sense philosophy of Scotland.[62] The ameliorative and pedagogical tone also may betray more general Enlightenment assumptions, but it hardly represents an American version of Lessing's *Education of the Human Race*. While TC speaks in juridical and egalitarian idiom of participating in this initiative by "universal right" and as "a duty equally belonging to every citizen of Zion,"[63] and while he may share cognitive and anthropological assumptions rooted in Scottish philosophy,[64] the language of "Zion" returns the reader quickly to the distinctively "religious" realm. Zion appears to be a favorite ecclesiastical term that refers to the eschatologically triumphant church. Thus, ministers, advocating a Bible-oriented polity along with a focus on the atonement and holiness, are also called "Zion's watchmen," for whom Campbell hopes—irrespective of their denominational identifications—that soon they "shall see eye to eye, and all be called by the same name."[65] AC, in his eschatological dictionary, begun around the time that his father wrote the *D&A*, defines "Zion" as "the christian church in her impregnable and triumphant character."[66] Such a church differs radically from the traditional state churches with their "unchristian hierarchy" in that their egalitarianism lacks any divinely instituted privileges.[67]

While such laboring on behalf of Zion involved rational communication and egalitarian participation, the Association's business was far from being a humanly generated and directed enterprise. TC acknowledged divine support even where he hoped for human solidarity. His ecclesiastical vision thus represents no secular utopia but a divinely blessed "heavenly enterprize."[68] The effort of "an entire union of all Churches in faith and practice" could not ultimately depend on human competence, but TC felt nevertheless a "bounden duty to make the attempt, by using all due means in our power to promote it."[69] According to Robert Frederick West, AC also later retained and defended, especially against Robert Owen, this "religious" nature of the millennium by arguing "that the controlling part is wrought by the hand of God in the affairs and development of human history, although man's cooperation or lack of cooperation could check or accelerate its arrival."[70] Smallness was no hindrance for initiating the unity effort, as God was able to give the increase. The measures suggested by the *D&A* were considered as "first fruits." They were "preliminary," in that they opened up "the way to a permanent scriptural unity among friends and lovers of truth and peace throughout the churches."[71] Far from dictating terms or representing edicts, TC's program represented an effort in communication. The rational, juridical, pedagogical, and pragmatic elements coexisted in a happy symbiosis with eschatology and divine purpose. We observe repeatedly how easily human effort and divine initiative are brought into harmony. TC, John Wesley, Count Zinzendorf, and many other eighteenth-century church leaders saw no intrinsic contradiction between reason and revelation, awakening and enlightenment, divine guidance and human progressivism.

TC also applies the notion of a "faithful remnant" to the ecumenical laborers, but without the separatist narrowness and exclusivism with which Puritans and sectarians at times claimed this biblical notion in the past.[72] The Association's self-understanding was that of a group preparing the way "for a permanent Scriptural unity among Christians." This was done by considering basics, "fundamental truths" and "first principles," and by engaging in a clean-up operation, where stumbling blocks and "the rubbish of ages" were to be removed. While such eliminations point to yet another Enlightenment presupposition, its antitraditionalism, the remedies were by no means viewed in a perfectionist manner but remained open to correction and amendment.[73] TC pointed out that the means recommended operated, unlike conciliar edicts, through rational persuasion. Throughout the *D&A* the divine will in history never overwhelms individuals but cooperates with rationality and purposive action that is informed by a knowledge of principles laid down in Scripture as the Word of God. For TC, even the "auspicious phenomena" that manifested themselves in European Christendom were after all "collateral arguments" that taught and convinced the laborers in the evangelical vineyard about the legitimacy and timeliness of their endeavor.

Much of this eschatological action plan fits into what Ruth Bloch has observed for American eschatology of the last decade of the eighteenth and the first of the nineteenth century. Extreme hopes and despair over the French Revolution and its accompanying francophilic and francophobic reactions had given way to an evangelicalism that included in particular a role for America in the shaping of religious events as well as a cooperative and "aggressive evangelical action," which focused on the conversion of the individual.[74] Revivals such as those in western Pennsylvania in 1799 and at Cane Ridge in 1801 reinforced the notion that God was moving with power in evangelical America. While TC did not share the assumptions of revivalists about the direct operation of the Holy Spirit, he nevertheless appreciated its effects and had been involved himself in cooperative endeavors in Ireland. He seems to have been well informed on ecumenical initiatives in evangelization and fellowship both in Europe and America, for he refers to the "printed documents, upon those subjects."[75] One can argue that both Presbyterians, Barton W. Stone and TC, during the same decade, were motivated in their vision of ecclesiastical unity by the same evangelical impulses, even where they differed on how the conversion in the believer was accomplished.

TC partook of this general evangelical optimism but was keenly aware of the obstacles and disunity among the churches, partly through his own recent experience in western Pennsylvania. One can argue that his personal situation added existential urgency to the evangelical and intellectual options more generally available in the culture of the Enlightenment and Second Great Awakening to promote unity for the sake of evangelization. In order to achieve the preconditions for uninhibited proclamation, scriptural unity, the Christian Association of Washington reached out and invited others into association with it. It is here that the Association and its charter document achieved also an eschatological significance of their own:

> Thus impressed, ye will find means to associate at such convenient distances, as to meet, at least, once a month, to beseech the Lord to put an end to our lamentable divisions; to heal and unite his people, that his church may resume her original constitutional unity and purity, and thus be exalted to the enjoyment of her promised prosperity—that the Jews may be speedily converted, and the fullness of the Gentiles brought in.[76]

In this passage we gain a glimpse into how TC envisioned the progression of his initiative. The voluntary association with its ecumenical purpose would return the church to her biblical unity and pure design and by so doing advance her to her triumphant completion. The anticipated developments also assumed the conversion of the Jews and the successful completion of the Gentile mission. In effect, yet another passage in the *D&A* shows that the presence of Jews and Gentiles in the millennial church mirrors the times of the beginnings:

> This we see was actually the case in the apostolic churches, without any breach of christian unity. And if this was the case, at the erection of the christian church from amongst Jews and Gentiles, may we not reasonably expect, that it will be the same at her restoration, from under her long antichristian and sectarian desolations?[77]

Interest in the conversion of the Jews was a feature of millennialism of the period after 1790 and resulted in the same year that the *D&A* was composed in the founding of the London Society for Promoting Christianity among the Jews.[78] This had been preceded by several publications specifically directed toward the conversion of the Jews, such as Joseph Priestley's *Letter to the Jews* and James Bicheno's *Friendly Address to the Jews*. Ruth Bloch observed for America, where the interest in the conversion of the Jews achieved greater popularity in the 1790s and thereafter, that the turn coincided with a period of political disenchantment and a religious turn toward remote exegetical interests.[79] In the case of TC, the typological proximity of Israel with the church invited speculation, and the recovery of the idealized early church envisioned conditions where Jews and Gentiles coexisted "without any breach of christian unity." AC voiced similar sentiments in his sermon held before the Christian Association of Washington at their annual meeting in 1810, which has been preserved in manuscript form. Here he employed the same texts, Is 57 and 62, that his father also used in the *D&A*.[80] The conversion and restoration of the Jews and completion of the Gentile mission remained an important millennial thought of AC's well into the 1840s[81] and may have driven as well his interest in supporting his son-in-law Dr. J. T. Barclay, the Disciple missionary to Jerusalem.[82]

While there was already a shared commitment to the Bible among all evangelicals, religious practice and life on the frontier were still governed by the differing confessional and theological norms and commitments of the historic churches. With his radical biblicism and exclusion of binding human inferences, however, TC was intent on sacrificing historical theological views where they created disunity and inhibited the establishment of the eschatological Zion. One can argue that in TC's understanding the sought-for Zion came close to what his son was to call the "millennial church," namely a recapitulation of its early Christian state. In such a coincidence of beginnings and end we have what Hermann Gunkel felt was a general characteristic of millennial thought: that *Urzeit wird Endzeit*.[83] Such is at least reflected in TC's language about the church, when he spoke in the *D&A* about the need to "restore to the church its primitive unity, purity and prosperity."[84] In yet another passage he asserted the "co-operation to promote the unity, purity, and prosperity of his church."[85] "Prosperity" refers here to the church's eschatological, triumphant, and successful status, which is insolubly linked and preconditioned by returning to what TC perceived to have been its early Christian character when unity and purity prevailed. He insisted on sacrificing subsequent ecclesiastical developments in the process and felt that once human beings recognized "truths demonstrably evident in the light of scripture and right reason," then "should our eyes soon behold the prosperity of Zion."[86] TC was a child of his time, and Michael W. Casey has shown convincingly how he modified his Reformed heritage to accomplish his end: "Campbell believed that by rejecting the binding nature of human inferences and by agreeing with the simple positive or express ordinances of scripture all division and discord between Christians would disappear and unity would result."[87]

TC's "Protest and Appeal" of 1808, in which he defended his actions in frontier Pennsylvania before the Associated Synod meeting in Philadelphia against the censure of his presbytery, anticipated what he would state one year later in the *D&A*. Here he rejected "human opinions and human inventions" as norms for faith and worship because of their absence in the Bible and supported this view with specific reference to similar views found in the irenic and mission-minded spokesman among dissenters, the Presbyterian Philip Doddridge. For TC the church is to be "in all things conformed to the original standard," and the empirical disunity he sought to remedy with "the Scriptural and apostolic worship of the church." The scriptural and apostolic model that he defended before the synod in 1808 appeared to TC "indispensably necessary to promote and secure the unity, peace, and purity of the Church." He refused "to acknowledge as obligatory upon myself, or to impose upon others, anything as of Divine obligation for which I cannot produce a 'Thus saith the Lord.'" In so doing he anticipated his later, often-repeated Proposition 5 of the *D&A*.[88]

The healing of divisions and recovery of ecclesial purity were for TC preconditions for the exaltation of the millennial church. AC voiced this same sentiment in 1830 when he wrote: "We assume it for a principle that the union of christians, and the destruction of sects, are indispensable prerequisites to the subjection of the world to the government of Jesus, and to the triumphant appearance of Christ's religion in the world."[89] TC elaborated on this "restoration of the ancient gospel and discipline," as he liked to distinguish it from his son's "restoration of the ancient order of things," in several articles in the *Christian Baptist*, which, although fifteen years removed from the *D&A*, continue that theme with the same language.[90] Here he also spoke of the church's "original constitutional unity and purity," which were still in need of recovery and a precondition for the triumph of Christianity and the fulfillment of its kerygmatic purpose. In a lengthy letter to the editor—AC—his father writes:

> Now, therefore, as professed restorers, as healers of the breaches, as faithful disciples, and followers of the apostles, we must, upon principles of fidelity and self-consistency, feel ourselves morally bound, by those high considerations to a strict and undeviating adherence to the letter of the divine testimony upon every article of faith and duty.[91]

Restoration appears to have been the method by which unity, purity, and prosperity were to be accomplished. While TC remained relatively vague in the *D&A* in formulating biblical specifics, the very bones of contention with which the subsequent movement would be plagued, in his later writings, notably in a lengthy essay on "Christian Union," he did specify the early Christian content. Here he also furnished—as complement to his 1809 rather formal program—an ecclesiology:

> We make this appeal to the understanding and practice of the primitive churches, not to authorize our faith and practice, but merely to show, that

> we understand the apostolic writings upon those subjects, just as they were understood from the beginning. And this we think all true Christian unionists are bound to do; because it is only upon the belief of the apostolic doctrine, that Christ has proposed and prayed for the unity of his people. John xvii. 20, 21.[92]

Such ecclesiological and "early catholic" language is still embedded in an eschatological context, for TC considers the recovery of scriptural faith and practice ultimately a method toward the establishment of the millennium. "And are we not all looking for a Millennium of universal peace and prosperity, in which truth shall universally triumph? These things being so, our grand concern and present duty is, to adopt the proper means for accomplishing this truly blissful and desirable object."[93] The *D&A*, after TC's defense before the synod, was the first public program to suggest such "proper means." The views espoused here, which linked unity, restoration, and the end-times, had an afterlife in the AC of the 1820s and 1830s. The observation of Richard T. Hughes regarding AC's thinking during this period could as well be applied to his father, when he writes, "One of the chief reasons Campbell based the millennium on primitive Christianity was that only the restored church, he thought, could produce the unity in church and society that the millennial age required."[94]

While Hiram Lester's form-critical observations led him to observe the ambivalent character of the *D&A* on account of the different intentions of the Declaration (proclamation and mission) and Address (unity), the restitutionist orientation can in my judgment not be divorced from the unity focus. Already the dual preconditions of "purity" and "unity" for the prosperity of Zion dictate such. Moreover, the persistence of Resolution 5 of the Declaration,[95] which TC reduced to the Old Testament formula "Thus saith the Lord,"[96] as a presupposition of unity in the later writings of TC, makes this early "restoration principle" an integral part of the *D&A*. One could assume that if the Declaration had the sole purpose of setting down the organizational specifics of a voluntary mission-minded society in the service of evangelical gospel preaching, later reflection upon the *D&A* would find the Declaration of little use, once the original *Sitz im Leben* had vanished, and would focus mainly on the Address. If there had been such a lack of an intrinsic thematic alignment between Declaration and Address, one can assume that TC would have had little reason ever to evoke again the Declaration part of the *D&A*. But this was not the case. TC reflected later in five significant passages on the *D&A* and its original purpose, and in all of these the principles of the

Declaration were still relevant and related meaningfully to union. The earliest retrospect took place in 1832, twenty-three years after the *D&A*'s composition, and the latest occurred in 1844, thirty-five years later.[97]

After perusing all the later statements by TC about the purpose of the *D&A*, it seems to me that he saw both Declaration and Address as devoted to the same purpose: the advancement of Christian Unity on a scriptural basis. It follows from this that AC did not single-handedly accomplish a theological refocusing of the early Disciples from Proclamation to Restoration, but that this was merely a developmental consequence of the dual heritage of the *D&A*. The insistence on a recovery of unity *and* purity via a restitutionist method distinguishes the *D&A* also from other eschatologically-driven evangelical cooperative enterprises of his day.

Conclusion

While the Second Great Awakening and its evangelical missionary and eschatological horizon provided the wider religio-historical context for TC's eschatology, it was the new American situation and the persistent Old-World discord that animated his action program for an effective and triumphant church. The apocalyptic "signs of the times" witnessed at a distance the judgment of the European state churches, notably the Beast of Revelation: the Roman Catholic Church. By their witness they compelled evangelical Americans to remove division and discord in their churches as barriers to successful evangelization, fellowship, and spiritual growth. The *D&A* became thus for TC an eschatological action plan to suggest means to accomplish these evangelical and ecclesiastical desiderata. By restoring to the church its original unity and purity, he hoped to create the irenic conditions for effective evangelization, which were eventually to prosper into a millennial Zion, when Jews would convert and the fullness of the Gentiles was to be completed. One may conclude that this also advanced the return of Christ, although neither the Parousia nor the millennium is mentioned in the *D&A*. The vision of TC, while drawing upon intellectual options furnished in contemporary Enlightenment philosophy, remained ultimately a religious one. The apocalyptic eschatology that embraced restoration and unity was otherworldly but had as its arena this earth and depended significantly on human cooperation. From the premillennialism of the nineteenth and twentieth centuries it distinguished itself by assigning a crucial role to human activity and by refraining from chronology and too specific a correlation of historical events with biblical prophecy. One is tempted to classify it as postmillennial in character, although its eschatological building blocks were hewn from eighteenth-century historic premillennialism. TC's eschatology provided no timeline toward Armageddon but hope for those who would work together to establish God's Zion on earth. The *D&A* became thus an optimistic eschatological action plan for the erection of a millennial Zion. This agenda eventually proved capable of development, when—under the leadership of AC—TC's views on how to further the evangelical Zion matured in the 1830s into a "millennial Church" and after additional cultural compromises into the vision of an Anglo-Saxon religio-cultural hegemony. What it did not accomplish was the unity it had sought in the first place. Instead it produced a fractured movement with a plethora of ecclesiastical factions once more badly in need of peace and unity. But this is to anticipate events not yet in sight from TC's second-story window on Brother Welch's farm in the summer of 1809.

Notes

1. Thomas Campbell, *Declaration and Address of the Christian Association of Washington* (Washington, Pa.: Brown & Sample, 1809), 7.7.
2. *D&A*, 7.5.
3. *D&A*, 7.3.
4. On the historical particulars of the heresy case against TC, as well as his dealings with his presbytery and synod, see the copious quotations from the original Presbyterian minutes and documents in William Herbert Hanna, *Thomas Campbell: Seceder and Christian Union Advocate* (Cincinnati: Standard Publishing, 1935; on-line). The standard biographical sources for TC remain the *Memoirs of Elder Thomas Campbell, Together with a Brief Memoir of Mrs. Jane Campbell* (Cincinnati: H. S. Bosworth, 1861; on-line) by his son Alexander, as well as Robert Richardson's *Memoirs of Alexander Campbell*, 2 vols. (Cincinnati: Standard Publishing, 1913). The most comprehensive modern biography of TC is Lester G. McAllister, *Thomas Campbell: Man of the Book* (St. Louis: Bethany Press, 1954).
5. *D&A*, 7.31-38 and throughout the text.
6. *D&A*, 8.1, 3.
7. *D&A*, 8.20-21.
8. *D&A*, 14.19-37.
9. *D&A*, 7.48-8.7.
10. *D&A*, 14.20-33.

11. Frederick D. Kershner, *The Christian Union Overture: An Interpretation of the Declaration and Address of Thomas Campbell* (St. Louis: Bethany Press, 1923; on-line), 76.

12. TC, "Christian Union," *Millennial Harbinger* (April 1839): 155.

13. TC, "A Synopsis of Christianity," *Millennial Harbinger* (November 1844): 481-91, esp. 490.

14. David Thompson, "The Irish Background to Thomas Campbell's *Declaration and Address*," *Discipliana* 46 (Summer 1986): 23-27. See also Hiram J. Lester, "Alexander Campbell's Millennial Program," *Discipliana* 48 (Fall 1988): 35-39.

15. Hiram J. Lester, "The Form and Function of the *Declaration and Address*," in this volume.

16. Lester, "Form and Function."

17. Peter Brooke, "Controversies in Ulster Presbyterianism" (Ph.D. diss., Cambridge University, 1981); David Miller, "Presbyterianism and 'Modernisation' in Ulster," *Past and Present* 80 (August 1978): 66-90; I. R. McBride, "'When Ulster Joined Ireland': Anti-Popery, Presbyterian Radicalism and Irish Republicanism in the 1790s," *Past and Present* 99 (November 1997): 63-93. I am grateful to Dr. David Thompson, Cambridge, for furnishing me with the relevant pages of the thesis by Peter Brooke.

18. McBride, "'When Ulster Joined Ireland,'" 68-85.

19. McBride, "'When Ulster Joined Ireland,'" 72.

20. Brooke, "Controversies," 27-28.

21. Brooke, "Controversies," 28.

22. McBride, "'When Ulster Joined Ireland,'" 90.

23. Alexander Campbell, "Opinions and Conjectures on Prophecy: Extracts from Diverse Authors," unpaginated manuscript, Disciples of Christ Historical Society.

24. Miller, "Presbyterianism and 'Modernisation,'" 79.

25. Miller, "Presbyterianism and 'Modernisation,'" 81.

26. An overview of this discovery as well as a preliminary finding aid can be found in "Original Early Campbell Manuscripts Discovered," *Discipliana* 24 (November 1964): 62-63; Claude E. Spencer, "The Long Voyage Home—Primary Campbell Materials Received from Australia," *Discipliana* 25 (November 1965): 69-72; D. G. Whyatt, "A Brief Detail of Manuscripts of A. Campbell," *Discipliana* 25 (November 1965): 73-74.

27. *Millennial Harbinger* (September 1832): 433-38; (October 1832): 493-96.

28. *D&A*, 7.47-8.4.

29. *Millennial Harbinger* (May 1832): 218-19.

30. Robert Frederick West, *Alexander Campbell and Natural Religion* (New Haven: Yale University Press, 1948), 194-96.

31. Kershner, *Christian Union Overture*, 76-77.

32. Kershner, *Christian Union Overture*, 76.

33. "Prophetic Iconisms (II)," *Millennial Harbinger* (October 1832): 496.

34. On the importance of James Bicheno for apocalypticism, see especially W. H. Oliver, *Prophets and Millennialists: The Uses of Biblical Prophecy in England from the 1790s to the 1840s* (Auckland and Oxford: Auckland University Press; Oxford University Press, 1978), 46-50.

35. AC, "Opinions and Conjectures on Prophecy."

36. AC, "Opinions and Conjectures on Prophecy."

37. Ernest R. Sandeen, *The Roots of Fundamentalism: British and American Millennarianism 1800–1930* (Chicago: University of Chicago Press, 1970), 7.

38. *D&A*, 8.24-27.

39. Richardson, *Memoirs of Alexander Campbell*, 1:337.

40. "Prophetic Iconisms (I)," *Millennial Harbinger* (September 1832): 435.

41. "Prophetic Iconisms (I)," 436.

42. "Prophetic Iconisms (I)," 437.

43. "Prophetic Iconisms (II)," 495.

44. *D&A*, 14.35-37.

45. *D&A*, 8.17-20.

46. *D&A*, 8.28-31.

47. See here especially David Thompson, "Irish Background," 23-27.

48. *D&A*, 14.15-19.

49. Thompson, "Irish Background," 23-25.

50. Thompson, "Irish Background," 25.

51. Thompson, "Irish Background," 25-26.

52. "Address of Thomas Campbell to the Synod of Ireland (1804)," in AC, *Memoirs of Elder Thomas Campbell*, 209-10.

53. *D&A*, 3.1-2.

54. *D&A*, 6.31-33.

55. *D&A*, 7:49-8.1.

56. Ruth Bloch, *Visionary Republic: Millennial Themes in American Thought, 1756–1800* (Cambridge: Cambridge University Press, 1985), 228.

57. *D&A*, 8.46-48.

58. *D&A*, 7.10-28.

59. *D&A*, 8.8-9.

60. *D&A*, 8.10-14.

61. *D&A*, 9.2-3.

62. On the influence of Scottish Common Sense philosophy on TC, see especially Edward R. Crowther, "Thomas Campbell: A Man of 'Common Sense,'" *Discipliana* 57 (Spring 1997): 13-21.

63. *D&A*, 9.16-17.

64. Crowther, "Thomas Campbell: A Man of 'Common Sense,'" 18.

65. *D&A*, 24.24-33.

66. "Prophetic Iconisms (II)," 496.

67. *D&A*, 9.16-29.

68. *D&A*, 9.44.

69. *D&A*, 9.45-10.4.

70. Robert Frederick West, *Alexander Campbell and Natural Religion*, 177.

71. *D&A*, 15.7-13.

72. *D&A*, 18.38-46.

73. *D&A*, 18.49-19.8.

74. Bloch, *Visionary Republic*, 219.

75. *D&A*, 8.31-32.

76. *D&A*, 20.30-36.

77. *D&A*, 28.7-11.

78. Sandeen, *The Roots of Fundamentalism*, 9-12.

79. Bloch, *Visionary Republic*, 144-49.

80. "Sermon propounded at the semiannual Meeting of the Christian Association 1810," unpaginated manuscript, Disciples of Christ Historical Society.

81. West, *Alexander Campbell and Natural Religion*, 181-82.

82. "Response to Dr. Barclay," *Millennial Harbinger* (February 1854): 90-91.

83. See Johann Michael Schmidt, *Die jüdische Apokalyptik: Die Geschichte ihrer Erforschung von den Anfängen bis zu den Textfunden von Qumran*, 2d ed. (Neukirchen-Vluyn: Neukirchener Verlag, 1976), 15, 221-25.

84. *D&A*, 10.14.

85. *D&A*, 15.45-46.

86. *D&A*, 19.31-33.

87. Michael W. Casey, "The Theory of Logic and Inference in the *Declaration and Address*," in this volume.

88. "Protest and Appeal" can be found in AC, *Memoirs of Elder Thomas Campbell*, 11-14.

89. "Millennium (I)," *Millennial Harbinger* (January 1830): 55.

90. On the terminological distinction between "ancient order of things" and "ancient order of the Gospel," see T. W. [TC], "To the Editor of the Christian Baptist," *Christian Baptist* 7 (7 December 1829): 108.

91. T. W. [TC], "To the Editor," 109.

92. TC, "Christian Union," *Millennial Harbinger* (April 1839): 163.

93. TC, "Christian Union," 154.

94. Richard T. Hughes, "From Primitive Church to Protestant Nation: The Millennial Odyssey of Alexander Campbell," in Hughes and C. Leonard Allen, *Illusions of Innocence: Protestant Primitivism in American, 1630–1875* (Chicago: University of Chicago Press), 173.

95. *D&A*, 16.43-17.5.

96. The formula occurs already six times in the *D&A* without specific quote but indicating the necessity for a scriptural warrant. See the "Scripture Index to the *Declaration and Address*" by Christopher R. Hutson in this volume.

97. See *Religious Reformation* (n.p., [1832]); *Millennial Harbinger* (August 1833): 421-22; (June 1835): 272-73; (March 1839): 142-43; (May 1844): 199.

Restoring the One, Holy, Catholic, and Apostolic Church: The Appeal of the *Declaration and Address* as Interpreted by Frederick Doyle Kershner and William Robinson

Paul M. Blowers

In the 1840s John Williamson Nevin, Philip Schaff's colleague at the German Reformed seminary in Mercersburg, Pennsylvania, criticized American Protestant denominationalism from an "Evangelical Catholic" perspective and issued one of the most potent criticisms of the Stone-Campbell movement in its early history. Willing to acknowledge the Campbellites as a self-proclaimed unity movement, Nevin nonetheless rebuked their ignorance of the sacramentality of the church and their attempt to rebuild the church and its unity through a rationalistic Commonsense hermeneutic centered on allegedly "self-evident" scriptural truths. Centuries of church history betrayed the project as naive.[1] The only hope for Christian unity was for Protestants to rediscover the organic oneness of the church as grounded in the mystery of the Incarnation and focused in the celebration of the Eucharist.[2] "Visible" as well as invisible unity, Nevin argued, was imperative for the church; but only the living Christ, mystically indwelling his Body, could sustain that visible unity. It could not be peeled off the pages of the New Testament or engineered by human reason.

I have found no hard evidence that Nevin's criticism was ever registered among major leaders of the Stone-Campbell movement in the nineteenth or early twentieth centuries; yet it merited a response. Indeed, Nevin's criticism already anticipated the kinds of tensions between broadly "Catholic" and broadly "Protestant" perspectives on Christian unity that would intensify in the developing ecumenical movement. Was the church or the Bible the authoritative matrix of Christian unity? What role should independent human reason play in the realization of unity? How could the "invisible" (spiritual) unity of the church find expression in a "visible" (organic) unity? Such questions thrust themselves on the Disciples of Christ as their ecumenical participation deepened in the twentieth century.[3] And as Disciple ecumenists conscientiously reflected on what their heritage uniquely had to offer the larger ecumenical movement, they were already engaged in lively reinterpretation of the original "plea" of their movement's founders—especially, of course, the appeal of Thomas Campbell's *Declaration and Address*.

In this paper I will focus on two distinguished Disciples leaders who, from the 1920s to the 1950s, sought to interpret the *D&A* for the emerging "Ecumenical Age." Frederick Doyle Kershner (1875–1953) and William Robinson (1888–1963) may justly be called theological moderates within the Disciples spectrum of their time. In their work we see two interesting dynamics simultaneously operative: first, the need to deal with internal ideological tensions among the Disciples over the direction of their movement; and second, the urgency, amid these tensions, to bring a *coherent* and *credible* Disciples voice to the ecumenical quest for Christian unity. Kershner's career especially exemplified the former,[4] while Robinson's manifested more the latter; yet both men aspired to a fresh reading of TC's first principles of ecclesial unity that would command attention from Christians both within and beyond churches of the Stone-Campbell heritage. Kershner and Robinson were "bridge" figures between liberals and conservatives in a Disciples communion that they hoped could itself be a bridge for the ultimate unity of Protestant and Catholic (and Eastern Orthodox) churches.[5]

Born in America, Kershner made his mark principally as an educator and editor. He was sometime president of Milligan College (1908–11) and of Texas Christian University (1911–15), editor of the *Christian-Evangelist* (1915–17), Book Editor of the *Christian Standard* (1918–20), Professor of Christian Doctrine at Drake University (1920–24), and Dean of the Butler University School of Religion (1924–44), where he continued teaching Christian Doctrine until retirement in 1952. Along the way he served on the Council on Christian Unity spearheaded by Peter Ainslie, was President of the International Convention of the Disciples in 1938 (while also supporting the North American Christian Convention), and, in one of his most significant roles, served as chairman of the Commission on Restudy of the Disciples of Christ (1934–49), a commission that probably represented the last, best hope for averting a second division in Disciples ranks.[6]

William Robinson was a pioneering leader among British Churches of Christ, serving as Principal of Overdale College in Birmingham (1920–49), editor of *The Christian Quarterly* (U.K., 1934–39) and later of the *Christian Advocate* (U.K., from 1940), Chair of Christian Doctrine and Philosophy of Religion at the Selly Oaks Colleges (from 1940), and Professor of Christian Theology and Doctrine at Butler University School of Religion (1951–56), where he was, briefly, Kershner's colleague. Beyond these duties, however, Robinson was one of the most accomplished Disciple ecumenical theologians and activists of his time, having represented British Churches of Christ in the World Conferences on Faith and Order at Geneva (1920), Lausanne (1927), and Edinburgh (1937), and having served on that organization's Continuation Committee (from 1934). Having further distinguished himself in Free Church ecumenism in Britain, Robinson also represented Churches of Christ in the World Council of Churches assemblies at Amsterdam (1948) and Evanston (1954). His visibility among American Disciples was greatly enhanced by his participation in the Disciples' World Convention, by an extensive United States lecture tour in 1947, and by his tenure at Butler School of Religion. His most prolific contributions to ecumenical ecclesiology were his *Essays on Christian Unity* (1921) and *The Biblical Doctrine of the Church* (1948; revised edition, 1955).[7]

In Kershner's case, we have the luxury of an entire commentary on the *D&A*, *The Christian Union Overture* (1923).[8] Moreover, allusions to and remarks on the text appear throughout his corpus of writings.[9] Robinson, like Kershner, viewed the *D&A* as the true charter document of the Stone-Campbell movement,[10] but we are forced to glean his interpretation from dispersed quotations and allusions. In my view, Kershner's and Robinson's appropriations of the document, notwithstanding certain differences of perspective, had a common thrust: to demonstrate precisely how, both theologically and pragmatically, the Disciples' plea—*unity, through restoration, for the sake of world evangelization*—was an agenda whose time had come. Sharing the optimism of many other Disciples leaders that there was a wider ecumenical consensus on the atrophying effects of creedalism and denominationalism,[11] and confident that a unity more substantial than cooperation or "federation" was increasingly promising, Kershner and Robinson sought to spell out the implications of TC's position for the modern churches in an irenic, catholic, but critical, spirit. This would be no easy task. Internally, Disciples were already, from the 1920s on, locked into controversy over the nature of unity and its reconcilability with the "restoration" commitment,[12] while the larger ecumenical movement was addressing the question of what kind of unity (simple cooperation? federal union? organic unity? "spiritual" unity?) could possibly be realizable for all of its participant churches.[13]

Thomas Campbell in a "High Church" Perspective: Proposition One, the *Una Sancta*, and "Organic Unity"

Without doubt the passage most quoted by Kershner and Robinson from the *D&A* is TC's first proposition in the Address, affirming the essential, intentional, and constitutional unity of the church.[14] This is the lens, as it were, through which the whole document must be interpreted and thereupon presented to the worldwide church. It is the principle which collapses the distance between the church past, present, and future and folds us into one communion of saints. It brings into immediate focus the nature and mission of the church. Kershner calls it perhaps the most famous statement in Christian union literature and remarked that "at this point Thomas Campbell is at one with the High Church interpretation which makes unity, along with catholicity, holiness, and apostolicity, one of the essential marks of the Christian ecclesia."[15] Kershner elaborates this connection with the *una sancta* ideal of the Nicene-Constantinopolitan Creed even more in his 1938 presidential address to the Disciples' International Convention, where he recommends these four universal attributes of Christ's church over against all denominational particularisms.[16] Robinson later echoes the same sentiment:

> The first proposition of the *Declaration and Address* was "That the church of Christ upon earth is essentially, intentionally, and constitutionally one." The main interest was in the visible church, and the sole purpose was that the scattered forces of Christianity might be gathered into "one holy catholic apostolic church." Schism, wherever it existed, was sin: "There ought to be no schisms, nor uncharitable division." This

document was almost a century before its time. In a sense it was a Catholic voice speaking from the Protestant fold.[17]

TC was a true "catholic," a "high churchman," precisely because, amid the Protestant sectarianism (and biblicism, Robinson would add) of his time, he and his early colleagues had rediscovered the ontological reality of the church. Yes, the church is *de facto* a free association of faithful and obedient believers, as TC indicates in the latter part of Proposition One ("consisting of all those in every place that profess their faith in Christ and in obedience to him in all things according to the Scriptures"); but it is first, *de jure*, an "objective, visible society" having a genuinely "priestly" nature and worship.[18] Kershner asserts that TC is intimating the underlying "mystical and sacramental" character of the church, not just the empirical features of its unity, in Proposition One.[19] Christ's own intention, his urgent will for its unity as set forth in his prayer for unity in Jn 17:19, imbues every aspect of the church's being and life:

> The underlying philosophy involved in Christian union is brought out in the word "essentially." The mystical and sacramental reality is brought out in the word "intentional," and the political and organizational elements in the word "constitutional."[20]

According to Kershner and Robinson, what placed the "high" ecclesiology of TC and his associates so far ahead of its time in relation to the ecumenical movement was *their identification of the truly "organic" nature of ecclesial unity*.[21] The term "organic," of course, became quite precarious in ecumenical usage, meaning different things to different groups.[22] But for Kershner and Robinson alike, TC had penetrated the original apostolic sense of the corporateness, the organic vitality of the Body of Christ. He had done so first and foremost by rediscovering the true life-giving principle behind the church (and likewise behind the New Testament): namely, the prevenient and all-pervasive personal authority of Christ himself, the Author of unity, the Head of the Body. Kershner asserts that the *D&A*'s thirteen propositions could be further simplified into seven, the first four betraying TC's profoundly Christocentric understanding of unity: (1) God as supreme authority; (2) Jesus Christ as the supremely revealed authority; (3) Jesus' will revealed in New Testament Scripture; (4) the church universal with Christ as its only Head; (5) the church's visible form embodied in local congregations submitting to Christ's authority; (6) Christ's will in the New Testament as interpreted by the consensus or common mind of intelligent Christians; and (7) the exclusion of all else as a binding authority for the life of the church.[23] Through this Christocentric ecclesiology, TC effectively paved a *via media* between the extremes of Catholicism and Protestantism—the tendency of the former to substitute a vicarious ecclesiastical authority for that of Christ, the tendency of the latter to reduce Christ's personal authority to the "verbally inspired" text of the Bible.[24]

In their respective writings, both Kershner and Robinson developed their own reading of this Campbellian-Catholic principle, the Christocentric basis of the church's organic unity. Kershner, for example, observes in the *D&A* a purposive tension between the "vital" (religious-ethical) principle of unity and the "formal" principle of unity (having to do with creed, ordinances, and organization): "Thomas Campbell desires to restore the original church. The restoration he has in mind is far more a matter of life than of form."[25] TC had explicitly said that "a manifest attachment to our Lord Jesus Christ, in faith, holiness, and charity, was the original criterion of Christian character, the distinguishing badge of our holy profession, the foundation and cement of Christian unity."[26] The *una sancta*, then, is at bottom a holy unity, a matter of "vital" righteousness, of "tempers and conduct," not of mechanical conformity.[27] As Kershner had argued in his first book, *The Religion of Christ* (1911), this unity is grounded in the Gospels' portrait of Christ, not just the Pauline pattern of the church. Jesus himself is its model.[28] Yet "Christ assuredly founded a church, specifying its requirements, and explaining its organic structure," even if much freedom remained for human actualization of its formal elements.[29]

Christ, then, is not merely the pioneer of a new morality, nor is his church solely an ethical community; Christ is the Word indwelling his Body mystically and sacramentally, the Life which brings order. Like Robinson, Kershner tended increasingly to think of the "ordinances" as *sacraments*, unique means of the grace and continuing efficacy of Christ.[30] In a fascinating 1940 essay in which he prognosticates about the ultimate "synthetic" unity of the church, Kershner suggests that the Catholic understanding of the Real Presence would, stripped of any magical or mechanical interpretation, survive as an *ecclesiological* first principle. "The essential thing is that through the corporate life of the church expressed visibly, as the Catholic understands the sacraments, the individual enters into that life of the Vine which can alone guarantee eternal salvation."[31] In further projecting some sort of progressive or developmental "synthetic" unity between the sacramental ecclesiology of Roman Catholicism and "Left-Wing" Protestantism's emphasis on the prerogatives of individual Christians and their critical reason, Kershner poses an interesting parallel to the "Evangelical Catholic" speculations of Philip Schaff, some of whose work was known to Kershner. Schaff, strongly influenced by German Romanticism, had envisioned a future glorious union that would absorb the best traits of Roman Catholicism, Orthodoxy, and the diverse Protestant traditions.[32] And yet Schaff shared his colleague Nevin's judgment on rationalistic and sectarian agendas like those of the Campbells.[33] Who knows how Schaff or Nevin might have reacted to Kershner's (or Robinson's) rereading of Campbellian ecclesiology?

Robinson's development of TC's "high church" principles is far more elaborate than Kershner's. Among the hallmarks of Disciples ecclesiology, based on the work of the movement's founders, he includes: (1) rejection of the theory of a purely "invisible" unity of the church; (2) rejection of an individualistic view of salvation for an ecclesial or corporate one ("they have a very high doctrine of the Church as the Divine Society"); (3) rejection of the "branch theory" of the church; (4) condemnation of sectarianism as sin; and (5) the embrace of organic unity rather than mere federation.[34] In his mature work, *The Biblical Doctrine of the Church*, Robinson justifies this high ecclesiology both biblically and historically, insisting, like Kershner, that Jesus indeed "founded" the church as a radically new bid for divine-human fellowship, not so much the "ark of salvation" as the "bringer of salvation."[35] The church is organic *qua* the organ by which the divine life penetrates the world, and can in this sense be called the "extension" of the Incarnation.[36] Thus, Robinson, even more than Kershner, emphasizes the genuinely *sacramental* efficacy of the full life of the Body, including its preaching, the ministry, and especially the sacraments proper—choosing, for example, in his elucidation of the Lord's Supper, to highlight the "Real Action" even more than the "Real Presence" of the living Christ in the church.[37] Overall, for Robinson, the church is God's means toward fully actualizing that fellowship of persons, divine and human, which is already, cosmically, the "hidden structure of reality."[38] This, I suggest, effectively represents his own extended gloss on TC's interconnection of the unity of the church and the unity of humanity in Christ: that the "grand design and native tendency of our holy religion is to reconcile and unite men to God, and to one another, in truth and love, to the glory of God."[39]

The Apostolicity of the Church and the Restoration Principle

Was TC, in the *D&A*, more a restorationist or a unionist? How intent was he on reconstituting an ancient apostolic order? How much room did he mean to allow for "good-natured accommodation"? Numerous Disciples leaders were asking these questions in the early decades of the twentieth century, amid competition between restorationist and ecumenical strategies for unity. The *D&A* took some hard hits from "liberals" of the time, anxious for a radical revision of "the plea." While acknowledging TC's charitable and humble spirit, Charles Sharpe criticized the *D&A* as

> a legalistic document in that it presents a legalistic conception of the Christian religion. It regards Christianity as essentially a once-for-all-delivered institutional order of "doctrine, worship, discipline and government expressly revealed and enjoined in the Word of God."[40]

Some later Disciples have expressed similar concerns. Ronald Osborn described TC's embrace of "restorationism" in the *D&A* as a "fatal definition" of the ideal of apostolicity.[41]

Both Kershner and Robinson were convinced that the restoration principle was a nonnegotiable in the *D&A*,[42] but were, like their more liberal Disciples friends, committed to keeping TC in "conversation" with current ecumenical issues, since the restoration principle needed further nuancing if it were to have catholic appeal. How "biblicistic" or "legalistic" was TC in his appeal to the "constitutional" authority of New Testament Scripture? Both Kershner and Robinson expressed reservations that TC, when he wrote the *D&A*, may still have been beholden to the doctrine of verbal inspiration and the "prooftexting" tradition of Protestant Orthodoxy:

> Then when he uttered these hopes [of Christian unity in the *D&A*], although he was feeling towards seeing the Bible as a historical book, he was still lingering in the orthodox post-Reformation conception of the Bible as verbally inspired in all its parts and containing the truth of God. It was to him, and to his fellow-Christians to whom he appealed, a source

> of dogmatic proof-texts, and it is amazing that with that background he discovered so much historical truth, especially about the Church on earth.[43]

TC may have still been rooted in Protestant biblicism but he was already, prophetically, pioneering a new sensitivity to the historical character of revelation, and had kept his focus on the authority of Christ himself. Kershner even suggests that in the *D&A* TC was adumbrating a Barthian emphasis on the centrality of the Word:

> Although Thomas Campbell doubtless believed in verbal inspiration, as did most of the theologians of his day, there is nothing in the Declaration and Address which requires the acceptance of such a dogma. It is Jesus who is authoritative and not the verbal text of any book. It is the Word of God, as Karl Barth would put it, expressed in and through the Incarnation which matters. Other details are extraneous and incidental.[44]

On the other hand, both Kershner and Robinson understood that the restoration principle, freed from biblicism and verbal inspiration theories, represented the one genuine contribution of the Stone-Campbell Movement to the ecumenical quest for unity.[45] It was imperative, therefore, to interpret it afresh, and in doing so they addressed three controversial dimensions of the restoration plea: (1) the precise nature of the authority of Scripture; (2) the issue of an "original pattern"; and (3) "apostolicity" as an attribute of the historic church as well as a signal of New Testament authority.

In the first place, Robinson in particular was insistent that for TC and AC, Walter Scott, and their associates, the real authority within the New Testament was the authority of Jesus Christ and his gospel,[46] just as the real authority of the Bible as a whole lay in the revelation of Person to persons, the "gospel facts" as the enactments of God's mighty deeds through Jesus Christ his Word.[47] Too many restorationists, Robinson argues, had been "bottle-fed" on the New Testament as a law book, a collection of prooftexts set out mechanically to reinstate "New Testament Christianity."[48] But the New Testament has the (derivative) authority of "witness." Altogether it is the testimony of the "creative Christian experience, and witnessed to the life, faith, and spirit of apostolic Christianity."[49] To say that, however, is not to drive a wedge between Christ (the gospel) and the authority of the New Testament, or for that matter, between Christ and the authority of the church, since his prior personal authority inheres—vitally or organically—in both.[50]

Yet TC clearly asserts in the *D&A* that an "original pattern" or "infallible directory" has been set forth in the New Testament as "constitution."[51] As Kershner notes, TC is fully confident, indeed overconfident, that such a platform is self-evident and will be obvious to all rational seekers after truth.[52] Be that as it may, both Robinson and Kershner take this pattern to mean a coherent and perdurable order(liness) of faith (confession of Jesus as the Christ), sacraments (immersion and the Lord's Supper), and ministerial organization (along congregational lines).[53] Such an order is not constraining or mechanical, since it is couched in the gospel and enduringly catholic. It is not, Robinson insists, a sheer "blueprint" complete in all details; rather, for TC and his associates, the order included

> things which naturally had a local and temporal manifestation, but their pattern was eternal in the heavens, and not subject to man's preferences. This Gospel and the character and genius of the Church were to be found in the New Testament, wherein what was of temporal and local significance must be clearly distinguished from what was of permanent significance—the very essence and principles of the Gospel and the Church.[54]

TC and AC are to be credited for their scrupulous insistence on expediency, their ability to distinguish what was gospel from what was culture-bound. Their restoration ideal was no "sterile uniformity, but strove after a unity that admitted of rich diversity."[55] The *D&A* is explicit on the idea that pure uniformity is not a desideratum in the unity of the church, in spite of the need for manifest conformity to the core standards of the gospel.[56]

Restoration of the apostolic "pattern," both for Kershner and for Robinson, presupposes the *una sancta*, the holiness and wholeness of the Christian *ecclesia* in its obedience to the person of Christ.[57] Immersion is indeed a mechanical action, mere submission to a primitive ordinance, if it is not a personal response to Christ and if it is not framed sacramentally in terms of the gospel, as an intimate identification with Christ's death, burial, and resurrection.[58] In taking a staunch stance in support of immersion in the debates over open membership, Kershner and Robinson both saw themselves as upholding less a restoration principle *per se* than a full evangelical ideal of the church.[59] The restoration project was one of ongoing communal discipleship, no better exemplified than in the life of the earliest Jerusalem community—constituted of "baptized believers who were disciples or pupils enrolled in the school where the Gospel of Jesus was taught"[60]—or again in the life of TC himself, who in his own experience matured toward an understanding of the fuller implications of the gospel.[61]

Apostolicity, especially for Robinson, is not merely a signal of the normativity of the New Testament, nor a byword for restoration, but a statement about the historic and missionary church as the extension of the Incarnation. It begins with the "apostolical character of Christ" himself as the eternal Lord penetrating the world; the "apostolicity" of the church unfolds, then, as the continuing actualization of the divine-human fellowship inaugurated by Christ.[62] What, however, marks out the true "apostolic" church in history? Robinson rejected any "mechanical" theory of apostolicity, be it in the formalism of the doctrine of catholic, apostolic succession of the episcopal ministry, or in the functionalist claims of restorationist sectarians that the apostolic church ceased to exist but can be started again from scratch.[63] We can also easily surmise that he rejected any idea of a covert "apostolic succession" of remnant "New Testament Christians" (bypassing the Roman Church) such as AC had advanced in his debate with Bishop Purcell.[64] Once again recalling the "organic" and personalist principle of the *una sancta*, Robinson argues that the apostles set in motion an order with structural consistency but with a built-in prerogative, or freedom, belonging to the whole community of the church to maintain regularity and orderliness in its ministry:

> That which constitutes the apostolicity of the church is her faithfulness to the apostolic tradition, and . . . the power of choice and ordination is within her own life, as she commits herself to the Head of the church and to the guidance of the Spirit.[65]
>
> That church is apostolic in which the apostles' doctrine is preached and taught, in which the sacraments are administered with the unfailing intention of the apostles, who delivered them to us from the Lord, and in which this is safeguarded by a ministry, freely chosen by the church as it is guided by the Holy Spirit, and bearing the apostolic commission.[66]

Along these lines, Robinson could concur fully with the Campbells that a basically congregational polity, with its presbyterial ministry, has the blessing of "apostolicity," but only so long as that polity and ministry truly upholds the "apostolic" ideal, bearing the burden of the whole *una sancta*, and not turning in on itself as a rigid independency or congregational solipsism.[67]

Catholicity, Creeds, and the Common Mind of the Church

Catholicity, too, is an essential mark of the *una sancta*. In what does its catholicity consist, and what is the guarantee of its catholicity? Kershner and Robinson were convinced that another of TC's greatest contributions to ecumenical Christianity was his thoroughly catholic principle of the "common mind" of the church such as keeps it to the apostolic truth and holds in check all unhealthy theological or interpretive particularisms. Indeed, it is for Kershner TC's preeminent contribution, becoming the most dominant theme of his commentary in *The Christian Union Overture*.[68] There were, however, as we shall see, perspectival differences between Kershner and Robinson on precisely how the universal *consensus fidelium*, or common mind, expresses and perpetuates itself.

Textually, their focus was on those passages in the *D&A* in which TC indicates the reality of a universal mind of the church capable of determining the "self-evident" truths of Scripture.[69] The divine mind is infallibly represented in Scripture, such that we do not need a "General Council" ("the voice of the multitude" or "majority vote") to locate it. It is a matter rather of divine truth identifiable through the exercise of "right reason" on the part of all conscientious Christians who can perceive the "manifest distinction between an express Scripture declaration, and the conclusion or inference which may be deduced from it."[70] The way to unity, after all,

> must be a way very far from logical subtilties [*sic*] and metaphysical speculations, and as such we have taken it up, upon the plainest and most obvious principles of Divine revelation and common sense—the common sense, we mean, of Christians, exercised upon the plainest and most obvious truths and facts divinely recorded for their instruction.[71]

It was precisely this ecclesial common sense that undermined privatism and the necessity of contrived creeds as means to impose unanimity of faith and practice.[72]

Yet was TC speaking principally of *assensus* or *consensus*, of assent to a set of self-evident constitutional truths or of broad agreement on the core evangelical truth? Or was he looking, in effect, to pave a *via media* between the two?

Kershner acknowledges that TC, grounded in the Common Sense/ Reidian philosophical framework of his time, is profoundly confident (risking overconfidence—but so be it!) in the transhistorical and transcultural universal reason that enables harmonious interpretation of Scripture.[73] TC upholds both the "substantial infallibility" of the scriptural platform of truth and the parallel "substantial infallibility" of the universal reason of all Christians, as God authors both.[74] Reason is a "divine gift" but is perverted by individualistic self-interest, the very basis historically for the tyranny of creeds.[75] Yet the church, in exercising this universal reason, is not a pure democracy of individual minds, and if TC denied the ecumenical council as assuring catholicity, he most assuredly would have leaned the burden of proof of the church's interpretation of Scripture on the "intellectual majority," "the overwhelming consensus of thoughtful scholarship of the world," "the consecrated common sense of Christian scholarship at large," knowing that this is the only viable means of authenticating and representing the universal mind of the church, and the only balance to individual "prooftexting."[76] Both have expressed themselves historically:

> The common mind for the [Protestant] group becomes the considered judgment of the General Council in the [Catholic]. The principle involved is the same. It is that the eccentricities of individual opinion shall be corrected by the judgment of a large number of similar opinions, and what appears to be the common judgment of all must be regarded as the true voice of "right reason," which St. Anselm and other scholastics looked upon as the voice of God.[77]

In his own time, in turn, Kershner finds evidence of this common mind in a recognizable consensus of scholars who have already come to judge that both immersion and the Petrine confession are genuinely catholic terms of Christian fellowship.[78]

Kershner sometimes describes TC's idea of the catholic mind of the church in quite cerebral and rationalistic terms, terming it a "broader intellectual fellowship of the universal reason," and suggesting that, down through the centuries, it acts as a clarification of prophetic revelation that "guarantees all civilization and progress."[79] Indeed, Kershner enthusiastically praises TC as a virtual "Socinian" in liberating reason and helping position the Disciples of Christ at the vanguard of "the scientific spirit" of the Ecumenical Age.[80] On the other hand, Kershner clearly understands that the exercise of the church's common mind is not some mechanical science of scholars downloading the truth from the Bible; it is still a quest, a heuristic process of seeking *authoritative*, not absolutizing, interpretation of Christian truth.[81] It necessarily expresses itself as an "appeal" or "plea"—exemplified in the heuristic method of the *D&A* itself[82]—and looks to the "gradual educational enlightenment" of the whole church.[83] It is a matter of discipleship and discernment. For catholicity, like apostolicity, is *a spiritual ideal for*, and not just a philosophical foundation of, the *una sancta*. The common mind cannot thrive without a "catholic spirit":

> The ground of catholicity is . . . the unity of the divine Mind and our duty and capacity for fellowship within it. This philosophical basis for the one catholic church is, however, not fundamental to our practical acceptance of the principle. That is quite independent of any metaphysical interpretation. It involves only the willingness to make what is universal in our faith the final test of fellowship in the church. This catholic ideal is the one and only way to unity and is all-important on that account.[84]

Robinson concurs with Kershner on a number of points in interpreting TC's idea of the common mind of the church, particularly as a response to Protestant individualism and creedalism:

> While stressing the importance of the New Testament and urging a return to New Testament Christianity, early Disciple teachers declared that no interpretation of the Scriptures was authoritative unless supported by the considered, qualified, scholarship of the church catholic. The great doctors and teachers of the whole church (now unhappily divided) in all ages must be appealed to. This meant that what they sought in the Scriptures was not a *final* and *absolute* interpretation, but an *authoritative* one. They set the Scriptures within the living institution and so allowed for development of thought and the spirit of inquiry. They recognized that subtle combination of freedom with loyalty to the church which was characteristic of the church of the early Fathers, but which has largely been lost sight of in the West.[85]

Robinson also concurs with Kershner in seeing the exercise of the catholic mind of the church as organic rather than mechanical, a consecrated intuition ("sanctified commonsense") which comes about only with an attitude of worship and submission to the ongoing judgment of the living

Word.[86] It is a questing mind, and, borrowing a phrase from AC, seeks ever to come within "the understanding distance" of God's truth.[87] Robinson parted from Kershner, however, in accentuating the *developmental* character of the common mind in the historic *consensus fidelium*. Although strongly supportive of the new role of historical criticism, he did not fully share Kershner's enthusiasm that the catholic mind of the church had been more or less ultimately liberated by the Christian enlightenment that had been unfolding since the time of the Campbells and Commonsense philosophy. Given the much broader audience of his writings, moreover, Robinson was far more ecumenically conscientious of the need to search for the *consensus fidelium* from within the whole historical spectrum of Protestantism, Roman Catholicism, and Eastern Orthodoxy.[88] We might say that "Tradition," understood in its proper role, was not a bad word for him.

Nowhere is the disparity between Robinson and Kershner as "Campbellian-Catholic" thinkers more pronounced than in their assessment of the role of creeds, historically and prospectively. For Kershner, the anticreedalism of the *D&A* (including its insistence on the simple Petrine confession as the only truly catholic creed) was one of its most significant contributions and was being vindicated in the ecumenical age.[89] For Kershner, TC's allowance for the catechetical utility of creeds was mainly a function of his conciliatory appeal and should not eclipse the fact that "the Campbells rejected all human creeds."[90] Robinson hardly intended to undermine the centrality and catholicity of the Petrine confession as a constitutive principle of the Stone-Campbell Movement, and he forcefully argued for it in his ecumenical involvements. But the militant repudiation of all "human" creeds on the part of the Disciples had burned certain vital bridges with the shared Christian past, and the anticreedal plea needed to be put in its proper perspective. Thus, unlike Kershner, Robinson chose to interpret TC's statements about the *educative* role of creeds as a constructive principle rather than as a temporary concession.[91] Instead of the Westminster Confession or other relatively late Protestant confessions, however, Robinson highlighted the utility of the great ecumenical creeds, particularly the Apostles' Creed (which AC had endorsed[92]) and the Nicene Creed, to the extent that, over and beyond their "metaphysical" glosses, they simply helped to elucidate the great gospel "facts" of creation, incarnation, and redemption, and provided a time-tested digest of the faith of the church catholic, into which individuals could "grow" after baptism.[93] They could also conceivably provide, in a liturgical context, a doxological rallying point for the reunited church.[94] At baptism, however, only one confession would suffice: the Petrine confession, a personal oath of allegiance, or faith directly in the person of Christ.[95]

The difference between Kershner and Robinson on creeds is patently illustrated in a 1921 essay in which Kershner reports, very favorably, that Robinson was one of the few advocates for the catholicity of the Petrine confession at the preliminary meeting of the World Conference on Faith and Order at Geneva in 1920:

> Unfortunately Mr. Robinson spoiled the effect of his statement a little later in his speech by saying that while he could not accept the Nicene creed as a formula to be enforced on candidates for entrance into the church, he did believe, to quote his exact language, that it "might form a statement of belief accepted by the unified and universal church. There is a difference between what we can demand of the individual and what the church might stand for."[96]

In the end Kershner admits that he cannot imagine Jesus of Nazareth making heads or tails of the Nicene doctrine; but if individual Christians want to adopt its tenets, they have that theological freedom:

> Nobody objects to individual tolerance of the finely spun Trinitarian formulae which characterize the Nicene symbol. The idea of requiring these out of date speculations of Neo-Platonic Alexandrism as essentials of salvation, however, harmonizes neither with the modern nor with the New Testament conception of the Church.[97]

Robinson, to my knowledge, never replied, but my suspicion is that he would have thanked Kershner for acknowledging that he had had no intention of making the Nicene Creed or any other historic confession a test of communion right along with baptism. Yet he would have chided him for ignoring the fact that, historically and ecumenically, the Nicene symbol has gone farther than most standards in helping the church express its *consensus fidelium*, its collective sense of an integral, enduring, and catholic faith. For it is, writes Robinson, "the result of the Church's experience and the summing up of its historic foundation."[98] Historic "orthodoxy" counts at least for something in the shaping of Christian identity.

Conclusion

I began this essay by noting the criticism of John Williamson Nevin, a self-avowed "Evangelical Catholic" who decried the biblicism, ahistorical restorationism, rationalism, and self-centeredness of American "sects," including Campbell's Disciples and Stone's Christians. He notes at one point, that "every sect, in spite of itself, is forced to acknowledge, at least indirectly, the necessary attributes of the Church, as one, holy, catholic, and apostolical," but then they go on to claim these marks only for themselves.[99] The remedy, then, for the Campbellites and others was this: "All redemption from the power of the sect plague must begin with a revival of true and hearty faith in the ancient article of the one holy catholic Church."[100] From there Nevin extols the "incarnational" mystery of this church and its creed:

> Peter's confession: "Thou art the Christ, the Son of the living God!" carried in itself in truth, potentially, the whole sense of the Apostles' Creed, though with no insight of his, at the time, into several articles of this, as afterwards evolved from its bosom. And just so, we may have a true faith in the article of the one, holy, catholic Church, while yet most incompetent in our minds to estimate, in full, the terms and conditions under which it may be required to manifest itself in the world. Such faith does not turn primarily on the presence of the Church, as a given corporation accredited by outward seal, but on the idea of Christianity itself, as necessarily requiring this constitution to make itself complete. Not only the word of Christ, but his life, demands its presence. The article flows forth, with inward necessity, from the Christological mystery itself.[101]

As I noted at the beginning, I have no evidence that Nevin's rebuke and recommendation was ever read by subsequent Disciples leaders, including Kershner and Robinson. But, as I hope this essay has revealed, these two "Catholic" thinkers, despite certain differences, effectively answered the criticism with as much substance and verve as any Disciples ecclesiologians of the twentieth century. Nevin may well have accused them of ultimately claiming the perennial attributes of the *una sancta* only for their own "sect," but it would be hard, especially in the case of Robinson—who has himself lately been called a "Catholic Evangelical,"[102] a "Reformed Catholic,"[103] and a "Free-Church Catholic"[104]—to make the charge stick. For here, in their "high church" reading of the *D&A*, are the makings of a genuinely catholic appeal that takes seriously the Incarnational mystery precisely as an ongoing and unfolding mystery in the visible, organic life of the one church. As we have seen, both Kershner and Robinson read TC with an eye to drawing out the fuller ramifications of his emphasis on the personal, perduring, all-pervasive authority of Christ, the "Real Presence" who indwells and graces the church in its historic and apostolic mission.

Critics may certainly question whether their "high church" reading is an accurate or legitimate reinterpretation of the *D&A*, but few are likely to come away from it without a new appreciation of the genuinely ecumenical appeal of this document, and the seriousness of its proposal for restoring the one, holy, catholic, and apostolic church in the "Ecumenical Age."

Notes

1. John Williamson Nevin, *Antichrist, or the Spirit of Sect and Schism* (excerpt), in *The Mercersburg Theology*, ed. James H. Nichols (New York: Oxford University Press, 1966), 95-113, and, on the Stone-Campbell Movement, especially 97-99, 101-102, 105, 106, 111, 112-13.
2. Nevin, *Antichrist*, 113-19.
3. See Douglas Foster, "The Many Faces of Christian Unity: Disciples Ecumenism and Schism, 1875–1900," in *Explorations in the Stone-Campbell Traditions: Essays in Honor of Herman A. Norton*, ed. Anthony Dunnavant and Richard Harrison (Nashville: Disciples of Christ Historical Society, 1995), 95-113; "The Disciples' Struggle for Unity Compared with the Struggle among Presbyterians, 1880–1980," in *A Case Study in Mainstream Protestantism: The Disciples' Relation to American Culture, 1880–1989*, ed. D. Newell Williams (Grand Rapids: Eerdmans, 1991), especially 237ff.
4. For an excellent recent assessment of Kershner's moderate position in the tensions between liberal and conservative Disciples, see Byron Lambert, *"The Middle Way" of Frederick D. Kershner* (Johnson City, Tenn.: Emmanuel School of Religion, 1998).
5. On this point, see especially William Robinson, "Editor's Notes," *The Christian Quarterly* [U.K.] 3, no. 3 (July 1936): 76; compare Robinson's *The Shattered Cross* (Birmingham: Berean Press, 1945), 81.
6. In the absence of a published biography, I have been greatly aided by Lloyd Knowles, "A Study of Dr. Frederick Doyle Kershner's Educational Thought" (M.R.E. thesis, Emmanuel School of Religion, 1971), and by Charles Gresham, "Frederick Doyle Kershner: A Bibliography Essay" (Restoration Archives, Emmanuel School of Religion, Johnson City, Tenn.).

7. Exceptionally useful for Robinson's biography and achievement are the collection of essays edited by James Gray (*W.R.: The Man and His Work* [Birmingham, Eng.: Berean Press, 1978]), and Anthony Calvert, "The Published Works of William Robinson: An Interpretive, Annotated Bibliography of a Catholic Evangelical" (M.A. thesis, University of Birmingham, 1984).

8. Frederick Doyle Kershner, *The Christian Union Overture: An Interpretation of the Declaration and Address of Thomas Campbell* (St. Louis: Bethany Press, 1923).

9. See especially Kershner's "Stars" series, chap. 2 ("The Message of Thomas Campbell"), *Christian Standard* 75 (1940): 245-46, 248, 263, 273-75.

10. See Kershner's pamphlet *The Churches of Christ (Disciples) and the Ecumenical Age* (St. Louis: Christian Board of Publication, 1951), 3, 5; also his introduction to the British reprint of the *D&A* (Birmingham, Eng.: Berean Press, 1951).

11. Both insisted that the *D&A*'s principles were being vindicated and that the Disciples provided the only coherent plan for ecumenical unity. See Kershner, "Historic Efforts in Behalf of Conciliation and Present Status of Christian Unity," *Christian Union Quarterly* 7, no. 3 (January 1918): 31; *Christian Union Overture*, 26, 27, 28; "The Effects of Our Plea Upon the Churches," *Christian Standard* 76, no. 14 (5 April 1941): 339-40. Compare Robinson, *The Biblical Doctrine of the Church*, rev. ed. (St. Louis: Bethany Press, 1955), 205; and Kershner, *The Churches of Christ (Disciples) and the Ecumenical Age*, 5ff.

12. The extended "open membership" controversy was, of course, the principal manifestation of this.

13. On this problem of variant definitions (and expectations) of unity, see the "Final Report" of the Second World Conference of Faith and Order (Edinburgh, 1937), in *A Documentary History of the Faith and Order Movement 1927–1963*, ed. Lukas Vischer (St. Louis: Bethany Press, 1963), 61-64 (para. 113-26).

14. Thomas Campbell, *Declaration and Address of the Christian Association of Washington* (Washington, Pa.: Brown & Sample, 1809), 16.9-10.

15. Kershner, *Christian Union Overture*, 81-82.

16. Kershner, "One Holy, Catholic and Apostolic Church," *Christian Standard* 73, no. 43 (22 October 1938): 1029-32.

17. Robinson, *Biblical Doctrine of the Church*, 7; compare Kershner, "Stars" (chap. 2), 274-75: "It is sometimes asserted that the *Declaration and Address* is more Catholic than it is Protestant, because of its constant and emphatic emphasis upon the unity of the church. Protestantism at this time did not have much to say about Christian union."

18. Robinson, *Shattered Cross*, 82.

19. Kershner, "One Holy, Catholic and Apostolic Church," 1030; compare "The Unanswered Prayer of Our Lord," *Christian Union Quarterly* 14, no. 1 (July 1924): 26-34.

20. Kershner, *Christian Union Overture*, 82.

21. Robinson, *Shattered Cross*, 82; compare Robinson, *What the Churches of Christ Stand For* (Birmingham, Eng.: Churches of Christ Publishing Committee, 1926), 72-78.

22. See "Final Report," 63 (para. 121ff).

23. Kershner, "Stars" (chap. 2), 273.

24. Kershner, "Stars" (chap. 2), 274, 275.

25. Kershner, *Christian Union Overture*, 158. Compare his *The Religion of Christ* (New York: Revell, 1911), in which Kershner develops the distinction, yet ultimate reconciliation, between "vital" and "formal" Christianity.

26. *D&A*, 36.30-33; compare 17.39-46.

27. Compare Kershner, *Christian Union Overture*, 83, 90-91, 158; "One Holy, Catholic and Apostolic Church," 1030.

28. Kershner, *Religion of Christ*, 15-80; compare "One Holy, Catholic and Apostolic Church," 1030.

29. Kershner, *Religion of Christ*, 38; compare Robinson, *Biblical Doctrine of the Church*, 35ff.

30. See Kershner, *Religion of Christ*, 125ff; more significantly, Kershner, "The Real Communion," *Christian Standard* 48, no. 21 (24 May 1913): 837; "This is My Body," *Christian Standard* 50, no. 31 (1 May 1915): 1016.

31. Kershner, "Toward a Synthetic Theology" (Presidential Address to the American Theological Society), *Shane Quarterly* 3, no. 4 (October 1942): 263-65.

32. See in particular Schaff's last great work, "The Reunion of Christendom" (1893), reprinted in *Phillip Schaff: Historian and Ambassador of the Universal Church: Selected Writings*, ed. Klaus Penzel (Macon, Ga.: Mercer University Press, 1991), especially 336-40.

33. See Schaff's reflection and expansion on Nevin's analysis of the "sect system" in America (which had, of course, included the Campbellites and Stone's "Christians") in his 1854 essay, "The Churches and Sects," reprinted in *Phillip Schaff*, especially 169ff.

34. Robinson, *What the Churches of Christ Stand For*, 73-75; compare William Robinson, *Essays on Christian Unity* (London: James Clarke, 1923), 28-62.

35. Robinson, *Biblical Doctrine of the Church*, 35-53; compare *Essays on Christian Unity*, 15-23.

36. Robinson, *Biblical Doctrine of the Church*, esp. 15-34, 115-19, 162; *Essays on Christian Unity*, 25, 173-74, 186.

37. On the general "sacramentality" of the church's life, see *Essays on Christian Unity*, 169-77, and on the sacraments proper (Baptism, Eucharist), see 177-202; compare *The Sacraments and Life* (Birmingham, Eng.: Christian Action Fellowship, 1949); "The Meaning of Anamnesis," *Shane Quarterly* 14, no. 1 (January 1953): 20-23; "Ordinance or Sacrament," *The Scroll* 45, no. 4 (Spring 1954): 42-43. See also Byron Lambert, *The Restoration of the Lord's Supper and the Sacramental Principle; with Special Reference to the Thought of William Robinson* (Los Angeles: Westwood Christian Foundation, 1992); Charles

Ashanin, "Sacramental Theology of William Robinson," *Encounter* 48, no. 1 (Winter 1987): 35-43.

38. Robinson, *Biblical Doctrine of the Church*, 15-18, 139-59.

39. *D&A*, 6.5-7.

40. Charles Sharpe, "The Idea of Doctrinal Progress," in *Progress: Anniversary Volume of the Campbell Institute*, ed. Herbert Lockwood Willett and others (Chicago: Christian Century, 1917), 84-86.

41. Ronald Osborn, "One Holy Catholic and Apostolic Church," in *The Reformation of Tradition, Panel of Scholars Report*, vol. 1 (St. Louis: Bethany Press, 1963), 316; compare Alfred T. DeGroot, *The Restoration Principle* (St. Louis: Bethany Press, 1960), 138-39.

42. The restoration principle, and specifically the notion of a fixed platform of truth, are more or less explicit in *D&A*, 10-11, 16-19, 35-36, 42, 45-47, 49-50; see also Kershner, *Christian Union Overture*, 29-30, 64-65, 67-68, 149, on restoration's importance for TC.

43. Robinson, "Three Recent Movements in the Field of Theology," *Shane Quarterly* 13, no. 1 (January 1952): 9-10.

44. Kershner, "Stars" (chap. 2), 274; compare *Christian Union Overture*, 27; also his critique of verbal inspiration theory in "Why Is a Fundamentalist?", *Christian-Evangelist* 61, no. 18 (1 May 1924): 547, 558. The emphasis on the enacted Word and on personal encounter as the content of revelation was an aspect of Biblical and Neo-Orthodox theology admired by both Kershner and Robinson. See Kershner, "Realities and Visions" ("How My Mind Has Changed"), *Christian Century* 56 (1 February 1939): 148-51; Robinson, "Three Recent Movements," 5-30; *Whither Theology? Some Essential Biblical Patterns* (London: Lutterworth, 1947), especially 35-41, 44. One recent historian has labeled Kershner among the "Neo-Orthodox": see William R. Hutchison, *The Modernist Impulse in American Protestantism* (New York: Oxford University Press, 1976), 304 n. 32.

45. See Kershner, *Christian Union Overture*, 47-48; "Unity and Restoration," *Christian Standard* 53, no. 17 (26 January 1918): 532; Robinson, *Churches of Christ (Disciples) and the Ecumenical Age*, 5ff.

46. William Robinson, "Introduction" to Thomas Campbell, *The Declaration and Address* (Berean Press reprint; Birmingham, Eng.: Berean Press, 1955), iii; compare *Shattered Cross*, 81: "What they meant was that behind and within the New Testament there was the objective thing 'the Gospel,' and as part of the Gospel there was the equally objective thing 'the Church.'"

47. See Robinson, "The Authority of the Bible To-day," *Expository Times* 62, no. 3 (December 1950): 76-79; compare *Churches of Christ (Disciples) and the Ecumenical Age*, 5-6.

48. Robinson, *Essays on Christian Unity*, 10.

49. Robinson, *Biblical Doctrine of the Church*, 149.

50. See *Biblical Doctrine of the Church*, chap. 7.

51. See *D&A*, 10.42-43; 16.26-30; 49.47.

52. Kershner, *Christian Union Overture*, 29-30, 149.

53. Compare Kershner, *Religion of Christ*, 117-40; Robinson, *Essays on Christian Unity*, 45-62, 63-202.

54. Robinson, *Shattered Cross*, 81-82.

55. Robinson, *Churches of Christ (Disciples) and the Ecumenical Age*, 6. On this standard of unity-in-diversity of the apostolic churches themselves, see Kershner, "The Imperative of Union," in *International Convention Disciples of Christ: Addresses and Sermons* [San Antonio, 1935] (St. Louis: Christian Board of Publication, 1936), 184-88.

56. See *D&A*, 37-38.

57. As Kershner put it, real restoration aimed at the spirituality behind the "forms": "The Real Restoration," *Christian Standard* 53, no. 27 (6 April 1918): 863.

58. Robinson, *Churches of Christ (Disciples) and the Ecumenical Age*, 11-12. See also his "The Nature and Character of Christian Sacramental Theory and Practice" (1941), reprinted in *The Lord's Supper: Historical Writings on Its Meaning to the Body of Christ*, ed. Charles Gresham and Tom Lawson (Joplin, Mo.: College Press, 1993), 213-27.

59. See in particular Kershner, "Open Membership and the Restoration Plea," in *The Watchword of the Restoration Vindicated* (Cincinnati: Standard Publishing, 1919), 43-72, especially 56 ff. Compare Robinson, "Christian Unity—A Survey," *Christian Union Quarterly* 14, no. 1 (July 1924): 35-40; "Submarine Membership," *The Christian Quarterly* [USA] 1, no. 3 (April 1955): 17-19.

60. Kershner, "The Church—A Disciple Point of View," *Christian-Evangelist* 74, no. 50 (12 December 1945): 1207.

61. See Kershner, "Open Membership and the Restoration Plea," 46-54.

62. Robinson, *Biblical Doctrine of the Church*, 157.

63. Robinson, *Biblical Doctrine of the Church*, 161-64, 169 ff, 181 ff. See also David Thompson, "Unity as Gift and Call: The Hidden Reality of the Church," *Mid-Stream* 20, no. 3 (July 1981): 307-8.

64. For this argument of a proto-Protestant lineage of true New Testament Christians, see *A Debate on the Roman Catholic Religion between Alexander Campbell, Bethany, Va. and the Right Reverend John B. Purcell, Bishop of Cincinnati* (Cincinnati: J. A. James, 1837), 65-68. The theory was further popularized by James DeForest Murch, *Christians Only* (Cincinnati: Standard Publishing, 1962), 9-18. Compare Robinson, *Essays on Christian Unity*, 11, censuring the outworn attitude of some Protestants that "the whole of Catholic Christianity has fundamentally gone astray from the gospel."

65. Robinson, *Biblical Doctrine of the Church*, 201.

66. Robinson, *Biblical Doctrine of the Church*, 204. Compare Kershner, "The Church—A Disciple View," 1208.

67. See Robinson's essay "Was Alexander Campbell a Congregationalist?", *Shane Quarterly* 15, no. 1 (January 1954): 5-12; *Churches of Christ (Disciples) and the Ecumenical Age*, 6-8; compare Kershner, "The Church," in *The Witness of the Churches of the Congregational Order: Papers Exchanged by Baptists, Congregational-Christians, and Disciples in 1940* (Anderson, Ind.: Association for the Promotion of Christian Unity, 1940), 42-47; *Christian Union Overture*, 46 (on how TC approved congregational polity but refused to "dogmatize" it).

68. See Kershner, *Christian Union Overture*, esp. 41-48, but also 67, 99-102, 104, 153, 155-56. See also Lambert, *"The Middle Way,"* 6-7.

69. See *D&A*, 12.15-16; also 16-17, where it is clearly presupposed; also 30.

70. *D&A*, 19, 60.

71. *D&A*, 47.4-9.

72. See the *D&A* passages restricting creeds, 17, 24-25, 42, 46.

73. Kershner, *Christian Union Overture*, 156, 157.

74. Kershner, *Christian Union Overture*, 44, 67-68, 153.

75. Kershner, *Christian Union Overture*, 45.

76. Kershner, *Christian Union Overture*, 44, 45, 100-1; "One Holy, Catholic and Apostolic Church," 1032; "Stars" (chap. 2), 274.

77. Kershner, "Toward a Synthetic Theology," 274-75.

78. Kershner, *Christian Union Overture*, 45-46.

79. Kershner, *Christian Union Overture*, 47, 48.

80. Kershner, *Christian Union Overture*, 83, 100, 148.

81. Kershner, *Christian Union Overture*, 46. Kershner comments that, according to Prop. 6, the process still includes room for disciplined theological interpretation, given the progressive historical character of the church, but only insofar as such does not violate the catholic terms of communion (*Christian Union Overture*, 87).

82. Kershner, *Christian Union Overture*, 99-100, 102-5, 148.

83. Kershner, *Christian Union Overture*, 102. Note again Kershner's image of the primitive Jerusalem church as a "school where the Gospel of Jesus was taught" and the fellowship of love inculcated ("The Church—A Disciple View," 1207).

84. Kershner, "One Holy, Catholic and Apostolic Church," 1031.

85. Robinson, *Biblical Doctrine of the Church*, 150; compare *Shattered Cross*, 83; "The Authority of the Bible To-day," 78.

86. Robinson, *Biblical Doctrine of the Church*, 151ff; *Shattered Cross*, 81, 83.

87. Robinson, *Biblical Doctrine of the Church*, 156.

88. Compare Robinson, *Essays on Christian Unity*, 10-12, passim; also his classic "The Eastern Church and the Unity of Christendom," *Christendom* 3, no. 3 (Summer 1938): 364-76.

89. Kershner, *Christian Union Overture*, 89; "The Effect of Our Plea Upon the Churches," 340.

90. Kershner, *Christian Union Overture*, 47, 88-9, 147-48, 153.

91. Robinson, *Churches of Christ (Disciples) and the Ecumenical Age*, 8-9.

92. See AC, "Reply to Barnabas," *Millennial Harbinger* 3, no. 12 (3 December 1832): 602.

93. Robinson, *Essays on Christian Unity*, 63-97. In the course of his argument here, Robinson discusses four approaches to creeds: (1) no creeds; (2) "No Creed but the Bible"; (3) no creed save the Nicene or Apostles'; (4) "Thou art the Christ" as a sufficient basis of union. Robinson rejects (1) as naively divorcing doctrine and ethics, and (2) as inviting an unrealistic and unhistorical biblicism; his final position is (4) while taking (3) into sympathetic consideration. For Robinson's view of creeds in a Disciple perspective, see *Shattered Cross*, 84-85; *Whither Theology?*, 21 n. 1.

94. Robinson, *Essays on Christian Unity*, 97.

95. Robinson, *Essays on Christian Unity*, 91-8; *What the Churches of Christ Stand For*, 65-71; *Churches of Christ (Disciples) and the Ecumenical Age*, 8-9.

96. Kershner, "Unity by Way of Nicea: A Question Now Before Christians of All Creeds and Classes," *Christian-Evangelist* 58, no. 20 (19 May 1921): 579.

97. Kershner, "Unity by Way of Nicea," 580. For Kershner, the use of such confessions invariably evoked precisely the "cheap and easy orthodoxy" that TC had repudiated in the *D&A*. Compare *D&A* (Appendix); 41; Kershner, *Christian Union Overture*, 154.

98. Robinson, *Essays on Christian Unity*, 95.

99. Nevin, *Antichrist*, 112.

100. Nevin, *Antichrist*, 114.

101. Nevin, *Antichrist*, 117-18.

102. Calvert, "The Published Works of William Robinson," 15-16.

103. Thompson, "Unity as Gift and Call," 308.

104. Alfred T. DeGroot, *Disciple Thought: A History* (Fort Worth: privately published, 1965), 270-76.

The Understanding and Impact of the *Declaration and Address* among Churches of Christ

Douglas A. Foster

Writing of the impact of the *Declaration and Address* on Churches of Christ seems at first quite strange. Born in a stronghold of Churches of Christ in northern Alabama, I was "in church" every time the doors were open from the age of three weeks on. I attended Mars Hill Bible School in Florence, Alabama, for twelve years, followed by four years at David Lipscomb University. Every school day for those sixteen years I attended a Bible class and chapel service. I never once heard any mention of the *D&A* nor any substantive mention of Thomas and Alexander Campbell. The only formal course that touched on Stone-Campbell history in the Lipscomb curriculum in the early 1970s was a speech course for ministerial students titled "Restoration Preaching." No church history courses were offered. The first time I studied my own heritage was in a church history course taken at the United Methodist Scarritt College while pursuing an M.A. in theology.

Though the situation is different at Lipscomb now and was already different in other places (Abilene Christian offered a church history M.A. as well as undergraduate courses with such professors as LeMoine Lewis, Everett Ferguson, and Bill Humble), the *D&A* has been and remains largely an unknown document among Churches of Christ.

This apparent paucity of knowledge made the question of evidence of a "reception history" of the *D&A* among Churches of Christ all the more intriguing. While initial searches revealed a number of references to the *D&A* in historical books and articles, they generally consisted of a brief acknowledgment, perhaps a choice quotation, followed either by no analysis at all or by one so superficial that it is of little use. Almost invariably the *D&A* is mentioned as a significant document for the beginning of the movement, once even being called a "Magna Carta."[1] High regard is given it, but little or no effort is made to understand it. What follows is a survey of what I believe are the most significant attempts written by members of Churches of Christ to analyze the *D&A*. With the two exceptions that immediately follow, all were written in the twentieth century.

Apparently the earliest, albeit brief, treatment of the *D&A* by a writer clearly identified with the part of the movement that would become Churches of Christ was written by Tolbert Fanning in 1866. Several weeks after hearing of AC's death, Fanning penned a series of four articles titled "Sketches in the Life of Alexander Campbell." Fanning's agenda in the series appears to be to show a Campbell amenable to, and the very source of, "conservative" positions Fanning and others in that part of the movement then held.

At the end of the first article Fanning describes TC's withdrawal from the Associate Synod and his writing in 1808 [*sic*] "A 'Declaration and Address' of the Christian Association of Washington, Pa." Quoting from the fifth resolution of the Declaration, Fanning then articulates what he saw as the essence of the document. "[H]e proclaimed eternal enmity to 'All human authority in matters of religion,' and declared that he would require nothing of others for which he could not find a 'Thus saith the Lord, either in express terms or by approved precedent.'" Fanning goes on to assert that TC had in this declaration "taken the ground that nothing short of the complete 'Restoration of pure, primitive, apostolic Christianity, in letter and spirit, in principle and practice,' could satisfy the honest enquirer after truth."[2] Given Fanning's biblicism and strongly restorationist theology, it is no surprise that he holds up those ideas as crucial. What is significant, however, is that Fanning gives no indication that the *D&A* had anything to do with the pursuit of Christian unity.

A second early treatment appeared in a series of articles written by David Lipscomb in 1890 and published as a booklet that year, with a reprint edition in 1916. Prompted by the attack of an unnamed Disciple writer on those responsible for the events at Sand Creek, Illinois, in August 1889,[3] Lipscomb lashed out at those whom he believed to be introducing opinions into the work and worship of the church to divide the movement. Lipscomb intended to show that religious opinions, which he defines as "impressions resting on human judgment, without clear and satisfactory testimony,"[4] were perfectly acceptable as long as they were never mentioned. In the chapter titled "The Voice of the Reformers," Lipscomb quotes from writings of TC and AC to show that his position is truly faithful to the founding ideals of the movement. He prefaces his remarks with the disclaimer that "the teaching of Mr. Campbell and the fathers is of small importance," but since others were invoking them on the other side of the issues, he felt it important to show what they really said.[5]

Lipscomb begins by identifying the *D&A* as the recognized beginning of "the present effort to restore the apostolic order." Quoting selectively from the first two sections of the document in which TC denounces human opinions as illegitimate in the church's faith and practice, Lipscomb concludes that "the original movers in this reformatory movement" believed the introduction of anything lacking a clear revelation of the divine will was the "universally acknowledged cause of all the corruptions and divisions that have taken place on earth."[6] In this article Lipscomb forcefully reverses the progressives' use of the movement's fathers by rallying them against "opinionism." The *D&A* is for Lipscomb completely supportive of the conservative position.

The most accessible material on the *D&A* is in the book-length histories of the movement written by members of Churches of Christ, eleven of which seem to me to deserve attention.

One of the first attempts in the twentieth century to articulate the place of Churches of Christ in Christian history was written by J. W. Shepherd, the person asked by David Lipscomb to gather data about Churches of Christ for the 1906 United States religious census. In 1929 F. L. Rowe published Shepherd's study that purported to survey the entire history of the church, its apostasy, and its restoration.

Shepherd first gives a short history of the founding of the Christian Association and the writing of the *D&A*. His initial evaluation was that the document was in substance, spirit, and style "the most notable historical production of the initiatory period of the effort to restore the apostolic church . . . ," and worthy of study now.[7] He goes on to note what he sees as the essential principles of the document by quoting the introduction to the Declaration and selections from the Address. Though Shepherd mentions the unity aspects of the document, he emphasizes its ideas of the restoration of the primitive model of the church. He quotes extensively from AC's comments on the *D&A* in *Memoirs of Elder Thomas Campbell*, in which the younger man focuses on the restorationist agenda. Shepherd closes his treatment by quoting the full text of the thirteen propositions with the judgment that "they need to be diligently and profoundly studied by the present generation."[8] Shepherd reveres the memory of the *D&A*, sees in it primarily the restorationist emphasis that is part of the essence of Churches of Christ, and contends that it deserves attention now. He gives no extensive critique of the document.

The second-longest treatment of the *D&A* in the books chosen for this survey (exceeded only by Leroy Garrett's discussion in *The Stone-Campbell Movement*) is found in Homer Hailey's *Attitudes and Consequences in the Restoration Movement*. Hailey spends eleven pages describing the *D&A* in his chapter on the birth of the movement. He calls it the movement's most important document and clearly attributes TC's motivation for writing it to his passion for unity. Hailey contends, however, that TC was convinced that unity could be found only in Christ and his simple Word.[9] He then illustrates three critical positions in the *D&A* gleaned from a list in Winfred Ernest Garrison's 1931 history *Religion Follows the Frontier*: (1) that the will of Christ includes a definite doctrinal and ecclesiastical program; (2) that the Scriptures give an "inerrant" report of the teachings of Jesus and his apostles and the procedure of the first-century church; and (3) that since the teaching authority of Christ passed to the apostles, their teachings and examples constitute a pattern that the church must permanently follow. Hailey strongly emphasizes the biblicist side of the document by quoting numerous short passages from it. While he always balances his treatment with references to TC's longing for unity, Hailey makes it plain that the one thing that would bring about the unity TC envisioned is "the adopting of the New Testament pattern."[10]

Hailey spends some time on TC's willingness to give up anything not clearly taught by precept or example to achieve full communion with other believers. That attitude, Hailey asserts, was different from the attitude of any other reformer. He quotes TC on his willingness to relinquish opinions and practices and points out that TC was not proposing to force beliefs on people, but rather urging them to cease pushing their opinions to the disruption of the peace of the church. Here, Hailey says, is where trouble eventually came to the movement—when people pressed matters that were neither expressly commanded nor forbidden to the violation of the command to maintain the unity of the Spirit in the bond of peace.[11] Though TC was convinced that his platform would lead to unity among Christians, Hailey insists that TC was committed to the side of truth rather than popularity and would stick with it even if no one else accepted it. Hailey concludes his treatment with the assertion that a complete restatement of these principles in the present time would be quite appropriate.[12] While Hailey highlights the restorationism of the document as crucial, the tone of his treatment is not as strident as some, and his overall evaluation of the document and its spirit of unity is wholeheartedly positive.

One of the most widely used and constantly in-print histories of the Stone-Campbell Movement among Churches of Christ is Earl West's four-volume *The Search for the Ancient Order*. West says very little about the *D&A*, treating it in one paragraph of his first volume. He describes the three-part structure of the document, and then says that TC's plan for unity was a "re-statement of Rupertus Meldinius [*sic*] famous maxim: 'In essentials unity; in non-essentials liberty; in all things charity.'" He goes on to explain TC's distinction between faith and opinion, with unity possible only on the "expressed declarations of the Bible" upon which faith is based. He concludes that "The important and timely enunciations of the Declaration and Address have given it a deserving place among the classics of restoration literature."[13] Just prior to this brief description, West assessed the formation of the Christian Association as "related more to denominationalism than apostolic Christianity" and explained that though the people involved had not yet reached a full knowledge of the ancient order, they were going slowly in that direction.[14] This is perhaps the most common early evaluation among those in Churches of Christ who attempted to deal with the *D&A* and the Christian Association. The explanation provided a way to embrace the document as essential to the formation of the movement while dismissing parts with which an author might be uncomfortable. West was certainly not the first nor the last to articulate such a judgment.

Bill Humble, in his remarkably succinct study, *The Story of the Restoration*, asserts that the importance of the *D&A* is its articulation in the most precise and detailed manner of the "restoration principle." This formulation, Humble asserts, gives the document its importance, and it is, therefore, necessary to know something about the *D&A* to understand properly this restoration principle.[15] While he clearly understands that the chief goal of the document is the unity of all Christians and that the concepts of unity and restoration are complementary in TC's mind, Humble places primary emphasis on the author's call for (1) recognition of the New Testament as the divine constitution for the church; (2) restricting church practices to those things expressly authorized by it; and (3) returning to New Testament faith and practice, which would "end the differences among denominations and restore the essential oneness of Christ's church."[16]

Humble sees this plan as sound though deficient, since its restoration principle was not immediately applied to any specific problems. When it finally was applied in the matters of Christian identity and church membership, the Campbells elected to immerse believers, a move that Humble contends set them on a course that increasingly pushed unity to the background in favor of searching for New Testament Christianity. Humble concludes with the familiar explanation adopted by many on both sides of the Disciples/Churches of Christ division, that "the goals of unity and restoration, complementary in theory, turned out to be antagonistic in practice."[17]

The first critical history of the Stone-Campbell Movement by a member of Churches of Christ was written by David Edwin Harrell, Jr. Harrell's *Quest for a Christian America*, as well as a second volume titled *The Social Sources of Division in the Disciples of Christ, 1865–1900*, constitute a masterful social history of the nineteenth-century movement. Harrell mentions the *D&A* twice in the first volume, describing it as a list of the problems with the Christianity of his day and an outline of "the steps necessary for the restoration of primitive Christianity."[18] Later Harrell cites the document as evidence that the early Stone-Campbell Movement "is perhaps the most striking American example of the legalistic and objectivistic sectarian expressions."[19] Harrell's brief depiction is of an exclusively restorationist document advocating a divine biblical pattern that would remedy the problems of the Protestant world if discerned and followed. There is nothing new here, though with Harrell's training at Vanderbilt and close association with the Disciples of Christ Historical Society one might have expected at least a mention of TC's unity agenda.

Leroy Garrett gives the most detailed examination of the *D&A* among the books examined here. He argues that without the *D&A* the Stone-Campbell Movement would likely not have survived as a viable movement.[20] It reads, he says, as if it had been written by a freedom fighter, though he worries that its verbosity might cause potential readers today to sell it short. To help avoid that pitfall, Garrett summarizes the essence of the *D&A* under ten headings: (1) divisions are sinful; (2) Christians must do something about them; (3) divisions are mostly over matters of opinion; (4) Christ and his Word are the only source and terms of unity; (5) the call to unite the church is reasonable and timely; (6) since Jesus prayed for unity it can be achieved; (7) we must be one on earth as we will be in heaven; (8) Christians must become less interested in their own party and associate with others; (9) the wars of Europe show the horrors of division; and (10) our efforts are a humble beginning needing the help of others.[21]

Garrett continues by quoting the first, third, sixth, and seventh propositions from the Address. Of those, Garrett asserts, the sixth may be the most insightful of all as TC rejects inferences and deductions as having any legitimate place in the church's confession. In contrast with subsequent evaluations, Garrett makes no distinction between what TC labels generically "inferences and deductions" and what some would come to identify as "necessary inferences."[22] He simply says that TC meant that no theological opinions and interpretations can be made terms of communion, and that his assertion reflected "the law of love that ruled in all of Thomas Campbell's thought."[23]

Garrett concludes that the *D&A* is permeated with the conviction that there is a law of unity and fellowship in the universe, the violation of which is as great a sin against God and humanity as the breaking of any other law that God has given. He lists three ideals he sees articulated in the *D&A* that seem to function for TC as universal laws: (1) no one has a right to reject a professing Christian brother or sister unless they stand condemned by the express letter of the law; (2) the law of unity and love ought not to be violated by making human opinions terms of communion; and (3) "The first and foundation truth of our Christianity is union with Christ, and the very next to it in order, union with each other in him."[24]

Garrett then raises a question about the nature of the *D&A:* Is it both a unity *and* a restorationist document? Though he admits that certain passages in the document read as if they were propounding a strict patternism, he insists that the text's overall thrust would be violated by such a rigid restorationist interpretation. TC at times overstates his case in his appeal to primitive Christianity, Garrett insists, for he obviously was pointing to the essentials of the ancient faith as the bond of union, not the myriad details that may or may not be relevant. Garrett ends his discussion with the assertion "that it is the unity motif that pervades the

Declaration and Address, with 'restoration' as usually conceived being of little moment."[25] This judgment dramatically reverses the general trend of interpretation in Churches of Christ, reflecting Garrett's own unity emphasis and part of the reason he was often ostracized by mainstream leadership.

Though Robert Hooper's *A Distinct People* is primarily a history of twentieth-century events, the first chapter lays out his view of the nineteenth-century background of Churches of Christ. He begins by explaining the *D&A* as TC's fleshing out of the principle delineated earlier in the Christian Association, "where the Scriptures speak we speak; and where the Scriptures are silent, we are silent." After quoting the first of TC's thirteen propositions from the Address, Hooper stresses that TC made a strong connection between unity and biblical truth. Yet Hooper moves abruptly to other matters, leaving readers with only this fleeting glance at the document and the relation between the two components unity and truth.[26]

Richard Hughes gives the *D&A* even less notice in his *Reviving the Ancient Faith.* As in Hooper's history, this is at least partly because the book's focus is on twentieth-century Churches of Christ. He mentions that TC had withdrawn from the Seceder Presbyterians and written the *D&A* before the arrival of his family in America. "This document, which calls for Christian unity through a return to the clear and unambiguous teachings of the New Testament, in many ways charted the course for the movement the Campbells led." Hughes then goes on to suggest that it was actually the *Christian Baptist* that had more importance for the theology of Churches of Christ.[27] Though Hughes spends a third of the book in a detailed examination of the setting for the twentieth-century events he chronicles, he deals with the *D&A* in two sentences. No historian can avoid making choices about what to deal with—one simply cannot do it all. But the fact that a leading historian of the movement did not think the *D&A* any more important than such a brief mention for a history of Churches of Christ is, I think, significant.

Again, neither Hooper nor Hughes pretends to give full histories of the movement. They are writing histories of the Churches of Christ. Yet that is precisely why their treatments are significant. Both reflect what I should label the long-standing general trend of acknowledging the relative importance of the *D&A* for the early part of the movement, but indicating (implicitly or explicitly) that it has little if any continuing relevance for

Churches of Christ. I believe that their historical judgment is correct; I believe that their theological judgment is wrong.

In his popular-level *Restoration Principles and Personalities,* Dabney Phillips summarizes what he sees as the basic points of the *D&A*: (1) the Holy Scriptures are the only rule of faith and practice; (2) sectarianism is evil since the church is essentially and constitutionally one; (3) divisions result when people neglect the revealed word and introduce human innovations; and (4) human expedience must not be given a place of authority in the church.[28] Phillips clearly continues the trajectory begun with Tolbert Fanning's treatment, with no indication that the document had anything to do with Christian unity.

Finally, two lesser-known histories of the movement written by members of Churches of Christ are Marvin Hastings's *Saga of a Movement* and David Roper's *Voices Crying in the Wilderness*. Neither holds any surprises. Roper, while admitting that TC was probably concerned most of all with unity, insists that TC understood unity coming only by "all going back to God's word and taking *that* alone (i.e., by restoration)."[29] Roper's final appraisal is that TC, like Job, had uttered things that he understood not, things too wonderful for him which he did not fully know (Job 42:3). Obviously so, for TC remained a pedobaptist for some years after. To interpret the *D&A* in light of TC's doctrinal positions at the time he wrote it, Roper insists, is to abandon the restoration concept for which TC himself was calling.[30] Hastings ignores the unity theme of the document entirely in his brief mention of it and implies that the *D&A* had been a speech given by TC that he closed with the aphorism "Where the Scriptures speak, we speak; where the Scriptures are silent, we are silent."[31]

With the exception of Garrett's interpretation, the book-length histories of the Stone-Campbell Movement written by members of Churches of Christ overwhelmingly see the *D&A* as restorationist in theme, some failing even to acknowledge its Christian unity message.

A search for journal material about the *D&A* in twentieth-century Churches of Christ does not produce overwhelming results. Relatively few entries appear in the indexes, and several that did proved to be reprintings of the thirteen propositions from the Address without commentary, leaving the impression that this was the sum of the document.[32]

There are, however, a couple of significant exceptions. By far the longest and most thorough treatment of the *D&A* in the literature of twentieth-century Churches of Christ was written by L. L. Brigance, longtime Bible and church history teacher at Freed-Hardeman College.[33] As part of a six-year, sixty-eight-article series titled *Studies in the Restoration*, Brigance wrote fourteen articles—more than 20 percent of the series—as an analysis and commentary on the *D&A*. Ten of the articles focus on the thirteen propositions of the Address. It is important to look at this series in some detail since it is perhaps the quintessential treatment of the *D&A* among Churches of Christ.

In the first article Brigance begins with a statement that can only be labeled hyperbolic. "Since the last 'amen' of Revelation was penned by John on the Island of Patmos, it is doubtful if another religious document of equal importance has been written."[34] This is certainly a remarkable accolade, even more so in light of some of Brigance's negative evaluations of parts of the document. He continues with a brief history of the document's origins, then ends by quoting a good portion of the "Declaration." In the second article, which appeared more than a month later, he begins with an interesting disclaimer. His writing of the articles is not to be understood as an approval of everything in the *D&A* nor an endorsement of the Christian Association. As Earl Irvin West would assert a decade later, TC and his associates were seeing "through a glass darkly" in this period, though they were, in general, traveling in the right direction.[35] The remainder of the article deals with a subject Brigance would broach twice more in his treatment of the *D&A*—the right of individual Christians to determine for themselves exactly what the Lord required of them. He thoroughly denounces intolerance as one of humanity's greatest weaknesses (using Roman Catholics and Presbyterians as examples). Nevertheless, he insists that it is the right and duty of Christians to insist on the plain teaching of Scripture and to urge all people to follow it. Only in matters of opinions, preferences, or judgments—things about which God had not spoken—is liberty to be allowed.

Based on the continued caveats Brigance includes in his articles, he evidently felt obligated to justify the series and to assure readers of his own soundness as he continued to hold up an uninspired document as worthy of considerable time. In the third article he clearly articulates a consensus view in the Churches of Christ of that era. Speaking of the Christian Association he asserts that in light of Bible teaching, "it is more than probable that none of them were Christians at this time, not even Mr. Campbell. . . . they were just a group of *religious*, not *Christain,* [*sic*] people, wandering around in the dark seeking the light."[36] He spends some time expressing amazement that they would, in the formation of the Christian Association itself, violate their own maxims of practicing simple Christianity and refusing anything for which they could not find a "thus saith the Lord." The truth is, Brigance concludes, that Campbell and those with him were blinded by the fogs of sectarianism and enmeshed in the wilderness of denominationalism. Finding their way out was a slow and tedious process. "It took years upon years, and perhaps they never completely emerged into the full, glorious light of the gospel."[37]

Brigance did not mean that last statement as a wholesale condemnation of TC's efforts. He went on to say in the same paragraph that while others after TC took up the trail that led back to Jerusalem, it was more than probable that the goal had not yet been reached even in Brigance's own day—not an uncommon sentiment among *Gospel Advocate* readers then, but ambiguous in the context.

As Brigance moves into a consideration of the Address in article four, he essentially reduces it to the thirteen propositions. Quoting the paragraph just before proposition one, he again moves into hyperbolic language. When TC proposed to come to the original ground and "take up things just as the apostles left them," he was, according to Brigance, advancing an absolutely new idea. "Since the great apostasy began in the first century, no such proposition had ever been made before."[38] He went on to make the then familiar distinction between attempts at reformation of existing religious bodies and TC's proposal of a restoration of the original church. TC was proposing to correct all errors once and for all "by jumping over the intervening centuries and landing in Jerusalem in the days of the apostles and taking up the work right there where they left it."[39] Brigance saw no difficulty whatsoever with such a proposal—it was patently achievable.

In the fifth article Brigance begins his lengthy treatment of the thirteen propositions, heartily agreeing with the strong unity sentiment of the first. "The perfect unity of all believers in Christ is taught, encouraged, and urged," he writes. "There is no justification in reason or revelation for religious parties, sects, or denominations."[40] In the bulk of the article he states and refutes what he sees as the chief arguments for denominationalism: the necessity of meeting different spiritual needs and temperaments, the need for different divisions in an army, and the classic "vine and branches" argument based in John 15. He also ridicules the economic inefficiency of having "five or six little one-horse, unqualified preachers" in every town, when if Christians were united, "They could have a strong, able gospel preacher, adequately supported to break unto people the bread of life," a remarkable economic argument for Christian unity.[41]

Most interestingly, Brigance asserts that after the movement had been fully launched, it became the object of a common hatred by "human parties, sects, and denominations." The perceived threat to their continued existence posed by the Restoration Movement, according to Brigance, forced the formerly warring denominations to "sympathize, tolerate, and fraternize with one another." A rather pretentious explanation of the beginnings of Protestant ecumenism!

In reading these first articles, Brigance's approach to the *D&A* appears much like that of the preacher who announced the text for the sermon, then "went everywhere preaching the gospel."[42] In fact, Brigance's style in the articles is homiletic. His purpose in writing the articles, he explains in the 11 January 1940 installment, was not to give a complete exposition of the document, but to develop some principle from each part of it for his readers.

Brigance's comments on the second proposition begin with an explanation of the two senses in which the word "church" is used in the New Testament—universal and local. While Christians were by necessity from the beginning divided into local groups, "they all wore the same names, had the same organization, preached the same gospel, did the same work and the same things in the worship of God."[43] Brigance appears, however, to have understood TC to include as part of the "church of Christ on earth" groups Brigance would have labeled denominational churches. In the moderate style of Fletcher D. Srygley that was generally characteristic of the *Gospel Advocate,* in contrast to papers like the *Firm Foundation*, Brigance simply states that TC spoke the truth in light of New Testament teaching, regardless of whom he had meant to include in the statement.

On the third proposition Brigance launches into a familiar argument against creeds. The one and only rule all professed Christians can agree on is the Bible. None would ever agree to give up his or her own creed to accept someone else's as the basis for communion. Yet, if pressed, all would admit that if one took the Bible alone and followed it faithfully through life, the person would be saved. "It is seen, therefore, that any of the denominations can give up its creed without surrendering anything it holds to be essential to salvation." Doing just that would unite believers in exactly the way TC explained in proposition two. Brigance concludes with the assertion that TC was right again. "His understanding of the Bible, his clear vision of the unity and fellowship of Christians, was far in advance 'of his day and generation.'"[44]

While Brigance takes TC to task for using the phrase "Old Testament church" in describing the Old and New Testaments as perfect constitutions for their respective ages (such usage leads some to confuse the New Testament church with the congregation in the wilderness, Brigance explained), he agreed fully with the thesis of proposition four. The Old Testament was nailed to the cross, its authority ended. The New Testament is Christ's law to govern his church.[45] Similarly Brigance agrees wholeheartedly with proposition five, quoting a statement of David Lipscomb that "it was as great a sin to make a law where God has made none as it was to ignore or disobey one he had made."[46] He proceeds to illustrate his point in several ways, only one of which seems to have any direct relevance to his readers. The disposition to make laws where God has none, he asserted, had troubled the disciples in recent years when some had denied the use of classes, Sunday school literature, and other such things on the basis that they were not specified in the Bible. They should have known, said Brigance, that these things were included in the word "teach," and that by denying teachers the right to use any method they think most expedient, they are doing precisely what TC says no human has a right to do.[47] I suspect that any supporters of the missionary societies who might have happened on this article would have been surprised to see such a strongly worded statement dealing with what they would have seen as precisely the problem with the anti-society people decades earlier.

Beginning with his treatment of proposition six, Brigance's evaluations of TC's ideas take on a more critical tone. Here he is forced to deal with TC's denial of any place for inferences and deductions as terms of communion in the church. Brigance begins by saying that it was generally admitted that the Bible teaches us our duty in three ways: commandment, approved example, and necessary inference. While the first two are easy to understand, he asserts, "the last one has given a lot of trouble."[48]

In the remainder of the article Brigance seems to offer mixed signals on the matter. First, he makes a sharp contrast between inferences and *necessary* inferences. After giving examples of each, he makes a remarkably strong statement. "It is safe to say that all *necessary* deductions and inferences are to be accepted as the teaching of God's word and are to be bound upon the consciences of men, but no one is required to accept an *unnecessary* inference because it may or may not be the truth."[49] Though he asserts later in the article that no one is bound by *any* inference or deduction unless he or she personally believes it was "fairly drawn," it seems he means only "unnecessary inferences." While he gives numerous examples of these "unnecessary inferences," he gives only one example of a necessary inference: if the Bible says that Jesus came up out of the water at his baptism, it is a necessary inference that he first went down into the water.

Brigance then launches an attack on those who try to force their unnecessary and unjustified inferences and deductions on others, "with all the cocksuredness of absolute certainty." His conclusion is that the Scriptures are either silent or obscure on "many things with which we have to do in this age." He lists smoking, drinking coffee, tea, or Coca-Cola, wearing jewelry, joyriding on Sunday, and playing cards as examples. Interestingly, all are issues that reflect a "holiness" style of personal morality. Brigance, however, asserts that each person must settle such matters for himself or herself and be tolerant of those who disagree.

Brigance's criticism of TC for not being clear enough in his treatment of inference in the sixth proposition becomes even stronger in the following article, where he appears practically to reverse his earlier praise of the author of the *D&A*. Dealing with propositions seven and eight Brigance asserts that TC's mind was "still beclouded by the mists and fogs of theology," his language reflecting the medieval scholasticism that concealed rather than revealed clear meaning. Brigance was particularly disturbed by TC's reference to people's knowledge "respecting their lost and perishing condition by nature and practice." The reference to nature, Brigance insists, refers to the Calvinistic doctrine of human depravity, an idea not in harmony with the gospel. Though Brigance does not dwell on this perceived flaw in TC's theology, he goes on to explain to readers that all the knowledge necessary to become a Christian was simple enough to be learned by "anyone intelligent enough to be responsible . . . in a few minutes from a good teacher of the gospel."[50]

Brigance continues the same train of thought in the following article on propositions nine and ten. TC, like all sectarians, seems to have been confused on the subject of salvation, Brigance wrote. Focusing on the phrase that speaks of persons enabled by grace to make a profession of faith in Christ, he assumed that TC meant that God works salvation in humans through some kind of direct action on them. Such an idea leads people to uncertainty about what should or should not happen in salvation and to doubt that it has happened after it is supposed to have happened. He goes on to say that the sectarians who believe themselves to have been saved by faith profess a kind of Christian fellowship with each other but are really rivals at heart. He again attributes the level of toleration experienced among other Christian bodies to their having formed a "mutual assistance compact" in the face of the assaults on sectarianism by the Campbell movement. Should this common foe be removed, Brigance insists, "they would soon be sniping at one another again and in the course of time would be engaged in a general conflict."[51] Once again, this is an astounding assertion that attributes the ecumenical movement to the continued existence of the Stone-Campbell Movement, particularly Churches of Christ.

In his commentary on the widely quoted proposition ten, which condemns division as a "horrid evil, fraught with many evils," Brigance makes two points. First, if the various religious sects were parts of the body of Christ it would be like the dismembered corpse of someone run over by a train whose body parts are strewn along the track. That is the picture, he contends, inherent in "the denominational idea." "If the different sects are parts of the body, then, indeed, is its visible unity destroyed. But they are no part of it."[52] Furthermore, while religious division is a sin for which those responsible must answer, those who teach or practice anything for which there is no authority in the word of God are the ones responsible. Here and in his comments in the third article of the series Brigance most clearly reflects the exclusivity then characteristic of Churches of Christ. Much like Moses Lard in his classic article "Can We Divide?," Brigance's concept of Christian unity sees all true Christians already united—those in the visible Churches of Christ.[53]

Omitting proposition eleven, Brigance moves to an analysis of the final two. In a long article on proposition twelve, Brigance discusses four topics under the heading "The Perfection and Purity of the Church." He asserts that regardless of what TC had in mind when he wrote that only those with a "due measure of scriptural self-knowledge" who profess faith in Christ and obedience to him in all things according to the Scriptures were to be admitted to membership in the church, it was the truth. What it actually meant, however, was that "only those who have believed in Christ, repented of their sins, confessed him before men, and been buried with him in baptism are saved. Consequently they are the only ones who should be received into the fellowship of the church."[54]

The final proposition elicited two articles dealing with expedients. In the first he defines faith as the belief of testimony, the acceptance of evidence from the Word of God. Matters of faith consist of anything spoken of in the Bible, he asserts, then proceeds to give a long list of such things. He also lists things that are not matters of faith because they are not mentioned in the Bible, including purgatory, extreme unction, transubstantiation, the Presbyterian Church, the Baptist Church, and missionary societies. He then proceeds to explain what he calls the implied law of expediency. This law says that some way of doing God's commands has to be employed when no way is specified, and it should be the most efficient way.[55] He concludes the article with a long list of expedients, including whether the bread of the Lord's Supper should be leavened or unleavened, or the cup fermented or unfermented.

Brigance ends his series on the *D&A* with a second article on expedients. While the "law of expediency" requires us to use the most efficient means of doing something, he asserts, who will decide what is the most efficient way poses the real problem, for there will always be differences of opinion. He suggests, quoting AC, that when two or more opinions exist, the younger should yield to the older, assuming that this will also usually mean yielding to the majority. The real issue for Brigance, however, is that in matters of faith, that is, things about which God has spoken, there can be no compromise even if it meant one standing alone against a thousand.[56] He goes on to explain exactly what he means. There are two types of commandments in Scripture, general and specific. When God said "Go into all the world" he did not say how to go, so we may go any way that is expedient. If he had said "Ride a horse into all the world," it would have left no room for expedients. If God had said "make music in the worship," we would have been open to making whatever music we thought best suited to our context. But God said "sing"; therefore no other form of music can be admitted. Furthermore, when God has given specific directions by command or example, and humans substitute something else, it is sin. A prime example of such substitution, Brigance argues, is the organization of the American Christian Missionary Society in which God's plan for missions was set aside and a human plan was substituted.[57]

This series by L. L. Brigance epitomizes the mainstream attitudes of traditional Churches of Christ toward the *D&A*—where it was known at all. TC, while beginning to move in a positive direction, was still a sectarian (and probably not even a Christian) when he penned the *D&A*.

While he was certainly right about the Bible as the only source for religious belief and practice, he was mistaken (or at least unclear) about matters such as God's role in salvation, the role of inferences in establishing doctrine, and the boundaries of the church of Christ on earth. Brigance's ambiguity about the document is reflected in the range of his evaluations of it, from arguably the most significant religious document since the inspired writings of the Bible to a text clouded with the mists and fogs of theology and sectarianism.

Possible reasons for this ambiguity are suggested in a short article by Jay Smith published in the July 1961 *Restoration Quarterly*. Smith analyzes the *D&A* under three headings: the overall purpose of the document, the method for achieving its purpose, and how the purpose and method could be seen in current Churches of Christ and Disciples of Christ. The purpose of the document, shouted on every page, Smith insists, is unity. The method of effecting unity was acceptance of the Bible as the only standard of faith and practice—which he labels restoration. These two represent the philosophy of the document, and any different alignment of the ideas will present a different outlook.[58]

As he begins his evaluation, Smith predictably accuses the Disciples of having kept the purpose but lost the method. Smith quotes TC's own words in the *D&A* that if Christians refused to accept the restorationist method of achieving unity he had spelled out, the only remaining way to accomplish it would be "voluntary compromise and good-natured accommodation," which Smith implies had been the case with Disciples.

When Smith moves to Churches of Christ, one expects the familiar evaluation that we, in contrast with the Disciples, had chosen the restorationism of the document to the neglect of the unity purpose. Smith, however, says that the difference between our stance and that of TC is more complex than that. It is here that Smith says he made a startling discovery:

> It was not what Thomas Campbell said that surprised me, it was his total ignoring of a subject which I had been "reading into" the document. Restoration is not preached among us primarily for the purpose of uniting the religious world, but as the only valid means of salvation. In other words, we feel that without the gospel restored to its N.T. purity salvation is impossible. To be sure, we still feel that unity is desirable and would come as a *result* of a return to N.T. practice by all; but salvation is the real objective; and disunity is preferable to risking salvation.[59]

While writing cautiously and noncritically, Smith articulates a key component of the historic reluctance of people among Churches of Christ to participate in unity efforts and even to embrace fully their own heritage represented by the unity effort inherent in the *D&A*. This was fundamentally a matter of salvation. The risk of going wrong on any point in the pursuit of unity and becoming lost was simply not worth it.

One other article will close this chronicling of treatments. Ross W. Dye's "Is the 'Declaration and Address' Heretical?" is actually more a critique of sectarianism among Churches of Christ than an analysis of the *D&A*. Dye first acknowledges the "sane and sensible plea for unity" put forth by TC, which allowed for a wide range of liberty on matters not specified in the Bible. Churches of Christ, while giving lip service to that unity plea, have in reality demonstrated a capacity for division unequaled in the religious world. This is the result, Dye asserts, of superficiality and sectarianism. Quoting propositions two and three of the Address, Dye focuses his criticism on the propensity in Churches of Christ to make opinions tests of fellowship, or at least to "write up" and abuse one another over them. The right to opinions, he declares, is not itself an opinion but a matter of faith and commandment—we must grant others the right to disagree with us (Rom 14). "Unless we 'restore' the right to think, we have made little progress in 'restoring' the New Testament church." He concludes by calling down shame on Churches of Christ for going around the world seeking proselytes to our views, but converting few people to Christ.[60]

These last two articles reflect a less dogmatic attitude toward maintaining traditional stances and a willingness to reexamine the *D&A* afresh. The seminar that generated the essays in this book is itself testimony to a rekindling of interest in this foundational statement. At least two lacunae remain in this survey—an examination of the *Christian Leader* and *Word and Work*. I suspect that nothing new would be found, but as early "alternative" journals their approach to the *D&A* might be expected to reflect a less hostile evaluation of the document than that seen, for example, in the Brigance series.

The basic epistemological assumptions on which TC based the *D&A* are not ones many would be willing to defend today. Nor would many of the judgments of L. L. Brigance about TC and the document be accepted as widely as they once may have been. The real problem for Churches of Christ, however, is that most of our people have not the slightest idea what this document is or what it said. Despite its flaws, the spirit of the

D&A and its major premises are still filled with power—not merely as inspiring history (though it is that), but as a place to focus as we rethink our self-understanding and mission for the next century. We need a new "Declaration and Address" that speaks to the needs of Christ's body in the world of A.D. 2000 as appropriately as the original did for the world of 1809.

Notes

1. J. M. Powell, "The 'Declaration and Address,'" *Gospel Advocate* 103 (7 December 1961): 778.

2. Tolbert Fanning, "Sketches in the Life of Alexander Campbell, No. 1," *Gospel Advocate* 8 (15 May 1866): 308-9. See *D&A*, 4.45-47; 16.26-30.

3. For accounts of the events see James DeForest Murch, *Christians Only* (Cincinnati: Standard Publishing, 1962), 216; and Leroy Garrett, *The Stone-Campbell Movement* (Joplin, Mo.: College Press, 1981; reprint, 1994), 390-95.

4. David Lipscomb, *Christian Unity, How Promoted, How Destroyed. Faith and Opinion* (Nashville: Gospel Advocate, 1890; reprint, Nashville: McQuiddy, 1916), 9.

5. Lipscomb, *Christian Unity*, 19.

6. Lipscomb, *Christian Unity*, 22.

7. J. W. Shepherd, *The Church, The Falling Away, and the Restoration* (Cincinnati: F. L. Rowe, 1929; reprint, Nashville: Gospel Advocate, 1961), 182.

8. Shepherd, *The Church*, 184.

9. Homer Hailey, *Attitudes and Consequences in the Restoration Movement* (Rosemead, Calif.: Old Path Book Club, 1945), 54-55.

10. Hailey, *Attitudes*, 57.

11. Hailey, *Attitudes*, 60.

12. Hailey, *Attitudes*, 62.

13. Earl Irvin West, *The Search for the Ancient Order*, 4 vols. (Nashville: Gospel Advocate, 1949), 1:49.

14. West, *Search*, 48.

15. B. J. Humble, *The Story of the Restoration* (Austin, Tex.: Firm Foundation, 1969), 19. See also Humble's essay "The Restoration Ideal in the Churches of Christ," in *The American Quest for the Primitive Church*, ed. Richard T. Hughes (Urbana: University of Illinois Press, 1988), 220-31.

16. Humble, *Story*, 21.

17. Humble, *Story*, 22.

18. David Edwin Harrell Jr., *Quest for a Christian America* (Nashville: The Disciples of Christ Historical Society, 1966), 6-7.

19. Harrell, *Quest*, 27.

20. Leroy Garrett, *The Stone-Campbell Movement: An Anecdotal History of Three Churches* (Joplin, Mo.: College Press, 1981), 136.

21. Garrett, *Stone-Campbell*, 146-50.

22. See Michael W. Casey, "The Development of Necessary Inference in the Hermeneutics of the Disciples of Christ/Churches of Christ" (Ph.D. diss., University of Pittsburgh, 1986).

23. Garrett, *Stone-Campbell*, 153.

24. Garrett, *Stone-Campbell*, 155-56.

25. Garrett, *Stone-Campbell*, 158.

26. Robert E. Hooper, *A Distinct People: A History of the Churches of Christ in the 20th Century* (West Monroe, La.: Howard, 1993), 3.

27. Richard T. Hughes, *Reviving the Ancient Faith: The Story of Churches of Christ in America* (Grand Rapids: William B. Eerdmans, 1996), 11.

28. Dabney Phillips, *Restoration Principles and Personalities* (University, Alabama: Youth in Action, 1975), 27.

29. David Roper, *Voices Crying in the Wilderness: A History of the Lord's Church with Special Emphasis on Australia* (Salisbury [Adelaide], South Australia: Restoration Publications, 1979), 50.

30. Roper, *Voices*, 51 n. 13.

31. Marvin W. Hastings, *Saga of a Movement: Story of the Restoration Movement* (Manchester, Tenn.: Christian Schoolmaster Publications, 1981), 16.

32. See, for example, *Christian Chronicle* 25 (12 January 1968): 48; *Firm Foundation* 93 (10 August 1976): 505; *Integrity* 10 (March 1979): 142.

33. For information on Brigance see H. A. Dixon, "Honor to Whom Honor is Due," *Gospel Advocate* 103 (12 January 1961): 22-23. He died in February 1950.

34. L. L. Brigance, "Studies in the Restoration," *Gospel Advocate* 81 (29 June 1939): 605.

35. L. L. Brigance, "Studies in the Restoration," *Gospel Advocate* 81 (3 August 1939): 719.

36. L. L. Brigance, "Studies in the Restoration," *Gospel Advocate* 81 (24 August 1939): 798.

37. Brigance, "Studies," 798.

38. L. L. Brigance, "Studies in the Restoration," *Gospel Advocate* 81 (7 September 1939): 846.

39. Brigance, "Studies," 846.

40. L. L. Brigance, "Studies in the Restoration," *Gospel Advocate* 81 (12 October 1939): 963.

41. Brigance, "Studies," 963.

42. N. B. Hardeman said Brigance was not that kind of preacher. Quoted in Dixon, "Honor," 23.

43. L. L. Brigance, "Studies in the Restoration," *Gospel Advocate* 81 (26 October 1939): 1011.

44. Brigance, "Studies," 1011.

45. L. L. Brigance, "Studies in the Restoration," *Gospel Advocate* 81 (16 November 1939): 1088.

46. L. L. Brigance, "Studies in the Restoration," *Gospel Advocate* 81 (30 November 1939): 1127.

47. Brigance, "Studies," 1127.

48. L. L. Brigance, "Studies in the Restoration," *Gospel Advocate* 81 (21 December 1939): 1208.

49. Brigance, "Studies," 1208.

50. L. L. Brigance, "Studies in the Restoration," *Gospel Advocate* 82 (11 January 1940): 31.

51. L. L. Brigance, "Studies in the Restoration," *Gospel Advocate* 82 (25 January 1940): 82.

52. Brigance, "Studies," 82.

53. Moses Lard, "Can We Divide?," *Lard's Quarterly* 3 (April 1866): 330-36. See also Douglas A. Foster, *Will the Cycle Be Unbroken?* (Abilene: ACU Press, 1994), 43-61.

54. L. L. Brigance, "Studies in the Restoration," *Gospel Advocate* 82 (8 February 1940): 129.

55. L. L. Brigance, "Studies in the Restoration," *Gospel Advocate* 82 (22 February 1940): 175.

56. L. L. Brigance, "Studies in the Restoration," *Gospel Advocate* 82 (4 April 1940): 326.

57. Brigance, "Studies," 326.

58. Jay Smith, "The 'Declaration and Address,'" *Restoration Quarterly* 5 (July 1961): 114-16.

59. Smith, "D&A," 117.

60. Ross W. Dye, "Is the 'Declaration and Address' Heretical?," *Gospel Advocate* 105 (6 June 1963): 356, 360-61.

The *Declaration and Address* among Independents

C. J. Dull

A priori the *Declaration and Address* should not be received sympathetically among Independents. A document penned by a maverick Presbyterian can at best claim within an Independent frame of reference to be "a good first step." Above all, the defining struggle in the formation of the Independents is the separation from what officially became the Christian Church (Disciples of Christ), and the overwhelming issue from the Independent perspective was the nature of baptism and open membership, however much it may have been affected by institutional changes. The *D&A* does not endorse baptism by immersion for believers; its major emphasis is unity, the Disciples theme in that struggle.

By "Independents," I refer to what is generally known as the Undenominational Fellowship of Christian Churches and Churches of Christ. Similarly, I use "Disciples" to refer to the Christian Church (Disciples of Christ). The term "Church of Christ" is the most widely used and, in the world context, has the most variety. I use "Noninstrumental" to refer to the noninstrumental Churches of Christ as defined by Mac Lynn. What follows is strictly my assessment. The reader may chafe at some background detail, but a number of aspects of Independent life are not well documented. Perhaps because we are dominated by a class—preachers—whose skills are oral rather than literary, a substantive oral tradition exists about personnel and institutions, but it is often incomprehensible to outsiders. "Preacher" and "minister" are used interchangeably.

The Influence of Preachers

Independents do not have editors for bishops but rather defer to prominent preachers, and understanding Independents is impossible unless one realizes that all effective power and influence beyond the congregation is wielded by preachers. In institutionally defined positions such as the continuation committee and the staff of the North American Christian Convention (NACC), the boards of colleges and seminaries, and the Standard Publishing committee, preachers overwhelmingly dominate. Most college and seminary teachers, even influential women, have significant congregational experience. Only one NACC president, Edwin Crouch, a lawyer, was not a preacher. We know Henry Webb and James North as Restoration Movement experts. For a Reflections series in *Christian Standard*, each biographical note took pains to describe the authors as "Christian."[1] The omnipresent reality is that very little happens among Independents not directed either by or in the interest of preachers. One of our more conservative periodicals, *Restoration Herald*, has published a series, "Restoring the Restoration," by Harold Ford, a retired professor of Restoration History, with this foreword: "This material was written at the request of a preacher who wanted material for his church newsletter that would help teach his people about the Restoration Movement." Among Independents, scholarship rarely exists outside pastoral applications.

An overwhelming predisposition against the *D&A* as simply not useful in the "nuts and bolts" of church life thus prevails. While numerous preachers have found two phrases in the *D&A* rhetorically useful—"the church of Christ on earth is essentially, intentionally and constitutionally one" and "nothing ought to be inculcated upon christians as articles of faith; nor required of them as terms of communion; but what is expressly taught and enjoined upon them, in the Word of God"—I have yet to find an example of a prominent preacher who has preached a sermon on it. When I posed the question to a prominent local minister, an NACC past president, he commented to the effect that we need more sermons on unity within a congregation; rarely are sermons on a wider unity helpful. This is not the viewpoint of a representative of the schismatic right but of a longtime trustee of Milligan College, a student of Henry Webb and Dean Walker.

Historically, the struggle between Independents and Disciples is often viewed from outside Independent circles as a struggle between diametrically opposed views of biblical scholarship, a position not uncommon among Independent scholars.[2] There is, however, an oral tradition that places the emphasis elsewhere. The practical redrawing of lines began in earnest during the late 1940s and continued until Disciple Restructure in 1968. During this period the most influential school was Lincoln Christian College and Seminary in Lincoln, Illinois. While its founder and longtime president, Earl Hargrove, was certainly not sympathetic to the emerging Disciples theological consensus, the school's origin is revealing and paradigmatic. Lincoln Bible Institute began in 1944 in the basement of the largest congregation in that area, Lincoln Christian Church, where Hargrove preached. It began because of a decided shortage of ministers in the area. Thus, two points need to be made. The vanguard of the opposition to the Disciples came from regional bible colleges that had been formed to recruit and train preachers; by implication the effective response to liberalism in colleges came from churches. Much of the *modus operandi* of Independent ministers was defined during this period. Lincoln was perceived as having succeeded because it met a need, training preachers, that Eureka College no longer could. In this way the theological meets the practical in that the function of such colleges is overwhelmingly to produce preachers; liberal theology is both identified and condemned because it will not produce such preachers. Thus, first of all, the effective opposition to liberal theology came from preachers, and the best defense against liberal theology is a strong, numerous cadre of preachers, not scholars. Second, Independent preachers tend to view and react to theological trends as they affect congregational growth. Perhaps two illustrative examples can clarify. I have heard a number of ministers state that they have some theological sympathy with the elevation of women to the eldership or pulpit, but they do not want to see that implemented because "groups that do it don't grow." Contrariwise, a movement toward more Evangelical positions has gained strength because they do seem connected with numerical growth.

A crucial characteristic of Independent ministers is circumscribed by the adjective "methodological," which may seem an odd choice, especially to Noninstrumentals. To Disciples, who know Herb Miller's work, this is more comprehensible. Noninstrumental preachers are often preaching elders or biblical scholars-in-residence; Disciple ministers increasingly liturgical worship leaders. Either may occasionally happen in Independent congregations, but mostly Independent preachers are church managers. The analogy is with city managers. They are methodologically sophisticated professionals hired by a congregation to manage its programs and operations. They may well be theologically and biblically sophisticated, but that is not required. Like CEOs of small businesses, they are leaders of congregations and apart from them. A fascinating irony about Independent ministers is that as a class they dominate church life outside the local congregation, have become indispensable for congregational growth, and yet have, generally, only a functionally defined congregational status. Independents can easily say what a preacher "does"; we often find it awkward to say what the biblical or theological basis for that action is.[3] Some more conservative congregations call their preachers "evangelists" or indicate that is the function. In some a preacher may be an elder *ipso facto* or perhaps *ex officio* because he is the preacher.[4] It is not unheard of in some larger congregations that the preacher is hired "to do the work of the church" or some specialized part of it. I have even heard a preacher's status described as "equivalent to an elder." Usually, for good public relations, ministers routinely transfer their membership when they begin work with a new congregation. Yet, it is not uncommon for congregations to have restrictions in their by-laws or constitutions that limit the voting privileges of ministers (and sometimes their families).

The status of preachers is connected to that of elders. Independent elders are hardly as powerful or influential congregationally as Noninstrumental ones. They usually are elected for specific terms, and a hiatus often is required after so many terms. Consequently, it is increasingly rare for an individual elder to dominate a congregation, but rather the whole group functions institutionally in a significant way. Noninstrumental elders have been characterized as upper management.[5] Independent elders are generally less "hands on," and most function as either a board of directors or a group of majority stockholders. They regularly have influence and often veto power over most major initiatives. Generally, elders make up a significant portion of, if they are not coterminous with, a ministerial search committee.[6] Typically, it is the elders' recommendation that presents a ministerial candidate to the congregation for hiring. Many elders can fire a minister apart from any congregational action. They may not do much but are institutionally capable of stopping ministerial initiatives. They are not outsiders and have no doubt of their biblical status. However powerful ministers may be beyond the congregation, they often have a precarious existence in the congregation, where their major interests are producing growth and avoiding conflict. Since their only accountability is local, interest in unity in a wider context generally exists only if a particular congregation endorses it.

In the course of acquiring the experience and techniques of managing growth, preachers commonly attend workshops or classes with other individuals across a wide theological and ecclesiastical spectrum. Frequently the most popular courses are offered by large congregations or megachurches. Since most preachers are more practically than ideologically defined, they tend to form bonds with these other individuals beyond theology, especially since, historically, there is a theological dimension to growth that tends to place other ministers who are successful in making congregations grow in the same category, subliminally if nothing else, as our ministers. While some conservative ministers have qualms about local ministerial associations, most do not. Yet the reader should not be too eager to interpret this as some incipient unity movement with the unimmersed or those with significantly differing theological views. This is a professional association in the truest sense. It resembles gatherings of accountants, real estate agents, software developers, lawyers, and such. Other members of the association share similar skills and may be useful in strengthening such skills. Remarkably little theology may be involved.[7]

Schools of Thought

While Independent discussion of the *D&A* is not voluminous,[8] it may be more varied and nuanced than in the other branches. In one sense, Independents are more uniform than the other two branches since individuals among us who disagree with the unofficial theological synthesis can find more congenial associations to the right or left. We perhaps preserve some of the tensions between the two to a greater extent, and this may be a good example. Significantly differing schools of thought among Independents do exist. Only by understanding what I call the intellectual geography of Independents can we assess the influence of the *D&A* and the reciprocal influences from them. The papers of Lee Snyder and Paul M. Blowers in this volume also illustrate this in greater detail. They are also unmixed in their education and teaching in Independent schools. Unlike North and Webb, who both have been educated in one Independent school of thought and have taught mostly in another, these men have been educated and have taught in the same circles (Blowers) or outside the movement (Snyder). Naturally, sometimes these schools' approaches overlap, although that seems less true here.

Independents had in their period of coalescing as a group basically three schools of thought,[9] and the *D&A* and the ideas contained in it are treated distinctly differently. The schools represent a "low" and two different "high" views of unity—or, rather, a restrictive, balanced, and expansive view of unity.

The low or restrictive view is generally held by what I call the fundamentalist segment.[10] Their graduate school is Cincinnati Bible College and Seminary (CBCS), a school formed in reaction to faculty embracing modernistic views at College of the Bible (now Lexington Theological Seminary). The major interest of the school, exemplified in the activities of R. C. Foster and his son Lewis, has been a conservative interpretation of the Bible. Both Fosters were experts in New Testament and dominated the intellectual life of the school during their tenure. Typically, this school and segment have been most concerned about being "Christian" as they understand that biblically. Restoration, not unity, is the overwhelming theme and purpose of the movement; if restoration is divisive, so be it. Still, while their concept of unity may seem quite restrictive, it is not anemic. Whoever shares with them (especially baptism by immersion as a believer) basically qualifies as a Christian. Reservations may exist about those insisting that baptism is not involved in the forgiveness of sins, but they rarely insist on rebaptism. Since the school began in 1924, when extracongregational structures were either in question or in tatters and traditional designations that had long been either acceptable or innocuous (for example, "Disciples") became negative, the insistence on having the same name—rather than doing the same thing—is much less. Sherwood Smith, a professor of Church History, has preached at a Congregational Church in Covington, Kentucky. One of CBCS's larger supporting congregations in the Cincinnati area is Lincoln Heights Missionary Baptist Church, a black congregation. Thus, the most conservative portion of the Independents is often quite active for unity within its particular framework. Ozark Christian College has been the major Independent player in the Restoration Forums with Noninstrumentals. Don DeWelt was both a professor there and the founder of College Press, and his connection needs comment.

The most austere Independent segment is a group usually referred to with the place name Ottumwa used as an adjective. The reference is to the Midwestern School of Evangelism in Ottumwa, Iowa. Generally, its adherents are known for not using television and makeup; more positively, it has congregations in some significant urban areas (Portland, Seattle), where they often set up adult schools and are quite biblically literate. It is known primarily for two individuals, Donald Hunt and Archie Word, the former a longtime professor at the school and the latter an evangelist, mostly on the west coast. Word's best-known convert was Don DeWelt; Hunt's best-known graduate is Victor Knowles.[11] It has published *One Body*, the major mouthpiece for unity efforts with Noninstrumentals and some conservative Disciples. Overwhelmingly, appeals for unity in these circles are based on New Testament passages. The basic idea that division is a scandal among Christians is something that resonates strongly even here. Aside from an editorial flourish by Knowles,[12] Independent use of the *D&A* in the Restoration Forums has been largely by historians. Overwhelmingly, the themes are the importance of unity, the evil of division, and the place of inferences.[13] While the definition of what is a Christian may seem restrictive,[14] within that framework there is an interesting similarity to what Thomas Campbell said about groups he considered Christians in his time.

The other end of the Independent spectrum belongs to what I call the "Old Disciples.[15] The primary schools are Milligan College, from which I hold a degree, and Emmanuel School of Religion. They are both the most liberal Independents and the most reactionary Disciples. Emmanuel faculty members are much more comfortable with critical scholarship and an expanded role for women. Emmanuel has advertised in *Christian Century*, held a retreat with Lexington Theological Seminary, and sent observers to Faith-and-Order meetings. Old Disciples are reactionary in that they wish to emulate, and to some extent restore, institutions, views, and practices more widespread among Disciples before the split. Their separation from the Disciples was reluctant and is not yet final. Northwest Christian College is jointly, officially, run by Disciples and Independents, as is at least one camp in Oregon. Most Emmanuel faculty are members of the Disciples Pension Plan, and a recent hire is an ordained Disciples minister.[16] Basically, their view is that the intellectual synthesis that existed at the Old Butler School,[17] from Frederick Doyle Kershner's founding of the school in 1924 until Henry Shelton's becoming dean, was basically sound and remains to a considerable degree definitive. A seminal document for them is Kershner's commentary on the *D&A*.

The towering personality among the Old Disciples was Dean Everest Walker. In the formation of the Independents he is both one of the most influential and least documented figures. Although writing only a short book and some articles,[18] he was a widely influential teacher with an extensive oral tradition and anecdotal history. The son of W. R. Walker, prominent minister at Indianola Church of Christ in Columbus, Ohio, he was expelled from Bethany College for leading a student revolt. He finished at Tri-State College in Angola, Indiana, and went to the Butler School of Religion, where he received a B.D. with a thesis on the challenge of the rural church, and an M.A. with a thesis on the portrayal of Jesus in the Ur-Markus. He did not finish a doctorate at St. Andrews University in Scotland but did form a friendship with William Robinson, who wrote the foreword to his book. Walker taught at Butler until becoming president of Milligan College in 1950 and later of Emmanuel School of Religion. Professor Blowers has appropriately discussed the two major influences on Walker, Kershner and Robinson, and, unlike most Disciples scholars, thinks they are more than transitional figures.

Unlike the previous group, the Old Disciples advocate the priority of unity as the movement's *raison d'être* while averring the movement's combination of unity and restoration as distinctive. More significant is who it defines as Christians. Unlike the fundamentalist element, for these Independents the immersed are not the only Christians. While the former would refer to a pious Lutheran, Catholic, or Presbyterian as at most a "believer," this camp has no difficulty calling them "Christians." However old this tension may be, it demonstrates the ecclesiological and theological distance between Independent poles. In practice—the hallmark of Independents—the difference may seem negligible, a matter of terminology, form, or even public relations. A fundamentalist congregation will require immersion of a candidate for membership who has been baptized in infancy; an Old Disciples congregation will do the same. Both usually have a high view of baptism, that it is for the remission of sins and makes one part of the body of Christ.[19] Characteristic of this group is the view that those baptized in infancy or not immersed generally have in some sense been baptized inadequately or defectively. Yet, generally citing Acts 19:1-7,[20] they consider them Christians. This obviously changes a number of things.

While a fundamentalist preacher or scholar considers a Baptist understanding of baptism inadequate or inaccurate, few if any would require someone baptized thus to be baptized again, unless there were some contributing factor such as an extremely young age. They may be in error, but they are at least Christians, while the unimmersed are not even Christians. The Old Disciples take on this is significantly different. Both a Baptist and an Episcopalian have defective baptisms; the former has the correct form and an incorrect understanding while the latter has the correct understanding and an incorrect form.[21] Thus, both need correcting; one is simply more concrete. Open communion with the unimmersed becomes not an embarrassment but a positive statement.[22] Consequently, since the more liturgical churches are often closer in other ways theologically, links with them become more comprehensible and desirable, and this segment regularly has served as something of an apologist for the more liturgical churches. These Independents identify baptism and the Lord's Supper as sacraments, terminology that others find at best questionable and sometimes appalling. For the fundamentalist element, ecumenical unity is out of the question if for no other reason than that most of the bodies represented, liberal theology aside, are simply not Christians; for the Old Disciples there may indeed be problems, but these bodies are conceptually not further away than many immersionist groups. For this segment the *D&A* has both an immediacy and applicability it does not have elsewhere among Independents.

Furthermore, unlike other Independents, Old Disciples believe in the priority of scholars. Scholars define the faith; ministers proclaim it. Not surprisingly, they easily have the best financed educational establishment at the graduate level and probably have produced more college professors and scholars than any other segment. They are the most middle-class, which contributes to their financial security and organizational efficiency. Their cosmopolitanism has also made them a major player in the missions community. Scholarly priorities obviously differ from ministerial priorities. Clearly a group educated largely in elite universities in the United States and Europe will have a different perspective from those whose status comes from their ability to motivate and administer programs among a more populist element. Yet in 1983 Emmanuel was forced to make a significant turn. In what is generally called the Beck-Owens affair, a footnote on a thesis title page suggested that the professor held a composite view of the authorship of Isaiah and Daniel. The fallout from that footnote and the way the administration handled the situation resulted in a quite extensive operating loss. The president, Fred Thompson, a preacher interested in being a scholar, was succeeded by Calvin Phillips, a preacher with a D.Min. and more than three decades of pastoral experience. By stressing the ministry and dealing tactfully and skillfully with its critics, he was able to recoup its fortunes to the extent it is now easily the most prosperous Independent seminary. While scholars obviously predominate there, they also are now quite aware that continued success means working within that ministerial framework, one only minimally interested in the *D&A*. In fact, the quandary of Emmanuel and the Old Disciples generally is that they are essentially anomalous compared with the majority of Independents. With success comes the imperative either to become more like other Independents or make the rest of the Independents more like them. Any significant initiative expanding the application of unity from this segment carries with it a corresponding danger of internal disunity.

The moderate schools are what I characterize as the regional methodological ones.[23] The model was essentially created by Lincoln Christian College in the 1940s and 1950s. The view was that a college strategically located would recruit and train ministers for that area and serve as a regional center for evangelism. A number of schools were created for exactly that purpose, and many older schools adopted that model. In fact, two of the strongest schools in that camp are Johnson Bible College, which originally was formed in 1893 to give poor students an education and has significant Disciple alumni, and Kentucky Christian College, originally a normal school. The major emphasis is method. The concern generally is not with the formulation or definition of the faith as an end but rather the methods by which it can be successfully propagated. To give one example, study of theology in the first two camps is more an end to help in understanding the faith, but in these circles study of theology is intended more to provide a helpful framework for making the gospel more comprehensible to others. Most Independent method experts, the professors of Education, Speech, Missions, Linguistics, and such, come out of this segment. Generally, they hold doctorates from the major state universities or seminaries in a particular region.[24] The influence of this segment has historically been dominant in the formation of the Independents, and especially the emphasis on the minister as a methodological expert seems its lasting legacy.

Given its emphasis on the ministry, Restoration History would not seem a priority within this group. Yet probably no segment takes it more seriously. The building housing the seminary faculty at Lincoln is called Restoration Hall, and its catalogue regularly features the four founders on its cover. Lincoln last reprinted the *D&A* and Knofel Staton, a Lincoln graduate, paraphrased it. In fact, to a greater degree than the others, the movement is "our tradition," a phrase very few would be eager to use. In the language of many adherents, both in this segment and more widely, the opposite of this movement is "denominationalism." These Independents generally share the view of the fundamentalist segment that the unimmersed are not Christians, although they are usually less likely to express it in those terms. Professor Blowers has given a paper on two interpreters of TC and the movement, and many Noninstrumental scholars have likewise commented on David Lipscomb and other such individuals. Professor Snyder is characteristic of many in this group in that he basically handles the source documents of the founders. What the Campbells especially, and Stone and Scott to a lesser extent, have said does matter. Finally, we are likely to see expressed in this segment what I call the balanced view—neither unity nor restoration is in itself sufficient. While restoration is clearly the more important, the combination makes for a correct understanding and evangelistic growth.[25] Professor North, a Lincoln graduate, sums this succinctly in the title of his book, *Union in Truth*, taken from the *D&A*.

A brief comment on the genealogy of Independent scholars on the *D&A* may be useful. The family tree of Independent restorationist scholarship all traces back to Kershner. Aside from his writings, Old Disciples scholars either studied under Kershner or his student and colleague Dean Walker. Even James DeForest Murch, who was educated outside movement schools, was influenced by Dean Walker, as was Henry Webb, a Southern Baptist doctorate. Those at Lincoln, including Professor North at CBCS, studied under two students of Kershner, Charles Mills and Enos Dowling, the latter having served as librarian at Butler. Robert Rea, now at Lincoln, studied under Dean Walker at Emmanuel.

Dean E. Walker

We start with a document written before the split, Dean Walker's lectures entitled *Adventuring for Christian Unity* (1935). Since the whole book is only fifty-five pages, Walker's treatment is terse. He begins:

> The *Declaration and Address* was over a century before its time. It repays our careful study to-day. Campbell here lays down a platform for Christian union, consisting of thirteen propositions, which may be condensed into five.[26]

These five headings are: (1) the essential, intentional, and constitutional unity of the Church of Christ; (2) the supreme authority of Scripture, especially the New Testament; (3) the relative value of theology and futility of human creeds; (4) the essential brotherhood of all Christians; (5) if human innovations are removed, Christians will find themselves united.[27] He calls the first "not Protestant, but Catholic or High Church," and states that "a divided Church is a self-contradiction," and "unity consists not in mere cooperation in service, but in rational agreement on things essential." The second he characterizes as "the ultimate and radical Protestant contention"; "creeds nullify this fundamental Protestant position." The third point is that theology and creeds may be good or valuable, but their conclusions or statements should not be tests of fellowship or communion. Point four he characterizes as Catholic, but not Roman Catholic, since he does not believe baptism is the *sine qua non*. Point five is that divisions are due to peculiarities—"discard these and universalities remain." That can only be done by restoring the church pictured in the New Testament.

Walker also sees two basic principles under the surface. The first is the Protestant position of private judgment. The second one puts him "on Catholic ground" by repudiating creeds and appealing to the infallibility of the universal reason.[28] He further elaborates this point: it is an assertion that in religion, revelation, as interpreted by full and honest scholarship, is the last word, and that unity must rest on truth thus arrived at, or be forever despaired of. He also stresses that the Campbells regarded members of denominations as Christians.

There is one other concept, which does not appear in that discussion but looms large in Old Disciples circles: the view that divine authority is personal:

> In short, our contention here is that authority by its very nature must be external to ourselves (though not alien) and hence, in religion, it must be personal. Authority is not statutory nor scientific. It is personal and religious. . . . If we are to attain at all to pure, new, and eternal life and so enjoy the divine fellowship, we must have that life given to us by Him who has the authority so to act. Christ's authority is His Lordship (inherent and proven possession and power) confirmed to Him by the Gospel, witness and pledge of God, over Nature and mankind to create, sustain, and recreate according to the will of God.[29]

The position of Walker is also fleshed out by the thesis of his student Adrian Fraley, who cites three purposes:

> [T]o call Christendom back to the Bible as its rule of faith and practice, to unite God's people and to evangelize those portions of every nation where the people had no opportunity to hear the gospel of Christ. [30]

Those opposed, "the denominations,"[31] are still Christians. Most significantly, the *D&A* becomes metonymically symbolic of the whole nineteenth-century restoration program.[32] Thus, Independents can later see in a change of baptismal practice—not mentioned in the *D&A*—a betrayal of that document.

James DeForest Murch

James DeForest Murch is the renaissance man of the early Independents. Among his achievements Murch served as acting president and faculty member at Cincinnati Bible Seminary in its earliest years; editor of *Restoration Herald* and president of the Christian Restoration Association; a founder of the Disciples of Christ Historical Society; member of the Commission on Restudy of Christian Churches; a cofounder of the NACC; editor of the *Lookout*;[33] a founder of the Christian's Hour Broadcasting Association; a cofounder of the National Association of Evangelicals; managing editor of *Christianity Today*; writer of hymns; and dabbler in architecture. Murch was familiar with the whole Independent spectrum: Cincinnati Bible Seminary and the Christian Restoration Association represent the right; Standard Publishing, the NACC, and his work with Christian Endeavor the middle; his friendship with Dean Walker and the Commission on Restudy the left. His book *Christian Education and the Local Church* (1943) established his methodological credentials, and his *Christians Only* was the only Independent history of the movement from 1962 to 1990. The central event in his life was the break with the Disciples. *Christians Only* is the first to describe Independents, his "centrist" branch.

Murch's view of the *D&A* is high and seminal. In the second paragraph of his preface he states:

> I have long had a secret desire to write such a volume in the frame of reference afforded by Thomas Campbell's *Declaration and Address*, a document as vital to this movement as the Declaration of Independence is to the United States of America.[34]

Similarly, he states:

> The *Declaration and Address* is so basic to the development of the American movement to restore New Testament Christianity that it needs to be presented and considered in its entirety. He sees four basic principles: (1) the authority of the Holy Scriptures; (2) the individual Christian's responsibility before God and the right of private judgment; (3) the evil of sectarianism; and (4) the way to peace and unity in the body of Christ is through conformity to the teachings of the Holy Scriptures.[35]

Murch thought that TC had no desire to set up a new denomination and assumed the existence of an inherent desire for a united church, but minimized the prevalence and power of bigotry among the rank and file of the people and their sentimental loyalty to denominational traditions. In his view the thirteen propositions "all . . . point toward the restoration of the New Testament church."[36]

Murch cites Kershner's summaries of the propositions and also points to TC's contention "that all human creeds must be constantly scrutinized to determine whether the doctrines they teach are true to the Bible."[37] He also refers in this section to TC's making clear that "fundamental orthodox Christian doctrine is essential to the fellowship of Christians." He then concludes with a quote from the Appendix, which begins, "The New Testament is the proper and immediate rule, directory, and formula, for the New Testament church, and for the particular duties of Christians."[38]

Murch further notes Alexander Campbell's "hearty approval" of all the propositions in the "masterly document" and his joining this "noble Christian enterprise."[39] It is perhaps revealing that his next mention of the *D&A* is in the chapter on Independents, and in fact this document defines us:

> In the broad sense the Center might be characterized as consisting of all those who continue to hold to the basic Biblical principles set forth in Thomas Campbell's *Declaration and Address* and Isaac Errett's *Our Position*. Let it be emphasized: to the basic Biblical principles—not to the historic documents themselves as such. Through one hundred years of history, Disciples had been Biblical inclusivists, and modern Centrists are of the same persuasion.[40]

This document thus is synonymous with the movement. When missionaries go to England, "the first intimations of the plea set forth in the *Declaration and Address* were carried to England in 1833."[41] In a discussion of the World Convention, the principles in the *D&A* become an umbrella for all groups arising from this movement. Regarding internal unity, he suggests a restudy of the spirit, motives, and precepts in TC's *D&A* and their elaboration in the Appendix. In a pairing that became common for him, Murch asserts "the principles of the *Declaration and Address* are still valid, and the truth of the Holy Scriptures is eternal."[42] Finally, he mentions the new meaning and relevance of the *D&A* for this ecumenical age.

Murch clearly has a high view of the *D&A*. He also sees it linked to a high view of Scripture. Unity is desirable, but its achievement seems inconceivable to him without a strong emphasis on the Bible. His book ends with a prayer for unity in which one paragraph begins, "Forbid, O God, that unity which would compromise thy eternal truth."[43]

H. Eugene Johnson

Eugene Johnson is, like Murch, something of a transitional figure, although a much less defining one. He was educated at Phillips and Vanderbilt, where he pursued a doctorate in theology. He became a lawyer, and Standard Publishing published his book *The Christian Church Plea*. His sentiments and education belong to the Old Disciples. Johnson's *The Declaration and Address for Today* (1971) is one of the few books written exclusively on this subject. By this time Restructure was a reality.

Johnson's work consists of a preface, introduction, and six chapters. In the preface, he states that the *D&A* is considered by many the fountain-head of the Campbell-Stone movement, and TC is still thought of in some areas as a pioneer for the movement and those advocating ecumenicity. Johnson characterizes TC as more prophetic than systematic and clearly attempts to revise Kershner. Alluding to the abandonment of restoration by some, he asserts that the principles of TC's plea still remain vital and summarizes "his dream": (1) unity of allegiance to the Christ of the Scriptures and (2) unity of demonstrable *agape*.

After the introduction, which mostly deals with the historical background to the *D&A*, Johnson's first chapter briefly summarizes the document. He finds three major influences: the covenant theology of Cocceius, the Commonsense philosophy of Thomas Reid, and the psychology of John Locke.[44]

Johnson's next chapter, "Organic Unity of Christians," begins his exposition. The church of the New Testament must be a united body of believers, separated only in geography. The church was a deliberate creation of God, not an accidental afterthought of the apostles. "Constitutional" is given an obvious meaning by TC, a fixed formula or appeal to final authority that undergirded the oft-repeated "constitutional unity" of the church.[45] The church is a "great visible professing body," and Johnson admits that TC may have gained insight from the new political documents of the United States.[46] The Campbells also were aware of the inadequacy of isolated congregations, a point on which he quotes Kershner and which remains an Old Disciples emphasis. Johnson then refers to restructure:

> It seems that the Disciples have capitulated to the Roman Catholic concept that Christ and His Spirit reside within the correct church structure. Form, not content, has been the emphasis. Restructure has now changed the historic horizontal type of church organization of the Disciples into a vertical pattern, with its inherent chains of command and levels of authority.[47]

Somewhat surprisingly, Johnson states that Faith and Order conferences have made the same "discoveries" on non-theological factors in the churches. Denominational leaders now are expressing "fresh ideas" of unity that were probed by Campbell 160 years ago. The nineteenth-century reformation is alive, although its adherents are unaware of the source of their ideas for unity. Yet TC would find little comfort in the Consultation on Christian Union (COCU). The basis of unity is in the New Testament alone. Johnson then condemns existentialism, demythologizing, and form criticism, which de-emphasize the Plea. The gospel must be heard in the church through the Scriptures.

Johnson's third chapter, "Campbell's Use of Scripture," mostly deals with literary usages. The interpreter must take into account TC's love of alliteration, adjectivial [sic] stairways, and the stringing together of nouns. TC also seemed to make a distinction between inspiration and authority when differentiating between the Testaments. Many of the controversies would have been avoided if the movement had more closely adhered to levels of New Testament authority recognized by TC, of which there were three. Johnson then talks about models and even quotes Ronald Osborn approvingly that "Restoration was a liberating, not a legalistic principle."[48] Johnson says that (1) Christians cannot fill silences with authoritative substitutes, and (2) silences do not command restrictions upon Christians. *Contra* Tertullian, faith is not blind obedience. *Vox populi, vox dei* refers only to enlightened followers of Christ, and TC actually advocated a *media via*.

In Chapter IV, "Christ of Scripture: The Foundation of Unity," Johnson begins by naming predecessors in the search for unity or restoration. He then moves to the issue of allegiance to Christ, even over the Bible. He then proceeds to a typical Old Disciples emphasis on the personal, especially in dealing with the concept of the Personal Word: "A careful reading of the *D&A* impresses one with the greater emphasis given to the Personal Word over that given to the written word of Scripture."[49] He then turns to the Bible and its relationship to Christ's authority. Johnson condemns Bultmann's distinction between the historical Jesus and the exalted Christ and closes by pointing out that the two ancient heresies of Docetism and Gnosticism are alive today.

In Chapter V, "Creedal Abuse to Unity," Johnson writes that TC did not oppose apologetics or defenses of the Faith. He cites examples of irony, tells us that TC refers to three creedal statements expressly, and that he was not averse to orderly procedures. Johnson then cites E. V. Zollars: "when a man knows only the Bible, he does not know the Bible."[50] Much of the rest of the chapter deals with plans to use creeds in COCU. At the end he quotes William Robinson in Dean Walker's book to the effect that the church needs the fullest room for theological and philosophical advancement. He also repeats the view that there are devout christians [sic] in the denominations.

In Chapter VI, "Latitudinarian Spirit of Love," Johnson refers to TC's laying the foundation for a larger and more irenic fellowship and comments that an amazing feature of the *D&A* is its lack of personal animosity. TC wrote seeking an encompassing fellowship of *agape* that would suppress, if not eliminate, pride and prejudice. Most of the rest of the chapter deals with TC's concept of love. Johnson also gives it an interesting twist: the spirit of *agape* is essential for those who believe that all revelation did not end with the apostolic age, who believe that the church is the expression of the Holy Spirit in living relationships. This true Love is our sign, our signature, our solution. The message is Christocentric; the Plea is not passé.

Knofel Staton

Knofel Staton left a career as an air-traffic controller at O'Hare to go to Lincoln Christian College. After some work on a doctorate at the

University of Iowa, he taught for a number of years at what is now Ozark Christian College. He taught for a year at the seminary at Lincoln, then returned to Ozark before assuming the presidency of what was then Pacific Christian College, from which he retired. He has been a prolific popular writer and taught mostly New Testament. His paraphrase of the *D&A* originally appeared in *The Compass*, Ozark's alumni paper, as installments, which College Press published as a book (1976). That it was originally published in the alumni periodical may be most significant. Ozark has often been where the regional schools meet the fundamentalist element, and this seems to indicate a growing attachment to unity.

Staton had earlier published a short article on the thirteenth proposition and on avoiding sectarianism. Most of the paraphrase is rather straightforward. His paraphrase of the first proposition is: "The Church of Christ on earth is indispensably, intentionally, and structurally one." There is no mention of baptism, but Staton does refer to liberalism:

> [S]ome will still insist that we ought to outline some definite creed to prevent liberalism from creeping in. But we reply that to insist upon what the Bible says is enough to prevent liberalism. But some will still object and say, "Both liberals and various sects claim to believe the Bible and practice it. According to your plan, you would receive them. You need to spell out what the Bible says in a creed." But we answer in this way—The Bible does not teach different things. If people are following it, they will believe and practice the same things. But if they are following their own interpretations and opinions, they stand rejected. For they claim to believe the Bible and yet practice their own opinions. There are too many people in this category.[51]

This seems a movement toward the more expansive view of unity generally held by the Old Disciples and a growing interest in unity on the Independent right.

Henry Webb

Henry Webb is retired from teaching Church History at Milligan College. His educational background is somewhat mixed. After undergraduate work at Cincinnati Bible College and Seminary, Webb attended Southern Baptist Theological Seminary, where he first heard that our movement was a unity movement. That caused him to seek out Dean Walker at Butler, who convinced him of it. Webb's book (*In Search of*

Christian Unity: A History of the Restoration Movement) clearly indicates his emphasis, as does his acknowledgment of the debt he owes to Dean Walker.

Webb begins by referring to the *D&A* as the most important literary product of TC's life and, "very probably, the most influential single document in the history of the Disciples."[52] He quotes the appeal in the Address, and comments that this hope was doomed. He sees an enduring issue: "[C]an proponents of undenominational Christianity advance their cause without becoming a denomination? This issue would have to be faced over and over in the years to come."[53]

Webb then quotes TC's indictment of the divided church, his interest in a church with discipline, and his appeal to join the union movement. He points out that TC took pains to note that his propositions are not a creed, by intent or nature. These propositions are the most significant part of the document; except for the first they are summarized. Webb alludes to his "common sense"[54] approach, a characteristic in the movement later, and then closes this section with TC's quote from the Appendix on liberty in the church.

Interestingly, Webb then turns to problems posed by the *D&A*. The first is the potential hermeneutical anarchy possible from the affirmation of the right of private judgment. This is resolved by appealing to the *consensus fidelium*, a concept common in Old Disciples circles;[55] the phrase *vox populi vox dei* with help from Kershner is transformed from referring to a populist segment to a scholarly elite:

> Alexander Campbell would often quote: "*Vox populi, vox dei*" . . . not in the sense that the majority was always right, but that the overwhelming consensus of the thoughtful scholarship of the church (the *consensus fidelium*) must be respected in the search for truth, as it is unlikely that all of the people could be wrong all of the time.[56]

Webb then comments that our appeal is "genuinely catholic." The second problem is the difficulty in defining what is "simple evangelical Christianity."[57] Like many in Old Disciples circles he refers here to "the ideal,"[58] which he understands primarily as the ideal of seeking biblical sanction for the activities of the church. The third problem refers to the divisive possibilities in trying to use restoration as a means of unity when there often is no consensus on what is to be restored. The fourth problem is the more recent insight that divisions are caused more by social, not doctrinal, factors even though TC was aware of the cultural basis for the divisions in his day. After a comment on TC's view of creeds, he closes this section with two condemnations: (1) of the empty reductionism that makes Christ, in some vague, emotional sense, the least common denominator; and (2) of the anti-intellectualism that regards theological inquiry as extraneous to faith and results in proof-texting. Both are easily found in aspects of church life, but, since Webb rarely if ever talks about the personal in theology, the first may indicate a slight departure from Walker.

Webb's final section deals with presuppositions of the *D&A*. He cites four. They are: (1) the authority of the Scriptures for everything pertaining to the church and individual Christians; (2) the belief it was possible to discern "simple evangelical Christianity" without an admixture of "human opinion"; (3) the appeal to reason and common sense as the means for extracting "truths" from the Scriptures; and (4) the possibility of extracting from the Scriptures "a simple, original form of Christianity."[59] In the notes and bibliography Webb cites only the original text of the *D&A* and Kershner's commentary.

James B. North

North was educated at Lincoln, the University of Chicago, and the University of Illinois. Thus, we should expect him to take the *D&A* quite seriously, to be aware of influences elsewhere, and to connect to American history. His allusions to the *D&A* begin with his book's title, *Union in Truth: An Interpretive History of the Restoration Movement*: "the phrase reflects both the commitment to Christian unity as well as the commitment to base that union on biblical authority (truth)."[60] After narrating TC's conversion experience and experience at Rich Hill,[61] North's treatment of Glas and Sandeman points to his basic "balanced" view. "But this emphasis on the restoration of New Testament teaching," he writes, "was not balanced by a concern for Christian unity, and the result was to see numerous divisions over various issues."[62] On the *D&A* proper, North starts by summarizing its nature and its value:

> The *Declaration and Address* is probably the most significant document that the Restoration Movement has produced. In it Thomas Campbell laid out the principles by which a reformation of the church according to the authority of the New Testament could be attained. Here is represented the distillation of a lifetime of thinking about the divisions that existed in the churches and what could be done about them. Campbell's ideas on unity

> and his observations on church history are brilliant insights into human nature and the applicability of the Word of God to the human situation. If more people followed Campbell's insights today, most troubles among churches would disappear.[63]

After again emphasizing that the author advocated "that simple original form of Christianity, expressly exhibited upon the sacred page,"[64] North then begins a short commentary on each of the propositions. One of TC's crucial concepts, unity, is found in Propositions 1 and 2; TC's other major commitment, the authority of the Bible alone for the church, is found in Proposition 3. Most of the propositions deal with secondary issues, of which 11 and 13 are commented on at the greatest length. Again, he emphasizes the balance inherent in the movement in his discussion of 11. "This is what the Restoration Movement is all about: unity and scriptural authority."[65] The last two pages basically compare similar sentiments between the *D&A* and John Locke's writings.[66]

Conclusion

I have yet to observe any hostility toward the *D&A* primarily because the major advocates of unity in our past (for example, "restructure") are also perceived as having repudiated it. The treatment of the *D&A* by Independents is perhaps somewhat schizophrenic. We have a large and influential population that considers it essentially irrelevant. A much smaller, but seminal, scholarly population generally takes it quite seriously and finds it a meaningful and useful model for the *raison d'être* of our movement. There are, indeed, significant, but as of yet not irreconcilable, differences in those interpretations. Perhaps more to the point, most of the competing interpretations are restatements or modifications of views that had currency in the past; few differences seem a result of new insights or trends.

Notes

1. Henry E. Webb, "Reflections on Christian Unity," *Christian Standard* 128 (20 June 1993): 525-26; Mark S. Joy, "The Restoration Movement in Recent Histories of American Religion," *Christian Standard* 130 (5 March 1995): 198-201.

2. Compare James DeForest Murch, *Christians Only* (Cincinnati: Standard Publishing, 1965), 237-45; Henry E. Webb, *In Search of Christian Unity: A History of the Restoration Movement* (Cincinnati: Standard Publishing, 1990), 249-61.

3. Compare Sam Stone, *The Christian Minister: A Practical Approach to the Preaching Ministry* (Cincinnati: Standard Publishing, 1978), 13-34.

4. Some ministers' contracts specify that they are elders.

5. The phrase is from Jon Jones of the Richland Hills Church of Christ in Fort Worth, speaking at the Canton Christian Conference in Canton, Ohio, in 1983.

6. Stone, *Christian Minister*, 99.

7. Stone, *Christian Minister*, 37.

8. I found only one short article (see n. 26) in *Christian Standard* since 1970 on the *D&A*. In *One Body* and the *Restoration Forum* volumes, I count seventeen references.

9. See my "Intellectual Factions and Groupings of the Independent Christian Churches," *Seminary Review* 31, no. 2 (June 1985): 91-117. The article is historical description, not contemporary analysis.

10. Dull, "Intellectual Factions," 104-11.

11. Don DeWelt, *Happy on My Way to Heaven!* (Joplin, Mo.: College Press, 1989), 42-43; Victor Knowles and William E. Paul, *Taking a Stand, the Story of the Ottumwa Brethren* (Joplin, Mo.: College Press, 1996).

12. Victor Knowles, "The Way to Christian Unity," *One Body* (Summer 1989): 23.

13. Dwaine Dunning, "A Compact Overview of the 'Argument from Silence' and Its Influence on the Restoration Movement," *One Body* (Spring 1986): 20; Dunning, "Are Our Subjects of Debate Important to God?" *One Body* (Winter-Spring 1987): 35; Robert O. Fife, "The Nature of Christian Unity,"*One Body* (Summer 1987): 22, 24; Thomas Thurman, "The Uniting of the Forces," *One Body* (Summer 1988): 39; W. Robert Palmer, "Two Abused Words: Implication and Inference," *One Body* (Autumn-Winter 1988): 14; Earl Grice, "The Forgotten Goal," *One Body* (Autumn 1992): 6; C. Robert Wetzel, "Confessions of a Misspent Youth," *One Body* (Autumn 1995): 5. Enos Dowling, "Restoring the Biblical Ideal of the Nonsectarian Spirit," in *Restoration Forum* , ed. Don DeWelt (Joplin, Mo.: College Press, 1989), 7:25-26, 31. James North, "What We Have Done Together from 1809 to the Civil War," in *Restoration Forum*, ed. Don DeWelt (Joplin, Mo.: College Press, 1988), 6:14.

14. Typically, Donald Hunt ("Doctrine," *One Body* [Summer 1988]: 19) comments on the lateness of TC in coming to baptism as immersion.

15. Dull, "Intellectual Factions," 95-98.

16. Rodney Werline, an Old Testament professor.

17. Webb, *In Search of Christian Unity*, 96 n. 5.

18. Dean E. Walker, *Adventuring for Christian Unity* (Birmingham, Eng.: Berean Press, 1935). See *Christian Standard* 108 (11 March 1973): 215-16, (18 March 1973): 233-34, for the same title.

19. For a fundamentalist approach, see Jack Cottrell, *Baptism: A Biblical Study* (Joplin, Mo.: College Press, 1989), 45-66. For Old Disciples views, see Robert O. Fife, "Our Future—As the Only Christians?" *Christian Standard* 120 (18 August 1985): 743-45, and John Greenlee, "The Galatian 'Legalism,'" *Christian Standard* 113 (5 February 1978): 127-28.

20. Fred Norris, "'Christians only, but not the only Christians' (Acts 19:1-7)," *Restoration Quarterly* 28, no. 2 (1985-86): 97-105. His first note cites Kershner's *Christian Union Overture*.

21. Robert O. Fife, "The Worshiping Congregation: Universality and Particularity," in *Essays on New Testament Christianity*, ed. C. Robert Wetzel (Cincinnati: Standard Publishing, 1978), 35-37, talks about "meaning" and "form."

22. C. J. Dull, "Report from Anderson," *One Body* (Summer/Fall 1990): 9.

23. Dull, "Intellectual Factions," 98-104.

24. At Lincoln the two professors teaching Restoration History in the seminary, Robert Rea and John Castelein, have their doctorates from Saint Louis University and the University of Chicago.

25. For the connection to evangelism see Robert Rea, "What Is the Restoration Vision?" *Christian Standard* 129 (11 September 1994): 786-87; Enos Dowling, *The Restoration Movement* (Cincinnati: Standard Publishing, 1964), 3; and James B. North, *Union in Truth: An Interpretive History of the Restoration Movement* (Cincinnati: Standard Publishing, 1994), 7.

26. Walker, *Adventuring*, 20.

27. Walker, *Adventuring*, 21.

28. Walker, *Adventuring*, 21-22.

29. Dean E. Walker, *The Authority of the Word* (Milligan College, Tenn.: Milligan College Press, 1950).

30. Adrian Fraley, "The Historical Setting and Some Influences of the *Declaration and Address*, As Reflected in the Religious Press from 1810 to 1860" (B.D. thesis, Butler University School of Religion, 1946).

31. Fraley, "Historical Setting," 74.

32. Fraley, "Historical Setting," 58-87.

33. Compare Webb (*In Search of Christian Unity*, 356) for Murch's firing at Standard.

34. Murch, *Christians Only*, v.

35. Murch, *Christians Only*, 42-43.

36. Murch, *Christians Only*, 44-45.
37. Murch, *Christians Only*, 49.
38. Murch, *Christians Only*, 50.
39. Murch, *Christians Only*, 57.
40. Murch, *Christians Only*, 293.
41. Murch, *Christians Only*, 329.
42. Murch, *Christians Only*, 366.
43. Murch, *Christians Only*, 375.
44. Eugene Johnson, *The Declaration and Address for Today* (Nashville: Reed Publishing, 1971), 12.
45. Johnson, *The D&A for Today*, 15.
46. Johnson, *The D&A for Today*, 17.
47. Johnson, *The D&A for Today*, 18.
48. Johnson, *The D&A for Today*, 33.
49. Johnson, *The D&A for Today*, 45.
50. Johnson, *The D&A for Today*, 55.
51. Knofel Staton, "Proposition Thirteen," *Christian Standard* 114 (27 May 1979): 479-80; "Oh No, Not Another Sect!" *Christian Standard* 107 (19 March 1972): 249-50.
52. Webb, *In Search of Christian Unity*, 77.
53. Webb, *In Search of Christian Unity*, 80.
54. Webb, *In Search of Christian Unity*, 84.
55. Fred Norris, "Apostolic, Catholic, and Sensible: The *Consensus Fidelium*," in *Essays on New Testament Christianity*, ed. C. Robert Wetzel (Cincinnati: Standard Publishing, 1978), 15-29. Norris mentions Kershner, Robinson, and Walker as mentors.
56. Webb, *In Search of Christian Unity*, 86.
57. Webb, *In Search of Christian Unity*, 87.
58. Compare Marshall Leggett, *Introduction to the Restoration Ideal* (Cincinnati: Standard Publishing, 1989).
59. Webb, *In Search of Christian Unity*, 90-91.
60. North, *Union in Truth*, xii.
61. Both North and Webb (*In Search of Christian Unity*, 71-72) apparently treat Rich Hill as almost the model Independent congregation; North even capitalizes "Independents" in the last paragraph.
62. North, *Union in Truth*, 76.
63. North, *Union in Truth*, 88.
64. North, *Union in Truth*, 89.
65. North, *Union in Truth*, 92.
66. Webb (*In Search of Christian Unity*, 96 n. 5) writes that the influence of John Locke is a primary emphasis of University of Chicago historians.

The *Declaration and Address* in a Postmodern World

Ronald Grant Nutter

Postmodernism is a Lon Chaney sort of word: it has a thousand different faces. In the hands of some scholars it is a powerful set of critical tools to analyze literary and historical texts, while in the hands of others it is a billy club inflicting an ideological pummeling on intellectual oppressors, and in the hands of still others it is little more than a jargon-laden screed of scholarly trendiness on the road to academic tenure. Some view it as a threatening "boogeyman" challenging those cultural verities that give our lives a sense of stable meaning, while others see it as a clarion call to rip away the unsuspected bias and injustice embedded in our cultural assumptions. In short, postmodernism represents a serious approach to an understanding of human knowledge that, like other intellectual movements in history, may also be used in inappropriate and at times thoroughly ridiculous ways.

In approaching the ways that Thomas Campbell's *Declaration and Address* might be read in the context of "postmodernism," it is first necessary to gain some understanding of just what is meant by the term. This is a difficult task in and of itself. Postmodernism is an umbrella that covers a variety of viewpoints, opinions, methods, and ideologies. Thus, any attempt to give a description of postmodernism in a short essay like this may be, and no doubt will be, attacked as being too narrow. So be it. What follows will say more about postmodernism than about TC's text.

But that's all right. Many essays in this volume analyze the *D&A*. The main attempt here is to play postmodernist advocate—and devilishly so—in an effort to describe those intellectual changes that have occurred in this century, changes that will challenge each of the presentations made so far about just what the *D&A* "means," or what TC is "saying," or how various backgrounds and historical contexts and theological issues are "important." In short, think of this essay as the "fly in the ointment."

In deliberately reading the *D&A* with a postmodernist mindset, what is immediately striking is the presence of certain assumptions on the part of TC that he obviously felt no need to justify. "As the Divine word is equally binding upon all," TC writes in the very first paragraph, "so all lie under an equal obligation to be bound by it, and it alone; and not by any human interpretation of it."[1] Aside from the logical point that the statement "begs the question" in that the claim for Scripture being equally binding should be argued rather than simply declared, one is left to wonder just how Scripture comes to mean anything at all without the "human interpretation of it."

Another assumption of TC's that strikes a postmodernist reader as questionable, to be polite, is the assertion later in the first paragraph that a rest from sectarian strife can come only "in Christ and his simple word, which is the same yesterday, today, and forever."[2] Our postmodernist reader wonders: what word, what text, is ever the same yesterday, today, and forever? For that matter, what word, what text, is ever the same at any one moment?

TC's first resolution speaks of a religious association promoting simple evangelical Christianity "free from all mixture of human opinions and inventions of men."[3] At this point our postmodernist reader, not a mean and callow person at all, simply dissolves into laughter. How can any such association of men (and women, she no doubt mumbles to herself) possibly exist? What human institution has ever been free of human "opinions and inventions"?

Laughter turns to a knowing and cynical nod as she reads at the end of the fifth resolution that the proposed association will support those ministers who exhibit a conformity only to that which may be supported by a "thus saith the Lord, either in express terms, or by approved precedent."[4] So much for words meaning the same yesterday, today, and forever, our postmodernist reader smirks, seeing that last phrase as a loophole even a guileless believer, much less a beguiler of believers, could walk through in justifying a variety of beliefs and behaviors.

Our reader continues to read, page after page, a chuckle or two along the way at the efforts of this poor, misguided Scotsman who makes claims that are simply insupportable, given what we know these days about knowledge and the accumulation of same. Then the smile leaves her face. There it is. The one statement that is the most recalcitrant hindrance in helping men and women to see the world aright. After a lengthy attempt to shake off the term "latitudinarian" in the document's Appendix, TC makes a last effort:

> Union in truth, among all the manifest subjects of grace and truth, is what we advocate. We carry our views of union no further than this, nor do we presume to recommend it upon any other principle than truth alone. Now, surely, truth is something certain and definite; if not, who will take upon him to define and determine it?[5]

Our postmodernist ponders: Who indeed?

TC published his *D&A* in 1809. The document contains phrases and words that make clear the author's Enlightenment belief both in the power of human intellect to ascertain truth and the efficacy of language to share truth with others. This is the simple method by which understanding is achieved among wide gatherings of men and women. It is this Enlightenment ideal that is a grounding belief behind notions of universal education, scientific progress, nationalism, and so many other aspects of western culture.

TC reflects an Enlightenment time when a proposition is taken to be true if it ultimately corresponds with the observable world around us. He reflects an Enlightenment time when a person commenting on his times is judged by the analytical and clarifying power of his argument rather than by his race, ancestry, sex, or sexual preference. He reflects an Enlightenment time when men and women take satisfaction in discovering a perceived "common humanity" that is more to be valued than whatever cultural differences may be discerned. TC recalls an Enlightenment time of optimistic hope that Reason, along with its progeny —Science, the Arts, and Religion—would usher in an age in which economic want and spiritual emptiness would be remedied, an age that would come to be dominated by common sense, clear thinking, and good will to all.

Such an optimistic view of the future will, for many, sound almost silly from our *fin de siècle* vantage point nearly two hundred years later. TC's *D&A* exemplifies an Enlightenment time when reality is seen as single and ultimately knowable, a time when truth is seen as verifiable and constant, a time when it is possible to speak of *the* meaning of a written text, a time when men and women see themselves as living in a *uni*verse. Today, of course, postmodernism speaks of many realities, of myriad truths, and of multivocal texts, as we each seek to wend our way in what Henry Adams comes to call a *multi*verse.[6]

TC worked in a pre-Darwin and pre-Freud world, and thus did not have to accommodate the enormously unsettling influences these seminal thinkers occasioned, chipping away as they did the certainties of humans as qualitatively distinct and superior to other forms of life, and of rational human individuals being in firm control of their own subjectivity and of their physical environment. Thus, TC's essay is full of confidence in the power of his logic to bring believing Christians around to his point of view. As far as TC is concerned, he is merely presenting an objectively compelling case for the union of Christians on the basis of a readily understandable series of propositions easily inferred from scriptural text. In today's postmodernist world, words just don't hang together so easily anymore.

Some of the early warnings of change, in addition to the work of Charles Darwin and Sigmund Freud, can be seen in the work of scientists in the late nineteenth and early twentieth centuries, seeking to accommodate the anomalies of a Newtonian, mechanistic determinism in physics. Max Planck, Albert Einstein, Jules Henri Poincare, Werner Heisenberg, and others began to revolutionize our understanding of the physical world by presenting at one moment the strange world of "relativity" and its warping of time/space, and at another moment proposing the truly bizarre and unpredictable world of quantum theory.[7] Though there have been attempts to come up with a "unified theory" that would explain natural physical phenomena at both the macro- and microcosmic level, such a theory has eluded physicists. What we see and experience of the physical world on one level, it appears, is quite a different reality from that of other cosmic perspectives.

It is certainly not new that men and women believe there to be levels of reality not immediately available to finite beings. An unseen spiritual realm, for example, has for centuries been an accepted part of reality for many. What has changed in the latter part of the nineteenth and twentieth centuries, however, are the kinds of metaphors used to talk about the unseen. In the hands of "modernist" thinkers, earlier metaphors of height (sky, mountains, storms, God, angels) have given way to metaphors of depth. For psychoanalysts like Freud and Carl Jung, the reality of one's subjective self is to be found in the psychological depths of one's psyche or in the shared reality of hidden archetypes. For Darwin, there is a hidden law of natural survival that dictates the variety and survivability of various species. For Karl Marx, there are hidden economic forces at work sustaining human political, aesthetic, and religious institutions. For an anthropologist like Claude Lévi-Strauss, there is a diachronic and synchronic "structure" of meaning hidden beneath all human mythical narratives. Put simply, reality is coming to be seen as more than that which is manifestly available to the physical senses and to common sense. What is needed, these modernists argue, are authoritative experts working as "intellectual geologists" in the various disciplines to strip away surface debris in order to uncover the more foundational realities that lie beneath the surface of things.

The "higher criticism" of the Bible at the turn of the century captures the same mood in that it, too, seeks for a "depth" of understanding. The contextualizing of Scripture by means of various forms of socio-historical and literary-critical approaches is welcomed by modernists as a liberation from an institutional church that has valorized certain uses and interpretations of Scripture while proscribing others.[8] To understand the full meaning of Scripture, modernist scholars would now argue, one must get below the manifest level of the text itself, identify its constituent parts, understand the historical context for each of those parts, and bring to the surface as much as one is able the motivations and ideological concerns of the final text's redactors. The biblical scholar, as a sophisticated interpreter of matters scriptural and historical, comes to be seen as one who can enlighten a lay public about what Scripture "really" means. The ideal the biblical scholar holds up for herself is an image of an objective investigator seeking an understanding of the truth of the matter.

Literature, too, develops its own modernist standards of objective and scholarly judgment in the form of semantic theories like the New Criticism and Structuralism. In the case of the New Criticism, practitioners do admirably well in excluding consideration of authorial intent, the world represented in a literary work, and the interaction of an implied reader with a text. This is done in an effort to allow the text—and only the text—to constitute an objective field of meaning, thereby opening the door for literary scholars to plumb the depths of literary works for metaphors, symbols, allusions, objective correlatives, and other sorts of hidden deposits of meaning and truth.[9] Structuralism, drawing from the fields of semiotics, semantics, and cultural anthropology, argues that literary texts are a projection of basic human structures of thought (binary opposition), which are recoverable through objective techniques.[10] Some concern is expressed, a warning of sorts, as it is realized that these approaches to literature, as exemplary as they are in maintaining the goal of deriving dispassionate insights into the meaning of a literary text, continue to draw from the subjectivity of "expert" literary critics making authoritative judgments about literary texts.

When we look at modernist intellectuals like Darwin, Freud, Marx, and Lévi-Strauss, as well as modern physicists, biblical scholars, and New Critics and Structuralists, what they all have in common is that they are interpreters. Nothing more, nothing less. All profess confidence that the interpretations they render are representations of truth, and as such their interpretations constitute stable reservoirs of knowledge. TC, though representative of an Enlightenment rather than modernist tradition, makes much the same claim in his *D&A*. The only difference would seem to be that whereas modernist thinkers believe truth is to be found hidden beneath the surface of things, behind what is otherwise manifestly obvious to all, TC believes the truth of the biblical message is just that: manifestly obvious to all.

This modernist confidence in the dispassionate objectivity of scholars and scientists, in the efficacy of value-neutral methods in the various disciplines of the arts and sciences, and in the stability of human knowledge, has been eroding throughout the twentieth century. With what has come to be known as postmodernism such notions are being attacked openly, primarily by academics in the humanities and the social sciences. Much can be learned from these challenges to modernist beliefs by looking at what has happened to the study of literature in university English departments.

French intellectuals were coming to exert influence in the 1960s with a series of guest lecturers at Johns Hopkins University. Jacques Derrida, in particular, created a stir with his philosophical hermeneutics of suspicion.[11] Essentially, Derrida rejects the notion that language is transparent to a world beyond the words themselves. He coins the term *différance* to convey two ideas: (1) an advocacy of the Saussurean (a reference to the linguist Ferdinand de Saussure) notion that meaning is a function of the contrasts and differences within a network of linguistic terms, and (2) a rejection of any privileged or centered position determining the relationship between a text and any extra-textual reality beyond the text. The desire for an epistemic center is what leads to certain "readings" of a text, which, it is claimed, says more about the reader's interests and ideological commitments than it does about the text being read. As text, Derrida sees writing as a symbolic playground full of interpretive possibilities in which any final rendering of "meaning" is deferred. His notion of "deconstruction" attempts to highlight through puns, plays on words, and the occasional argument how a text might be interpreted in many different ways. Hence the heteroglossic, or "many-tongued," character of any text. What Derrida clearly wants to move away from is the notion that there is any sort of privileged interpretive position—whether that be the intention of an author, a contact with external reality, or the expertness of a literary critic—that can provide *the* meaning of a text.

Derrida—along with other French intellectuals like Roland Barthes, Michel Foucault, Julia Kristeva, and Jacques Lacan—opens a door to challenging any privileged position in adjudicating truth.[12] Echoing Friedrich Nietzsche a century earlier, these critics argue that such privileged positions claiming objective knowledge are, in fact, disguised expressions of cultural power or authority. What passes as rational thought is, they argue, an imposition of a limited perspective that generally serves the interests of a limited few. It is this sort of approach that has led to works of cultural criticism that seek to identify how objectivist claims to knowledge are used to marginalize certain ideas and people while benefiting others.[13]

This approach has become the philosophical rationale for opening up the canon of western literature. Thus, marginalized literary works, previously ignored by those cultural gatekeepers protecting the vested interests of an earlier time, are now coming to be read. While traditionalists may howl, and point to the "greatness" of classic works of literature, postmodernists will simply respond by saying a work's "greatness" merely reflects the interests and biases of the privileged few. Even libraries, though filled with tomes studying and appreciating the greatness of classic works of literature, are institutions that reify the attitudes and interests of a privileged class, thus giving these attitudes and interests an "objective" character. Also, under the rubric of "reader-response criticism," a postmodernist approach allows for the reinterpretation even of classic literature from differing perspectives, including that of Marxism, Feminism, Gay/Lesbian Studies, or any other interpretive perspective that had previously been dismissed by those "experts" who had wielded their authority to keep certain interpretive voices on the margins.

What has resulted, in the minds of many, is a cacophony of textual interpretation that appears to have ended any hope of objective literary standards. While one certainly can argue that the postmodern approach to literary interpretation has led to a kind of silliness that seems a waste of almost everyone's time (one of the truly funny lines in the television show *Law and Order* is when one of the detectives picks up a paper written by a college English professor titled "The Whale Is Red: A Marxist Interpretation of *Moby Dick*"), the postmodernist concern with interpretive authority being used to marginalize other perspectives is an important consideration that must be taken seriously.

The postmodernist mood, if that be what it is, spread from English departments into other disciplines of the academy. Under the guise of the "sociology of knowledge" all human endeavors to ascertain and articulate truthful knowledge have come to be seen as purely social constructions reflecting the political and economic interests of the producers of knowledge.[14] History has certainly felt the sting of the postmodernist challenge. Hayden White, in *Metahistory*, severely undercuts the notion of "objectivity" in historical understanding. While no historian seriously thinks that subjectivity is completely removed from historical representations, modernist historians have nonetheless believed that proper historical method can render a generally objective and truthful account of the past. White, for his part, throws the entire enterprise of history onto the shores of ideology and narrative theory.[15] In his notion of "emplotment" he argues that certain ideological decisions are made before a single word of history is written. The resultant history will merely embody the assumptions and attitudes of the historian in a narrative form. The very act of choosing what is a significant historical fact, and of deciding how it is significant, is to make certain kinds of ideological commitments. Historical implications of antebellum slavery, for example, will take on much different significance for a Marxist historian than, say, a Darwinian.

Frank Kermode comments on history from a literary-critical perspective in his book *The Genesis of Secrecy*, which examines the sorts of interpretations that are written about the Bible. According to Kermode, readers of history are mistaken when they see history as transparent to "what actually happened." Rather, he suggests, more attention needs to be paid to the biblical narrative, to the kinds of assumptions and attitudes embodied in the narrative itself. There are many examples of the Bible giving different descriptions of the same historical event. Such differences are better explained, Kermode suggests, as literary fulfillments of writerly desire than as historical renderings of fact.[16]

In writings such as those of White and Kermode, the interpretation of history appears as fluid as that of literature. These approaches claim that access to *the* meaning of a text or historical event is unattainable. Any effort to attain such certainty is seen by postmodernist critics as an attempt to privilege only certain perspectives and interpretations, thus protecting the interests and authority of those who are doing the privileging.

A skeptical stake has even been driven into the heart of the physical sciences. Indeed, this is where bitter debates are fought over notions of "truth" and "knowledge." For example, science has come to be seen by many postmodernists as a male-dominated mode of inquiry that replicates a world from a limited, male perspective. Writers like Hélène Cixous and Luce Irigaray explore the construction of sexual difference in philosophy and psychoanalysis, and conclude that males seek to manipulate the world-as-given by positing authoritative categories that are static, while women approach the world with a joyous wisdom and faith that is more accepting of the fluidity of the world-as-given.[17] For this reason, the knowledge that is the fundamental basis of physical sciences like chemistry and physics has been called into question, suspected as they are of masking the culturally privileged positions of power enjoyed by men in the constructions of so-called "objective" scientific knowledge.

So sensitive is postmodernism to issues of privilege and hegemony in rendering objective "matters of fact," that the very notion of the "self" is being defaced. Rather than seeing the self as an existing reality that acts as a self-contained adjudicator of truth by rational or empirical means, postmodernists lean heavily on a psychoanalytic dissolution of the self. For them, the self is merely a cultural enabler in the replication of privileged authorities. There isn't an "author" existing as a stable consciousness conveying independently weighed and adjudicated objective knowledge.[18] Instead, what we call the "author" is a social construction that, drawing on already accepted authorities and knowledge as contained in social institutions like universities and libraries, merely replicates the already existing constructions of knowledge along with the biases and prejudices and "blindness," to use Paul de Man's term,[19] endemic to any privileged perspective. The danger, as seen by postmodernists, is that those perspectives privileged in western culture carry with them an unwanted and oppressive bias against women, minorities, homosexuals, and others. By decentering such privileged positions of cultural power, postmodernists hope to open up human understanding of knowledge to include those voices and perspectives that previously had been silenced.

So how might one, given this postmodernist mood, read TC's *D&A*? One aspect of TC's essay that would become obvious to a postmodernist reader is the distinction TC makes between "us" and "them," with "us" being all those Christians "that love our Lord Jesus Christ, in sincerity,"[20] while "them" is saddled with terms like "weak,"[21] "subject to bigotry,"[22] "slothful and reluctant,"[23] "man of sin,"[24] "hirelings,"[25] "idle shepherds,"[26] "artificial and superficious characters,"[27] "little beholden to" the Bible,[28] and unable to "distinguish truth from error."[29] The postmodernist reader would also note those passages where TC claims that "we have humility, faith, piety, temperance, justice, charity, etc.,"[30] with the implication being that those who resist his call have none of these Christian dispositions. Seeing how certain people are marginalized, our postmodernist reader would no doubt be on the lookout for whatever "objective" club TC uses to beat his opposition into intellectual submission. And the "objective" criterion TC uses is what he calls the "truth" of Scripture, easily and manifestly known by any reader. "With you all we desire to unite in the bonds of an entire Christian unity," he writes, "Christ alone being the head, the centre, his word the rule—an explicit belief of, and manifest conformity to it, in all things—*the terms*" [TC's emphasis].[31] This statement, and another like it—"our confidence is entirely founded upon the express Scripture and matter-of-fact evidence, of the things referred to,"[32]—become a kind of "metanarrative" by which to judge others' motivations and standing as Christians.

This privileging of a certain interpretation of Scripture as manifestly obvious, which TC rhetorically claims is beyond challenge, is precisely the kind of privileging authority that postmodernist critics wish to unmask. That "objective readings" of what TC says is manifestly obvious in Scripture has led to the fragmenting of groups within the "unity" of the Restoration Movement is an irony over which postmodernist critics would no doubt chuckle. But they would also recognize these rifts within the Restoration Movement as instances of new "objective readings" being wielded so as to approve of certain activities and practices while proscribing others.

Those postmodernists representing certain ideological camps (Marxists, feminists, and others) would no doubt work toward unmasking TC's project as just another social construction working to limit and further oppress whatever group or perspective that particular postmodernist happens to be championing. Someone like Derrida, though, would probably have more fun playing deconstructive linguistic games with TC. For example, one can admire the cleverness as well as take in the interpretive turn when advocates of Derrida's approach use parentheses in titles to redirect attention in a text, or perhaps identify hidden motivations and meanings in a text. In about thirty seconds I managed to come up with this rendering of TC's title:

DE(CLA)RATIO(N AND) AD(D)RES(S)

Taking that portion of the title not in parentheses, we are left with a Latinesque statement about the rational nature of things. On one level, this is certainly what TC is arguing for. However, taking that portion that is in parentheses, we have another level of meaning, namely that the essay isn't about Christian union at all, but about "clan," about a group of "us" seeking to establish our own unique identity in a sea of competing Christian groups, with our "objective" standard distinguishing "us" from "them" being our acceptance of Jesus Christ and the manifestly obvious reading of Scripture that TC valorizes. Of course, the full line of that which is in parentheses says "clan and ds." It is at this point I might wish TC were a Methodist and we could say something about district superintendents. Alas, deconstructive punning and jokes are limited by the creative abilities (or lack of them) of the deconstructive punner and jokester. I, for one, am at my deconstructive best around 3 a.m., as the irrationalities of an oxygen-depleted brain frolic within my aching-to-sleep body. For postmodernists, though, whatever fun or *jouissance* may be derived in the interplay between reader and text, it is a serious business nonetheless.

While some postmodernists would read TC cynically, seeing him as attempting to establish an authoritatively privileged position in order to enhance his own argument while marginalizing or discounting other perspectives, other postmodernists would simply see in TC the naïveté of an earlier time. We live today in an age of indeterminacy, when the pluralism of the age, as Richard Ruland and Malcolm Bradbury write in *From Puritanism to Postmodernism*, "has multiplied theories of art, reading and culture" leading "to disputes that for the moment seem irresolvable." They go on to say that "we live in a world of symbol systems, that we are largely the artists of our own realities, that we all build fictions, provisionally 'adequate,' never 'supreme.'"[33]

The most grave danger postmodernism presents is from those who draw from its premises the conclusion that any interpretation is as good or bad as any other. Such a move is an insult to anyone who has changed her mind when confronted with a better argument. It is not at all clear that this is the goal of serious postmodernist thinkers. Rather than think of postmodernism as a programmatic attempt to flatten all interpretations, think of it rather as a corrective to those attempts to privilege only certain kinds of interpretations, especially as these privileged interpretations appeal to some objective ontological criterion as an epistemic guarantor of "the truth of the matter." Here is precisely where postmodernists will take TC's *D&A* to task, advocating as it does a union of Christians in truth. Postmodernism would make Pontius Pilates of us all. "Truth!" our postmodernist exclaims. "What is truth?"

While this paper attempts to describe some of the issues and concerns of postmodernism, as well as give a brief indication of how TC's *D&A* would be read in the context of postmodernism, it should be pointed out that there are severe critics of the postmodernist movement as well. Indeed, there seems to be a growing backlash, particularly among the public at large, as postmodernism makes its way from the isolated groves of academe to more public venues. The recent flap known as the "Sokal Affair," in which a New York University physicist named Alan Sokal successfully perpetrated a hoax on the postmodernist academic journal *Social Text*, highlights the backlash.[34] Basically, Sokal wrote an article challenging standard and accepted "knowledge" in science, an article replete with names and quotes of innumerable postmodernist critics strung together in what Sokal later admitted was "absolute gibberish" with absolutely no point or sustained argument. He wrote it just to see if an unintelligible article that claimed to criticize science using the language of postmodernism could be published. To his surprise and amusement, it was. For many, it is an episode showing that the postmodernist emperor has no clothes.

Indeed, much of what passes as postmodernist criticism is, not to put too fine a point on it, crap. That said, there is an earnest and important challenge presented by postmodern concerns about the bases of knowledge and truth, and with the controlling of knowledge and truth in such a way as to exert cultural authority. We should be well advised to acknowledge these concerns and take them seriously. To the extent postmodernism makes us aware of such issues we should be grateful to it, even if it leads us to challenge some of the icons of our own religious tradition.

Notes

1. Thomas Campbell, *Declaration and Address of the Christian Association of Washington* (Washington, Pa.: Brown & Sample, 1809), 3.13-15.
2. *D&A*, 3.36-38.
3. *D&A*, 4.12-13.
4. *D&A*, 4.46-47.
5. *D&A*, 45.46-46.2
6. Henry Adams, *The Education of Henry Adams* (New York: Library of America, 1983), 1066-76; 1112-17; 1132-41. Adams doesn't really use the term until page 1141, but all of his discussions in the previously cited pages clearly are expressions of this paradigm shift toward a multiverse, a "modern force" from which he recoils, holding on as he does to a nostalgic universe of the past.
7. Stephen Toulmin, *The Return to Cosmology: Postmodern Science and the Theology of Nature* (Berkeley: University of California Press, 1982), 237-74. Toulmin gives a nice overview of a changed view of the world, especially as to our claims to know the world "objectively."
8. Martin E. Marty, *Modern American Religion* (Chicago: University of Chicago Press, 1986), 37-41.
9. William E. Cain, *The Crisis in Criticism: Theory, Literature, and Reform in English Studies* (Baltimore: Johns Hopkins University Press, 1984), 85-121. These two chapters from Cain's book provide both a nice summary of the rise of the New Criticism as well as a prescient discussion of how the New Criticism has become institutionalized in universities. He also makes a compelling case for the New Criticism's emphasis on "close reading" as an important element in the rise of both structuralist and, later, postmodernist criticism.
10. Claude Lévi-Strauss, *Structural Anthropology*, trans. Claire Jacobson and Brooke Grundfest Schoepf (Garden City, N.Y.: Anchor Books, 1967), 202-27.
11. Jacques Derrida, "La Structure, le signe et le jeu dans le discours des sciences humaines," published as "Structure, Sign and Play in the Discourse of the Human Sciences," in *Writing and Difference*, trans. Alan Bass (Chicago: University of Chicago Press, 1978), 278-93. Many mark this lecture by Derrida, delivered at the International Colloquium on Critical Languages and the Sciences of Man on 21 October 1966 at Johns Hopkins University, as the beginning of the continental (particularly French) influence on American critical theory. The flavor of his radical shift in interpretive priority can be seen in this brief section (292) from his lecture:

> There are thus two interpretations of interpretation, of structure, of sign, of play. The one seeks to decipher, dreams of deciphering a truth or an origin which escapes play and the order of the sign, and which lives the necessity of interpretation as an exile. The other, which is no longer turned toward the origin, affirms play and tries to pass beyond man and humanism, the name of man being the name of that being who, throughout the history of metaphysics or of ontotheology—in other words, throughout his entire history—has dreamed of full presence, the reassuring foundation, the origin and the end of play. The second interpretation of interpretation, to which Nietzsche pointed the way, does not seek in ethnography, as Lévi-Strauss does, the "inspiration of a new humanism."

12. Frank Lentricchia, *After the New Criticism* (Chicago: University of Chicago Press, 1980), 157-210. Lentricchia, in this broadly erudite volume, gives an excellent survey of the continental influence among literary critics in the United States in the chapter titled "History or the Abyss: Poststructuralism." Poststructuralism is an earlier term for what has come to be known as postmodernism.

13. Edward W. Said, *Orientalism* (New York: Vintage Books, 1979), 272-73. This is but one passage making an argument identifying the "imperialistic" use of "objective knowledge" to maintain cultural and ideological advantage over, in this case, the "Orient." This passage is particularly instructive. After noting that the "West" has fundamentally misrepresented Islam, Said writes that

> the real issue is whether indeed there can be a true representation of anything, or whether any and all representations, because they *are* representations [emphasis his], are embedded first in the language and then in the culture, institutions, and political ambiance of the representer. If the latter alternative is the correct one (as I believe it is), then we must be prepared to accept the fact that a representation is *eo ipso* implicated, intertwined, embedded, interwoven with a great many other things besides the 'truth,' which is itself a representation. What this must lead us to methodologically is to view representations (or misrepresentations—the distinction is at best a matter of degree) as inhabiting a common field of play defined for them, not by some inherent common subject matter alone, but by some common history, tradition, universe of discourse.

14. Karl Mannheim, "Ideology and the Sociology of Knowledge," in *Readings in the Philosophy of the Social Sciences*, ed. May Brodbeck (New York: Macmillan, 1968), 114-23. Though somewhat dated—it was originally published in English in his *Ideology and Utopia* in 1936—this essay is still a classic statement of the relativistic thrust of the "sociology of knowledge."

15. Hayden White, *Metahistory: The Historical Imagination in Nineteenth-Century Europe* (Baltimore: Johns Hopkins University Press, 1975), 5-38.

16. Frank Kermode, *The Genesis of Secrecy* (Cambridge, Mass.: Harvard University Press, 1979), 122.

17. Luce Irigaray, "Is the Subject of Science Sexes?" trans. Carol M. Bové *Hypatia* 2 (Fall 1987): 65-87; and Hélène Cixous, "The Laugh of the Medusa," *Signs: Journal of Women in Culture and Society* 1 (Summer 1976): 875-93.

18. Michel Foucault, "What Is An Author?" in *Language, Counter-Memory, Practice: Selected Essays and Interviews by Michel Foucault*, ed. and trans. Donald Bouchard and Sherry Simon (Ithaca, N.Y.: Cornell University Press, 1980), 113-38.

19. Paul de Man, *Blindness and Insight: Essays in the Rhetoric of Contemporary Criticism* (New York: Oxford University Press, 1971), ix.

20. *D&A*, 23.41-42.

21. *D&A*, 12.4

22. *D&A*, 12.4-5.

23. *D&A*, 14.16-17.

24. *D&A*, 19.29.

25. *D&A*, 24.35.

26. *D&A*, 24.36.

27. *D&A*, 36.29.

28. *D&A*, 36.41.

29. *D&A*, 36.47-48.

30. *D&A*, 47.15-16.

31. *D&A*, 11.10-13.

32. *D&A*, 21.40-42.

33. Richard Ruland and Malcolm Bradbury, *From Puritanism to Postmodernism: A History of American Literature* (New York: Viking, 1991), 418.

34. Alan Sokal, "Transgressing the Boundaries: Toward a Transformative Hermeneutics of Quantum Gravity," *Social Text* 46/47 (Spring/Summer 1996): 217-52. Almost simultaneous with its publication was the appearance of "A Physicist Experiments with Cultural Studies," *Lingua Franca* 6, no. 4 (May/June 1996): 62-64, in which Sokal admitted the *Social Text* article was a complete hoax, an attempt to pass off as brilliant analysis what is little more than scientific nonsense. His *Social Text* article is weighted with heavy doses of actual writings from postmodernists as ballast, not to mention his parody of the often opaque writing style of postmodernist theorists. He claims in the *Lingua Franca* article that he just wanted to see if editors at a postmodernist journal critical of the sciences could be snookered by postmodern-sounding gibberish.

The *Declaration and Address* as "Countercultural Agenda": Then . . . and Now[1]

Don Haymes

The hand of the Lord was upon me,
and he brought me out by the Spirit
of the Lord, and set me down in the
midst of the plain; it was full of bones.

And he led me round among them;
and behold, there were very many
upon the plain; and lo, they were
very dry.

And he said to me, "Son of man, can
these bones live?" And I answered,
"O Lord God, thou knowest."

—Ez 37:1-3

In the year of our Lord 1809 a lonely man far removed from his own country—a country of stark certainties and violent passions—found himself despised and rejected in the new land of hope to which he had come. Thomas Campbell, traversing land and sea in the middle of life, came to his own—the Scots-Irish Seceder Presbyterians of Western Pennsylvania—and his own received him not. Yet out of the turmoil that accompanied his rejection by the Chartiers Presbytery emerged a faithful remnant, drawn to the Irish preacher's irenic temper and the conviction of his teaching.

In Robert Richardson's "gospel" account, most members of the little remnant that gathered around TC were, like him, immigrants from the North of Ireland and reared in some sort of Presbyterian sectary. In the American West of 1809 they were at large in newly found liberty, exultant and yet alarmed. They longed for the leeks and onions of the Egypt from which they had come, and yet they chafed when the faithful Calvinist clergy caught up with them and attempted to reimpose the miscellaneous tyrannies of creed and clerical order. They were "pious and intelligent," these Scots-Irish pioneers, so Richardson tells us (he does not find any contradiction in that description, nor should we). They found, we might suppose, fresh air, the pure oxygen of the gospel, in TC's plea "to put an end to partyism, and to induce the different religious denominations to unite together upon the Bible as the only authorized rule of faith and practice, and to desist from their controversies about matters of mere opinion and expediency." Yet according to Richardson these wanderers in the American wilderness

> naturally experienced some misgivings as they felt themselves slowly drifting away from the well-known shores and landmarks of their respective religious systems into the wide ocean of Divine truth, which seemed to them so boundless and as yet but imperfectly explored.

In the beginning, then, these disparate immigrants and exiles from a far country were drawn into tenuous relation to one another "by a vague sentiment of Christian union and by the personal influence and character of Thomas Campbell." They soon found need for a "formal understanding or agreement" on which they could unite in principle and action.

Richardson is writing "gospel," not "history"; he is plainly not an *eye*witness to these pilgrims and their progress, but he is our earliest witness, and he writes from personal acquaintance with TC in his old age. Whatever other "sources" he may have had to hand are now lost. We cannot know *exactly* what happened or *precisely* what was said when the solemn assembly convened to seek "formal understanding," but we can believe that distinctions rather than affinities came to the foreground in that meeting. Did TC propose "that WHERE THE SCRIPTURES SPEAK, WE SPEAK; AND WHERE THE SCRIPTURES ARE SILENT WE ARE SILENT," with all the solemnity that Richardson's capitals imply? We cannot be certain that he did. Can we believe that Andrew Munro, "shrewd" Seceder of Canonsburg, immediately saw the consequences for "infant baptism"? We can be certain that, before long, someone did. Did then an emotional Thomas Acheson leave the room in tears, proclaiming that he would never deny welcome to the "little children" whom Jesus had welcomed, while the stalwart Independent James Foster reminded him that "in the portion of Scripture you have quoted *there is no reference, whatever, to infant baptism*"? Surely we may, with Richardson, imagine such scenes and exchanges as these. It may be that Richardson is reading back into this primordial event the questions and struggles of later times, but it is surely possible—given the known origins and likely character of the participants—that even in the beginning such issues and answers could have dominated discussion. Yet in the end the assembled agreed to "form themselves into a regular association" that they would denominate as "The Christian Association of Washington." Twenty-one members—the adult males present, perhaps?—were set apart as a committee "to determine upon the proper means to carry into effect the important ends of their association." In this work they were to have "the assistance of Mr. Thomas Campbell, minister of the gospel."

"Assistance," indeed! Pursuant to this meeting, in August 1809, TC repaired to an upstairs room at the house of "a respectable farmer," a Mr. Welch, where, we are told, he composed our *Declaration and Address* in something less than three weeks. What contribution the committee of twenty-one may have made to this composition we have no way of knowing, although we may think that TC had listened to them and had taken their positions and their passions into account. We know, or think we know, only a few of their names: Andrew Munro, the Canonsburg Seceder; Abraham Altars, the friend whose house provided an early place of meeting; that Mr. Welch who sheltered TC as he wrote; James Foster, the "Independent" of strongly held opinions; and that warm-hearted lover of the very young, Thomas Acheson, who in the end, with TC, signed the final draft of the document. Despite this signature there is no suggestion by any one at any time that any hand other than TC's wrote a line of the *D&A*; we may rather suppose that these hands were busily engaged in hastily erecting that nearby "log building on the Sinclair farm"—is Mr. Sinclair yet one more of the anonymous twenty-one?—that would serve the nascent Association as meeting house and common school. That labor, and the fund they would raise "to support a pure Gospel ministry," are the most likely and most important contributions of the twenty-one: they are paying TC to think for them, and providing a place to hear what he thinks.

(In the first printing of the *D&A*, Acheson is identified as "Treasurer," while TC is "Secretary.")

So we may imagine TC at his writing desk, in that upstairs room, in the heat of August, scribbling with ink and quill on whatever material came to hand, seizing the moment toward which all his learning and teaching and preaching had propelled him. The *D&A* is his composition, surely, and yet it is composed, from the first sentence onward, in the first person *plural*: not I, but *we*.

Robert Dee Colvett, the sage of Florence, Alabama, has remarked to me in conversation that the *D&A* may be "an 'I' document, enlisted in the search for a 'we.'" This is, it seems to me, a useful, even important insight. The *D&A* as we have it is conducted throughout in the first person *plural*; it is signed by TC *and* Thomas Acheson; and yet no learned commentator or authoritative witness, to my knowledge, regards Acheson or any member of the committee of twenty-one as other than a vestigial appendage in the composition of the *D&A*. What our brother Acheson in fact does—along with all of the committee of twenty-one and the entire membership of the Christian Association of Washington, if it be possible to distinguish one from the other—is to provide a tangible and literal "we" for the *D&A* that is not an "editorial we" or (surely!) a "royal we" or a "wee-wee all the way home." Acheson is, with all of the committee and the Association that he most surely represents, the communal context of the *D&A*; the "we" of the *D&A*, though it be the composition of a solitary individual, is a communal "we," and so *we* must regard it. And yet, dear hearts, it must be said that little as *we*—the community of students and scholars concerned with the *D&A*—know of TC, *we* know even less of Acheson and his tribe, who are the real Christian Association of Washington, if that entity ever existed beyond words "on paper."

They were "immigrants," most of them from Ireland and Scotland, and they were "pioneers" in an "unsettled" country. That much we know of them, and that much is a beginning; perhaps it is enough. The clergy of the Chartiers Presbytery and their counterparts in the other "denominations" of Europe were eager and ready to impose "settlement" and "order," but only on terms that denominate and divide these immigrants from one another on the basis of forgotten formulae and ancient antagonisms that were largely if not entirely irrelevant to their new condition in their new land. They were, with so many of their kind in that Western frontier, detached from whatever roots in the old world that might previously have constrained them, economically, socially, or religiously.

They had come far from whatever conditions that might have impelled them to seek a new life. They were at liberty to choose what suited them in a new country that they had chosen, perhaps for just that reason. They were engaged in a daily struggle for necessities of life, working each day from dawn to dusk and beyond, but still it seemed then that only their intelligence, their energy, and the will of God would limit what they could achieve. TC, we know, had his own reasons—"sad experience"—to decry "religious controversy among christians" and "the bitter jarrings and janglings of a party spirit." We may not doubt that his new collaborators were as "tired and sick" of these things as he, and we may be sure that they heard gladly his plea for "such measures as would give rest to our brethren throughout all the churches; as would restore unity, peace, and purity, to the whole church of God." Here was a call for a new order that was, in fact, an old order: "Christ and his simple word; which is the same yesterday, today, and forever." TC's program promised freedom with stability, unity with purity, that would issue in rest and peace, all to be found "in Christ and his simple word." How simple, indeed, and how utterly irresistible! And, we may think now, how utterly impossible!

Were they hopelessly naïve, these seekers of "unity, peace, and purity"? It must seem so now. How could they possibly imagine "unity" and "purity" in the same space at the same time with the same cast of characters? Is it not always so, that we achieve *unity* only at the cost of *purity*, and *purity* only at the sacrifice of *unity*? Is not *unity* the child of compromise? How may we compromise *purity* and remain . . . pure? And how are we to "restore," on the basis of the Bible alone, a condition—"unity, peace, and purity"—that demonstrably, on the evidence of the Bible itself, has never existed "in the whole church of God" or anywhere else? The *D&A* surely expresses a truly wonderful ideal, the ideal of the New Testament, but the condition of the church, even in the New Testament, is always something less than ideal. We may admire such idealism, and we may revere the *D&A* as we revere, say, the Sermon on the Mount; but as for making it happen in a living community . . . well, now, let's be practical!

Indeed. The *D&A* is nothing if not practical. The hardy tradesmen and farmers who are the cause of its composition are no longer burghers or peasants; the categories of the Old World no longer apply. In the American West of 1809, the new citizen (in the words of Henry Nash Smith) "had to work as hard as a common laborer or a European peasant, and at the same tasks," and "his economic status was not necessarily higher." These yeomen, although they embody what becomes (again in Smith's words) "*the* myth of mid-nineteenth-century America," are, in their ideas and actions, relentlessly practical, indeed pragmatic. On the American frontier, *praxis* is everything; theory "ain't worth a hill of beans." Hills of beans are made by action—hard labor. Christians may be "saved" by faith, but American yeomen are sustained by works. Everywhere in the West it is what one does, not what one thinks, that really matters. Hence, the preoccupation of these practical reformers with matters of *form* rather than of *substance*, with *what* is done and *how* it is done rather than *why* one should do it or what it "means."

The learned gentlemen of Boston and Cambridge—having the leisure of their fathers' fortunes made in textiles, shipping, and the slave trade—turn to Scripture as their "only rule of faith and practice" and find no warrant for the Trinity. For the practical yeomen of Western Pennsylvania, God is God: Father, Son, and Holy Spirit. In the Bible it is so. They have no taste, and no time, for "speculation." The Idea of God as handed down in the classical creeds is not something about which they can *do* anything, but baptism is. They and their descendants wrestle endlessly with *how* baptism is administered, *who* is to be baptized, and *when*. The question of *why* one should be baptized is moot; one is baptized "to be saved." But what it means to "be saved" is largely unexplored, beyond escape from the threat of hell. Who may "observe" the Lord's Supper ("that great ordinance of unity and love"), when and where one may eat it, how its "elements" may be served, and how frequently—these "issues" are continually examined. *Why* one should eat the bread and drink the "fruit of the vine" is, once again, moot. They do what they do because, in the New Testament, the earliest Christians did it, and *they* did it because Jesus appears to have given a vague instruction, repeated and reinforced by Paul. Lacking any more specific directions, these yeomen and their heirs argue about frequency and containers and the qualifications of those who eat and drink, but they rarely if ever address the nature of the "presence" of Christ in the Lord's Supper. (Indeed it may be said, justly, that the inheritors of the *D&A* most often serve a Supper distinguished by a *Real Absence*.)

Members of the community of the *D&A* celebrate human intelligence—they impute to every human mind the awesome power to discern the will of God in the pages of the Bible—but they are hardly naïve about human integrity and human intention. They have escaped the tyranny of king, clergy, and creed, but in the distance they can hear the devil's hounds sounding on the scent, "even in this highly favored country, where the sword of the civil magistrate has not as yet learned to serve at the altar." How many volumes of experience are contained in those two little words, *as yet*! They know that the devil will sign any creed that humankind can devise, and sign it all the more gladly in the knowledge that the purpose of any creed is not to unite believers but to divide them. They are not without irony. They are passionately concrete, eschewing all forms of abstraction—thereby saving themselves and their heirs from endless palaver with the theological Blind Men of Indostan, who (the poet reminds us):

> Rail on in utter ignorance
> Of what each other mean,
> And prate about an Elephant
> Not one of them has seen.

And yet these stalwart partisans depose that they can and will "put an end to our hapless divisions and restore to the church its primitive unity, purity, and prosperity." This noble goal they intend to pursue on the "model" and "practice" of "the primitive church, expressly exhibited in the New Testament." Leaving abstract theological "speculation" to the *Luftmenschen* in Cambridge, New Haven, Princeton, and Philadelphia, our heroes vow to pursue a unity and purity of ecclesiology:

> Were we, then, in our church constitution and managements, to exhibit a complete conformity to the Apostolic church, would we not be, in that respect, as perfect as Christ intended we should be? And should not this suffice us?

It all seems so simple, really. Since "all the churches of Christ, which mutually acknowledge each other as such" (already the field is narrowing!) agree "in the great doctrines of faith and holiness" and also "as to the positive ordinances of Gospel institution," it seems so clear "that our differences, at most, are about the things in which the kingdom of God does not consist, that is, about matters of private opinion or human invention." Truly it is a "pity" that God's kingdom is so divided! Surely, once we realize the reasons of our divisions, we should at once abandon our divisive "opinions" and "inventions" for the "peace" of "purity" and "unity":

> Who, then, would not be the first among us, to give up with human inventions in the worship of God; and to cease from imposing his private opinions upon his brethren; that our breaches might *thus* be healed? Who would not willingly conform to the original pattern laid down in the New Testament, for *this* happy purpose?

Just about everybody—that's who. *What* "human inventions" are to be abandoned? *Whose* "private opinions" about *what* are in question? One person's human invention is another's inspired tradition; what seems to one person a private opinion is to another a matter of faith. The *D&A*, seeking to be inclusive and timeless, is notably vague about specific causes of schism. As a comprehensive call for an end to division of the Kingdom of God, the *D&A* presents a most attractive program—but the division is in the details. In the *D&A* the New Testament is "perfect" as "a constitution for the worship, discipline and government of the New Testament church" and "perfect" as "a rule for the particular duties of its members." Yet human readers and interpreters of this "perfect" collection of documents are, demonstrably, something less than perfect. Whatever the powers of the human mind to discern the will of God in this "perfect" book, wherever there are two human beings or more there are two minds or more. According to the *D&A*, the "particular and distinct societies" that make up the "essentially, intentionally, and constitutionally one" church ought "all to walk by the same rule, to mind and speak the same thing; and to be perfectly joined together in the same mind, and in the same judgment."

It ought to be so simple. We begin with "all those in every place that profess their faith in Christ and their obedience to him in all things according to the scriptures"; this is indeed a "particular and distinct" population, for "none else can be truly and properly called christians." Already we have something less than the *oikoumene*. These particular and distinct believers in their particular and distinct societies are called to unite on "what is expressly enjoined" in the perfect New Testament, "either in express terms, or by approved precedent." No human authority can intervene where the New Testament has not spoken or supplement what the New Testament has not provided. "Inferences and deductions from scripture premises" are allowable, and "may be truly called the doctrine of God's holy word," but only insofar as Christian believers "perceive the connection, and evidently see that they are so."

But what happens when you "perceive the connection," and I don't? Whose "inference" is "necessary"? According to the *D&A*, no inference is ever necessary

> unless we suppose, what is contrary to fact, that none have a right to the communion of the church, but such as possess a very clear and decisive judgment; or are come to a very high degree of doctrinal information; whereas the church from the beginning did, and ever will, consist of little children and young men, as well as fathers.

And young women and mothers, we may well add; we find them in the New Testament, although not all of us have been able to see them there in the same way. There are so many connections that we are not able to perceive with one mind; so many "inferential truths" for which we are not able to perceive the same necessity or value. We can agree that "division among christians is a horrid evil" but we more rarely understand its precise cause in exactly the same way. Among the putative heirs of the *D&A* there are those who value the sound of the organ more than the voices of their dissenting sisters and brothers, and there are those for whom the sound of the organ drowns out the voices of their assenting sisters and brothers. We may admit that "each is partly in the right," but the *D&A* would have us to see that "all are in the wrong." That admission is more difficult, for it requires us to give way or forbear. When inferences conflict, we cannot enforce them. But more usually we take our text from 1 Kings 9:32:

> *Who is on my side? Who?*

It is ever so. Writing a quarter of a century after the publication of the *D&A*, in the preface to the first edition of his *Christian System*, Alexander Campbell fondly recalled "the first piece that was written on the subject of the great position" and summed up "a controversy of *twenty-five years*" that followed it. "Every inch of it," AC reported, "was debated, argued, canvassed for several years in Pennsylvania, Virginia, and Ohio." So much for "peace." The "progress" of the movement spawned by the *D&A*—so no less an authority than AC can argue—"corresponds with the history of every other religious revolution," and is to be, appropriately, couched in martial metaphors:

> We began with the *outposts* and *vanguard* of the opposition. Soon as we found ourselves in possession of one post our artillery was turned against another; and as fast as the smoke of the enemy receded we advanced upon his lines.

Did the army enlisted in this cause march out to meet the "enemy" on feet "shod with the preparation of the gospel of *peace*"? We may wish it so. The professed objective of their campaign is to "restore unity, peace, and purity, to the whole church of God." But that is not what happened. We may wonder why. Yet how could it be otherwise?

The *D&A* is a "countercultural agenda"; sure and it's true. It is as "countercultural" as the vision of the "church of God" it sets out to "restore" in all its "unity, peace, and purity." That vision runs counter to every recorded tendency of human culture since the emergence of the phenomena that lie behind the myth of Babel in Genesis 11 and the "confusion" of human language. Yet is it not to end such barriers between human beings—barriers of language and understanding, barriers of race and class and nation, barriers of sex—that the "gospel of God" proclaims the "church of God," in which all human beings shall be reconciled to one another and to God? Yes, that is so. Why, then, are we not reconciled to one another in that one church, as the *D&A* so devoutly desires? Even among the heirs who claim the *D&A* as a "foundation" of their existence, the confusion and division are everywhere to be seen. In a crude caricature that, we may ruefully admit, reveals all too much of the truth, we may say that the Disciples of Christ have pursued the "unity" of the *D&A*, while the Churches of Christ have sought "purity," and the Independent Christian Churches and Churches of Christ—true to the denominator they have adopted for themselves—have attempted, quite unsuccessfully, to have it both ways. I write of human phenomena in a human way—but that is precisely the problem. The Kingdom of God on earth is not to be achieved by human beings according to the devises and stratagems of the human political order. We find "unity" with "purity" to be an internal contradiction, and so we choose sides, we attempt to subdue the "enemy," and when that fails, in the interest of some kind of "unity," we attempt compromise. Compromise is the essence of "unity" in the human order, but it makes for fragile alliances easily undone, and for the Kingdom of God there is no *theology* of compromise. When and where shall "purity" be compromised? How and by whom? By what authority?

Why, then, does the Lord Jesus pray, in the Gospel of John, "that they may all be one"? He knows well the human tendency. But this saying is not a "command," even though it is often taken to be one. It is a prayer, addressed to the source of any real "unity" or "purity" that humankind shall ever possess. Unity and purity of humankind begin with the unity of God, expressed in the ancient confession of Israel:

> *Shema Yitzrael, Adonai Elohenu, Adonai echad.*

This is indeed the first and greatest of the commandments, repeated by the Lord Jesus in the Gospel of Mark:

> *Hear, O Israel, the Lord our God, the Lord is One.*
> *And you shall love the Lord your God*
> *with all your heart, and with all your being,*
> *and with all your mind, and with all your strength.*

And then Jesus adds its corollary:

> *You shall love your neighbor as yourself.*

Surely this is where any "unity" and "purity" that we shall ever have must begin, with our love for the One God, with the devotion of our entire being—that love which issues in our love for one another. That is the recipe for "peace"; there is no other. If we are determined to *do* something, this is it. It is, indeed, all that we can do. But it is easier said than done.

Is it hopeless then? For us it is marvelous; we are historians, and therefore connoisseurs of irony. The *D&A* is a feast of irony. The bones of the *D&A* litter the plain of history, and with them the bones of all the great movements to "restore unity, peace, and purity." They are scattered all around us, and we walk round among them, and—would you believe?—they are *very dry*:

> *Son of man, can these bones live?*

That is the question. And the answer, the only one we can give, is the same answer that came to Ezekiel so long ago:

> *O Lord God, thou knowest.*

Life for these dry bones, for the bones of the *D&A* and the movement it brought into being, will come from the breath of the Spirit of God, and from nowhere else. It is God who gives life, God who gives unity. We must believe, we must trust, we must commit to the power of the Spirit of God to transcend all human barriers and distinctions. Are, then, our "unity, peace, and purity" merely an *eschatological* hope? Not "merely." But surely it is resurrection that we seek. If Jesus did not get up on Sunday morning, and we cannot rise with him, then the unity, peace, and purity of the church of God shall have no meaning, for there are no "Christians." We are, then, of all humankind most to be pitied. But if Jesus is risen, then even the *D&A* may rise again, to confound our fear and confirm our hope.

Will there then be a "church of Christ upon earth . . . essentially, intentionally, and constitutionally one"? *O Lord God, thou knowest*! Of whom shall it consist? It shall include "all who are moved by the Spirit of God." And who are they? *O Lord God, thou knowest*! Just as the dry bones scattered about Ezekiel's plain become the people Israel, reborn from the dead, so might we also live to join that numberless throng, gathered from the ends of the earth, lifting our voices in the anthem everlasting:

Salvation belongs to our God,
Who sits upon the throne,
And to the Lamb.

In that day there shall be unity and purity and peace, in a world beyond history. And what shall we have in history? *O Lord God, thou knowest*!

Note

1. This essay proposes to read and, indeed, to *revive* the *D&A*: to understand "what it meant" that we may learn "what it means." In that light the usual scholarly apparatus of annotation has not been used. Its mission is to impart "meaning," not "information." Yet surely some debts should be acknowledged. Its author has read the *D&A* closely, and also the Bible, most especially the prophet Ezekiel; he owes some things to Robert Richardson's *Memoirs of Alexander Campbell* and also to AC's *Christian System*; and of course the historian Henry Nash Smith's *Virgin Land* and John Godfrey Saxe's poetic vision of the blind men and the elephant have contributed beyond measure to the author's understanding and now, perhaps, to that of the reader as well. To God be all glory forever and ever. *Amen.*

Thomas Campbell: A Bibliography of Primary Sources

Ernest C. Stefanik, compiler

This bibliography of the works of Thomas Campbell has been compiled from the card catalogue of the Disciples of Christ Historical Society, Nashville, Tennessee; Claude E. Spencer's *An Author Catalog of Disciples of Christ and Related Religious Groups* (Canton, Mo.: Disciples of Christ Historical Society, 1946); *The National Union Catalog of Pre-1956 Imprints*; "Thomas Campbell, 1763–1854. Books by and about Him," *Discipliana* 20 (January 1961): 80-81; David I. McWhirter's *An Index to the Millennial Harbinger* (Joplin, Mo.: College Press, 1981); Gary L. Lee's "Index to the Burnet Edition of the *Christian Baptist*" in *The Christian Baptist* (Joplin, Mo.: College Press, 1983); and William Herbert Hanna's *Thomas Campbell: Seceder and Christian Union Advocate* (Cincinnati, Ohio: Standard Publishing, 1935; reprint, Joplin, Mo.: College Press, 1986). The online catalogues of Abilene Christian University and Pepperdine University libraries have been consulted to verify and clarify information. Only a few of the books have been examined by the compiler. TC's contributions to a few books are not specifically identified in the catalogues.

The bibliography is arranged chronologically by date of publication and alphabetically by publisher within each of the six major headings.

Thanks to Elaine Philpott for providing copies of the cards for holdings of the Disciples of Christ Historical Society. Thanks to Dr. Hans Rollmann, who first suggested the project and then freely offered his advice and assistance throughout the writing process. Thanks to R. Jeanne Cobb, Archivist and Special Collections Coordinator, for providing information regarding the letters by TC held at T. W. Phillips Memorial Library, Bethany College, Bethany, West Virginia.

I. Separate Publications

Declaration and Address of the Christian Association of Washington. Washington, Pa.: Brown & Sample, 1809.

Prospectus of a Religious Reformation, the Object of Which Is the Restoration of Primitive Apostolic Christianity in Letter and Spirit—in Principle and Practice. [Cincinnati, Ohio, 1829.]

On Religious Reformation. [Richmond, Va. ?: ca. 1832.]

II. Reprintings, as Separate Publications

Declaration and Address of the Christian Association of Washington. 1809. Pittsburgh, Pa.: Centennial Committee, 1908. Zinc etching reprint issued in a limited edition for the Pittsburgh Centennial. Shows corrections made by the author and revision marks of Alexander Campbell.

Declaration and Address of the Christian Association of Washington. 1809. St. Louis, Mo.: Christian Board of Publication, 1908. Limited edition, zinc etching reprint.

Declaration and Address. 1809. Centennial ed. Pittsburgh, Pa.: Centennial Bureau, 1908. Reprint, including a facsimile reproduction of the original title page. On title page: "Twentieth Thousand."

Declaration and Address. 1809. Centennial ed. Pittsburgh, Pa.: Western Pennsylvania Missionary Society, 1908. Reprint, including a facsimile reproduction of the original title page. On title page: "Twentieth Thousand."

Declaration and Address. 1809. Centennial ed. Cincinnati, Ohio: Centennial Department of the American Missionary Society, 1908. Reprint, including a facsimile reproduction of the original title page. On title page: "Twentieth Thousand."

Declaration and Address. 1809. Centennial ed. Cincinnati, Ohio: Centennial Department of the American Missionary Society, 1909. Reprint, including a facsimile reproduction of the original title page. On title page: "Twenty-fifth Thousand."

Declaration and Address. 1809. Centennial ed. Pittsburgh, Pa.: Centennial Bureau, 1909. Reprint, including facsimile reproduction of the title page. On title page: "Thirtieth Thousand."

Declaration and Address. 1809. Cincinnati, Ohio: Standard Publishing, 1909. Cover title: *A Plea for Christian Union: A Century of Effort to Restore the New Testament Church, in Name, in Ordinances, and in Life.* Reprints text of First Edition, from new setting of type; omits Postscript.

Principles of Christian Union, Proposed by the Disciples of Christ, from a Declaration on the Subject by Thomas Campbell, Published in the United States in 1809. St. Louis, Mo.: Christian Board of Publication, 1927. Contents taken from *Declaration and Address.*

Declaration and Address and The Last Will and Testament of the Springfield Presbytery. 1809 and 1804. With an introduction by Frederick D. Kershner. Indianapolis, Ind.: International Convention of Disciples of Christ, 1949. Reprints text of Centennial Edition (1909).

Declaration and Address. 1809. With an introduction by William Robinson. Birmingham, Eng.: Berean Press, 1951. Reprints text of First Edition; omits Appendix and Postscript. Produced from a first edition preserved in the Library of Overdale College, Selly Oak, Birmingham.

Declaration and Address by Thomas Campbell, and The Last Will and Testament of the Springfield Presbytery by Barton W. Stone and others. 1861 and 1804. With a brief introduction by F. D. Kershner. St. Louis, Mo.: Bethany Press, 1955. Reprints text of Second Edition; introductory note is reproduction from Facsimile Edition; omits notes by Alexander Campbell.

Declaration and Address by Thomas Campbell, and The Last Will and Testament of the Springfield Presbytery by Barton W. Stone and others. 1861 and 1804. With a brief introduction by F. D. Kershner. St. Louis, Mo.: Mission Messenger, 1972.

The Paraphrase of Thomas Campbell's Declaration and Address, by Knofel Staton. Joplin, Mo.: College Press, [1976].

Declaration and Address. 1861. Lincoln, Ill.: Lincoln Christian College, 1983. Cover Title: *—Reprint—Original: Washington, Pennsylvania: Brown and Sample, 1809.* Reprints text of Second Edition; omits notes by Alexander Campbell; includes introductory note and Postscript from Centennial Edition.

III. First-Appearance Contributions to Books

"English Classical School, or Mercantile Academy." *Scholastic Theology*. (ca. 1815.)

Letter to Sidney Rigdon (February 4, 1831). In *Mormonism Unvailed* by Eber D. Howe. Painesville, Ohio: Eber D. Howe, 1834, 116-23. First published in the *Painesville Telegraph* (15 February 1831): 2.

"Family Education: The Nursery." In *Family Culture, or, Conversations at the Carlton House* by Alexander Campbell. London: Hall and Co., 1850, 335-43. First published in *Millennial Harbinger* ns 4 (August 1840): 340-45.

"Protest and Appeal." In *Memoirs of Elder Thomas Campbell* by Alexander Campbell. Cincinnati, Ohio: H. S. Bosworth, 1861, 12-15.

"Address on Withdrawing from the Associate Synod of North America." In *Memoirs of Elder Thomas Campbell* by Alexander Campbell. Cincinnati, Ohio: H. S. Bosworth, 1861, 17-18.

"Letters of Thomas Campbell." In *Memoirs of Elder Thomas Campbell* by Alexander Campbell. Cincinnati, Ohio: H. S. Bosworth, 1861, 141-93. Thirteen letters to Mrs. Jane Campbell, Dorothea Bryant, A. S. Hayden, Alexander Campbell, Brother and Sister Bakewell, Margaret Campbell, and the Editor of the *Gospel Advocate,* as well as an album note to Mrs. Julia Bakewell.

"Thomas Campbell's Diary, Anno Domini, 1800." In *Memoirs of Elder Thomas Campbell* by Alexander Campbell. Cincinnati, Ohio: H. S. Bosworth, 1861, 194-204.

"Notes of a Sermon." In *Memoirs of Elder Thomas Campbell* by Alexander Campbell. Cincinnati, Ohio: H. S. Bosworth, 1861, 205-6.

"Method of Discoursing." In *Memoirs of Elder Thomas Campbell* by Alexander Campbell. Cincinnati, Ohio: H. S. Bosworth, 1861, 207-9.

"Address of Thomas Campbell to the Synod of Ireland, Met at Belfast, County Down, 1804." In *Memoirs of Elder Thomas Campbell* by Alexander Campbell. Cincinnati, Ohio: H. S. Bosworth, 1861, 210-14.

"Farewell Discourse of Thomas Campbell." In *Memoirs of Elder Thomas Campbell* by Alexander Campbell. Cincinnati, Ohio: H. S. Bosworth, 1861, 215-34. First published in *Millennial Harbinger* 4th ser. 4 (March 1854): 133-45.

"Christianity Is Neither a Theory Nor a Philosophy." In *Memoirs of Elder Thomas Campbell* by Alexander Campbell. Cincinnati, Ohio: H. S. Bosworth, 1861, 235-52.

"Circular Letter" (1816). In *Memoirs of Alexander Campbell* by Robert Richardson. 2 vols. Philadelphia, Pa.: J. B. Lippincott, 1868, 1:539-55.

"Extract of a Letter to His Family" (April 1807). In *Memoirs of Alexander Campbell* by Robert Richardson. 2 vols. Philadelphia, Pa.: J. B. Lippincott, 1869, 1:80.

"Extract of a Letter to His Family" (27 May 1807). In *Memoirs of Alexander Campbell* by Robert Richardson. 2 vols. Philadelphia, Pa.: J. B. Lippincott, 1869, 1:85-86.

"Extract of a Letter to His Family" (1 January 1808). In *Memoirs of Alexander Campbell* by Robert Richardson. 2 vols. Philadelphia, Pa.: J. B. Lippincott, 1869, 1:88-90.

"Extracts of Two Letters to Alexander Campbell" (1811). *Memoirs of Alexander Campbell* by Robert Richardson. 2 vols. Philadelphia, Pa.: J. B. Lippincott, 1869, 1:413-21.

"Extracts of Two Letters to Alexander Campbell" (1812). In *Memoirs of Alexander Campbell* by Robert Richardson. 2 vols. Philadelphia, Pa.: J. B. Lippincott, 1869, 1:447-55.

"Letter of Dismission" (1 August 1823). In *Memoirs of Alexander Campbell* by Robert Richardson. 2 vols. Philadelphia, Pa.: J. B. Lippincott, 1869, 2:69.

"Extract of a Letter to Alexander Campbell" (9 April 1828). In *Early History of the Disciples in the Western Reserve, Ohio* by A. S. Hayden. Cincinnati, Ohio: Chase & Hall, 1875, 148-49.

"Obituary." In *Restoration Readings.* Ed. Oram Jackson Swinney. Rosemead, Calif.: Old Path Book Club, 1949, 16-22. First published in *Millennial Harbinger* 6 (June 1835): 284-87.

"Some Pioneer Answers—1824 thru 1861." In Restoration Readings, ed. Oram Jackson Swinney. Rosemead, Calif.: Old Path Book Club, 1949, 60-61; 73-75. First published as "Queries" in *Christian Baptist* 7 (7 September 1829): 581; and as "Queries by A. S. H." in *Millennial Harbinger* 3d ser. 2 (May 1845): 220-22.

IV. Reprintings, as Contributions to Books

"Declaration and Address." In *Memoirs of Elder Thomas Campbell* by Alexander Campbell. Cincinnati, Ohio: H. S. Bosworth, 1861, 25-109. Second Edition, with emendations and notes by Alexander Campbell.

"Extract of a Letter to Sidney Rigdon" (4 February 1831). In *Early History of the Disciples in the Western Reserve, Ohio* by A. S.

Hayden. Cincinnati, Ohio: Chase & Hall, 1875, 217-20. First published in the *Painesville Telegraph* (15 February 1831): 2. First book appearance in *Mormonism Unvailed* by Eber D. Howe. Painesville, Ohio: Eber D. Howe, 1834, 116-23.

"Declaration and Address" (1861). In *The Message of the Disciples for the Union of the Church, Including Their Origin and History*, ed. Peter Ainslie. New York: Revell, 1913, 145-210. Reprints text of Second Edition; omits introductory note and Alexander Campbell's notes.

"Declaration and Address" (1809). In *That They May All Be One*, ed. Thomas Jefferson Gore. Melbourne, Australia: Austral Publishing, 1914, 195-221. Reprints text of First Edition; omits some paragraphs, Appendix, and Postscript.

"Declaration and Address" (1861). In *Historical Documents Advocating Christian Union*, ed. Charles Alexander Young. Chicago: Christian Century, 1904, 71-209. Reprints text of Second Edition.

"Declaration and Address" (1861). In *The Christian Union Overture: An Interpretation of the Declaration and Address of Thomas Campbell* by Frederick D. Kershner. St. Louis, Mo.: Bethany Press, 1923, 31-34, 51-55, 59-62, 70-73, 81, 83-99, 105-8, 113-45. Reprints text of the Second Edition, except pp. 105-8, which is from the Centennial Edition.

"Declaration and Address" (1861). In *Pioneer Sermons and Addresses*, ed. F. L. Rowe. 3d ed. Cincinnati, Ohio: F. L. Rowe, 1925, 14-104. Reprints text of Second Edition.

"Prospectus of a Religious Reformation, &c." In *Memoirs of Elder Thomas Campbell* by Alexander Campbell. Cincinnati, Ohio: H. S. Bosworth, 1861, 253-64.

"Address on Withdrawing from the Associate Synod of North America." In *Thomas Campbell: Seceder and Christian Union Advocate* by William Herbert Hanna. Cincinnati, Ohio: Standard Publishing, 1935, 106-9.

"Interpretation of the Scriptures" (Propositions 3-6), "Faith vs. Opinion" (Propositions 7-11), and "A Statement on the Church" (Propositions 1-2). In *Great Pioneer Papers*. Selected by the Editorial Committee. Rosemead, Calif.: Old Path Book Club, 1949, 128-29, 138-39, 159. Reprints Propositions 1-11 from *Declaration and Address*.

"Farewell Discourse of Thomas Campbell, Sr." In *Restoration Readings*, ed. Oram Jackson Swinney. Rosemead, Calif.: Old Path Book Club,

1949, 26-40. First published in *Millennial Harbinger* 4th ser. 4 (March 1854): 133-45.

Movimento de Restauracion Historia y Documentos [de] Thomas Campbell, Barton W. Stone, Juan Antonio Monroy. Madrid, Spain: Editorial Irmayo, 1987.

V. Contributions to Periodicals[1]

"To the Editor of the Christian Baptist." *Christian Baptist* 1 (1 September 1823): 11. Signed "T. W."[2]

"Essay on the Proper and Primary Intention of the Gospel, and Its Proper and Immediate Effects." *Christian Baptist* 1 (1 September 1823): 11-13. Signed "T. W."

"To the Editor of the Christian Baptist." *Christian Baptist* 1 (7 June 1824): 65-66. Signed "T. W."

"To the Editor of the Christian Baptist." *Christian Baptist* 2 (4 October 1824): 98. Signed "T. W."

"Essay on the Religion of Christianity." *Christian Baptist* 2 (4 October 1824): 98-101. Signed "T. W."

"To Mr. D., A Sceptic.—Replication No. V." *Christian Baptist* 4 (4 December 1826): 296-97.

"Constitution of a Congregation in Ohio." *Christian Baptist* 5 (7 July 1828): 456-57. Extract of a letter. Unsigned.[3]

"To the Religious Public." *Christian Baptist* 7 (3 August 1829): 573-74.

"Queries." *Christian Baptist* 7 (7 September 1829): 581. Unsigned.[4]

"Reply to the Above" [A Constant Reader's Letter to the Editor]. *Christian Baptist* 7 (2 November 1829): 597-98. Signed "T. W. *alias* Thos. Campbell."

"Query." *Christian Baptist* 7 (2 November 1829): 598. Signed "T. W."

"To the Editor of the Christian Baptist." *Christian Baptist* 7 (7 December 1829): 608-11. Signed "T. W."

"To the Editor of the Christian Baptist." *Christian Baptist* 7 (7 December 1829): 611-13. Signed "T. W."

"Reply to 'A Constant Reader.'" *Christian Baptist* 7 (1 February 1830): 625-26.

"The Mormon Challenge." *Painesville Telegraph* (15 February 1831). Consists of Letter to the Editor of the *Telegraph* and Letter to Sidney Rigdon.

Letter to "Mr. Alexander Campbell." *Millennial Harbinger* 3 (April 1932): 169-71.

"A Word to the Disciples of the Ancient Gospel, in Behalf of the Reformation, and for the Consideration of Opponents." *Millennial Harbinger* 3 (December 1832): 584-86. Signed "T. W."

"Worcester on the Atonement," Letter to William Z. Thompson. *Millennial Harbinger* 4 (June 1833): 256-62.

Letter to Barton W. Stone. *Millennial Harbinger* 4 (August 1833): 421-25.

"To Barton W. Stone." *Millennial Harbinger* 4 (September 1833): 439-45.

"To B. W. Stone." *Millennial Harbinger* 4 (October 1833): 503-9.

"To B. W. Stone." *Millennial Harbinger* 4 (November 1833): 548-53.

"To B. W. Stone." *Millennial Harbinger* 4 (December 1833): 594-98.

Letter to J. R. Howard. *Millennial Harbinger* 6 (May 1835): 206-11. Signed "T. C."

Reply to M. Winans's "Offences." Millennial Harbinger 6 (May 1835): 218-20. Signed "T. C."

Reply to "The Term Evangelist." *Millennial Harbinger* 6 (May 1835): 238-40. Signed "T. C."

Obituary of Samuel Marshal. *Millennial Harbinger* 6 (May 1835): 240. Signed "T. C."

Editorial Note to "M. Winans to Elder Henry Grew." *Millennial Harbinger* 6 (June 1835): 272-73. Signed "T. C."

"Obituary" [of Jane Corneigle Campbell]. *Millennial Harbinger* 6 (June 1835): 284-87.

"To the Editor of the Millennial Harbinger." *Millennial Harbinger* 7 (May 1836): 214-18.

"Answer to Query" [of M. Winans]. *Millennial Harbinger* ns 2 (November 1838): 524-25.

"The Divine Order for Evangelizing the World." *Millennial Harbinger* ns 3 (January 1839): 25-30.

"The Direct and Immediate Intention of the Christian Institution. Essay I." *Millennial Harbinger* ns 3 (January 1839): 41-43.

"The Direct and Immediate Intention of the Christian Institution. Essay II." *Millennial Harbinger* ns 3 (February 1839): 92-93. Signed "T. C."

"Christian Union." *Millennial Harbinger* ns 3 (March 1839): 134-44.

"Christian Union." *Millennial Harbinger* ns 3 (April 1839): 155-64.

"The Direct and Immediate Intention of the Christian Institution. Essay III." *Millennial Harbinger* ns 3 (May 1839): 216-20.

"On Personal and Family Devotion." *Millennial Harbinger* ns 3 (September 1839): 392-95.

"Prospectus, &c." *The Evangelist* 7 (July 1839): 149-53. Reprints first four sections of *Prospectus of a Religious Reformation* (Introduction, "Queries," "Conclusion," and "Reflection").

"Church Edification." *Millennial Harbinger* ns 3 (October 1839): 462-66.

"Remarks upon the Above" [James Shannon's "Ordination"]. *Millennial Harbinger* ns 3 (December 1839): 569-75.

"Reply to M. Winans." *Millennial Harbinger* ns 3 (December 1839): 576-77.

"Church Edification." *Millennial Harbinger* ns 3 (December 1839): 591-93. Signed "T. C."

"Remarks upon the Above" [Chas. D. Hurlbutt's "Self-Education"]. *Millennial Harbinger* ns 3 (December 1839): 596. Signed "T. C."

"Communication" [on Christianos's "Our Name"]. *Millennial Harbinger* ns 4 (January 1840): 19-21. Signed "T. C."

"Church Edification." *Millennial Harbinger* ns 4 (February 1840): 56-60.

"Animadversions on the Above" [M. Winans's "Faith Alone"]. *Millennial Harbinger* ns 4 (August 1840): 338-40.

"Family Education: The Nursery." *Millennial Harbinger* ns 4 (August 1840): 340-45.

"A Scriptural View of Christian Character and Privilege." Section 1. *Millennial Harbinger* ns 4 (August 1840): 345-49. Signed "T. C."

"A Scriptural View of Christian Character and Privilege." Section 2. *Millennial Harbinger* ns 4 (September 1840): 396-98. Signed "T. C.

"Proceedings of the Board of Trustees of Bethany College." *Millennial Harbinger* ns 4 (November 1840): 508-10. Signed by Thomas Campbell, President pro tem., and W. F. M. Arny, Secretary.

"A Scriptural View of Christian Character and Privilege." Sections 3 and 4. *Millennial Harbinger* ns 5 (March 1841): 135-37. Signed "T. C."

"A Scriptural View of Christian Character and Privilege." Section 4 (concluded). *Millennial Harbinger* ns 5 (April 1841): 182-87. Signed "T. C."

"Remarks" [on T. H.'s "Order"]. *Millennial Harbinger* ns 5 (April 1841): 190. Signed "T. C."

"Answer to Query by 'A Disciple in Prince Edward.'" *Millennial Harbinger* ns 5 (April 1841): 192. Signed "T. C."

"A Scriptural View of Christian Character and Privilege." Section 5. *Millennial Harbinger* ns 5 (May 1841): 201-4. Signed "T. C."

"A Catechetical and Analytical Index to the Study and Teaching of the Bible." *Millennial Harbinger* ns 5 (September 1841): 421-24. Signed "T. C."

"A Scriptural View of the Agency of the Holy Spirit in the Conversion and Salvation of Sinners—According to the Gospel." *Millennial Harbinger* ns 5 (November 1841): 496-99. Signed "T. C."

"A Scriptural View of Christian Character and Privilege." Section 6. *Millennial Harbinger* ns 5 (December 1841): 556-57. Signed "T. C."

"A Scriptural View of Christian Character and Privilege." Section 7. *Millennial Harbinger* ns 6 (January 1842): 26-29. Signed "T. C."

"Reply" [to "Figurative Allusions to Baptism"]. *Millennial Harbinger* ns 7 (June 1843): 275-76. Signed "T. C."

"Extract of a Letter from T. C. to S. R. J." *Millennial Harbinger* 3d ser. 1 (March 1844): 102-5. Signed "T. C."

"Letter from T. C. to D." *Millennial Harbinger* 3d ser. 1 (March 1844): 121-25. Signed "T. C."

"An Address to All Our Christian Brethren, Upon the Necessity and Importance of the Actual Enjoyment of Our Holy Religion." *Millennial Harbinger* 3d ser. 1 (May 1844): 199-203. Postscript signed "T. C."

"Christianity." *Millennial Harbinger* 3d ser. 1 (November 1844): 481-91.

"Elder Thomas Campbell's Views of Slavery." [Letter to Cyrus M'Nealy, 11 August 1841.] *Millennial Harbinger* 3d ser. 2 (January 1845): 3-8.

"Reply to 'A Disciple' on the Subject of Slavery." *Millennial Harbinger* 3d ser. 2 (May 1845): 196-200. Postscript signed "T. C."

"A Brief Scriptural Exhibition of the Laws and Duties of Matrimony." *Millennial Harbinger* 3d ser. 2 (May 1845): 204-5. Signed "T. C."

"Queries by A. S. H." *Millennial Harbinger* 3d ser. 2 (May 1845): 220-22.

Letter to N. H. Finney [in "Mission to New England"]. *Millennial Harbinger* 3d ser. 2 (May 1845): 229-32.

"Letter from Elder Thomas Campbell." *Millennial Harbinger* 3d ser. 2 (December 1845): 561-65.

"Baptism." *Millennial Harbinger* 3d ser. 4 (June 1847): 322-28.

"Christian Society." *Millennial Harbinger* 3d ser. 4 (July 1847): 394-401.

"The Means of Enjoying Our Holy Religion." *Millennial Harbinger* 3d ser. 4 (August 1847): 443-50.

"An Address, to the Brethren to Meet at Matthews the 21st Instant." *Millennial Harbinger* 3d ser. 4 (September 1847): 491-503.

"The Disease, the Cure, and the Means of Enjoying It." *Millennial Harbinger* 3d ser. 4 (December 1847): 661-75.

"Advice to an Evangelist." *The Christian Union and Religious Review* 1 (April 1851): 112-15. Reprinted as "Ancient and Modern Evangelists—No. I." *Millennial Harbinger* 4th ser. 1 (August 1851): 450-53.

"Letter to an Evangelist, by Father Campbell." *Millennial Harbinger* 4th ser. 2 (February 1852): 94-97.

"Christian Training." *Millennial Harbinger* 4th ser. 3 (April 1853): 214-17.

"Farewell Discourse of Elder Thos. Campbell, Delivered June 1st, 1851." *Millennial Harbinger* 4th ser. 4 (March 1854): 133-45.

"Personal and Family Devotion." *Millennial Harbinger* 5th ser. 3 (November 1860): 628-31.

VI. Manuscripts

Letter. Author: Thomas Campbell, Loyds, Virginia, 24 December 1831. Recipient: Alexander Campbell, Bethany, Brooke County, Virginia. ALS. Original. Campbell Family Papers, T. W. Phillips Memorial Library, Bethany College, Bethany, West Virginia.

Letter. Author: Thomas Campbell, 1832. Recipient: Jane C. Mooney. ALS. Original. Campbell Family Papers, T. W. Phillips Memorial Library, Bethany College.

Letter. Author: Thomas Campbell, Spottsylvania County, Virginia, August 1, 1832. Recipient: Alexander Campbell, Bethany, Brooke County, Virginia. ALS. Original. Campbell Family Papers, T. W. Phillips Memorial Library, Bethany College.

Letter. Author: Thomas Campbell, Bethany, Virginia, April 29, 1835. Recipient: Alexander Campbell. ALS. Original. Campbell Family Papers, T. W. Phillips Memorial Library, Bethany College.

Notes

1. In preparing the contributions to periodicals section, the following reprints have been consulted: *The Christian Baptist* (Joplin, Mo.: College Press, 1983); a reprint of the edition revised by D. S. Burnet from the second edition (Cincinnati, Ohio: D. S. Burnet, 1835); *Millennial Harbinger* (Joplin, Mo.: College Press, 1976).

2. See signature on p. 598, "T. W. *alias* Thos. Campbell."

3. Gary L. Lee, in his "Index of the *Christian Baptist*" (in the College Press reprint, 1983), attributes this unsigned extract of a letter to Thomas Campbell. I have not been able to determine Lee's source for this information; however, it is a reasonable attribution inasmuch as Thomas Campbell is named as one of the witnesses to the constitution.

4. See Alexander Campbell's "Contents" to the bound volume, p. ix.

Name Index

Subject Index

About the Editors

Thomas H. Olbricht received his S.T.B. with a focus on church history from Harvard Divinity School, and his Ph.D. in rhetoric and early church history and his M.A. in speech communication from the University of Iowa. He has published scholarly materials on the history of the Stone-Campbell movement, the history of biblical studies, biblical theology, and rhetoric. He has taught and occupied administrative posts at Harding University, University of Dubuque, Pennsylvania State University, Abilene Christian University, and Pepperdine University. He is distinguished professor of religion, emeritus, Pepperdine University, and lives in retirement in South Berwick, Maine.

Hans Rollmann received his Ph.D. in biblical studies from McMaster University, Hamilton, Ontario, Canada, his M.A. in history of religions from Vanderbilt University, and his B.A. *magna cum laude* from Pepperdine University. He has published widely in the areas of religious and intellectual history, the history of biblical studies, and the religious history of Newfoundland and Labrador. He has been on the faculty of the University of Toronto and is presently Professor of Christian Thought and History at Memorial University of Newfoundland. In 1986, he received the President's Award for Outstanding Research and has also been an adjunct faculty member in the Faculty of Theology at Queen's College, St. John's, Newfoundland.